LEO PANITCH is a member of the Department of Political Science at Carleton University.

The Canadian State is a powerful collection of essays. Leo Panitch's theme essay, dealing with the theories of recent neo-Marxist thinkers such as O'Connor, Miliband, and Poulantzas on the nature and role of the state and sketching their relevance to Canada, sets the tone and interpretation of the whole work, which thus has a rare unity and cohesion. Reg Whitaker and Garth Stevenson provide papers offering profound analyses of the history and functioning of the federalized state in Canada. The twelve further contributors develop this theme, dealing with such topics as the aspirations of those behind the governments of Alberta and Quebec, relations between the government elites and Canada's classes and ethnic groups, the management of the economy through budgets and welfare state policies, and the management of culture through education, the arts, and citizen participation. Together they illuminate various aspects of the way the bourgeois state organizes our society, above all, for the accumulation of capital and the legitimation of capitalism and, at times, uses coercion to these ends.

The work as a whole brings together Canada's economics and politics in a new and penetrating way.

EDITED BY LEO PANITCH

The Canadian state: political economy and political power

UNIVERSITY OF TORONTO PRESS
Toronto and Buffalo

◉ University of Toronto Press 1977
Toronto and Buffalo
Printed in Canada

Canadian Cataloguing in Publication Data

Main entry under title:

The Canadian state

ISBN 0-8020-2285-5 bd. ISBN 0-8020-6322-5 pa.

1. Canada – Politics and government – Addresses,
essays, lectures. 2. Canada – Economic policy –
Addresses, essays, lectures. 3. Socialism in
Canada – Addresses, essays, lectures. I. Panitch,
Leo, 1945–

JL65 1977.c35   320.9′71   c77-001588-3

This book has been published during the
Sesquicentennial year of the University of Toronto

Contents

vi **Contents**

Editor's preface

There has emerged recently among students of politics a notable revival of interest in the study of the state from a Marxist perspective. Various reasons might be adduced for this development, at least as regards Western societies. It might be attributed in part to the increasingly large and visible role the state has come to play in the post-war era of advanced capitalism. Relatedly, the marked failure of social democracy in the post-war period – not its failure to get elected, which it has done with regular success in a significant number of countries, but its failure to effect fundamental changes in the social order once elected – has given new impetus to an attempt to uncover the connections between state and class structure, between the formal political equality of liberal democracy and the socio-economic inequality of capitalist society. Yet again, the increasing expression of industrial class conflict has reinvigorated 'class analysis' and pushed it far beyond the narrow confines of voting behaviour research. In Canada, these kinds of factors have been compounded by an additional and crucial one: the need for a theory that could systematically address Canada's unevenly developed and dependent capitalist economy, and that would attempt to come to terms with a state which has all the formal attributes of sovereignty and independence but which presides over a society increasingly dominated by American capital. In short, concrete historical developments have altered the milieux within which social scientists operate, and this has led, to some extent, to an attempt to attend to certain 'significant problems' which not so long ago were dismissed as archaic in the name of 'pluralism,' or the 'embourgeoisement thesis,' or the 'end of ideology' ideology. The renewed interest in a Marxist theory of the state reflects a sense that the concepts and theories of modern political science, and the hypotheses that are derived from them to appropriate reality, are incapable of even addressing, let along explaining, many of the major political questions of our time.

The search for alternative frameworks for analysis was initially impeded by a certain excessive concern, even among radical scholars, with criticizing existing approaches to the detriment of developing and applying new theory. A fundamental problem in this regard was the marked absence in Canada of a strong indigenous Marxist tradition in politics or intellectual life. Nevertheless, the groundwork for the development of a Marxist body of thought in Canada had long been present in a rich political economy tradition. This tradition, long associated with the name of Harold Innis, had paid attention to historical research, to material factors of life, and to the international and domestic conditions of imperialism and colonialism. Above all, it had rejected narrow disciplinary boundaries in favour of investigation into the relationship between economy, politics, and culture. The revival in recent years of this tradition – which had been cramped but not extinguished even in the 1950s and 1960s – was both cause and effect of the widespread interest in Marxism among students of state and society.

The origins of this book are directly located in a number of fledgling structures created to support and encourage the growing body of young intellectuals who are pursuing a Marxist-oriented political economy approach to Canadian society. My article 'The Role and Nature of the Canadian State,' which serves as an introduction and general framework for the book as a whole, was initially presented (in February 1975) as a lecture to the Marxist Institute, a Toronto-based organization designed to foster Marxist education through series of public lectures and courses. Immediately after this lecture was presented, I was asked by SPEC (Studies in the Political Economy of Canada) to consider editing a collection of essays on the Canadian state. SPEC was founded by former members of the University League for Social Reform (ULSR) who were committed to the struggle for an independent socialist Canada and to promoting radical studies in Canadian political economy. The group had by this time already sponsored Gary Teeple's immensely successful collection, *Captialism and the National Question in Canada* (1972). This commission by SPEC would, in its turn, have been very difficult to undertake but for the existence at Carleton University of the interdisciplinary faculty-student 'Seminar on Contemporary Socialist Problems,' which a number of the contributors to this book had established a few years previously. This seminar, which had already provided an arena for the exchange of ideas and the presentation of research on many of the concepts and issues raised in this book, became the focal point for work on this volume. Almost half of the contributors were at one time or another active in the seminar, and over half of the articles were originally presented as papers to the seminar during 1975 and 1976.

From the very beginning this book was seen as more than a mere collection of original essays on the state in Canada. It was conceived, and finally emerged, as a collaborative effort among the contributors. The initial debate around 'The Role and Nature of the Canadian State' helped to crystallize a number of questions and problems to which the other contributors addressed themselves, from various perspectives within Marxism, in the course of their own research and writings for the book. Moreover, as far as was possible within specific time constraints, first drafts of the other articles were also distributed among the contributors as they became available, and comments and suggestions for revision were solicited. This was not done with a view to easing the task of the editor (indeed, it added to his concerns, by making it necessary to avoid the 'too many cooks' syndrome). Nor was it done to produce a rigid common 'line.' On the contrary, this process was adopted to stimulate productive criticism and thereby provide a collective learning experience for all those engaged in the project. Thus, the cross-references that will be found in many of the articles to others in the book (noting points of both agreement and disagreement) are not the product of 'post hoc' editorial work but rather of genuine and substantive intellectual collaboration.

The result of this process now before you stands as an attestation to the vitality of Marxist intellectual life. The jaundiced view of Marxism being inherently monolithic, dogmatic, and closed was always ridiculous. It is even more bizarre today when Western Marxism is producing an outpouring of writings reflective of serious and critical debate on class, culture, and epistemology, as well as on the state. As the reader will see from the following articles, much of this debate has been taken up in Canada as well. The differences in approach will be seen to span a wide range of issues, from the question of the breadth of the definition to be properly accorded to the state as a concept, to the use of a structuralist approach to state policy versus the utility of employing more specific analysis of the social backgrounds and ideological orientations of state elites, right down to such a tactical question as whether artists or citizens groups are inevitably co-opted by state funding.

The theoretical innovation taking place within Western Marxism today is in itself a factor attracting more intellectuals to it. It would appear, indeed, that there is at present more room for wide-ranging and meaningful debate *within* Marxism as a theoretical *cum* political practice than within any of the contending liberal/conservative frameworks. The creativity and openness of this debate (within Marxism as well as between contending frameworks) was immediately apparent at the panels held by the new political economy section of the Canadian Political Science Association meetings in Quebec City in 1976. These panels, which included some of the papers prepared for this book, were by far the liveliest and best attended sessions at the annual meetings.

One must of course cautiously avoid the illusion that by virtue of its strengths alone a Marxist theory of the state will gain prominence. The rise and fall of theories is not merely the product of intellectual competiton with the most fruitful coming out on top. The acceptance of any particular theory and its conceptual elements rests on some consensus among intellectuals with regard to the importance of the 'significant problems' it identifies. On the identification of those problems, questions of interest as well as objectivity, ideological hegemony as well as academic freedom, will inevitably play their part. Most important of all will be the question of whether the generation of Marxist theory itself will continue to be by and large divorced from the working class in Canada. For without a working class helping to identify the 'significant problems' by its own actions, and taking up cultural as well as political and economic struggle by re-examining its history and developing a theory and practice for future change, Marxist theory will lack a social base, which is finally the *sine qua non* for the sustenance of any body of ideas. Whether Marxist theory in Canada will prove capable of generating its own further development will in no small measure depend on the future development of the Canadian working class.

The production of this book at a time when the capitalist economy is still in the throes of its most serious recession for forty years must be related to the possibilities and necessities of working towards a mass revolutionary socialist practice in Canada. Of course, theory and practice must never be simplistically reduced to one another, and, if they are, the results are usually detrimental to both. But just as knowledge of and participation in current struggles of the working class will help to ground the theorists' awareness of the social forces actually at work in society, so will theoretical work help create a working-class alternative to the hegemony of capitalist ideas, as well as foster among activists a deeper understanding of our society, its history, and the possibilities for reaction and change within it. Thus, while itself no substitute for theoretical consideration of revolutionary organization, strategy, and tactics, and the practice associated with them, this book is at the same time by no means merely academic. It is an intellectual contribution to the continuing and difficult struggle for an independent socialist Canada. In so far as it has any influence abroad, it is also a modest contribution to the larger struggle of which our Canadian project is inevitably a part.

Apart from my fellow contributors, who took part in this collective project with responsibility and enthusiasm, a number of other acknowledgments are due. In particular, the student and faculty members of the Carlton seminar made important critical contributions. Allan Moscovitch worked particularly closely on the project and Jane Jenson and Glen Williams provided helpful comments on particular papers. The secretaries at the Political Science Department of Carleton University, especially Pearl Fisher, provided invaluable technical assistance. Willadean Leo, Mordy Bubis, and Nina Stipich helped me with editorial work during the final stages and Gerry Hallowell picked up many of the finer points in preparing the manuscript for publication. R.I.K. Davidson of the University of Toronto Press, a key figure himself in the revival of Canadian political economy, helped not only by speeding this book's production along but also by sage advice and substantive comments on the manuscript. Finally, Danny Drache and Ian Lumsden of SPEC did far more than initiate the project; they took an active, indeed invaluable, part in the project by reading many of the papers, providing critical comments, and bolstering the morale of the editor. Those of you who buy this book should know that all royalties will go to SPEC in order to promote further research in the political economy of Canada.

Leo Panitch
Ottawa
May 1977

PART I
THEORETICAL AND HISTORICAL
PERSPECTIVES

1
The role and nature of the Canadian state

LEO PANITCH

The concern of this essay is to identify the framework of a Marxist theory of the state, to explore some of the basic requisites of such a theory, and then to make an attempt to apply it to the study of the Canadian reality. Unfortunately, an undertaking of this kind is all too often dismissed out of hand without much appreciation for what it actually entails. For when one goes back to the *Communist Manifesto's* famous formulation – 'the executive of the modern State is but a committee for managing the common affairs of the whole bourgeoisie'[1] – this often conjures up a grotesque image in certain minds. It is assumed that what one *really* means, in the modern Canadian context, is that E.P. Taylor, after having eaten two or three babies for breakfast, calls Pierre Trudeau every morning and, amidst satisfied belches, gives the prime minister instructions on what the government should accomplish that day. To be sure, the idea that the modern state acts at the behest of the dominant class in our society has often seemed much more plausible than the pluralist and social-democratic view of the state as a neutral arbiter between competing groups or classes. A cartoon in the *Grain Growers' Guide* of 1910[2] showed a House of Commons in which the benches were occupied by 'fat cats' representing the 'meat combine,' the 'cotton combine,' and the 'cement trust,' led by the man from the 'railroads combine.' They are sending Laurier and Borden, dressed as parliamentary messengers, out of the House to carry the message of the 'real rulers' to the people. This cartoon alone, entitled 'How the Country Is Governed,' tells us more about the Canadian state of that period than many of our history texts. But the real point that must be made in this respect is that an interpretation of the Marxist theory of the state as claiming that the state merely acts on the direct instructions of the bourgeoisie is a crude caricature of the concept of the modern state as 'a committee for managing the common affairs of the whole bourgeoisie,' a caricature which fails to distinguish between the state acting on *behalf* of the bourgeoisie and its acting on their *behest*. As Ralph Miliband has put it: '... the notion of common affairs assumes the existence of particular ones; and the notion of the whole bourgeoisie implies the existence of separate elements which make up that whole. This being the case, there is an obvious need for an institution of the kind they [Marx and Engels] refer to, namely the state; and the state *cannot* meet this need without enjoying a certain degree of autonomy. In other words, the notion of autonomy is embedded in the definition itself, is an intrinsic part of it.'[3] For the state to act only at the behest of particular segments of the bourgeoisie would be dysfunctional to it managing the common affairs of that class. For it to accomplish this task, it needs a degree of independence from that class, a 'relative autonomy'. A crude economistic interpretation of the state makes it in fact impossible to understand the real functions the state performs for the capitalist class.

The notion of the state managing the *common* affairs of the *whole* bourgeoisie, even incorporating as it does the idea of autonomy, is only the starting point for a Marxist theory of the state. And in going beyond that starting point, it is true to say that there is in Marx's own writings no systematic examination of the state to match his work on the capitalist mode of production itself. To be sure, a careful reading of Marx – and not only of his explicitly political tracts, such as the *Eighteenth Brumaire*, but of *Capital* itself – gives us very important insights. When Marx observed in the third volume of *Capital* that despotic states perform both the general function of undertaking 'common activities arising from the nature of all communities, and the specific functions arising from the antithesis between the government and the mass of the people,'[4] he was clearly noting the co-ordinating role of the state in all societies, which is undertaken apart from specific class interests, although of course framed within the boundaries set by the mode of production and the relations of production of a given society. And when analysing the intervention of the state in the economy in the nineteenth century in the form of ten-hour day legislation and the Factory Acts, Marx showed that the state was by no means immune from the pressure of classes other than the bourgeoisie. He identified two factors that led the English state, ruled directly by capitalists and landlords, to forcibly limit the working day by state regulations: first, the demands of 'the working class movement that daily grew more threatening'; and, second, the need for the state to save the bourgeoisie from itself, as the individual capitalist in his relentless drive for profit, far from being protected by some invisible hand, threatened to destroy the very basis of bourgeois wealth and accumulation by 'the passion of capital for a limitless draining of labour power' – just as 'the same blind eagerness for plunder ... exhausted the soil' in the era of commercial farming. The state's role in the class struggle over the ten-hour day was to make the issue resolvable without revolution, and at the same time promulgate the bourgeoisie's common interest, constituting thereby its political unity, so as to prevent blind competition from undermining its dominance. And Marx followed this with an incisive analysis of how the state's action here produced a reactive response in the economy. For to maintain the extraction of surplus value at the same rate as previous to the ten-hour day legislation, capital immediately introduced further mechanization to increase labour productivity per hour. Marx was suggesting here a dialectical relationship between base and superstructure: the state acts out of contradictions produced in the economic base, and once it acts it produces modifications in the economic base.

Finally, we should note the extent to which Marx presaged the growth of the state's role in the economy. Indeed, those who would deny the validity of the Marxist analysis on the basis of modern conditions not fitting with laissez-faire would do well to read *Capital*. For Marx showed clearly there the dynamic of state intervention in the context of an analysis of the regulation of child labour. As soon as the state intervenes at one point by introducing an exceptional law relating to one branch of industry (mechanical spinning and weaving), the necessity for the generalization of factory regulation, for 'a law affecting social production as a whole,' arises. 'There are two circumstances that finally turn the scale: first, the constantly recurring experience that capital, so soon as it finds itself subject to legal control at one point, compensates itself all the more recklessly at other points; secondly, the cry of the capitalists for equality in the conditions of competition, i.e., for equal restrain on all exploitation of labour.'[5]

Despite these insights, it nevertheless remains true that the Marxist theory of the state is underdeveloped and, although Lenin, Gramsci, and others have added contributions, there remains much work to be done. It appears that a fully developed theory of the state in capitalist society must meet at least three basic requirements. It must clearly delimit the complex of institutions that go to make up the state. It must demonstrate concretely, rather than just define abstractly, the linkages between the state and the system of class inequality in the society, particularly its ties to the dominant social class. And it must specify as far as possible the functions of the state under the capitalist mode of production. It must undertake these tasks, moreover, not in an ahistoric way but in relation to the way the state's organization, its functions, and its linkages with society vary with the changes in the capitalist mode of production itself, and also vary with the specific conditions of a given social formation. Marxism may give us a method of analysis, but, as Marx himself pointed out in the third volume of *Capital*, this method has to be applied not as an overgeneralization but in a manner that will illuminate concrete empirical and historical circumstances: 'The specific economic form, in which unpaid surplus-labour is pumped out of direct producers, determines the relationship of rulers and ruled, as it grows directly out of production itself and, in turn, reacts upon it as a determining element. Upon this, however, is founded the entire formation of the economic community which grows up out of the production relations themselves, thereby simultaneously its specific political form. It is always the direct relationship of the owners of the conditions of production to the direct producers – a relation always naturally corresponding to a definite state in the development of the methods of labour and thereby its social productivity – which reveals the innermost secret, the hidden basis of the entire social structure, and with it the political form of the relation of sovereignty and dependence, in short the corresponding specific form of the state. This does not prevent the same economic basis – the same from the standpoint of its main conditions – due to innumerable different empirical circumstances, natural environment, racial relations, external historical influences, etc., from showing the infinite variations and gradations in appearance, which can be ascertained only by analysis of the empirically given circumstances.'[6]

Before turning, with this in mind, to an examination of the specific role and nature of the Canadian state in light of the 'empirically given circumstances' of our own society, a few comments are necessary with regard to each of three requisites of a theory of the capitalist state which were mentioned above. One of the very important contributions of Ralph Miliband's *The State in Capitalist Society* is to stress the importance of delimiting clearly the institutions of the state.[7] As Miliband points out, the state is not merely the government, far less just the central government. The state is a complex of institutions, including government, but also including the bureaucracy (embodied in the civil service as well as in public corporations, central banks, regulatory commissions, etc.), the military, the judiciary, representative assemblies, and (very importantly for Canada) what Miliband calls the sub-central levels of government, that is, provincial executives, legislatures, and bureaucracies, and municipal governmental institutions. Although the point itself seems simple once stated, its importance is paramount. It is important, first of all, because of what it leaves out. It leaves out political parties, the privately owned media, the church, pressure groups. These other institutions form part of the political system and no doubt part of the system of power in a liberal-democratic capitalist society, but, unlike the fascist case, they remain autonomous from the state. This is of crucial importance not only theoretically, in the sense that it requires us to explain how these other institutions form part of the system of power through their contribution to political socialization, political recruitment, and social control, but also because it means, in practice, that within the rubric of bourgeois democracy, as opposed to fascism, class conflict does obtain political and industrial expression through the voluntary organizations of the working class. At a general level both forms of the state may be seen as capitalist in their nature, but a specific understanding of the political sphere in each must follow different guidelines.

A second reason for delineating clearly the institutions of the state is that it leads us away from assuming, as social democrats consistently do, that election to governmental power is equivalent to the acquisition of state power. This is, of course, not necessarily true and in most cases is simply untrue, as the example of the Allende regime in Chile demonstrates and as Allende himself understood quite well. In what was probably his last public interview, Allende was asked whether he was turning Chile into a traditional Marxist-Leninist state. Allende's response was to the point. His election, he explained, had not of itself transformed Chile into a socialist country, nor did the fact that a Marxist occupied the office of head of state and leader of the government make the Chilean state socialist or Marxist. He was vice-president of the Senate for four years, and the Senate was not Marxist. He was president of the medical school and nobody could say that the medical school was Marxist.[8] The point here is that the extent to which a government effectively controls the power of the state, indeed even the extent to which it can speak authoritatively in the name of the state, will depend on the balance of forces within the various institutions of the state, such as the bureaucracy, the judiciary, and the military, in terms of the classes *they* represent and the values *they* hold. This will determine how far governmental power is circumscribed by state power.

The second requisite of a theory of the state – that of specifying linkages between the state system and the class structure – is also of key importance. Nicos Poulantzas, whose book, *Political Power and Social Classes*, has already had a substantial impact in the field, has tended to play down the utility of tracing the ties between state personnel and the capitalist class, suggesting that the state's activities on behalf of the capitalist class are determined by deep structural relations rather than by the similar class backgrounds and social positions of state personnel and businessmen. In this way he is able to grant the state 'relative autonomy' from the capitalist class while at the same time defining an 'objective relation' between the state and the bourgeoisie which automatically determines that state activities are the expression of the power of the dominant class. The most efficient capitalist state, for Poulantzas, is one that has the *least* direct personal ties to the bourgeoisie, both in terms of mystifying the relationship and in terms of acting as a cohesive factor for the whole bourgeoisie.[9] The problem with this approach, however, is that it tends to remove from the theory of the state a concrete empirical and historical orientation. By establishing by definition the relationship between state and bourgeoisie, one leaves out the central question, to be determined empirically in each instance, of the *extent* to which the state is acting on behalf of the dominant class. As Miliband has put it, in a critique of Poulantzas' 'structuralist abstractionism': ' ... one of the main reasons for stressing the importance of the notion of the relative autonomy of the state is that there is a basic distinction to be made between class power and state power, and that the analysis of the meaning and implications of that notion of relative autonomy must indeed focus on the forces which cause it to be greater or less, the circumstances in which it is exercised, and so on.'[10]

Turning finally to the question of the specific functions of the capitalist state, a useful framework has been suggested by James O'Connor: 'Our first premise is that the capitalistic state must try to fulfill two basic and often mutually contradictory functions – *accumulation* and *legitimization* ... This means that the state must try to maintain or create the conditions in which profitable capital accumulation is possible. However, the state also must try to maintain or create the conditions for social harmony. A capitalist state that openly uses its coercive forces to help one class accumulate capital at the expense of other classes loses its legitimacy and hence undermines the basis of its loyalty and support.'[11] A number of points should be noted in this respect. First of all, there are really three distinct functions identified here: in addition to policies that will foster capital accumulation (for example, subsidies to private industry), and in addition to policies that will foster social harmony (for example, the ten-hour day legislation or social welfare legislation), there is a *coercion function*, that is, the use by the state of its monopoly over the legitimate use of force to maintain or impose social order. The capital accumulation function does not *normally* rely on the coercion function, but operates independently of it. Secondly, the legitimization and capital accumulation functions are by no means necessarily mutually contradictory. A taxation policy aimed at income redistribution for the purpose of legitimization may be contrary to short-term accumulation, but necessary for maintaining accumulation in the long run, indeed even for accelerating it. It should be stressed, finally, that the emphasis given here to the concept of functions need not, if properly employed, give rise to the same problems as are found in other structural-functional approaches. As Eric Hobsbawm has observed: 'Marxism is far from the only structural-functionalist theory of society, though it has good claims to be the first of them, but it differs from most others in two respects. First, it insists on a hierarchy of social phenomena (e.g. "basis" and "superstructure"), and second, on the existence within any society of internal tensions ("contradictions") which counteract the tendency of the system to maintain itself as a going concern ... The importance of these peculiarities of Marxism is in the field of history, for it is they which allow it to explain – unlike other structural-functional models of society – why and how societies change and transform themselves ... Today, when the existence of social systems is generally accepted, but at the cost of their a-historical, if not anti-historical analysis, Marx's emphasis on history as a necessary dimension is perhaps more essential than ever.'[12]

It should be obvious, in this light, that the exercise of the various state functions is by no means uniform in all periods and in all societies, and that the size and prominence of any one of the three state functions must be examined in light of the 'empirically given circumstances' of a particular society. Indeed, what is striking as one turns to an analysis of the Canadian state is how at each point the Canadian state reflects *particular* characteristics which mark it off in a comparative sense from other capitalist states. On the question of state organization one sees that the federal form has always been, and remains, of crucial importance in terms of the power of the provincial segments of the state vis-à-vis the central government. One sees as well that the linkages between the state and the dominant class have been, and remain, not general and abstract but particularly close and intimate. And one sees in terms of state functions that, from its very beginnings, the Canadian state has played a tremendously large role in fostering capital accumulation. Each of these will be looked at in turn. What follows, however, must in no sense be seen as anything more than a tentative and necessarily incomplete approach towards employing Marxist theory to understand the Canadian state.

The utility of delimiting the institutions of the Canadian state, along the lines suggested by Miliband, is clear. Although no such spectacular examples of the distribution of state power as afforded by the Allende case exist in Canadian history, an appreciation of the balance of powers among various state institutions can give us the handle to grasp the limitations placed by the bureaucracy on CCF-NDP governments, and even the tensions between the Diefenbaker government and the federal civil service in the 1957 to 1962 period.[13] Moreover, by drawing the differences between the state system and the broader political system, we can begin to trace more clearly the worrying ways in which there is occurring within Canadian liberal democracy an increasing 'statisization' of the political sphere. Specifically relevant here are such developments as state subsidies to political parties' election campaigns or the recent attempts to involve trade unions in the government's 'consensus' incomes policy. Although the foray by the state into the regulation of party financing is progressive in the sense that it ostensibly seeks to limit the influence of corporate money on the electoral arena, the introduction of state financing as a substitute, carrying as it does a bias in favour of the existing parties and against new parties, may tend to freeze the extremely limited party alternatives presently available. Similarly, the attempt to incorporate trade unions in an incomes policy is clearly designed to ensure that these working-class organizations, however defective at present as representatives of workers' demands, will be obliged to act explicitly as agencies of social control over their members.

But in following Miliband's suggestive outline of the state system thus far, it is necessary immediately to depart from him in one crucial respect with regard to the Canadian state. For while Miliband argues that amongst Western societies there has been a tendency towards the centralization of state power at the expense of sub-central institutions, this does not hold for Canada where provincial state power has historically been important and has become increasingly more so in recent years. Unfortunately, Marxists in Canada have avoided dealing with this in a serious way, with perhaps the crucial exception of C.B. Macpherson, whose *Democracy in Alberta* remains the best political analysis in the Marxist tradition undertaken in Canada. To be sure, the federal factor has often been used by Canadian politicians to pass the buck on the introduction of progressive social legislation, as a rationale for inaction, and as a means of dividing the working class. Nevertheless, without an understanding of Canada's federal nature the Canadian state cannot be properly analysed.

The reasons for this dispersion of state power in Canada are complex and many of them hark back to the racial, geographic, and historical factors that Marx spoke of as necessitating a concrete examination of specific societies: the binational nature of Canadian society, the fact that the state was formed as an amalgam of British colonies, and the fact that within Canada there emerged a quasi-colonial relationship between regions, a relationship dominated by central Canada and its bourgeoisie although it itself was dominated from the outside. Moreover, the persistence of provincial state power is to be understood in terms of the differing class structures of various Canadian regions and in terms of the regional fractions of the bourgeoisie. The dominant classes, or rather class fractions, in the provinces, often unable to constitute a unity with their counterparts either through political parties or in economic coalitions, have used the provincial state to express their interests. This was shown by Macpherson with regard to the petite bourgeoisie of Alberta of the 1930s and it has been brilliantly demonstrated by Hubert Guindon with regard to the new middle class of Quebec in the 1960s.[14]

The relentless striving and competition on the part of provincial governments for American investment in the last two decades, which has been a large factor in the balkanization and quasi-colonialization of Canada as a whole, is a product of such factors. Moreover, this perspective is required to understand the Alberta–federal government dispute over oil, which reflects a clear difference of interest within the bourgeoisie between oil and gas interests and manufacturing interests (often both comprador in their nature). That the Ontario, Alberta, and federal governments could come together in an agreement on the Syncrude rip-off is an attestation to the important role the state plays in providing a unity for the bourgeoisie, which cannot be obtained through other mechanisms. This political unity is increasingly being achieved, however, not within the traditional federal institutions but by new and *ad hoc* federal-provincial conferences two or three steps removed from any sort of popular control, even in the liberal-democratic sense of that term.[15] The point, however, is that these developments can only be understood in terms of the fragmented representation of regional bourgeois interests in a federal system.

When we turn from the organization of the state to the second requisite of a Marxist theory, that of specifying the concrete linkages between a state formally based on political equality and a society dominated by the capitalist class, we again immediately note a particularly striking characteristic of the Canadian state – its very close personal ties to the bourgeoisie. Whatever the merits of Poulantzas' contention that the most efficient state is that with the least direct ties to the dominant class, it is a rather academic point as applied to Canada. Without indulging in fantasies of E.P. Taylor and P.E. Trudeau on the telephone, let us remember that the relationship between the first post-confederation cabinets and the financial bourgeoisie and the railway enterpreneurs was not only close – they were often the same people.[16] To take but one example among many, a list of the board of directors of the Grand Trunk Railway reads like a list of the Fathers of Confederation, including Galt and Cartier. T.W. Acheson's study of Canada's industrial elite at the turn of the century reveals that no less than one-third of the members of that elite held political office at some time in their careers.[17]

The story is a repetitive one extending through Mackenzie King, adviser of the Rockefellers, to St Laurent, the corporation lawyer, to Wallace McCutcheon, managing director of Argus Corporation, to the Pearson-Trudeau cabinets on which Drury, Sharp, and Richardson sat as members of the corporate elite in their own right. John Porter's demonstration of the degree of co-optation from business to government and of exit from cabinet to business makes the very concept of an autonomous political elite in Canada a highly tenuous one. The political recruitment role played by political parties in this respect is important. This was evident from the origins of the dominant nineteenth-century party – the Conservatives – out of the bosom of the Montreal business establishment.[18] And it is no less evident from an examination of the activists in the Liberal and Conservative parties today. A study of these parties' leadership conventions in 1967 and 1968 reveals that these great exercises in participatory democracy were attended by delegates 'drawn from a strikingly narrow socio-economic base.'[19] Two-thirds had annual incomes of $10,000 or more as compared with 7 per cent of the Canadian population in this income bracket; 40 per cent earned $15,000 or more – only 2 per cent of Canadians had such incomes; 25 per cent earned $20,000 or more – as against one per cent of all Canadians. As one would expect from this, 60 per cent of the delegates were executives or professionals, while only 8 per cent were drawn from clerical and other white-collar occupations or from the ranks of skilled or unskilled manual workers.

When we turn to the bureaucracy, we find again particularly strong linkages, with a major tendency, despite the development of a civil service based on the merit principle rather than patronage, for the co-optation of businessmen from the outside. The classic example is that of C.D. Howe's 'boys.' This architect of federal industrial and commercial policies during the war and in the formative post-war years, according to Mitchell Sharp, 'knew every important business man in Canada, and they seemed to have made a practice of talking to "C.D." whether they wanted anything from the Government or not.'[20] Howe brought to Ottawa a large number of businessmen to 'manage' the Canadian economy and to head publicly owned enterprises, and a number of these men maintained private corporate positions at the same time. As Porter observed: 'It was not surprising that a close relationship should develop and career lines become confused between the corporate world and the public service in and around departments which, through planning, regulations, and defence contracts, came into close contact with industry. The result was a growth of a penumbral area of power in which the political, bureaucratic, and corporate elites met, and became linked in such a way as to become a minor power elite.'[21] With the recommendations of the Glassco Commission in the early 1960s that these ties and interchanges between business and the civil service be encouraged and the consequent actions in this respect on the part of Liberal governments, this 'penumbral area of power' does not appear to have been attenuated. Wally Clement has indeed recently shown that there has been 'an increasing interpenetration between the corporate elite and both the state and political systems in the last twenty years,' and the 'a total of 39.4% of the current economic elite members either were themselves or had close kin in the state system.'[22]

The point to be drawn from all this is not that the state in Canada would be independent of the capitalist class without these specific linkages, given the balance of class forces within which the state operates. It certainly does suggest, however, 'a confraternity of power' of such dimensions as to permit the clear employment of the term 'ruling class' in the political as well as the economic sense in the Canadian case. It suggests, above all, an ideological hegemony emanating from both the bourgeoisie and the state which is awesome, which is reflected in the sheer pervasiveness of the view that the national interest and business interests are at one, and which certainly ensures the smooth functioning of the relationship between the state and the capitalist class. This was clearly evidenced in a frank statement by Jack Pickersgill from his position as head of the Canadian Transport Commission to the Canadian Manufacturers' Association in 1970: ' ... the public generally, and business men specifically, must come to realize that it is just as moral, and just as praiseworthy to operate a railway, an airline, or a trucking firm at a profit as it is to make a profit manufacturing motor cars or packing meat or making steel.' Not surprisingly, this statement was questioned by the Canadian Railway Labour Association as showing no little bias in favour of the rate hikes for Canadian Pacific, which Mr Pickersgill's CTC was supposed to be regulating. Pickersgill, however, was utterly amazed that anyone could take exception to his apologia for profit: ' "I must say," he said, "that I thought that that statement was as safe as saying one was in favour of motherhood as one could come and not be accused of banality ... What I was seeking to do was to remove all bias of any kind, without raising a very large question, which I have no intention of raising, as to whether it is moral to make a profit on anything. I am sure that no one wants to debate this subject." '[23] This disposition to see profit as motherhood, so widely spread throughout the operations of the Canadian state, lends particular credence to the concept, sometimes used in political science, of the 'non-decision.' The problem is not that political and bureaucratic officials *decide* to favour capitalist interests in case after case; it is rather that it rarely even *occurs* to them that they might do other than favour such interests. The problem is indeed a systemic one.

What must be understood, however, as we move to examine the functions of the Canadian state, is that this ideological hegemony that extends across the state-corporate sphere in no way inhibits a very large role for the state in the society; indeed, if one can distinguish between the capital accumulation function on the one hand and the legitimization function on the other, one can easily see how such close ties would promote a major role for the state in the former respect. In terms of the capital accumulation function, the Canadian state has generally undertaken four main tasks. It has provided a favourable fiscal and monetary climate for economic growth via private enterprise. It has underwritten the private risks of production at public expense through grants, subsidies, fast write-off depreciation allowances, etc. (Confederation itself was produced by the desire to facilitate capital accumulation by guaranteeing loans from London to build the railways.) It has played a crucial role, via control of land policy and immigration policy, in creating a capitalist labour market and, especially in recent decades, in absorbing the social cost of production of capitalist enterprise through sanitation services, medicare, unemployment insurance, educational facilities. And it has directly provided the technical infrastructure for capitalist development when this was too risky or costly for private capital to undertake itself. State ownership of railroads and public utilities and state construction and operation of airports were never undertaken as ends in themselves with the aim of managing or controlling the economy, but always with a view to facilitating further capital accumulation in the private sphere to the end of economic growth.[24]

What is particularly noteworthy about these activities is how large they bulked for the Canadian state long before the concentration of capital in the monopolistic stage found this function duplicated to this extent in other, more developed, capitalist countries. The Canadian state was *never* a laissez-faire state and, although it was not always the case that a spade was called a spade, Canadian economists and historians have well recorded this function. Indeed, Lord Durham in his famous *Report* of 1839 noted that, whereas in Europe the main role of the state was defence, in North America it was active engagement in the construction of communication links in the new societies.[25] But given the particular nature of the Canadian economy, this function became much more developed in Canada than in the United States. Writing almost twenty years ago, C.B. Macpherson observed:

... one of the main achievements of Canadian economics has been to show in more detail the close interdependence of political and economic structure. The constitutional structure of Canada has been to a large extent determined by the need to secure capital at favourable rates of interest and to promote the expansion of the economy: 'Constitutional changes are a part of market operations.' (Innis). In turn the political authorities, federal and provincial, have as a matter of course assumed large powers of control and protection, encouragement and regulation of economic life.

This embrace of private enterprise and government is not at all unusual in new countries. In Canada it is the direct result of the fact that the natural resources, abundant but scattered, have always afforded the prospect of highly profitable exploitation and could most rapidly be made profitable by concentrating on the production of a few staples for export – fur and fish in the early days, wheat, forest products and minerals today. This required a heavy import of capital and heavy government expenditure in railways, power developments, irrigation, land settlement, and so on. To support such investment, governments have been driven to all sorts of further encouragement of various industries and regions, notably by way of protective tariffs. They have also been driven to monetary and other regulatory policies to offset the extreme swings of an economy so dependent for its revenue on the unstable demand for and prices of a few staples, and so burdened by the fixed costs of interest on its capital indebtedness. And because the different regions of Canada, being unevenly developed, feel these problems at different times and to different extents, there is constant struggle both within federal politics and between federal and provincial governments for more favourable consideration for every region. In addition, the fact that governments still own or control many rich natural resources, leads to a continuing high degree of government manipulation and regulation.

All this flows directly from the demand of private enterprise; the economy as a whole remains fundamentally a private-enterprise system, but the pattern of prices, markets, and profits is perennially complicated by the manifold involvement of governments and by the pressures on governments which their involvement invites. Just as the Canadian economy is in an exposed position due to its dependence on world prices for staples, so the political system has from the beginning been exposed, to an unusual extent, to the pressures of economic interest groups.[26]

The Canadian bourgeoisie, moreover, has not shied away from considerable public ownership as an acceptable means whereby the state could perform the accumulation function. Indeed, the state's activities in this respect

were developed so early and in such large proportions that social-democratic politicians in Britain in the 1920s, with a characteristic inability – no
less remarkable then than now – to understand the true significance of
events, actually took inspiration from such public ventures as Ontario Hydro and the CNR as expressions of 'the great socialist experiments of the
Dominions.' This was the view of Arthur Greenwood upon the eve of his
entering Ramsay MacDonald's Labour government in 1929. He saw these
ventures as 'two enterprises [which] stand to the credit of a people whose
policy has been decided on grounds of public advantage.'[27] A rather more
realistic assessment has recently been offered by the historian H.V. Nelles
in his masterful account of government-industry relations in Ontario:
'From the outset the crusade for public power was a businessmen's movement; they initiated it, formed its devoted, hard-core membership and, most
importantly, they provided it with brilliant leadership. By the phrase "the
people's power," the businessmen meant cheap electricity for the manufacturer, and it was assumed that the entire community would benefit as a result. The socially and politically influential manufacturers turned readily to
public ownership primarily because the private electric companies at Niag-
ara refused to guarantee them an immediate, inexpensive supply of a commodity on which they believed their future prosperity depended.' Not surprisingly, the operation of Ontario Hydro has always looked more like state
capitalism than anything else, ' ... run by businessmen, for businessmen, in
what was always referred to as a "businesslike" manner.' Unlike so many of
our political analysts, Canadian capitalists have been good at distinguishing
between a large state with major accumulation functions and a socialist
state. As Nelles puts it: ' ... the positive state survived the nineteenth century primarily because businessmen found it useful. The province received
substantial revenue from the development process and enjoyed the appearance of control over it, while industrialists used the government – as had the
nineteenth-century commercial classes before – to provide key services at
public expense, promote and protect vested interests, and confer the status
of law upon private decisions. If public functions such as the distribution of
hydro-electricity were to the advantage of industry, this expansion of political control was eagerly sanctioned; whereas, if businessmen resented interference (mineral royalties and forest protection regulations, for example),
then the scope of government intervention narrowed ... the structures established to regulate business in the public interest ... contributed to a reduction of the state – despite an expansion of its activities – to a client of
the business community.'[28]

It has been the very lack of relative autonomy of the state, the sheer depth of its commitment to private capital as the motor force of the society, which, when combined with a weak indigenous industrial bourgeoisie and a strong financial bourgeoisie cast in the mould of an intermediary between staple production in Canada and industrial empires abroad, explains the lengths to which the state has gone in promoting private capital accumulation not only for the domestic bourgeoisie but for foreign capitalists as well. However persuasive the arguments by R.T. Naylor and Clement with regard to the Canadian financial bourgeoisie being particularly suited and willing to make a profit by acting as a conduit for American ownership of Canadian industry, it appears unlikely that the role of the Canadian state in fostering direct American investment is to be understood in terms of the dominant financial fraction of the bourgeoisie having 'captured' the state to the detriment of indigenous industrialists. T.W. Acheson has shown that in 1910, at the crossroads of the major growth of American direct investment, manufacturers were much more involved in politics at both the provincial and federal levels than were financiers.[29] A more general, yet more convincing, explanation might be suggested: Macpherson in his study of Social Credit observed that the Alberta petite bourgeoisie supported a strong state with a view to protecting itself against big eastern capital, but because of the strength of its commitment to private property in an age of monopoly capitalism it found the state inexorably drawn into the latter's orbit. We might suggest in a similar way that the Canadian bourgeoisie, both industrial and financial, seeks to build with the aid of a large and strong state a viable national economy on the northern half of the continent, but because of the commitment to private accumulation it comes to rely on American direct investment as the readiest source of capital. This produces the very opposite of the stated intention – not a viable independent bourgeois society, but a dependency of the American Empire. The National Policy, which has been pursued with unwavering commitment by Canadian governments from the time of John A. Macdonald and the CPR to the time of Donald Macdonald and Syncrude, has been based on shifting sands. It involves relying on foreign capital for staple extraction on the assumption that this will create the surplus out of which industrialization in central Canada will grow; and it involves the further assumption that foreign branch plants may take the lead in this industrialization behind tariff walls as good corporate Canadian citizens.

In the case of the earlier reliance on British portfolio investment, given the non-perpetuating character of control involved since loans can be paid off, and given the waning of British imperial power generally, this alone did not provide tremendous difficulties for the development of Canadian independence. But this independence from Britain, told so often in our school textbooks as the story of 'From Colony to Nation,' was but a temporary one, occasioned by a situation in which Britain had lost and America had not yet gained the ability to rule Canada. For as American direct investment permeated Canada with the help of the Canadian state and the financial bourgeoisie, the economic basis of independence was lost. The guiding ideology and function of the Canadian state remained that of providing the basis for capital accumulation to facilitate national economic development, with some discrimination in favour of central Canada in terms of the location of investment, but without discrimination with regard to the origin or nature of the investment. As C.D. Howe succinctly put it in a speech in Boston in 1954: 'Canada has welcomed the participation of American and other foreign capital in its industrial expansion. In Canada foreign investors are treated the same as domestic investors.'[30] The result of this policy was economic growth indeed, but a distorted growth which removed from the Canadian state, given the sheer dominance of foreign capital over the economy, much of the substance of its political sovereignty. It is the economic basis for a new colonial relationship with the American Empire which, through a foreign policy of 'quiet diplomacy,' 'special status,' and an 'ear in Washington,' resembles very closely the neo-colonial relationship offered to Canada at the turn of the century by Britain in the form of an 'imperial cabinet.' This was rejected by Laurier on the grounds ' ... that a method of consultation obviously defective and carrying with it in reality no suspensory or veto power, involves by indirection the adoption of that very centralizing system which it had been his purpose to block ... the policy of consultation gave the Dominions a shadowy and unreal power; but imposed upon them a responsibility, serious and inescapable.'[31] In Canada's voyage from colony to nation to neo-colony, we seem to have exchanged the 'shadowy and unreal' independence offered within the British Empire for the 'shadowy and unreal' independence tolerated by the Americans.

Turning now to the other functions of the Canadian state, it should be noted – although there is not the space to discuss this here – that in respect of the coercion function the state's use of its coercive powers to maintain or impose social order has also been much in evidence in Canadian history. To this, attest such famous examples as the tight central control of western expansion, the suppression of the Riel Rebellion, the employment of troops against strikers in Winnipeg and mounties against the unemployed in Regina, as well as the ready use of the War Measures Act more recently. What has been least developed, however, is the state's legitimization function. In contrast with the accumulation function where the Canadian state has been a forerunner, at least among the Anglo-American countries, in terms of legitimation the state's role has not been comparatively active, imaginative, or large. Legitimation is being used here not in the sense of state propaganda or statements by politicians that seek to rationalize capital accumulation in terms of its benefits for the whole community, but rather in the sense of concrete state activities such as welfare measures, anti-combines legislation, redistributive taxation, union protection, and governmental consultation with labour representatives. We are speaking of policies directed at the integration of the subordinate classes in capitalist society either through the introduction of reforms which promote social harmony or through the co-optation of working-class leaders via tripartite consultations with government and business – giving them the semblance of power without the substance – so as to employ them as agencies of social control over their members.

Noting that the legitimization function is relatively underdeveloped in Canada does not imply its total absence – it is a requisite of every state. With respect to union rights, it was clearly employed in Canada shortly after Confederation when Macdonald defended the right to strike of the Toronto *Globe*'s printers as against the newspaper's owner – the Liberal party leader – George Brown. Macdonald's Trade Union Act of 1872 was a Canadian variant of Disraeli's 'aristocratic embrace,' conceived in the hope of finding conservative angels within the hard marble exteriors of the working class. But what has been particularly notable about Canadian labour legislation, in comparison with the British and even in comparison with the American, is the extent to which the rights of unionization and free collective bargaining have been hedged around by, even embedded in, a massive legal and penal structure. This places such tremendous statutory restriction on labour and gives such a large role for the law and the courts to play, that the legitimation aspect of labour legislation in Canada's case seems at least balanced, if not actually overshadowed, by the coercive aspect.

In terms of state regulatory policies over business, Canada's first anti-combines legislation (1889) appeared in fact a year before the American Sherman Act. This legislation has never made much of an impact on Canada, however. As Michael Bliss has said of the pre–First World War period: 'Canadian anti-combines legislation during these years was insignificant and ineffectual; it did not reflect a serious desire by legislators to resist economic consolidation or restore the forces of the free market.'[32] Precisely the same conclusion has been reached for the post–Second World War period by Hugh Thorburn and Bert Young.[33] It is hard to believe that such a policy has garnered much legitimacy for the capitalist system. If it is important, it is in that it indicates so clearly the particular strength of the financial bour-geoisie of this country in that their banking institutions have been largely spared even the embarrassment of investigation, let alone actual 'trust-busting' by the state.[34]

In the field of social services the Canadian state has again been a laggard in comparison with its pathbreaking performance in the field of capital ac-cumulation. The 'welfare state' was late in coming to Canada, and once it came did not outrun by any means the provision of benefits or redistribu-tion of incomes of other capitalist societies.[35] This is in one sense surprising in view of the fact that the major political figure in Canada in this century, Mackenzie King, presaged the welfare state and the neo-corporatist devel-opment of union integration within liberal democracy in his *Industry and Humanity* in 1918, and was one of the first writers clearly to do so in the Western world. *Industry and Humanity* made the case for wide dissemina-tion of welfare benefits with a view to laying the basis of labour, capital, and state collaboration in the economy and industry. 'Let Labor and Capi-tal unite under the ideal of social service,' he exhorted; 'the work of mate-rial production will go on; not only will it vastly increase, but the whole complexion of Industry will become transformed. No longer will Industry be the battle-ground of rival and contending factions; it will become the foundation of a new civilization in which life and happiness abound.'[36] This fundamentally social-democratic view, very similar to that of Ramsay Mac-Donald in Britain – in fact, more fully developed and more concrete – had virtually no effect on Canadian legislation for the following quarter century, however, despite King's being prime minister for much of that period. Why? The reason is that ideas, if they are socially disembodied in the sense of not correlating with the nature and balance of class forces in a society, can themselves have little impact. The fact that in the pre–Second World War period the petite bourgeoisie was the largest subordinate class in Canada[37] and that there was less need on the family farm for the kind of benefits associated with the welfare state, was a major factor in explaining Canada's retardation in this respect. Another key factor was that labour did not pose a *centralized* threat with which the state was forced to deal. The major conflicts of the inter-war years were regionally isolated. It was only during the Second World War, with the tremendous growth of popular radi-calism and union consciousness, that the Canadian state turned in a delib-erate way towards welfarism. On the night in August 1943 that the Commu-nists won the Cartier by-election (over the CCF's David Lewis) and the CCF won two other by-elections, King wrote in his diary that he hoped that the victory might cause ' ... some of our people to realize that labour has to be dealt with in a considerate way. In my heart, I am not sorry to see the mass of the people coming a little more into their own, but I do regret that it is not a Liberal party that is winning that position for them. It should be, and it can still be that our people will learn their lesson in time. What I fear is we will begin to have defection from our ranks in the House to the C.C.F.'[38]

Canada's 'welfare state' legislation was much influenced by Britain's famous *Beveridge Report*,[39] and upon hearing Sir William Beveridge speak in Ottawa in 1943 King proudly noted how his *Industry and Humanity* had anticipated Beveridge's program. This was less true of specific policy proposals than of the philosophy behind them. Beveridge's main concern was with ensuring that the provision of social benefits and the guarantee of full employment would lead to wage moderation as well as political moderation on the part of the working class and particularly to the adoption of a 'responsible' accommodative stance by union leaders, who would discipline their members in the context of a more 'humane' society. This increased social role for the state combined with a role for unions as agencies of social control over their members – what a prescient London *Times* correspondent in 1943 called a 'middle course between Socialism and Fascism'[40] – was indeed central to King's thinking. In a visit to Germany in 1937 King had been above all impressed with the corporative element in German fascism, almost to the total neglect of its effects on the autonomy of working-class institutions and the freedom of working people. After his meeting with Hitler, King wrote in his diary: 'Like Henderson, the British Ambassador, I feel more and more how far reaching in the interests of the working classes, are the reforms being worked out in Germany, and how completely they are on the right lines. They are truly establishing an industrial commonwealth, and other nations would be wise to evolve rapidly on similar lines of giving to labour its place in the control of industry; its leisure, its opportunities for education, recreation, sharing, in all particulars, the life which hitherto had been preserved for the privileged classes only. Of all that I have seen on this trip abroad, I have been more impressed and more heartened by what seems to be working itself out in Germany in these particulars than on almost anything else.'[41]

These sentiments may give us some insight into the motives behind the introduction of the welfare state in Canada, together with the legal framework established for collective bargaining in the post–Second World War period. Yet, despite these developments, what is in fact surprising about post-1945 Canada is the fact that, unlike almost all western European capitalist states, it has not evolved an institutional mechanism for the integration of the unions in state policy. Whereas other states developed systems of indicative economic planning and incomes policies under which unions are expected to act as agencies of social control over the wage demands of their members, Canada did not. Many reasons might be adduced for this, but a crucial one, raised by the Economic Council itself in its third report, was that there did not exist effective 'corps intermédiaires' in Canada for such a system to operate. It was referring to its doubts that bodies like the CLC and CNTU had the requisite authority over its members to enforce a policy of wage restraint.[42] Rather than union integration, the Canadian state relied on a higher level of unemployment than in Europe to ensure wage moderation.

To be sure, we have seen in recent years an explicit attempt by the federal government at union integration, in the context of an economy beset by high inflation even at levels of unemployment double their post-war rate. That the Canadian labour movement was one of the few in the Western world that turned down participation in a voluntary prices and incomes policy when it was first offered to it (in John Turner's 'consensus' talks), indicates, however, the high degree of scepticism with which Canadian labour has come to view the alleged neutrality of the Canadian state between the classes. It is indeed an indication of a crisis of legitimacy that has come to attend a state that has given as much weight to the function of accumulation, to the neglect of its legitimation role, as has the Canadian. While federal and provincial governments stumbled over one another in rushing to hand out subsidies and grants to foreign subsidiaries, total Canadian social security spending as a percentage of GNP in the post-war period was consistently lower than that of any western European country with the exception of Switzerland, and by the mid-sixties was almost half that of West Germany, the Netherlands, France, and Sweden. And although Canadian social expenditure since that time has increased, so that Canada moved from what one scholar termed a 'welfare state laggard' to a 'middle-range spender,'[43] this has nevertheless taken place in the context of a tax system which while nominally progressive on income tax is in fact regressive when all taxes are taken into consideration. You pay less the more you earn up to $8000 (1969 dollars) when the tax system then becomes, at best, proportional.[44] At the same time there has been a clear trend for revenues on corporate taxation to fall and for taxes on individuals to rise.[45] This means at a time of fiscal squeeze a situation in which the ratio of state benefits received to taxes paid is declining. When one adds to this the effects of inflation on working people, it is perhaps not surprising that we find that days lost in strikes in Canada per 1000 workers has recently been higher than in any country in the West with the exception of Italy, amounting to an average of some five million working days lost and 400,000 strikers per year in the 1970s.

The developing contradictions in the role of the Canadian state are seen at another level in the fact that the folly of promoting national development through foreign ownership is also beginning to catch up with the state. This is seen not only in the recent statement by the president of Chrysler Canada, on the question of whether plants will be shut down in Canada to compensate for falling auto sales in the United States, that tells us that 'blood is thicker than water' and that any decision in this regard will be a 'corporate decision; not a Canadian one';[46] it is also seen in opinion polls which indicate that a majority of the Canadian population favours nationalization of oil and gas production. This too suggests a crisis of legitimacy for a state which, as Syncrude shows, in trying to extricate itself from the dilemma of foreign control, enmeshes itself deeper in it, so that its Foreign Investment Review Agencies are revealed for the empty symbolic exercises they really are.

Both the Canadian oil and gas policy and the highly restrictive statutory incomes policy introduced in the aftermath of the failed 'consensus' talks,[47] indicate the continued emphasis being given by the Canadian state to the accumulation and coercion functions. Moreover, the unity that the Canadian state has been able to forge among the provincial fractions of bourgeoisie around Syncrude, and particularly around the incomes policy despite the incursion it makes into provincial jurisdiction, suggests that the Canadian bourgeoisie is supportive of the state in this regard. Nevertheless, the extent and nature of the opposition of the organized working class to the incomes policy also indicates that class conflict in this country, which has largely been expressed at the industrial level heretofore, is beginning to take on an important political dimension, as evidenced in 1976 in the 22 March mass demonstration on Parliament Hill and the first political nation-wide general strike in Canadian history on 14 October. Although conclusions at this stage must necessarily be highly contingent on many factors, it does appear that the large role played by the state in Canadian society, in the context of industrial militancy, is beginning to lay bare the inconsistency between the apparent legal and political equality of liberal democracy and the socio-economic inequality of a capitalism protected and maintained by the state. But whether this will have immediate radical consequences, rather than stand as the basis for the development of conservatizing corporatist structures, will only be answered in light of the ensuing struggle.

24 Role and nature of the state

NOTES

1 Karl Marx and Friedrich Engels, *Selected Works* (Moscow 1969), I, 110-11
2 Reprinted in Robert Chodos, *The CPR: A Century of Corporate Welfare* (Toronto 1973), between 54 and 55
3 'Poulantzas and the Capitalist State,' *New Left Review*, 82 (Nov.-Dec. 1973), 85
4 *Capital* (Moscow 1959), III, 376-7
5 *Capital* (Moscow 1961), I, 239, 410 ff., 490
6 *Ibid.*, III, 772
7 *The State in Capitalist Society* (London 1969), 49-55; cf. Miliband, 'The Capitalist State: Reply to Nicos Poulantzas,' *New Left Review*, 59 (Jan.-Feb. 1970), 59-60
8 Interview with John P. Wallach, in *Genesis*, I, 3 (Oct. 1973), 117
9 See *Political Power and Social Classes* (London 1973), especially 275-321.
10 'Poulantzas and the Capitalist State,' 87-8. For the full debate between them, see the articles by Poulantzas and Miliband on 'The Problem of the Capitalist State' in R. Blackburn, ed., *Ideology in Social Science* (London 1972), 238-62; also E. Laclau, 'The Specificity of the Political: The Poulantzas-Miliband Debate,' *Economy and Society*, IV, 1 (Feb. 1975), 87-110; and Poulantzas, 'The Capitalist State: A Reply to Miliband and Laclau,' *New Left Review*, 95 (Jan.-Feb. 1976), 63-83.
11 *The Fiscal Crisis of the State* (New York 1973), 6
12 'Karl Marx's Contribution to Historiography,' in Blackburn, *Ideology in Social Science*, 273-4
13 See, in this regard, S.M. Lipset, *Agrarian Socialism: The Cooperative Commonwealth Federation in Saskatchewan* (rev. ed., New York 1968), chap. 12; and John Porter, *The Vertical Mosaic: An Analysis of Social Class and Power in Canada* (Toronto 1965), Chap. 14.
14 On Alberta, in addition to C.B. Macpherson's *Democracy in Alberta: Social Credit and the Party System* (2nd ed., Toronto 1962), see J.R. Mallory, *Social Credit and the Federal Power in Canada* (Toronto 1954); on Quebec, see H. Guindon, 'Social Unrest, Social Class, and Quebec's Bureaucratic Revolution,' *Queen's Quarterly*, LXXI, 2 (Summer 1964).
15 See, in this regard, D.V. Smiley, *Canada in Question: Federalism in the Seventies* (Toronto 1972), and R. Simeon, *Federal-Provincial Diplomacy: The Making of Recent Policy in Canada* (Toronto 1972).
16 See Gustavus Myers, *A History of Canadian Wealth* (Toronto 1972), 265-6; R.T. Naylor, 'The Rise and Fall of the Third Commerical Empire of the St Lawrence,' in Gary Teeple, ed., *Capitalism and the National Question in Canada* (Toronto 1972), 17-18; and Chodos, *CPR*, 20-1.

17 'The Changing Social Origins of the Canadian Industrial Elite, 1880-1910,' in B. Porter and R. Cuff, eds., *Enterprise and National Development* (Toronto 1973), 72

18 See G. Hougham, 'The Background and Development of National Parties,' in H.G. Thorburn, ed., *Party Politics in Canada* (Scarborough 1972), 2-3; cf. M. Duverger, *Political Parties* (London 1964), xxxiv.

19 J. Lele, G.C. Perlin, and H.G. Thorburn, 'The National Party Convention,' in Thorburn, *ibid.*, 107-8

20 Quoted in Porter, *Vertical Mosaic*, 430

21 *Ibid.*, 431

22 *The Canadian Corporate Elite*: *An Analysis of Economic Power* (Toronto 1975), 346

23 Quoted in Chodos, *CPR*, 16-17

24 See especially R. Deaton, 'The Fiscal Crisis and the Revolt of the Public Employee,' *Our Generation*, VIII, 4 (Oct. 1972), 11-51.

25 See H.G.J. Aitken, "Defensive Expansionism: The State and Economic Growth in Canada,' in W.T. Easterbrook and M.H. Watkins, eds., *Approaches to Canadian Economic History* (Toronto 1967), 183-4.

26 C.B. Macpherson, 'The Social Sciences,' in Julian Park, ed., *The Culture of Contemporary Canada* (Toronto 1957), 200-1

27 *The Labour Outlook* (London 1929), 32

28 *The Politics of Development: Forests, Mines & Hydro-Electric Power in Ontario, 1849-1941* (Toronto 1974), 248-9, 490, ix

29 'Changing Social Origins,' 72

30 Quoted in David Wolfe, 'Political Culture, Economic Policy and the Growth of Foreign Investment in Canada, 1945-57,' unpublished MA thesis, Carleton University, Ottawa, 1973, p. 120

31 J.W. Dafoe, *Laurier: A Study in Canadian Politics* (1922, Toronto 1963), 53

32 'Another Anti-Trust Tradition: Canadian Anti-Combines Policy, 1884-1910,' in Porter and Cuff, *Enterprise*, 39

33 See H.G. Thorburn, 'Pressure Groups in Canadian Politics: Recent Revisions of the Anti-Combines Legislation,' *Canadian Journal of Economics and Political Science*, XXX, 2 (May 1964), 157-74; G. Rosenbluth and Thorburn, 'Canadian Anti-Combines Administration, 1952-1960,' *ibid.*, XXVII, 4 (Nov. 1961); and Bert Young, 'Corporate Interests and the State,' *Our Generation*, X, 1 (Winter-Spring 1974), 70-83.

34 One must, of course, be careful not to minimize this aspect of the Canadian state's behaviour. For instance, the federal government established in 1919, amidst the economic dislocations and labour unrest of the immediate post-war period, a Board of Commerce to regulate price increases and curb unfair trade

practices. There is little reason to doubt T.D. Traves' view of the board's success: 'Preservation of the basic components of the existing economic order and integration of disruptive social forces in the established political economy were, broadly speaking, its tasks. In these aims it was partially successful. As a contemporary observer said, " ... in a general sense public opinion was soothed and the people carried more smoothly over the rocky road of war prices and reconstruction problems than would otherwise have been the case." The expansion of the Canadian state then, in this case, was intended, and in fact operated in a manner which was fundamentally conservative.' 'The Board of Commerce and the Canadian Sugar Refining Industry: A Speculation on the Role of the State in Canada,' *Canadian Historical Review*, LIV, 2 (June 1974), 174-5. No less significant, however, was the fact that the Board of Commerce failed to become a permanent element on the political scene, having been allowed by the government to wither away barely a year after its establishment.

35 For a history of Canada's snail-like progress in the field of social welfare legislation, see Kathleen Herman, 'The Emerging Welfare State: Changing Perspectives in Canadian Welfare Policies and Programs, 1867-1960,' in D.I. Davies and K. Herman, eds., *Social Space: Canadian Perspectives* (Toronto 1971), 131-41.

36 *Industry and Humanity* (1918, Toronto 1973), 336

37 See, in this regard, Leo A. Johnson, 'The Development of Class in Canada in the Twentieth Century,' in Teeple, *Capitalism and the National Question*, 142-53.

38 Quoted in J. Pickersgill, *The Mackenzie King Record, 1939-1944* (Toronto 1960), I, 570-1

39 *Full Employment in a Free Society, A Report* (London 1945). For an attestation to Beveridge's impact on Canada, see A. Brady, 'The State and Economic Life in Canada,' in K.J. Rea and J.T. McLeod, eds., *Business and Government in Canada* (Toronto 1969), 66.

40 'Planning Full Employment,' *The Times*, 23 Jan. 1943

41 29 June 1937, quoted in the *Citizen*, Ottawa, 11 Jan. 1975

42 Economic Council of Canada, *Third Annual Review: Prices, Productivity and Employment* (Ottawa 1966), 160-1; cf. Gilles Paquet, 'The Economic Council as Phoenix,' in T. Lloyd and J. McLeod, eds., *Agenda 1970: Proposals for a Creative Politics* (Toronto 1968), 135-58

43 See Harold L. Wilensky, *The Welfare State and Equality* (Berkely 1975), Table 2, pp. 30-1, and Table 4, pp. 122-4; and his 'The Welfare Mess,' *Society*, XIII, 4 (May-June 1976), 12-16, 64. I am indebted to Professor Wilensky for making his findings on recent changes in Canada's relative expenditure position available to me in advance of publication.

44 See Allan M. Maslove, *The Pattern of Taxation in Canada* (Ottawa 1972).

45 See Deaton, 'Fiscal Crisis,' Table 6, p. 33.

46 Ronald Todgham, quoted in the *Financial Post*, 25 Jan. 1975

47 For a fuller discussion of the Canadian incomes policy and the ambiguous CLC response to it, see Leo Panitch, *Workers, Wages and Controls* (Toronto 1976), reprinted in *This Magazine*, x, 1 (Feb.-March 1976); and 'The CLC Labour Manifesto: Is Corporatism a Strategy for Labour?' *ibid.*, x, 5-6 (Nov.-Dec. 1976).

2
Images of the state in Canada

REG WHITAKER

To understand what the state has been and is becoming in Canada it is necessary to understand what Canadians have thought the state to be. To develop a Marxist analysis of the Canadian state it is necessary to understand what the social classes generated by capitalist development have thought the state to be. To those, Marxist and non-Marxist alike, with a vulgar understanding of materialism, these statements may appear paradoxical. They are not at all paradoxical, in truth, but basic and crucial.

It is obvious that Marxist analysis must be made concrete in the historical specificity of particular nations and particular political economies. The mechanical application of concepts drawn exclusively from the European historical experience quickly comes to grief in the North American environment even at the level of economic structures. More importantly, for my purposes, is the fact that historical specificity is a *cultural*, as well as an economic, phenomenon. To analyse the objective economic interests of a class leads in no automatic sense to a grasp of the actual historical behaviour of that class. The crucial intervening variable is the individual perception by members of that class of their objective interests, as well as their capacity to develop appropriate collective forms of behaviour to achieve concrete objectives set by their conception of their class interests. And it is precisely at this point that cultural, ideological, and political factors assert a certain irreducible autonomy. To argue that the individual's behaviour is merely a reflection of his position in relation to the economic base is altogether unscientific, in the absence of any demonstrated concrete linkages between the base and the behaviour of individuals.

One never sees the world innocently or naïvely. How we interpret the sensory data upon which we base our actions is the product of our past experience; that experience structures and filters what we perceive. Historical specificity resides not only in the particular economic structures thrown up by particular geographic factors, historical timing, technological levels, and world market conditions, but also in the peculiarity and uniqueness of particular cultural mixes – national experiences – which prestructure the perceptions by classes and individuals of the objective economic factors. The point is that an inquiry into the specificity of any particular nation and its unique set of class forces must be approached with a truly open mind; forms of class behaviour cannot be presumed. It is instead necessary to understand the totality of determining factors, cultural, ideological, and political, as well as the material forces (determining in the 'last instance' as Louis Althusser puts it[1]), which bear on any specific historical situation. Hence the quest for 'images' or conceptualizations of the state in Canadian historical development, the glass through which Canadians have looked in understanding their collective organization as a nation, their definition and delimitation of the public realm from the private, and the meaning of the public realm for their own, class, interests.

One further theoretical point must be made at the outset. O'Connor's functions of the capitalist state – accumulation and legitimation, along with the coercion function identified by Panitch in the preceding essay – do not lend themselves equally to the same forms of analysis. Coercion is a classical state function, central to the very definition of the state by Max Weber, among others.[2] It is particularly in areas outside the state system as such, in the identification of the coercive nature of market relations of production and in the subjugation of the working class to the exploitation of the labour market, that Marxist analysis diverges strikingly from liberal thinking.[3] The accumulation and legitimation functions require more specific attention.

First, for accumulation: Marxist economic science demonstrates that there is a developmental logic of capitalism and that it is possible to situate specific state activities in relation to that logic. In retrospect it becomes clear that such and such an action did, or did not, contribute to capital accumulation, and thus did, or did not, contribute to the unfolding of the logic of capitalist development in history. In this sense, when examining accumulation, the perceptions of the individual actors are of lesser significance than the actions themselves. To this extent the accumulation function is objective and measurable in quantitative terms. There is another sense in which this breaks down. For example, accumulation policies which fail to maintain business confidence, however irrational that elusive state of mind may be, will undoubtedly fail. Thus subjective consciousness becomes a factor intimately involved in an objective process, objectively measurable.

This is even more pertinent when discussing legitimation. To understand the concept of legitimation one must understand what people *believe to be true*. To understand the legitimation component of the state's interventions, we must deal with motives, beliefs, forms of consciousness, all of which means resorting to historical evidence which is squarely 'ideological' in nature – what people said as well as what people did. To push the point further, what people held to be true must be taken with considerable seriousness, not because this is truth in a scientific sense, but quite simply because they believed it to be true, and acted upon it. Finally, it is manifestly impossible to separate the accumulation and legitimation functions into two insulated spheres. It is precisely in the interrelation of these functions that the specificity of the Canadian state may be discerned.

The enterprise I am thus proposing is a type of intellectual history of the successive images or conceptualizations of the state in Canada. It is intellectual history inasmuch as it rests upon articulated statements of historical actors, yet it is, I think, also Marxist to the extent that I situate these intellectual developments within the context of changing class forces and the development of capitalist market structures. Marx himself wrote that man makes his own history, but only with such materials as are at hand. Perhaps Claude Lévi-Strauss has posed the problem best: 'The sense in which infrastructures are primary is this: first, man is like a player who, as he takes his place at the table, picks up cards which he has not invented, for the card-game is a datum of history and civilization. Second, each deal is the result of a contingent distribution of cards, unknown to the players at the time. One must accept the cards which one is given, but each society, like each player, makes its interpretations in terms of several systems. These may be common to them all or individual: rules of the game or rules of tactics. And we are well aware that different players will not play the same game with the same hand even though the rules set limits on the games that can be played with any given one.'4

Canada was in its origins not merely a *new* society, but a *transplanted* society. The so-called 'fragment' theory of new societies developed by Louis Hartz and applied to Canada by Gad Horowitz and Kenneth McRae,5 while hopelessly idealist from a Marxist perspective, does offer some insights into the importance of the inherited ideological legacy, the political baggage, which the founders of the colonies brought with them, whether directly from France, England, or America, or indirectly through the heavily imperialist socialization and educational process in the colonial era. New France, with its feudal and authoritarian structures, protected by the barrier of the French language and the hegemony of the Catholic clergy in educational and cultural matters, diverged from its earliest beginnings in significant ways from the rest of English-speaking North America, a divergence to which the English Conquest gave only a particular form. Yet as early as 1789, with the French Revolution and the triumph of bourgeois and anti-clerical forces within the former motherland, Quebec was in many important ways to be isolated from the currents of thought and development in the French-speaking world of Europe. In the English-Canadian colonies, on the other hand, the influence of British culture and ideas, not to speak of the American impact, remained at a surprisingly high level throughout the nineteenth century. Thus in the case of English Canada, to which I intend to devote most of my attention, the images of the state were deeply indebted to the old world, as well as to the new world rising to the south. English Canadians saw themselves most often in borrowed mirrors.

In the English-speaking world of the late eighteenth and nineteenth centuries, the concept of the state was undergoing a major transformation under the combined impact of the political changes released first in the American Revolution and, more importantly, the French Revolution, and then in the Industrial Revolution in England. This change has been seen most characteristically, but not very illuminatingly, in liberal terms: the emancipation of the productive energies of the bourgeoisie from mercantilist economic controls and the remnants of feudal privilege, and the securing of an ever-increasing share of political liberties from the encroachments of autocratic state power. In fact, the triumph of laissez-faire and free-trade ideology in England can now be seen as the coincidence of classical political economy as a science and the interests of England as the first industrial nation, with everything to gain from maintaining other national competitors in a position of inferiority on the world market. By the late nineteenth century it was becoming apparent that the English concept of the state and its role in national economic life was peculiarly limited and idiosyncratic. Yet the 'English model' was itself somewhat less monolithic from the beginning than standard liberal treatments might lead us to believe. Indeed, an important variant in the English tradition was of unusual importance in Canada in helping to shape the ultimate Canadian rejection of free trade and laissez-faire as the defining image of the state. That variant has been most often termed 'Toryism.'

The concept of the state as it emerged in the era of political and industrial revolution was always bound up with two other concepts, sometimes openly but more often, in England, surreptitiously; *nation* and *class*. In historical retrospect the French Revolution may as importantly mark the emergence of modern nationalism and the centralizing features of nationalist sentiment as it did the emergence of radical democratic and egalitarian

ideas. The sweeping away of local particularisms by the centralist nationalism of the Jacobins and Napoleon, and the burst of political and military
energies unleashed in this process, rearranged the map of Europe and set
change and renovation in motion everywhere it touched. The power of the
nation-state, the integral identity of the cultural, linguistic, and ethnic community with the apparatus of a centralized state with its unified political,
economic, and military arms, was posed as an unanswerable challenge to
the ramshackle edifice of particularisms which was the Europe of the time.
But if the integration of the concepts of the state and the nation emerged
from the French Revolution, so too did the concept of class conflict and the
challenge from the dominated classes to the established order. This challenge, still somewhat diffuse and inarticulate in revolutionary France, took
concrete form in England with the creation of a working class in the factories of the Industrial Revolution and the growth of indigenous working-
class organizations to defend and advance the interests of workers within a
capitalist system which enforced wage-slavery upon all who were compelled
to sell their own labour power to the profit of the owners of industry. The
appearance of class conflict, as a structural contradiction of capitalist society, posed the question of *whose* nation and *whose* state?

Despite the hegemony of laissez-faire liberalism in England in the nineteenth century, the Tory tradition differed significantly over the very questions of nation and class. Common ground within the English-speaking
world lay in the fundamental distinction made since at least the seventeenth
century between *society* and *state*. 'Society' was not necessarily the same as
'nation,' but was a broader concept including the economic relations, social
institutions such as church and school, and even elements of the legal system, such as common law and prescriptive rights such as *habeas corpus*. All
of these were set against the concept of the state, which was a narrower construct involving the government – monarch, lords, and commons – and the
administration. This distinction took concrete form in the American constitution, embodying as it did the concept that the people (society) contracted
to form a government (state) while reserving for themselves certain rights
which were to remain beyond the reach of the state thus created. This state-
society dichotomy tended to distinguish the English-speaking world from
that of the European continent, where the idea of the state as the summation of the economic, social, cultural, as well as political, spheres was more
generally prevalent, as is best exemplified in the universal homogenous state
in the thought of Hegel. In the English-speaking world, universalism gave
way to more individualist and even particularist conceptions of man-
versus-the-state.

Yet an emphasis on individualism and particularity left open a considerable range of controversy concerning the question of the linkage between the individual interest and the national interest. There is a sense in which the chief problematic in the confrontation between liberalism and Toryism in the nineteenth century lay in this question. To good liberals, schooled in the Manchester mode of classical political economy, there was the miraculous intervention of the invisible hand of the market mechanism which meshed individual and national interest into a seamless web of economic progress and political stability – so long as the state maintained strictly defined limits of activity. Tories were, to be sure, no less admirers of the market or of the capitalist mode of production; England, after all, had witnessed a smoother transition from aristocracy to bourgeoisie than most European countries were to enjoy, the transition taking the form of class merger which turned traditional conservatism into market conservatism. But what did distinguish Toryism was a less than automatic reliance on the ability of the market to regulate the society without a certain discretionary role for the state.

Moreover, while liberalism experienced no end of trouble with the concept of *class* in an era when liberal thought underwent a subtle change towards more liberal-democratic forms under the pressure of rising working-class demands, leaving unsolved a fundamental contradiction between the political values tending towards egalitarianism and the economic values of the market which were ineradicably inegalitarian,[6] Tory thinking tended to skirt this problem by a more open acceptance of the concept of inequality as a positive political value as well as an economic necessity. Rooted in the older feudal past of hierarchy and the authoritative allocation of roles in society, Tories tended to be much more explicitly in favour of class inequality as an end as well as a means. Liberals were more ambivalent and, in a sense, more deceptive about the inequality of capitalism. Hence the bad faith in which a thoughtful liberal like John Stuart Mill attempted to rationalize the subordination of the working class, a subordination which unsettled his conscience even as it spurred his apologetics.

On the question of the *nation*, liberals were again more ambivalent than Tories. Certainly the English nation was the forum or framework within which capitalist development took place, and liberalism became a sort of national ideology of a triumphant industrial England selling its high-priced manufactured goods in world markets. Yet at the same time free trade and laissez-faire did have certain internationalist implications, and there was one school of thought which saw the market as a kind of universal solvent of human differences.[7] Tories, again rooted in a more particularist past, were inclined to view the English nation as the highest stage of political development, a fusion of the social and economic hierarchy with the cultural particularity of the English language and English traditions.

It is easy to generalize too far about differences which were not always classifiable into polar camps. But the central area of contention – the question of the linkage between individual and national interest – was a serious problem of a market society, about which the bourgeoisie itself could readily disagree without in any sense calling into question the capitalist mode of production. The Tory view, reflecting the persistence of aristocratic, pre-industrial elements, with its emphasis on the need for more conscious order and control over the processes of a market society, was rather easily dismissed in the nation which experienced the first Industrial Revolution amid the sundering of the older mercantilist restrictions on trade and anachronistic feudal residues in legislation and custom. When Mill termed the Tories the 'stupid party,' he only echoed much respectable opinion among his educated countrymen. But in the transfer of cultural and political baggage to the British North American colonies, Toryism found an environment in which, rather paradoxically considering the absence of a feudal past, it was to play a more important role as a legitimizing ideology of capitalist development than it ever did in its English homeland. In colonial Canada, both inherited Tory images and the learned experience of development in the peculiar circumstances of that time and place led to a domination of the Tory image of the state over the more liberal laissez-faire concept prevalent in the imperial metropolis.

The first and perhaps most crucial point to be made is that in English Canada, and particularly in Upper Canada, which was to play the most dynamic role in national development well into the twentieth century, the bourgeoisie was not a class which emerged out of a struggle with feudalism and then recreated the world in its own image in the aftermath of its triumph, as had happened in Europe; the emergence of the bourgeoisie was instead itself the result of a conscious policy or plan, enacted through the agency of the imperial and colonial state apparatuses. The indigenous roots of the Canadian bourgeoisie were from the beginning linked closely to the imperialist-mercantilist framework which nurtured the exotic plant in new soil. The history of colonial Canada may be seen as an interaction of a series of plans, dreams, and prefabricated 'societies' with the realities of the actual human and economic resources which alone could give concrete shape to these blueprints. As Gilles Paquet has written: 'In fact the word "dream" catches one of the basic ingredients of Canadian economic development. Canada has been significantly influenced in its evolution by a series of "dreams" ... by a long list of these magnificent projects and ideas, many of which also proved magnificent failures.'[8]

The point which needs emphasizing, at a time when everyone – from popular historians of the 'national dream' to self-proclaimed progressives who laud the 'public enterprise' culture of Canada – has done his utmost to mystify the actual tradition of state activity,[9] is that from the earliest beginnings the dreams and plans which were applied to the raw material of British North American society had far more to do with the creation of a viable national bourgeoisie with all its attendant paraphernalia of privilege and luxury than it had to do with a 'public sector.' In this process the public domain had a role to play, but it was always a decidedly ancillary role.

Not only did the early Loyalist settlers bear with them the usual bitterness of émigrés towards the ideas and symbols of the revolutionary nation from which they had fled – nurturing an anti-Americanism, not to speak of anti-democratic sentiments, which were to remain persistent features of Canadian political life – but this basic strain was consolidated and encouraged by the ideological mission of the Colonial Office. As S.F. Wise has strikingly demonstrated, the new generation of colonial administrators following the American and French revolutions represented a new hardened and rationalized conservatism.[10] Faced with the radical and democratic implications of the French Revolution in particular, English opinion turned sharply rightward, especially during the Napoleonic wars when a blanket of McCarthyite-type conformism and anti-revolutionary zeal settled over political debate. The colonial administrators came to Canada armed with a mission to build a conservative, un-American, and undemocratic society in the northern half of the continent. In this mission the conservatism of Edmund Burke, who had alerted the opinion of right-thinking Englishmen, noble and bourgeois alike, to the dangers inherent in the revolutionary enterprise in Paris as early as 1790, proved to be a most valuable resource.

To understand the power of Burkean conservatism, it is first necessary to disabuse oneself of much conventional nonsense on the subject. Burke was in no sense a traditionalist who harked back to a defunct feudal past. On the contrary, it was Burke whom Adam Smith singled out as the only man to have come independently to the same conclusions about the workings of the market economy as Smith himself. Indeed, Burke was a Malthusian enthusiast for the abolition of all state charity and the final triumph of the 'great wheel of commerce' as the sole organizing principle of economic life.[11] But Burke also quickly discerned the inherent contradiction concerning liberty and equality concealed within the assumptions of market society, and became the most influential opponent of the egalitarian and democratic tendencies within the French experiment in liberal revolution. Burke's solution to the dilemma was to resurrect the idea of traditional authority ('the bank and capital of nations and of ages') as a kind of shell, within which the new subordination of wage-labourer to employer would be masked by the customary subordination of peasant to lord ('the coat of prejudice' as Burke nicely put it).[12] Although Burke himself was rarely quoted directly, it was the spirit of his rationalized, hard-nosed philosophy with its fusion of market liberalism and anti-democratic conservatism which served early colonial Canada as a blueprint for the nature of the society to be created.

The 'better America' to be erected to the north of the United States would be one which pursued economic growth with all the enthusiasm of market man unbound by tradition, yet at the same time sought, as a positive goal of public policy, the creation of a hierarchical society where privilege was resistant to the demands of those less fortunate. The 'state,' such as it was, would be an instrument of economic development, understood always as both the growth of production and the consequent differentiation of society into classes specializing in the different aspects of the productive process, with vastly differentiated rewards. The conventional wisdom of the colonial administrators and the dominant local forces in strictly political terms was the so-called balanced Whig constitution of the eighteenth century, with its division of power between monarch, lords, and commons. In fact, it quickly became apparent that, given the 'immaturity' of the frontier population, the subordination of the colony to Britain, and the thinness of local 'aristocracy,' the balanced Whig constitution would turn out to be rather unbalanced in the direction of the executive. Upper Canada thus began its constitutional history in an atmosphere of considerable executive authority, buttressed by deep ideological hostility to the principle of popular representation and the urgent sense of a need to create a dominant class of privilege and power to which colonial interests could be entrusted. In the blank slate of North American frontier development, this obviously meant a bourgeoisie without any particular stamp of tradition or birth – capital and wealth alone would be its emblem. In the particular circumstances of Canada it further meant a bourgeoisie which would be parasitic upon the colonial state apparatus from which its privileges arose. It was a peculiar combination.

Land distribution policy was a major instrument in the implementation of this Burkean blueprint. Land was, of course, at this time the chief economic resource of a frontier colony and the chief attraction to draw immigration from Europe. Both the reservation of extensive tracts of land to the clergy (as a means of providing an economic base for an established church which would act as an authoritative centre of control over moral and educational development) and the attempt to maintain artificially high land prices (to help create a landed bourgeoisie), had the long-range goal of creating a landless proletariat which would have to sell its wage labour to the nascent bourgeoisie. As Marx pointed out in refutation of the land theories of Gibbon Wakefield, a figure of some significance in colonial Canadian thinking, the necessity of colonial regimes to intervene in the land market to keep the lower orders landless was 'the secret discovered in the new world by the Political Economy of the old world, and proclaimed on the house-tops: that the capitalist mode of production and accumulation, and therefore capitalist private property, have for their fundamental condition the annihilation of self-earned private property; in other words, the expropriation of the labourer.'[13] Proclaiming the secret from the house-tops was an activity quite congenial to the dominant Tory figures in the colony who never made much attempt to hide their design for creating hierarchy and preventing equality. But shouting does not in itself achieve the purpose. The land scheme turned out to be one of the failed social blueprints, of which there were to be many more. The intractably mobile nature of the population, the inability to control a factor of production as abundant as land in the new world, the failure of the emergent bourgeoisie to provide employment for landless labourers, and not least the decided tendency of the privileged 'aristocrats' to turn land into a quick and easy source of profit by selling their landed interests to the highest bidder, all contributed to the early demise of the entire scheme, as it was at first envisioned.[14]

By the 1820s and 1830s there had emerged in Upper Canada a locally based ruling clique attached to the state apparatus. The Family Compact was a summation of both economic and political power in the rudimentary forms in which these elements appeared. By no means lacking in political talent, in the person of such conservative operatives as Bishop Strachan (the Richelieu of colonial clerical politics) and John Beverley Robinson, the Family Compact was not averse to economic enterprise, especially of an infrastructural nature such as the Welland Canal project or the Bank of Upper Canada. Despite the romanticizations of liberal and left-wing historians, the unanswerable fact remains that the Tories were able to mobilize popular sentiment and votes just as often as their opponents. The image of the Family Compact as an unpopular minority foisting itself upon a hostile mass of citizenry simply does not fit the facts. Toryism had roots in the population; the Tory image of the state had resonance and persistence, not simply

among the ranks of the privileged but among the poorer citizenry as well.
The emergence of a ruling alliance of political and administrative notables
with nascent mercantile and commercial capital, the latter dependent upon
the former and often synonymous with them, with widespread popular support from below, whether based on ethnic-religious identification – as in the
case of the Irish Protestants mobilized into the Orange Lodges – or on a de-
ferential interpretation of economic self-interest, all begin to give flesh and
blood to a type of Tory hierarchical society which, while different from the
original blueprint, was nevertheless strikingly divergent from the American
model.

Toryism thus demonstrated a kind of Hamiltonian model of national
economic development, within an imperialist framework, at the very time
when Hamiltonianism was crumbling under the assaults of laissez-faire capitalist development in the United States. Politically, moreover, the Tory
model specifically called for a state apparatus and a governmental superstructure which would directly reflect the inegalitarian social structure
which capitalist development was slowly consolidating, in sharp contrast to
the rise of Jeffersonian and later Jacksonian democracy to the south.

Toryism was not reducible simply to an economic doctrine masquerad-
ing as a philosophy. The Tory mind involved certain elements which fitted
it well for the exercise of national economic development, even while undermining the effectiveness of Tories in industrial Britain. The emphasis on
control of the processes of national development, the element of the collective will of the dominant class expressed through the public institutions of
the state, while seemingly anachronistic in an increasingly laissez-faire Britain, was crucially relevant to a thinly settled frontier colony struggling on
the fringes of a growing economic and political power to the south. A quotation from a letter written by Bishop Strachan in 1830 on the subject of an
established church perhaps indicates best the quality of this Tory paternal-
ist mission: 'In regard to Christianity, it may be remarked, that the sponta-
neous demand of human beings for a knowledge of its truths, is far short of
the actual interest which they have in them ... it is just as necessary to create a hunger as it is to minister a positive supply ... Nature does not go
forth in search of Christianity, but Christianity goes forth to knock at the
door of nature, and, if possible, to awaken her out of her sluggishness.'[15] In
short, Toryism began with an acceptance of man's fallen nature which led
to a type of activism on the part of national leaders to counteract this en-
tropic nature by control and direction. It is in the will and purpose of the
leading elements that the state and the nation find definition.

The emergence of a ruling group around certain privileged economic interests was bound to rouse the opposition of elements which felt excluded from the process. The fact that opposition reached such proportions by 1837 that an attempted revolution was mounted is certainly evidence of discontent. Yet the rapid and, it must be said, somewhat ignoble collapse of the 'revolutionary' forces points in another direction, one which sits very poorly with the current revisionist school of left-wing nationalist history. The class base of the grouping led by William Lyon Mackenzie and his associates is not easily placed within a simple framework of social conflict. Small property-holding farmers and landless elements from the towns and villages employed as artisans or labourers appear to have made up the ranks. Yet these class elements themselves were drawn from the larger population in a somewhat complicated manner. Cross-cutting cleavages of religion and ethnicity, not to speak of locality, do little to clarify the picture. An examination of the ideas with which the rebels armed themselves results in yet more confusion. Mackenzie himself, now a hero of the nationalist left, managed to lead a strike-breaking cartel of employers against an attempt by his own printers at his newspaper to organize themselves, as well as to call for the virtual annexation of Canada to the United States in 1838. In fact, the ideological incoherence of Mackenzie is such that, like Thomas Jefferson, he can be quoted every which way on every issue. It would not be difficult, although scarcely illuminating, to devote an entire volume to selections of his writings which would create an image of his thought altogether opposite to that put forward by some currently fashionable selections.[16] At best one may surmise both from Mackenzie himself, and from some of the popular resolutions and other documents which emerged at the time of the rebellion, that the radicalism of Upper Canada centred around a Jeffersonian subspecies of laissez-faire, based on a perception of a simple market economy of independent commodity producers striving for self-sufficiency but ensnared in the meshes of financial and merchant capital and the privileges of those whose class positions allowed them close association with the state apparatus. There were indeed powerful reasons for making such a case. The fundamental basis of any rejection of Tory capitalist hegemony in the new colony would naturally rest on the one significant class force whose interests could not be accommodated within the projected scheme of economic and class development: the independent family farmers, who made up the vast bulk of the colonial population and who were the crucial factor in the colonial mode of production, which was mainly agricultural.

To the extent that 1837 represented the first and most violent confrontation between the grande bourgeoisie and the petite bourgeoisie, it set the tone for a century of class conflict in English Canada. Mechanical replica-tions of particular European class struggles tend to miss the specificity of this peculiarly North American situation.[17] The frontier theory of North American development has long since disclosed its limitations, but an emphasis on the frontier does point to one crucial factor for Marxist analysis: the development in a context where land was inevitably cheap and labour inevitably dear – at least by European standards – of a mode of production reliant on the family farm as a productive unit and thus on the farmers as the most significant subordinate class. Ideologically, this class confrontation took on a form which was altogether different from the European experience. Since the struggle was mainly between different *forms* of property rather than between the propertied and the unpropertied, the complexities of ideological conflict are particularly difficult to disentangle.

Most importantly, one may distinguish a crucial and profound ambiguity in the world-view of the farmer, derived directly from the ambiguity of his class position as both proprietor of his own means of production and the source of the labour required for production. The farmer in a sense combined the class antagonists of capitalism within his own person. To the colonial farmer this ambiguity was manifested in his vulnerability to the money economy and the penetrative power of financial and mercantile capital over his simple market society. From the beginnings of colonial agricultural production, the credit market was a factor tending towards class conflict. Farmers were more often than not debtors. The money economy was thus the fatal flaw in the idealized image of the yeoman colony. Paper currency, manipulated by a shadowy and privileged class of finance capitalists, was a mechanism whereby the fruits of the labour of independent farmers were appropriated by idle speculators and predatory pseudo-aristocrats. An obsessive concern with currency questions has always been a characteristic of petit-bourgeois radicalism in this country. When Mackenzie's draft constitution for an independent Upper Canada included a clause forbidding mercantile and banking corporations, this in a sense summed up the strivings of independent commodity producers attempting, albeit in a mystified manner, to gain full control over the conditions of their own production within a restored simple market economy.[18]

Yet to the extent that it was financial capital and the state, rather than capitalism itself, which they identified as the enemy, the farmers could never hope to control the real forces which held them in thrall. Witness the débâcle in the United States, where the Jacksonian Democrats destroyed the Bank of the United States – a Hamiltonian fusion of economic power and political privilege – under the banner of hard currency theories and petit-bourgeois resentments, only to bring about the proliferation of state banks whose inflationary paper currencies not only contributed to destabilizing business cycles but formed the basis for the triumph of unchecked speculative capitalism. Mackenzie himself, in American exile following the defeat of 1837-8, conceived a strong revulsion against the face which Jacksonian democracy presented by the 1840s. The point is that the farmers were confused, and that their confusion arose more from their class position than from their own tactical mistakes. This ambiguity is further demonstrated by the weakness of the revolutionary mobilization, and the deep cleavages which ran through the subordinate class. In Lower Canada, the reinforcement of ethnicity and culture transformed the struggle into a much more serious patriotic upheaval of the French against their English conquerors. In Upper Canada the lines were not drawn so clearly, and in the absence of a 'national' struggle by a local mercantile elite against restrictive imperial controls over commerce – as had happened in the Thirteen Colonies to the south in 1776 – class confrontation which would transform the political economy could not take shape. In the Maritime colonies there was not even a movement, let alone an actual armed struggle. Toryism emerged triumphant from Canada's one near-revolutionary situation.

The triumph of Toryism in Lower Canada meant the defeat of liberal French-Canadian nationalism and the reconfirmation of the reactionary elites which had dominated Quebec society in alliance with the Tory merchants and the British administrative class. It also meant a reconfirmation of the tacit bargain struck between these English and French elites following the Conquest, whereby economic development was left to the English capitalists and the spheres of culture and education were left to the Catholic church, which could be expected to preach political quietism and a safe inward-looking cultural nationalism that left the structures of English economic and administrative power untouched. More specifically, this bargain contributed to a long-standing distrust of the state among the Quebec masses. Given the identification of Quebec nationalism with political reaction, the state would appear in two contradictory guises: either it was an instrument for the maintenance of English power and oppression, or if it fell into the hands of French Canadians it could do no more than protect the place of those non-state institutions, particularly the church, whose task was to preserve French culture and identity. In neither case could the state have a positive role in directing the society; it could never be a vehicle for the collective realization of popular national goals. On the other hand, the merchant class of Montreal saw the state confirmed as an instrument for their conquest of the 'empire of the St Lawrence.'

In Upper Canada, the defeat of the rebellion once again demonstrated the power of conservative elitism, although in this case an elitism which had stronger popular roots than the English upper class of Quebec. The emergent concept of the state was one in which accumulation took priority, since the forces which had directed their energies towards the goal of capitalist development around the state as an instrument had been victorious. The Reform demand for economy in government with its somewhat Jeffersonian image of that government which governs least governing best had been expelled from the political stage. In its place was an ideology which benevolently gazed upon the distribution of special privileges, pay-offs, and other forms of corruption, through the instrumentality of the state, to the emergent capitalist interests as a means to accumulation. In one sense, accumulation was legitimation. The two functions cannot be separated in the nineteenth century. The Tory triumph also involved a great deal of secondary non-economic legitimation as well: British loyalty, the identification of conservative elitism as British, and reform as American and hence treasonous. Toryism moreover was illiberal: the state under Tory auspices would be willing to practise coercion at a high level. Indeed, there is a Hobbesian flavour about the Tory notion of the state and the nature of state sovereignty. The power of Toryism was such that there has always been a distinctly Hobbesian flavour to the English-Canadian concept of the state as well. Certainly the readiness of the Canadian state to exercise illiberal powers – as witness the War Measures Act – has deep roots in early colonial history.

This state, focused on accumulation, would play a central role in continental economic development, but the border between the state system and the political system, in Miliband's terms, is exceedingly difficult to draw in this period. The personnel of the state and the personnel of capitalist enterprise were often enough the same. Public office and private profit were two sides of the same phenomenon. One need go no further than Gustavus Myer's *History of Canadian Wealth* to discover how difficult it was to disentangle the 'public' from the 'private' spheres. Given the task of creating a national bourgeoisie, this state of affairs is scarcely surprising. Yet to the extent that such a bourgeoisie was actually developing, a certain amount of differentiation and specialization of labour may be discerned. In the light of Miliband's maxim that in capitalist societies the ruling class rules but does not govern, Canadian experience is paradoxical. While the state was helping bring to birth an indigenous economic ruling class, the state itself was slowly becoming a branch of this same bourgeoisie. In his study of pre-Confederation Canadian bureaucracy, J.E. Hodgetts points out that the leading state personnel in the person of ministers of the Crown were mainly lawyers by profession. Journalists and businessmen were a poor second. Business-men were too dogmatic and self-righteous to be successful in politics: '... the businessman was not embarrassed by his dogmas but clung to them with such tenacity that he was distrusted, even ridiculed, by the lawyers who always outnumbered him in the cabinet. The businessman was always convinced that the problems facing Canada could be easily solved by the application of a few standard policies ... The subtleties and subterfuges of the legal brotherhood who largely dominated the political scene were be-yond his comprehension. He did not understand that in Canadian politics the shortest distance between two points is not a straight line.'[19]

The point is hardly that the state was neutral or independent of business, but rather that there was a functional division of labour involved. At the same time lawyers in politics often used their state positions to gain entry into the higher levels of the bourgeoisie. Moreover, in examining this spe-cialist role for the state in economic life it is important not to mistake the appearance for the substance. The state as such was far too poorly organ-ized, far too ridden with political patronage and inefficiency, and far too en-meshed with the private sector, to allow for an autonomous role in direct economic activity. Instead, the state offered an instrumentality for facilitat-ing capital accumulation in private hands, and for carrying out the con-struction of a vitally necessary infrastructure; for providing the Hobbesian coercive framework of public order and enforcement of contract within which capitalist development could alone flourish; and, finally, for commu-nicating the symbols of imperial legitimacy which reinforced the legitimacy of unlimited appropriation in a small number of private hands. The basic engine of development in Canada was to be private enterprise, but it was to be *private enterprise at public expense*. That is the unique national feature of our Tory tradition.

The hegemony of mercantile and financial capital after 1837 did not en-joy a serene reign. Most important, the British were in the very process of abandoning their colonial agents. The campaign against the Corn Laws and the victory of free trade was a devastating blow for the Montreal merchants, as they watched the entire mercantile imperialist framework being casually torn to shreds by the motherland itself. Moreover, the gradual growth of re-sponsible government and the continued resistance of the French-Canadian representatives in the legislature of the united Canadas to assimilation meant that the internal position of Toryism was weakening at the same time. When the Baldwin-Lafontaine Reform ministry was called to office after winning a majority in an election, it was the Tory merchants of Mon-treal who in 1849 rioted and burned the legislative buildings. They then demonstrated their deep allegiance to the British Empire by seeking annexation to the United States.

Despite the apparently darkening horizon, the merchants protested too much. Neither the abandonment of protection by Britain nor the acceptance of responsible government meant the end of capitalist domination. North American colonies when ethnic deadlock in the united Canadas, military fear of the United States, and, above all, the crisis in the capital this time as a modernized version of the old party with strong popular roots both in English Protestant Canada and in French Catholic Quebec. Perhaps the best single characterization of the Macdonald Conservative party is that of Frank Underhill: 'government of the people, by lawyers, for big business.'[20] In any event, it was this party, and its traditional Tory concept of the state, which emerged as the instrument of confederation of the British North American colonies when ethnic deadlock in the united Canadas, military fear of the United States, and, above all, the crisis in the capital markets which demanded a consolidation of all the colonial debts and a political framework which could guarantee future British investments, together called for a fundamental reconstruction of the colonial situation.

The major features of the British North America Act which bear on the shape of the federal state are as follows. The federation was to be highly centralized, in contrast with the United States which had just experienced a civil war. In this connection almost all important economic powers were given to the federal government, as well as all important sources of revenue. Its major role was to provide economic infrastructure, expecially railways. The federal government would in addition have significant constitutional superiority over the provincial governments, including the right to veto provincial legislation. The economics-culture trade-off with French Canada was consolidated in the new Confederation. The recognition that there would be two languages and two cultures had important implications for the concept of the Canadian state. The federal government, as the instrument of national development, was primarily concerned with economics; Canadian nationalism, as such, would be economic nationalism more than any other kind of nationalism. The BNA Act gave official form to a fact which had already been accepted in practice: the Canadian state and the Canadian nation were not one and the same.

The weakness of the instruments of national power may be seen in another way. The manner in which the BNA Act was passed speaks volumes about the political legitimacy of the new 'nationality.' There was, of course, no democratic or popular authority. Canadians never expressed their preferences in the matter; indeed any recourse to popular ratification was assiduously avoided. Only in the province of New Brunswick was there anything like a referendum on Confederation and here the Confederationists lost. This expression of popular will was promptly ignored. There were no 'we, the people' as the authors of state sovereignty. Instead, the BNA Act was an act of the British Parliament, passed on the advice of a small elite of colonial politicians. In fact, the overwhelming bulk of these colonial politicians were strikingly anti-democratic in sentiment, viewing democracy as an American heresy. Macdonald perhaps summed up best the conventional wisdom of the dominant political elites with his clever aphorism that 'the rights of the minority ought to be protected, and the rich are always fewer in number than the poor.'[21] The basic source of authority and legitimacy for the new nation was to be found in the traditional Tory notion of historic continuity with the British Crown. While the Americans had founded a new nationality out of a revolution against the Crown on behalf of popular sovereignty, there would be no such break in Canada. In striking contrast to the Lockean declaration of 'life, liberty, and the pursuit of happiness' as the inalienable rights for which Americans had rebelled against tyranny, the BNA Act in its general grant of powers to the federal government spoke instead in authentically Hobbesian terms of 'peace, order, and good government.'

The political working-out of the constitutional arrangements of Confederation was entrusted to Macdonald's Tory party. To Macdonald a near one-party state would be the best device for integrating the provinces into this heavily centralized system.[22] Patronage, under the personal direction of the prime minister in Ottawa, would be the instrument for building an integrated Tory party and the latter would be the instrument for channelling energies and interests towards the national state. The old Tory notion of a strong central authority linking the private self-interest of the wealthiest and most influential citizens with the national interest would thus be accommodated within the federal state operated by the Conservative party.

The first phase of this plan was the political unification of the colonies. The second, economic, phase was inaugurated with the National Policy of 1878-9. Within a world context of growing challenge to the domination of Britain, which about this time was assuming the form of tariff protection and extensive government activity in Prussia and France, Canada openly broke with British free-trade dogma under a protectionist national development plan which saw the sponsorship of an east-west economy linked by a national railway, industrialization being protected by tariffs, with a captive market in the western prairie hinterland which would provide foreign exchange through wheat exports. Political patronage, pay-offs, and corruption were all central parts of this strategy. For example, tariffs were raised in response to campaign fund donations from manufacturers, thus linking party and state in a single development strategy.

The National Policy represented a clear rejection of liberal laissez-faire in two important senses. The refusal to accept the free-trade dogma of Manchester liberalism was predicated on the grounds of national interest. Macdonald had read and rejected the ideas of the classical political economists. Tories were never in fact sycophantic to liberal Britain when the interests of the Canadian bourgeoisie conflicted with those of the capitalists of the imperialist metropole. A strategy for the industrial development of an emerging economy could not be based on free trade; even the United States had adopted protectionism. Second, the Tories rejected the Victorian liberal conception of public morality, intimately bound up with the notion of the strictly delimited state. To the Grits, the Tories were the 'corruptionists.' A case can be made that to Macdonald corruption was not so much an end in itself but a means to an end, that of national development. Corruption served the function of accumulation.

The Tory state was thus tinged by peculiarities of the Tory tradition, the strengths of which may help to explain the extraordinary success of that party throughout the late nineteenth century. There was a significant strain within the Liberal party which saw the world as a grim Newtonian universe of inexorable laws, mainly derived from the Manchester school of the dismal science of economics. To Macdonald it was rather a universe of contingencies, one in which men could make their own history, in defiance of the 'inevitable' laws of historic development. It was that element of will and purpose which perhaps commended Macdonald to the electors of a developing nation.

The system which Macdonald helped create was given its ultimate compliment when the Liberals under Laurier assumed national office in 1896: they simply took it over and in fact made it work better than it ever had under the Conservatives. World conditions happened to be more encouraging at this time, and the Liberals benefited from this happy circumstance to extend the National Policy into a wider imperialist framework, with an imperial preference system as an added inducement to industries to locate in Canada in order to sell to the extensive hinterland regions of the empire under preferential rates. By the turn of the century such was the extent of the industrialization and prosperity that Laurier could echo a mood of naïve national confidence: 'the twentieth century belongs to Canada.' A more inept prediction could scarcely be found anywhere in our history.

Although Canada did not dominate the twentieth century, the National

Policy was nevertheless a qualified success; it did, however, have some unexpected consequences. As a 'national' policy it failed to develop a nationalist basis for the state system. And as a strategy for the consolidation of a secure national bourgeoisie it generated, as a dialectical result of its very success, significant class opposition from the farmers and the emerging working class.

The singularly *economic* basis of the instruments of the new nationality which emerged out of Confederation has already been noted. The forced recognition of French language and cultural autonomy and the accommodative relationships established between the political elites of English and French Canada through the dominant party and the federal cabinet – albeit a very unequal accommodation from the point of view of Quebec, bearing in mind the nature of the tacit bargain struck – involved a central ambiguity in the national definition. But this was only one side of the problem. That the new nation remained in a state of partial subordination to Britain and a part of the British Empire meant that in its external status it was equally indeterminate. The Canadian 'nation' was thus curiously indistinct both internally and externally. Yet every attempt to define the nation more clearly in either its internal or external dimensions tended to be divisive.

The first major demands for a new nationality came from the Canada First group. The call for a new identity which would lift the minds of Canadians beyond crass material considerations to a higher cultural plane came mainly from displaced class elements such as artists and intellectuals, many of them attached directly or indirectly to the state apparatus. This later became a major strain of Tory social criticism, amplified into the Imperial Federation movement of the late nineteenth and early twentieth centuries. Again, the leading figures of this movement tended to be those in positions which were 'ideological' – ministers, teachers, writers, such as G.M. Grant, George Parkin, and Stephen Leacock. Economic nationalism and the sordid pay-offs associated with it did not excite the imagination of intellectuals, nor did it offer a secure and prestigious place to those who worked with their minds. But when the Imperialists looked to a cultural or national identity above materialism they looked to their Britishness and their place within a world-wide empire.

Their attempt to found a sentimental or cultural nationalism on imperial ties involved a concept of nationalism which could only alienate French Canada. The emphasis on legitimation through the historical tradition of British rule was bad enough, but much worse were the claims for British racial superiority and the celebration of militarism and the longing for war which characterized much of the imperialist writing and agitation.[23] In advocating some form of imperial federation the Imperialists placed Canada within a larger system of sovereignty. Even if, with the misplaced confidence of the time, they may have believed that Canada would one day rival Britain within the empire, this scheme still left the national question in a state of ambiguity. At the same time, the symbols used to raise national sentiment at home were the very symbols calculated to repel French Canadians.

On the other side of the national question in English Canada in this period, the situation was even worse. Goldwin Smith's *Canada and the Canadian Question* (1891) may be taken as the most reasoned expression of the continentalist response to imperialism. Smith was if anything even more racist and anti-French than the Imperialists. Indeed, one of the most striking charges he could find against the idea of imperial federation was the inclusion of Anglo-Saxons in a system which teemed with non-whites. Smith's alternative was some form of union with the United States which would finally sink the French Canadians into a powerless minority status and pave the way for an eventual 'moral federation' of all the white English-speaking peoples of the world. The Imperialists' overblown sense of the superiority of the British way of life and of British institutions may have blinded them to the advance of American influence through branch-plant investment; Smith positively welcomed the absorption of Canada by the American Empire or at least its reduction to the status of Scotland within the United Kingdom. Neither the imperialist nor the continentalist argument saw Canada as an autonomous and distinctive nation in its own right. What is just as striking is the lack of strongly and consistently argued nationalist positions in this latter sense. Paradoxically enough, the closest one can find to a truly nationalist position in the national debate came from Henri Bourassa, excoriated as a traitor and seditionist by the self-proclaimed patriots of English Canada during the Boer War and the First World War. Repelled by the anti-French sentiments of his English-Canadian countrymen, he looked to a binational, bilingual political association which would be free of foreign entanglements and divisive external loyalties. Such an association would comprise a federal state system based on a fundamental cultural duality.

What is most interesting about the various schools of thought in the national debate is the underlying structural similarity of almost all the arguments. The *nation* and the *state* were not coterminous concepts in Canadian discourse. The concept of cultural nationality and the concept of political or state sovereignty were distinct and analytically separate. Moreover, the idea of differing cultural nations coexisting under a wider political sovereignty – whether French and English within Confederation, or Canada within a wider empire, or the 'moral federation of the English-speaking peoples' – was at the root of most thinking about the national question. Integral nationalism in the European sense, or even in the American sense, in which state sovereignty is synonymous with a single cultural, ethnic, and linguistic nationality, never took decisive shape in this country. The Canadian national state thus lacked one of the most powerful reinforcements known to the modern state – national sentiment and collective cultural identity. What weakened the Canadian state yet further was the fatal trap that every attempt to grasp such a collective definition only drove the internal divisions yet deeper. Even within English Canada itself, the late nineteenth century witnessed a growing regionalism and a drawing-away from national integration under the banner of 'provincial rights.'

This complex of factors came to a head in the 1911 general election. The defeat of reciprocity and the Liberals by a resurgent Tory imperialist wave of jingoism was aided by the Bourassa *nationalistes* in Quebec, the latter financed with New York money. Six years later there was fighting on the streets of Quebec City when the same Tories, in conjunction with Unionist Liberals, imposed conscription upon an unwilling French population. Tory imperialism created the worst internal crisis in Canada since the Riel affair in the 1880s. At the same time, Bourassa *nationalistes* drove English Canadians to an anti-French fury by their insistence upon the bicultural and bilingual nature of Canada. The political force which finally emerged out of this chaos was the Liberal party led by Mackenzie King who was unswerving in his determination to avoid any political innovation or initiative on the part of the federal state if there were the slightest hint of possible division on English-French lines.

The 1911 election was a watershed in another sense as well. The beginnings of massive class confrontation were manifest in the circumstances of an election in which the manufacturers intervened decisively to defeat an attempt at reciprocity with the United States and to reconfirm the National Policy. The full emergence of a national bourgeoisie, not merely financial and commercial but industrial as well, was indicated by the determined manner in which this class threw its weight behind the Conservatives and drove the suddenly heretical Liberals from office. Yet while its fears were centred around the development of free trade and a north-south pull to the east-west economy of the National Policy, the bourgeoisie was at least equally concerned about the rise of western farmers as a viable and vociferous force of opposition to the hegemony of this central Canadian ruling class. In fact, the defeat of the traditionally free-trade Liberals when they finally attempted a move towards reciprocity after fifteen years in office only demonstrated to the farmers that traditional party politics were hopeless. When Union government in 1917 further demonstrated the sham of party rivalry, the farmers were ready to make an epochal break with the old parties and begin the long tradition of third-party protest politics in this country.

It is important to place these developments in some perspective, since so much of the writing on third-party politics has been obscured by the liberal urgency to call these movements 'regional' or 'protest' or 'deviant' – or anything but what they most importantly represented, *class* politics in rejection of the so-called brokerage two-party model. It is also important to realize that the development of class opposition to the national bourgeoisie did not emerge out of nowhere. Rather it emerged from the same process which had created the bourgeoisie itself. The National Policy had envisioned the settling of the prairies and the development of a wheat economy. The creation of a vast agricultural hinterland in the prairies producing a staple export commodity meant the creation of a large concentrated farm population engaged in similar activity with similar interests – the latter distinctly at variance with those of the central Canadian bourgeoisie who wished to exploit the hinterland for its staple crop and for its captive, tariff-protected market for the finished manufactured goods of industrial central Canada. Moreover, to the extent that central Canada – and its hinterland satellites like the mini-metropolis of Winnipeg – did industrialize, at the same time an industrial working class was created which would inevitably develop forms of class consciousness to call the dominant values of the capitalists into question, as well as challenge their interests directly through trade union organization and action. If the Canadian bourgeoisie did not exactly dig its own grave it certainly gave shovels to its opposition. None of this is, of course, in any way surprising from a Marxist perspective. But the elements were worked out in a unique way within the specificity of the Canadian political economy in the peculiar circumstance of historical timing.

The first point is to reiterate the importance of the independent commodity producer class as the major opposition force at this historical conjuncture. Urbanization was steadily cutting into the dominance of rural over urban and agricultural over blue-collar occupations in the labour force. Ironically, at the very moment when the farmers burst on the political scene as an organized force at the end of the First World War, they were just dipping below the urban labour force as the leading sector. Indeed, in Ontario, where rural depopulation had become a major concern to the farming sector, the United Farmers of Ontario came to office in 1919 as the representatives of a class whose back was pushed to the wall and which was fighting back out of desperation – a familiar enough role for petit-bourgeois elements in Europe, often with pernicious connections to fascism and authoritarian movements. But this obscures the fact that on the western prairies the farmers were not being pushed into the cities but were the leading class element uniting an entire region around grievances of a colonial nature vis-à-vis the dominant external forces of central Canada. Particularly in the West, the farmers developed a remarkably lucid and wide-ranging ideology which represented their specific class position. The same arguments suggested earlier in this essay, for the particular position developed by independent commodity producers who idealize a simple market type of economy in which the owner-operated farm is the model of property relations, remain valid for this most fertile period of farmers' movements. Besides the characteristic obsession with monetary control by bankers and financial capital over lands and equipment, which gave a mighty thrust to the emergence of Social Credit as an expression of the farmer ideology by the 1930s, there was by now an additional element: demands for the collective control – either through co-operative enterprise or by state ownership – of the various factors intervening between the farmer and the marketing of his staple product, that is, grain elevators, railways, grain exchanges, and the tariff structure.

The farmers' movements also developed a political theory of far greater ideological coherence than that of the farmers' revolts of 1837. The political theory was in fact radically divergent from that of the dominant forces in Canadian life, which had used representative and parliamentary governmental institutions to divide and mystify the subordinate classes. The farmers' attack on the party system was an attack on all the instruments which distorted direct democratic expression. Such ideas as initiatives, referenda, and recalls were innovative devices to short-circuit the manipulation of government by wealth and influence. Moreover, the farmers looked beyond this to a form of group government which would replace cabinet and party rule by direct exchange between economic or occupational groupings. The farmers, due to their unique position as owners of their means of production and as workers of their own fields, had, it was widely believed, a special role to play in bringing about class co-operation between capital and labour. The weakness of this theory arose just as certainly from its class origins as did the strengths. The failure to understand the dynamics of the world capitalist system and the inevitable penetration of the power of monopoly capital into the simple market economy of the western farmer left them helpless before the onslaught of corporate might. Yet their own position prevented them from becoming radical opponents of capitalism as such. They were, after all, themselves property-owners, however small. Their insistence on co-operation as a means as well as an end and their fundamental hostility to a disciplined party as the arm of the movement rendered them politically impotent in the face of the continuing partisan coherence of the Liberal and Conservative parties.

As economic development and class differentiation continued apace, new elements entered the political stage in loose alliance with the farmers. The specialization of the professions led to a new middle stratum. Many of the professionals, particularly lawyers, doctors, and engineers, played a role which was largely ancillary to and supportive of the hegemony of capital. But there were also elements, particularly to be found among the teachers and preachers, whose ambiguous class position, suspended between the dominant bourgeoisie which had associated itself with all the symbols of the 'cultural heritage' and the people whom they served on a day-to-day basis, left them in a state of ideological ambivalence. Although many continued to play the traditional role of agents of political socialization and bourgeois hegemony, there were a few who became loose, agitational elements, ideological leaven in an already fluid situation. The Social Gospel movement, with roots in English Methodism, became a vehicle for the expression of radical, sometimes even anti-capitalist, sentiment. The Social Gospel was the dominant ideological hegemony of capitalism turned upside-down. Instead of individual salvation and political quiescence, Social Gospellers preached social salvation and political activism. Instead of turning the attention of the poor towards the afterlife, Social Gospellers turned them to this life and its tasks. Social work, social science, and social engineering were the staples of this movement, within which may be discerned the germ of the social-democratic image of the 'social service state,' an apparatus operated by technical experts motivated by a desire to do good and tuned to the amelioration of the conditions of modern life.

At the same time, there were deep contradictions embedded within the Social Gospel ideology, which reflected deep contradictions in its social base. Both its strength and its weakness came from its fusion of cultural conservatism and political radicalism. Nowhere is this contradiction more manifest than in the feminist movement which was closely associated with Social Gospel preaching. Nellie McClung's feminism arose directly out of a wholehearted acceptance of the Victorian image of woman as more 'spiritual' and 'civilizing' than the male; she turned this image upside-down and argued that if women were indeed morally superior they should be allowed to vote and take a leading role in political life in order to elevate the debased standards set by men. Since the movement touched on all the fundamental symbols of ideological hegemony – Christianity, the family, motherhood – but gave them a radical twist, there was a certain difficulty in confronting the challenge; yet, by the same token, the challenge was self-limiting. This cultural conservatism made it difficult for the early feminists in Canada to theorize the sexual liberation of women as well as their political enfranchisement. Given the vote, women simply drifted back into familial and maternal quietude. Moreover, the Social Gospel, always a minority movement within Christianity, was never able to free itself from a contradiction inherent in Christianity itself: the confusion between social reformation (possibly eventuating in socialism) and moral reformation of the individual (most often taking the form of an idiosyncratic obsession with the prohibition of alcohol). Finally, the weak class position of the Social Gospel, its base in the middle-class professions, left it extremely vulnerable to changes in the more important class confrontations. When the farmers' movements dissipated themselves and labour radicalism declined in the 1920s, the Social Gospel underwent a prolonged deterioration. Marginal middle-class elements were not enough to sustain a major radical confrontation of the established order. In this sense the Social Gospel movement was strictly an ideological vehicle for deeper rooted class antagonisms, giving a particular form of expression to these antagonisms.

The significance of this ideological vehicle for the formation of socialist opposition in Canada can be seen by an examination of the first major challenge posed by the emergent labour movement to the power of capital which also took shape in this same period. Canada's industrial revolution from the 1890s through the first decades of the twentieth century, accelerated by wartime industrial production, telescoped stages of industrial development which took place over longer periods of time in the United States and Britain. For example, the introduction of assembly-line production and the mechanization of the work place, with the consequent degradation of workers from craft status to mere semi-skilled labour, was largely coincident in Canada with the major surge of industrialization. When labour, pent up by wartime restrictions on wages while inflation raged unchecked, finally burst onto the stage in 1919, it was in the unforgettable form of the Winnipeg General Strike, the single most important working-class confrontation of capitalism ever staged in this country. This, together with sympathetic strikes in other western cities, posed the spectre of socialist revolution to the capitalist state. Yet the major ideological thrust of workers was much more social democratic and trade unionist than revolutionary. The leadership of the strikers was heavily drawn from the Social Gospel movement. Sincere dedication to the cause of the working class and a commitment to social democracy did not in itself lead to revolutionary politics when it was expressed through doctrines of class harmony and Christian fellowship. In another sense, radical working-class action was emerging at the very moment when the larger confrontation was being carried out between the grande bourgeoisie and elements of the petite bourgeoisie, especially the farmers. In this struggle, which found its expression in the 1921 federal election when the Conservatives were reduced to third-party status by the farm-based Progressive party and in a series of provincial elections in Ontario, Alberta, and Manitoba which brought farmers' parties or farmer-labour coalitions to office, the working-class elements seeking participation as a class in the political process had to choose between sides already formed. Too weak organizationally, demographically, and ideologically to act decisively on their own, the workers had to choose the side of the petite bourgeoisie under the ideological guidance of middle-class leadership elements whose views were in some senses much closer to the independent commodity producers than to wage labour. Thus a historical conjuncture of class forces with profound consequences for the development of socialist opposition was struck at this crucial moment.

Whatever the exact class conjuncture, it was the class question itself which had been unmistakably posed by the subordinate classes in revulsion against the concentration of power and wealth in the hands of the national bourgeoisie. This challenge to the domination of central Canadian capital precipitated a political and ideological crisis of such proportions as to call for revisions of the dominant ideology. Moreover, the transformation of nineteenth-century entrepreneurial capitalism to modern corporate capitalism, with monopolistic or oligopolistic control over the market by a few highly organized and bureaucratized giant corporations, created an internal dynamic within capitalism itself towards 'modernization' and 'rationalization,' which, as in the case of the United States during the so-called Progressive era, would inevitably lead to a growing role for the state as a device to consolidate and stabilize the market on behalf of corporate capital. The nationalization of private power companies in Ontario by a Conservative provincial government in the first decade of the century was a leading example of the state acting on behalf of one section of capital against another in the long-term interests of a rationalized power grid system as industrial infrastructure.[24] Robert Borden as national Conservative leader espoused 'progressive' policies of state intervention and national conservation of natural resources. The first major intervention of the federal state into direct ownership came with the nationalization of private railways into the Canadian National system under a Tory administration. Borden also presided over the modernization of the federal state apparatus itself with the introduction of the merit system of appointment and efficiency studies of government operations, at the direct behest of his capitalist supporters who demanded a strong and effective state apparatus to act as their agent, especially in external trade and the search for foreign markets.[25] In short, the logic of capitalism was tending to increase the role of the state at the same time as class opposition to bourgeois domination was making political demands on the state for policies more appropriate to the subordinate classes. It was a fateful conjuncture which presented capitalism with a crucial historical opportunity.

The bourgeoisie itself was incapable of seizing this opportunity; the state, under enlightened leadership, could play a certain entrepreneurial role in acting on behalf of the larger interests of capitalism even against particular interests. The coming of William Lyon Mackenzie King, grandson of the rebel of 1837, to the leadership of the Liberal party in 1919 was an important step in this political solution to the crisis of capitalism. With King's victory in 1921 the class struggle generated by the process of capitalist development entered a new stage: thesis, antithesis ... mystification. King represented another face to the middle-class radicalism of the Social Gospel with which he flirted. A university-trained political economist who was willing to sell his skills to the highest bidder, whether this was the federal bureaucracy in Ottawa where he had been the first deputy minister of the fledgling Department of Labour, or the private empire of the Rockefellers for whom he had acted during the war as a labour relations consultant during the bloody Colorado coal-mining strike, King represented a new kind of twentieth-century man: the technocratic intellectual. Drawing on the Social Gospel rhetoric of social service and Christian conscience, he at the same time developed a theory of the integration of class opposition into the capitalist system and a leading role for precisely the kind of 'expert' which King fancied himself. His book, *Industry and Humanity*, leapt past the conjuncture of 1918 to a future when the petite bourgeoisie had passed from sight and the fully industrialized world was divided fundamentally into capital and labour. Like Galbraith, King attempted to break down the functions of ownership and control by distinguishing a managerial technostructure allegedly separate from capital. He then introduced the state as a neutral bridge between capital, management, and labour, emphasizing the role of the state as a legitimizing force for the stabilization of class harmony. Since organized economic groups were directly represented within the processes of decision-making, with the political state only one of the four 'partners to industry,' one is justified in terming this a liberal-corporatist theory, although King himself never used the term corporatism, which had then distinctly Catholic and non–Anglo-Saxon origins. State and economy tend to fade into one another in this scheme, and the process of conflict becomes bureaucratized and thus denatured.

The state had demonstrated its capacity to intervene with direct coercion against working-class opposition in the smashing of the Winnipeg General Strike. Against the farmers and middle-class progressives it would instead shift its forms of legitimation. The coincidental identity of King's liberal-corporatism with the class co-operation theory of the farmers' movements allowed the new Liberal government the ideological capacity to slowly swallow the Progressive members of Parliament to the point that the party was a spent force within one term. It is indeed an ironic commentary on the weakness of the farmers' movements that they should have been thus co-opted by a man who cared so little for their world. Yet King was also able to draw the support of enough trade union elements over the long years of his stay in national office to decharge much of the momentum of the labour movement as well. One must not, however, confuse King's legitimizing ideology with actual restructuring of the state apparatus. Corporatism was to be symbolic, not structural. Capital at this stage showed little enthusiasm and strong elements of the labour movement, to their credit, have always been suspicious of such an arrangement. More importantly, the continued, albeit declining, influence of petit-bourgeois elements did not offer the real economic and class base for a corporatist bargain. Furthermore, this same persistent influence also militated against the adoption of social welfare legislation which was a concern for working-class people but only of marginal importance to farmers who were more self-sufficient by the nature of their occupation. Thus the only social legislation passed by the Liberals during the decade of the 1920s was the old-age pension program, virtually forced down King's throat by J.S. Woodsworth at a crucial time for the minority Liberal government.

Yet however much the King Liberals were engaged in reshaping the image of the state without changing the substance, there was a long-term change in the role of the federal state which dates from the period of crisis at the end of the war. Some observers have identified a new national policy, emphasizing regional pay-offs and a slow turn towards welfarism as a phase succeeding that of the old National Policy with its emphasis on continental development and economic growth.[26] There was such a shift, in part, but it is somewhat misleading to point away from the accumulation function. Pay-offs to regions and classes were the *price* which capitalism was willing to pay for the social and political peace which would allow accumulation to continue. The focus on the class question in the post-war years also obscured the older national question. It was not that the Liberals were anti-nationalist so much as their preoccupation with settling class conflict which blinded them to the takeover of the Canadian economy by American capitalism. Indeed the pork-barrel involved in the new national policy could be paid for out of the dividends of new foreign capital investment. Thus, once again accumulation and legitimation came together, with disastrous long-term results for the Canadian nation.

The Great Depression renewed the crisis of capitalism which had seemingly lessened during the 1920s. Canada, as a nation strongly dependent upon primary export production, was particularly hard hit by the world-wide decline in prices. The evident failure of capitalism to produce the goods was just as surely a failure of the capitalist state to carry out its accumulation function. On the one hand, Canadian capitalism was divided and confused about the nature of the crisis; on the other, the state system, battered by a profound fiscal crisis brought on by enormously increased relief expenditures at the same time as tax revenues were drastically declining, was apparently incapable of generating ideas, let alone responses. Political opposition was just as weak and confused. It must be remembered that the depression had very *uneven* effects: since prices were falling, those who retained jobs were often able to maintain a standard of living which was equal to or even surpassed that which they had enjoyed earlier; while those who were unemployed suffered inconceivable hardship without adequate state welfare.

The birth of a social-democratic party alternative, the CCF, was an ambivalent event, incorporating as it did elements of working-class radicalism, western farmer populism, and the Fabian socialism of eastern university intellectuals. The CCF critique of capitalism was largely premised on the assumption that the system had failed in practical terms – an assumption which was to cost the party dearly when capitalism later recovered – and leaned very heavily on the idea of central economic planning and centralized social engineering by elite corps of technical experts in the bureaucracy as the solution to the crisis. In other words, with the CCF came the full emergence of the modern social-democratic image of the state in capitalist society: public ownership of key sectors, extensive regulation and control of economic activity, a welfare minimum, and the integration of the organized working class within the structures of the state system, all this to be accomplished by peaceful, evolutionary, and parliamentary means without recourse to coercion. The state, and particularly the federal state, took on an aura of neutrality, as an instrument which could allegedly be used against capitalism's excesses and on behalf of its victims. The myth that any extension of state activity is a victory of 'socialism' was fostered both by unreconstructed fundamentalists of business and by the partisans of social democracy. The traditional Tory image of corporate state welfare could slide into the so-called 'Red Tory' image of the welfare state for all, with few realizing the optical illusion, and the mystification, involved.

In any event, even this ambiguous new turn was, during the depression at least, a minor event. The farmer and populist elements within the CCF itself remained somewhat restive about the trend towards *étatisme*, and in many parts of the country agrarian discontent drifted into other political forms, from a return to traditional party politics in Ontario to the emergence of right-wing monetarist populism in Alberta with Social Credit. Both the Conservative and Liberal governments in Ottawa in this decade did extend the role of the state to a degree, particularly in direct ownership of transportation and communication infrastructure (CBC and Trans-Canada Airways) and regulation and control through such devices as the Bank of Canada. Contrary to the social-democratic belief, however, it was not so much popular pressure from below which was largely responsible for these ventures into 'socialism' as the logic of capitalism and its needs. For example, the Bank of Canada was necessary to stabilize financial operations as well as to create a mechanism for national monetary policy, none of which was contrary to the interests of Canadian bankers. Indeed R.B. Bennett's Bank of Canada was literally a 'bankers' bank' directed by the directors of the chartered banks. The Liberals, with greater sensitivity to the need for public mystification, changed it into a supposedly neutral state institution, although its role continued to be highly supportive of financial capitalism.

It was the experience of the Second World War which brought the crisis to at least a temporary resolution with a new role for the federal state emerging out of both the needs of capitalism and the sudden appearance of strong popular pressures. The perception on the part of the subordinate classes that laissez-faire economic policies during the depression had meant unemployment and misery while extensive government controls and mobilization of resources for the war effort had brought about full employment and stability, meant a dawning fear of the end of controls following the war and the re-emergence of depression conditions with the restoration of the old order. The CCF enjoyed a sudden upsurge of popularity, even the Communist party won a few seats here and there, and public opinion swung sharply to the left, evidenced in polls which suggested majority support for the nationalization of industry.[27] At this conjuncture both the accumulation and legitimation functions were thus in question. 'Reconstruction' involved a package of economic, social, and constitutional policies which formed the basis of a successful transition to a peacetime economy, a period of renewed economic growth of capitalism, a revised and highly centralized federalism, and the continued hold of the Liberals on national office. It was Keynesian economics which formed the logic of the policies while at the same time allowing for a vastly expanded role for the federal state. In effect, the new apparatus of fiscal and monetary control guaranteed accumulation through the maintenance of full employment and the protection of a stable economic environment which would attract capital investment, much of it American. At the same time, Keynesian policies offered a neat solution to the legitimation crisis. Welfarist policies of redistribution, such as the famous family allowances scheme, placed purchasing power in the hands of the people, which provided demand for the goods and services of capitalist enterprise, which in turn kept employment up. It is interesting to note that not only did the national state emerge much stronger out of this transformation, but the state itself played a certain autonomous role in bringing these policies into being, even against the opposition or indifference of some elements of Canadian capitalism. One might cite in this regard the lack of any important voice from the corporate sector in the framing of the new policies which originated entirely from within the senior civil service with some input from important Liberal party officials as well. One might also point to a certain amount of alienation exhibited by big business towards both major political parties in their moderate leftward policy turn.[28] Certainly the senior civil service of the 1940s and 1950s maintained a fund of expertise and technical mastery over details of economic management which far surpassed earlier stages of bureaucratic development and which certainly outweighed the provincial administrations. As capitalism regained its equilibrium, and under the deadening blanket of anti-communist Cold War ideology, the social-democratic image of the state became obscured within a Liberal state which appeared to offer apolitical, technical, bureaucratic solutions to the problems of conflict within capitalist society.

It is necessary to pause before this 'end of ideology' image of the Liberal state. A number of considerations call the image into serious question.

First, there is the undeniable fact that once the pressure of popular demands abated with the Liberal victory in 1945, almost all initiatives in social welfare legislation ceased: the curious death of the national medical plan is the best example. In considering the long career of Mackenzie King as prime minister one judgment at least is clear: the Liberal state would be moved just so far as popular demands forced it, and never a step further. Minimal legitimation was always the maximal program. Second, as a study by David Wolfe has documented, capitalists remained highly suspicious of Keynesian economics and accepted the new role for the state only so long as economic growth continued. Stabilization, and thus accumulation, were still the focus of business interest.[29] Finally, accumulation was maintained largely through the importation of American direct investment, the ownership aspects of which were beginning to reach critical proportions by the 1950s, and by the headlong rush into the exportation of unprocessed raw materials.

The Liberal party, like the Conservative party before it, fashioned its own profitable relationship with the capitalist sector out of its domination over political office. To the extent that the state intervened on a wider basis in the private sector, it became intimately involved in purchasing goods and services from the private sector on a contractual basis. The Liberal party financed itself by levying a percentage on government contracts, or by straight patronage rake-offs where tenders were not involved.[30] In short, the Liberal state, even at its zenith of prestige, begins in retrospect to appear as little more than the old Tory state writ large, but no longer in possession of any directing national principle other than economic growth at any cost, even if the capital accumulation from the profits of growth accrued more to American multinational corporations than to the Canadian national bourgeoisie. The old weakness of the Canadian state, the lack of national identity, was even more pronounced in an era when even the economic aspects of state activity became as involved in the logic of American capitalist profitability as in the national elements of Canadian development. The Liberals had bested the Tories by their superior understanding of class conflict and of the techniques of co-opting left-wing opposition generated by the success of the old National Policy, and by their ability to integrate the Quebec political elite into the state system. They ended by losing sight altogether of the loss of national integrity consequent on their pursuit of accumulation at any cost.

During the brief Diefenbaker interlude of 1957-63 and the renewed Liberal domination since, one may discern with little difficulty a general unravelling of the system built up in the 1940s. Some of the major developments salient to the history of the state system in Canada since the late 1950s may be summarized as follows: the increasing domination of the industrial and resource sectors of the economy by American direct ownership with the consequent weakening of the national government's ability to control and manage the national economy; the continued peripheralization of the economy towards regional resource-based economies with north-south connections with the United States surpassing east-west connections within the Canadian economy; the striking failure of Keynesian economic policies which became obvious earlier in Canada than elsewhere but which is now a general phenomenon of the Western world, reflected in the persistent association of inflation with unemployment; the inability of federal programs to generate significant economic growth in poor regions of the country; the emergence for the first time of a sustained basis of trade union militancy which, beginning in the mid-1960s, raised the man-hours lost through strikes to unprecedented levels and began to bring pressure to bear on the profit margins of capitalist enterprise; the transformation of Quebec nationalism into an *indépendance* movement organized around a political party with widespread support among the political, administrative, media, and professional elites of Quebec, thus directly challenging the elite accommodation basis of the Liberal party's Quebec connection. All these factors taken together have altered the basis upon which the Canadian state system rests and have tended, although not without contradictions, to contribute to a deterioration of the importance of the federal state, and the emergence of stronger provincial state power amid a general balkanization of the Canadian nation.

The picture is a complex one. One demand made by the logic of corporate capitalism in the 1960s tended towards a renewal of federal strength. A rationalization of welfare plans on a national basis would be of benefit to corporate capital which was increasingly mobile: prosperity in the mid-1960s seemed to offer the economic surplus from which social security rationalizations and extensions could be financed. Welfarism also seemed to be a popular legitimation policy. But provinces could not be expected to undertake isolated initiatives in such areas without other provinces following suit. Thus a certain innovative role in the introduction of such schemes as medicare, the Canada Pension Plan, national minimum standards, and increased transfer payments from rich to poor provinces, was undertaken by the federal government. But the limitations of welfarism as legitimation became apparent when the increase in labour militancy demonstrated that class conflict, far from being defused, had been instead inflamed. When the present economic crisis struck the Western world in the early 1970s, the overall fiscal position of the state deteriorated and consequently its social security programs fell under attack. Thus both the legitimation and accumulation functions were seriously undermined at the same time. In the wake of this crisis there appears to have been a definitive abandonment of the welfarist role of the national state. With continued inflation and rising pressures from corporate capitalism for retrenchment, the federal government has ceased any significant extensions of welfare programs, is cutting back on others, and has most recently been attempting to turn back to the provinces responsibility for financing some of the very programs which the federal government had earlier persuaded, and in some cases virtually coerced, provinces to undertake.

The rise of labour militancy has had the effect of drawing the federal state into direct confrontation with the working class. The demands that federal action be taken against inflation had become so irresistible by 1975 that the Liberal government was forced to reverse its own campaign policy of 1974 and institute the so-called 'anti-inflation' program. It is important to realize that the labour militancy has been almost entirely apolitical, being largely focused on industrial relations and wage negotiations with employers and scarcely at all upon global political demands which would develop a broader ideological critique of capitalist society. Even the social-democratic NDP, with its direct organizational affiliations with industrial unions, has been unable to better its political position significantly. The intervention of the federal government into the worsening relations between capital and labour was in a sense a 'nationalization' of labour relations on behalf of capital. The focusing of wage demands on the state rather than the employer might seem to constitute a politicization of the labour struggle. There were indeed marked tendencies in this direction, the most spectacular being the 14 October 1976 national day of protest, the first nation-wide grassroots labour action in the history of this country. The moment appears to have passed, however, and the most likely results at this time are either a general defeat for the working class with resultant apathy and resignation, or the securing of some sort of liberal-corporatist arrangement between the CLC, the federal government, and big business – which from a socialist perspective is scarcely preferable to the first alternative. It remains to be seen whether long-term delegitimation of the state in the eyes of the working class will result from the wage control intervention.

Working-class pressure on profits will undoubtedly push the federal government towards intervention, even to coercion if the crisis of capitalism demands illiberal measures. At the same time the current shift in federal spending priorities away from health and welfare programs towards defence projects – under the pretext of a Soviet 'threat' to Canadian sovereignty – indicates a further abandonment of legitimation policies and a deepening of the emphasis on state activities directly beneficial to industry.[31] One may confidently expect that the thunderous orchestration of propaganda through the mass media in recent years attacking 'big government,' 'bureaucracy,' and 'waste and inefficiency' will not be extended to a massive growth in armament expenditures.

There is another aspect to the anti-government propaganda which bears examination. Much of the campaign, whether inspired by the giant corporations or by such ideological excrescences as the small businessmen's association, has focused almost exclusively on the federal state. The Conservative party has adopted this assault on Ottawa as its prime partisan obsession, along with the demand for more give-aways and tax bonuses to big business. The identification of the federal government as the source of economic deterioration is understandable at one level, given the primary role played by Ottawa in the post-war world. But the failure to include the provincial governments within the same *obiter dicta* suggests a less innocent orientation. There is strong reason to argue that the major thrust of contemporary capitalist development in Canada, primarily in the extraction of natural resources, is towards the weakening of the national state system and the balkanization of the country into regional dependencies of the American Empire. The Conservative call for the 'decentralization' of Confederation, clothed in the self-serving rhetoric of freedom and local initiative, has now been given further impetus by the spectre of the Quebec *indépendance* movement enshrined in office in Quebec City and the precipitous crisis of Trudeau's federalism. It may well be that 'decentralization' is an ideology whose time has come, with very powerful interests in support.

Visions of the total dismemberment of the nation are no doubt overdrawn. The national state manifestly performs functions still necessary to capitalism, which provincial states cannot perform on their own. Moreover, the question of centralization versus decentralization within the context of constitutional federalism tends in one very important sense to obscure the main issue. The state system in Canada, of which the federal and provincial governments are merely aspects, has become a complex, many-layered, and multidimensional phenomenon. Federal-provincial conferences and particularly the growth of vast, and literally uncharted, machinery for intensive and sustained interbureaucratic consultation between levels of government has created what some observers have called a new branch of the state. Perhaps the disintegration of the central political authority may be discerned in the weakness of any central command over this fragmented and unwieldy apparatus, where horizontal accommodations between loosely interdependent bureaucratic empires may be more important than control from Ottawa. Needless to say, such a situation offers increasing opportunity for fractions of the bourgeoisie to capture parts of the apparatus and to carry on conflicts with other fractions through the competing sections of the state system – the conflict between Alberta and Ontario over oil prices is one example. Yet the same example indicates that some unification will also be necessary for capitalism – the interests of the whole bourgeoisie – and thus some central co-ordination of oil price policy is undertaken by Ottawa. A point made by Panitch in the preceding essay may usefully be reiterated again: the fact that such decisions are taken at levels of interbureaucratic and intercorporate negotiation remote from any direct popular influence – levels literally *irresponsible* to the voters even under the normal definition of responsibility in liberal democracies – means that capitalist dictation to the state is even further insulated from possible oppositional class criticism.

At another level the state system in Canada has been moving towards yet closer relationships with the private sector. Senior civil servants are now encouraged as part of an official career planning program to spend periods of time in the corporations; the old career civil service model followed in the days of the Liberal mandarinate in the 1940s and 1950s is being replaced by a 'cross-pollination' between executive positions in both sectors. There is the proliferation of advisory councils to departments made up of big business executives with interests closely connected with the particular department concerned. And, perhaps most significant of all, there has been a very conscious move towards blurring the line between public and private enterprise. The Canada Development Corporation, originally the nationalist brainchild of Walter Gordon, has become instead a device for taking Crown corporations out of the direct ownership of the state and into a curious half-life of mixed public-private control. The development of government-corporate consortia, such as Panarctic, is another device for integrating the capacity of the state to mobilize capital investment with the desire for profit by capitalist enterprise. And, of course, such devices are ideal for the capitalist whose profits will be guaranteed by the state itself as a partner. Only those mesmerized by the myth that state intervention is a form of 'socialism,' or those who perpetuate the Canadian folklore that socialism is the highest stage of Toryism, should react with shock and indignation when the suggestion is made, as it was recently, that since Canadian National has finally made a profit, after over a half-century of subsidization by the taxpayers, it should be turned over to the private sector. That is directly in the Canadian tradition – the state exists to mobilize financial support for neces-

sary but unprofitable enterprises. Even in those areas where direct ownership has been undertaken, especially transportation and communication infrastructure, the normal pattern has been for public-private sector duality,
not state monopoly: CN competes with CP, Air Canada with Canadian
Pacific, the CBC with CTV. And even within the state sector itself this dualism
is perpetuated, with regular departments paralleled by Crown corporations
whose operations are encouraged to be as much like private corporations as
possible.

The gradual merger of the state and corporate sectors ought not to surprise anyone conversant with the dominant image of the state in Canadian
history. The Syncrude deal suggests a kind of archetype of state capitalism
for the future: an arrangement made under the gun of the multinational oil
companies involving the federal state and two provincial governments with
divergent economic bases together forming a stabilizing minority interest in
a foreign-controlled project for the extraction of a crucial non-renewable
natural resource. The old Tory image of the state remains operative: private
profit at public expense. The rationale of the old Tory image has, however,
been discarded by events. A bourgeoisie has indeed come to birth long
since, has even reached maturity (in some cases senility), but it is a national
bourgeoisie only in part, and its private interests are not linked with the national interest, even if one defines this in the minimal terms of liberal capitalist concepts of the national interest. Even bourgeois nationalist figures
like Walter Gordon and Eric Kierans have departed political life, unable to
acquiesce in the further destruction of the bourgeois basis of a national
state.

The fatal continuity of the image of the state from nineteenth-century
Toryism to twentieth-century Liberalism, a continuity founded on capitalism without a viable national basis, is deepened by the weakness of an alternative, socialist, image. At this stage in our history there is little point in discussing a Marxist revolutionary critique as a dominant aspect of mass
working-class politics. Marxism exists more importantly as an analytical
tool and an academic mode of interpretation, as in this book. Yet even the
social-democratic image, however ambivalent and accommodative with
capitalism it has proved to be in countries where social democracy has been
electorally successful, is extremely enfeebled and rests on a profoundly fragmented base. The defeat of the NDP government of British Columbia after a
single, and by social-democratic standards innovative, term is a haunting
sign of the political impotence of social democracy. The failure of mass
working-class opposition to wage controls, especially the astonishing ideological confusion of the trade union leadership, is even more disquieting.

At this conjuncture, the election of the strongly social-democratic and union-backed Parti Québécois in Quebec on 15 November 1976 is an event fraught with the deepest irony for English-Canadian socialists. The rise of integral nationalism in twentieth-century Quebec finally destroyed the old monopoly of the national identity by the traditional elites. The bourgeois renovation of the structures of Quebec society under the Lesage Liberals' so-called Quiet Revolution in the early 1960s established the demand that middle-class Quebec become *maîtres chez nous* through the instrumentality of the Quebec provincial state. With the traditional aversion to *étatisme* thus broken, events were set in motion eventuating in the release of some of the most militant working-class energies yet seen in Canada. There is no doubt that the Parti Québécois represents the more progressive elements of Quebec society, with a strong working-class constituency. This constituency is, however, only one of its bases, and it is balanced by the same new middle-class technocratic-bureaucratic *étatiste* elements which gave thrust and direction to the Quiet Revolution. The overarching commitment to nationalism, which may be seen not so much as a goal opposed to class politics but rather as a vehicle for the class interests of the new middle class, may very well serve to submerge working-class interests once again. Yet even if the progressive aspect of social-democratic *indépendantisme* is not lost, the tragic irony for English-Canadian socialists is that even a partial victory for progressivism in Quebec may be bought at the price of the breakup of the Canadian nation.

The outlook is not bright. Yet the task for socialists in Canada must be to understand reality, as a first step to changing that reality. We must strive to understand the capitalist state in its Canadian specificity, to purge the mystifying layers of ideology from the image of the state and see it for what it really is. Toryism built it, Liberalism consolidated it, social democracy misjudged it. With our backs turned to the future and our eyes fixed upon the wreckage of the past, the question is, as always: what is to be done?[32]

NOTES

1 'Ideology and Ideological State Apparatuses,' in *Lenin and Philosophy* (London 1971), 127-88
2 It is interesting that Weber specifically cited Trotsky in formulating his definition. Weber, 'Politics as a Vocation,' in H.H. Gerth and C. Wright Mills, eds., *From Max Weber: Essays in Sociology* (New York 1958), 78
3 See C.B. Macpherson, *The Real World of Democracy* (Toronto 1965).
4 *The Savage Mind* (Chicago 1966), 95

5 Hartz, *The Founding of New Societies* (New York 1964), especially articles by Hartz and K.D. McRae; Horowitz, *Canadian Labour in Politics* (Toronto 1968), chap. 1

6 Macpherson, *Real World of Democracy*, and his *Democratic Theory: Essays in Retrieval* (London 1973)

7 See Tom Nairn, 'The Modern Janus,' *New Left Review*, 94 (Nov.-Dec. 1975), especially 8-11, for a Marxist interpretation of the fate of this concept.

8 'Some Views on the Pattern of Canadian Economic Development,' in T.N. Brewis, ed., *Growth and the Canadian Economy* (Toronto 1968), 41-2

9 Herschel Hardin's *A Nation Unaware: The Canadian Economic Culture* (Vancouver 1974) is the most fully developed statement of the argument.

10 See his 'Upper Canada and the Conservative Tradition,' in Ontario Historical Society, *Profiles of a Province* (Toronto 1967), and 'Conservatism and Political Development: The Canadian Case,' *South Atlantic Quarterly*, LXIV (1970), 226-43.

11 D. Barrington, 'Edmund Burke as Economist,' *Economica*, NS XXI, 83 (1954). Burke's economic views come out most clearly in his 'Thoughts and Details on Scarcity' and 'Speech on Economical Reform' in *The Works of Edmund Burke* (London 1826), III and VII.

12 Burke, *Reflections on the Revolution in France* (London 1907), 95

13 *Capital* (New York 1967), I, 774

14 Gary Teeple, 'Land, Labour, and Capital in Pre-Confederation Canada,' in Teeple, ed., *Capitalism and the National Question in Canada* (Toronto 1972)

15 J.L.H. Henderson, ed., *John Strachan: Documents and Opinions* (Toronto 1969), 109-10

16 Greg Keilty's *1837: Revolution in the Canadas* (Toronto 1974) is a good reflection of the left nationalist image of Mackenzie. Rick Salutin's script for the Theatre Passe Muraille's performance of *1837: The Farmers' Revolt* is another example of this currently fashionable interpretation. Margaret Fairley's *Selected Writings of William Lyon Mackenzie* (Toronto 1960) is a more scholarly collection and one reflecting an older left-wing image of the rebel of 1837.

17 Stanley Ryerson's *Unequal Union* (Toronto 1968) tends, in my opinion at least, to see the conflict in somewhat exogenous terms.

18 The clause in question reads: 'There shall never be created within this State any incorporated trading companies, or incorporated companies with banking powers. Labor is the only means of creating wealth.' S.D. Clark, *Movements of Political Protest in Canada, 1640-1840* (Toronto 1959), 429

19 *Pioneer Public Service* (Toronto 1955), 67

20 *The Image of Confederation* (Toronto 1964), 25

21 Bruce Hodgins, 'Democracy and the Ontario Fathers of Confederation,' in

Hodgins and Robert Page, eds., *Canadian History since Confederation: Essays and Interpretations* (Georgetown, Ont. 1972), 27

22 Ramsay Cook, *Provincial Autonomy, Minority Rights, and the Compact Theory, 1867-1921* (Ottawa 1969), 9-13

23 See Carl Berger's masterful intellectual history, *The Sense of Power: Studies in the Ideas of Canadian Imperialism, 1867-1914* (Toronto 1970).

24 See Viv Nelles, *The Politics of Development: Forests, Mines & Hydro-Electric Power in Ontario, 1849-1941* (Toronto 1974).

25 J.E. Hodgetts *et al.*, *The Biography of an Institution: The Civil Service Commission of Canada, 1908-1967* (Montreal 1972), 46-7; Paul Stevens, *The 1911 General Election: A Study in Canadian Politics* (Toronto 1970), 69-70

26 V.C. Fowke, 'The National Policy – Old and New,' in W.T. Easterbrook and M.H. Watkins, eds., *Approaches to Canadian Economic History* (Toronto 1967), 237-58

27 Reginald Whitaker, *The Government Party: Organizing and Financing the Liberal Party of Canada, 1930-1958* (Toronto 1977), 137-43

28 *Ibid.*; J.L. Granatstein, *The Politics of Survival: The Conservative Party of Canada, 1939-1945* (Toronto 1967)

29 Davld Wolfe, 'Political Culture, Economic Policy and the Growth of Foreign Investment in Canada, 1945-1957,' unpublished MA thesis, Carleton University, 1973

30 Whitaker, *Government Party*, 102-11, 402-6

31 See the *Financial Post* special supplement, 'What Canada's New Defence Policy Means for Business,' 19 Feb. 1977.

32 The final image is drawn from Walter Benjamin's extraordinary vision of the 'angel of history': 'his face is turned toward the past. Where we perceive a chain of events, he sees one single catastrophe which keeps piling wreckage upon wreckage and hurls it in front of his feet. The angel would like to stay, awaken the dead, and make whole what has been smashed. But a storm is blowing from Paradise; it has got caught in his wings with such violence that the angel can no longer close them. This storm irresistibly propels him into the future to which his back is turned, while the pile of debris before him grows skyward. This storm is what we call progress.' Benjamin, *Illuminations* (New York 1968), 257-8

PART II
CAPITALISM AND FEDERALISM

3

Federalism and the political economy of the Canadian state

GARTH STEVENSON

Analyses of the state from a Marxist perspective have given little attention to federalism, a fact which reflects the rather limited contribution that federal countries have made to recent Marxist theory.[1] In *The State in Capitalist Society*, Ralph Miliband includes 'the various units of sub-central government' among six elements of the state system, the others being government, bureaucracy, coercive apparatus, judiciary, and parliament. He notes that in advanced capitalist countries sub-central government is more than an administrative agency of central government, having also a representative function and, in some cases, remaining a power structure in its own right.[2] This formulation, however, does not adequately describe the situation in a federal state such as Canada. In a federal state the sub-central units in fact reproduce, in miniature as it were, each of Miliband's other elements of state power, having their own governments, bureaucracies, and parliaments as well as, in most cases, their own courts and coercive apparatus. In dissecting the structure of the state system the state-at-the-provincial-level can be viewed for some purposes almost as a self-contained complete system, although one that is strongly influenced from outside. In practice, we must analyse three related phenomena – the state-at-the-provincial-level, the state-at-the-central-level, and the relationships between the two, sometimes conflicting and sometimes collaborative – which constitute a vitally important aspect of the exercise of state power in a federal system.

Canada is an interesting case for those intending to construct a theory of federalism, since it seems to constitute an exception to a general trend towards centralization and the erosion of local power in advanced capitalist countries, including those that are formally federal. Miliband draws a parallel between this trend and the tendency of parliaments to lose power to the executive, which likewise appears inexorable in advanced capitalist systems.[3] In one of the very few books providing valuable insights into federalism from a Marxist perspective, James O'Connor sees sub-national units of government in the United States as fighting a desperate rearguard action: 'There has been a gradual erosion of the traditional federal system in the United States. Monopoly capitalist groups and the federal executive have been working together to increase federal power in local affairs and, step-by-step, to dismantle local government.'[4]

Whether measured in terms of revenues, expenditures, or the effective distribution of legislative and coercive power, the dominance of central government in the United States indeed seems assured, and the sub-national governments appear to have meekly accepted their fate. At least one perceptive student of American politics argues that for all practical purposes there is no longer any reserved area of 'states' rights' in which Congress cannot legislate.[5]

The situation in Canada is clearly very different, as over the past generation the provinces have actually gained in power and vitality. Not content merely to defend their existing powers and resources against the central government, they have taken the offensive and sought to shift the balance in their favour with considerable, although not invariable, success. Unlike their American counterparts, the provinces still have important reserved areas of legislative jurisdiction, and they intrude constantly into areas of activity which every other advanced capitalist country leaves to the central authorities. In Canada it is the central government which seems to be perennially on the defensive, and which can hardly act in any sphere of activity without taking the wishes of the other level of government into account. The first task of any serious analysis of Canadian federalism must be to explain why this is so.

Canadian Marxists could hardly ignore federalism, and have not in fact done so, but little systematic work has been done in Canada towards developing a theory of the federal state. The question of federalism has arisen in a tactical context: What courses of action should socialists follow, given the fact that Canada is a federal state? What position should socialists take in regard to controversies over the future of federalism? While some implicit assumptions concerning the reasons why federalism operates as it does may underlie the answers that have been supplied to these questions, the assumptions, if any, do not seem to have been derived from any very impressive analytical efforts.

Such efforts, however, must be made, because it is not possible to understand the political economy of Canada without understanding the dynamics of federal-provincial relations. A theory of the state which ignores this essential dimension is useless for Canadians seeking to understand, or to change, their society. In the absence of anything better, there is a tendency to accept uncritically the 'explanations' which are offered by politicians and the media and which form part of the prevailing ideology. An example would be the recent assertions by many bourgeois political scientists that the distinctive 'identities' and 'cultures' of the various provinces both explain and justify the increasing power and authority of the provincial governments in relation to Ottawa.[6] The varying popularity over the years of this particular notion, which John Porter has aptly described as 'hallowed nonsense,'[7] could probably tell us something about the importance which dominant economic interests have attached at different periods to provincial autonomy. Its resurgence over the last few years is certainly remarkable enough to invite suspicion; one critic has even suggested that the recent academic enthusiasm for provincial autonomy may not be unrelated to the fact that the provinces are now solely responsible for distributing grants to universities.[8] Whether or not this is so, Canadians, and Canadian socialists in particular, should be wary of ideas that may be no more than rationalizations for vested economic and institutional interests.

Marxists in particular ought to be sceptical of theories that lean too heavily on ethnic and 'cultural' differences as explanatory variables, even when those differences are as genuine as in the case of English Canada and Quebec. While Quebec is not a province like the others, this fact is not enough to justify the romantic enthusiasm for Quebec nationalism that has come to be typical of the Anglo-Canadian intelligentsia.[9] It certainly is no excuse for a failure to examine the real causes of conflict between the politico-bureaucratic elites of Ottawa and Quebec City, or to admit that the behaviour of the latter often resembles, both in motives and consequences, that of their counterparts in Toronto, Edmonton, and Victoria.

This essay aims to provide the brief outline of an explanation both of the historical evolution of Canadian federalism and of its present situation, an explanation that seeks to draw attention to the economic factors that contribute to political phenomena. It is also an attempt to discover how successfully insights derived from Marxist writings on the capitalist state can be adapted to the peculiar circumstances of Canada's decentralized federalism. As the starting point for this exercise it is necessary at least briefly to consider the nature and circumstances of Confederation.

ECONOMICS AND THE BNA ACT

Different historians have emphasized a variety of reasons why Confederation gained the necessary support to become a reality in 1867, and it is likely that there is some truth in all of their explanations. Stanley Ryerson, for example, emphasizes the role of the rising industrial capitalists, seeking a wider market for their products.[10] A similar analysis was made in the Communist party's brief to the Rowell-Sirois Commission, which attributed the retention of provincial governments after Confederation to a compromise with 'semi-feudal influences' seeking to preserve landlordism and feudalism in the provinces.[11] By this interpretation centralization, and Confederation itself, were viewed as progressive, and resistance to them as reactionary. More recently Tom Naylor has taken an opposite view, arguing that Confederation was promoted by a mercantile bourgeoisie of merchants, bankers, and railway promoters who sought to stultify the growth of indigenous industrialism and the free market.[12]

Whatever the truth of these assertions (and the present writer finds the Ryerson thesis more persuasive) it is certain that support for Confederation was not confined to the Canadian bourgeoisie, either industrial or mercantile. The farmers of Canada West (Ontario), at that time a very numerous and important property-owning class, strongly supported Confederation because it promised to open up the West as a new agricultural frontier. Mercantile interests in Nova Scotia and New Brunswick viewed Confederation as a means to protect the fishing industry from American competition following the end of reciprocity.[13]

Confederation was not really the establishment of a new state, but rather the adaptation of an existing state to new purposes and new circumstances. The Canadian state had been established by the Act of Union in 1841, complete with its government, bureaucracy, courts, and legislature. Municipal institutions and a volunteer militia were added in 1849 and 1855 respectively, thus completing Miliband's six elements of a state system. Ottawa was selected as the capital in 1857 and actually assumed that position two years before Confederation. Confederation changed neither the essential character of this state nor its legal relationship to the United Kingdom. It merely devolved certain state functions onto the newly created (or re-created) sub-national units of 'Quebec' and 'Ontario,' as well as providing for the expansion of the state to encompass New Brunswick, Nova Scotia, and subsequently the remainder of British North America. Aside from the expansion of its territorial boundaries the state was not much different after Confederation from what it had been before. Its institutional structure, its personnel, and its relationship to the ruling class remained substantially unchanged. It is difficult to justify Naylor's odd assertion that 'Liberal democracy in Canada was thus set back three decades' by the restriction on the taxing powers of the provincial legislatures in the BNA Act.[14] Apart from the fact that the Ontario and Quebec legislatures had not existed at all under the Act of Union, and were revived by Confederation, there is no apparent reason to consider a provincial legislature a more shining incarnation of liberal democracy than a federal parliament.

The functions which were devolved onto the new provinces of Quebec and Ontario, and retained by the old provinces of New Brunswick and Nova Scotia, were mainly what we would describe today as 'legitimization' functions, for example, hospitals, charities, education, municipal government, property and civil rights, and the solemnization of marriage. Since these were inexpensive and relatively undeveloped, few sources of revenue were provided to perform them. The accumulation functions represented by jurisdiction over railways, shipping, money and banking, the tariff, and major public works, were retained in Ottawa where, as previously noted, they were already being performed prior to 1867. The coercive functions were divided: Ottawa was responsible for the militia, the criminal law, and penitentiaries, but the provinces organized the courts, were given control over 'public and reformatory prisons,' and were responsible for whatever municipal police forces existed at the time.

Federal-provincial conflict did not take long to develop after 1867, and to some extent it assumed the character of a class conflict between the bourgeoisie and the independent commodity producers.[15] The former understandably concentrated their attentions on Ottawa in the early years, since it performed the accumulation functions in which they were primarily interested. The independent commodity producers were largely shut out at the federal level.

It is instructive in this connection to examine the changing perceptions of federalism on the part of the Reform or Liberal party in Ontario, which represented the interests of the independent commodity producers. In contrast to similar parties in the other provinces, these people were strong supporters of Confederation, and prior to 1867 they were in full agreement with Macdonald's view that the provinces should be little more than glorified municipalities, destined to wither away in due course. After Confederation, however, Macdonald's Conservatives no longer needed or wanted to maintain a coalition with their erstwhile Liberal opponents. The Liberals were excluded from power and patronage at the federal level, and were left with only the provincial government of Ontario, which they had previously considered too insignificant to be worth their notice. In this situation they changed very quickly from centralists into strong supporters of provincial autonomy.[16] In the last decades of the nineteenth century Liberal-dominated Ontario was by far the most militant of the provinces in defending its 'rights' against the federal power.

At a later period that role was assumed by the Prairie provinces, and especially by Alberta, since this region had replaced southwestern Ontario as the bastion of the independent commodity producers. Manitoba was increasingly an exception as the mercantile bourgeoisie of Winnipeg came to dominate the province. In this period the class basis of federal-provincial conflict was even more obvious than it had been earlier in Ontario, and since the subject has been extensively treated elsewhere, there is no need to discuss it any further here.[17]

Had the centrifugal forces in Canadian federalism continued to represent nothing more than the interests of the declining class of independent commodity producers, they would long since have diminished to the point of insignificance, leaving the Canadian provinces in much the same position as the American states. This, however, was not to be. In placing the accumulation functions in the hands of Ottawa, the Fathers of Confederation had made one apparently insignificant exception that was to prove the undoing of their plans. Section 109 of the BNA Act deserves to be quoted in full:

All Lands, Mines, Minerals, and Royalties belonging to the several Provinces of Canada, Nova Scotia, and New Brunswick at the Union, and all Sums then due or payable for such Lands, Mines, Minerals, or Royalties, shall belong to the several Provinces of Ontario, Quebec, Nova Scotia, and New Brunswick in which the same are situate or arise, subject to any Trusts existing in respect thereof, and to any Interest other than that of the Province in the same.

The importance of Section 109 today may be indicated in part by the fact that more than three-quarters of Canada's land area, outside of the territories, consists of provincial Crown land. Only in the three Maritime provinces is more than half of all land under private ownership. Federal land, mainly national parks and military bases, amounts to less than 2 per cent of the total.[18] Even more important is the fact that all minerals belong to the Crown (that is, the province) including those found under private land. In the United States, by contrast, most land and most minerals are privately owned, while most public land comes under the federal Department of the Interior.[19]

In 1867, Section 109 seemed relatively unimportant. Mining was almost non-existent, except in Nova Scotia where coal royalties provided about 5 per cent of the colonial government's revenues just prior to Confederation.[20] Forestry was important only in New Brunswick, since the accessible forests of Ontario and Quebec had been almost completely cut down and shipped to the United States during the period of reciprocity. The technological developments that gave economic significance to sprucewood pulp, nickel, hydro-electric power, oil, and natural gas still lay in the future. Most of the land suitable for agriculture in the original provinces had already passed into private ownership.[21]

The resources under provincial jurisdiction began to acquire major economic, and therefore political, significance before the turn of the century. An important effect of this development was to increase the revenues of provincial treasuries, particularly that of Ontario, making them less dependent on the federal subsidies provided by the BNA Act. As early as 1891 the lumber industry, which depended on American markets, had become such an important source of revenue for the Ontario treasury as to make the provincial government a strong supporter of continental free trade. It was the Ontario Liberals (in office) who persuaded the federal Liberals (in opposition) to propose the renewal of reciprocity in the federal election of that year.[22] The Conservatives, aided by the CPR, had no trouble remaining in office. Already at this early date a characteristic relationship between different sections of the bourgeoisie and different levels of government can be observed in action, with the provincial government speaking for the embryonic resource industries while Ottawa represents the interests of railways, banks, and tariff-protected secondary manufacturing. Laurier had to abandon his free-trade principles to gain office five years later, although unaccountably he forgot the lesson once again in 1911.

The one area where the Fathers of Confederation had expected lands and resources to be important was in the territory purchased from the Hudson's Bay Company in 1869. Although the province of Manitoba came into existence almost immediately, and the other two Prairie provinces in 1905, the federal government retained control of Crown lands and natural resources in all three provinces until 1930, when Mackenzie King finally gave in to years of demands by the three provincial governments and surrendered them.[23] By this time the Prairie provinces, like the original provinces in 1867, had ceased to be an agricultural frontier, and their mineral resources appeared to be of modest proportions. Only later, in 1947, did Alberta reveal the potential to become a major producer of petroleum.

The reader may note that relatively little has been said up to this point about Quebec. The reason, perhaps surprisingly, is that there is relatively little to say. Until after the Second World War the Quebec government was rarely in conflict with the federal government, and its role in federal-provincial relations was usually passive and unobtrusive. Unlike Ontario, Quebec was usually governed by the same party that held office in Ottawa (Conservative in the nineteenth century, Liberal in the twentieth) and this reflected the more significant fact that both the federal state and the Quebec state were largely dominated by the anglophone bourgeoisie of Montreal. Like Winnipeg, Montreal was more mercantile than industrial and depended for its prosperity on the east-west movement of trade and commerce. To adapt the famous phrase of Sir Allan MacNab, railroads were its politics. Arthur Meighen's *lèse-majesté* in establishing a state-owned competitor to the CPR had as much, if not more, to do with his political weakness in Quebec as his support for wartime conscription.[24]

As Harold Innis pointed out at the time, the changing nature of the Canadian economy in the inter-war period was beginning to place strains on the federal structure.[25] Montreal and Winnipeg, the strongholds of the mercantile bourgeoisie whose interests required a strong central government, began to decline, relatively speaking, after the First World War, and continued to do so even more rapidly after the Second World War. The rise of Toronto, Vancouver, and later Calgary as the new strongholds of economic power reflected the shift to an economy, or rather a collection of regional economies, based on natural resources under provincial jurisdiction and relying heavily on American direct investment. The newer ruling classes had less need of a strong central government than their predecessors, but their interests necessitated control of the provincial states and their strengthening vis-à-vis Ottawa.

Enough has been said to indicate the basic difference between the class basis of Canadian and American federalism. In the United States, as O'Connor points out, the common interests of monopoly capital call for the strengthening of the central government and the completion of national unification. Only the declining local petit-bourgeois elements, especially in backward states like Arkansas and Mississippi, resist the increasing centralization of power in Washington. In Canada, on the other hand, important sections of the ruling class have an interest in strengthening the provinces in relation to Ottawa. The primordial basis of the distinction is the existence in Canada of a largely resource-based economy, plus the provincial jurisdiction over the resources themselves. The relationship between resources and provincial power is, however, somewhat more complex than this statement might suggest. Provincial jurisdiction over resources makes control over the provincial state apparatus important to certain sections of the bourgeoisie, and gives them an interest in strengthening the provincial state and providing it with the wherewithal to carry out its functions effectively. The increasing effectiveness and power of the provincial state, as well as its revenues from resource royalties, give it the means to assume new functions and acquire new assets. These in turn make it still more essential for the bourgeoisie – no longer simply those elements directly interested in resources – to solidify their relationship with the provincial state on which they increasingly rely to promote their common interests. The process thus continues indefinitely.

There is another and related reason for the importance of the provinces and the relative weakness of Ottawa, namely the regional specialization of the economy. Oil and gas are concentrated in Alberta, lumber in British Columbia, automobile manufacturing in Ontario, and so forth. The common interests of the whole Canadian bourgeoisie, which would have to be pursued through a strong federal state, are relatively limited, particularly since the ruling class does not face any domestic or external threat serious enough to make it more cohesive.[26] On the other hand, the common interests of the bourgeoisie in a particular province are clearly defined by the predominant industry of that province, and may place them in opposition to the bourgeoisie of other provinces. Ontario wants cheap natural gas while Alberta wants a high price. Ontario wants protection from Japanese imports and access to the American market, while British Columbia knows that Japan is overtaking the United States as a market for its own exports. Ottawa's economic policies, if it has any, can reflect little more than a lowest common denominator of consent among regional fractions of the ruling class jockeying for advantage. These regional class fractions rely on their provincial states to promote their specific interests and to speak on their behalf in federal-provincial or even, in some cases, international negotiations.[27]

An observation by Dr J.A. Corry, in one of the studies he did for the Rowell-Sirois Commission, goes a long way towards explaining the weakness of central government in Canada, as compared to other advanced capitalist countries: 'The inner logic of the demand for severe limitations on state action is that the diverse interests in society cannot agree on any broad programme and each interest fears a strong state which may be captured by other interests jockeying for advantage. When large areas are predominantly concerned with some single industry, that logic does not apply and it is relatively easy to get agreement that the state should help people to help themselves.'[28]

Ironically, Corry in this passage was attempting to account for the growth in the functions of the Canadian federal state, which he attributed to the dominance of a one-staple wheat economy. With the growth of specialized regional economies since he wrote, and the relative decline of the old wheat economy, the 'large areas ... predominantly concerned with some single industry' are now the individual provinces. This fact explains the extremely rapid growth of the public sector at the provincial level in recent years, and its relative lagging at the federal level. It also explains in part the curious fact that complaints from the business community against 'big government' and demands to 'cut spending' are invariably directed against the *federal* government, even though Ottawa's taxing, spending, ownership of enterprises, and regulatory jurisdictions have all increased much less in recent years than those of the provincial states. In particular, the provincial state of Ontario, which directly serves the most important sectors – aside from the oil industry – of American monopoly capital in Canada, appears virtually exempt from this kind of criticism.

GROWTH OF THE PROVINCIAL STATES

In all advanced capitalist countries there has been a general tendency in recent years for the functions of the state to multiply. As a result, state revenues and expenditures have increased more rapidly than the overall growth of the economy. Except in the United States it has not been the coercive function of the state that has grown most dramatically, but rather its contributions to promoting economic growth and lessening social conflict. In Canada, as we have seen, the accumulation function of the state was important even in the nineteenth century, but it has continued to grow in recent years. The legitimization function, in the development of which Canada lagged behind western Europe, although not behind the United States, has also grown vastly in recent years.

Canada differs from other advanced capitalist countries in the unusual extent to which this growth in state functions has occurred at the sub-national (provincial) level. This is reflected in the changing distribution of government spending. Contrary to a widespread belief which has been deliberately fostered by the business community, state expenditure at the federal level in proportion to GNP has increased only slightly over two decades. In 1955 it was 17.5 per cent of GNP and in 1974 it was 19.9. Almost all of the increase in the percentage was accounted for by the huge increase in payments to the provincial governments, which accounted for almost a quarter of federal spending in 1974 compared to less than a tenth in 1955. Provincial government spending increased sharply from 6.4 per cent of GNP in 1955 to 16.0 in 1974, while municipal and school board expenditure in proportion to GNP remained stable. The provinces and municipalities together now spend more than the federal government.[29]

Most government expenditure in Canada today consists of transfer payments to individuals, such as pensions and family allowances. Spending on goods and services by all levels of government, a more reliable indicator of the size of the public sector in proportion to the economy, declined slightly in relation to the GNP from 17.6 per cent in 1955 to 16.9 in 1974. In 1955 more than half of government spending on goods and services was by the federal level, where it amounted to 9.2 per cent of GNP; by 1974 the federal level accounted for less than a third of such expenditure, or 5.3 per cent of GNP. In the same period provincial expenditure on goods and services increased from 3.1 to 5.2 per cent of GNP and local government expenditure from 5.3 to 6.4 per cent of GNP. Hospital expenditures (about 2.5 per cent of GNP in 1974) are additional to these figures.[30]

During the Second World War the state at the federal level exercised vast powers over the economy as well as maintaining military forces of unprecedented size. As a result it accounted for about five-sixths of all state expenditure. In 1944 the federal level alone spent more in proportion to GNP than all three levels of government do today, despite the absence in 1944 of health insurance and other costly services. Undoubtedly, it was expected and hoped by some elements in the federal bureaucracy that this predominance of Ottawa over the provinces would last indefinitely into the post-war period, but this was not to be. Ottawa fought a rearguard action to maintain the wartime system whereby the provinces had 'rented' their right to impose direct taxes, but finally surrendered in 1960. In the sixties federal taxes were substantially reduced to make room for the increasing demands of the provinces, although each reduction only stimulated the insatiable appetites of the provinces for more. The federal surrenders were the result, as much as the cause, of Ottawa's political weakness vis-à-vis the provincial states.

There were a number of reasons for the post-war strength of the provinces. First and foremost, the resource industries under provincial jurisdiction expanded enormously, mainly in response to American needs and with the aid of American direct investment. Iron ore, oil, and gas were added to the older staples of copper, nickel, lead, gold, and pulp and paper. Vast quantities of hydro-electric power, also under provincial jurisdiction, were used in refining and smelting resources. The direct export of hydro-electric power to the United States, which had previously been prohibited by federal statute, began on a large scale after the precedent-setting Columbia River Protocol was signed in 1964. Over all, the share of the provincial resource industries in Canada's exports, which had been 32 per cent in 1910 and 40 per cent in 1930, increased to 51 per cent in 1950 and 56 per cent in 1960.[31]

This shift in the nature of the economy was associated with increasing integration between Canada and the United States, as measured by trade, capital flows, and American ownership and control of Canadian enterprise. The trend in the direction of a single North American economy resulted in the Canadian bourgeoisie looking increasingly to Washington, rather than to Ottawa, to perform many of the functions of a central government, ranging from the manipulation of interest rates to the protection of their investments in the Third World. At the same time continental integration increased the balkanization of the national economy, as the provinces became more closely tied to corresponding regions in the United States and less integrated with one another.[32]

These developments have had a particularly strong impact on Quebec, and have both contributed to and been reinforced by the neo-nationalism of the francophone petite bourgeoisie since 1960. Montreal's importance as a seaport, railway terminus, and financial centre declined with the shift to a north-south trading pattern, a fact which explains why the declining anglophone bourgeoisie of Montreal have been able to put up only the feeblest resistance to resurgent Quebec nationalism. The economic policies pursued by the provincial state over the last two decades have used New York and Boston as counterweights to Toronto and Ottawa, and have contributed to north-south integration. The James Bay project, financed by American capital and designed to rescue New York from the incompetence of its privately owned electric power utility, was launched by the provincial Liberals and endorsed, after a short period of hesitation, by the Parti Québécois. The continentalist implications of the Quiet Revolution were carried to a bizarre conclusion in the proposal for a Quebec-us common market, which was endorsed by a former finance minister, Mario Beaulieu, as part of his campaign for the leadership of the Union Nationale. The originator of the proposal, an economist named Rodrigue Tremblay, was subsequently appointed minister of industry and commerce when the Parti Québécois formed a provincial government at the end of 1976.[33]

The resource industries provided the original impetus for the expanding economic functions of the provincial states, but the process did not end there. For a while the continuing inflow of new investment from the United States could apparently be taken for granted, but with the recession of the late fifties it began to slow down. This contributed to an increasingly ferocious competition among the provincial states to attract direct investment from outside the country or to lure it away from one another with the aid of tax concessions, subsidies, and the provision of infrastructure and services out of the provincial treasury.[34] Substantial, although unevenly distributed, resource royalties and the 'tax room' vacated by the federal government in the sixties increased the ability of the larger provinces to play this game.

The smaller ones were kept in the race with various forms of federal assistance, although barely enough to enable them to hold their own.

The institutions and structures of the provincial states underwent considerable development in the post-war period, reflecting the increasing importance of their functions. Legislatures, hitherto the preserves of the independent commodity producers, were redistributed to the benefit of the urban bourgeoisie. Political patronage gave way to the merit principle in provincial administrations, since the functions of the provincial state now required various forms of expertise. State ownership of hydro-electric utilities and various other enterprises was instituted or extended. The line between public and private sectors became increasingly blurred as a variety of institutional links were forged between the business community and the state apparatus. Quasi-public 'boards' or 'funds,' staffed by leading businessmen, were established to distribute the largesse of the provincial treasury among private investors. Advisory councils of various kinds were set up. Intergovernmental relations multiplied, and machinery was established whereby the provinces could deal with one another, with Ottawa, and increasingly with foreign governments as well.

The effect of these changes was threefold. In the first place, and most obviously, the modernized provincial state was a far more effective instrument for the promotion of bourgeois interests than the primitive small-scale state of earlier years. Secondly, ties between the provincial state and the bourgeoisie were strengthened, particularly by the merit system which in a capitalist economy almost ensures a circulation of elites between the corporations and the state, as well as the isolation of state administration from the influence of political parties that may represent other classes. Thirdly, a vast number of state functionaries at the provincial level emerged, and their interest in supporting the power of their provincial state vis-à-vis Ottawa reinforced, and was often even stronger than, the interest of the bourgeoisie in doing likewise.

Owing to the uneven development that has always been a feature of the Canadian political economy, these changes did not occur simultaneously in all provinces. In Ontario they had begun long before the Second World War, while in Newfoundland and Prince Edward Island they were barely underway by 1970. For most of the provinces, however, the fifties and sixties saw this process of institutional development proceeding rapidly. In Quebec it was described as the Quiet Revolution, but the innovations associated with Manning in Alberta, with Roblin in Manitoba, with Robichaud in New Brunswick, and with Stanfield in Nova Scotia were no less 'revolutionary' than those presided over by Jean Lesage. Expenditures by all of the provincial states increased enormously in these years, so that by 1971 they were more than ten times as great as they had been in 1950. Although health and welfare spending contributed substantially towards the increase, especially in the late sixties, most of the growth was in the costs of functions related to capital accumulation, such as hydro-electric power, transportation, industrial subsidies of various kinds, and, above all, education.

Increasing provincial expenditure had two important consequences. In the first place it contributed greatly to conflict between the provinces and Ottawa. Resource revenues, although rising rapidly, were never enough even in Alberta to pay for the increasing functions of the provincial state. Rather than increasing provincial taxes, which might drive away investment as well as annoy the electorate, it was politically more expedient to press for the reduction of federal taxes or the total withdrawal of Ottawa from certain tax fields, leaving the provinces to fill the vacuum. Quebec and Ontario, which had the most to gain by fiscal decentralization, led the onslaught but were supported by most of the other provincial governments, with only occasional and sporadic resistance by a few of the smaller ones. Ottawa was obliging enough in 1955 to separate equalization payments from the tax rental system, thus ensuring that there would be no real resistance from even the poorest provinces to the abandonment of the tax rental system five years later. In the sixties Quebec, Ontario, and later British Columbia demanded massive withdrawals by the federal government from the direct tax fields, and were partially successful. By 1966 Ottawa had agreed to surrender 28 per cent of the income tax it might have collected in all provinces except Quebec, which received 50 per cent of the take in return for agreeing to assume full responsibility for hospital insurance and a number of other programs. Following this, Ottawa became somewhat more intransigent, but it discontinued its estate tax in 1970 with the result that all provinces except Alberta promptly moved into that field as well. Efforts by Ottawa to extricate itself from medical insurance and university grants, in return for which it would make yet another abatement, were unsuccessful in 1973 because the concession offered was not considered generous enough by the provinces. Presumably they believed a better deal might be forthcoming later, and in 1975 Ontario was again predictably howling for 'tax points.' A further federal-provincial conference in 1976 failed to reach agreement, even though the federal offer had been modified in response to the objections of the larger provinces.

The second major consequence of escalating provincial expenditure was to drive the provinces heavily into debt. By 1973 interest charges on all provincial debts amounted to nearly $1.2 billion, substantially more than the total of *all* provincial expenditures in 1950. Borrowing was particularly favoured as a means to cover the costs of investment in electric power developments, or the costs of compensating private owners when these were brought under state ownership. However, borrowing also contributed heavily to meeting the everyday expenditures of provincial government. Only the government of W.A.C. Bennett succeeded in manipulating its accounts to the point at which all borrowing was attributed to various Crown corporations, while the province itself was declared to have no debts at all!

In the early days of the Canadian state the central government borrowed heavily abroad, and both the Act of Union and Confederation were motivated in part by a desire to improve the colonial credit rating in London. In recent years Ottawa has been able to finance all its needs from domestic sources, but the provinces continue to borrow heavily from foreign sources. Of $11 billion worth of provincial bonds and debentures outstanding in 1970, approximately $2.5 billion represented borrowing in the United States and $500 million represented borrowing in other foreign countries.[35] In 1963 the borrowing of $300 million in Boston to compensate the owners of the private power companies taken over by Hydro-Québec prompted the Kennedy administration to impose an 'interest equalization tax' on foreign securities to protect the American balance of payments. This caused such alarm in official Ottawa that a delegation was dispatched to Washington to seek the exemption of Canadian borrowers from the tax. The Americans agreed but understandably asked a heavy price: a ceiling on Canada's foreign exchange reserves which could only be maintained by surrendering control over monetary policy to Washington. The episode illustrates, as does the Columbia River affair, how the pursuit of their own priorities by the provinces can contribute to continental integration and the weakening of Ottawa vis-à-vis the United States.

Another political consequence of provincial dependence on borrowing is the extent to which the freedom of action of the provincial state is circumscribed by the need to make a favourable impression on potential lenders. This is probably not the least important reason why CCF-NDP provincial governments have been less radical in performance than in promise. Jacques Parizeau, who had been the principal economic adviser to Quebec governments in the sixties, charged in 1970 that a consortium of Toronto financial houses had put pressure on the province throughout the decade by threatening to prevent the sale of Quebec bonds on the Canadian money market. Among the consequences he attributed to this pressure were delays in setting up the General Investment Corporation, abandonment of plans for a state-owned steel industry, appointment of the ultra-reactionary Marcel Faribault as an economic adviser to the cabinet in 1968, and the passage of Bill 63 to protect English-language education.[36] Thus the provincial state, while growing in importance relative to the federal state, involving itself more and more deeply in the lives of those ruled by it, and enjoying a certain autonomy vis-à-vis the provincial bourgeoisie on behalf of whom it acts, is itself subject to certain restraints from outside its territorial jurisdiction.

FEDERAL AND PROVINCIAL FUNCTIONS

It may be asked, in the light of this account of the growth of the provincial states, what functions are performed by the state at the federal level. At the risk of some oversimplification it may be said that while the major accumulation functions have increasingly been assumed by the provincial states, the legitimization and coercion functions have continued to be performed to a much greater degree at the federal level. At a rough estimate about three-fifths of total spending by both levels of government on the accumulation function is now done by the provincial states. The proportions are approximately reversed for spending on the legitimization function. This is a reversal of the situation at Confederation, when accumulation was considered the *raison d'être* of the federal state while legitimization was left to the provinces. In addition, Ottawa now spends four times as much as the provincial states on 'protection of persons and property,' a euphemism for the coercive function.[37]

Ottawa's accumulation function has not, of course, disappeared. It still retains its traditional economic responsibilities, such as jurisdiction over railways, canals, banks, and the post office, to which airlines and communications were added as they developed. It finances a large proportion of industrial research and development, as well as assisting exporters through the Department of Industry, Trade and Commerce, the Export Development Corporation, the Canadian International Development Agency, and the Wheat Board. In recent years it has become involved in the petroleum industry through Petro-Canada, Panarctic Oils, and the participation in the Syncrude project.[38] It distributes massive industrial subsidies through the Department of Regional Economic Expansion, although the activities of this department may perform a legitimization function as well. Its manpower and immigration policies provide a supply of skilled labour. In addition, the tariff is still, of course, a significant subsidy for large sections of the industrial economy, particularly in Quebec.

All of these are important functions, but regardless of what the BNA Act may say on the subject, very few of them are performed exclusively at the federal level. The provincial states participate in making federal policy through federal-provincial conferences, through the countless intergovernmental consultative or co-ordinating committees, and through the increasing practice of submitting federal legislative proposals for provincial 'input' before Parliament has the opportunity to consider them. If Ottawa decides to act alone it may not be successful; for example, the Ontario government has apparently frustrated federal plans for a second Toronto airport by refusing to build the necessary access roads.

In addition, the provincial states have moved directly into many of the fields of activity that are normally considered to be under federal jurisdiction. Ontario and British Columbia own important railway systems. Alberta holds a controlling interest in the country's third largest airline (purchased with surplus resource royalties), and three other provinces are involved in commercial aviation as well. Federal legislation has been amended to allow provincial states to own shares in chartered banks. As already noted, the provinces are heavily involved in industrial subsidy programs. Several of them have agencies or programs to assist exporters in penetrating foreign markets. Even functional equivalents of the tariff are not unknown at the provincial level.

Turning to the coercive function it was noted that Ottawa spends four times as much in this area as the provincial states, leaving aside the substantial amount spent at the municipal level for local police forces. This does not, however, give a fully accurate picture of the coercive activities of Ottawa and the provincial states, because the former to a large degree acts as the agent of the latter, and indirectly of the provincial fractions of the dominant class. Most RCMP personnel are in effect rented out to the provincial attorneys-general as provincial police forces, except in Ontario and Quebec which have their own forces. The role played by the RCMP at the behest of Premier Smallwood in violently suppressing the Newfoundland woodworkers' strike of 1959 is an example of how this works in practice.[39] Similarly, the Canadian armed forces can give 'aid to the civil power' only at the request of the attorney-general of the province in which their assistance is required, although unlike the RCMP the armed forces remain under federal command when performing such a function. Even the proclamation of the War Measures Act in October 1970 was a response to demands from the government of Quebec and the mayor of Montreal. Far from being an assertion of federal power against a provincial state, it was a case of Ottawa acting as the agent of a provincial state, and threatening the liberties of all Canadians in the process.

Dealing with labour militancy has been mainly a responsibility of the provincial states since 1925, when the Judicial Committee of the Privy Council in the *Snider* case ruled that federal efforts in this direction violated the provincial jurisdiction over property and civil rights. The federal government has jurisdiction only with respect to airlines, railways, shipping, and its own public service. Because most industries and firms are concentrated in a single province the Judicial Committee's ruling has created no serious difficulty for ruling-class interests. During the Second World War it temporarily ceased to have effect and even in peacetime it could be circumvented, if necessary, by use of the federal power to declare 'Works ... for the general Advantage of Canada' under Section 92-10c of the BNA Act. Although federal governments have certainly not hesitated to crack the whip on occasions when their view of 'the national interest' demanded it, provincial jurisdiction over most of the labour force has probably made the coercion of labour by the state in Canada even more repressive than would otherwise have been the case. Competition among the provinces to attract investment and retain business 'confidence' has led provincial governments to vie with one another in demonstrating their harshness towards labour, even to the point of calling unnecessary elections to secure a 'mandate' for this purpose, as in British Columbia in 1975 and Quebec in 1976. In the poorer provinces the fact that the working class is docile, poorly organized, and underpaid may be among the few inducements that can be offered to potential investors. The imposition of federal wage controls in October 1975 may or may not represent the beginning of a long-term trend to centralize control over labour. Business support for the controls appeared to be much less solid a year later than it did at the time they were first imposed.

The legitimization function in Canada is divided between the two levels of government, with Ottawa responsible for meeting the larger share of the costs. This function was slow to develop in Canada and even today it accounts for less state expenditure overall than the accumulation function. Shared-cost programs or conditional grants have been an important means of performing this function, largely because, as already noted, the BNA Act left it almost entirely to the provinces on the assumption that little expenditure would be required. When the legitimization function became costly the provincial states could not, or would not, perform it without federal assistance. Welfare and health insurance are federally assisted but provincially administered programs, which means that the provincial states probably benefit from whatever gratitude is forthcoming from the recipients. In the case of family allowances Ottawa provides all the funds, but the provinces now have some control over their distribution. Other social programs, such as pensions, OFY, LIP, New Horizons grants, etc., are exclusively the responsibility of the federal level. The list of programs connected with legitimization should also include the many forms of state support for cultural and recreational activities. These have multiplied at the federal level in recent years, although the provincial states have by no means ignored them. Only Quebec, however, argues that such programs should be an exclusive provincial responsibility. This is one of the very few instances in which the Quebec state takes a position vis-à-vis Ottawa which is not supported by the other provincial states. Except possibly in Quebec, the provincial states appear generally much more vigorous in expanding their accumulation function. This reflects the fact that the Canadian bourgeoisie have more regionally specific and heterogeneous needs in regard to accumulation, as a result of the different types of economic activity that predominate in different regions, than they have in regard to legitimization. A family allowance or a pension serves its purpose equally well regardless of whether the recipient works for Macmillan-Bloedel or for General Motors and thus it may as well be provided by Ottawa. This division of functions has the effect that the individual businessman may tend to see more direct and immediate benefit to himself in the activities of the provincial state than in those of Ottawa, however important the latter may be to bourgeois interests in general.

An important task of the state at the federal level is the transfer of funds directly to the provincial states. The collection of provincial corporation and income taxes by Ottawa acting as the agent of the province is not really an example of this, since the taxes in question are levied by the provincial state on residents within its own territorial boundaries. What is meant is rather two distinct phenomena: conditional transfers, whereby Ottawa subsidizes particular provincial programs of its own choice, and unconditional transfers, which are contributions to general provincial revenues. As noted above, conditional transfers have been extensively used to persuade the provincial states to undertake social programs. Given the rigidity of the BNA Act, this was the only possible response to the common interest of the Canadian ruling class in the legitimizing effects of such programs. The recent attempts by Ottawa to unload the entire responsibility for health insurance and welfare onto the provincial states illustrate the tendency for each level of government to prefer spending its scarce funds on accumulation rather than on legitimization, since the former has a greater pay-off both in terms of political support from the bourgeoisie and in partially paying for itself through eventually greater tax revenue.

Unconditional transfers have a history as long as Confederation, but in their predominant modern form of equalization payments they originated in the 1950s. Seven of the ten provinces receive equalization payments. In Newfoundland they account for about one-third of provincial gross general revenues and in each of the Maritime provinces about one-quarter. These payments can perhaps be viewed mainly as performing the function of legitimization, and it is on those grounds that federal politicians argue in favour of equalization, but obviously they contribute indirectly to accumulation in the provinces where they are received. As in the case of DREE subsidies, the beneficiaries are not only the local fractions of the bourgeoisie but also the Ontario and foreign capitalists who extract profits from the underdeveloped hinterlands of Canada.

FEDERAL-PROVINCIAL CONFLICT

Conflict between Ottawa and one or more of the provincial states has been an endemic feature of the Canadian political scene. To discuss it in detail would be virtually to write the history of Canadian politics. All of the provincial states have at one time or another been in conflict with Ottawa, and the catalogue of the issues over which they have contended would be a lengthy one. However, federal-provincial conflict can usefully be divided into several types, an exercise that may contribute to the demystification of this much-discussed but little-understood subject.

Federal-provincial conflict that results from class conflict appears for the moment at least to be almost obsolete, but in the past it was of very considerable importance. As already noted, early conflicts between the Ontario government and the federal government had elements of class conflict, and it was even more pronounced in some later conflicts involving the Prairie provinces, particularly those occasioned by Premier Aberhart's attempts to alleviate the effects of the depression in Alberta.

A much more common type of federal-provincial conflict, especially in recent years, has been based upon conflicts between different segments of the ruling class. The specialized nature of many provincial economies and the concentration of industries in particular provinces is highly conducive to this kind of conflict. To cite the most obvious case, Alberta since 1947 has been the spokesman for the oil industry, and conflict between Alberta and the federal government, as in 1974, may reflect conflicts of interest between the oil industry and other sections of the bourgeoisie. Ontario acted as the spokesman for the gold-mining industry in the thirties, and for the insurance industry in the sixties when Premier Robarts unsuccessfully opposed the establishment of a national pension plan and medical insurance.

In all the cases cited above – and many more could be cited – the provin-

cial state spoke on behalf of the narrow and parochial interest of one segment of the bourgeoisie, while Ottawa spoke on behalf of the more general
and long-term interests of the ruling class as a whole. Narrow and specific
interests can more easily recruit a provincial state to act on their behalf than
they can capture the federal state, which is exposed to a much wider range
of influences, but it would be misleading to assume that this is the invariable pattern. At the turn of the century Laurier's government spoke for the
Orford Copper Company (predecessor of INCO) when it used a threat of dis-
allowance to prevent the proclamation of an Ontario act designed to encourage the processing of nickel in the province.[40]

In Quebec from the 1950s onwards the rapidly growing francophone petite bourgeoisie, whose opportunities in both the federal state apparatus and
the private sector were limited until very recently, developed an ideology of
Quebec nationalism that identified their own interests with those of Quebec
as a whole, and whose logical conclusion was the demand for a fully sovereign Quebec state. These developments, which are more fully treated elsewhere in this volume, added a new dimension to federal-provincial conflict
at the same time as the disintegrative impact of American economic penetration on the Canadian federal state was becoming most acute. Despite the
distinctiveness of the Quebec situation, it is not entirely lacking in similarity
to developments in other provinces (see Pratt's article in this volume) nor
has the Quebec state failed to find allies against Ottawa in other provincial
states, particularly Ontario, whose interests in many respects parallel its
own.

Conflicts between classes, conflicts between different elements of the ruling class, and conflicts between nationalities exist in many political systems
that do not have federal institutions. Even in Canada, federal-provincial
conflict is only one form in which these types of conflict may appear. Class
conflict may appear and run its course within a province, and often does,
given the provincial jurisdiction over industrial relations between labour
and management. National conflict within a province is also not unknown;
the controversies over language legislation in Quebec are an illustration.
Conflict between different sections of the bourgeoisie also appears at the
provincial level, especially in Ontario which has a fairly diverse economy.
(This explains why Ontario can support two viable bourgeois political parties, while Alberta has only one.) Thus one effect of institutional federalism
is that it keeps many conflicts out of the arena of national politics, by
confining them within a province. This is particularly true of class conflict
for a variety of reasons: provincial jurisdiction over matters that are most
likely to provoke class conflict; the predominant federal role in legitimiza-

tion which makes the federal state appear less class-oriented; the greater ability of the federal state to make concessions, especially as compared to the poorer provincial states; and the weakness of workers' and farmers' organizations at the national level.

Even conflicts that are not confined within a province need not take the form of an intergovernmental confrontation. Indeed, the Fathers of Confederation probably assumed that conflicts between different elements of the bourgeoisie and conflicts between the two nationalities would continue to arise and be resolved mainly as they had done from 1841 until 1867: that is to say, within and through the institutions of central government. To some extent, of course, this expectation has been fulfilled, aided by the deliberately representative nature of the federal institutions such as the cabinet, Parliament, and the administrative departments. Conflicts between English Canada and French Canada have often been successfully resolved within the institutions of central government, particularly when the Liberal party was in office. Even when they have been more intractable they have not always become federal-provincial issues: the provincial state of Quebec did not play a significant role in either of the conscription crises. It is equally true, although less celebrated by our liberal historians, that economic conflicts of interest between different segments of the bourgeoisie have sometimes been resolved within the institutions of central government, just as they are in other advanced capitalist countries.

In Canada, however, there is a tendency for these two types of conflict, particularly the latter, to find expression in the form of conflicts between different levels of government, and this tendency may be increasing. Part of the reason for this is institutional: the Canadian parliamentary system cannot accommodate economic conflict within the ruling class as effectively as the American congressional system. The main reason, however, is that economic conflicts within the Canadian ruling class are unusually pronounced as a result of regional specialization, tension between metropolis and hinterland, and the predominance of foreign direct investment. Thus they cannot be easily accommodated at the federal level, and this fact both creates a functional necessity for federalism from the point of view of bourgeois interests and ensures that conflict will be a normal condition of federal-provincial relations.

Not all federal-provincial conflict, however, can be explained in these terms. A very large part of it simply results from the existence of the federal institutions themselves. Organizations, whatever interests they may represent and whatever socio-economic bases they rest upon, develop a dynamic of their own. For the hundreds of politicians and the thousands of functionaries involved in one or the other level of government, promoting the acquisition of power and money by 'their' level of government becomes an end in itself, even if at the same time it may objectively serve the interests of one or another segment of the ruling class.[41] Without this fact, the usefulness of the provincial states to those elements of the ruling class that benefit from their existence would be greatly reduced. It would be difficult to measure how much federal-provincial conflict results from this institutional tendency to self-extension, but much of the conflict over financial aspects of intergovernmental relations admits of no other explanation. Certain jurisdictional controversies, such as the one over cable television in 1974-5, appear to result from the same cause.

The increasing size and complexity of the state apparatus at both levels, particularly the provincial, have increased the likelihood that this type of conflict will occur, and simultaneously economic trends have increased the likelihood of conflict over economic issues. The size and complexity of the state apparatus and the decline of party patronage in public administration also have the effect that intergovernmental conflicts can no longer be resolved, as they once were, on the basis of personal and political relationships among a handful of office-holders. Federal-provincial conferences, councils, and committees have proliferated, but the record of conflict resolution through such means has been unimpressive. Deadlock and stalemate are often the results. The state grows bigger at both levels, but its ability to resolve problems, even in the interests of the ruling class, does not improve. Increasingly one hears of the 'crisis' of Canadian federalism.

PRESENT AND FUTURE TRENDS

Federal states are normally assumed to be of two types. The classic Anglo-Saxon model, described by K.C. Wheare and based on the constitution of the United States, is a system in which two levels of government each perform their own functions more or less in isolation from one another, with a supreme court to define the jurisdictional boundary between them.[42] The central European model, represented particularly by West Germany but towards which the United States is clearly moving in practice, is a system in which the establishment of basic priorities is highly centralized but in which administration is decentralized; in effect, the states are administrative units which carry out centrally determined objectives.

Canada resembles neither of these models. Instead, it is a system reflecting the fragmented and regionalized nature of the economy, in which clear jurisdictional boundaries are absent, in which the provincial states strive constantly to expand their freedom of action, in which priorities at the centre are established only after negotiation with the provincial states, and in which Ottawa acts as the instrument of one or more provincial states as often as it acts independently. Such a system presents a complex picture of collaboration and conflict that seems to defy the standard categories of political science. Robert Bourassa's favourite description of Canada as a 'common market' is hardly that of a disinterested observer, but at times the operation of Canadian federalism does bear a certain resemblance to that of the European Community institutions in Brussels.

Supporters of western European integration have often, and correctly, maintained that until capital is internationalized to a much greater degree little progress is likely in the development of stronger supranational political institutions. They point out that there are corporations located in the individual nation-states, as well as American corporations operating in Europe, but no 'European corporations,' in other words no transnational bourgeoisie that could lay the foundations of an emerging superstate as the instrument of their common purposes.[43]

Although the parallel should not be overstressed, this diagnosis has considerable relevance to the situation of Canadian federalism. There is not in Canada at present a dominant national bourgeoisie whose common purposes require a centralized Canadian state as their instrument. Noting the erosion since Confederation of this essential basis for a 'National Policy,' Donald Smiley refers to a speech delivered in 1971 by Norris Crump, then chairman of the CPR, in which Crump called for an end to all centralized economic policies, setting the provinces free to link up with their 'natural' markets in the United States and overseas.[44] The fact that the CPR, which profited so greatly from the original National Policy, should now call for its antithesis appears paradoxical, but the paradox is easily explained. Canadian Pacific has diversified its operations, and today derives as much profit from investments in the resource industries as from transportation; in addition, the mining and pulp and paper industries and the continentally integrated automobile industry account for most of its railway freight revenue. Balkanization would benefit the CPR of Crump and Sinclair as much as economic nationalism benefited the CPR of Shaughnessy and Van Horne.

The functions which a modern state performs for a capitalist class are performed, as far as Canada is concerned, in part by the American state and in part by the provincial states, leaving a fairly limited, although not negligible, role for the Canadian federal state. Thus for the most part the present decentralized character of Canadian federalism suits the purposes of Canadian – and American – capitalists. This is not to say that complete homogeneity of interest and outlook prevails. Crump's views are probably characteristic of the resource industries, whether Canadian- or American-owned. Even if the United States should take a diminishing share of Canada's resource exports, which is quite likely to be the case, this would not change. A strong central state is not needed to sell raw materials to resource-hungry Europe and Japan, as Norris Crump well knows.[45] Strong provincial states, on the other hand, are useful spokesmen for the resource industries in their conflicts with other economic interests in Canada, a role which Alberta, Saskatchewan, and Newfoundland played effectively in the federal-provincial energy conferences of 1974 and 1975.

The interests of secondary manufacturing are somewhat different and not homogeneous. The automobile industry is a special case because it is completely integrated on a continental basis as a result of the Automotive Products Treaty in 1965. It is true that the treaty itself resulted from the temporarily coinciding interests of Ottawa and of the corporations, and that Ottawa still performs certain functions for them, notably that of protecting them from European and Japanese competition by means of a tariff substantially higher than that imposed by the United States. In general, however, the automobile industry can find a far more reliable instrument in the provincial state of Ontario, since the industry is overwhelmingly concentrated in Ontario and dominates that province's economy to almost the same extent that the petroleum industry dominates Alberta's. Revealing evidence of how reliable the instrument is can be found in the fact that in July 1975 the Ontario government announced the exemption from provincial sales tax of automobiles 'assembled in North America from North American parts.'[46] The purpose of the last four words was to exclude from this exemption the Swedish cars assembled in Nova Scotia, which from the Ontario government's point of view are apparently more 'foreign' than American cars assembled in Michigan or Ohio. In effect, one province, acting on behalf of an American-owned industry, raised a tariff barrier against another province, a practice explicitly forbidden in Section 121 of the BNA Act.

Action of this kind is not welcomed by all sectors of American-owned secondary manufacturing in Canada. In a 1972 speech the chairman of Canadian General Electric, J. Herbert Smith, referred to a new system of power transmission developed by his firm with the aid of a grant from Ottawa and noted that its commercial success would depend on 'the degree to which the provincially-owned utilities use the new system for their power transmission needs.' One province, however, had already opted for a foreign system. From this episode he drew a general conclusion: 'Unfortunately for this national strategy, the Canadian market is not a single economic unit but is, in reality, ten separate "countries," each with its own purchasing policies related to provincial, not national, objectives ... Industrial strategies can be successful when national policy is implemented on the basis of integrating the Canadian market into a single economic unit of twenty million people. Strategies are at risk when that market is not so integrated, and in fact is divided by ten.'[47]

Mr Smith did not suggest any basic modification of Canadian federalism; indeed he argued that incentives to the provinces and 'imaginative' use of Ottawa's existing legislative powers could overcome some of the difficulties inherent in the system. His conclusion that industrial strategies should be developed 'in concert with the private sector and provincial governments' indicated his acceptance of, and could even be interpreted as an encouragement to, the pretensions of the provincial states to involve themselves in every area of economic policy.

None the less, it appears that certain elements of the industrial bourgeoisie have an interest at least in preventing any further erosion of federal power, and possibly even in strengthening Ottawa vis-à-vis the provinces. Those firms which conduct extensive research and development in Canada, and which aspire to sell manufactured end products in overseas markets, clearly require the assistance of the state both in financing the research and in penetrating the markets. For the moment at least, Ottawa is better equipped than any province to perform these particular functions. This reasoning does not apply to industries that are integrated on a continental basis, or to those 'miniature replica' branch plants that are content to operate in domestic markets behind the barrier of the tariff. In short, it applies to what is still a rather small minority sector of the Canadian economy.

There are, however, signs that this sector may be growing, in other words that a fraction of the bourgeoisie may be emerging that would rely very heavily on the federal state and operate in large part through public or quasi-public institutions, more or less on the French or Italian model. The establishment of the Canada Development Corporation, the efforts to sell CANDU nuclear reactors on foreign markets, the force-feeding of an indigenous aircraft industry through the state-financed STOL project, and the repatriation of control over the Montreal Locomotive Works after its previous American owners attempted to block sales to Cuba are all indications of a trend. The remarkable growth in the activities of the Export Development Corporation and the Canadian International Development Agency also seems to indicate the emergence of this fraction and its use of state institutions for its own benefit.

The weakness of this pro-centralist fraction of the Canadian bourgeoisie, however, was revealed by the less than vigorous response to the electoral victory of the Parti Québécois on 15 November 1976. With few exceptions the political and journalistic spokesmen for the Anglo-Canadian bourgeoisie had no better response than to suggest a further erosion of federal powers to reinforce the powers of all ten provincial states within a 'Confederation' that would become little more than a common market. Such inanities neither appease the petit-bourgeois nationalists who want a formally sovereign Quebec nor offer anything to the working class and the farmers of Quebec, who would gain little or nothing from *indépendance*. The no longer negligible francophone bourgeoisie (Bombardier, Marine Industries, Power Corporation, etc.) is in many ways more dependent on a strong federal state than its counterparts in the West or even Ontario, but its political instrument, the Liberal party, is in disarray both federally and provincially.

At the time of writing the future of the federal state is difficult to predict with much assurance. It is apparent that the Anglo-Canadian ruling class is no longer deeply enough interested in 'national unity' to resist Quebec's departure by force. Some fractions of the ruling class, particularly in the West, might even favour Quebec's departure on the grounds that it would remove much of the burden of high tariffs, equalization payments, and Ottawa's regional development policies. In these circumstances, the future of Quebec – and of Canada – is likely to be decided within Quebec itself.

What form of Canadian federal state, if any, could survive the departure of Quebec is difficult to foresee. Analysis of the Canadian bourgeoisie and its economic interests lends little support to the notion, fashionable in the 1960s, that English Canada would become more centralized and cohesive after severing its ties with Quebec. More likely, Quebec's departure would be followed by further fragmentation as regional fractions of the ruling class sought to make their own arrangements with external centres of economic power. In the long term, the most likely outcome of these developments would be the formal annexation of the English-speaking provinces by the United States. Since few Americans would wish to annex Quebec, it would presumably survive as an 'independent' republic, albeit safely within the informal hegemony of US imperialism.

NOTES

1 Although Charles A. Beard denied that he was a Marxist, every Marxist interested in federalism should read his classic study, *An Economic Interpretation of
  the Constitution of the United States.* First published in 1913 and reissued in pa-
  perback in 1965, it shows clearly the class interests at stake in the struggles between federalists and anti-federalists over the adoption of the constitution.
2 *The State in Capitalist Society* (London 1969), 52-3
3 *Ibid.,* 171
4 *The Fiscal Crisis of the State* (New York 1973), 90
5 Michael Reagan, *The New Federalism* (New York 1972)
6 For example, John Wilson, 'The Canadian Political Cultures,' in *Canadian Journal of Political Science,* VII, 3 (Sept. 1974), and Edwin R. Black, *Divided Loyalties*
  (Montreal 1975)
7 *The Vertical Mosaic* (Toronto 1965), 382
8 Frank Mackinnon in a review of Black, *Divided Loyalties,* in *Canadian Journal
  of Political Science,* IX, 3 (Sept. 1976), 499-501
9 For a criticism of contemporary political scientists along these lines, see Donald
  V. Smiley, *Canada in Question* (2nd ed., Toronto 1976), 220-8.
10 *Unequal Union* (Toronto 1968), *passim,* especially chaps. 16 and 18
11 Royal Commission on Dominion-Provincial Relations, *Report of Hearings,* p.
  9718
12 'The Rise and Fall of the Third Commercial Empire of the St Lawrence,' in
  Gary Teeple, ed., *Capitalism and the National Question in Canada* (Toronto
  1972), 1-41
13 Harold Innis, *The Cod Fisheries* (New Haven 1940), 350-64
14 'Rise and Fall,' 14
15 Most Canadian farmers have been independent commodity producers. For a
  discussion of this fact and its consequences, see C.B. Macpherson, *Democracy in
  Alberta* (2nd ed., Toronto 1962), especially 10-20 and 221-30.
16 See Bruce W. Hodgins, 'Disagreement at the Commencement: Divergent Onta-
  rian Views of Federalism, 1867-1871,' in Donald Swainson, ed., *Oliver Mowat's
  Ontario* (Toronto 1972), 52-68.
17 Two excellent works that explore this theme are Macpherson, *Democracy in
  Alberta,* and J.R. Mallory, *Social Credit and the Federal Power in Canada* (Toronto 1954).
18 See the table in *Quick Canadian Facts* (29th annual ed., Toronto 1973), 172.
19 The monarchical basis of Canadian resource law, and the contrast with the
  United States, are discussed by H.V. Nelles, *The Politics of Development* (Toronto 1974), 1-49. See also G.V. Laforest, *Natural Resources and Public Property
  under the Canadian Constitution* (Toronto 1969).

20 D.G. Creighton, *British North America at Confederation* (Ottawa 1939), Table I, p. 98

21 *Ibid.*, 55-6

22 Nelles, *Politics of Development*, 335-46

23 The transfer of these resources to the provinces is described in Chester Martin, *'Dominion Lands' Policy* (Toronto 1973), chap. 12.

24 See Roger Graham's biography of Meighen, vol. I, *The Door of Opportunity* (Toronto 1960) and vol. II, *And Fortune Fled* (Toronto 1963); see also Porter, *Vertical Mosaic*, 542-4, and W.L. Morton, *The Progressive Party in Canada* (Toronto 1950), 140.

25 *Essays in Canadian Economic History* (Toronto 1956), 209, 236, 251, 279, 317-18. The essays cited were originally published between 1937 and 1941.

26 The competition from US capitalism was viewed as a threat in the days of Macdonald, and a strong federal state was established for this reason. Today US capitalism is viewed as a partner rather than as a threat.

27 In October 1976 the premier of Alberta said he would ask US senators and congressmen and the US ambassador in Ottawa to lobby the Canadian government to change Canadian tariff regulations to benefit the petroleum industry. *Globe and Mail*, Toronto, 22 Oct. 1976

28 'The Growth of Government Activities since Confederation,' a study prepared for the Royal Commission on Dominion-Provincial Relations (Ottawa 1939), 5

29 Data derived from *National Accounts, Income and Expenditure*, 1955-7, and *National Income and Expenditure Accounts* (quarterly) for 1974

30 *Ibid.*

31 Derived from the table in *Canada One Hundred, 1867-1967* (Ottawa 1967), 260

32 This relationship has been more extensively explored by the present author in 'Continental Integration and Canadian Unity' in Andrew Axline *et al.*, eds., *Continental Community? Independence and Integration in North America* (Toronto 1974), 194-217.

33 See Tremblay, *Indépendance et Marché Commun Québec-Etats Unis* (Montreal 1970).

34 Interesting case studies illustrating the operation of this process are found in Philip Mathias, *Forced Growth* (Toronto 1971).

35 *Canada Year Book* (1973), 829

36 *Globe and Mail*, 7 Feb. 1970

37 'Coercive' expenditure on national defence, which has recently increased quite sharply, is largely designed to secure trade concessions from the United States and the European Community, which expect Canada to contribute its share to defending 'the free world.' Thus the real purpose served is one of accumulation.

38 Not all of the ruling class support these initiatives. The new leader of the opposition, a good friend of the petroleum industry, has promised to dispose of Petro-Canada if he wins office. *Globe and Mail*, 3 Nov 1976

39 For a brief account, see Peter C. Newman, *Renegade in Power; The Diefenbaker Years* (Toronto 1963), 112-18.

40 H.V. Nelles, 'Empire Ontario: The Problems of Resource Development,' in Swainson, *Oliver Mowat's Ontario*, 189-210

41 A useful discussion of the organizational dynamic of bureaucracy and its usefulness to the ruling class may be found in Nicos Poulantzas, 'On Social Classes,' *New Left Review*, 78 (March-April 1973), 40-8.

42 *Federal Government* (4th ed., London and New York 1963)

43 A fascinating Marxist analysis of this whole subject may be found in Ernest Mandel, *Europe vs. America: Contradictions of Imperialism* (New York 1972); see in particular chap. 9, 'The Future of Supranational Institutions.'

44 Donald V. Smiley, 'Canada and the Quest for a National Policy,' *Canadian Journal of Political Science*, VIII 1 (March 1975), 40

45 Although Canadian-based resource companies are increasingly international in scope, this does not imply that they need a strong central government in Canada. In the last analysis they will look to Washington, not Ottawa, to protect their interests in the Third World. When Alcan's holdings in Guyana were nationalized, it was the American government that protested, not the Canadian. Ottawa could never have the ability to intervene effectively in such a situation.

46 *Globe and Mail*, 15 July 1975

47 'Industrial Strategy and Canadian Sovereignty,' remarks to the 79th annual meeting, Canadian General Electric Company Limited, Toronto, 1972

4

The decline and fall of the Quebec Liberal regime: contradictions in the modern Quebec state

HENRY MILNER

The question addressed in this essay in its simplest form is: why is Quebec different? Why the constant turmoil and crisis – the whole gamut of political changes, declarations, strikes, scandals, confrontations – that seem to make contemporary Quebec different from Canada and elsewhere?[1] What might be called the 'culturalist fallacy,' which at its most basic says that as a group Les Québécois are just not like other Canadians, may be dismissed as uninformative. Its common though often unarticulated acceptance helps explain why there has been relatively little serious analysis of this question. Moreover, the rather frequent assertions, especially on the left, that Quebec is different because it is seeking national independence or because the Quebec working class is 'revolutionary' should be recognized as in themselves insufficient. For one thing, much of the revolutionary content is merely rhetoric: radical change expressed in the words of trade union leaders but not in actions or events. It becomes evident that, if a useful contribution is to be made, the first requirement is an appropriate theoretical framework.

The theoretical framework used here is in large part the Marxist conception of the state, a framework which even today remains relatively undeveloped, though in the past few years some notable progress has been made. For Marxists the function of the state in a capitalist society is to serve the *long-term* interests of the *whole* ruling class. The state is understood to serve the interests of the bourgeoisie not so much in its day-to-day activities as to ensure the continuity of capitalist relations of production, and not only in the face of the fundamental challenge potentially posed by the proletariat but also, at times, against short-term threats posed by fractions within the bourgeoisie whose immediate interests pit them against the global interests of their class. Consequently, the actual form of the role of the state will differ under different conditions of capitalism, though the ultimate content remains unchanged.

In recent years the most far-reaching (as well as most noted) economic transformation has been the transition from 'market' to 'monopoly' capitalism. While the Marxist analysis of this phenomenon shares certain common elements with the most widely known formulations of contemporary prophets of the 'technological society,'[2] the former is more concrete and thus serves our needs better. Marxists generally understand the transition to monopoly capitalism to comprehend the following characteristics: (1) a significant increase in the size of the basic productive units, the corporations; (2) a noticeable shift among these corporations from being national to international in scope; (3) the domination on the part of these huge corporations or 'multinationals' of key industries which, combined, form the monopoly sector of Western economies; and (4) the monopoly sector is characterized by the replacement of market instability by corporate planning through: (a) the manipulation of consumer demand through advertising rather than price competition;[3] (b) increases in productivity through increasing dependence on a highly sophisticated technology and a mobile and relatively skilled work force; and (c) the integration of corporate decision-making through intercorporate ownership, interlocking directorships, etc.

This transition presupposes and hence entails a far more decisive role for the state in relation to corporate planning. Among its functions[4] are (1) the politically structured guidance of capital into sectors neglected by the market through subsidies, 'regulation,' fiscal and taxation policy, etc.; (2) the improvement of the material infrastructure (transportation, education, health, vocational training, urban and regional planning, housing, etc.); (3) the improvement of the non-material infrastructure (promotion of science, research and development, granting of patents, etc.; (4) increasing the productivity of labour (universal education, manpower retraining, etc.[5]); (5) unproductive state consumption (military spending, etc.); and (6) 'strengthening of national competitive capacity' (creation of supranational economic blocks, imperialistic safe-guarding of international stratification, etc.).

With this expanding economic role of the state, it becomes necessary and useful to speak of three sectors of the capitalist economy: the monopoly sector, the competitive sector, and the 'state' sector, each employing, very roughly, about one-third of the work force. Furthermore, it has been cogently argued, though not yet substantiated, by James O'Connor and his students[6] that it is the 'state sector' that experiences the fiscal crisis of contemporary capitalism most directly, a crisis predicted in its general form by Marx. A concise statement of this argument is found in an excerpt from a recently published article – although it deals specifically with the case of the United States its application is far wider:

The corporate [that is, monopoly] sector has squeezed small business through its greater productivity and consequent ability to pay higher wages; yet it has employed a declining portion of the nation's work force. As a result, the public sector has been forced to take up the slack, providing jobs where the private sector will not, providing assistance and welfare where no jobs are available, and supplying the services needed by the unemployed and the 'working poor' in the low-wage competitive sector ...

The government's fiscal crisis is a direct consequence of these economic forces: Government revenues decline as employment in the high-wage, high-profit corporate sector declines (relatively) and incomes and profits in the small business sector are reduced still further.

At the same time, government expenditures rise, as more and more pressures are imposed on it, both to meet the needs of the corporate sector and to take care of those people and small business which corporate action has squeezed out of economic life ...

As workers are driven from decaying small towns into the cities, or into the sprawling suburbs, the public sector must provide more roads, more recreation facilities, more mass transit, medical facilities, child care, and urban renewal ...

The declining quality of life leads to growing demands on government, especially from city-dwellers, for social services, better public service jobs, and so on. To keep social peace, government at all levels has acceded to these demands with the result that taxes have risen to pay these growing social costs while the costs have risen even faster. This creates a simultaneous fiscal crisis at all levels of government.[7]

While this thesis has been subjected to serious critical evaluation, its central argument remains convincing on the whole. If nothing else, it serves to draw the attention of political economists to the state, though unfortunately the definition of exactly what is meant by 'the state' has been insufficiently examined. Turning to this question, we find Marxists presented with two main approaches, both fraught with conceptual difficulties. The first, proposed notably by Ralph Miliband and adopted by Leo Panitch in an essay in this collection, is one that on the surface appears the most reasonable: that is, the state is that complex of institutions exclusively limited to the public sphere.[8]

The opposing definition is put forth by Louis Althusser and taken up by Nicos Poulantzas. Althusser notes: 'In order to advance the theory of the State it is indispensable to take into account ... reality which is clearly on the side of the (repressive) State apparatus, but must not be confused with it. I shall call this reality by its concept: *the ideological State apparatuses ...*' Althusser readily admits that some of his state institutions fall into the 'private' as opposed to the 'public' domain, but adds that 'Gramsci ... had the "remarkable" idea that the State could not be reduced to the (Repressive) State Apparatus, but included, as he put it, a certain number of institutions from "*civil society*": the Church, the Schools, the trade unions, etc. ... Much the larger part of the Ideological State Apparatuses (in their apparent dispersion) are part ... of the *private* domain. Churches, Parties, Trade Unions, families, some schools, most newspapers, cultural ventures, etc., etc., are private ... The distinction between the public and the private is a distinction internal to bourgeois law, and valid in the (subordinate) domains in which bourgeois law exercises its "authority." The domain of the State escapes it because the latter is "above the law": the State, which is the State *of* the ruling class, is neither public nor private; on the contrary, it is the precondition for any distinction between public and private. The same thing can be said from the starting-point of our State Ideological Apparatuses.'[9]

Poulantzas' definition follows directly on that of Althusser: '... the system of the State is composed of *several apparatuses or institutions* of which certain have a principally repressive role, in the strong sense, and others a principally ideological role. The former constitute the repressive apparatus of the State ... (government, army, police, tribunals and administration). The latter constitute the *ideological apparatuses of the State*, such as the Church, the political parties, the unions (with the exception of course, of the *revolutionary* party or trade union organizations), the schools, the mass media (newspapers, radio, television), and, from a certain point of view, the family. This is so whether they are *public* or *private*.' His inclusion of these 'private' institutions within the state follows directly upon Althusser's formulations, though his clarification in relation to parties and trade unions as well as his back-pedalling on the family is a welcome addition. In a sentence, Poulantzas defines the state as 'the instance that maintains the cohesion of a social formation and which reproduces the conditions of production of a social system by maintaining class domination.'[10]

Poulantzas contends that, although given greater room to maneouvre, ideological state institutions are ultimately dependent on the repressive state apparatus. In support of this position we may point to examples of this dependent relationship such as the customary exemption of churches from property taxation, the certification of trade unions and professional associations, the licensing of broadcasting, and the subsidization of political parties and 'private' schools (in Quebec to a tune of up to 80 per cent). Finally, as Poulantzas notes, revolutionaries, in organizing to 'smash' the state, know (or should know) that the institutions to be overturned are ideological as well as repressive and extend far into the 'private' domain.

For these reasons the broader conceptualization above seems more useful than the Miliband/Panitch version. Nevertheless, as Miliband pointed out in his criticism of Poulantzas' formulation,[11] it becomes difficult to apply: how and where are we practically to draw the line that separates the state from the remainder of social reality? This criticism is not fatal, however, for what matters is its conceptual clarity in explaining the functioning of capitalist institutions generally; the term 'public' will be used to denote that subset of institutions encompassed in the Panitch formulation. Most simply, institutions within the public sphere are those where the main employer is one or another level of government. Within the public sphere are many institutions that carry out the functions of the state, but not all. In differing proportions, each of the state functions – that is, repression (or coercion), legitimation (the ideological function), and accumulation[12] – is carried on both within and outside the public sector. The nurse in both public and private hospital, the teacher in public and private school, the bureaucrat in a reformist trade union and his counterpart in the Ministry of Labour; the broadcaster with the CBC and with CTV; the social worker employed by the state and the one working for a 'private' agency – all serve the state. O'Connor, when seen from this perspective, is really speaking of the fiscal crisis of the public sector. The crisis of the state, at least in so far as this analysis of Quebec is concerned, is both wider and, in its immediate implications, more limited in scope.

A final element that contemporary Marxism adds to the discussion is a structural definition of social classes enabling us in principle to link particular classes and strata with given state fuctions.[13] For example, we can clarify the specific differences among the workers of the three sectors under contemporary capitalism and still see them as fundamentally united by the basic oppression common to them.[14] Because this paper is only indirectly concerned with the working class we leave this point in its general form and turn to the application of Marxist class analysis to the group that directly concerns us, which is the petite bourgeoisie and a specific stratum within it, the 'state middle class.'

The traditional petite bourgeoisie is to be found employed in the competitive sector, which itself has been noted to be declining in importance in the capitalist economy. This declining group, like the peasantry under early capitalism, serves mainly to provide the 'foot soldiers' of the ruling class (in Quebec these foot soldiers often take the form of Liberal party cadres). The second stratum of the petite bourgeoisie, sometimes referred to as the 'new middle class' or more narrowly as the 'new professionals,' is more important, its steady recent growth coinciding with the expansion of the public sector where it is mainly employed. The term 'new professionals' focuses on a key characteristic of this stratum, namely the tendency for its members' skills to be defined through certification by a professional or semi-professional organization (itself in turn usually certified by the state). It is 'middle' class in the sense that its members tend to play intermediate roles in the economic system. Terrence Johnson notes: 'Specialist occupational tasks may include either the typically fragmented and routinised tasks of the collective labourer or functions of coordination and unity which are equally a product of the labour process and therefore the collective labourer ... Such professionals may be regarded agents of the collective labourer and their incomes derive from labour in the form of wages. On the other hand specialist occupational tasks may be associated with the global functions of capital particularly in respect of the work of control and surveillance, and including the reproduction of labour.'[15] In this sense, the new professionals are 'middle class,' as Carchedi has employed the term, located by their intermediate and contradictory economic class position: 'In locating certain professional occupations in the "new middle" class we may follow Carchedi in viewing them as agents of both the collective labourer and global capital. They are, then, part of a class which carries out the global functions of capital without owning the means of production ... while at the same time and in various ratios carry out the functions of the collective labourer – they are then both labourer-non-labourer, exploited and exploiters.'[16] And the state is directly implicated, as we have noted:

As the state has become more active in this process [of reproduction of the social conditions necessary for the maintenance of class relationships], state heteronomy as an institutionalized form of the control of occupational activities has become increasingly important ... heteronomy refers to the intervention of the state to remove from both the occupation and the client ... the authority to determine the content and manner of practice. There are variations in the extent of this intervention. At one extreme the state may attempt to ensure a desired distribution of occupational services of a determinate kind through the creation of a state agency which is the effective employer of all practitioners who have a statutory obligation to provide the service. Social work is an example of this ... State heteronomy may be more limited however; involving, at the other extreme, a minimal encroachment on an existing, institutionalized system of colleague control ...

Whatever the balance of this intermeshing of state and 'profession,' determining the institutionalized forms by which occupational services are controlled, the very services themselves represent mechanisms of control in the processes of reproduction. State heteronomy refers to a situation where occupational definitions of, for ex-

ample, success and failure in education, sickness and health, deviant and normal be-
havior, are subordinated to or derived from 'official' definitions.[17]

Utilizing a broad functional definition of the state with the above insights into the role of the middle class, we can begin to speak meaningfully
of the *state middle class*. The state middle class comprises those 'new
professionals' engaged in directly or indirectly carrying out the three functions of the state in a specialist or co-ordinating role.

Before continuing, let us summarize the key theoretical points made
above: (1) the state serves the long-term interests of the whole bourgeoisie;
(2) under emerging conditions of monopoly capitalism, its role has widely
expanded so that we may speak of three very roughly equal sectors: monopoly, competitive, public; (3) the state (which is wider than the public sector)
serves three essential functions: repression, legitimation, and accumulation;
(4) the increasing pressures upon the state involved in carrying out these
functions are understood to cause an escalating fiscal crisis and lead to
mounting working-class discontent, both notably in the public sector; and
(5) monopoly capitalism brings into existence a state middle class which
must co-ordinate and carry out the vital collective or cohesive tasks of the
system.

Finally, in so far as legitimation is concerned, one may speak of several
'models' through which the co-operation or at least passivity of the working
class may be won (excluding fascism – where the risks and high costs[18]
make it an instance of last resort). For our purposes the key models are two,
with the second having two variants:

1 *The European model:*[19] The existence of classes is socially acknowledged
and both manifested and moderated through the party system as well as
trade union declarations and actions. Through these institutions limited
bargaining takes place between the classes, resulting in the winning of inter-
mittent concrete 'welfare state' gains for the working class but also its co-
optation through 'social compacts,' economic planning boards, and the like.

2 *The North American model:* The existence of classes and the class role
of the state is both obfuscated and sublimated through selective articulation, diffusion, and incorporation of national, regional, racial, and religious
interests by the various state institutions. There are two major variants:
(*a*) *liberal nationalism:* the gradual development and consolidation of an
essentially unchallenged link between private property, national consciousness, and state allegiance – as in the United States where 'socialism is

"un-American" '; (b) *liberal consociationalism*: the mystification of the monopoly capitalist system and the subordinate role of the state within it through decentralization of administrative powers and through domination of the national political arena by elite groups expressing 'regional' demands and grievances – as in Canada.[20]

The above models are extremely sketchy, but will serve our purposes here. Let us first note that inherent in each of these models are built-in contradictions in the system of legitimation itself. In the Canadian variant, contradictions are revealed most dramatically in endless Quebec-Canada and federal-provincial wrangling, in problems of mobility associated with the 'vertical mosaic,'[21] and in the nation-wide inability to effectively oppose foreign economic and cultural domination. Contradictions in the American variant are manifested in the exploitative decay of the natural environment, the general alienation that characterizes urban life, recurrent outbreaks of senseless violence, and continuing racism. Within the European context, manifestatations of contradictions are more direct than sublimated; class divisions are reopened in sometimes serious contestations (for example, France 1968) and then renegotiated and temporarily resolved (usually through the election of social-democratic regimes).

In the North American variants, legitimation (obfuscation) is clearly a major institutional task given over primarily to the state middle class. The relative autonomy of this stratum from the repressive apparatus serves to enhance its ability and willingness to carry out its ideological tasks. In the European setup, elements from this stratum regularly hold direct political (though not state) power through 'labour' governments. In this situation the role of the state middle class remains important, but its place within the social formation, politically and culturally, is more assured. It is one thing merely to sell capitalist class relations; it is another to have the power and status to negotiate and 'settle' their particular forms (within parameters of course set out in advance by the system of production).

With this last point made, this section can be ended by setting out how the thesis is to be applied to Quebec and establishing the definition of a few of the key concepts to be used:

1 The fiscal crisis of the state as well as other (international) factors have led to increasing militancy (though, except for a small minority, not revolutionary consciousness) among workers in Quebec, especially in the public sector.
2 This crisis, coinciding as it does with the expanded role of the state under

monopoly capitalism, has placed great pressures upon the state and hence, and in particular, upon the state middle class to perform its required functions.

3 The state middle class, however, due to general factors and especially due to certain ones specific to Quebec in the years 1966-76, has itself been increasingly unwilling to accept the legitimacy of the regime (and to defend it) along the lines of liberal consociationalism. This has been most clearly evident in the continuously increasing adherence of key elements in the state middle class to a specific form of Quebec nationalism.

4 The American variant is ruled out for Quebec,[22] leaving only the possibility of a change to the European model of legitimation as class obfuscation becomes increasingly unsuccessful and costly in the face of the above developments.

5 While this alternative is objectively appropriate in Quebec at this time, especially in so far as it conforms to the interests of the state middle class, its indissoluble link to national independence (a) has made it far more difficult to win than is objectively necessary due to built-in electoral obstacles, and (b) has added an intensity to the struggle which extends beyond the actual differences in interests between the state middle class and the regime it is expected to serve.

The general class and political formation of contemporary Quebec is set out in Figure 1. For the purposes of this analysis the key terms are defined as follows:

The regime is the 'ruling class' or rather stratum of the state: it consists of cabinet ministers, top civil servants, key political and economic advisers, and the individuals and groups that link the state with the bourgeoisie (for example, the directors of public corporations).

The state middle class consists essentially of those 'professionals' who are expected to carry out the global or collective functions of the monopoly capitalist state, especially legitimation, usually under conditions of relative autonomy from the repressive apparatus. The list, in no special order, would likely include teachers and professors, psychologists, technicians, journalists, planners, economists, broadcasters, nurses, social workers, trade union officials, professional athletes, artists, entertainers, ministers, scientists, as well as members of the 'older professions' (medicine, etc.) employed directly or indirectly in the public sector.

Figure 1

Class, industry, and the state in Quebec

SECTOR:	PUBLIC	MONOPOLY Heavy industry, manu- facturing, finance	COMPETITIVE Primary, light secondary, construction, services
Ruling class	*Regime*	*Bourgeoisie* American and English Canadian and small French Canadian Liberal	*Moyenne bourgeoisie* English and French Canadian and immigrant Mainly Liberal
	←——— link ———→		
Middle class	*Public and para-public middle class* Expanding Increasingly unionized – CNTU and CEQ PQ supporters French Canadian	*'New middle class, new professionals'* Increasingly PQ Mainly French Canadian	*Petite bourgeoisie* Small business, sales distribution, some 'older' professions Some third party, mainly Liberal
	←——— state functions ———→		
Working class	*State workers* Increasingly unionized – mainly CNTU Mainly PQ French Canadian *State clients:* students – PQ, plus others	*Organized working class* Mainly French Canadian Generally unionized – QFL Increasingly PQ	*Unorganized working class* French Canadian and immigrant Liberal and some third party

The state apparatus is composed of identifiable governmentally controlled institutions and those employed in them. Its breadth and activities provide a minimal approximation of corresponding aspects of the state; and changes in the former signal corresponding changes in the latter.

THE DEVELOPMENT OF THE QUEBEC STATE

Three points should be noted initially: (1) The main thrust of the transition from market to monopoly capitalism with its concomitant social and political changes took place very late in Quebec – in the early 1960s with the coming of the Quiet Revolution. (2) The nationalism or *indépendantisme* which became a *cause célèbre* in the 1960s was itself not new to Quebec. Nationalism, as Léon Dion has explained,[23] has been fundamental to all Quebec ideologies throughout its history. What was new was the clear link between the national aspirations of Québécois and the perceived and actual role of the Quebec state since 1960. (3) The Quebec state apparatus grew remarkably in size and in its share of public attention during this period. Staffs and budgets multiplied but so did scandals in the regime. The government constantly was called upon for resolution of economic and cultural issues of virtually all kinds; it became the prime, sometimes seemingly the only, focus of public concern.

To comprehend the significance of these general developments, one must place them in the context of the 'ancien régime' that preceded the Quiet Revolution. The view of the state in Quebec has traditionally been a negative one which consociational theorists call 'nation-saving.' Throughout most of its history the Quebec state apparatus never took on a positive identification with the nation. The Quebec nation as a cultural entity was there before the emergence of industrial capitalism, and long before the possibility of political independence presented itself in the middle of the nineteenth century. The opportunities to participate in Canadian statehood and to elect representatives to a provincial government with limited powers were not enthusiastically embraced in Quebec, as they were elsewhere in Canada where they were given a certain positive national meaning. The nation was identified in the early days with the traditional way of life the Québécois had developed. For the most part, participation in the federal government and the selection of provincial administrations, apart from the avenue it provided to jobs and contracts, was seen negatively – viewed as a distasteful necessity for defence of the nation from external, particularly cultural, challenges. The tasks of the nation were not economic – these lay essentially elsewhere, among the English-speaking owning class – but were rather cultural and social. These latter tasks lay in the domain of the traditional Québécois institutions (left to them after the British conquest) built around the church and parish; the job of the state apparatus was merely to defend them from encroachment. This was as true of the Québécois' view of their relation to the federal state as of the provincial government's 'proper' role, and accounts, at least in part, for the success of seemingly different politicians like Duplessis and St Laurent. Of course, during this period the state did its part towards accumulation when called upon by the business class, but these were 'private' transactions conducted in English by gentlemen – of 'no interest' to any but those directly concerned.

By the late 1950s Quebec society found itself under increasing pressure to develop an economic and technological infrastructure in keeping with the needs of advanced capitalism, yet lacking the necessary basic institutional network. Most notable in its absence was a well-defined new professional stratum able and willing to manage a state apparatus in keeping with the economic requirements placed upon it. Given the constitutional and cultural realities of Quebec, there was no alternative; the Quebec state had to serve this purpose. During the Quiet Revolution the infrastructure rapidly developed, not simply because Jean Lesage and the revitalized provincial Liberals willed it – Paul Sauvé would have had to do much the same had he lived to lead a Union Nationale government throughout the early 1960s – but because the changing socio-economic conditions dictated it.

In Quebec, since the transition was later, it was also more rapid than in Canada or in the Western world in general. In a few years Quebec developed not only the administrative and technical structure of a modern state but also much of its cultural apparatus – in education, mass media, the arts, etc. Without going into any detailed description of the well-known changes brought about, it is useful to cite a few statistics to give a sense of their extent: (1) Quebec government revenues from all sources including state expenses and services went from $758 million in 1961 to $3383 million in 1970; income taxes accounted for 41.7 per cent in 1970, up from 16.4 per cent in 1961; (2) between 1961 and 1970 provincial government expenditures quadrupled, while federal government expenditures in Quebec merely doubled, with the result that in 1970 the provincial government was spending roughly $4 billion to the federal government's $3 billion in Quebec; (3) the total government budget (including provincial and federal state-owned enterprises, school boards, municipalities, hospitals, etc.) tripled in revenues and expenditures from 1961 to 1970, while the Quebec GNP only doubled in the same period – this means that while the entire public sector accounted for one-third of all expenditures and 30 per cent of all revenues in 1961, these figures rose to 43.4 per cent for revenues and 45.9 per cent for expenditures in 1970.[24]

For the federal government in Canada, the expansion of its role under monopoly capitalism took place relatively easily, based on the nation-building precedents of the past. The transition in Quebec, on the other hand, has been anything but gradual and its consequences indeed significant.[25] With the coming of the Quiet Revolution the Quebec state was transformed from a secondary national institution to a primary one; the Quebec nation and the Quebec state became inseparably linked. Many of the political struggles which have resulted from the Quiet Revolution may best be seen as manifestations of the contradictions inherent in this dramatically new role of the state. These contradictions comprise certain elements of a general nature, that is, intrinsic to monopoly capitalism, and others specific to Quebec. In reviewing the latter aspect, four points stand out:

1 *Rapidity of transformation*: as pointed out earlier, development of the modern Quebec state in such a very brief period of time resulted inevitably in problems of efficiency, personnel, etc., which might not have otherwise occurred.

2 *Timing*: this important transformation took place in Quebec at a time when world-wide economic developments threatened monopoly capitalism's economic position in general.

3 *Nationalism*: once the Quebec state apparatus became the primary institution of the Quebec nation, the question of political independence and therefore separation from Canada became central. This was far different from the past when the question of independence was raised by the Québécois essentially as a camouflage – a political threat to protect the things that really mattered which were not political but social, cultural, and religious.

4 *Economic control*: not only was it still the case but it now became a public fact that the economy of Quebec was essentially owned and managed by English-speaking Canadians and Americans. Hence the Quebec state bureaucracy was kept at a distance from the corporate elite by national/linguistic divisions, and the habit of collaboration through close social contacts, regular shifts of personnel between sectors, etc., required by the logic of capitalism, did not develop. Even up to today this is evident in recruitment, as skilled university and college graduates in Quebec divide quite strikingly, with the English-speaking going into higher positions in the corporate sector, and the French entering those of the public sector.[26]

The fiscal crisis described above is one cause of the public sector having become a key focus of worker militancy in the past decade. Furthermore, it is plausibly argued that under monopoly capitalism the corporations have in fact become less vulnerable to working-class militancy because of their multinational nature which places the working class at a disadvantage in regional or national industrial struggles. Of course multinational corporations can and do easily pass wage increases on to the consumer in increased prices. Under these circumstances the fiercest economic battles often take place at the political level between the regime and state workers.

One result of this general situation is stepped-up pressure on the state to perform. This pressure is of three kinds: the first as noted is syndical – public or para-public service unions' increased militancy is directed at the state/employer; the second comes from the corporate elite which becomes increasingly uncomfortable with the regime the more it finds itself relying upon the state; the third is of a cultural or 'public opinion' nature with the attention constantly focused (by the mass media) on the government to resolve every kind of 'public' issue. Each of the specific circumstances noted about Quebec, as we shall see, exacerbates these general tendencies and, in particular, brings into question the 'loyalty' of the state middle class under conditions when that loyalty is especially needed. In another time and place such a loss in allegiance might be less than significant and only temporary – to be regained, say, by putting another party of the same stripe into power or even by a cabinet shuffle. In Quebec, given the rapid development of the positive state and the linguistic divisions between the public and private sectors, this situation is more serious. It is intimately related to the major factor leading to the present crisis, the national issue. Because the nation has remained so deeply rooted since long before the state apparatus was created, it could not be manipulated at will. Amidst the tumultuous changes that have rocked Quebec since 1960, the increasing contradiction between what we have termed the state middle class and the regime has tended to escape notice, as have its effects on current political practice. Let us briefly outline the development of the former over the past fifteen years before turning to examples of the latter in the next section.

The years 1960-5 can be seen as a period of relative success for the new nation-building state. The Liberal victory in 1961 soon brought with it many administrative and technical changes, some of which improved working conditions in Quebec and also gave rise to a greater sense of freedom of cultural expression. During this period, with Premier Lesage's deft manipulation of the Ottawa 'enemy,' the close relationship of the corporate elite with the state bureaucracy presided over by the Liberal party appeared established, especially since the part played by the corporate elite was little in evidence. In evidence instead was the seeming openness of the regime towards union leaders (like Jean Marchard), progressive journalists (like René Lévesque), and intellectuals (like Paul Gérin-Lajoie).

However firm it may have been, cracks in the system soon became apparent. Breakdown came less with the unexpected electoral victory[27] of Daniel Johnson's Union Nationale in 1966 than with the schism of the Liberal party which followed. The expulsion of Lévesque and his supporters, coupled with the resultant unification of the various independentist groups under the banner of the Parti Québécois, loosened the bonds of many within the state middle class to both the economic elite and the Liberal party and drew them towards this emerging alternative. This shift in allegiance continued in response to what was seen as the pitiable capitulation by Premier Robert Bourassa before the federal state in October 1970.

The period from 1966 through at least 1970 was one of transition and uncertainty – among the Liberals (and the other parties as well), within the trade unions, throughout the educational system, and in Quebec generally. While this was captured most dramatically by events 'in the streets' such as the series of 'Québec français' demonstrations, the campaign to free Vallières, Gagnon, and other political prisoners, and of course the October 1970 events, the change in political party alignment and support is more telling. The PQ emerged onto the scene, the UN headed towards extinction, and the provincial Créditistes first rose and then fell dramatically. When the dust settled in the early 1970s the political composition of Quebec had been fundamentally altered. The next section looks at the new political alignment of Quebec in some detail but its broad outlines may be readily stated.

The apparent grand coalition of the Quiet Revolution between the corporate elite and the state bureaucracy had been fractured. The Liberal party, though, was able to replace its lost state middle class elements in sufficient numbers drawing upon petit-bourgeois elements – many of them former 'Blues' (UN supporters) – while retaining its anglo-immigrant base. During the early seventies these elements added up to a powerful Liberal electoral constituency, and this electoral strength served to conceal its profound political weakness. Opposing the Liberals, the Parti Québécois had gathered the support of the great bulk of the state middle class: intellectuals, some younger and more progressive professionals, as well as many trade union officials and militants – groups which had formed the active base of support for the Quiet Revolution – as well as an increasing working-class and student vote. (The PQ's original inability to translate this growing support into significant electoral breakthrough resulted mainly from its built-in weakness in the anglo-immigrant sector.[28])

The Bourassa Liberals' resolute federalism and repudiation of vague nationalistic goals for '100,000 jobs' and other concrete economistic goals thus both signified and symbolized the end of the Quiet Revolution. The new regime could not alienate the forces of positive nationalism, however, without serious long-term costs. In practically discarding the collective national aspirations of the Quiet Revolution the Quebec Liberal party of the 1970s in the short term probably gained votes, but ultimately weakened its link to the legitimacy demanded of the nation-building state. The Parti Québécois arose as a natural result of the consequent political vacuum and laid claim to the ideological basis for nation-building, thereby progressively winning the allegiance of key segments of the state middle class. It was, after all, this stratum that the new nation-building state had virtually created and which in turn created it – both in its day-to-day acts and in the national–socio-political hopes that it nourished.

THE LIBERAL REGIME IN THE SEVENTIES

Looking more closely at the basic composition of the active Liberal party supporters and cadre we see the corporate bourgeoisie[29] (mainly English and consequently 'low profile') and a few high-level technocrats, combined with a large part of the petite bourgeoisie including most of those employed in the traditional professions, proprietors of small businesses of all kinds, real estate and insurance agents, and salesmen. The importance of the petit-bourgeois elements was notable, for example, at Liberal party conventions, and apparent in the content of some of the resolutions the party adopted.[30]

The policies of the Trudeau government in Ottawa should also be seen in this light. A central thread running through its thinking, its structure, and its legislation has been selling the federal government to the French-Canadian (Quebec) state middle class, through direct employment, job creation, 'bilingualism' in the federal civil service, etc. Apart from the fact that the pursuit of such politics inevitably leads to an anti-French-Canadian backlash[31] (which in typical Canadian fashion was in 1976 expressed as anti-Trudeaumania), there is little indication that cash from Ottawa bought any significant conversions in loyalty from the state middle class. For example, in the November 1976 election the Parti Québécois won the two Quebec ridings which are closest to, and comprise the main French-speaking suburbs of, Ottawa. These ridings are increasingly populated, it should be noted, with francophone civil servants recruited by the federal government. The vote should be seen here for what it was – a painful bite out of the hand that feeds. One might also suggest that the presence in the French CBC of 'a majority of separatists,' as Prime Minister Trudeau stated in February 1977, is another such example.

Within the Parti Québécois one can discern essentially two relatively distinct groups: (1) the Quiet Revolution refugees, many of whom left the Liberals with Lévesque in 1967-8 – an older group including some professionals and former middle- and higher-level state bureaucrats, whose leaders hold some of the major cabinet positions in the new government, and (2) its amorphous left wing that tends to dominate the local leadership of the party, oriented towards administrative decentralization, anti-parliamentary in style, and more radical on economic questions – a group well represented at the lower and middle levels of the state middle class – among local union officials and militants, intellectuals, artists, and students.[32] In fact, the existence of these two groups has been a factor since the founding of the party. The *modus vivendi* of the two groups was briefly threatened in late August 1976 by the *Le Jour* affair. In temporarily closing that paper, the 'technocratic' wing[33] of the party showed unusual bitterness towards the *Le Jour* editors and the left wing of the PQ they tended to represent.

From the point of view of the regime, the PQ was not a 'loyal opposition,' but a contaminating political force. It had to be defeated not only at the polls but in the hearts and minds of the Québécois and rooted out of the state. Hence the loyalty of prospective members of the state middle class, especially for individuals in politically sensitive posts, became a *sine qua non*. Ideally one hired well-known Liberals (recommended by MNAs, etc.) or, failing that, one hired individuals known not to be Péquistes. This latter could be easily found among supporters of other political parties, especially well-known old-line 'Blues.' While it is impossible to document such a tendency within the state bureaucracy, impressionistic evidence is quite convincing. On this last point, there were indications that sensitive posts in the regime (the top bureaucrats, the cabinet, and the Premier's Office) were being cleared of progressive figures (who had served since the time of the Quiet Revolution) and were being filled by more conservative people, some of them brought back from the Duplessis period and retaining a basic antipathy to the aspirations of the Quiet Revolution.[34]

The wariness on the part of the regime towards the loyalty of the state middle class, if we are to accept its very narrow conceptions of loyalty, was well founded – if our analysis is correct. For example, the quotation that follows is taken from a report on the position of the Quebec Government Professionals Union (CNTU) on one item of a collective agreement then under negotiation; it shows both the 'disloyalty' in question and the reaction of middle-class state workers to the regime's paranoia:

Always do what your conscience recommends; even if the State asks for contrary, said Albert Einstein.

It is the government's Professionals Union's (4,300) firm intention to apply this great scientist's maxim during the present negotiations, by laying the following contractual clause to the governments:

'No disciplinary measure can be laid down on an employee who refuses to sign a technical document or stand up for an employer's politic (the government), which he approves, in all conscience.'

By this clause, the government's Professionals; lawyers, architects, agronomists, veterinaries, engineers, etc. ... want to deny the government of their professional competence support, without any risks.

If they win their case they will no longer fear ... and at the same time really serve the population instead of risking their reputation in defending a questionable political scheme of some party in power. Several times in the past, professionals have been forced to do government's low tasks at their credibility's expense.

Let us just quote the 'Dignity' operations in Lower St. Lawrence ... Four years ago, Bourassa decided to close villages, regroup lands and rationalize wood cutting in Lower St. Lawrence. Against their own beliefs, professionals have been forced to tell the local population it would be more advantageous for them to shut down their cooperative pulpmills, to let CIP have the wood cutting monopoly and live on 'welfare,' at Matane.

The Lower St. Lawrence proud population has evidently resisted to this governmental scheme. This resistance gave birth to Dignity Operation, demonstrations, clergy's support, etc. ... Unintentionally, professionals have been forced to struggle against the population in order to realize a governmental scheme which, the majority of them could not approve, in all conscience.

If professionals win their case during the present negotiations, the conscience cases where, in the professionals's mind, the population's interest opposes a governmental scheme, will not happen again.[35]

Evidence of 'disloyalty' and regime efforts to counter it were not lacking. The former seems evident both in terms of evidence from polls, from studies of participation in PQ and trade union conventions,[36] from the unionization of the state employees at many levels (most notably in the CNTU), and finally from continual leaks of information by bureaucrats prepared to risk job security in order to embarrass the government. The latter may be seen in this excerpt from a February 1976 letter sent by the Quebec Ministry of Education to provincial co-ordinators of committees of teachers in the various disciplines taught in Quebec junior colleges (Cegeps):[37] 'Il arrive que certains d'entre vous utilisent leur titre de coordonnateur ou du papier à correspondance pour laisser croire que c'est comme employé de la DGEC qu'ils exercent des pressions politiques. Vous conviendrez avec moi, j'en suis sûr, que de telles pratiques sont tout à fait inadmissibles de la part *de personnes qui travaillent directement pour l'Etat.* Vos droits de citoyens peuvent s'exercer par les moyens habituels ... J'ose croire que cette simple mise au point suffira à corriger des pratiques qui desservent la crédibilité de l'ensemble des coordonnateurs.'[38]

Similar considerations are evident in the August 1975 statements of federal Treasury Board president Jean Chrétien on the relative merits of the federal and Quebec bureaucracies and the controversy that followed thereupon. Chrétien was quoted in a Treasury Board release as saying, among other things, that the Québécois had more faith in federal civil servants than their provincial counterparts. And he went on: 'I think that one of the factors, which we cannot see at the provincial level, at least in Quebec is that Ottawa civil servants have a better sense of what is the state. They work for the state ... This is probably the cause for the fact that the administration in Ottawa is better than the one to which I've just referred.'[39]

The minister was publicly taken to task by, among others, Robert Burns of the Parti Québécois, former Quebec civil service minister Oswald Parent, and editorialists in the French-language Quebec papers. The response of Jacques Doré, president of the Quebec Government Professionals Union, in a letter addressed to the minister and published in *La Presse* on 12 August 1975 is most instructive. Below are several excerpts in translation:

... It is perhaps true that provincial civil servants *appear* to lack what you call the 'sense of the state' ... However ...

It must be said that almost unanimously the civil servants have concluded that the work asked of them and on which they often laboured for months has found its way to the bottom of drawers to be forgotten.

They have also concluded that the normal form of organization and work in their ministries have been short-circuited by the 'special occasional staffers hired by the ministers' ... cabinets.'

They have also concluded the Quebec government programs have usually been tied to the man who conceived them and not integrated into the structures ...

They have also concluded that the government has a weakness for 'contractual' firms that generally repeat the work already done in the ministries ...

They have concluded as well that the work and organization of their ministries were centred on the imperatives of the party in power and not the state ... As we learned from Mr Louis P. Lacroix, Liberal party whip ... 'all appointments are political' ... In the Industry and Commerce Ministry a political inquiry was undertaken before according tenure to a public servant ...

They have concluded that the Quebec state apparatus was being lost in 'tight controlitis'; to such a point that many suggest that 50 per cent of civil servants are there just for surveillance over the other 50 per cent … When one comes to understand all this, one has the right to ask who lacks the 'sense of the state,' the civil servants or the government?

No doubt the regime's evident paranoia made it hard to measure just how clear was the case to which it was (over?) reacting. The studies and polls that were conducted reveal enough empirical evidence to suggest that a 'trahison des clercs' was in fact materializing elsewhere than merely in the minds of Liberal ministers. For example, the most thorough study of the Parti Québécois' electoral strength previous to the 1976 election found that the two strongest correlates of PQ support among francophones were education (directly) and age (inversely). It takes no unusual powers of deduction to see that the group which is both young and well-educated (and francophone) corresponds quite closely to what we have termed the state middle class. In addition, the next two strongest factors – professional/semi-professional occupation status versus others, and size of the population of locality, both of which varied directly with PQ support – demonstrate the same correspondence.[40] As the authors note, the key factor is not that the PQ is a middle-class party; in fact, it has more working-class support than it has from all segments of the middle class other than those in the professional/semi-professional category. Nor is it, as they also note, a question of the PQ supporters simply as 'technocrats,' as has often been stated, since the 'professional' knowledge on which the PQ supporters' new middle class status tends to be based is more often general than specific. In our terms, the PQ supporters are concentrated in the state middle class, a stratum having distinct legitimation functions requiring 'generalists' as well as administrative ones requiring 'specialists.'[41]

This general state of affairs was manifested even within the higher echelons of the Quebec bureaucracy. For example, Premier Bourassa's chief adviser, Paul Desrochers, told the Cliche Commission of the frustrations encountered (in his unstated but obviously central role as a key corporate representative in the government) when dealing with the bureaucracy. He cited one instance concerning a senior official in the Quebec Department of Industry, Trade and Commerce who told an important potential American investor: 'Quebec does not need your investments, sir.' Some Quebec officials apparently saw themselves as loyal to Quebec but not therefore necessarily obedient to the dictates of the Liberal government when the two appeared to conflict. The Cliche Commission revealed that some key civil servants were often willing to do what they were told only if there was something in it for them – and that Desrochers and other high officials, unable to change the situation, were prepared to tolerate it. The commissioners' report made it apparent that the government did not attempt to seek enforcement of many laws relating to the construction industry at least partly because it could not depend on the public servants to provide such enforcement. An analogous problem existed in the difficulties encountered on many occasions by the government in efforts to implement provisions for testing the language of school children under Bill 22, to bring juries to convict political-social offenders, and sometimes even to get judges to issue injunctions against strikers.

In light of all this it would appear that the knowledgeable francophone population in Quebec harboured few illusions concerning the class role of the Quebec state under the Liberal government. Understanding the crisis for what it is, most Québécois were not surprised by (and, if status-quo oriented, often favoured) extreme and repressive measures that violate basic democratic conventions and accepted principles of collective bargaining. Furthermore, those who made up the large extra-parliamentary opposition, while clearly disgusted by governmental repression, were seldom surprised by it, since they had come to understand the class role of the state. The anglophones were less well aware of Quebec's political condition. Their federal orientation and cultural distance from provincial political developments allowed them a much larger capacity to be shocked at publicly reported instances of bald partiality and disregard for niceties by the Liberal government. Bill 23, hastily passed in April 1976 to force teachers back to work, was a good example of this. First, the polls showed more anglophones than francophones opposed to it;[42] second, reaction of most anglophone teachers (and many parents) was that of great emotional revulsion directed against the law itself. The francophone teachers' unions, on the other hand, reacted far less vocally to the law. Their attitude was generally one of: what else can you expect from a class regime? Their position generally was: to win a just settlement to our claims we must simply continue our strategy of one- and two-day strikes just as though the law did not exist.

In this context it should not be surprising to find that English-language journalists and broadcasters were often even more assiduous than their French-language counterparts in exposing facts leading to the scandals which so often beset the Bourassa government. A brief look at a few of these scandals provides another useful illustration of points made above. The most common charges levelled were of preferential use of state grants, funds, and appointments. These charges included: (1) the existence of lists

of lawyers, notaries,[43] engineers, and architects[44] designated as Liberal supporters who were the only ones to be handed state assignments and contracts; (2) the awarding of contracts for lotteries' distribution,[45] construction, building maintenance, government advertising, business forms, and
'importation of Liquors' to firms with close Liberal connections; (3) a Liberal party intimacy with underworld figures as revealed for example by the
Cliche Commission, and the tie-in of these figures with highly dubious election practices; (4) the selective hiring for public service jobs on political
(Liberal) criteria, including parallel hiring at James Bay;[46] (5) the rigging of
'open line' shows by using civil servants to phone in anonymously and defend the government.[47]

Apart from the usual explanations which apply to all capitalist democracies, it is suggested that, rather than simply blaming 'dishonest' individuals,
the specific analysis of Quebec provided helps to explain this proliferation
of scandals. In many cases, the regime was forced to use such methods to
ensure that its directives were carried out and that its messages were com-
municated to the population. In this way it secured, through resort to various forms of pay-offs if necessary, the loyalty of the persons involved, a loyalty otherwise sometimes impossible to obtain. Adherence to the Quebec
Liberal party was thus often more than a favour deserving a reward; it was,
here too, an indication of support for the system – support which (if necessary) came at a price the regime had to be willing to pay.

Beneath a surface of apparent electoral strength, the Liberal regime thus
revealed itself to be weak indeed. Beset by a state middle class it was unable
to depend on, by the related scandals and intensified public criticism this
produced, and by a working class which was increasingly militant for general international reasons as well as those specific to Quebec, it reacted continually with repressive legislation which was enacted almost at the first sign
of strike action.[48] The effect was frequently the opposite of the intent. The
civil disobedience which such precipitous action must and did evoke further
weakened governmental legitimacy. Even the corporate elite grew nervous
at the failure of the state to maintain the stability without which monopoly
capitalism cannot function. A poll in early 1976, for example, found that
less than 10 per cent of members of the high-powered Conseil du Patronat
were satisfied with the Liberal regime.[49]

The clearest manifestation of this state of events lay in the cyclical but
intensified confrontation between the Quebec state and those unions representing its public and para-public employees, most notably the Common
Front first in 1972 and again in 1976, each round resolving nothing but
merely setting the stage for the next one. In the process the sometimes

'social-democratic' stance of Premier Bourassa[50] rapidly evaporated, and the issue became defined as one of confrontation – the regime versus the trade unions.

It is clear that the bread and butter – 'Quebec back to work' – strategy of the Liberals, while successful in the short term, ultimately did not work. In the heady years of the Quiet Revolution, the enlarged and high-profile state could effectively carry out its essential techno-democratic tasks by associating its actions with national goals which appeared to override class interests. But in the 1970s such an appeal carried with it political and economic consequences unacceptable to the Liberal constituency. Focus remained on the actions of the Quebec state, but in the context of significant polarization which took place in the intervening period and which could not be undone. The regime had few options, none of them likely to succeed for very long.

A note of caution. The impression that outsiders, too often including English-Canadian radicals, often get – that Quebec is posed for a revolutionary transformation in the name of the working class and led by the trade unions – is inaccurate. The major forces which in the mid-1970s mobilized for action to effect concrete changes do not consist of a class with revolutionary potential but rather comprise a stratum whose interests could well be accommodated by creation of an independent 'leftish' Quebec within a Canada-wide common market along the lines of European social democracy. The failure of both the electoral system and the regime to accommodate these interests engendered a situation of deep confusion in which reconcilable conflicts appeared irreconcilable. The result was that fertile ground was laid for mobilizing the working class beyond economism mainly through escalation of rhetoric by certain elements within what we have called the state middle class, among them some union leaders, intellectuals, etc. The strong opposition to the Liberal regime took on the language of class conflict when in many cases class conflict was neither intended nor realistic. Such rhetorical escalation occurred despite the fact that the trade unions were often still structurally weak and badly divided.

The best organized and most radical of the three main trade union centrals, the CNTU, continues to struggle with financial and membership problems. The largest teachers' union, the Corporation des enseignants du Québec (CEQ), while radical and militant in its outward appearance, as for instance in the publication of the *Manual for the First of May* in 1975 which put forth Marxist alternatives to the contents of traditional school texts, is in fact divided and as a whole quite cautious when it comes to taking collective action. This became evident in the weak part played by the CEQ within the public sector Common Front actions of 1976. The Quebec Federation of Labour (QFL), the third and largest of the three, while keeping up with the other two in its rhetoric, is not all that different from other provincial federations within the CLC (no more radical, for example, than the BC Federation of Labour), partially due to its fragmented structure which leaves much power in the hands of its international union affiliates. Hence, the Marxist analysis of Quebec, and particularly of the role of the state and the unions' relationship to it that is to be found in the unions' recent position papers, gives one an impression at least partially at odds with the facts.[51] Beyond all this is the general question of how politically radical one can expect a trade union as a trade union to be, since its role is ultimately to sign contracts. For English-Canadian socialists this has not been a question since the CLC was nowhere near this possible theoretical limit. But in Quebec, in the CNTU in particular, the question is being asked – and the answer is not all that clear.[52]

Although the working class was on the whole still unprepared to reject the system, class conflict rhetoric struck many responsive chords because the mediating structures were not doing their job. And militant actions in themselves, though far from constituting the revolutionary advances their rhetoric portrays, did provide valuable experience of collective solidarity and strength for the workers of Quebec.[53] The state middle class was not supporting the system through what it did and what it said. Instead, even its own members unionized, and increasingly identified with, and even initiated, attacks upon the regime. Under these conditions, the serious and potentially revolutionary mobilization that *is* taking place among certain elements of the working class, especially in the public sector, is likely to remain secondary – until a significant change occurs on the left in Quebec.

The evidence as gathered here points to the primary political conflict being that between the regime and the state middle class. But under changed conditions this contradiction might be overcome through winning the loyalty to the state of this crucial stratum. These conditions amount essentially to independence for Quebec as a European-style common market social democracy. The coming to power of the Parti Québécois in late 1976 thus surely marks a large step in this direction.

EPILOGUE: THE NEW REGIME

The above analysis was substantially completed several months before the Quebec election of 15 November 1976. Looking at unfolding developments, several months later, a few suggestive points can be added for their interpretation in light of our analysis. Any fuller treatment will have to be a separate one.

The result of the November election requires little repeating. The Parti Québécois captured 71 of 110 seats in the National Assembly with 41 per cent of the popular vote, a net gain of 11 per cent since 1973. Many of the factors contributing to the erosion of the strength of the Bourassa Liberals have already been noted and were clearly manifest, though practically everyone, especially in the PQ, was caught by surprise by its rapidity and extent. The victory was celebrated as a triumph and collective achievement by many more than 41 per cent of the Québécois. The state middle class, public enemy number one of the former regime, suddenly and without warning, found itself holding the reins of government.

A few major developments since 15 November should be briefly noted. Premier René Lévesque has taken pains to reaffirm the government's commitment to Quebec's independence (which he soft-pedalled during the campaign) at the same time asssuring non-francophones that the project will be placed before the people in a referendum with the fullest and widest participation. In addition, the government appears to be attempting to live up to its promised social-democratic reforms. It has effectively ended wage and price controls, raised the minimum wage to $3.13, provided generous subsidies to the workers' co-operative knitting mill Tricofil, freed Dr Morgentaler, brought in anti-scab legislation.

The government has also served notice that it will bring in a series of laws to protect the working conditions of non-unionized workers, democratize Montreal's Charter, as well as bring changes of policy in the areas of agriculture, environment, tenant rights, electoral laws, and a few others of the type one would expect from a moderate social-democratic government. All of these changes, it must be noted, take place in the context of an increasingly difficult economic situation: heavy debts, high unemployment, industries threatening to close down and pull out, and a general slowdown of economic activity – facts already publicly noted by the new government on several occasions and which will no doubt affect its ability to manœuvre. In the midst of all this a new policy of language for education and business is being introduced, provoking angry debate and providing additional elements of the 'uncertainty' that editorialists love to declaim.

Another major development is notable in the trade unions, where there are signs of a counter-offensive against 'Marxist influence.' For example, Jean Gérin-Lajoie, well-known péquiste head of the Quebec steelworkers, made this much publicized denunciation in his address to his union's congress in December 1976. Hubert Sacy, press attaché to the Quebec teachers' central, released a paper in January 1977 suggesting that the time had come for the union to move away from its Marxist viewpoint and towards a pé-quiste orientation. A similar stand can be seen in the position of the 'moderates' in the Montreal Citizens' Movement, led by city councillors such as Paul Cliche (also of the CNTU) and Nick Auf der Maur with their well-publicized attacks on the party's dominant radical, that is, socialist, wing.

While this kind of debate is healthy if it remains confined to these organizations – for there is no doubt, as noted above, that much of the radicalism of the trade unions was too frequently more a matter of new-middle-class posturing than revolutionary workers' consciousness – the political question of concern is what will be the role of the state in this struggle, which focuses the question squarely on the PQ. Lévesque, for example, was the honoured guest of the steelworkers and his presence during Gérin-Lajoie's speech was noted by the speaker himself as well as the journalists who reported and the editorialists who commented on it.

It is editorialists, especially in the Power Corporation–owned *La Presse*, who have not only jumped on the anti-Marxist bandwagon but who seemed to be leading it. *La Presse* editorials roundly applauded these attacks on the unions and the MCM, in the process, of course, distorting and exaggerating them, and attempted to pressure the PQ to publicly distinguish itself from these 'go-gauchistes' (a term formerly used to describe 'Marxist-Leninist' sects) like Marcel Pépin (former CNTU president) and Yvon Charbonneau (president of the CEQ). So far, the PQ has seen fit to remain on the sidelines of this struggle, preferring to let the sides fight it out among themselves, understanding surely that the trade unions are less likely to engage in militant actions if thus divided. As long as this remains the case, then, we can predict the not entirely unwelcome development of less outward militancy from the Quebec unions in the next few years but a deepening ideological debate so that where militant action does emerge it will be based on a clearer conception of class interests and divisions.

What will happen when the economic impact of the PQ's reforms become evident? Will the bourgeoisie play it cool[54] and accept short-term losses of various kinds, or will it get caught up in anglophone petit-bourgeois hysteria on independence and language, and tighten the economic screws on the government? In the first case, we may see the realization of the new middle class' goal, common market social democracy; if the latter, then the PQ will have to come to some decision with regard to the position represented by the trade union left. It may choose to try to prove itself to the bourgeoisie by joining in on the attack and publicly cleansing its program and structures of 'Marxist influence,' or it may find itself, in spite of itself, moving towards the trade unions and the left for its only firm ally and base of support in its confrontation with the economic ruling class.

This hypothesis flies in the face of all those who would dismiss the PQ as nothing but 'petit-bourgeois nationalists' or social-democratic reformers.[55] They wish to be the latter, indeed, but for them this requires national independence; they are indeed petit bourgeois but of a specific kind, that of the state middle class. Cut off from the monopoly and competitive capitalist sectors by language, age, occupation, and attitude, this by no means revolutionary class is not, due to the particularities of Quebec's national development, the most dependable group with which to entrust the capitalist state apparatus. What they will do with it seems at least in part uncertain, dependent not so much on what the PQ government itself does, but what is done, and what it perceives to be done, to it by other forces.

While far too early to say in any but speculative form, it may be that Quebec is moving (either slowly or rapidly) towards a stage where the active contradiction no longer centres around the new middle class but instead reflects the fundamental class division in monopoly capitalism. The victory of the PQ represents a definite advance in an historical process that has been in progress for many years and clearly manifest since 1960; the referendum and its results, among other events, will represent another stage in that process. Those who wish to understand such events in themselves are certain to be mistaken in their conclusions; no static analysis will explain a dynamic collectivity.

NOTES

1 In an earlier work, H. and S. H. Milner, *The Decolonization of Quebec* (Toronto 1973), this topic was explored in a general historical manner. This paper advances and somewhat modifies the arguments presented there.
2 Jacques Ellul, *The Technological Society* (New York 1964); Daniel Bell, 'Notes on the Post-Industrial Society,' *The Public Interest*, VI *and* VII (Winter and Spring 1967); Amitai Etzioni, *The Active Society* (New York 1968); Paul Baran and Paul Sweezy, *Monopoly Capital* (New York 1966); Zbigniew Brzezinski, 'America in the Technotronic Age,' *Encounter*, XXIX (Jan. 1968). See also Maurice Duverger, *Modern Democracies: Economic Power versus Political Power* (Hinsdale, Ill. 1974), for a quasi-Marxist portrayal that is quite interesting.
3 John Kenneth Galbraith, perhaps most notably among other observers, Marxist and non-Marxist, sets out this development; see his *The New Industrial State* (Boston 1971).

4 This classification is a modification of one proposed by J. Habermas in 'What Does a Crisis Mean Today or Legitimation Problems in Late Capitalism,' *Social Research*, XL (Winter 1973), 646-7.

5 'The increasingly significant role of the state in reproduction of agents is related to the concentration of capital in the monopolistic stage of capitalist development, whereby the ensuing rationalization of production and mobility of capital sets in train the demand for a labour force which is itself characterized by its mobility or transferability. The state, in centralizing and formalizing processes of reproduction, such as education, creates a labour force less tied to local and particularistic cultures; sharing in a common (yet hierarchically organized) formal socialization process. The state takes on a function, therefore, which cannot be effectively carried out within the confines of a single productive enterprize.' Terrence Johnson, 'Professions, Class, and the State,' paper presented to 1976 meeting of the Canadian Sociology and Anthropology Association, Quebec, May 1976

6 *The Fiscal Crisis of the State* (New York 1973). For a Canadian application, see Richard Deaton, 'The Fiscal Crisis of the State in Canada,' in D. Roussopoulos, ed., *The Political Economy of the State* (Montreal 1973). See Ian Gough, 'State Expenditure in Advanced Capitalism,' *New Left Review*, 92 (July-Aug. 1975), for a useful critical evaluation.

7 Leonard Rodberg, 'Caught in the Fiscal Squeeze: Government as Corporate Servant,' Institute for Policy Studies, Washington, *Transnational Link*, no. 10 (Oct. 1975)

8 Miliband, *The State in Capitalist Society* (London 1969), and Panitch, pp. 6-7 above

9 *Lenin and Philosophy* (London 1971), 136-8

10 'The Problem of the Capitalist State,' in R. Blackburn, ed. *Ideology in Social Science* (London 1972), 251, 246

11 Miliband argues in addition that such an all-encompassing definition of the state is unacceptable given that it does not allow for the distinction between fascism and liberal democracy since what distinguishes the former is the very absorption of intermediate bodies by the state. Yet this argument is falsely premised. What distinguishes liberal democracy from fascism is the relative autonomy of both private and public intermediate institutions from direct day-to-day repressive control by what can be called 'the regime.' The extent of the state (or public sector) *per se* is not itself a determining factor. If it were, it would logically follow that social democracy equals social fascism, an incorrect position far less likely to be attractive to Miliband than to Althusser. See Miliband, 'Poulantzas and the Capitalist State,' *New Left Review*, 82 (Nov.-Dec. 1973).

12 'Accumulation' simply means to create the conditions where profitable capital accumulation is possible; the term is thus not very apt but neither is any alternative term such as 'reproduction.'

13 See Poulantzas, 'On Social Classes,' *New Left Review*, 78 (March-April 1973), and G. Carchedi, 'On the Economic Identification of the New Middle Class,' *Economy and Society*, IV, 1 (Feb. 1975).

14 'Even though, strictly speaking, we cannot talk of exploitation of unproductive workers because these workers do not produce, and thus cannot be expropriated of, surplus-value, we can talk of economic oppression of these workers. The value of their labour-power is determined in the same way as the value of the labour-power of the productive workers, i.e. by the value of the goods and services going into the culturally determined subsistence minimum. The application of this labour-power, even if it does not create value and thus surplus value, is, just as in the case of the productive worker, by no means limited by the value of the labour-power itself ... Suppose the value of this labour-power is the equivalent of five hours of the working day. He does not produce value but provides the capitalist with unpaid labour. That is, while the productive worker is expropriated of his labour in the form of value, the unproductive worker is subjected to a direct expropriation of labour.' Carchedi, *ibid.*, 20

15 'Professions, Class, and the State,' 35-6

16 *Ibid.*, 37; cf. Carchedi, 'Economic Identification'

17 *Ibid.*, 54-6

18 See Habermas, 'What Does a Crisis Mean'; see also Claus Offe, 'Theses on the Theory of the State,' *New German Critique*, 61 (Fall 1975), 137-47.

19 It is clear that the 'European' model does not refer to each and every western European state. There are exceptions such as Belgium which could best be termed consociational.

20 See the article by Garth Stevenson in this collection.

21 See John Porter, *The Vertical Mosaic* (Toronto 1965); Gad Horowitz, 'Mosaics and Identity,' in C.W. Gonick and B. Finnigan, *Making It: The Canadian Dream* (Toronto 1972); Wallace Clement, *The Canadian Corporate Elite* (Toronto 1975).

22 The American version requires a 'frontier-style' political culture emanating from a specific economic historical development. See Louis Hartz, *The Liberal Tradition in America* (New York 1955), and *The Founding of New Societies* (New York 1964). The major Canadian applications are Gad Horowitz, 'Conservatism, Liberalism and Socialism in Canada,' *Canadian Journal of Economics and Political Science*, XXXII, 2 (May 1966), and Kenneth McRae, 'The Structure of Canadian History,' in *The Founding of New Societies*. While McRae and Horowitz disagree on whether English Canada qualifies as a 'liberal fragment,' both agree that Quebec does not.

23 *Nationalismes et politique au Québec* (Montreal 1975). Dion's book provides many insights and his analysis in some instances tends to parallel my own.

24 These figures are based on those compiled by Kemal Wassef of the CNTU research department in 1971. See B.R. Lemoine, 'The Growth of the Quebec State,' in Roussopoulos, *Political Economy*.

25 The comparison is with the growth of federal government. No doubt some other provinces experienced similar expansion during the same period. The point here is not the expansion itself but its combination with other factors, especially the national question, and it is this that accounts for Quebec's uniqueness.

26 André-E. Leblanc, 'Bill 22 and the Future of Quebec,' *Canadian Forum*, LIV, 646 (Nov.-Dec. 1974)

27 The UN victory was achieved with a smaller popular vote than the Liberals due to a number of factors including malapportionment and unexpected support for 'separatist' parties. After the initial shock wore off, most Québécois, including Premier Johnson, understood that the result did not signify a repudiation of the Quiet Revolution and a call for a return to the 'ancien régime.'

28 A useful study of PQ support was recently published on the premise that the anglophone support was so negligible as to merit being left out of an analysis of voting data. See R. Hamilton and M. Pinard, 'The Basis of Parti Québécois Support in Recent Quebec Elections,' *Canadian Journal of Political Science*, IX, 1 (March 1976).

29 See Pierre Fournier, *The Quebec Establishment* (Montreal 1976), for a study of the close relationship of the Liberal regime to the bourgeoisie.

30 At their 23-25 April 1976 congress, the Quebec (provincial) Liberals (1) strongly defeated a resolution in favour of free university education; (2) rejected public day-care; (3) called on the government to plug up leaks of secret documents to journalists; and (4) came out against no-fault automobile insurance. 'Le Parti Libéral en congrès,' *Le Jour*, 26 April 1976

31 See, for example, C. Arpin, 'The Bilingual Backlash,' an excellent series of articles in the *Montreal Star*, beginning 2 Oct. 1976.

32 The strength of the more radical elements of the PQ were revealed at its January 1976 congress. See 'L'aile parlementaire, mis en minorité; le PQ condamne la loi 253 sur les services essentiels,' *Le Jour*, 26 Jan. 1976.

33 Vera Murray in her recent competent study of the PQ describes its two major wings as the 'technocrats' and the 'participationists.' *Le Parti Québécois* (Montreal 1976)

34 See Greta Chambers, 'The Senior Mandarinate Is Not Like the Rest of Us,' *Gazette*, Montreal, 1 May 1975; see also 'Bourassa Keeps Lid On in Quebec,' *Montreal Star*, 9 Oct. 1976.

35 Intercommunication Bulletin no. 10, Common Front, Public Sector, Sept. 1975; the grammatical errors in the quotation are (unfortunately) not this author's.

36 At the fall 1973 congress of the Quebec Federation of Labour, delegates were polled on party preference. Of the 849 delegates, 66 per cent responded. The results were: PQ 76 per cent, Liberals 11, others 5, no response or vote 8. The PQ ran strongest among younger delegates as well as those representing unions in the public sector. The only group of delegates which gave a majority (53 per cent) to the Liberals were the anglophones. *Québec-Presse*, 18 Nov. 1973

37 The provincial co-ordinators are Cegep teachers released from part of their teaching duties to aid in curriculum development.

38 Letter from Léonce Baupré, directeur du service des programmes, Ministère de l'Education, Gouvernement du Québec, 13 Feb. 1976, reference no. 03-01-04 (emphasis added)

39 'Chrétien est bien fier de son monde,' *La Presse*, 12 Aug. 1975 (my translation)

40 Hamilton and Pinard, 'Parti Québécois Support'

41 Murray found that 53 per cent of PQ candidates in 1970 and 54 per cent in 1973 could be clearly categorized as 'new middle class.' *Le Parti Québécois*, 34

42 'Les francophones appuient majoritairement la loi 23,' *La Presse*, 19 April 1976. The anglophone attitude is symbolized in this quotation from a story appearing in the *Gazette*, 14 May 1976: 'Charging that the present Quebec government seems to be playing into the hands of those who would destroy our democratic system, Anglican Bishop of Montreal Reginald Hollis, last night told the annual synod of his diocese to "encourage men and women with Christian concern to run for public office." "How terrifying it is that politics have come to be equated with corruption," he said, after referring to the Quebec government handling of its labor disputes with the teachers.'

43 'Liberals Confine Legal Work to Favorites,' *Montreal Star*, 23 March 1976; 'Grits Admit Favored Notaries List,' *Gazette*, 21 April 1976

44 See James Leeke, 'La Plus ça Change: Patronage in Québec,' *Canadian Dimension*, XI, 1 and 3 (July-Aug. 1975 and Feb. 1976).

45 Claude Arpin, 'Loto Firm Paid into Parti Fund,' *Montreal Star*, 18 June 1976

46 Leeke, 'La Plus ça Change'

47 'Civil Servants Phone Open-Line Shows: Liberals Manipulate Broadcasts,' *Gazette*, 28 Nov. 1975

48 'En six ans, 45 lois dont 15 visent des conflits de travail,' *Le Jour*, 29 April 1976

49 For a useful description of the various employers organizations in Quebec, see Fournier, *Quebec Establishment*, 50-68. See Dominique Clift, 'Business Poll Reveals Pessimistic Outlook,' *Montreal Star*, 24 Jan. 1976.

50 For example, the following is from the *Gazette* interview with Bourassa, 16 Feb. 1976:
Q: The Parti Québécois has accused you of working out a package deal in which you trade repatriation of the constitution for federal help in paying for the Olympic deficit.

A: That's ridiculous. As Mao Tse-tung said, politics is war without blood and the PQ will fight with anything it can.

Q: That's the first time we've heard the premier of Quebec quote Mao Tse-tung, is this an indication of the direction in which we are heading?

A: Well, we are all social democrats, aren't we?

51 For a useful anthology of the major union documents, see D. Drache, ed., *Quebec – Only the Beginning* (Toronto 1972).

52 For a valuable statement of where the CNTU is now, see Marcel Pépin, *Prenons notre pouvoir*, rapport du président de la CSN, 47e congrès, Quebec, June 1976.

53 This solidarity may be seen in the annual May Day activities in Montreal and in other Quebec centres and in the readiness of Quebec workers to take part in protest marches, one-day general strikes, etc., especially when compared to workers elsewhere in Canada.

54 This seems to be the position of Alex Hamilton, president of Domtar; see David Lord, 'Give PQ a Choice, Domtar President Advises,' *Montreal Star*, 26 Feb. 1977.

55 Those so quick to dismiss 'petit-bourgeois nationalists' might look at the social background, for example, of Fidel Castro and his campaneros of the 1950s.

5
The state and province-building: Alberta's development strategy

LARRY PRATT

But how long can it last? In my view, not very long; perhaps a decade at the most, unless we're able to put in place a more balanced economy for that inevitable day, Mr. Speaker, when oil and gas no longer provide such a large number of our jobs, when production begins to decline, and resource revenue falls off. But it will not be easy to do so. There are going to be some failures and setbacks. It's not a place for timid people ... We can't rely on the federal bureaucrat or the establishment in Toronto to do it for us. For our objective means a fundamental change in the economy of Canada, a shift in the decision-making westward, and essentially to Alberta. Because of that, it will be vigorously opposed ...
Premier Peter Lougheed, Alberta legislature, 13 October 1976

This is an interpretative essay in the private purposes of public government.[1] Its themes are the role of the state in planning and promoting Alberta's economic development since the advent to power of the Conservative government in 1971 and the synthesis of business and politics in the new West. The proposition is advanced that the powers and resources of an interventionist, 'positive' government are being employed to nurture the development, and to defend the province-building interests, of an ascendant class of indigenous business entrepreneurs, urban professionals, and state administrators. The objectives of this nascent class are to strengthen its control over the Albertan economy, to reduce Alberta's dependence on outside economic and political forces, and to diversify the provincial economy before depleting oil and natural gas reserves are exhausted.

Driven by the dual fear of economic stagnation and encroachments by a federal government dominated by central Canadian interests, Alberta's business-state alliance supports a strong, interventionist provincial government which can perform the following functions: first, intervene in the market place to secure higher prices and returns for oil and gas producers, thereby creating room for the Crown to capture part of the windfall through higher royalties – which can in turn be used to subsidize industrial diversification; second, increase its control over the supply and pricing of feedstocks, so as to gain leverage for the promotion of 'forward linkage' effects; third, stand as a bulwark of provincial rights, intervening where necessary to block incursions by the federal government into Alberta's economy, especially into its resource base; fourth, secure local control over transportation routes and systems as part of an effort 'to correct the mistakes of history' and to overcome the disadvantages of geography; and, fifth, use the resources of the state to arrange joint ventures between multinational corporations and Alberta-based businesses, thereby increasing local ownership of the economy and giving Alberta companies an entry into high-growth industries such as petrochemicals and access to know-how, new markets, and technologies. It is essentially the province-building imperatives of business that lie behind the expansion of state activities in Alberta since 1971.

The leading role of the state in support of indigenous business, professional, and administrative elites has manifested itself in a variety of policy areas since about 1972. Several of these will be discussed later in the paper. Here, in the interest of avoiding misunderstanding about the argument, it is advisable to make three important generalizations about the methods and purposes of state intervention in Alberta. First, except in circumstances of last resort Alberta has eschewed public ownership as a mode of intervention, preferring to intervene through its unique quasi-state corporations and through joint ventures with the private sector. With this has come an ideological emphasis on the development of 'people's capitalism' and more local participation by Albertans in province-building. None the less, the activism of the state has given rise to conservative anxieties in a community where property rights and fear of socialism are virtually a secular religion.

Second, underlying the specific instances of state intervention in Alberta, we can discern a coherent strategy of development which can be described as the provincial equivalent of economic nationalism – the ideological emblem of a rising middle class. Closely resembling Ontario's old 'manufacturing condition,' Alberta's development strategy is to encourage local industrial processing of its energy resources and to negotiate a transfer of secondary industry, high-income jobs, and decision-making from central Canada to the West. The cornerstone of this strategy is the province's attempt to foster an Albertan world-scale petrochemical complex; indeed, a failure in this area would mean that the brave rhetoric of the new West can be dismissed.

Third, it must be stressed (and the case of petrochemicals well illustrates the point) that the target against which this development strategy is primarily directed is central Canada. That Alberta perceives its development struggle as being essentially an intra-Confederation affair, and that its main quarrel is with what Premier Lougheed calls 'the Toronto-Montreal establishment' and 'its' federal government – these are obviously true. But (and this seems to be a good deal less apparent to some observers) *within* the province the old alliance of interests and outlook between the major petroleum companies and the government of Alberta has been yielding to a much more fluid and ambivalent relationship. In part this is the predictable consequence of Alberta's declining potential as an oil-producing region; in part it results from the province's aggressive pursuit of its own development plans. To argue that the Lougheed government is merely the instrument of outside capital is a serious error.

The remainder of this essay concerns the purposes and methods of state intervention in Alberta since the Second World War. The first section focuses on two important examples of intervention in the oil and gas industries during the Social Credit years. The next part – much of which is based on interviews with selected Alberta 'elites'[2] – attempts to explain the development policies of the Lougheed government as a response to post-war social changes in the province. The purposes of state intervention are examined through an exposition of four policy themes in a third section, and the conclusion summarizes part of the argument. This essay, it should be noted, is an early and still tentative report of work in progress; and the interpretation of Alberta's policies which follows is offered less as a final argument than as an invitation for further debate.

THE LAW OF THE JUNGLE AND THE POSITIVE STATE

It is as well to begin by noting that, although the Crown has a strong ownership position with respect to minerals in Alberta, historically the province has rejected the option of developing its resources through government departments or Crown corporations. The norm has been public regulation of private development. When the province has seen the need to create new corporations to fulfil some social purpose, in the area of mineral resources it has invariably placed control of such enterprises in private hands: 'The Crown in right of the province owns some 80 per cent of minerals in the ground, including oil and gas. Nevertheless, in many respects the Crown has been the passive partner of private enterprise in the development of these resources. The influence of private ownership of minerals has been disproportionately strong, perhaps because the earliest discoveries were made in areas where such ownership was significant, and certainly because experience in the development of these resources was gained from Texas, Louisiana, Oklahoma and California, where private ownership was the norm. Alberta has maintained an unbroken tradition of reliance upon private enterprise for the conduct of exploration and production operations for Crown minerals as well as for those subject to private ownership, and when problems have arisen requiring government intervention, the protection of private rights has been paramount in any solution adopted.'[3] Yet oil and gas are resources whose peculiar characteristics in many ways compel state intervention and regulation, and Social Credit proved to be no exception to this rule. In the struggle for conservation of resources, in the need to regulate markets, and in the fear of encroachments by outside monopoly or the federal government, Social Credit found sufficient rationale for intervention. Since space is limited, discussion of antecedents will be limited to the origins of two of Alberta's most important economic institutions – the Energy Resources Conservation Board (ERCB, formerly the Petroleum and Natural Gas Conservation Board) and Alberta Gas Trunk Line Company Limited (AGTL), each of which continues to play an important role in shaping the province's development.

Conservation came to Alberta in the 1930s at a moment when the oil and gas industries were still in their infancy and struggling in chaotic conditions of overproduction, inadequate markets, and unstable prices. In the Turner Valley natural gas field, where a host of small producers and royalty owners had for years waged a hopeless fight against Imperial Oil and its entrenched subsidiaries, unregulated drilling and production and the flaring of natural gas resulted in a disastrous rate of depletion and a scandalous waste of energy: 'The fearful flares burned night and day and turned the country into what was referred to as "Hell's Half Acre," a yawning chasm that spouted flames for 14 years until Alberta established a conservation board in 1938 with enough legal powers to force operators to produce naptha and then crude oil in an orderly fashion. Until that time it proved very difficult to persuade numerous small independent operators to adopt the scientific methods of production urged by the large companies and their personnel. The latter had difficulties in applying such methods to their own properties since oil and gas are migratory and come to the surface in whatever holes are drilled in a field; the independent operators were anxious to get their investments back in as short a time as possible and drilled wells accordingly.'[4]

This situation, combined with a perverse legal tradition ascribing ownership of oil and gas only when reduced to possession (that is, the so-called 'rule of capture' which, by giving ownership rights to the person who can first bring the oil or gas to surface, gives every lease-holder a legal incentive to rob his neighbour before his neighbour robs him – thus sanctioning the kind of resource development which is both profoundly anti-conservationist and the antithesis of Adam Smith's maxim about each man working for the common good by working for his own gain[5]), had reduced the Turner Valley field by the 1930s to what a disapproving provincial royal commission later described as 'a law of the jungle.'[6] Problems in the field were exacerbated in June 1936 with Alberta's first major crude oil discovery, the Turner Valley Royalties well; and two years later, following bitter public outcry against Imperial Oil's monopolistic practices in the field, the Aberhart government created the Petroleum and Natural Gas Conservation Board[7] to fix production quotas and to prevent waste, but also to stabilize an industry which seemed on the verge of open war. Populist pressures and a widespread demand in Alberta for a takeover of part of the industry resulted in October 1938 in the setting up of a royal commission charged to investigate the entire oil industry; but when the commissioners reported in April 1940 they seemed far more concerned to press home the need to eliminate 'the evils of over-production' through state regulation. They commented in their report, *Alberta's Oil Industry*, 'that free competition and the so-called law of supply and demand would not have served, without government intervention, to prevent shameful waste of a natural resource and to keep the industry itself from complete demoralization.' While rejecting the idea of a government takeover of the industry, the commissioners argued that unrestricted competition in the oil industry 'is an economic absurdity which must every so often lead to chaos and to a cry for government intervention by those who are the first to decry government intervention in normal times. We believe in unrestricted competition but not at the price of economic stability, waste of a great natural resource and a disregard for reserves in nature's reservoir.' Here, in a convenient conjunction of society's interest in conservation and the industry's interest in stabilization, was a classic liberal rationale for positive government.

Greatly influenced by American ideas and legislation concerning petroleum conservation – much of which had been evolved by the major US companies[8] – the Alberta board was thus in a position to regulate production and to stabilize relations within the Canadian industry in the wake of the great discoveries which commenced at Leduc in February 1947. Once again, the industry's oldest bogey – the spectre of overproduction, falling prices, and cut-throat competition – reared its ugly head; and, when a voluntary system of market sharing broke down following the discovery of the giant Redwater field northeast of Edmonton in December 1950, the conservation board, acting upon the urgent request of the industry, introduced the controversial practice of prorationing oil according to market demand. Market demand prorationing, first begun in Texas and Oklahoma in the 1930s, is designed to keep prices high and to promote equitable sharing of markets; in Alberta it is buttressed by the board's legislative mandate to prevent not only the physical waste of resources but also 'economic waste' – defined as 'the production of oil, gas or crude bitumen in excess of proper storage facilities or of transportation and marketing facilities or of market demand.'[9] That conservation has greatly prevented physical waste is not in question, but, as has frequently been noted, market demand prorationing is also a form of public subsidy to producers, since the most important effect of controlling the quantity of oil entering the market is to stabilize prices. And the board's role is more complex than simply that: '... "market demand" prorationing is essentially a price maintenance device, designed to protect producers against downward movements in price. The institution of "market demand" prorationing in 1950 has effectively cartelized Alberta's crude oil industry. The Board's role is essentially that of a cartel secretariat. It has two main functions. The first is to determine the quantity the industry should produce in a given time period in order to obtain its objective ... The second is to distribute this output among the industry members in what [sic] they will accept as fair and equitable.'[10]

As this suggests, another crucial function of the board has been to provide a forum within which conflicts and grievances within the Canadian oil and gas industries, particularly those dividing the small independent producers and the large integrated majors, can be aired and legally resolved. This 'secretariat' function now extends beyond the confines of the petroleum industry. The board's mandate was broadened by Social Credit in 1971 when it was reconstituted as the Energy Resources Conservation Board and given regulatory authority over all provincial energy resources; and it was extended again in 1974 when the Lougheed government – as part of its overall strategy of development – empowered the board to issue industrial permits[11] and thereby to regulate development of the province's petrochemical industry. Traditionally tied to the interests and outlook of oil and gas producers, Alberta's most important regulatory agency is now playing a broader role in shaping the province's economic development. As competition intensifies among conflicting business interests for control of scarce, depleting energy reserves, the ERCB will be expected to adjudicate disputes between, for instance, integrated gas producers and petrochemical concerns over such issues as the availability and pricing of feedstocks, and its decisions will presumably be expected to reflect the government's broad development priorities. The expanding responsibilities and powers of the ERCB thus extend well beyond 'conservation' matters and are themselves a useful yardstick for measuring the growth of government in the new West.

Alberta Gas Trunk Line had its origins in the tangled and controversial politics of natural gas exports in the 1950s. Gas export had long been a recurring and volatile issue in Alberta before exploding into the national arena in 1956 at the time of the Trans-Canada Pipe Lines affair. That episode, which was so revealing of the inner workings of the federal political economy and of the complex demands placed upon the state at both the national and provincial levels by the rapid post-war development of Alberta's oil and gas, is far too tortuous a tale to justify another discussion here. What is worth noting, however, is that the prospect of large-scale sales of surplus gas set in motion a sweeping expansion of provincial powers over Alberta's gas reserves between 1949 and 1954, of which the formation of AGTL was but one important step. It is in part because of this strongly interventionist legacy that the Lougheed government is in the position today to use natural gas as the cornerstone of its industrial development strategy.

No issue was so contentious, so loaded with potential friction, in post-Leduc Alberta as the question of exporting gas from the province. On no other policy matter did Ernest Manning's Social Credit government move with such extreme caution and trepidation. And with reason: ' ... gas kept the street lights on and the barn warm and the house cheerful. The vast caverns of natural gas beneath the farm or the thousands of cubic feet running by in a pipe was part of the everyday life and folklore of Alberta. God had put it there for the enjoyment of His people. Woe betide the politician who sold such a birthright.'[12]

Natural gas was now widely understood to be both a cheap, clean fuel and an important industrial feedstock, and there was virtually unanimous opposition within the province to any further wastage of the resource, and much popular resistance as well to the various pipeline promoters who planned to ship it out in large quantities to eastern Canada and the United States. Both of the small but vocal opposition parties, the Liberals and the CCF, opposed gas exports and the Alberta legislature saw several fierce shouting matches and mêlées over the issue between 1949 and 1954 (it was the main issue of the 1952 election campaign). But it cut more deeply than this. The president of the University of Alberta was speaking for an important segment of the community when he privately informed one pipeline promoter that 'I may have a bit of prejudice against the proposal to export natural gas because I have always felt that this resource represented for Alberta what hydro-electric power represented to the St. Lawrence Valley. On this view it would seem unwise to sacrifice for immediate gain our long-range potentialities for industrial development.'[13] During hearings by the Dinning Natural Gas Commission, appointed by the province in November 1948 to investigate Alberta's gas reserves and requirements, the cities of Edmonton, Calgary, Medicine Hat, and Lethbridge, the Union of Alberta Municipalities, the provincial utility companies, the Edmonton Chamber of Commerce, the Coal Operators' Association of Western Canada, the Alberta Federation of Agriculture, the Alberta Research Council, the Alberta branch of the Canadian Manufacturers' Association, and a variety of manufacturers and small businessmen all expressed varying degrees of opposition and outright hostility to the plans of the American pipeline promoters, and most insisted that Alberta's requirements be assured for at least fifty years before exports were approved[14] (the government eventually settled for thirty years' protection). Business spokesmen wanted cheap gas protected as a catalyst for industrial growth; the Research Council anticipated major petrochemical developments; consumers in the cities and municipalities already dependent on gas wanted their supplies assured and worried that exports would increase prices; more remote communities insisted that they be supplied before outside markets were served – in vain did the government plead that this would be wildly uneconomic; while the coal industry was fearful of the effects that gas exports could have on its already dwindling markets. Much of the opposition was expressed in strong nationalist language and the *Lethbridge Herald* was voicing popular sentiments when it argued in July 1949: 'Albertans want no wastage of this invaluable resource. There has been too much wastage already in the Turner Valley. The flares that lighted the skies for years over the Valley told their own story. More of our communities want natural gas for fuel. The demand for this clean fuel is growing and the Herald wants to see our needs guarded. If it is allowed it should be permitted only under strict control and not for the enrichment of absentee capitalists who have no real interest in the country.'[15]

Given this protectionist opinion, a good portion of it emanating from the local business community, it is not surprising that the Manning government moved warily in dealing with the interests lobbying for early approval of gas exports. Unsure of its consitutional position and fearful that federally incorporated pipeline companies would attempt to make individual arrangements with the major producers, in July 1949, at a stormy session of the legislature, the government greatly strengthened its well-head control

over gas by enacting legislation protecting Alberta's requirements, prohibit-
ing waste, and empowering the conservation board to control export
permits.[16] The board itself moved very cautiously and only recommended
exports when established gas reserves were conservatively estimated at 6.8
trillion cubic feet, substantially in excess of the province's thirty-year needs.
Nevertheless, the opposition parties bitterly attacked the cabinet's decision
to approve gas exports to the Pacific Northwest via the Westcoast Transmission project in early 1952, and Manning evidently felt free to support
the much-larger Trans-Canada scheme only when he had fought and won
an election on the question. Interestingly, whereas the Liberals and CCF argued that gas sales would have a negative effect on Alberta's prospects for
industrialization, Social Credit argued that such industrialization would be
impossible *without* gas exports: Alberta's best opportunity, Manning argued, lay in petrochemicals, an industry which would utilize the by-prod-
ucts extracted from natural gas before export. Failure to approve exports
was 'restricting an important phase of potential industrial growth,' he
charged, adding that with the completion of Trans-Canada 'we may antici-
pate a program of gas exploration, development, processing and industrialization that may equal or exceed the development of our vast oil resources.'[17]
The debate about Alberta's industrial development is thus an old one.

Impending approval of the Trans-Canada project in early 1954 necessitated a further controversial intervention by Alberta into the natural gas
business. A precondition of new gas exports was the creation of a corporate
instrument to defend the province from encroachments into its resource
base by the federal government – to appropriate a well-known concept of
Aitken's,[18] what was required was a new round of 'defensive expansion' by
Social Credit. On constitutional grounds, the Manning government had
long worried that federally incorporated and regulated pipeline companies,
by extending their gathering lines into Alberta's major gas fields, could
thereby also extend Ottawa's jurisdiction into Alberta and give the Dominion authorities well-head control over the province's reserves; this in turn
could undermine Alberta's emphasis on local priority in regard to supply
and price. Fear of a marketplace under federal regulatory authority was
partly behind some of the earlier interventionist legislation discussed above,
and it was clearly the dominant consideration underlying the idea (first
mooted in the 1949 report of the Dinning Commission) to create a provincial monopoly over gas-gathering within the province. A single grid or integrated gathering system would act as a common carrier inside Alberta, distributing pooled gas to export companies at the border. This would keep gas
pipelines within Alberta under exclusive provincial jurisdiction, and such a

grid or trunk line could also serve the secondary community-building objective of supplying gas to outlying areas of the province.

The nature of the vehicle created by Social Credit was highly revealing of the specific ideological boundaries of post-war public enterprise in Alberta. On the one hand, the government rejected an application by the two major provincial utilities and their parent, International Utilities of New York, to build such a grid, apparently because of the concern that it would be reluctant to perform the relatively uneconomic function of supplying gas to small communities. On the other hand, the cabinet also rejected legal advice that it create a Crown corporation to shield Albertan interests: 'public ownership is bad in principle, worse in practice,' Manning told the legislature, adding that a Crown corporation would impinge on industry rights and disturb the province's business climate.[19] As a half-way house, the cabinet had formulated the ingenious structure of Alberta Gas Trunk Line Company. Incorporated by an act of the legislature in April 1954, the company was confined exclusively to the business of gathering and transmitting gas and was expressly forbidden to enter into arrangements with gas exporters which could give the latter indirect control of the company. Two types of common stock, Classes A and B, were authorized: non-voting Class A shares numbering eight million; and voting Class B shares totalling 2002 and divided among four groups – producers, gas exporters, Alberta utilities, and the Alberta government (holding two shares). The Class B shares were divided and appointments to the board of directors defined so as to give an overwhelming preponderance to the producers, utilities, and government-appointed directors and to make it virtually impossible for the privately owned company to pass into the hands of external interests such as Trans-Canada.[20] A large block of non-voting Class A shares were sold in 1957: restricted to bona fide residents of Alberta, the issue was so heavily oversubscribed that brokers and bankers had to ration sales. The emphasis on 'people's capitalism,' which was of course central to the ideology of Social Credit, was justified as the market value of the shares increased markedly.[21] And, as Trans-Canada's historian noted: 'By forming this organization Premier Manning avoided the distasteful prospect of using a government department or crown corporation to control the direction and price of Alberta gas, while at the same time he effectively achieved the same thing by keeping jurisdiction over gas-gathering pipelines within Alberta.'[22]

Reflecting the new development priorities of Alberta in the 1970s, Alberta Gas Trunk has now evolved well beyond its original conception. Since 1972-3 the company has embarked on a sweeping program of corporate diversification whose long-term objective is to make the company an Alberta-based and Alberta-controlled multinational enterprise while at the same time creating 'a Canadian presence in the Canadian oil and gas industries.' Through its affiliate, Foothills Pipelines Limited, Alberta Gas Trunk has been at the forefront of the debate over northern natural gas development as the main rival to the large US-oriented Arctic Gas consortium proposing to bring Alaskan and Canadian gas to southern markets down the Mackenzie Valley. Working in close co-operation with the Lougheed government and gas producers, AGTL created in 1972 a subsidiary brokerage-company, Pan-Alberta, to gather natural gas not already committed to contract and to offer it for sale at prices substantially higher than those then being offered by TransCanada Pipelines (because of National Energy Board rulings against new gas exports in November 1971, Trans-Canada was in the position of a monopolistic buyer). As gas prices began to rise in Canada in response to changing market conditions and new government policies, AGTL determined to use its own lucrative monopoly over gas-gathering and transmission within Alberta as a base for diversifying into petrochemicals, an industry much in favour with the Lougheed government. In 1974 the government amended AGTL's act of incorporation, giving the company legal sanction to diversify, and Premier Lougheed also gave his blessing to the firm's plans for an Alberta-based petrochemical complex on the grounds that it would 'involve many new jobs for Albertans and opportunities for small business in Alberta,' had 'a high degree of Alberta and Canadian ownership potential,' and was thus 'a major step in our plan to diversify our economic development.'[23] A privately owned enterprise pursuing public, as well as business, objectives, AGTL has thus adapted itself to the changing circumstances of the 1970s while preserving its close historic relationship with Alberta's political leadership.

The origins of Alberta's oil conservation system and of its gas trunk line monopoly nicely illustrate some of the determinants, and also the limits, of state intervention in the oil and gas industries in post-war Alberta. The rule of capture, market failures, and the need to cartelize an unstable industry and to prevent waste led the state to intervene in order to regulate oil production in the name of conservation, while the fear of federal encroachments and pressures to give priority to local interests were the most important variables influencing the growth of government management of the natural gas industry. Unquestionably, this process contributed to the expansion of the executive arm of government – placing enormous powers in the hands of administrative agencies – and weakened the system of ministerial responsibility and accountability in Alberta. Yet it is also true that the pressures to intervene were balanced by a strong determination on the part of Social Credit to protect property rights and to ensure the kind of business stability necessary to attract outside capital. 'Businesslike management' of resources was the hallmark of the Manning era. Crown corporations were carefully avoided and so too was the sort of draconian intervention which, at least from the standpoint of rational resource management, might well have improved the efficiency of Alberta's development policies (for example, as an alternative to market-demand prorationing, Alberta could have enforced compulsory unitization of oil pools, but this would have involved a large degree of interference with property rights). The fear of disturbing Alberta's stable business climate – a factor which Premier Manning considered to be the province's strongest suit in competing with other oil-producing areas for new capital[24] – and the unwillingness of the cabinet to dispute the property rights of producers weakened the position of the Crown vis-à-vis private interests who used the powers of the state to invest business preferences with the authority of the law. Consequently, when the province finally emerged from the Social Credit era in 1971, its oil and gas industries were operating in an environment which was at once highly protective of the interests of private enterprise but was also characterized by extensive government regulation of all phases of development.

THE LOUGHEED ERA: THE GENESIS OF ALBERTA'S
DEVELOPMENT STRATEGY

Alberta's large and growing urban middle classes, nurtured by twenty-five years of oil and natural gas development, acceded to political power in the provincial election of August 1971. In retrospect that election, which saw Peter Lougheed's revived Progressive Conservative party take forty-nine seats and thereby write *finis* to the thirty-six-year dynasty of Social Credit, represented an inevitable, though much delayed, response of the electoral system (delayed, in part, by Social Credit's careful gerrymandering and the deliberate under-representation of the cities in the legislature) to post-war population growth, urbanization, and secularization – demographic and social trends that were underway before Leduc and accelerated by the dramatic effects of rapid oil and gas development on the provincial economy and labour force. Ironically, Social Credit's resource management policies and its discretionary spending of oil and gas rents in such areas as secondary education and the growth of municipalities helped to undermine the party's own social and political base – the rural, small-town, petite bourgeoisie described in C.B. Macpherson's *Democracy in Alberta* at the opening of the oil boom.[25]

By 1971 Macpherson's socially homogeneous province of independent commodity producers was an anachronism. Rapid population growth and the steady migration of Albertans and other Canadians to the province's major urban centres in search of jobs commenced during the Second World War and has continued to the present. In 1941 approximately half the people of Alberta lived on census farms and less than a quarter in Edmonton and Calgary; by 1971 less than 20 per cent of the population was still on farms while better than half the population was concentrated in the two major urban centres.[26] By the opening of the 1970s, much of Alberta's population worked in white-collar occupations for large private or public institutions and rejected Social Credit's blend of agrarian populism and fundamentalism in favour of the secular values of the 'new middle class.' The failure of the Social Credit party to adapt itself to these changing social circumstances following Manning's retirement in 1968 sealed the party's fate.[27]

Under the impact of the heavy capital expenditures of the oil and gas industries, Alberta's economic base shifted in the 1950s and 1960s from its traditional dependence on agriculture to a new dependence on mineral extraction (accounting for about 35 per cent of annual productivity) and oil-related construction and manufacturing. The striking impact of the new staples on the work force can be gleaned from a recent study which estimates that oil accounted for *half* the jobs created in Alberta during the 1960s, and that of the 87,000 oil-created jobs more than half were in the services and trade. By contrast, relatively few jobs were created in manufacturing, and these have been concentrated in satellite industries of the foreign-controlled petroleum industry. The activity of the oil and gas industries did not provide a spur for the creation of large-scale manufacturing or for Alberta's industrialization.[28] The province's generation of prosperity has been dependent, in large part, on the extraction and sale of non-renewable natural resources – as have the fortunes of its business community.

The predominant position of a few very large international companies in the development of Alberta's oil industry is well known and requires no further emphasis here. Eight companies, all of them foreign-owned, have fully integrated operations in Canada, involving exploration, production, transportation, refining, and marketing. What is less well known, however, is that by the late 1960s these major companies had shifted their exploratory operations away from Alberta to frontier regions of Canada in search for new 'elephant' pools, while the 200-plus minor operators (or independents), which tend to be involved only in exploration and production, had begun to account for up to 75-80 per cent of new exploratory work in the province.[29] This was not due to any change in Alberta's policies or business climate; rather, it represented a collective decision by the 'majors' that the limits of

Alberta's oil-producing potential had been reached and that new exploratory work would bring diminishing returns. The upshot of this was that by
the early 1970s it had become apparent that the majors' interest in Alberta
was falling off and that the small independent companies would have to
take up much of the slack if the province's prosperity was to be maintained.
This fact must be constantly borne in mind when assessing Alberta's resource policies.

The dominant status of the majors notwithstanding, the many smaller
operators are by no means an insignificant part of Alberta's business community. The capital spending of the majors on exploration, development,
production, and pipeline equipment stimulated the growth of many oil-related businesses in the province, including drilling companies, oil service
and supply companies, small manufacturers, transportation firms, and so
on. Unlike the majors, such companies earn virtually all their income in Alberta and their own future is literally tied to the province's economic prospects. In addition, the expenditures of the petroleum industry spawned the
development in Alberta's urban centres of a large body of educated professionals – corporate lawyers, geologists, engineers, landmen, consultants, accountants, etc. – providing services of a technical and specialized nature to
the oil industry and government. Another important segment of this urban
elite occupies administrative positions within the public sector, particularly
in government departments and regulatory agencies, such as the ERCB,
charged with the job of supervising and managing the development of
Alberta's resources. Confident of its administrative competence to manage
the huge revenue surpluses of the 1970s and committed to provincial economic planning, this state-bureaucratic elite sees the province as the logical
arena for the advancement of its career opportunities and, like its counterparts in the private sector, it is fiercely loyal to the province as a semi-sover-
eign economic and political unit and deeply engaged in the process of province-building. Much of the pressure to use Alberta's remaining energy
resources as a catalyst for industrialization appears to originate within the
public bureaucracy.

It is no exaggeration to suggest that these business-professional-
bureaucratic elites have begun to make arrangments for their own future by
preparing for the inevitable day when the international oil industry pulls
out of Alberta. Committed to 'Alberta first' in virtually all questions, these
elites found many of their aspirations and fears being articulated politically
for the first time by the provincial Conservative party, revived by Calgary
corporate lawyer Peter Lougheed and a small coterie of professionals and
businessmen in the mid-1960s. Preaching the need to reduce Alberta's de-

pendence on outside forces, to modernize and diversify the province's economic base, and to enhance employment and investment opportunities for Albertans, the Conservatives and their slogan, 'It's time for a change,' 'offered the electorate continued free-enterprise conservatism, but with the added bonuses of urban middle-class respectability, a comfortably vague social conscience and a little political excitement.'[30] In 1967 Lougheed's party won a handful of seats in the upper-income districts of Calgary and Edmonton and four years later, following Manning's retirement, swept the cities (and part of the disaffected rural north) to take power. A shrewd political organizer who is highly sophisticated in his use of television and his approach to public relations, Lougheed's image of the dynamic, successful conservative leader is said to have been modelled on the campaign of two American politicians, John F. Kennedy and Ronald Reagan. Affluent, ideologically to the right, and the grandson of Sir James Lougheed – CPR lawyer, R.B. Bennett's business partner, and a pioneer of frontier capitalism in Alberta – Peter Lougheed is the embodiment of the values and aspirations of a rising urban middle class impatient for change. His two cabinets have been dominated by corporate lawyers and successful small businessmen, most of the senior portfolios going to representatives of Calgary and Edmonton constituencies. More important than the location of state personnel, however, has been the direction of the government's development policies.

Since taking power in 1971 the Lougheed administration has proven itself to be markedly activist and interventionist in its economic policies. To cite but a few examples, oil and natural gas royalties have been increased dramatically; the government has increased its controls over the pricing, marketing, and utilization of energy resources; Alberta has acquired its own regional airline; the Lougheed cabinet has created the Alberta Energy Company and invested equity in the giant Syncrude oil sands project; the government is diverting a portion of surplus revenues into the Alberta Heritage Fund for economic diversification; and the province is attempting to foster its own world-scale petrochemical industry, a venture that has led the Lougheed government into negotiation for special tariff arrangements with the United States. More significant than these, however, is the emergence in Edmonton of a province-building administration committed to long-range economic planning, policy co-ordination, and a consistent strategy of economic development. Professor Smiley has ably summarized the latter: 'On the basis of its existing circumstances Alberta has evolved a relatively coherent industrial strategy with these elements: the preservation of provincial autonomy in resource matters against federal influence; the creation of a strong petrochemical industry within the province; the establishment of arrangements by which Albertans are given preferential treatment in terms of employment and investment opportunities in the development of Alberta resources; the dispersal of economic development outside the Edmonton and Calgary metropolitan areas; adjustments in federal transportation and tariff policies to serve Alberta needs.'[31]

The essentials of this strategy were evolved by Peter Lougheed and his closest political associates while in opposition in the late 1960s. Perceiving that the province was near maturity as an oil-producing region and that its position as a land-locked, thinly populated hinterland far from distant markets was impeding industrial growth, the Conservatives accepted the need for an activist government to steer the province's development. Rejecting the 'industrialitis' syndrome that has plagued so many of the poorer provinces, Lougheed argued the necessity of fostering 'natural' industries – such as petrochemicals and agricultural processing – out of the province's strong resource base. An internal government memorandum on this subject, dated 1974, states that the province is at the point of transition 'from a primarily extractive economy, where our resources are exported for processing to other parts of Canada and the rest of the world, to an industrialized economy which will see further processing of our raw materials, increased manufacturing and ... satisfying employment opportunities for Albertans.' But, the document cautions, unless the government manages growth and steers the economy in desired directions, this transition might not occur and the province could become even more dependent on its natural resources.[32] Alberta's industrial strategy seems to be partly rooted in the implicit assumption that regional economic growth typically occurs in a unilinear sequence of stages, the region evolving from a subsistence economy through the exploitation of its resources to the early and advanced stages of industrialization. A failure to make the transition to a modern industrial economy, according to this viewpoint, dooms the region to stagnation and decay as emigration occurs and living standards fall.[33]

Where should one seek the determinants of Alberta's push for industrialization in the 1970s? A major source appears to lie in the status and occupational drives of dissatisfied elites who would transform the province from a periphery into an industrial core area where power, wealth, and attractive careers are located. These elites view the West as an exploited dependency of central Canada: Confederation and its political and economic arrangements are perceived to be the instruments of Ontario and Quebec interests, the heritage of Macdonald's National Policy. Discontent with such issues as the lack of secondary industry on the prairies, the practices of Canada's financial institutions, national freight rates, tariffs, and federal taxation of the resource industries, comments one observer, 'can be seen as a mixture of dissatisfaction with the inevitable fate of a small region in a market economy, and unhappiness with distortions in such a system initiated or at least tolerated by the federal government.'[34] Prairie economic alienation is essentially a hinterland quarrel with a market economy, but, probably inevitably, regional protest tends to focus on federal policies that are believed to buttress distortions and on demands for various kinds of remedial state intervention. A familiar western grievance, for example, is that national tariffs, federal purchasing policies, freight rates, etc., conspire to obstruct the normal evolution of economic development on the prairies. 'The real request of the West is not special privilege,' Premier Lougheed commented at the Western Economic Opportunities Conference in August 1973, 'but the removal of unnecessary obstacles to growth': 'To use a Western term – "Don't fence us in!" The concerns of the West are more than a matter of dollars, or job security, or even economic opportunity, important as these are, it's a feeling of Western Canadians that we have a great deal going for us in the West but that we feel frustrated in reaching out for our potential ... we are thwarted by Federal Government policies.'[35]

Underlying Alberta's quarrel with the market economy and with Ottawa is an assumption – verified by historical experience – that the West's narrow economic base, its vast distance from the major population centres of North America, and its dependence on outside capital, communications, transportation, and volatile commodity markets, have produced a society whose well-being and security are precarious, always at the mercy of decisions taken by outsiders. This is compounded by an acute awareness of Alberta's reliance on the oil and gas industries. 'Since entering public life over nine years ago,' Lougheed told the Calgary Chamber of Commerce in 1974, 'my theme has been that this province's economy is too *vulnerable*, it is too dependent upon the sale of depleting resources, particularly oil and natural gas for its continued prosperity.' Alberta had a decade to diversify, Lougheed argued, adding that the government's development strategy was rooted in three fundamental objectives: 'The first one is to strengthen the control by Albertans over our own future and to reduce the dependency for our continued quality of life on governments, institutions or corporations directed from outside the province. Secondly, to do this as much as possible through the private sector and only to move through the public sector if the private sector is not in a position to move in essential new directions and then only in exceptional and very specific circumstances. And thirdly, to strengthen competitive free enterprise by Albertans which to us means giving priority to our locally-owned businesses. Our basic guidepost [is] to maximize the number of our citizens controlling their own destiny.'[36]

This 'economic provincialism' has great political appeal among local businessmen and professionals and, taken to its extreme, manifests itself in the activities and studies of the neo-separatist Independent Association of Alberta. Lougheed's declared intention to shift economic power to the West from central Canada should be interpreted, in part, as an expression of the desire of the Alberta business community to be liberated from its traditional dependence on eastern financial interests. 'Half the businessmen you meet,' comments one journalist of Alberta, 'from Carl Nickle, whose father was a Calgary shoe salesman who became enormously rich during the first oil strikes of the 1940s, to Don Getty [minister of energy and natural resources in Lougheed's second cabinet], who was born in the East but made his millions in oil in the 1960s before turning to politics – talk bitterly of how they were treated by officials in banks and investment houses on Bay or St. James Streets when they went there seeking development money.'[37] This hostility has been strongly reinforced by new federal resource taxation policies which have been generally interpreted in Alberta as thinly disguised attempts by Ottawa to undermine the province's jurisdiction and to gain indirect control of its energy resources. Business anxiety over further federal encroachments and interventions into the oil and gas industries provides the Alberta government and its regulatory arms with a powerful base of support for market interventions undertaken in defence of provincial rights. Businessmen support a positive, strong state at the provincial level as a buffer against a predatory national government.

Fear of economic stagnation provides a second crucial support for state intervention. Alberta's elites are well aware that the booming economic conditions of the 1970s are essentially a consequence of rising demand for non-renewable oil and gas reserves; and the knowledge that production from most of the province's major conventional oil fields will soon begin to decline and that large new discoveries are improbable has created some anxiety among businessmen and professionals – many of whose families, certainly Peter Lougheed's, were hard hit by the Great Depression. Uncertainty about the future gives Alberta business an incentive to overcome its conservative dislike of bureaucracy and 'big government' and to support a regime dedicated to the planning and promotion of an economy less dependent on resource extraction and less under the control of outside institutions. On condition that the province resists the temptation to set up Crown corporations to compete with private enterprise (the purchase of Pacific Western Airlines and the creation of the Alberta Energy Company each produced some uneasy stirrings in local business circles), the Alberta business community perceives that it has much to gain by supporting an activist government which is willing to use its powers in support of such province-

building objectives as: ensuring 'fair market value' for oil and gas producers; diverting a share of rising resource revenues into capital funds for diversification; processing of more resources in Alberta; securing control over
western transportation routes; offsetting the costs of geography by holding
down provincial gas prices; establishing a tax incentives system favourable
to small businesses; and maintaining a business climate favourable to new
foreign investment while insisting on various forms of 'participation' by Alberta businesses and investors in the ownership and control of new projects.

Closely resembling turn-of-the-century Ontario's 'manufacturing condition,'[38] as mentioned earlier, the strategy of development being pursued in
Alberta puts great emphasis on the processing and upgrading of resources
at the source. By increasing its control over the pricing, supply, and utilization of feedstocks (particularly natural gas), the state can reduce the export
of raw materials – and jobs – to markets in eastern Canada and the United
States and promote forward linkages in the Alberta economy. A viable
manufacturing sector, based on the processing of resources at the source,
will attract new advanced technologies to the province, assist the development of a skilled industrial labour force and stimulate the growth of related
industries. Alberta's leaders believe that the world energy crisis, and the
shift in bargaining power from consumers to producers, gives the province
the leverage it requires to make the transition to a modern industrial economy. Using Alberta's large but depleting conventional reserves of oil and
natural gas as bargaining tools, in a situation of energy scarcity with consumers increasingly concerned about the availability and security of future
supplies, an aggressive government can negotiate a transfer of industry,
high-income jobs, and power from the central Canadian heartland to the
West. This is what lies behind Alberta's lengthy struggle with Ottawa and
Ontario over the future of the petrochemical industry in Canada. Lougheed
has argued that here Alberta has 'a natural economic advantage over other
areas since the importance of assured feedstocks under current energy conditions is becoming as significant as proximity to markets,' and that the
chemical industry offers the province the promise of high-income jobs and
important opportunities for small businessmen.[39] However, Ottawa's support for a rival Sarnia-based project (Petrosar) jeopardizes Alberta's petrochemical plans and constitutes, in the eyes of Premier Lougheed and his
supporters, yet another sorry episode in the historical exploitation of the
West.

'ALBERTA FIRST': THE USES OF THE STATE

Within the context of these economic development plans, the Lougheed
government has exploited its constitutional powers to the fullest possible ex-

tent since about 1972-3 in an effort to impede aggrandizing moves by Ottawa and to protect its control over its natural resource base. Fear of federal encroachments and distrust of a market economy under outside control have manifested themselves in a series of interventions, virtually all of which have been justified in the name of Alberta private enterprise. The objectives of state intervention are best understood through a brief exegesis of four related policy themes.

First, 'Alberta first' is the key to understanding the province's highly protective natural gas policies. Albertans tend to view natural gas as a special birthright or natural endowment and since 1949 the province has strictly controlled the production, sale, and utilization of gas through such legislation as the Gas Resources Preservation Act. The strong opposition in Alberta to the wastage or export of the resource after the Second World War was a logical precursor to the policies of the present administration. These policies begin from the premise that Albertans have hitherto been denied a just return for the depletion of their gas reserves, including the opportunity to utilize the resource as a catalyst for industrial development, and that outsiders have earned a disproportionate share of the benefits from the exploitation of the province's gas.

Following a comprehensive study of the field pricing of Alberta natural gas, the Energy Resources Conservation Board concluded in 1972 that prevailing prices were substantially below commodity value (that is, the value of equivalent energy in competing forms, such as oil, in the same markets), and argued that a lack of competition among gas purchasers was the vital cause of underpricing.[40] Acting on the board's recommendations, the Lougheed cabinet quickly intervened on the side of gas producers to challenge TransCanada Pipelines' monopsonistic position. Approval was withheld from new applications to remove gas from the province until prices increased substantially, and the province amended its arbitration legislation governing the redetermination of gas prices paid by pipelines to producers: such prices are now to be redetermined every two years on the basis of full commodity value.[41] These steps, which were vigorously opposed and protested by Ontario – the target of Alberta's interventions – have had an enormous impact on gas pricing in Canada, but the Lougheed government has thus far sheltered Alberta consumers from the full effects of the increases through its two-price policy of natural gas rebates.[42]

Natural gas is regarded as the basis of Alberta's future industrialization, and this has shaped the province's attitude to the use of feedstocks. Alberta's world-scale petrochemical complex, involving Alberta Gas Trunk Line, Dome petroleum, and Dow Chemicals in a complicated joint venture, is to be based on ethylene manufactured from ethane, a natural gas by-product. Under legislation enacted in 1974 the ERCB now has the power to issue industrial development permits, subject to cabinet approval, and thus can control the utilization of gas within Alberta. The board also retains the authority, again subject to cabinet approval, to issue permits for the removal of gas judged to be surplus to the province's own thirty-year needs, and there is every reason to think that these powers will be exploited to the full as Alberta bargains for concessions and trade-offs in the area of industrial development in return for its approval for new sales of natural gas.

Second, Alberta has sought to increase its share of the revenues from its depleting stock of natural resources in the interest of diversification. The province's dependence on outside capital can be mitigated by a more aggressive acquisition of resource rents. One of the earliest initiatives of the Lougheed government – its 1972 'Natural Resource Revenue Plan' – sought to raise petroleum royalties fixed at a maximum of 16⅔ per cent in long-term leases. Concerned over rising government expenditures, the shift of the majors into the frontier regions, and a declining life-index of reserves, the province determined to raise its royalties by imposing a new tax on mineral rights; this was combined with a new system of drilling incentives 'designed to benefit those operators who actually undertake exploration for crude oil in Alberta.' The incremental revenues would be used 'to stimulate substantial diversification of the Alberta economy over the next 10 to 15 years': 'The Government is aware that, as the conventional crude oil industry reaches maturity in Alberta, economic growth of the Province may tend to level off unless new and imaginative programs are initiated soon to diversify the Alberta economy along logical courses ... Diversification of a significant nature will be difficult for a number of reasons, not the least of which are our relatively "thin" consumer markets and transportation hurdles which affect the cost of inbound material and outbound products. It is the position of the Government that, in the Alberta public interest, significant expanded sources of Government revenues must begin to flow into the provincial treasury now in order to provide part of the funds for new programs specifically designed for such diversification to help finance industry for Albertans. Clearly, revenues from a depleting natural resource are an appropriate source of such funds.'[43]

However, the prospect of increased federal taxation of Alberta's resources – first through the oil export tax, later in the elimination of provisions allowing resource companies to deduct provincial royalties when calculating their federal income tax – jeopardized these development plans. Predictably, federal encroachments resulted in a vigorous, albeit defensive, expansion of the province's own powers. In a decision that startled the oil industry, the Lougheed cabinet in the fall of 1973 suddenly abandoned its new royalty plan – the subject of months of careful negotiation with industry – and announced that royalties would henceforth rise with international oil prices.[44] The province's objective was evidently to force Ottawa to withdraw its oil export levy by squeezing the oil industry; damage done to the industry could be repaired by Alberta later on. In a striking departure from the long-established practice of prior consultation, this decision was taken with no advance discussion with representatives of the oil industry.[45] In December 1973 the province also created the Alberta Petroleum Marketing Commission, a Crown corporation with broad powers relating to oil pricing. To date, the commission has had little influence on prices – which are presently set through federal-provincial agreement – but its powers could be called upon in the future.[46]

Not surprisingly, Alberta's aggressive defence of its jurisdiction and its development plans set the province on a collision course with the international oil industry. A major source of the industry's grievance with the province (and Ottawa) can be seen in Table 1. Between September 1973 and September 1975 the average well-head price of Alberta crude oil increased from $3.80 a barrel to $8.00 a barrel. Alberta's percentage take on an average barrel (royalties plus provincial income tax) increased from 24 per cent to 39 per cent, while the private producer's share of revenue declined from 51 per cent to 34 per cent. That many companies increased their net income in these two years does not alter the fact that the lion's share of the incremental revenues from rising prices went to Alberta – a point which the consuming provinces have often noted in opposing new price increases.[47] Following Ottawa's 1974 decision to eliminate the deductability of royalties in the calculation of taxable income, the major petroleum companies confronted the producing provinces with a well-co-ordinated capital strike – withdrawing drilling rigs, cancelling new investments, and laying off employees. In Alberta this campaign, which culminated in the near-collapse of the giant Syncrude project over the winter of 1974-5 (rescued through vast federal subsidies to Alberta and the private participants), threatened many of the province's small oil-dependent businesses with sudden recession. The Lougheed government came under severe pressure from the province's business community and the media and was forced in December 1974 to reduce its royalties through a new exploration incentives scheme.[48] While it confirmed the vulnerability of Alberta to pressure from the international oil industry, perhaps the most revealing fact about this conflict was that the majors found it necessary to use such harsh methods in dealing with the

Table 1
Distribution of revenue per barrel of Alberta oil[a]

	September 1973		September 1975		Increase
Operating costs	$0.67	18%	$0.85	1%	$0.18
Taxes:					
Federal income tax	0.27	7	1.28	16	1.01
Alberta royalty and provincial income tax	0.92	24	3.12	39	2.20
Industry cash flow	1.94	51	2.75	34	0.81
Average price	3.80	100	8.00	100	4.20

[a]of 'old' Alberta Crown oil sold in Canada; Alberta produced 86 per cent of Canadian oil in 1974.
Source: compiled from federal, Alberta, and *Financial Post* data. Does not include federal oil export tax, which is not a net transfer from the industry to government.

Lougheed regime. The province's royalty policies, its stress on the local up-grading of hydrocarbons, its attempts to influence the supply and pricing of feedstocks within Alberta – all of these have led to friction with the inte-grated operators who regard such practices as contrary to good business logic. The comfortable assumption that the interest of the major oil compa-nies and Alberta's interests are identical is now questioned on both sides, and this divergence of outlook could well increase as competition for scarce resources intensifies.

Third, the Lougheed government has striven to nurture the development of a strong indigenous class of business entrepreneurs and to hoist its devel-opment strategy on the petard of 'people's capitalism.' Far from being aber-rations in social democracy, Alberta's recent experiments in state enterprise should be understood as a form of public works undertaken for the benefit of the province's business community and urban middle classes. For in-stance, Pacific Western Airlines was purchased by Alberta in 1974 to enhance its control over transportation – 'the key to diversification,' accord-ing to Premier Lougheed – and to meet a challenge to the province's status as 'gateway to the North' prior to anticipated northern pipeline develop-ments; but the airline has been placed under the control of some of the government's closest business allies and in future will be operated 'by an in-dependent board of successful Alberta businessmen as directors charged with continuing to develop a profit.'[49] Similarly, the Alberta Energy Company – a 50-50 venture between the Alberta government and private investors – was incorporated in September 1973 as a vechicle for the province's direct participation in the Syncrude oil sands project and is designated to play a leading role in providing seed capital for economic diversification. The AEC, according to Mr Lougheed, 'is intended to be a unique partnership concept between public and private ownership': he advised the company's first president in 1974 that 'Substantial direct citizen ownership will provide added stimulus and accountability for results that are inherent in the private enterprise system ... Modern society is challenging the concept of private investment and ... the behaviour of corporations. It may well be that the Alberta Energy Company, by creating widespread ownership and corporate participation in the province, will foster better understanding between our citizens and our economic system.'[50]

This philosophy manifested itself in a remarkable two-week period in November 1975 when Albertans were offered their first chance to buy AEC shares: some 60,000 agreed and the issue was oversubscribed. 'Street hawking of stock at a pitch unseen in Calgary since the 1914 oil boom heralded the debut of Alberta Energy Company Ltd. into the Canadian investment community ... Within a two-week period reserved for Albertans to exclusively purchase the $10 priced shares of the 7.5 million share offering, brokers deserted their plush swivel chairs to hustle pedestrians at shopping centres, downtown department stores and public institutions. From humble, knocked-together wooden stands, they shilled the promises of A.E.C. in a gut reaction to the competition of banking institutions.'[51]

Much of the entrepreneurial drive of the Alberta business community can be located on the boards and managements of companies like PWA, AEC, and AGTL – all of which are creatures of state intervention. These quasi-state enterprises are seen as the breeding-ground of a western Canadian bourgeoisie and as a logical area for the career advancement of hundreds of young Alberta professionals.

Fourth, it must be noted that the success of Alberta's development strategy is by no means assured. There are important economic and institutional factors impeding the industrialization of western Canada, and the constitutional limits of the province's capacity to overcome these obstacles have probably been reached. Doubts have already been expressed about the constitutionality of some of Alberta's petroleum marketing legislation,[52] and the prairie provinces have also made little headway since the 1973 Western Economic Opportunities Conference in reforming national transportation policies. The Lougheed government seems determined to push ahead with its own world-scale petrochemical complex in spite of the awkward facts that its federally backed nemesis, Petrosar, is likely to absorb much of the Canadian market, that it has been unable to deny Petrosar feedstocks, and that the US market is virtually closed by high tariffs. Alberta's protestations to the contrary notwithstanding, it is hard to see how the province can avoid heavily subsidizing its petrochemical industry – unless an unexpected breakthrough is made in the area of tariffs. Tariffs, of course, are a matter under exclusive federal jurisdiction, but the Lougheed government has been actively pursuing negotiations in the United States in the attempt to find continental allies to use against an unsympathetic Ottawa. The nature of the deal Alberta is sponsoring is a limited edition of the old continental energy pact: in return for easier access to the US market for the products of its petrochemical industry, Alberta would undertake (again, subject to Ottawa's approval) to increase gas exports to the US Pacific Northwest.[53] However, it is not clear why the federal government – which reportedly is concerned about possible domestic shortages – would be interested in supporting such a bilateral agreement. It thus seems likely that, having literally willed its new petrochemical projects into existence, Alberta will now be forced to use various types of subsidies to keep them alive.

The cause of Alberta's difficulty with the petrochemical industry would appear to lie less with Ottawa's policies than in the questionable economic philosophy underlying its own development strategy. 'Processing resources at the source' has undoubted political appeal among businessmen and professionals eager for industrialization, but the failure of Ontario's old 'manufacturing condition' and similar provincial policies suggests that as a criterion for locating industry it may be something less than sound economics. It is not at all plain that Alberta *does* have a 'natural economic advantage' in petrochemicals or that 'the importance of assured feedstocks' *is* now as significant as 'proximity to markets.' The blunt conclusion of a comprehensive study of the industry undertaken for the province in 1973 was that 'there are no chemicals that can be made competitively in Alberta';[54] and the situation has only worsened (because of Petrosar) since those words were written. The apparent irrationality attending Alberta's development policies is clearly not to be explained by textbook economics.

Alberta's economic provincialism, with its stress on the use of the state to foster an indigenous industrial-technological core, must be interpreted as the frustrated reaction of elites in a hinterland region to the uneven diffusions of growth that are characteristic of a market economy. In a capitalist setting, where the regional distribution of industry is a question essentially resolved according to profit-maximizing principles, the normal tendency is for industry, ecomomic activity, and wealth to concentrate around growth centres, and for the rate of growth of wealth and economic activity at these centres to be faster than the diffusion of growth to peripheral regions. According to one student of economic location, this uneven development 'will normally be accompanied by a series of displacements, from the periphery to the center of the principal factors of production: labor, capital, entrepreneurship, foreign exchange, and raw materials in unprocessed form.'[55]

Such unevenness and its accompanying displacements often have important political implications as well, producing a frustrated sense of dependency and subordination among elites in the periphery which aspire to the top but feel blocked. This frustration typically vents itself in some variant of economic nationalism, which, as Karl Polanyi pointed out, emerges historically as a protective response to market forces.[56] Economic nationalism reflects the desire of a peripheral political, cultural, or ethnic group to possess and enjoy an industrial core of its own where wealth, attractive careers, and power are located. 'Its objective is to transform this division of labor through industrialization and to transform its territorial base into a relatively independent industrial core.'[57]

Viewed from this perspective, the industrial underdevelopment of western Canada is the normal fate of a small and thinly populated region in a market economy. And Alberta's interventionist development strategy is a predictable rejection of market forces that have created a division of labour between an industrialized core and the 'hewers of wood and drawers of water' of the periphery. Its present policies reflect the anxieties and aspirations of a dependent business community and an ascendant urban middle class, neither of which seek the elimination of the market economy – merely promotion within it. It is the relentless pressure of these dissatified groups, combined with the impact of the international energy crisis on the Canadian political economy, that makes Alberta in the seventies 'une province pas comme les autres.'

NOTES

1   I am grateful to Allan Tupper, L.C. Green, Jim Lightbody, and John Richards
     for comments and criticisms. On the theme of 'province-building,' see E.R. Black
     and A.C. Cairns, 'A Different Perspective on Canadian Federalism,' *Canadian
     Public Administration*, IX, 1 (March 1966), 27-45.

2 Fifty-one selected 'elites' were interviewed during the summer of 1976. These included leading provincial politicians (cabinet ministers, opposition party leaders, and former cabinet ministers); several civil servants at the deputy minister
level in departments responsible for economic affairs; officials at the Energy Resources Conservation Board; the chief executive officers of several important
Alberta-owned oil and gas 'independents'; and the Alberta managers of a small
sample of multinational enterprises in the petroleum and chemical industries.
The interviews were conducted (except where otherwise noted) on an off-the-
record basis by Mr Barry Wilson, a professional political journalist and writer. I
am indebted to Mr Wilson for his invaluable assistance.
3 M. Crommelin, 'Government Management of Oil and Gas in Alberta,' *Alberta
Law Review*, XIII, 2 (1975), 146
4 E.J. Hanson, *Dynamic Decade* (Toronto 1958), 47
5 The rule of capture and related theories of ownership of oil and gas are discussed in the large body of writings on petroleum law, property rights, etc. A
useful analysis is in D.F. Lewis and A.R. Thompson, *Canadian Oil and Gas* (Toronto 1971), I; also E.J. Hanson and E.H. Shaffer, 'Economics of Oil and Gas,'
Canadian Perspectives on Economics (Toronto 1972).
6 *Alberta's Oil Industry: The Report of a Royal Commission Appointed by the Government of the Province of Alberta under the Public Inquiries Act to Inquire into
Matters Connected with Petroleum and Petroleum Products* (April 1940); chairman: Hon. A.A. McGillivray
7 The Oil and Gas Resources Conservation Act (1938), *Alberta Statutes* (1938)
8 American influence on Alberta's thinking about petroleum conservation can be
seen in the McGillivray Commission's report of 1940. On the us history, cf. R.
Engler, *The Politics of Oil* (Chicago 1961), especially chap. 6; H.F. Williamson
et al., *The American Petroleum Industry: The Age of Energy, 1899-1959* (Evans-
ton 1963), chaps. 9 and 15; H.M. Larson *et al.*, *New Horizons: History of Standard Oil Co. (New Jersey), 1927-1950* (New York 1971), 80-93; and L.M. Logan,
Jr., *Stabilization of the Petroleum Industry* (Norman, Okla. 1930).
9 The board was given the power to proration to market demand in amendments
to conservation law, passed by the legislature in July 1949, and instituted it in
1950. Alberta's conservation policies are discussed in *Alberta Law Review: Petroleum Law Supplement*, VII, 3 (1969); and in M. Crommelin *et al.*, *Management
of Oil and Gas Resources in Alberta; An Economic Evaluation of Public Policy*,
University of British Columbia, Department of Economics, Discussion Paper
no. 76-19.
10 E.H. Shaffer, 'Energy Conservation Boards,' University of Alberta, Faculty of
Business Administration, mimeo., 1972
11 *Ibid.*, and R.C. Muir, 'Utilization of Alberta Gas,' *Alberta Law Review: Petroleum Law Supplement*, XIII, 1 (1975), 66

12   W. Kilbourn, *Pipeline* (Toronto 1970), 18-19
13   R. Newton to J. Walker (Northwest Natural Gas Co.), 31 Jan. 1949, University of Alberta Government Publications. *Report of the Province of Alberta Natural Gas Commission* (1949); chairman: R.J. Dinning
14   Cf. summary of hearings by the Dinning Commission – *ibid.*, 12-17.
15   11 July 1949. The same day the *Medicine Hat News* argued that 'consent to export might well open industrial development elsewhere which could set back similar progress within the province for 50 to 100 years ... Let American export be held as a last resort, because once the flurry of field exploitation is over ... all the increment that will be left within our borders will be watchmen's wages to supervise the "liquidation of our empire." '
16   For accounts of this debate, much of which centred on the growth of cabinet powers and the accountability of the regulatory agencies, cf. *Calgary Herald*, 5, 6, 7, 9 July, *Edmonton Bulletin*, 5 and 7 July, *Edmonton Journal*, 7 July 1949. The controversial legislation, the Gas Resources Preservation Act (1949), is in *Alberta Statutes* (1949).
17   *Edmonton Journal*, 6 March 1954
18   H.G.J. Aitken, 'Defensive Expansionism: The State and Economic Growth in Canada,' reprinted in W.T. Easterbrook and M.H. Watkins, eds., *Approaches to Canadian Economic History* (Toronto 1967), 183-221. Aitken, of course, used his concept to explain the behaviour of Canadian governments faced with external threats, especially from the United States. Alberta's obsession with federal encroachments in the post-war era must be seen in the context of the disallownce of most of its Social Credit legislation in the late 1930s. See J.R. Mallory, *Social Credit and the Federal Power in Canada* (Toronto 1954).
19   *Edmonton Journal*, 1 and 8 April 1954, and information obtained from interviews and correspondence
20   The Alberta Gas Trunk Line Company Act (1954), *Alberta Statutes* (1954)
21   Hanson, *Dynamic Decade*, 247
22   Kilbourn, *Pipeline*, 56
23   Statement by Premier Lougheed re Petrochemicals, 16 May 1974; Wilson interviews with S. Robert Blair, president, Alberta Gas Trunk Line Co., on-the-record, 13 Aug. 1976; and AGTL *Annual Reports*, 1970-5
24   On-the-record interview with Senator E.C. Manning, 28 July 1976
25   *Democracy in Alberta: Social Credit and the Party System* (Toronto 1953)
26   Cf. T.E. Flanagan, 'Electoral Cleavages in Alberta during the Social Credit Reign, 1935-1971,' University of Calgary, Department of Political Science, mimeo., 1971; also Flanagan, 'Stability and Change in Alberta Provincial Elections,' *Alberta Historical Review*, XXI, 4 (Autumn 1973), 1-8.
27   Cf. J. Barr, *The Dynasty* (Toronto 1974), for some details of Social Credit's declining years.

28 E.H. Shaffer, 'The Employment Impact of Oil and Natural Gas on Alberta 1961-1970,' University of Alberta, Faculty of Business Administration, mimeo., 1976

29 Government of Alberta, *Tentative 'Natural Resource Revenue Plan'* (April 1972), 14-15

30 H. and T. Palmer, 'The 1971 Election and the Fall of Social Credit in Alberta,' *Prairie Forum* (Fall 1976)

31 D.V. Smiley, 'The Political Context of Resource Development in Canada,' in Anthony Scott, ed., *Natural Resource Revenues: A Test of Federalism* (Vancouver 1976), 67

32 Alberta, Department of Industry and Commerce, 'Management of Growth,' mimeo., 29 May 1974

33 This view of growth is discussed and criticized in D.C. North, 'Location Theory and Regional Economic Growth,' *Journal of Political Economy* (June 1955), 243-58; see also J.C. Stabler, 'Exports and Evolution: The Process of Regional Change,' *Land Economics* (Feb. 1968).

34 K.H. Norrie, 'Some Comments on Prairie Economic Alienation,' *Canadian Public Policy*, XI, 2 (Spring 1976), 212

35 Western Economic Opportunities Conference, 24-26 July 1973, *Verbatim Record*, morning session, 24 July

36 'Alberta's Industrial Strategy,' speech to the Calgary Chamber of Commerce, 6 Sept. 1974, Alberta Office of the Premier

37 C. Newman, 'The New Power in the New West,' *Saturday Night* (Sept. 1976)

38 Cf. H.V. Nelles, *The Politics of Development* (Toronto 1974), chap. 2.

39 Statement re Petrochemicals, 16 May 1974

40 'Field Pricing of Gas in Alberta,' ERCB Report 72-E-OG (Aug. 1972)

41 Crommelin, 'Government Management of Oil and Gas,' 194-200

42 Muir, 'Utilization of Alberta Gas,' 67

43 *Tentative 'Natural Resource Revenue Plan'* (April 1972)

44 *Oilweek*, 10 Oct. 1973

45 Based on interviews with petroleum industry and government officials

46 H.R. Ward, 'Marketing and Pricing Legislation,' *Alberta Law Review: Petroleum Law Supplement*, XIII, 1 (1975)

47 Alberta's net non-renewable resource revenues (excluding funds allocated to the Alberta Heritage Savings Trust Fund) increased from $560.7 million in 1973-4 to an estimated $1.3 billion in 1976-7, and now constitute 45.4 per cent of Alberta's total budgetary revenue. Hon. M. Leitch, *Budget Address 1976*, 19 March 1976

48 L. Pratt, *The Tar Sands: Syncrude and the Politics of Oil* (Edmonton 1976), 152-64

49 Lougheed, 'Alberta's Industrial Strategy'; see also the speech by Dr H. Horner, minister of transportation, 18 Aug. 1976, reprinted in *Business Life in Western Canada* (Sept.-Oct. 1976)

50 Lougheed to D. Mitchell, 9 Oct. 1974, Alberta Office of the Premier

51 *Business Life in Western Canada* (Nov.-Dec. 1975)

52 Crommelin, 'Government Management of Oil and Gas,' 196

53 *Financial Post*, 19 June, *Calgary Herald*, 25 June, *Edmonton Journal*, 20 Oct. and 8 Dec. 1976

54 Associated Engineering Services Ltd., *Petrochemical Report Prepared for the Government of Alberta Department of Industry and Commerce* (Oct. 1973). This study nevertheless recommended that Alberta foster a world-scale petrochemical complex.

55 J. Friedman, *Regional Development Policy – A Case Study of Venezuela* (Cambridge, Mass. 1966), 12-13

56 *The Great Transformation* (Boston 1944), chaps. 17-18; cf. also A. Breton, 'The Economics of Nationalism,' *Journal of Political Economy*, LXXII, 2 (1964), 376-86

57 R. Gilpin, 'Integration and Disintegration on the North American Continent,' *International Organization*, XXVIII, 4 (Autumn 1974), 857

PART III
CLASS STRUCTURE AND STATE STRUCTURE

6

Canadian public policy: the unequal structure of representation

RIANNE MAHON

A critical Marxist understanding of the Canadian state system constitutes a basic component of a strategy for fundamental social change. In Canada, the state has assumed from the outset a particularly active and visible role in facilitating the development of capitalist relations of production. Confederation itself can be seen as the first step towards the implementation of the National Policy – the development strategy, elaborated through the state, which served to establish the conditions Canadians confront today.[1] Since the 1930s the Canadian state, like the state in other advanced capitalist formations, has assumed an even more explicitly 'interventionist' character. In this context, the development of a means of understanding the 'state in action' – the state as it intervenes (and is called upon to intervene) in the daily life of the nation – has become essential.

Recent developments in Marxist theory have shed considerable light on the role of the capitalist state.[2] However, less attention has been devoted to the development of an analysis of the public policy process. The thesis of this paper is that a Marxist method of public policy analysis can be developed by identifying the way in which the class struggle is expressed through a complex system of representation inside the state. That is, once the unequal structure of representation which has evolved over time in a given social formation has been identified, it becomes possible to link a particular policy instance to the effective 'national policy' by tracing the relation of the forces involved to the broader structure of representation.

This kind of approach is consistent with the main tenets of the Marxist problematic of the state. It is based on the concept of the 'relative autonomy' of the capitalist state – a relative autonomy which is essential if the state is to function as organizer of the hegemony of the bourgeoisie. It is also historical: the structure of representation is not conceived in a static, mechanical way but rather as the product of the class struggle as this has developed and is developing within a particular social formation. Finally, it is concrete in that it calls for a specification (and a reading) of the institutional matrix of which the state is comprised. The multiplication of agencies and institutions typical of advanced capitalist states, and the additional complication posed by Canadian federalism, however, necessitate a certain selectivity. In this paper the focus will be on the federal civil service. Thus the party system, the legislature and cabinet, and the federal-provincial network will not be dealt with. These latter constitute important areas of the Canadian state system. Yet much of the literature on policy formation in Canada points to the key role of the senior federal bureaucracy. Further, although the provincial governments have assumed a considerable importance in the Canadian state system since the 1920s, the federal government has retained jurisdiction over key policies and it performs the critical function of 'co-ordinator' in many of the areas of 'shared jurisdiction.'[3] For these reasons, the federal administrative apparatus constitutes a legitimate institutional referent in the elaboration of a method for analysing the public policy process (a process of 'compromise') from the perspective of the role of the state as organizer of hegemony.

This paper, then, presents a proposal for a Marxist method of public policy analysis – one centred on the notion of the 'unequal structure of representation.' In addition, it provides an initial reading of the unequal structure of representation inscribed in the federal administrative apparatus – a structure which facilitates the functioning of the federal government as organizer of the hegemony of the bourgeoisie as a whole and of a definite fraction of the bourgeoisie (Clement's 'indigenous elite') in particular. The reading will begin with a theoretical clarification of the notions of 'relative autonomy,' 'hegemony,' and 'structure of representation.' This will be followed by a utilization of these concepts in analysing key parts of the federal administrative apparatus.

THE STATE AS ORGANIZER OF HEGEMONY

From the perspective of public policy analysis there are five major characteristics of advanced capitalist formations: the organization of a significant fraction of the working class; the plurality of capitalist interests; substantial direct state intervention in the economy; the 'transfer' of state power to the 'executive'; and the concomitant development of a professional or 'bureaucratic' civil service. In combination, these characteristics determine the necessity of, and the structure for, the state as organizer of hegemony.

That is, the state is forced to organize the consent of the subordinate classes to bourgeoise domination and, at the same time, to arrange a consensus uniting the bourgeoisie in order to facilitate capitalist accumulation and to permit the bourgeoisie as a whole to remain the dominant class. This increasingly involves the state in specific forms of economic intervention. In order to intervene effectively, the state has centralized authoritative decision-making in the hands of the executive (which includes senior civil servants) who command a hierarchically ordered group of career civil servants recruited on the basis of their 'expertise.' Inscribed in this hierarchical arrangement is the unequal structure of representation which permits the state to organize hegemony. This notion of the unequal structure of representation inside the administrative apparatus is sufficiently complex to warrant some clarification.

Hegemony and the role of the state
Bourgeois hegemony has been organized through the state since the advent of capitalism: 'The revolution which the bourgeois class has brought into the conception of law, and hence into the function of the State, consists especially in the will to conform (hence the ethicity of the law and of the State). The previous ruling classes were essentially conservative ... their conception was that of a closed caste. The bourgeois class poses itself as an organism in continuous movement, capable of absorbing the entire society, assimilating it to its own cultural and economic level. The entire function of the State has been transformed; the State has become an "educator." '[4] That is, the extension of the capitalist market generated a contradiction: on the one hand, the disintegration of the locally based social system in which each class (landlord, serf, bourgeois-merchant, and artisan) comprised a closed group bound to the others by a system of mutual obligations 'sanctified' through the church; on the other hand, integration of a national territory at the level of the economy. The creation of the nation-state under the aegis of the absolute monarchy established a new political unity, coincident with the economic territory, and counterposed to a fluid, disintegrating socio-cultural structure. The Industrial Revolution, in the stage of competitive capitalism, created a new contradiction: the atomized individual selling his/her labour time on the 'free market' and the combination of exploited workers in an urban factory setting. Working-class organization and rebellion against the common experience of exploitation helped to transform the state from 'liberal monarchy' to 'liberal democracy': the government of the nation by (the consent of) the people. In this form, the state became an 'educator' through the promulgation of positive laws which are agreed to (in

advance) by the people qua electorate. Further, working-class opposition to capitalist exploitation, particularly in times of severe economic crisis and in the context of the rise of 'monopoly' capital,[5] provided the conditions conducive to the development of the welfare state: that is, to the state's intervention in the market, granting concessions to the working class by 'redistributive' programs and policies. Thus, in advanced capitalist societies the state's active participation in the economy, qua welfare state, forms an important aspect of its role as organizer of the consent of the dominated classes to capitalist relations of production.

The plurality of capitalist interests in advanced capitalist formations – and hence the role of the state in organizing the unity of the bourgeoisie – stems from the uneven development of capitalism. In societies where capitalism succeeded feudalism, remnants of the upper classes of feudal society (the aristocracy, church officials, etc.) and of the transitional society (mercantile interests) may still constitute dominant classes, at the ideological level, if not the economic.[6] In addition, the uneven development of capitalist relations of production has as an effect the creation of divisions between 'competitive' capital and 'monopoly' capital – divisions which may coincide with regional, linguistic, or ethnic cleavages in a social formation. Further, inasmuch as 'monopoly' capital is actually oligopolistic in structure, competition between firms still persists, even though it does not extend to price competition. Most importantly, uneven development in the state of monopoly capital has produced imperialism – the penetration of national economies by multinational corporations which organize a complex international division of labour.

These divisions – foreign/indigenous, commercial/industrial/financial, competitive/monopoly, and intra-industry – pose a dual problem: the need for unity among the dominant classes and fractions vis-à-vis the dominated classes, and the need for co-ordination of economic decision-making if the general conditions for the continued and expanded accumulation of capital are to obtain. An alliance of the dominant classes in the power bloc – 'a contradictory unit of *politically dominant* classes and fractions *under the protection of the hegemonic fraction*'[7] – is achieved partly through 'private' agencies like national manufacturers' associations and 'core institutions' (corporations whose boards bring together representatives of a variety of leading corporations). In fact, the character of the latter can be seen as an approximate identification of the hegemonic, or 'leading,' fraction of the power bloc.[8] Tradition, inculcated through family, educational, and socio-cultural institutions, also helps to cement the power bloc. Yet such institutions lack the authority to enforce a collective or complementary mode of behaviour.

The state – as the institution which possesses a 'monopoly on the legitimate exercise of force' – thus becomes an agent for ensuring an effective (if contradictory) unity by forcing any particular fraction to make concessions in the common interest of the bloc as a whole. The increasing intervention of the state in the economy must, therefore, be seen not only as the result of working-class struggles but also as the consequence of conflict within the power bloc and the need to maintain the hegemony of a particular fraction of the bloc – the 'weighty, authoritative part.'

The question of 'representation'
If the state is to perform the role of organizer of hegemony it cannot be the 'instrument' of any one class or fraction but rather must possess a 'relative autonomy' in relation to the immediate (short-term) interests of the dominant class(es). Most Marxist theorists of the state recognize the relative autonomy of the capitalist state. Some, like James O'Connor, see this as the result of the contradictory functions of legitimation and accumulation which the state performs.[9] While O'Connor's approach is useful in analysing the character of state expenditures, he tends to fall back on instrumentalist explanations when analysing the formation of any particular policy. Thus, although he asserts that the interests of monopoly capital 'emerge within the state administration "unintentionally," ' O'Connor is unable to specify the way this is achieved. Nicos Poulantzas has provided the most adequate theorization of the meaning of the 'relative autonomy' of the capitalist state in the context of its function as organizer of hegemony – and has provided an important clue as to how this conceptualization can be utilized in the development of a Marxist method of public policy analysis. Poulantzas argues that '... the relative autonomy of the capitalist state stems precisely from the contradictory relations of power between the different social classes ... in the final analysis, a "resultant" of the relations of power between classes within a capitalist formation – it being perfectly clear that the capitalist State has its own institutional specificity ... which renders it irreducible to an immediate and direct expression of the strict "economic-corporate" interests ... of this or that class or fraction of the power bloc ...' Thus, the state is a relation, an expression of the antagonistic and contradictory relations among classes and fractions: it does not possess power ('the state is not a subject'). The structure of the state is nothing but the mediated expression of basic socio-economic inequalities as these are manifested politically, in the various forms and levels which the class struggle assumes at a particular point in time in a given society. This means that the state, in its concrete, institutional manifestation, does not constitute a sim-

ple homogeneous unity: ' ... conceiving of the capitalist State as a *relation*, as being structurally shot through and constituted with and by class contradictions, means firmly grasping the fact that an institution (the State) that is destined to reproduce class divisions cannot really be a monolithic, fissureless bloc, but is itself, by virtue of its very structure ... divided.' That the state, as a relation, forms a 'contradictory unity' holds certain implications for policy analysis.

First, its activity cannot be analysed in terms of a logically consistent definition of the 'national interest.' To begin with, the latter assumption would only produce an ideological understanding. The state's role as organizer of hegemony means that its activity will reflect inter- and intra-class contradictions – contraditions which are likely, however, to be 'resolved' in such a manner that the 'general political interest' of the power bloc is maintained. Therein lies the effective definition of the 'national interest.'

Second, the state's activity as organizer of hegemony does not consist of negotiations between private forces (interest groups) and 'the State.' Rather, such negotiations largely occur through the state, for its organs and branches 'represent' the various social forces: 'The various organs and branches of the State (ministries and government offices, executive and parliament, central administration and local and regional authorities, army, judiciary, etc.) reveal major contradictions among themselves, each of them frequently constituting the seat and the representative – in short, the crystallisation – of this or that fraction of the power bloc, this or that specific competing interest.'[10] Yet the nature of 'representation' inside the state is quite different from 'interest group' representation. The function of the latter is primarily to represent one particular interest; the former simultaneously 'represent' a particular interest and are bound by a commitment to reach a compromise, to see beyond the particular to the 'general' or 'national' interest. In addition, the claims of interest groups do not possess 'authority' whereas representatives inside the state, once a compromise has been reached, are empowered to force the compromise on the very forces they 'represent.' In this way, they carry all the weight of the state's authority – an authority backed, in the last instance, by its monopoly on the legitimate use of force.

It is important to recognize, however, that all 'representatives' are not equal: the unity of the state is ultimately based on the long-term interests of the hegemonic fraction. The inequalities as between the power bloc and the subordinate classes and various members of the power bloc and the hegemonic fraction are expressed in the quality (or functions) of their respective representatives. Thus, the dominant classes and fractions which belong to the power bloc are likely to have a more 'positive' role – able to negotiate concessions which enhance the ability of those they represent to perform their leading role in the economic and social spheres. Conversely, the representatives of subordinate social forces are likely to have a more limited mandate – for example, to extract 'concessions' limited to the sphere of consumption rather than that of production. In addition, the coercive aspect of the relation, represented/representative, is likely to be more prominent or normal.

The distinction between the quality of representation accorded the hegemonic fraction and that of other members of the power bloc is also marked, carrying with it an extremely important consequence: 'The functioning of the state system is assured by the *dominance* of certain apparatuses or branches over others: and the branch or apparatus which is dominant is generally that one which constitutes the seat of power of the hegemonic class or fraction.'[11] That is, various branches of government may, as a result of their specific function, establish a particular relation with different social forces. However, that branch which is in a position of authority vis-à-vis the other branches guarantees the long-term interests of the hegemonic fraction. In negotiating the compromises which constitute public policy, that branch is empowered to limit the concessions made to other social forces through their representatives in the state. The core interests around which the unity of the power bloc is constructed (the long-term interests of the power bloc) are thereby expressed in public policy and lend to the activity of the state a functional, effective, but 'contradictory,' unity.

The notion of the unequal structure of representation provides an important clue for public policy analysis. It suggests that a particular policy can be analysed by identifying the forces directly and indirectly (the hegemonic fraction) involved in relation to a reading of the overall structure of representation. Through this approach, policies no longer appear as merely fragmented responses to the power of this or that group of corporations. Rather, it becomes possible to show precisely how the interests of the power bloc as a whole, and of the hegemonic fraction in particular, 'emerge within the state administration "unintentionally." ' The characteristics of the state administrative apparatus in advanced capitalist formations provides a useful illustration of the way this occurs.

The administrative apparatus
In advanced capitalist formations, coincident with the expanding role of the state, the administrative apparatus of government has assumed an impor-

tant place in the policy process. In fact, with the move to 'depoliticize' and 'render more efficient' the activities of the state, the administrative apparatus has come to play a key role, not only in the 'implementation' but also in the 'formation' of public policy. It is, therefore, essential to understand the way in which this apparatus is structured to enable it to arrange the compromises that reproduce hegemony. Poulantzas provides the following clue: '... in the case of the administrative bureaucracy, the internal hierarchy of delegated authority characteristic of the state apparatuses, the particular status attributed to functionaries, the specific internal ideology circulating within the state apparatuses (the "neutral state" as an arbitrator above classes, "service to the nation," "general interest," etc) allow the bureaucracy to present a unity of its own in certain conjunctures ...'[12] Although Poulantzas does not generalize here, it would appear that these factors will in fact normally give the civil service relative autonomy from society, enabling it to participate in the negotiation of compromise. Its unity is a biased unity which functions, ultimately, to secure hegemony or consent to a particular structure of domination. The 'relative autonomy' of the civil service is related to the ideology of the 'national interest': a conception of 'duty' which involves reference to the common interest 'above' the interest of any one class or group. It is the civil service which must discover the common interest in the particular claims articulated by diverse social forces. However, the way in which the common or national interest is perceived is biased (though this bias is cloaked in ideological terms).

A key ideological notion which serves this purpose in advanced capitalist countries is the notion of 'the economy': 'Governments may be solely concerned with the better running of "the economy." But the descriptions of systems as "the economy" is part of the idiom of ideology, and obscures the real process. For what is being improved is a *capitalist* economy; and this ensures that whoever may or may not gain, capitalist interests are least likely to lose.'[13] In other words, government policies may be elaborated by civil servants in order to 'stimulate,' 'cool,' or 'improve the health of ' the economy. But the economy is not an abstract or natural phenomenon. It possesses a particular structure. In advanced capitalist societies it is an economic order in which large corporations hold the commanding heights. In 'taking measures to assist the economy,' civil servants are acting to assist the corporations that dominate that economy. However, by defining such measures abstractly, they overlook the significance of the character of 'the economy' and, therefore, accept the structural constraints imposed by that economy. This bias does not mean that no concessions are extracted from the dominant class through the state. On the contrary, in articulating a conception of the 'national interest' the civil servant becomes somewhat removed from any particular interest. Yet it is precisely because of this relative independence that the civil servant is able to negotiate the compromises essential to the maintenance of the basic interests of the dominant class.

The internal hierarchy of the civil service constitutes a vital element in the reproduction of hegemony. The civil service is a hierarchically ordered institution: each unit is responsible for that below it and to that above it. In addition, the particular character of the hierarchy (the principle from whence its order derives) reflects and gives operational significance to the ideology of the whole. Donald Gow, who has produced an interesting analysis of the Canadian federal state system, makes this point concretely: 'Each bureaucratic organization looks at the world through its own framework of values. These values give meaning to the world as the department faces it. A department cannot see everything – it must discriminate in order to make sense of the booming buzzing confusion around it. Thus, in looking at the world, it takes information of a certain type and disregards everything else. It selects, and shapes this information according to the values it holds significant.'[14] Gow is referring to one department or branch. Yet his analysis can be extended to inter-branch relations. As Poulantzas notes, 'What is involved is a process of structural selectivity by one of the organs from information provided and measures taken by others: a contradictory process of decision and also of partial non-decision ... of structural determination of priorities and counter-priorities (with one organ obstructing and short-circuiting others); or immediate and mutually conflicting "compensating" institutional reactions in the face of the falling rate of profit, of "filtering" by each organ of the measures taken by other organs ... '[15]

Yet 'anarchy' does not prevail: the administrative apparatus, too, is characterized by a contradictory unity. Authority is not distributed evenly among departments. Certain departments have precisely delimited mandates; other departments have a broader mandate which renders them more powerful; and, normally, one department and/or branch is placed in a position of authority vis-à-vis the remainder. This hierarchy reinforces the ideological bias. That is, the hierarchical relationship within and across departments reflects a hierarchy of values. To cite Gow: 'Hierarchy is not essentially a matter of someone telling someone else what to do. It is an arrangement, or a system of roles which link up with one another in such a way that values are subordinated to one another. Thus the outcome of the work of the hierarchy is predictable ... '[16]

The ordering of values through the hierarchical arrangement of roles assumes a wider significance on consideration of the external linkages established; that is, the relations between the civil service and the social structure. Certain subunits within the civil service form relations with particular sections of society. These derive from the specific functions assigned to these administrative units. Through these relations, the subunits form a certain understanding and sympathy for 'their' group. Thus, when the negotiation of compromise takes place within the state system, these subunits act as representatives of a particular interest – but representatives bound by a commitment to arrive at a definition of the 'national interest' transcending the particular. In addition, the hierarchy within the civil service renders this structure of representation biased, providing operational support for the bias engendered by the acceptance of ideological notions like 'the economy.'

THE STRUCTURE OF REPRESENTATION INSIDE THE FEDERAL
ADMINISTRATIVE APPARATUS

The discussion of the way in which the state is structured to perform its role as organizer of hegemony – and, more particularly, the system of representation inside the administrative apparatus – suggests a useful approach for analysing the public policy process in advanced capitalist formations like Canada. Once a reading of the general structure of representation has been made, it should be possible to examine any specific policy instance, showing concretely how that policy is consistent with the effective 'national interest' – the 'national interest' which coincides with the hegemony of a particular class fraction. That is, the decision-making structure for a particular policy can be interpreted in relation to the broader structure of representation.

In the following sections a tentative reading of the structure of representation inscribed in the federal administrative apparatus will be advanced. The reading will not attempt to be comprehensive but rather will single out four important examples, beginning with an identification of the 'seat of power' of the hegemonic class fraction. This will be followed by a discussion of an example of the mode of representation accorded other members of the power bloc ('secondary industry'). Finally, two examples of subordinate forces – the organized working class and native peoples – will be examined as a means of illustrating the differences in the quality of representation as between these and the power bloc.

All of these examples will be analysed from a historical perspective. This should show that a structuralist reading is not (nor can it be) mechanical or primarily synchronic: the structure of representation is conditioned by the class struggle as this develops over time. That is, the structure of representation inside the state is ultimately determined by the class struggle. The state possesses only a 'relative' autonomy vis-à-vis the class struggle as this develops at the level of civil society.

Seat of power of the hegemonic fraction
Authorization of the negotiation of compromises frequently stems from political agents: the cabinet or the legislature. Yet, in the actual negotiations it is the civil service that acts as a 'custodian' of the basic power structure. This maintenance function is specifically served by the dominant position of one branch within the civil service. That branch can be identified in relation to three characteristic features: its internal superiority vis-à-vis other departments; its connection with other important points in the state system (for example, the provincial governments and the co-ordinating institutions of the international system); and its relationship to social forces. In the Canadian federal government it is the Department of Finance which has traditionally constituted the 'seat of power' of the hegemonic fraction. As Gow has pointed out: 'The Department of Finance is one of the chief integrative mechanisms of the Canadian political system. Through its influence in fiscal, economic, monetary, and commerical matters, it is one of the institutions which can give coherence to government policy.'[17] Its position of dominance over the other departments is specifically achieved through its domination of the budgetary process[18] and its role in 'training' those who later head other important departments.

Thus, the department's pace-setting role, derived from its mandate in critical policy areas, is complemented by the influence which Finance exercises over the programs developed in other departments through its control of the budgetary process. This has led to the practice whereby all new legislation with financial implications is discussed with the Department of Finance at some time prior to its submission to cabinet for approval in principle. This places officials in the department in a decisive position vis-à-vis the other departments and the social forces they represent. This relationship is reflected in a statement made by R.B. Bryce before the House Committee on Finance, Trade and Economic Affairs. Bryce, then deputy minister of finance, told the committee: 'we frequently are cast in the role of sort of an internal opposition ... if we do not get them [other departments] while they are in the process of crystallizing [their policies] then we have them presented to us for discussion, either at a Cabinet committee or occasionally inter-departmental committees. They could go up to a Cabinet committee which could refer them back to a group of officials to try to reach an agreed view. This is done in order that ministers will not have to waste their time and tempers in trying to reconcile things between themselves. If the officials can do it and get an agreed view it helps ministers carry on their work, but if we cannot do it any other way, we have to go and give our opinion before a group of ministers collectively, perhaps in opposition to or in criticism of a particular item a minister has brought forward.'[19] Bryce's statement testifies to the facts that senior officials do carry out most of the detailed negotiations and that Finance officials play a decisive role in shaping the consensus.

The practices associated with Finance's budgetary role permit the department to exercise a strong influence on the programs elaborated by the other departments. This is complemented by the role Finance performs in training senior civil servants,[20] a practice which dates from the thirties when the state assumed a more explicitly interventionist role in the Canadian economy. At that time, the need for a professional civil service (whose authority derived from an ability to provide 'objective' economic advice, not from personal links to influential members of society), led R.B. Bennett to appoint W.C. Clark as the deputy minister of finance. Clark, a leading economist at Queen's University, recruited many bright young economists – imbued with Keynesian ideas and a nationalism based on a rejection of ties to Britain – to the Department of Finance.[21] It was these 'experts' who subsequently came to occupy posts in other parts of the federal civil service. By training senior personnel, Finance was able to disseminate a particular perspective on Canada, its problems and potential, throughout the policy departments. The dissemination of a concept of the national interest through Finance's training function has created a level of ideological coherence in government policy, ensuring that those who 'represent' non-hegemonic forces basically accept the development philosophy that serves the fundamental interest of the hegemonic fraction.

The co-ordinating function of Finance is further cemented by its links with other decisional centres. For example, since the thirties Finance has played a critical role in relation to the provinces. The department was responsible for developing the tax rental agreements which permitted the federal government to co-ordinate provincial social welfare services. The department's links with the provinces now extend to questions of resource development and other key areas of national policy. In addition to this, the department is linked to co-ordinating institutions of the international economic system. It performs an important role in international negotiations through its Tariff, Trade and Aid branch. In these, the department deals primarily with Canada's major trading partners – the United States, Britain, Japan, and France.[22] More importantly, Finance is that part of the government which defines Canada's role in relation to the International Monetary Fund (IMF) and the World Bank.

Finally, the Department of Finance interacts with most organized interests through its role in the formation of central policies like tax and tariff policy and its 'overseer' role in monetary and financial transaction. This gives it an appearance of relative autonomy, independent of any one interest or group of interests: an appearance which is essential to its role as guardian of the 'national interest.' However, Fred Schindeler's analysis suggests that the dominant corporations are likely to orient primarily to the Department of Finance. Based on a survey of the major demands of large corporations, Schindeler concluded: 'The considerations they sought from Government were preferential access to natural resources, tariff adjustments, government guarantees for corporate bond issues, subsidies and subventions, tax concessions and even trade treaties.'[23] Finance is directly responsible for several of these policy areas and has a marked influence in the other areas. Most importantly, through the Bank of Canada and parts of the department which oversee the operations of financial institutions, the department has a close functional relationship with the economic institutions of the hegemonic fraction. For example, Finance plays an important role in the negotiations surrounding the decennial revision of the Bank Act. This 'regulatory' relationship has resulted in protection of the particular position of the leading Canadian banks. Considering Poulantzas' criterion for the definition of the 'seat of power of the hegemonic class or fraction' – 'by noting the dominance of one apparatus or branch over others and by also noting the specific interests served by that apparatus in a dominant fashion'[24] – it would appear that the Department of Finance indeed constitutes the 'seat of power' of the hegemonic class.

This does not mean that other branches do not perform important co-ordinating functions. At least two other departments – External Affairs and Trade and Commerce – form a part of the 'inner circle' of top civil servants.[25] They do not, however, possess the same authority that Finance does. It is the Department of Finance which establishes relations with all important sectors in the Canadian political economy. Finance, therefore, is characterized by a greater 'relative autonomy.' In addition, Finance is the leading department in developing/containing the federal government's economic policies. It is through this control function that Finance is empowered to limit concessions to other social forces. External Affairs and Trade and Commerce do not have the authority to do so.

Since the sixties, other potential 'control' centres have been developed – in order to render more efficient the structures of internal cohesion.[26] For instance, following the Glassco Commission's report the Treasury Board was separated from Finance. It is now the Treasury Board which engages in active negotiations over the allocation of internal resources with all departments. However, Finance's primacy seems assured through its control over revenue policy – which not only determines how much government will have to spend but also constitutes an important factor in the decision-making environment of the private sector. A more serious 'threat' may be the enhancement of the power of the Prime Minister's Office (PMO) and the Privy Council Office (PCO). Since the Pearson regime the latter two offices have acquired a sizeable professional staff empowered to review departmental policies. In theory, the revamped PMO and PCO give cabinet access to political and technical advice independent of the consensus worked out by the established departments.[27] More recently, it was disclosed that Trudeau had used the PMO to recruit a group of economists to provide economic advice to 'counter' Finance. These economists were recruited from several ideological associations (like the C.D. Howe Institute), core institutions (the Canadian Imperial Bank of Commerce), and parts of the ideological apparatus that are linked to the business community (the University of Western Ontario's business school).[28] This initiative prompted the former superintendent of insurance (Department of Finance), K.R. MacGregor, to allege that the Trudeau government was seeking to concentrate power in the PMO. This, he argued, would jeopardize the balance of power once maintained by the departmental structure. These consultations preceded the government's introduction of wage and price controls – a policy which the then deputy minister of finance opposed. However, the introduction of controls placed the Anti-Inflation Board under the Department of Finance – a department whose new deputy minister seems to be able to work within the general strategy of the Trudeau government. In fact, the current deputy minister chairs the senior interdepartmental committee which is negotiating the terms of 'post-controls' policy. Despite the broadening of the range of branches with a co-ordinating function (like the PCO), Finance still seems to be the 'regular' seat of power of the hegemonic fraction.

Modes of representation: the power bloc
While Finance constitutes the 'seat of power' of the hegemonic fraction in the federal government, other fractions of the dominant class are represented in the administrative appartus. The various modalities of representation and the interrelation of the parts in the policy formation process can be illustrated by an examination of the relationship between Finance, Trade and Commerce, and the secondary manufacturing sector. This example

gives an indication of how the tension between various fractions of the power bloc have been resolved by government. In particular, this serves to point up the difference in the mode of representation as between the dominant fraction of the power bloc and a 'junior partner.' At the same time, it shows how structural changes (the increasing significance of the manufacturing sector and of the corporations within it) have resulted in a change in the mode of representation.

Until the late 1930s the Department of Finance constituted the undisputed centre of the federal government's planning network. Certainly, for manufacturers Finance was critical due to its responsibility for tariff and other import policies. However, its centrality appeared to be challenged with the advent of the 'Howe era.' In 1935 C.D. Howe entered the cabinet and was given responsibility for an important sector of the Canadian economy: transport.[29] During his twenty-two years in cabinet Howe recruited a number of experts from Clark's Department of Finance and from the private sector. With them, he formulated the series of policies which shaped post-war Canadian development. For example, it was Howe (on the advice of W.A. MacKintosh[30]) who presented the *White Paper on Employment and Incomes* in 1945. Phrased in Keynesian terminology, the white paper became the symbol of government policies which collectively represent Fowke's second ' national policy.'

Although in practice this policy is most closely identified with the stimulation of rapid growth in the new resource sectors (petroleum, iron ore, uranium) and the 'free-trade' orientation of post-war Canadian commercial policy, an important component of this strategy was to promote the establishment of new import-substituting manufacturing industries. For instance, during the war the Department of Munitions and Supply established factories to produce essential goods such as aircraft, machine tools, and electrical goods. At the end of the war Howe's department disposed of $200 million in productive assets which were bought by private concerns at one-third of their value. In 1947 the Emergency Exchange Conservation Act imposed temporary import controls which encouraged further import substitutions: 'At least 42 manufacturing firms which commenced operations in Canada between 1948 and 1950 were established because of import controls or with the aid of the Import Control Division of the Department of Trade and Commerce.' Later, the Industrial Development Branch of Trade and Commerce (which grew out of the import control division) actively encouraged the import substitution process.[31] Incentives ranged from tariff reduction on inputs for final manufacture to approaches to provincial governments on behalf of the corporations for provincial and municipal tax concessions. In addition, the Department of Defence Production (established in 1951) used its substantial resources to foster the establishment and expansion of industries such as aircraft, electronics, and steel. Alcan, Stelco, General Dynamics, the Iron Ore Company of Canada, and A.V. Roe are only a few of the dominant corporations which benefited from the tax concessions, accelerated depreciation allowances, and tariff manipulations carried out by Howe and his civil servants.

Although many of these measures were formally under the jurisdiction of the Department of Finance, the force of Howe's personality had permitted him to restructure the pattern of state-corporate linkages in order to actively encourage the type of development which had begun in the twenties. In this Howe was assisted by persons recruited from Finance. None the less, the locus of industrial policy formation shifted from Finance during the 'Howe era.' In the short run, the 'energy and single-mindedness' of Howe and his support staff produced this change. However, it was the structural change – the increasing importance of the secondary sector associated with the larger size of the corporations controlling production, as well as an absolute growth in manufacturing – that had the effect of removing direct responsibility for the manufacturing sector from Finance. This process culminated in the creation of the Department of Industry in 1963. J.E. Hodgetts' comment on this development is instructive: ' ... a belated recognition (according to then Prime Minister Lester Pearson) of the importance of the manufacturing industries to the economy of Canada which for so long had been dependent upon natural unprocessed resources; it was to be "for the manufacturing industry what the Department of Agriculture is for farmers" ... Clearly this was not the first administrative recognition of the importance of manufacturing in Canada ... It is clear from the debate that arose in connection with the creation of this department that the government expected it to remain a very modest size, concentrating on co-ordinating, informational, and possibly inspirational functions with respect not only to its clients but also to the resource-oriented departments and other departments that might have certain peripheral concern for secondary industry.'[32]

This statement captures the rationale underlying the creation of the department and hints at its real subordination to 'other' departments (primarily Finance and Trade and Commerce). Yet, to some extent, it distorts the issue. First, according to one of the original members of the department, it was felt that the Industrial Development Branch in Trade and Commerce was dominated by the remainder of the department.[33] The primary concern of Trade and Commerce was with export promotion. Given the import-substituting character of the Canadian manufacturing sector, it was felt that little could be done to assist 'industry' in a department committed to the 'free-trade' policies that were the logical extension of its concern with export promotion. The creation of a separate Department of Industry would permit the articulation of the development philosophy of the secondary sector in government policy formation. Second, in later years the branch had become largely confined to aiding small business. This inhibited the development of relations with the large companies in the dynamic industries, making it difficult for the branch to develop a 'real industrial mandate.' In addition, departmental status (with the resources to support it) would permit government to provide positive incentives to larger firms in the newer areas and thus (it was hoped) encourage 'rationalization.'

Although the intent was genuine – reflecting the increased importance of that sector which was further enhanced by the marked imbalance of trade in manufacture and the related problem of unemployment – the Department of Industry remained subordinate. Apparently this was partly the result of the government's decision to staff the new department primarily with persons drawn from the private sector. The Treasury Board actually classified positions in the new department at one level higher than corresponding positions in other departments in order to assist the core of officials in the new department to fulfil the guidelines of no more than 5 per cent drawn from the public service.

In relation to the role of the ideology specific to the government apparatus, it is interesting to consider this explanation of the department's weakness. According to Lance Howie, the new officials experienced some difficulty in making the transition from the perspective of a particular industry to that of the government. Their obvious pro-industry, 'protectionist' bias, untempered by the general ideology which prevailed throughout the civil service, inhibited the establishment of a good working relationship with the other departments.[34]

Though the department remained relatively subordinate, it did produce one major policy. Under the guidance of career civil servants such as the then deputy minister of Industry, Simon Reisman (recruited from the international division of Finance), and Lance Howie, the department negotiated the continentalization of Canada's auto industry: the Auto Pact. That this first industrial policy was oriented to the establishment of a continental system of manufacturing is quite significant. It indicated an attitude to the manufacturing sector that eventually led to the reunification of Industry and Trade and Commerce.[35] As one commentator enthusiastically remarked, the reintegration of these departments showed that 'the transition to the new freer-trade economy should not only be smoother but should follow a course that will produce maximum benefits to the Canadian economy.'[36] The officials in the industry section of the new department were not quite so committed to this philosophy. However, reintegration (which implies that development to the secondary sector is dependent on a shift to production for export) reflects the ideology of senior officials in departments concerned with economic policy. For example, in his study of Canadian adjustment assistance policy, Klaus Stegemann found: 'Officials claim that expansion in export markets is the most effective way of increasing the productivity of Canadian industry: this emphasis on exports is consistent with the philosophy that the limited size of the domestic market constitutes a chief obstacle to the development of efficient manufacturing industries in Canada. The officials also claim that the practical implementation of support schemes such as the AAA, GAAP, DIP, PAIT, and STAP [all administered by Industry, Trade and Commerce] encourage the utilisation of export opportunities almost exclusively.'[37] Trade and Commerce shares this perspective with the Department of Finance. For example, the assistant deputy minister for the international division, Rodney de C. Grey, has stated that access to foreign markets is the key issue for the manufacturing sector.[38]

Several points may be drawn from this analysis. First, the integration of the two departments enhanced the position of Trade and Commerce vis-à-vis Finance in developing economic policy. Yet rather than viewing this as a defeat for Finance, it would seem that the new department is empowered to assume a practical responsibility, thereby freeing Finance to develop general strategy and monitor the activities of other departments. Second, as Gow indicated, the locus for decision-making shifted temporarily due to the role played by a particular minister. Long-term change, however, reflects a change in the importance (in absolute or relative terms) of a group. Finally, the 'junior partner' status of the manufacturing sector (or, all but the 'high productivity' industries) means that their representatives in the civil service will be subordinated to the dominant departments associated with the interests of the hegemonic fraction and the large exporters. Although manufacturing became more important in the post-war era, winning departmental status for its representatives, the department itself remained subordinate. Reintegration into the Department of Trade and Commerce occurred after the Department of Industry had developed greater skill in negotiating within the civil service network. The quality of representation had improved. However, Trade and Commerce holds a superior position within the new 'superdepartment.'

The Department of Labour: containment of the subordinate classes
Members of the power bloc are not the only classes 'represented' in the ad-

ministrative apparatus. Subordinate classes, too, can be said to be 'represented' by certain departments, notably Labour, Health and Welfare, and Indian Affairs and Northern Development. However, there are significant differences in the mode of representation. The representatives of all social forces perform two roles: representation of the specific interests of their respective groups in the negotiation process and regulation – the attempt to 'persuade' and/or coerce their group into accepting the compromise. Relationships like that of the Bank of Canada to the banks and of the National Energy Board to the companies involved in the production and distribution of energy are characterized by this dual aspect. This dual character of representation constitutes a critical factor in the functioning of the state as the central focus for the maintenance of the unity of the power bloc under the hegemonic fraction. The maintenance of the hegemony of the power bloc demands that the interests of the dominated classes, too, be taken into account – yet their subordinate position in civil society poses definite limits to their participation in general policy development through their representatives. The regulatory aspect of this relationship is, accordingly, more pronounced. This is well illustrated in the relation of the Department of Labour to the working class.

The Department of Labour's relationship to the working class has traditionally been, and continues to be, mediated through the trade unions. That is, the department's jurisdiction is largely confined to the third of the Canadian working class which is organized in trade unions. In order to understand the representation/regulation character of the relationship, it is important to begin by clarifying the nature of trade unions.

In capitalist societies trade unions have a contradictory character: they are organizations to defend the working class (primarily at the level of production, although trade union congresses can come to play a role in defending labour's interests in the wider political arena) and they are institutions of domination of the working class. That is, on the one hand unions organize workers giving them some bargaining power in the determination of wages, working conditions, and other work-specific matters. On the other hand, unions frequently have a political function which contradicts this inasmuch as they function as institutions to 'win the consent' of the working class to its subordinate, exploited position. C. Wright Mills has captured something of this contradiction in his description of the role of the union leader: 'even as the labor leader rebels, he holds back rebellion. He organizes discontent and then he sits on it, exploiting it in order to maintain a continuing organization; the labor leader is a manager of discontent. He makes regular what might otherwise be disruptive, both within the industrial routine and within the union which he seeks to establish and maintain.'[39] That is, the role definition of the trade union leader, the central agent in defining the immediate activity of the union, carries with it a dual aspect. In carrying out his responsibilities to his members, the trade union leader must articulate their interests. At the same time he must express these interests in a 'responsible' fashion if the union is to survive as a legitimate organization within the present system; in other words, he must contain discontent.

This 'contradictory' character is a feature common to the trade union movements of all advanced capitalist countries. However, the degree of 'contradiction' and the specific ways in which this is expressed vary in accordance with factors peculiar to each social formation.[40] The significance of such differences – not only for the working class as represented in the unions but also for the rhythm and tone of development within each formation – suggests the importance of analysing the specific character and history of each. Studies done for the federal Task Force on Labour Relations have pointed to the relatively high incidence of strikes in Canada and have attempted to provide explanations.[41] One of the factors mentioned is the dominance of mercantile capital, the widespread acceptance of its 'short-sighted' mentality which emphasizes immediate gain over long-run profitability partly secured through stable industrial relations. In addition, the political power of the traditional small-town petite bourgeoisie, particularly at the provincial level where jurisdiction over labour policy resides, has produced labour legislation reflective of their economic interest in holding the line against labour's demands. Yet, as John Porter argues, unions do function to neutralize working-class rebellion. Labour leaders function in terms of a norm of 'responsible' behaviour particular to unions: 'Trade union power is judged by other elites in terms of its responsibility. No other institutional elite has had to measure up to this peculiar test of responsibility ... The responsible labour leader is one who does not make too great demands on the system or whose activities do not interrupt the processes of production.'[42] Despite general employer intransigence in disputes with labour, Canadian unions have gradually been integrated into the system, facing up to the 'test' of responsibility. The federal Department of Labour has played a significant role in achieving this.

The Department of Labour's role can be analysed in terms of three phases of interventions. The first, from 1900 to 1944, was largely limited to resolving disputes which threatened the implementation of the National Policy. The second, from 1944 to the present, gave more positive support to the development of 'responsible' unions – to unions functioning as instruments of domination by consent. The third, which is in the process of emerging, seeks to win the unions' active commitment to the development strategy of the hegemonic class.

The federal Department of Labour was established as a result of the passage of the Conciliation Act of 1900. The spread of capitalist relations of production in that decade led to an expansion of its role which initially had been limited to the collection and publication of labour statistics. Between 1900 and 1910 the number of workers employed in manufacturing rose by approximately 200,000 and union membership increased by 50,000 to 175,799. The decade had seen a concomitant rise in union activity, defending the new working class in the face of the growing strength of capital as the first merger movement reached its peak. Charles Lipton notes that 'between 1900 and 1915, 377,234 workers were involved in 1,519 strikes with a total time lost of 1,712,262 man work days.'[43] Yet although several important strikes occurred in the manufacturing sector, the most important occurred in industries like railways and coal which were central to the success of the National Policy. Accordingly, the federal government, under the leadership of then deputy minister of labour Mackenzie King, intervened. In 1903 the Railway Labour Disputes Act was passed. This was followed by the more comprehensive Industrial Disputes Investigation Act (IDIA) of 1907. Both acts, administered by the federal Department of Labour, have conditioned the department's relation to the working class.

Central to the IDIA – which applied to all public utilities until 1925, and to all industries under federal jurisdiction until 1944 – was a concept of the 'public interest,' a concept which continues to inform the actions of the department. The 'public interest' served to limit private rights 'when they became public wrongs.' Concretely, the 'public interest' was identified with conditions necessary to the realization of the National Policy. That is, the objective of the IDIA was to: 'aid in the prevention and settlement of industrial disputes in so far as the same affect any form of public utilities. Such disputes obviously affect the public interest more closely than those concerning any other class of industry ...'[44] The government's intervention was designed to curtail, and possibly prevent, work stoppages in industries considered essential to the National Policy. This was to be achieved through the imposition of compulsory conciliation, assisted by conciliators appointed by the minister of labour, and through the provision for no work stoppage prior to the completion of the dispute investigation and conciliation process.

The IDIA thus established a role for the Department of Labour in containing labour's power: the use of the strike to force management to make concessions. Capital, too, had to compromise – it was forced to negotiate with workers. Yet, capital's *de facto* recognition of labour's collective power was in its own interest. That is, the 'public interest' coincided with the stability needed to implement the development strategy of the power bloc (the National Policy). The IDIA, however, did not formally recognize unions – which would have constituted an important step towards the reinforcement of unions as institutions of the hegemony of the power bloc. While employees could belong to unions and could bargain through these, the right to recognition was not legitimized. That 'recognition' was important to containing working-class rebellion was realized by the department from the outset. For example, the *Report* of the Royal Commission on Industrial Disputes in the Province of British Columbia stated: 'it is better that they [the workers] be encouraged to establish legitimate unions which will be clothed with responsibility for the exercise of power, and which will, therefore, be more readily recognized and dealt with by employers, than that they should join secret organisations, some of which are really nothing more than a conspiracy against society in general and employers in particular.'[45]

The department was aware, then, that recognition of 'responsible' unions, whose demands could be met within the framework of capitalist relations of production, was essential to the maintenance of industrial peace. Yet the conditions were not yet ripe. The shift from agriculture to mining (and the expansion of manufacturing); working-class unrest in the thirties; the aggressive but 'responsible' (instrumentalist) objectives of the Congress of Industrial Organisation (CIO) campaign, particularly during the war; the passage of the Wagner Act in the United States – these developments created the conditions conducive to recognition. Privy Council (order-in-council) 1003 of 1944 and the Industrial Relations Disputes Investigation Act (IRDIA) of 1948 included the right of recognition, giving the unions status approaching that of a 'corporation.' At the same time, unions became liable before the courts. This gave the government a means for enforcing 'responsible' behaviour among trade unions. In specific terms, this permitted the government to enforce the prohibition of strikes over the question of recognition and throughout the duration of the contract. Subsequent legislation passed by the provinces incorporated the dispute settlement, nonwork stoppage, and recognition principles.

The system established by IRDIA (and subsequent provincial legislation) has helped to neutralize the impact of the labour movement. It would be misleading to argue that this is solely or even primarily due to government intervention. Yet the federal Department of Labour has played a leading role in influencing capital to become more sophisticated in its industrial relations and, more importantly, in encouraging the development of 'responsible' unions.

The present relationship of the Department of Labour to the working class is still conditioned by the perspective of the IRDIA. This limits its representational character and stresses its containment function. At the same time, there are pressures to enlarge the scope of its activities. Inasmuch as the responsibility of the union movement has been established and the uneven development of capitalism requires the state to play a more active role in the accumulation process, organized labour's active consent to the global economic strategy must be sought – through specific policies and programs developed by the Department of Labour to win that commitment.

According to a former official in the department, the main purpose of the department remains conciliation and arbitration work in industries which, like the railway industry, fall under federal jurisdiction.[46] This places a strong pressure on the department to act in such a way as to enhance its image as an 'honest broker,' impartial between labour and capital. This, in turn, prescribes the type of linkage relation of both the minister and his officials to the unions.[47] Linkages between the unions and officials are minimal – despite the fact that certain union officials are recruited to the department's conciliation service and act as labour attachés abroad.

At the ministerial level, it is instructive to contrast the attitudes of the minister of labour with those of the minister of industry. The first minister of industry, C. Drury, described his role in the following terms: 'As the importance of secondary industry has grown over the years, it has become increasingly apparent that the viewpoint of the industrial sector of Canada's economy should be represented when government policy is being formulated ... [the minister's role] is to represent that viewpoint and to be the spokesman in government for Canada's manufacturing concerns.'[48] Clearly, Drury saw his role as representative of his constituency – members of the power bloc engaged in manufacturing. Consider, on the other hand, former labour minister Bryce Mackasey's description of his role as a 'go-between' between labour and management. His duty – and that of his officials – was to bring to the realization of labour and management *'that they have a common interest, a common destiny in our system of private enterprise.'*[49] The minister of labour is certainly not labour's spokesman in cabinet in the same way that the minister of industry (now industry, trade and commerce) is spokesman for the manufacturing sector. Rather, his task is to prevent 'industrial unrest' from disrupting 'our economic future' by mediating between capital and labour.

As might be expected from its non-representational role linkages, the department's role in the formation of economic policy is still limited. The department does possess substantial research capacity – collecting data on wages, working conditions, strikes, settlements in major industries. However, this is designed merely to monitor the industrial relations front. Discussions with officials in the department indicate that their research is not intended to provide a basis for participation in economic policy formation. This type of research has generated contacts of a limited nature between labour and the department. Officials interact with labour representatives primarily in the context of formal arbitration and conciliation procedures.

Despite this, the department's role in general policy formation may be expanding to develop policies which are designed to win labour's commitment to the development strategy of the hegemonic fraction. H. Waisglass, former director of research, described the policy research function (which still forms but a small part of the department's research) in the following terms: '– to prepare situation reports and recommendations on significant current and prospective developments in Foreign Trade (Exports and Imports) Policies and Conditions, as they affect employment labour incomes and working conditions, and as they may be affected by labour disputes; – to study the industrial relations implications of proposed changes in tariff and trade policies, and to forecast their effects on the needs for labour adjustment and income maintenance programs; – to study the social and labour obstacles and effects of the general trend towards free world trade, and to develop policy proposals designed to alleviate hardships and to facilitate adjustments among workers, and simultaneously to encourage expansionary trade policies; – to develop and evaluate policy alternatives, with emphasis on their labour aspects, that would strengthen the competitiveness of Canadian industry and facilitate labour and management adjustments to changing international circumstances, including multi-lateral reductions of tariffs and trade barriers.'[50] The department's policy role is still limited. However, the development ideology elaborated in the central departments (and the economic developments which are rendering these necessary) is creating pressure for the department to expand its concern in order to negotiate the compromise with labour necessary to the realization of these objectives. This has become particularly clear in the discussions surrounding the Trudeau government's new (corporatist) society with its complex of 'multipartite' and 'tripartite' councils.

The involvement of the Canadian Labour Congress in these deliberations is likely to be complemented by the inclusion of the Department of Labour in economic policy discussions. The department is already included on the interdepartmental committee of senior officials on inflation. The new importance of organized labour may also be seen in the federal government's possible assumption of responsibility for organized labour in industries like steel, auto, packing, and textiles under Section 92,10(c) of the BNA Act which authorizes the federal government to declare local works and undertakings 'to be for the general Advantage of Canada.'[51] In the face of the increasingly apparent structural crisis of advanced capitalism, the response of the state is to try to win the active consent of the most powerful section of the working class. The form which this has taken in Canada specifically includes a new role for the Department of Labour in negotiations involving social and economic policy. This does not, however, imply that 'labour' has gained (or is likely to gain) entry to the power bloc. Its objective interests as part of the working class are fundamentally antagonistic to capitalist development. The contradictory character of unions is, in fact, likely to become apparent as the state attempts to use the compromise struck between top union officials, government, and capital to discipline the rank and file. For fractions of the subordinate classes, the coercive aspect of 'representation' predominates.

Integration of marginal groups: Indian Affairs and native peoples in the North
The (changing) relation of the Department of Labour to the organized fraction of the working class bears certain similarities to departments and branches 'responsible' for other fractions of the subordinate classes. The character of representation is more limited in scope than is that of the branches representing the power bloc. The latter are 'authoritative decision-makers' in the sphere of production: the mandate of their representatives reflects this. Conversely, the working class (including the surplus population on welfare rolls) occupies a subordinate position in the social relations of production. The mandate of its representatives reflects this status. However, divisions in the subordinate class established at the level of production relations and reinforced at the level of consumption are also reflected in the differential role of their representatives. A brief consideration of the role of the Department of Indian Affairs and Northern Development in the context of the drive to develop northern energy resources serves to illustrate some of these differences.

The formation of the National Policy followed the decline of the fur trade – a staples economy in which native peoples had played a key role. The new Canadian state's commitment to the establishment of a national economy based on urban and rural settlement (or, the spread of commercial agriculture and urban industry across the continent) led to the marginalization of native peoples. Their marginal position – the creation of a system of reservations – was legitimized through the Indian Act. The reserve system effectively sealed treaty or 'status' Indians off from the modern capitalist economy. The 'protection' of their pre-capitalist economy through this system has necessitated increasing support through the extension of welfare programs.

The department responsible for administering the entire Indian Act, including the welfare aspect, has altered over the years. Since the late 1950s (when the North appeared as Canada's new frontier) the Department of Indian Affairs and Northern Development has assumed responsibility for native peoples. The department's relation to native peoples has been determined by two factors of particular relevance for native peoples in the North.[52] First, the terms of the Indian Act itself have conditioned the relationship. Under the act native peoples were defined as a colonial people, incapable of self-development and dependent on the largesse of the colonial authority. This dependency relationship reinforced the integration of native peoples to Canadian society as 'marginals.' The second factor – the department's 'province-like authority' over the North – has been of particular relevance to Indians and Innuit in the North. The Northern Development Branch, with its mandate to encourage large corporations engaged in resource exploitation to develop the North, has held primacy over Indian Affairs. This has meant that the department's role in the North has differed in an important respect from that of a provincial government. According to a study done for the Science Council of Canada in 1975-6 the department's 'personnel view the two northern Territories as vast sparsely populated areas, containing important natural resources which should benefit all Canada. In contrast, the provinces see their resources as first, benefiting their own citizens and second, other Canadians.'[53] In other words, unlike provincial governments which represent the particular social forces within their territory, the department's role in the North reflected the emerging alliance of the federal government and the large corporations with actual (or potential) interests in northern resource development. Thus, when northern development accelerated after the discovery of oil in Alaska in 1968, the governmental agency established to elaborate this strategy (the Task Force on Northern Development) included no representative from the Indian Affairs Branch: the department saw no need to consult with native peoples. However, the radicalization of native peoples in the south, the pending land claims settlement in Alaska (December 1971), and the emergence of northern native peoples' movements, supported by southern environmentalists and nationalists, forced the government to try to forestall any threat to their northern development strategy.

In June 1972 the Social and Environmental Committee was added to the task force. The new committee was to be headed by a director drawn from

Indian Affairs and to be chaired by the same branch. It was allocated a budget of $15 million to be expended on research over a three-year period. The committee was linked to the departments of the Environment, Indian Affairs, Energy, Mines and Resources, and the two territorial governments through co-ordinating committees. In addition, an advisory group was established, bringing together political representatives of the various social forces: native peoples, southern environmentalists, and the corporations. As Edgar Dosman noted, the advisory group had little practical effect. It met but twice a year and only on the request of the chairman of the Social and Environmental Committee. The $15 million budget merely indicated the degree of the government's commitment to a Mackenzie Valley natural gas pipeline. The budgetary allocation was based on the assumption that 'Ottawa could and should oblige industry by clearing away outstanding obstacles as quickly as possible.' The committee produced the *Expanded Guidelines* (tabled in the House, June 1972) – yet these were but a 'list of concerns that Canadian Arctic Gas Consortium would have to take up in its submission [to the National Energy Board].'[54] The main government document which voiced an alternate (or complementary) development strategy for the North – one which reflected a more 'socially-oriented' development – was prepared by the department: *Canada's North, 1970-1980*. This document emphasized environmental concerns, the need to develop renewable resources, to establish light industries, and to educate and train the native population. Indian Affairs officials had submitted the basic outline to the cabinet in January 1970. In July 1971 the cabinet approved the document. It was tabled in March of 1972 – and then only after strong public pressure had been applied. Again, Dosman correctly noted that the government's reluctance to table the document was based on its intention of deferring land claims negotiations until after the pipeline had been approved.

Canada's North did not represent government policy. It did, however, indicate that Indian Affairs officials had begun to redefine their role – from 'custodians' of native peoples to 'representatives.' In the dynamic context of the post-1968 North, the opposition of native peoples to a development process which would effectively destroy their way of life but which did not offer any clear alternative was predictable. Some accommodation of the interests of native peoples was necessary if their opposition were not to prove obstructive. Some officials in Indian Affairs realized this and took action. Yet the 'development' orientation of the department precluded effective action. Approval of the pipeline was clearly the priority: 'In both areas, native people and the environment, protection could take place only at the margin

... after the framework of development was already established by the central resource and pipeline decisions worked out in confidence between private executives and senior officials in Ottawa.'[55]

The sudden change in the politics of the North left the department and the government unprepared to cope with the increasingly effective opposition of northern native peoples who had developed links with southern groups. In March 1973 the government reversed its earlier decision to settle the rights-of-way question without a public hearing. Justice T. Berger, a member of the judiciary with a record of some understanding of native peoples, was appointed to lead a commission of inquiry, and undertook extensive hearings in the North. While the government indicated its preparedness to proceed with the pipeline (should the National Energy Board recommend) prior to the settlement of the land claims, the Berger Report was nevertheless a victory for the native people – whose objective it is to gain political control of the Territories within the Canadian state system – and may place them in a better position to negotiate future development policy.

The contrast between the representatives of native people and of organized labour reflects their different economic and political positions. In the post-war Canadian political economy, organized labour has gained a degree of 'recognition.' Although the Department of Labour has been slow to adapt to this, organized labour has officially been represented on quasi-governmental agencies like the Economic Council of Canada and, more recently, the Canadian Labour Relations Council. In addition, the formation of the New Democratic Party – an alliance of organized labour and the petite bourgeoisie under the leadership of the latter – has given labour a means of articulating its concerns (albeit in a manner which can be accommodated within the existing system). In contrast, Canadian native peoples have only recently begun to organize and struggle for their claims. The structure for negotiating their 'consent' to domination expressed their colonial or marginal status. Although certain officials in Indian Affairs were able to recognize the potential challenge the rise of northern native peoples' movements posed, the policy-making structures (and the values and relations embedded therein) could not. The Berger inquiry, in combination with the land claims negotiations, are likely to produce a new compromise with native peoples. The form this compromise will assume depends on the success northern native peoples have in forging an alliance with dissident forces in the south.

TOWARDS A MARXIST METHOD OF PUBLIC POLICY ANALYSIS

Identification of the determinants of public policy depends on assumptions concerning the structure of society and the relation between civil society and the state. There are two main tendencies: liberal and Marxist. For liberal political scientists, society is composed of a plurality of groups whose existence springs from the diverse economic, socio-cultural, and geographic characteristics of a society. The state is seen as autonomous, as the neutral arbiter of inter-group conflict. The outcome of a particular conflict thus depends directly on the relative power of the groups involved at any point in time. Marxist theory – which is historical, dialectical, and materialist – conceives of 'society' in terms of a definite mode of production which is characterized by relations of domination/exploitation that, in turn, produce antagonistic social classes. In a class society, the state functions to maintain these relations. In its liberal-democratic form, however, the state assumes a 'relative autonomy' vis-à-vis the class struggle. It is a class state and yet its legitimacy derives from its appearance as representative of the 'nation-people.' The structural determinants of public policy in a liberal-democratic state are the (ultimately) contradictory functions of facilitating private accumulation and creating the conditions for social cohesion by functioning as 'neutral arbiter.'

Liberal political scientists are unable to comprehend the contradictory 'facts' – that the liberal-democratic state appears neutral even while its actions (policies) perpetuate social inequalities. Yet while Marxists are able to offer an analysis of public policy which is at once more intelligible and critical, a problem has tended to arise when confronted with the need to explain specifically how the bias emerges. The instrumentalist perspective – which views the state as an instrument in the hands of the bourgeoisie – then seems to hold appeal even for sophisticated analysts like James O'Connor. It is possible, however, to arrive at a Marxist method for analysing the public policy process – a method which gives full recognition to the 'relative autonomy' of the capitalist state vis-à-vis the class struggle. The preceding pages suggested one such alternative.

In the method presented, the notion of the unequal structure of representation played a central role. It is this structure of representation which facilitates the functioning of the state as organizer of hegemony – of the series of compromises which seek to win the consent of the subordinate classes to the capitalist system. To argue that an unequal structure of representation exists inside the state is not, however, to argue that the state is an instrument in the hands of the dominant class. All social forces achieve a form of representation – although the relations among the representatives express the inequalities established in civil society. Further, this structure of representation is quite clearly distinguished from 'private' political representatives such as interest groups inasmuch as the former simultaneously 'represent' and 'discipline' the represented in the name of the national interest, backed by the might of the state.

In addition, this approach facilitates a dynamic analysis of specific policy instances – unlike O'Connor's which is largely geared to the effects (or 'function') of government policy. Finally, the notion of the unequal structure of representation draws attention to the 'contradictory unity' of the state, demystifying the fragmentation of its institutional manifestation.

More specifically, this perspective suggests a promising approach to the 'politics' of policy formation and implementation. From this perspective, the analysis of public policy, considered as a means of subordinating particular interests to the long-run interests of the hegemonic fraction, is seen to involve several key questions. First, what compromise had previously obtained between the relevant social force and the hegemonic fraction and how was this expressed in the state? Second, which factors account for the breakdown of this compromise? Third, what structural arrangements were made for renegotiation? Finally, what kind of compromise does the new institutional arrangement represent and what mechanisms are there to ensure that this compromise is effectively integrated with the 'global compromise'? These kinds of questions serve to relegate 'interest group' analysis (the focus of pluralists and instrumentalists alike) to its appropriate place, requiring the analyst to consider the ways in which the long-run interests of the hegemonic fraction bear on the 'issue' and are protected in its resolution.

There are, of course, important gaps in the reading of the structure of representation inside the Canadian state. Further research on the particular role of the different provincial governments is needed to supplement the suggestive studies done by Larry Pratt and Pierre Fournier.[56] In addition, the network designed to produce a level of cohesion among the provinces and between them and the federal government warrants greater attention. Finally, given the growing international interdependence of capital, it seems crucial to explore the ways in which the Canadian state functions to reproduce the conditions for Canadian integration. It is hoped, however, that this paper has provided a convincing argument to encourage such research.

NOTES

1 See Vernon Fowke, 'The National Policy – Old and New,' in W.T. Easterbrook and M.H. Watkins, eds., *Approaches to Canadian Economic History* (Toronto 1967).

2 The three major Marxist approaches to the state are best exemplified by the work

of Ralph Miliband, *The State in Capitalist Society* (London 1969, 1973); James
O'Connor, *The Fiscal Crisis of the State* (New York 1973); and Nicos Poulantzas,
Classes in Contemporary Capitalism (London 1975). While all are useful, the latter
has exercised a greater influence on the argument presented in this paper.

3 See Richard Simeon, *Federal-Provincial Diplomacy: The Making of Recent Policy
in Canada* (Toronto 1972).

4 Antonio Gramsci, 'The State,' reprinted in *Selections from the Prison Notebooks
of Antonio Gramsci*, ed. and trans. Quintin Hoare and G. Nowell Smith (New
York 1971), 260

5 The contemporary phase of capitalism is frequently called 'monopoly capitalism'
– a term which will be used in this paper. None the less, it is important to bear in
mind that 'oligopoly' – limited competition among a few – is the norm, rather
than 'monopoly' in the strict sense – a single producer, the absence of competition.

6 See Perry Anderson, 'Origins of the Present Crisis,' *New Left Review*, 23 (Jan.-
Feb. 1964), 26-53.

7 N. Poulantzas, *Political Power and Social Class* (London 1973), 239

8 In Canada, the merchant-financier fraction has historically constituted the hegemonic fraction whose long-term interests were realized through the National
Policy. The coincidence of two developments since the war – concentration of
capital and substantial penetration of the Canadian economy by American-
based multinational corporations – has led some to question the continued hegemony of this group. However, W. Clement's data – *The Canadian Corporate
Elite* (Toronto 1975) – show that the indigenous bourgeoisie of central Canada
possesses an ideological and political homogeneity, autonomy of economic base,
and control of the 'core institutions' of the Canadian economy. This suggests that
the central Canadian bourgeoisie remains the hegemonic fraction. A second
question concerns the composition of the power bloc. Inasmuch as the power
bloc constitutes a special kind of alliance – one marked by 'the relative homogeneity of their relations at all levels,' that is, ideological, political, and economic
– it can be argued that it is composed of the various fractions of monopoly capital (large enterprises in traditional and new areas and small enterprises in areas
created by the central needs of monopoly capital such as advertising and special
financial services). These, in turn, are divided along the lines of function, region,
and nationality.

9 *Fiscal Crisis of the State*

10 Poulantzas, 'The Capitalist State: A Reply to Miliband and Laclau,' *New Left
Review*, 95 (Jan.-Feb. 1976), 73, 75

11 Poulantzas, 'On Social Classes,' *New Left Review*, 78 (March-April 1973), 48

12 *Ibid.*, 40-1

13 R. Miliband, 'Reply to Poulantzas,' in Robin Blackburn, ed., *Ideology in Social Science* (London 1972), 255

14 'Canadian Federal Administrative and Political Insitututions: A Role Analysis,' unpublished PH D dissertation, Queen's University, Kingston, 1967, p. 90

15 'The Capitalist State,' 75

16 'Canadian Federal Administrative,' 63

17 *Ibid.*, 267

18 Budgetary responsibilities are shared with the Treasury Board; this has been the case since the 1960s.

19 Taken from 'The Cabinet and the Public Service Establishment,' in *Apex of Power: Prime Minister and Political Leadership in Canada*, comp. T.A. Hockin (Toronto 1971), 118-19; originally printed in House of Commons Committee on Finance Trade and Economic Affairs, *Minutes and Proceedings*, 24 April 1969

20 Canada, Royal Commission on Bilingualism and Biculturalism, *Documents*: 'Bureaucratic Careers: Anglophones and Francophones in the Canadian Public Service,' C. Beattie, J. Desy, and S. Longstaff (1972)

21 See John Porter, *The Vertical Mosaic* (Toronto 1965), particularly the section on federal bureaucracy; Peter C. Newman, 'The Ottawa Establishment,' *Maclean's Magazine*, 22 Aug. 1964.

22 Beattie *et al.*, 'Bureaucratic Careers,' 42

23 'Prime Minister and Cabinet: The History and Development,' in *Apex of Power*, 36

24 'On Social Classes,' 48

25 Beattie *et al.*, 'Bureaucratic Careers,' Newman, 'Ottawa Establishment,' and J.E. Hodgetts, *The Canadian Public Service: A Physiology of Government, 1867-1970* (Toronto 1973), all refer to the 'inner circle' of the federal bureaucracy. Some include other departments but all agree to the primacy of these three.

26 G.B. Doern, 'Development of Policy Organizations in the Executive Arena,' in *Structures of Policy Making in Canada*, ed. Doern and Peter Aucoin (Toronto 1971)

27 The PCO, however, remains dependent on the regular departments for detailed knowledge.

28 Ronald Anderson, 'Group of 7,' *Globe and Mail*, Toronto, 28 Feb. 1975

29 Howe held the portfolios of Munitions and Supply, Reconstruction, Trade and Commerce, and Defence Production during his lengthy career in the cabinet.

30 MacKintosh was one of the 'bright young men' recruited by Clark from Queen's.

31 David Wolfe, 'Political Culture, Economic Policy and the Growth of Foreign Investment in Canada, 1945-57,' unpublished MA thesis, Carleton University, Ottawa, 1973, p. 98. Wolfe notes that, although Canadian interests were approached first, branch officials were certainly far from reluctant to turn to foreign capital if Canadian producers could not be found.

32 *Canadian Public Service*, 103
33 Interview with Lance Howie, Ottawa, 19 Nov. 1974. Howie was with National Revenue in the fifties when the department had a policy role due to its deputy minister's membership in the 'inner circle.' The then deputy minister, D. Sims, was one of the 'Finance trainees.'
34 *Ibid.*
35 Announced July 1968, implemented in 1969
36 R. Beamish, 'Why Not a Federal Department of Commerce?' *Executive*, x, 10 (Oct. 1968), 34
37 *Canadian Non-Tariff-Barriers to Trade*, sponsored by the Canadian Economic Policy Committee, Private Planning Association (Montreal 1973), 96
38 From comments made at the Conference Board of Canada's 'Conference on the Problems and Potential of Canadian Manufacturing' (1972)
39 From *New Men of Power*, cited in Cy Gonick, *Inflation or Depression* (Toronto 1975), 365
40 Michael Mann, *Consciousness and Action among the Western Working Class* (London 1973)
41 Stuart Jamieson, *Times of Trouble: Labour Unrest and Industrial Conflict in Canada, 1900-66*, Federal Task Force on Labour Relations (Ottawa 1968); H.C. Pentland, 'Study of the Characteristics of the Economic, Social, and Political Background of the Canadian System of Industrial Relations,' Task Force study no. 1 (1968)
42 *Vertical Mosaic*, 312
43 Charles Lipton, *Trade Union Movement of Canada* (Toronto 1973), 99
44 Section 2(c), cited in H.D. Woods, *Labour Policy in Canada* (2nd ed., Toronto 1973), 54
45 Cited in Bradley Rudin, 'Mackenzie King and the Writing of Canada's Anti Labour Laws,' *Canadian Dimension*, VIII, 4-5 (Jan. 1972), 46
46 Interview with Alan Portigal, Research Division, Department of Labour, Ottawa, 11 Feb. 1975
47 The areas of jurisdiction are defined in such a way that the department has no contact with unorganized workers, who constitute nearly two-thirds of the working class.
48 Address to the Annual Meeting of the Canadian Textile Institute, reprinted in the *Canadian Textile Journal* (June 1964), 38
49 'Interview with Bryce Mackasey,' *Executive*, x, 10 (Oct. 1968), 26 (emphasis added)
50 'Labour and Management Adjustment to the Changing International Environment,' *Industrial Relations* (Quebec), XXIX, 3 (1974), 587
51 See the *Globe and Mail*, 22 Oct. 1976, where the Ontario deputy minister of labour, T. Armstrong, is cited on this point.

52 See Edgar Dosman, *The National Interest: The Politics of Northern Development, 1968-1975* (Toronto 1975), and R.F. Keith *et al., Northern Development and Technology Assessment Systems,* Science Council of Canada, background study no. 34 (Jan. 1976). This section mainly interprets the data which these two studies have provided – an interpretation which utilizes the method outlined in this paper.
53 Keith *et al., ibid.,* 61
54 *National Interest,* 166, 169
55 *Ibid.,* 114
56 Fournier, *The Quebec Establishment* (Montreal 1976), and Pratt in this volume

7
The state elites

DENNIS OLSEN

A theory of the state in Canada must build upon and integrate an answer to the factual question of who holds state power. In a Marxist analysis we are interested neither in the cult of personality nor in the great man theory of history; consequently 'who,' in the first instance, means which social classes and which other politically significant social categories? Since Canadian history includes the French regime, a conquest, a period as a British colony, and finally a buildup of the labour force through immigration from many countries, the other politically significant social categories, whose role must also be understood, are ethnic categories – particularly British Canadians and French Canadians but also the politically dispersed other (non-British, non-French) ethnic categories. An 'ethnic category,' to use a Poulantzian approach, is a grouping politically organized across social classes, which can be a social force in the society. The 'members' of an ethnic category do not, however, exist 'outside' of social classes but are simultaneously members of different social classes.[1] As with other ex-British colonies (Jamaica, South Africa) one finds that the Canadian corporate elite still has a British complexion, but the state is shared with the other ethnic categories.[2] The Canadian state developed through an ethnic alliance of the British and the French, which Ryerson called an 'unequal union.' To some extent this ethnic alliance coincided with the division of labour between the 'private and economic' (capital) and the 'public and political' (the state), a fact which should not be overlooked in any serious attempt to grasp the nature and role of the Canadian state or its current contradictions.

In this paper the term 'British' is used to refer to those Canadians whose ethnic origins are in the British Isles. The British ethnicities (English, Irish, Scottish, and Welsh) are more popularly known as 'English Canadians,' an identification which tends to confuse language with ethnicity. In most contexts today they tend to identify themselves as simply 'Canadian' (unhy-phenated). The term 'ethnic' in the popular press rarely refers to either British or French Canadians, but, almost invariably, refers only to one of the many other ethnic categories, that is, Canadians whose origins are German, Italian, Ukrainian, etc. British and French Canadians, as members of the two charter ethnic groups, are by implication the only 'true Canadians' who somehow mysteriously have no ethnicity.

It can be assumed that the institutional framework of the Canadian state system is understood to include the appropriate Canadian version of the set of institutions which were delineated by Miliband and again by Panitch in this volume; that is, federal and provincial governments or cabinets, their representative assemblies, federal and provincial bureaucracies, public corporations, regulatory boards and commissions, the courts, and the military and police.[3] For practical research purposes, the question of which social classes and ethnic categories provide the personnel who are typically 'in charge' of the state apparatus on a day-to-day basis can be answered by identifying a set of positions at the top of these institutions whose incumbents constitute a national state elite, and by examining the social composition of that elite over a period of time. In this paper some findings will be reported from a more detailed study examining leading state personnel from the federal part of the state system and from all ten provinces, with some extra consideration given to the four most economically powerful and populous provinces: Quebec, Ontario, Alberta, and British Columbia. Analytically, this can be thought of as an attempt to 'slice off' the top positions in the state system and examine the social background of those who occupy the 'heights' of the state.

In *Political Power and Social Classes* Nicos Poulantzas has argued that the state is the cohesive factor in unifying the various modes of production which coexist in a modern nation.[4] In order to do this, the state must have a degree of 'relative autonomy' from the economic interests of the capitalist class, precisely in order to express their general political interests, which often necessitates their entering into alliances and creating compromises with other classes in order to achieve an overall political hegemony. Elsewhere, Poulantzas pushes this as far as suggesting that 'the capitalist State best serves the interests of the capitalist class only when the members of this class do not participate directly in the State apparatus, that is to say when the *ruling class* is not the *politically governing class*.'[5] He cites as examples the role of the landed nobility in the state in 'nineteenth-century England and Bismarkian Germany,' and mentions Bonapartism in France and the social-democratic governments of some modern European states. As long as the capitalist class retains the private right to accumulate and invest wealth, this right being guaranteed by the state, the public state apparatus can be manned by personnel from other classes, who may in fact be better suited to achieving the compromises, concessions, and ideological hegemony which are necessary to reproduce and advance the whole bourgeois order through time. The state becomes involved in a dynamic 'unstable equilibrium of compromises' in order to create the political unity of the whole social formation.[6]

Generally, it can be argued that these observations by Poulantzas apply also to the Canadian state and its personnel; a fact which is not well understood throughout the Canadian left where some authors, understandably perhaps, have been so anxious to expose all the bourgeois connections and functions of the state and its elite that they have overstated the case. This could lead to the conclusion that the Canadian state is at once an important power in the society and yet at the same time completely dominated by the capitalist class with little or no relative autonomy of its own. Not only would this conclusion be false, not to mention contradictory, but it would seriously underestimate the ability of a working-class political movement to fracture the existing alliances and compromises of the state. In keeping with these remarks, evidence will be produced in the following pages to document three assertions:

1 The Canadian state elite is mainly composed of British and French Canadians of middle-class origins.
2 At the same time it is important to realize that (even internally) the state system is not controlled solely by personnel from the middle classes; other social classes – the capitalist class and the working class – also make their appearance here as do elements of the non-British, non-French ethnic categories, only in these other cases the proportions are much smaller. Internally the state elite is composed of a rough alliance of social classes and ethnic categories as one might expect from Poulantzas' remarks; however, it is by no means an equal alliance as the next assertion will indicate.
3 Because of the federal nature of the Canadian state system it contains within it centres with differing degrees of power: federal and provincial cabinets, federal and provincial bureaucracies, larger provinces and smaller provinces, etc. The further one moves away from the higher centres of power within the state the lower the social class origins of the state elite tend to be; and, conversely, the closer one moves towards the higher centres of power the higher the social class origins of the elite. Similarly, the higher centres are more likely to be occupied by British and French Canadians.

These are empirical generalizations, which means there are individual exceptions to the assertions.

Several qualifications are in order at this point. First, there is no need to assume that the *social origins* of a state elite are necessarily congruent with its *social functions*. The day-to-day operations of the state in a society whose economic formation is primarily determined by a dominant economic class follow a logic of necessity which is to a very great extent independent of the interests of the social classes and ethnic categories from which the elite was drawn. At the same time, the state does have a degree of relative autonomy; so that it can be expected that at least the elected members of the elite will try, within these limitations, to direct state advantages in a way which upholds their own base of support. The role of French-Canadian cabinet ministers in promoting bilingual and bicultural policies in the last decade provides a clear example in the Canadian case.

An elite study helps to specify the linkages which develop between various classes or between various ethnic categories, linkages which are historically and regionally variable within capitalism. An elite study also helps us to form an opinion about the nature of the alliance which is perpetually being created and recreated between the dominant class and other classes through the mediation of the state. An elite study should be a complement to, but not a substitute for, a more detailed class analysis.

METHOD

The state elites are those who occupy controlling positions within the state system. For purposes of statistical comparison the findings have been grouped and presented in terms of two elite categories: first, a 'political-judicial elite'; and, second, a 'bureaucratic elite,' which also includes the heads of the Canadian military and police. Social background data were gathered on these elites from a number of sources.[7] Because the method used to gather and classify the data is comparable to an earlier study of the same groups – John Porter's *The Vertical Mosaic,* 1965, Chapters 13 and 14 – the composition of the political-judicial elite can be reported on over a thirty-three-year period, from 1940 through to the end of 1973. In the case of the bureaucratic elite, the federal elite of 1953 can be compared to its equivalent twenty years later, and the federal bureaucrats of 1973 can also be compared to a set of provincial bureaucrats who held office in the same year.

STATE ELITES: THE POLITICIANS AND JUDGES

The statistical group taken to be the leading edge of these sections of the state system included all federal cabinet ministers, all provincial premiers, all justices of the Supreme Court of Canada, the president of the federal court, and the ten provincial chief justices. In addition, eighty-one of the most important provincial cabinet ministers from Quebec, Ontario, Alberta, and British Columbia are reported on separately. Data were obtained on a total of 240 cases which included 98 federal cabinet ministers, 28 provincial premiers, 81 provincial cabinet ministers, and 33 federal and provincial judges, all of whom held office during the period beginning January 1961 and ending December 1973. The tables which follow present these cases in two groups: first, 159 people who held the same positions as those studied by Porter in the period from 1940 to 1960, and, second, the eighty-one provincial cabinet ministers who are grouped and reported on separately.

Ethnicity
The first table distributes the 159 cases of politicians and judges according to their 'ethnicity.' 'Ethnicity' in this table has to be understood only as an indicator that the individual belongs to an 'ethnic category,' as previously defined – that is, one that is politically organized. In some cases this assumption is tenuous, especially among those of non-British and non-French ethnicity, who may be assimilated to the point that they defend, and in a personal sense 'stand for,' the institutions of one or the other of the two dominant ethnic categories. John Diefenbaker (for the British) and Claude Wagner (for the French) provide examples of this kind of identification. Comparing the political-judicial elite in 1973 to the 1971 population figures reveals that the British are still greatly over-represented, the French slightly under-represented, and all the other ethnic categories combined very heavily under-represented with only 7.6 per cent of the elite positions and 26.7 per cent of the population. The British-French alliance at the top of the state thus remains for the most part intact. It is also clear that there has been a shift in this alliance in favour of the French. The British in the elite have declined more rapidly than their proportion of the population (7.2 per cent compared to 3.2 per cent), while the French have actually reversed the population trend by increasing their representation in the elite. At a deeper level, the figures reflect the entry into the elite of a vanguard of cabinet ministers from the French-Canadian middle class, who were pushed into power not only by the various threats of separation and the demands for bureaucratic and linguistic space made by a middle class with blocked mobility

Table 1
Political-judicial elite by ethnicity (percentages)

Ethnic category	Elite			Canadian population	
	1960	1973	Change	Change 1951-71	Distribution 1971
British Isles	75.1	67.9	− 7.2	− 3.2	44.7
French	21.7	24.5	+ 2.8	− 2.2	28.6
Other	3.2	7.6	+ 4.4	+ 5.4	26.7
N	157	159			

The 1960 percentages are from Porter, *Vertical Mosaic*, 389; population changes calculated from the Canadian census 1951 and 1971. 'British Isles' category includes English, Irish, Scottish, and Welsh. 'Ethnicity' refers to descent group traced through the father's line: various criteria were used to determine ethnicity including the person's name, religion, and place of birth; parents' name and place of birth; spouse's name; and language of primary schooling.

but also by the strike activities of a militant Quebec working class.[8] At the purely political level, the figures reflect the return of the Liberals to power in 1963 and the advent of the Trudeau regime in 1968. Among other things, the table tells us that elite composition is by no means automatically determined by the size of the population base; the key factors are the degree of political mobilization and political clout that the base can deliver. All the other ethnic categories combined have not quite kept pace with their population increase; their dispersion, their political fragmentation, and the necessity to assimilate to one or the other of the two dominant categories, probably are the main reasons, along with their generally less favourable economic position.

The British-French alliance at the federal level of the state splits sharply apart when the provincial level is examined. Table 2 shows the sharp ethnic differences which exist among provincial political elites; with Quebec predominantly French, Ontario predominantly British, and the British dominant also in the two western provinces. Only the British and the French, the two 'charter groups' as Porter called them, have legal and linguistic systems guaranteed and enforced by the state. Given these, plus the provinces' control of natural resources and other state assets, ethnic *political* dominance is an *economic* advantage of no small consequence. Despite the multi-ethnic composition of cities such as Montreal and Toronto, only in the western provinces do members of the other ethnic categories get a share of the top

Table 2
Ethnicity of provincial cabinet ministers by province of main career, 1961-73

	Quebec	Ontario	Alberta	British Columbia	Total	%
British	4	18	10	12	44	54
French	25	1			26	32
Other	1		4	6	11	14
Total	30	19	14	18	81	100

The eighty-one provincial cabinet ministers included above are not the full complement of ministers who served in the four provinces during the period under examination, 1961-73. Most of them held a number of portfolios during their career, but they were selected because they held the more important ones: Finance or Provincial Treasurer, Justice or Attorney-General, Natural Resources, Education, Health, Labour, Welfare, Industry and Commerce. They were important enough to be considered part of a national 'state elite.'

state positions. The same pattern, even more sharply drawn, shows up later in Table 6 where the ethnicity of the bureaucrats from these four provinces is examined.

Social class origins
The political-judicial elite tend for the most part to be middle class in their origins. The trend in this direction has, if anything, increased since the previous study, especially among the federal cabinet ministers. Table 3 should not, however, be interpreted in a way which would suggest that nobody enters the elite from the corporate world or from wealthy family backgrounds; only that, statistically, it is far from being the typical case. As can be seen, those with 'upper-class' origins have formed a fairly constant proportion of the elite since 1940. In a separate calculation it was concluded that a minimum of 16 per cent of the *elected* members of this elite were connected to substantial family wealth before they entered politics. Federal cabinet ministers with inherited wealth included Charles Drury, Walter Gordon, George Hees, Pierre Trudeau, and James Richardson. Those who were connected to family fortunes by marriage before they entered politics included Walter Benidickson, Donald Fleming, and John Turner. Gordon, Fleming, and Turner were all ministers of finance in the federal government; between them, they held this key economic post for eleven of the eighteen years between 1957 and 1975. Provincial premiers with inherited wealth included Richard Hatfield, Frank Moores, Peter Lougheed, and Robert Stanfield, while Robert Bourassa married into the wealthy Simard family eight years

Table 3
Political-judicial elite: social class origins of the Canadian-born members (percentages)

Social class	Elite			
	1960	1973	Change	Population (approximate)
Upper	24.0	22.4	−1.6	1-2
Middle	65.7	69.0	+3.3	15
Below middle	10.3	8.6	−1.7	85
N	146	152		

Porter reports the upper-class percentage for 1960 in *Vertical Mosaic*, 394. His original data was re-analysed for a finer breakdown in order to compare his findings with the present study. Indicators of social class follow: *Upper*: (1) previous elite in the family, where 'elite' refers to the set of elite positions defined by Porter in 1965 – the corporate elite, political elite, bureaucratic elite, and the ideological elite – no relatives of the labour elite were found in the study; (2) father's occupation: owners of substantial businesses, judges and prominent members of the bar, directors of large but not dominant corporations – those near the elite but not in it.
Middle: (1) attendance at a private fee-paying school – most of the schools were either part of the classical college system of Quebec or members of the Headmasters' Association of Canada – members of the elite who attended these schools would have done so before 1940; (2) father's occupation: middle-class occupations – doctors, lawyers, ministers, merchants, mayors of middle-sized towns, and middle-level managers; (3) if none of the above criteria were met the person was considered middle class if he attended university. Only about 8 per cent of the male population in the same age group as the elite attended university.
Below middle: members of the elite in this category have none of the above attributes from the evidence available, or else they had fathers with definite working-class occupations; for the most part they are considered to be *possibly* of working-class origins.

before he was elected to the Quebec legislature. The wealthy may not be the typical case among members of the political elite; nevertheless, there are enough of them, with enough continuity in office, to ensure that the institutional arrangements which protect the private ownership and accumulation of wealth are safely preserved. In general, however, the economically powerful have not had to seek directly political office themselves, their interests being well served by the middle-class politicians who are already in office. As Porter remarked: 'In the corporate world both major political parties, the Liberals and the Conservatives, are seen as being favourable to the interests of corporate power.'[9]

As Table 3 indicates, those who come from working-class origins, or else from very small farm families, hardly show up at all in this elite; in fact, they have declined slightly since the previous study. At the political level their absence is due to the failure of a labour-based party, or for that matter any third party, to win control of the federal government. On the other hand, ministers whose origins are from below the middle class do have better representation at the provincial level than they have at the federal level; 23 per cent of the (eighty-one) provincial cabinet ministers were drawn from below the middle class as against only 8.6 per cent of those included in the main political-judicial elite. Among these provincial cabinet ministers, those coming from below the middle class are twice as likely to have risen to the top through a third party (CCF-NDP, Social Credit, Union Nationale) and much more likely to serve in the two western provinces rather than in the two central provinces. Provincial cabinet ministers from Ontario and Quebec greatly resemble the federal cabinet ministers in their class and ethnic attributes and tend to be drawn from somewhat higher in the class structure than the western ministers. There is a tendency for social class origins among the elite to decline as one moves west from the centre and down from the federal level to the provincial. This is a tendency only because the vast majority of the elected ministers, whether federal or provincial, are middle class in their origins.

The use of the particular indicators of social class origins found in Table 3 is partly dictated by the availability of data and also by the need to ensure comparability with Porter's previous study.[10] One can, however, examine the previous occupations of cabinet ministers, that is, those they had prior to entering politics, in order to get at their current class positions rather than their class origins: 83 per cent of the federal cabinet ministers were lawyers, businessmen, farmer-owners, physicians, or other independent professionals, as were 76 per cent of the provincial ministers. Most of these people (not *all*) came from a petit-bourgeois background – the 'old middle class' – in that they were independently organized producers or sellers of services who were not significantly involved in the labour market. The rest of the ministers came from occupations which can be called 'new middle class' – that is, the educated but essentially propertyless stratum of bureaucratized professionals. This second group, which included lesser managers, civil servants, teachers and academics, social workers, and other salaried professionals, made up 20 per cent of the provincial ministers (including the premiers) and 17 per cent of the federal ministers. There is a thin but detectable line of change in the data, from the previous study, towards an increase in the proportion from the new middle class, but it is very small and tends to be associated with the NDP provincial governments in the western provinces. More remarkable than the small increase of the new middle class is the amazing ability of the old middle class to monopolize political positions. The numerical decline of the old middle class, particularly the independent commodity producers, was discussed by Leo Johnson, who argued that politics in Canada has traditionally been dominated by the struggles and alliances of the petit-bourgeois and capitalist classes.[11] Despite the concentration of capital and the growth of the state in advanced capitalist societies, the petit-bourgeois class nevertheless seems to be both reproduced and transformed on the margins of the highly organized economy. As Miliband put it: 'The political history of these countries would undoubtedly have been radically different had the concentration of economic power been as rapid and as relentless as Marx thought it must become.'[12] As far as one can detect from the background data on Canadian cabinet ministers who served in the 1961 to 1973 period, the petit-bourgeois – capitalist alliance is still being reproduced within the state.

There has been a definite increase in the interconnection between the federal cabinet and business from one study to the next. In the 1960 study 18 per cent of the federal cabinet ministers came from business and 9 per cent of those who left politics went directly back to business.[13] In the 1973 study 27 per cent of the federal cabinet came from business and 19 per cent of those who exited (in the period from 1961 to 1973) went directly to business. Other ministers, those who went back to law firms or to the Senate, subsequently took up corporate directorships as well; so that, altogether, 27 per cent of those who exited in this period became involved in business or corporate decision-making. In short, about 27 per cent of the volume of circulation through the federal cabinet involves those who have had, or will have, business or corporate roles, and this volume appears to be half again as much as it was in the previous study, which is not surprising given the long period of post-war economic expansion in Canada. In any case, whether one uses indicators of social origins, as in Table 3, or previous occupation as an indicator of class position prior to politics, most of the members of the elite originally come from the middle class rather than from the grande bourgeoisie or the working class. At the same time, one should immediately add to these remarks the observation that many cabinet ministers who *began* in the middle class nevertheless wind up in the dominant class *after* their stint in politics.

STATE ELITES: THE BUREAUCRATS

Politicians tend to come and go, having a fairly rapid rate of turnover in the elite, but the bureaucracy is more permanent and, in this sense, the more important operating arm of the state system. In order to examine the composition of this branch of the state elite social background data were gathered on 318 bureaucrats. Of these, 224 were federal bureaucrats who held positions of the rank of deputy minister or assistant deputy minister (or their salaried equivalents) in all the main state departments and agencies including Crown corporations, regulatory boards, and commissions. A more detailed breakdown of the elite can be found in the Appendix. In addition, data were gathered on 94 provincial bureaucrats who held the rank of deputy minister or were heads of important Crown corporations or regulatory boards in the provinces of Quebec, Ontario, Alberta, and British Columbia. All of the bureaucrats in the present study held their positions in the state system during the year 1973. As before, the federal bureaucrats of 1973 are presented in the following tables alongside the 1953 bureaucratic elite studied by Porter, and the provincial bureaucrats are shown separately.

Ethnicity
In this elite, as with the previous group, it is apparent that British are still heavily over-represented, the French slightly under-represented, and all the other ethnic categories combined the most heavily under-represented, compared to the 1971 population distribution (see Table 4). In the case of this elite, however, the amount of change is more dramatic than in the political-judicial elite. The proportion of French Canadians more sharply reverses this category's population decline and the British-Canadian decline is larger than in Table 1. At the political level, these changes reflect the ethnic change in composition and tenure of the federal cabinet in the 1960s; the return of the Liberal government to power; the implementation of recommendations of the Royal Commission on Bilingualism and Biculturalism concerning the civil service; and, at a deeper level, the class forces operating in Quebec in the post-war period.

As for the other ethnic categories, while their rate of increase exceeds the corresponding population increase, it should be remembered that they began from an extremely low level of 'representation' at only 3 per cent. The fact that a few members of these other categories are being absorbed into the elite is important for the legitimation function of the Canadian state, which can then be presented as 'open,' 'tolerant,' and 'multicultural,' despite the obvious ethnic inequalities. In the case of these other ethnic categories, unlike the British and French, 'representation' is more properly called 'assimilation' – at least that appears to be the price that has to be paid to be in the elite. There was clear evidence of 'Anglo-conformity' among the statistical group studied – that is, an Anglicization of the last name and the sending of sons on to Oxford or to English-Canadian private schools.

In Table 5 the departmental members of the federal bureaucratic elite

Table 4
Federal bureaucratic elite by ethnicity (percentages)

	Elite			Canadian population	
	1953	1973	Change	Change 1951-71	Distribution 1971
British	84	65	− 19	−3.2	44.7
French	13	24	+11	−2.2	28.6
Other	3	11	+8	+5.4	26.7
N	202	224			

Porter reports the French-Canadian percentage for 1953 in *Vertical Mosaic*, 441; his original data was re-analysed to obtain a finer breakdown for comparative purposes.

are distributed by their rank within the bureaucracy and by place of birth and ethnicity. It should be noted that the Canadian-born of British ethnicity have by far the highest overall representation with 105 of the total 190 (55 per cent), and it should also be noted that in terms of actual numbers the Canadian-born British have the highest number of people in each of the three ranks. It is when we turn to the percentage distributions that we find some interesting relationships (the absolute numbers in the case of the foreign-born and the Canadian-born of non-British, non-French ethnicity are very small). For example, the few foreign-born members of the elite tend to have a higher-rank profile than the Canadian-born British (36 per cent in the top two ranks against 28 per cent). This is interesting because four-fifths of the foreign-born are themselves British, or were born overseas of British parents. Given that a person has a fixed ethnicity and is in the elite in the first place, the chance of being at the top rather than the bottom is somewhat different. In short, ethnicity does make a difference in one's rank. Although there are fewer French Canadians in the elite than British Canadians the French do have the best chance of being at the top (28 per cent) and the British Canadians have a smaller chance (15 per cent). Again, if we assume that a person has a certain fixed ethnicity and is in the elite, the chances of being in the top *two* ranks in descending order are: French Canadians first, other (non-British) Canadians second, foreign-born third, and British Canadians last. At the same time the chances of being in the larger bottom rank of the elite completely reverse this order with British Canadians first, foreign-born (mainly British) second, other (non-French) Canadians third, and French Canadians last. The reason for this ordering is that

Table 5
Federal bureaucratic elite by elite rank and ethnicity, 1973 only

| Elite rank | Canadian-born | | | | | | Foreign-born | | Total | |
| | British | | French | | Other | | | | | |
	%	N	%	N	%	N	%	N	%	N
Higher	15	16	28	12	12	2	16	4	18	34
Middle	13	14	26	11	41	7	20	5	19	37
Lower	72	75	46	20	47	8	64	16	63	119
Total		105		43		17		25		190

The 'higher' rank refers to those who were classified as Deputy Minister 3 or Deputy Minister 2 on the civil service scale; 'middle' refers to those who were classified as Deputy Minister 1; and 'lower' refers to those who were classified sx3–see the Appendix for a more detailed breakdown of this elite. The total N of 190 refers to those employed in the main government departments and excludes thirty-four who were Crown corporation executives or heads of autonomous regulatory boards.

Table 6
Provincial bureaucrats by ethnicity and province, 1973 only

	Quebec	Ontario	Alberta	British Columbia	Total	%
British		29	21	17	67	71
French	23		1		24	26
Other			1	2	3	3
Total	23	29	23	19	94	100

the elite's composition is a product of two kinds of forces; in the lower rank we are seeing the results of the pool of available candidates and the mobility pressures they exert from lower down in the system; and, at the same time, in the top two ranks we are seeing the results of the cabinet's political efforts to correct ethnic imbalances by appointment from above, cabinet in turn being pushed by the class forces already discussed.[14] Essentially, the results here reveal a struggle between the French and British middle classes for high state positions.

Provincial bureaucrats tend to be ethnically homogeneous within their centres. Table 6 points out an even sharper separation by ethnicity than was the case with provincial cabinet ministers. For elected politicians public visibility, and hence their 'representativeness,' is more important than it is with bureaucrats who operate behind the scenes. In half of the ninety-four cases

Table 7
Federal bureaucratic elite: social class origins of the Canadian-born members (percentages)

| | Elite | | | |
	1953	1973	Change	Population (approximate)
Upper	18	10	−8	1-2
Middle	69	75	+6	15
Below middle	13	15	+2	85
N	182	202		

The 1953 percentages are reported by Porter in *Vertical Mosaic*, 445-6. Social class indicators are the same as those used in Table 3. The approximate population figures are those for 1941, when most of the elite would have been entering the labour force. The total N of 202 for 1973 excludes twenty-two members of the elite who were born outside of Canada and also received their primary education outside of the country.

classified in Table 6 there was enough background information to apply the same criteria of ethnicity used in the previous tables; however, in the other half of the cases only the bureaucrat's name was available as an indicator of his ethnicity. Despite the inadequacy of the information it seems clear enough that provincial bureaucrats are divided along ethnic lines. While the federal elites (both politicians and bureaucrats) form a rough ethnic alliance, the same cannot be said of the large central provinces, where the ethnicity of both cabinet ministers and top bureaucrats represents mainly the provincial majority ethnic group. Since this ethnic separation coincides with the 'possession' by each elite of a provincial power base, this gives ethnicity a strong *political* expression within the Canadian state system, something which the federal elites are constantly trying to smooth over. As before, the two western provinces give more representation to the other ethnic categories than the two central provinces; nevertheless, it is very slight, and the British are heavily over-represented in both cases.

Social class origins
The bureaucratic elite is predominantly middle class in its origins. If the figures in Table 7 are compared to those in Table 3 it is clear that the bureaucratic elite is drawn from lower in the class system than the political-judicial elite, which in turn is drawn from lower in the class system than is the corporate elite studied by Wallace Clement. As was the case in Table 3, the middle class again has had the greatest increase over the twenty years. Whereas Clement found that the Canadian corporate elite is increasingly becoming upper class in its origins, Table 7 and the earlier tables on the

Table 8
Federal bureaucratic elite: elite rank by social class origins, 1973 only (percentages)

Elite rank	Upper	Middle	Below middle	Total
Higher	35	24	19	25
Middle	15	21	26	21
Lower	50	55	55	54
N	20	151	31	202

The rank categories are discussed in Table 5; social class indicators are the same as previous tables.

class origins of the political elite reveal that the state has been absorbing a lot of the slack by providing mobility chances for the middle class, which they cannot otherwise find within Canadian capitalism. The small increase from below the middle class is largely explainable through the mobility created by service in the armed forces during the Second World War. The war was probably the greatest single shakeup of personnel in recent Canadian history. After the war veterans were given government assistance for university education and preferential treatment in civil service recruitment. This allowed some sons of working-class people to obtain an education and a *few* have come up through the civil service exams into the elite.

The effects of social class origins on the rank attained within the bureaucracy are examined in Table 8. To begin with, it must be noted that the vast majority of bureaucrats (151 out of 202) have middle-class origins and the numbers in the other class categories are very small. Nevertheless, class does have its effect. The upper class has a better chance of being in the higher rank than either of the other classes and the middle class in turn has a better chance of being in the higher rank than those who come from below the middle class. The middle and lower ranks reverse this relationship with the middle class having higher representation than the upper class, while those few people drawn from below the middle are in turn distributed slightly higher than the middle class. Once again, it appears that the reversal reflects the lessening political influence of the cabinet as one declines in the ranks and the increasing influence of the internal civil service merit procedures. In an advanced capitalist society the successful performance of state functions requires educated expertise, which is more broadly available a little lower in the class system than it is in the tiny upper class.

Further support for these interpretations can be found by examining

Table 9
Federal bureaucratic elite: career profile by social class origins, 1973 only (percentages)

Career profile	Upper	Middle	Below middle	Total
Outside appointment	37	30	27	30
Career civil servant	63	70	73	70
N	19	142	30	191

The total N of 191 excludes another eleven members of the elite whose career pattern was too mixed to fall into either of the above categories. 'Outside appointment' refers to those who were not civil servants when they took up their present position or their previous position; 'Career civil servant' refers to those who have spent half or more of their working life in the civil service.

how the different classes enter the elite in the first place. This is shown in Table 9 which can be interpreted in a fairly straightforward manner. The higher the class background, the more likely the person entered the bureaucracy as an 'outsider'; and, conversely, the lower the class background, the more likely they are to have entered the elite after a lengthy career in the civil service. Every entry in the table supports this generalization.

The higher the class background, the more one resembles the elite doing the selecting, and the more connections and accumulated advantages one can bring to bear for a rapid rise to the elite level. Conversely, the lower the class background, the less one is like the elite doing the selecting, and, consequently, the fewer of the 'right' kinds of advantages one possesses. Those who come from below have to spend more time working their way up through the internal promotions of the bureaucracy, in the course of which, as Miliband has pointed out, a rough diamond will have his working-class edges considerably smoothed: 'What is involved here is rather a process of "bourgeoisification" of the most able and thrusting recruits from the subordinate classes. As these recruits rise in the state hierarchy, so do they become part, in every significant sense, of the social class to which their position, income and status give them access.'[15]

It is also important to realize that bureaucracy provides an important channel of upward mobility for talented and able people from the middle class and, far more rarely, from the working class. Not only does this help to legitimate a system which has far less opportunity than is commonly believed, but it also provides an important mechanism for renewal of the dominant class. As Marx pointed out in the third volume of *Capital*: 'The more a ruling class is able to assimilate the foremost minds of a ruled class, the more stable and dangerous becomes its rule.'

Table 10
Federal bureaucratic elite: cross-classified by ethnicity and social class origins, 1973 only

	Upper	Middle	Below middle	Total
British	9	99	19	127
French	9	37	6	52
Other	2	15	6	23
Total	20	151	31	202

For 'ethnicity' and 'social class' criteria see the notes to Tables 1 and 3. The total of 202 excludes twenty-two members of the elite who were born outside of Canada and also received their primary education outside the country.

Table 10 provides, at a glance, the kind of alliance that the Canadian state, or at least the bureaucracy – its more permanent arm – has put together. Clearly it is an unequal alliance for both classes and ethnic categories and hence harbours its own tensions and contradictions. The British-Canadian middle class has the greatest representation, and, given the British dominance in the corporate elite, this should mean they are relatively complacent about the arrangement. There are equal numbers of upper-class British and French Canadians, so that, at this level, there seems to be a straightforward sharing of power rather than proportional representation. The working class is under-represented whatever their ethnic origins, although this is less true for the British than for the other two categories. The upper and middle classes, as previously noted, are over-represented and this also seems to be true regardless of ethnicity, although it is very clear that the British Canadians are the most advantaged.

In fact, of course, the upper and middle classes of any of the three categories are over-represented. In order to see this point it is necessary to remember that these origin characteristics apply to the social structure some thirty or forty years ago. At that time a *very* generous estimate would place about 20 per cent of the Canadian population in the upper and middle classes (as those terms are used here). Assuming that this 20 per cent were distributed evenly between the British and the non-British ethnicities, about 10 per cent of the Canadian population would be both British Canadian and upper or middle class at the same time. Yet 108 of the 202 (53.5 per cent) in Table 10 have these two characteristics. Similarly, about 10 per cent of the population might have been upper or middle class and had a non-British ethnicity, but Table 10 reveals that 63 of the 202 (31 per cent) in the

Table 11
Provincial bureaucrats: social class origins by size of province, 1973 only (percentages)

	Largest Quebec and Ontario	Medium Alberta and British Columbia	Total
Upper	12.5		8
Middle	65	60	63
Below middle	22.5	40	29
N	40	25	65

Of the original N of ninety-four bureaucrats, twenty-nine (31 per cent) could not be classified as to social class origins due to lack of information on parental background.

elite have these two characteristics. Thus, in all cases, the upper and middle classes are over-represented. This point is often missed because spokesmen for an ethnic category will often claim that a member of the elite represents the whole category, whereas in fact they are drawn from the dominant classes' fraction within that ethnic category rather than the working class.

The internal composition of this elite seems to reflect the external task of the state; that task, as Poulantzas has argued, is to create the unity of a people-nation by organizing an unstable equilibrium of compromises.[16] As Poulantzas puts it, the state is a 'factor of cohesion,' but we see that within that 'cohesion' there is still an unequal distribution of the top positions in favour of the dominant classes and dominant ethnic categories.

Finally, the class origins of the provincial bureaucrats are examined in Table 11. Information on their origins was more difficult to obtain, which probably indicates that they are drawn from even lower in the class structure than the federal bureaucrats. Of those cases that were classifiable, 29 per cent came from below the middle class, compared to 15 per cent of the federal bureaucrats. Once again it should be noted that representation from below is related to provincial size in a centre-periphery sense. No members of the upper class were found among the bureaucrats from the two western provinces, and the proportion drawn from below the middle is almost double that of the two central provinces. It also is important to note that these few key provincial bureaucrats are mainly middle class in origin, as has been the case with all the statistical groups discussed in this paper. Table 11, together with the previous tables on federal bureaucrats and the tables on the class origins of cabinet ministers, all support the interpretation that the further one moves away from the centres of power within the state system, the lower the social origins of the elite are likely to be, and, conversely, the closer one moves towards the centres of power, the higher the social origins are likely to be. This can be taken as a summarizing generalization concerning the relationship between social origins and the occupancy of positions of state power in Canada.

In answer to the initial question of who directly holds the key positions of state in Canada the following answers have been given:

1 The Canadian state elite is primarily an elite composed of middle-class Canadian males of British and French ethnicity.
2 Representation in the elite has increased for French Canadians and for those who have middle-class origins.
3 The upper class maintains an advantaged position in the elite, while the working class has a very low level of representation.
4 British Canadians have declined but remain heavily over-represented, while all other ethnic groups are under-represented.

The question of the *social origins* of the state elite should not, however, be confused with issues regarding the *social functions* of the elite, which are discussed elsewhere in this volume. For example, it would be a mistake to assume that because the elite does not in the main have its origins in the capitalist class it is in any way an anti-capitalist elite. In the first place, there is an increased interconnection between private capital and the state in the post-war period. In the second place, the elite ensures in a general way the perpetuation and advancement of capitalism by organizing the framework of a nation-state and managing the general affairs of the economy. The mainly bicultural middle-class elite creates an unstable equilibrium of compromises in an effort to continually readjust the different sectors of the nation to capitalism and its developments. In this sense, the elite does what the capitalist class (with its own internal divisions and mainly upper-class British-Canadian composition) cannot do for itself.

Nor should the fact that the elite is nominally drawn from different social classes and ethnic categories be used to legitimize assertions that the Canadian state is 'democratic,' or that liberal-democratic institutions are thereby guaranteed. In the first instance, the elite for the most part is drawn from a very narrow slice of the Canadian population, with very little direct representation for the working class, women, and non-British, non-French ethnicities. It should also be remembered that in other countries middle-class state elites have just as often suspended liberal-democratic institutions and followed a policy of state repression in support of capitalism. The middle-class military elite in charge of the Brazilian state provides a good contemporary example.[17]

Finally, although the Canadian state has grown in scope, size, and power in the post-war period, it is by no means monolithic. Indeed, it is possible to argue that it is in many ways a rather fragile structure of alliances, one that is shot through with contradictions. The elite itself contains within it various classes and ethnic categories in an unstable alliance. There is the division among eleven different governments at the federal-provincial level; the division between and among all the various branches and departments of the state; and, finally, the division between the large and growing body of state workers and the small state elite. For all these reasons, it would be a serious political mistake to regard the Canadian state as immutable.

APPENDIX

Federal bureaucratic elite by department and civil service rank, 1973*

	DM3	DM2	DM1	SX3	Total
Agriculture		1		3	4
Communications			1	3	4
Consumer and Corporate Affairs		1	1	2	4
Energy, Mines and Resources		2	1	5	8
Environment		1	1	7	9
External Affairs	1		1	16	18
Finance	1	1	5	2	9
Health and Welfare		2	1	5	8
Indian Affairs and Northern Development		1		5	6
Industry, Trade and Commerce		1	1	4	6
Justice		2	3	3	8
Labour			3	2	5
Manpower and Immigration		1		6	7
National Defence		3	1	7	11
National Revenue		1	1	2	4
Post Office			1	2	3
Prime Minister's Office	1	2	3	2	8
Public Works		1		3	4
Regional Economic Expansion		1		6	7
Science and Technology		1		2	3
Secretary of State		3	2	9	14
Solicitor-General			3	6	9
Supply and Services			1	6	7
Transport		1		3	4
Treasury Board	1		2	1	4
Urban Affairs			1	2	3
Veterans' Affairs			1	2	3
Non-departmental†	2	2	3	3	10
Sub-total	6	28	37	119	190
Crown corporations					34
Total					224

* Annual salary ranges as of October 1973 were as follows: DM3 $50,000-$60,000; DM2 $44,000-$54,000; DM1 $37,500-$47,500; and SX3 $32,500-$41,500
† Includes the Auditor-General, Chairman of the Public Service Staff Relations Board, Chief Electoral Officer, Dominion Archivist, Master of the Mint, and various other non-departmental positions

220 **The state elites**

The following boards and commissions are included with the appropriate departments in the preceding list:

Department	Boards, commissions, or councils
Consumer and Corporate Affairs	Food Prices Review Board
Energy, Mines and Resources	National Energy Board
External Affairs	International Joint Commission
Finance	Tariff Board
Health and Welfare	Medical Research Council
Indian Affairs and Northern Development	Northwest Territories Council
Industry, Trade and Commerce	Metric Conversion Commission
	Statistics Canada
	Textile and Clothing Board
Justice	Tax Review Board
Labour	Canadian Labour Relations Board
	Information Canada
	Unemployment Insurance Commission
Manpower and Immigration	Immigration Appeal Board
National Defence	Defence Research Board
Prime Minister's Office	Economic Council of Canada
	Science Council of Canada
Secretary of State	Canada Council
	Canadian Radio-Television Commission
	National Arts Centre
	National Gallery
	National Library
	National Museum of Man
	Public Service Commission
Solicitor-General	Canadian Penitentiary Service
	National Parole Board
	Royal Canadian Mounted Police
Transport	Canadian Transport Commission

221 Dennis Olsen

The following units are included in the Crown corporations category:

Included in both the 1953 and 1973 studies

Atomic Energy of Canada
Atomic Energy Control Board
Bank of Canada
Canadian Broadcasting Corporation
Canadian Wheat Board
Central Mortgage and Housing Corporation
Crown Assets Disposal Corporation
Export Development Corporation
National Film Board
National Harbours Board
National Research Council

Added to 1973 study

Air Canada
Canadian Development Corporation
Canadian International Development Agency
Canadian National Railways
Canadian Transport Commission
Cape Breton Development Corporation
Eldorado Nuclear Limited
Farm Credit Corporation
National Capital Commission
St Lawrence Seaway Authority
Telesat Canada

Dropped from the 1953 list‡

Canadian Arsenals Limited
Canadian Commercial Corporation
Defence Construction Limited
Defence Production Limited

‡ Defence Production Limited no longer exists as a separate legal entity. In the other three cases, either those heading the corporation had a salary below the sx3 cut-off point or they were already included in the departmental list and held the Crown corporation position simultaneously.

Provincial bureaucratic elite,
sample by department* and province

	Quebec	Ontario	Alberta	British Columbia	Total
Agriculture	1	1	1	1	4
Consumer and Commercial Relations	2	1			3
Cultural Affairs/Recreation	1		1	1	3
Education	1	2	2	1	6
Environment		1	1		2
Finance/Intergovernmental Affairs	1	1			2
Health/Welfare†	1	2	3	2	8
Industrial Development/Trade/Tourism	1	1	1	2	5
Justice/Attorney-General	1	2	1	1	5
Labour/Manpower	1	1	1	1	4
Municipal Affairs	1		1	1	3
Natural Resources/Mines/Forests	2	2	2	2	8
Police	1	1			2
Premier's Office/Executive Council	1	2	1	1	5
Public Works/Government Services	1	1	1	1	4
Solicitor-General		1			1
Transportation/Communications	1	1	1	1	4
Treasury/Management Board	1	2	1		4
Crown corporations/Commissions/ Regulatory boards‡	5	7	5	4	21
Total	23	29	23	19	94

* The four provinces do not all have equivalent departments, or group functions together in the same way

† Welfare is called Social Development in some provinces

‡ This category included the following: Quebec – Quebec Hydro-Electric Commission, Quebec Securities Commission, Sidbec, Workman's Compensation Commission; Ontario – Civil Service Commission, Hydro-Electric Power Commission, Liquor Control Board, Ontario Energy Board, Ontario Municipal Board, Ontario Securities Commission, Workman's Compensation Board; Alberta – Alberta Government Telephones, Energy Resources Conservation Board, Hospital Services Commission, Workman's Compensation Board; British Columbia – Civil Service Commission, B.C. Hydro and Power Authority, Insurance Company of British Columbia, Workman's Compensation Board

NOTES

1 Nicos Poulantzas, 'On Social Classes,' *New Left Review,* 78 (March-April 1973), 42
2 Wallace Clement, *The Canadian Corporate Elite* (Toronto 1975), 232
3 Ralph Miliband, *The State in Capitalist Society* (London 1969), 54
4 (London 1973), 284-7
5 'The Problem of the Capitalist State,' in Robin Blackburn, ed., *Ideology in Social Science* (London 1972), 246
6 Poulantzas, 'The Capitalist State: A Reply to Miliband and Laclau,' *New Left Review,* 95 (Jan.-Feb. 1976)
7 The principal sources were: *Canadian Parliamentary Guide* (various years), *The Canadian Directory of Parliament, 1867-1967, The Canadian Who's Who* (various years), *Who's Who in Canada* (various years), other biographical dictionaries and encyclopaedia. In addition, biographical clippings from newspapers and periodicals were used along with biographical sketches obtained from the various government offices and departments.
8 For a good discussion of the ideologies and class fractions involved, see Gilles Bourque and Nicole Laurin-Frenette, 'Social Classes and Nationalist Ideologies in Quebec, 1760-1970,' in Gary Teeple, ed., *Capitalism and the National Question in Canada* (Toronto 1972), 194-200; but see also Hubert Guindon, 'Social Unrest, Social Class, and Quebec's Bureaucratic Revolution,' *Queen's Quarterly,* LXXI, 2 (Summer 1964).
9 *Vertical Mosaic* (Toronto 1965), 296
10 I have not tried to make direct comparisons with the Canadian corporate elite studied by Wallace Clement (1975). This would require a more detailed examination and discussion of the data. For those who are interested, Clement and I agree privately that the ethnic indicators are used equivalently and the following figures are a valid comparison of class origins: corporate elite, 49.4 per cent upper class; political-judicial elite, 22.4 per cent upper class; and federal bureaucratic elite, 10 per cent upper class.
11 'The Development of Class in Canada in the Twentieth Century,' in Teeple, *Capitalism and the National Question,* 141-83
12 *State in Capitalist Society,* 12
13 Porter, *Vertical Mosaic,* 391-2
14 The pool of candidates immediately below the elite level has mainly been British Canadian. The analysis of a lengthy question in the House of Commons in late 1966 showed the following distribution: of 1174 top public servants, 83 per cent were English mother tongue, 11.5 per cent were French mother tongue,

and 5.5 per cent had another mother tongue. The reply referred to public servants earning over $17,000 a year at the time. The data covered all the main de-
partments, agencies, and Crown corporations of the federal government; see
Chris Beattie, *Minority Men in a Majority Setting* (Toronto 1975), Table 5.1. It
should also be obvious by now that the cabinet's attempts to correct this imbalance by making order-in-council appointments from above – that is, by
'parachuting' in French Canadians at the top – does not solve the binational
contradictions in Canada but only recreates them within the state. On this
point, see especially Claude Morin, *Quebec versus Ottawa: The Struggle for Self-
government, 1960-72,* trans. Richard Howard (Toronto 1976), chap. 13.
15 *State in Capitalist Society,* 64
16 'The Capitalist State,' 71
17 For an interesting discussion of this, see Hermano Alves, 'Brazil: Martial
Mythologies,' in C. Harding and C. Roper, eds., *Latin American Review of Books*
(London 1973).

8
The corporate elite, the capitalist class, and the Canadian state

WALLACE CLEMENT

The corporate elite is the most powerful fraction of the capitalist class; it is the group of people who own, control, and manage the *largest* corporations in Canada. The capitalist class includes the individuals and their families who own, control, and manage (at a senior level) *all* corporations in Canada. In terms of an empirical analysis, it is practical to focus on the corporate elite for some purposes since they are more readily identifiable than the capitalist class as a whole; and, more significantly, they are the most powerful part of the capitalist class and control most of the privately owned capital in this country.

There are important fractions within the capitalist class and the corporate elite which require specification. The most important division is between corporations controlled indigenously by Canadians and those controlled by foreign capitalists through branch-plant operations. Related to this is the sector or activity of the economy the capitalists control – whether it is in finance, transportation, utilities, or the mass media where the indigenous fraction dominates or whether it is in secondary manufacturing or resources where the foreign-controlled fraction dominates. This paper will analyse, in a variety of ways, the relationship between these fractions of the capitalist class and the state in Canada, between 'public' and 'private' power.[1]

Before specific ties between various fractions of the capitalist class and the Canadian state are explored, the general character of this relationship merits some discussion. Initially, the structural relationship between the state and capitalism will be explored, followed by an empirical examination of connections between those who run the state and Canada's capitalists. The empirical material includes several levels on which this relationship is based: personal ties between state elites and the capitalist class, advisory boards established by the state, and a systematic analysis of previous and contemporary ties between members of the economic elite and the state system. Having done this, a number of different types of relations will be examined: state regulation of the economy, a case study of the recently established Royal Commission on Corporate Concentration, and the role of corporations in political party financing. The thesis of this paper is that the capitalist class and the state in Canada have enjoyed a very close association. In terms of fractions of the capitalist class, large foreign and Canadian capitalists have been effective in using the state apparatus to aggrandize their own power in their respective spheres of concentration while smaller national capitalists have often been left to 'fend for themselves.'

CAPITALISM AND THE STATE

One of the essential roles of the state in capitalist society is to create and protect the 'rights' of private property. These 'rights' are the basis of capitalist society for they sanction the claims of some classes to control others. Thus the institution of private property is predicated on the protection afforded it by the state. But the state itself has been shaped by private property in capitalist society. To change the economic functions of private property would be to alter radically the fundamental role of the state.

Since it is the capitalist class whose continued privileges depend upon the state remaining a capitalist state, it follows that this class will take actions to ensure its continuing existence. This principle has long been acknowledged by political economists. Writing in *The Wealth of Nations,* Adam Smith argued: 'It is only under the shelter of the civil magistrate that the owners of that valuable property, which is acquired by the labour of many years, or perhaps of many successive generations, can sleep a single night in security ... The acquisition of valuable and extensive property, therefore, necessarily requires the establishment of civil government.'[2] While the state would protect property, Smith believed that the forces of the market, the 'invisible hand' of many property holders, would protect the public from the power of property. This was an understandable argument given Smith's role in the struggle against the state-granted monopolies of mercantilism in favour of laissez-faire capitalism, but it is no longer a reasonable assumption in the era of corporate capitalism where a few dominant corporations are the seats of enormous power which negate the forces of the market.

Adam Smith was looking back to the emancipation of the bourgeoisie from the constraints of feudal society, and thus lauding the capture of the state by capitalist interests. On the other hand, Karl Marx identified the major roles of this newly formed state. In *The German Ideology,* written in 1845 and 1846, he maintained: 'By the mere fact that it is a *class* and no longer an *estate,* the bourgeoisie is forced to organize itself no longer locally, but nationally, and to give a general form to its mean average interest. Through the emancipation of private property from the community, the State has become a separate entity, beside and outside civil society; but it is nothing more than the form of organisation which the bourgeois necessarily adopt both for internal and external purposes, for the mutual guarantee of their property and interests.' While the state in capitalist society is essentially an instrument to ensure the 'rights' of capital and expedite its operation, there are a variety of ways this can be carried out, and, indeed, the state can have many different roles in regulating the specific relations between various capitalists and between the capitalist class and other classes. The particular character of the state is variable in Marx's framework, as the passage quoted earlier by Leo Panitch from the third volume of *Capital* makes quite evident. Only through empirical analysis can these qualities be identified for different states and different capitalist societies. This task is particularly important today since the size and scope of the state in all capitalist societies has expanded enormously. It is crucial to understanding the contemporary capitalist state to see that this expansion has not been undertaken at the expense of capitalism but rather to provide the conditions for its continued existence. Moreover, the state must take into account all the forces and movements in capitalist society if it is to maintain the stability required for the reproduction of capital.

At its most fundamental level capitalist society is shaped by the process of surplus creation and extraction – hence the focus of Marxism on the point of production and the major classes associated with the capitalist mode of production. These are the underlying features of capitalist society which shape class relations and determine the role the state will have in reproducing these relations. Again in *The German Ideology* Marx wrote: 'The material life of individuals, which by no means depends merely on their "will," their mode of production and form of intercourse, which mutually determine each other – this is the real basis of the State and remains so at all the stages at which division of labour and private property are still necessary, quite independently of the *will* of individuals. These actual relations are in no way created by the State power; on the contrary they are the power creating it ... Their [individuals who rule] personal power is based on conditions of life which as they develop are common to many individuals, and the continuance of which they, as ruling individuals, have to maintain against others and, at the same time, maintain they hold good for all.'[3]

Thus the actions of individuals and the role of the state are conditioned by the material conditions of the society. The paradox of the state in capitalist society is that it must strive to maintain its legitimacy and with that the legitimacy of capital by portraying itself as representing the common will of all its citizens, while at the same time upholding the right of some to extract the surplus created by others. As C.B. Macpherson has argued: 'political power, being power over others, is used in any unequal society to extract benefit from the ruled for the rulers. Focus on the *source* of political power puts out of the field of vision any perception of the necessary *purpose* of political power in any unequal society, which is to maintain the extractive power of the class or classes which have extractive power.'[4] This is certainly contrary to the commonly held view, presented by the state and by capitalist ideology, that the state acts simply as a 'sounding board' for all interests in society and that all citizens are responded to equally. In fact, if capitalists' rhetoric is to be accepted at face value, the state has become a threat to their 'free' operation.[5]

Given the dominant ideology in Canada of a state equally accessible to all and acting in the common interest, it remains an important task to analyse empirically the actual nature of the relationship between the capitalist class and the state. Even though theoretically it can be contended that the state must act to ensure the rights of capitalists in liberal democracies, it is by no means a widely accepted view among Canadians that this is the case. Thus it remains an important task to destroy the dominant ideology that shrouds the role of Canada's state and to explore the real nature of that relationship. But, in doing this, it remains important to keep two things in mind: first, the purpose of the state in capitalist society is to create the conditions for the extraction of surplus by some classes for the aggrandizement of others; and, second, one must avoid falling into the argument that the state acts simply as a front for capitalists. As Panitch's article has already pointed out, it is necessary 'to distinguish between the state acting on *behalf* of the bourgeoisie from its acting on their *behest.*' That is, the state does not act at the command of the capitalist class but for its interests or, more correctly, in its *general interest.* Since the capitalist class in Canada is a fractionalized one in terms of size and control, it is also important to understand the particular as well as the general interests being served. Moreover, in its attempt to provide the conditions for capital accumulation, the state is the major instrument for creating class harmony. Thus, a great deal of state policy is directed at moderating the glaring inequalities of capitalism towards this end, but it draws the line at the greatest inequality, that of the private power of property.

PERSONAL TIES BETWEEN THE CORPORATE WORLD AND THE STATE

The period of simultaneous direct participation in state offices and the corporate world is past (except for the dinosaur institution of the Senate). The increasing complexity of an industrial society has required a relatively autonomous state capable of responding to various capitalist class fractions and other demands from the society to provide necessary conditions for stability. However, this has not prevented other types of connections – career-switching, kinship ties, and advisory posts – all of which reflect an affinity and community of interest between the top of the state and corporate worlds. Personal ties are social indicators of relationships based on the structural relationship already discussed between the state and economy in capitalist society. These ties have been particularly intimate in Canada; an interesting exchange gives an unusual indication of this intimacy: 'A conversation last week about the issues raised when businessmen go into government and then have to deal with people from their former field eventually got around to Jack Austin. Mr. Austin, a mining promoter and lawyer, became deputy minister of Energy, Mines and Resources (before moving on to the Prime Minister's Office). When the subject of a possible conflict of interest came up, he was fond of saying that "you can't get virgins with experience." When this quote was tossed back to a senior civil servant working on the current problem he replied: "Yeah, but we don't want prostitutes with an air of innocence either." '[6]

In these terms there have been few 'virgins' (not to take the implication to the opposite extreme) in the highest state offices in Canada. A review of Canada's prime ministers from Robert Borden to Pierre Trudeau indicates the strength of business connections in this highest political office.[7] The most conspicuous links are with the dominant corporations in Canada.[8] Borden was a corporation lawyer, director of the Bank of Nova Scotia, and founder, with Sir Charles Tupper (an earlier Conservative prime minister), of the Crown Life Insurance Company before becoming prime minister from 1911 to 1920. After leaving politics he became president of Barclay's Bank (Canada) and president of Crown Life. Borden was succeeded in office by Arthur Meighen who was a prime minister between 1920 and 1921 and again in 1926. Meighen was also a lawyer allied with the Toronto financial community and managed to hold numerous financial offices. William Lyon Mackenzie King, prime minister from 1921 to 1926, 1926 to 1930, and 1935 to 1948, a total of over twenty-one years, was a grandson of the 'rebel leader' William Lyon Mackenzie. Before entering electoral politics he had become a wealthy man, largely through gifts and payments from corporations. Not the least of his sources of wealth was the Rockefeller family, with King serving as an adviser to John D. Rockefeller and becoming deputy minister of labour and labour minister before becoming prime minister.[9] From 1930 to 1935 Richard Bedford Bennett was prime minister. He was a lawyer and financier before entering politics and later became president of Calgary Power, owner of the E.B. Eddy Match Company, and a director of Imperial Oil and the Royal Bank (the latter position he also held before entering politics). Louis Stephen St Laurent was a corporation lawyer and before entering politics was a financier and director of Metropolitan Life and the Bank of Montreal. After acting as prime minister from 1948 to 1957, he became chairman of Rothmans of Pall Mall Canada and a director of IAC Limited.

Unlike the previous five prime ministers, John George Diefenbaker, in office from 1957 to 1963, Lester Bowles Pearson, in office from 1963 to 1968, and the current prime minister, Pierre Elliott Trudeau, did not have extensive corporate careers. Diefenbaker is a criminal lawyer without a business career and remains in politics today (thus not having a post-political business career). Pearson's early career was with the Department of External Affairs, later acting as Canadian ambassador to Washington. His political career was financed by big capital, most notably by Walter Gordon, and his post-political career included a directorship on Crown Life (a dominant corporation). Trudeau's father made a fortune of $1.4 million in 1933 by selling his chain of gas stations and automobile association to Imperial Oil, thus leaving the present prime minister independently wealthy. Although marrying late, he married well. His father-in-law is James Sinclair, a former minister in the St Laurent cabinet, and currently deputy chairman of Canada Cement Lafarge and a director of Alcan Aluminium, Canadian Industries, Sun Life, and the Bank of Montreal; all five are among Canada's largest 113 corporations. Apart from having surrounded themselves with cabinets heavily laden with businessmen, there have been no shortages of direct and family links between Canada's prime ministers and its corporate elite. Indeed, four members of the current economic elite are directly related to these prime ministers (Meighen's and St Laurent's sons, Borden's nephew, and Sinclair), between them holding no less than twenty dominant directorships!

David Nock has summarized the relationship between federal cabinets and big business. For the Conservative cabinet of the Bennett government, sixteen of twenty-three members (70 per cent) 'had a close relationship to some form of business,' as did twenty-one of the thirty-four members (62 per cent) of the Diefenbaker cabinet, 'either before or after their cabinet tenure.' For the Liberal government between 1935 and 1957, thirty-seven of fifty-eight cabinet members (64 per cent) 'held some important business position before or after their tenure of office.'[10] Using a different approach to this issue in his article in this volume, Dennis Olsen's analysis of the political elite in Canada between 1961 and 1973 finds that 'a minimum of 16 per cent of the *elected* members of this [political] elite were connected to substantial family wealth before they entered politics.' Focusing on changes over time, Olsen finds that 'about 27 per cent of the volume of circulation through the federal cabinet involves those who have had, or will have, business or corporate roles.' This represents an increase from 18 per cent of those in the federal cabinet between 1940 and 1960 who had prior business careers to 27 per cent of those in this office between 1960 and 1973. Of those leaving, 9 per cent during the earlier period and 19 per cent during the latter have left for full-time business careers.

Within the Trudeau cabinets the prominence of kinship ties to the current corporate elite are readily apparent: Jeanne Sauvé's husband, Maurice (himself a former minister in Pearson's government), is a vice-president of Consolidated-Bathurst and a director of BP Canada; C.M. Drury's son, Chipman, is chairman of Montreal Life Insurance; James Richardson's brother, George Taylor, is president of James Richardson and Sons, governor of the Hudson's Bay Company, and a director of the Canadian Imperial Bank of Commerce, Hudson's Bay Gas and Oil, and the International Nickel Company of Canada. Moreover, some of the departed members of the Trudeau cabinet quickly found their way into Canada's most powerful boardrooms. Before being recalled to head the Anti-Inflation Board, Jean-Luc Pépin was welcomed into the boardrooms of Bombardier, Canada Steamship Lines, Celanese Canada, Westinghouse Canada, and the biggest boardroom of all, Power Corporation. As if to upstage his former Department of Consumer and Corporate Affairs colleague, John Napier Turner, former minister of finance and cabinet minister from 1965 to 1975, immediately became a partner in the Toronto law firm of MacMillan, Binch and was recruited to the boards of Crown Life Insurance, Crédit Foncier, Marathon Realty, Canadian Investment Fund, and, to round it off, Canadian Pacific (CP). This caused the *Globe and Mail* on 22 March 1976 to herald his 'instant adoption into the corporate fraternity,' noting that 'Turner's knowledge of how a Cabinet is likely to approach a problem or how the civil service is likely to present it to its ministers will be of considerable value to CP or any other company with a major interface with government without one door being opened or one telephone call made.' Still other members of the Trudeau cabinets had their careers in dominant corporations before their political careers. Mitchell Sharp, for example, was closely associated with James Richardson and Sons before joining the Department of Finance and becoming deputy minister of industry, trade and commerce. Leaving this bureaucratic elite post after the Liberal defeat in 1958, he joined the corporate elite as a vice-president of Brascan where he stayed until 1962, after which time he served in Liberal cabinets as minister of finance, industry, trade and commerce, and external affairs.

Intimacy is not a quality confined to Canada's political elite – Canada's bureaucratic elite has done quite well itself in the corporate world.[11] For example, Michael Pitfield, 'one of Canada's most powerful civil servants – clerk of Privy Council, secretary of the federal cabinet and key advisor to Prime Minister Pierre Trudeau,'[12] is brother to Ward Chipman Pitfield, president of Pitfield, Mackay and Ross and a director of M. Loeb Limited and Husky Oil (as well as chairman of the Investors Dealers Association, 'the national self-regulating body of the securities industry'), as well as brother-in-law to Ross T. Clarkson, chairman of Caribonum (Canada) and a director of National Trust. Like politicians, many senior bureaucrats are 'instantly adopted' by the corporate world upon leaving. For example, Simon Reisman was immediately 'snatched up' by George Weston Limited and became a director of Burns Foods after leaving his post as deputy minister of finance, also setting up a consulting firm in Ottawa with James Gundy who happens to be the former deputy minister of industry, trade and commerce.

Of course, the Senate – that institution established to represent directly business in the state – is rampant with connections with the economic world, but they would be too numerous to list. Suffice it to say that seventeen members of the current economic elite have enjoyed the privilege of Senate membership. This is a time-honoured tradition. For example, of the 308 senators between 1925 and 1962, 62.4 per cent were found to be from law, manufacturing, commerce, or finance while only two (0.6 per cent) represented labour.[13] Louis Giguere, the Liberal senator involved in the Sky Shops scandal, is reported to have said: 'What's wrong with having a senator do a little business now and then? ... Do Canadians expect senators to be drawn from the ranks of the Salvation Army or something?'[14]

The importance of the close relationship between the Canadian state elite and the capitalist class is not that all positions in the state elite are 'snatched up' by members of the capitalist class. Indeed, many capitalists expressly avoid the kind of public exposure that goes with any elected office. (But, as will be shown, election is a prerequisite for only a small proportion of important state positions.) The important point is that an understanding of the ties between the economic elite and the state as a whole challenges the postulate that the state performs an unbiased role as manager of society for the benefit of all. The Canadian case illustrates that the highest levels of the state include many members who are directly from the corporate elite or are connected with them through close kinship ties. From this it would seem reasonable to deduce on empirical grounds alone that the state in Canada does not operate autonomously from the capitalist class.

Dennis Olsen's study deals with the relationship between the state and the economic world from the perspective of the state. The data here examine the relationship between those holding senior executive positions and directorships in Canadian dominant corporations (the economic elite) and various positions within the state system from the perspective of the economic elite. Table 1 demonstrates that one-third of the 1975 Canadian-born members of the economic elite held in the past, or continued to hold, positions directly within the state system. Moreover, 47 per cent were either themselves or had close kin who were in the state system at a senior level.

As the data illustrate, members of the Canadian economic elite had in the past, and many frequently still, operated directly within the state system. Thirty-seven members of the 1975 Canadian economic elite were recruited from political or bureaucratic elite posts while seventeen had been or continued to be senators. As well, there were another seventy-five who had served in other political or bureaucratic posts for the state, bringing the total proportion who had served the state in a full-time capacity to 18 per cent of the economic elite. Besides full-time positions within the state, there were a series of part-time advisory and decision-making roles such as Crown corporation boards, royal commissions, and other boards and commissions all directly within the state system which brings to one-third the proportion of the 1975 economic elite who had or continued to have direct positions within the state system. Of the over three hundred positions within the state system held by members of the economic elite, a mere handful have involved submitting themselves directly to election; the vast majority have been appointed positions.

The importance of these direct and kinship ties between the economic elite and the state system cannot be overstressed. They mean that this set of people, more than any others, are those taken into account by the state. Indeed, they are very often those directly establishing policy on behalf of the state. In periods of crisis this has been particularly apparent. During the Second World War the senior ranks of the state bureaucracy swelled with members of the economic elite drawn in to run the state machinery and guide the process of rapid industrialization. Within the current economic

Table 1

The economic elite of 1975 and the state system

Economic elite with state affiliations (current and past)	N	Cumulative[a] N	%
Direct personal affiliations:			
From political or bureaucratic elite	37	37	5
Senators	17	49	7
Wartime bureaucracy	53	88	13
Other political or bureaucratic posts	38	124	18
Crown corporations	45	160	23
Royal commissions	26	170	25
Boards or commissions	84	219	32
Party executive[b]	13	225	33
Kinship ties:[c]			
In political or bureaucratic elite	91	278	40
Senate	23	293	44
Member of Parliament	38	315	46
Lieutenant-Governor	12	318	47

This table is based on an updated sample of the 1972 Canadian-born economic elite (N = 683): this revised sample represents an 84.4 per cent coverage as opposed to 81.9 per cent used in *The Canadian Corporate Elite,* chaps. 5 and 6, pp. 259-63. In addition to the increased coverage, the quality of the data used in this table is better than that of the earlier sample because of the availability of additional material. See my *Continental Corporate Power: Economic Elite Linkages between Canada and the United States* (Toronto 1977).

[a] Does not include those already mentioned in an above category

[b] While party executive is not a position directly within the state system as identified by Miliband, it does provide a particularly close individual tie to the state apparatus.

[c] Includes fathers, fathers-in-law, brothers, grandfathers, and, in a few cases, uncles

elite there are fifty-three members who held senior positions within the wartime bureaucracy. Not only did they control the state machinery during this period, they established important connections most useful for later business ventures. As Peter Newman has noted, 'When the dollar-a-year men fanned out at the close of World War II to run the nation they had helped to create, the attitudes, the working methods, and the business ethic they took with them determined the country's economic and political course for the next three decades.' Their experience forged them into an intimate set of people, well acquainted with one another and the operation of the state. Newman says: 'They had come to Ottawa as individuals; they left as an elite.'[15]

When the state elite wants advice it turns to the most powerful members of society. One of the formalized ways this occurs today is through advisory boards to various ministers. For example, a July 1976 *Financial Post* article, 'The People Who Have Jamieson's Ear,' says: 'Industry, Trade & Commerce Minister Donald Jamieson has come to count heavily on his high-level Advisory Council.' Jamieson said: 'World competition is getting tougher and tougher. But we in the government tend to use funds to help the faltering companies. It becomes more and more clear that we need to decide which of our industries – which sectors of industry – can do best in the world.' With the state elite deciding which corporations it will be feeding through its loans and subsidies, it is important for members of the economic elite to be in touch to ensure that a share is directed their way. In the same article Clive Baxter says: 'Jamieson appears delighted with the flow of information he is getting through the council – he says that some of it helped a lot in drafting parts of the federal budget last month.'[16]

Just who are the thiry-seven men who make up this advisory council to Industry, Trade and Commerce, who have Jamieson's ear, and who are involved in drafting federal budgets? It is clear that the economic elite has the greatest access to the board. Of the thirty-seven members, twenty (54 per cent) are directly from the economic elite, between them representing forty dominant corporations. What kind of dominant corporations are represented? The most heavily represented sector is finance, with sixteen of the forty dominant directorships from this sector, including nine from Canada's top five banks (all of which are represented) with four from the Bank of Montreal alone. Eight are from the transportation/utilities sector (including three from Canadian Pacific), eight from manufacturing, six from resource companies, and two from trade. The dominant companies represented are mainly Canadian-controlled (twenty-seven), followed by six from the United States, and only one each from the United Kingdom and elsewhere, while another five are joint Canada-United States consortia. Similarly, the elite members themselves are mainly indigenous Canadian capitalists (thirteen), with five US compradors (that is, whose main affiliation is with a us-controlled company), and one each are UK and other compradors. Besides the twenty members of the economic elite who clearly dominate this advisory board, there are another seventeen capitalists from smaller companies. They are even more likely to be indigenous Canadian capitalists and associated with Canadian companies. Of the seventeen, fourteen are from Canadian companies, two from us-controlled ones, and one is associated with a UK-controlled company. Of all thirty-seven members, twenty-seven are indigenous Canadian capitalists while the other ten owe their main power position to foreign capital.

Canada's capitalists are certainly given ample opportunity to have their wishes heard within the Canadian state, especially those from finance and transportation which account for 60 per cent of all dominant directorships represented on the advisory council. It would be wrong, however, to think that their collective wish is to inhibit the entry of foreign capitalists. Rather, from the beginning of the Canadian state, Canada's capitalists have encouraged the state to stimulate the entry of foreign capital. The largest Canadian capitalists are not in conflict with foreign capitalists but in alliance, an issue to be returned to later.

Before leaving the subject of advisory boards, one further example illustrates economic elite dominance in these kinds of forums. It also indicates another bias of both the state and economic systems in Canada. Of all the advisory boards, the one most likely to provide an avenue for women's views in the corporate world would be one on 'the business community's progress on status of women issues' created by Marc Lalonde, as minister responsible for the status of women. Reflecting the lack of women in the economic elite – that set of people the state seems insistent on consulting – there is only one woman on the eight-person board. Six of the eight are members of the economic elite, with one of the others a former president of the Canadian Broadcasting Corporation and the other a president of RCA Limited.[17] Half of the members of this advisory board hold directorships in one of Canada's dominant banks, but there is room made for only one woman. Quite a reflection on whom the state elite perceives as their most important constituency, even when the issue is women in business!

STATE REGULATION AND INVESTIGATION

On another front, it is important to examine the increasing role of the state in regulating business. While it is certainly correct that there is increasing state regulation of business, it is important to be careful how this is interpreted and whose interests are being served. In a perceptive passage columnist Geoffrey Stevens writes: 'The prospect of greater use of regulatory powers ought, I submit, to cause real concern. But not concern on the part of corporation presidents. Concern, rather, on the part of ordinary workers and consumers who look to the 100-plus federal regulatory agencies to protect their interest and who are too often disappointed. Surely it is time to explode the myth that government regulation is antithetical to the interest of business. With few exceptions (and the CRTC may be one of them), regulation operates mainly for the benefit of the industry which is regulated.'[18]

Stevens goes on to examine the case of the Canadian Transport Commission and its relationship with Bell Canada which trades off its monopoly position for guaranteed profits through government regulation. Recently the CTC granted Bell Canada its full request for a $110.3 million rate increase. Bell has been known to spend upwards of $1 million on an application which, ironically, is tax-deductible and actually calculated into the rates. Compared to Bell's army of accountants and lawyers, 'there was only token public representation at the 26 days of CTC hearings and it was, in the Commission's judgement, too weak or too ill-informed to merit serious consideration.'

But the problem runs deeper than this question of unequal resources for all parties to appear before regulatory boards. The basic assumption of the board is a 'fair rate of return' on capital invested. The state gives the company a monopoly over a certain territory (in Bell's case most of Canada's industrial heartland) thus restricting the consumers' choice to either use Bell or go without a telephone. But, in return, Bell makes the 'sacrifice' of having its profit return guaranteed. Quite a sacrifice. Moreover, only part of its operation is regulated, while the production end – through its subsidiary Northern Telecom which supplies Bell's equipment – is able to make whatever it can selling to its parent.

Given this, it is little wonder, as Michael J. Trebilcock, chairman of the Consumers' Association of Canada's advocacy committee, notes that 'most of the extensively regulated industries, at least, prefer being regulated to competing and actively seek and sustain accommodating regulatory regimes.' Trebilcock goes on to quote John Turner when he was minister of consumer and corporate affairs as saying: 'I've looked at a lot of regulatory agencies, and the longer I'm around here, the more I believe that every one of these tends, in a period of time, to reflect the interests of the industry it is supposed to be regulating.'[19]

Turner's observations certainly fit for the Foreign Investment Review Board. At least publicly, opposition to the FIRB was recorded by the dominant capitalists in Canada (through the Bankers' Association of Canada, the Canadian Chamber of Commerce, the Canadian Manufacturers' Association, and the Mining Association of Canada) when the scheme was first announced. Thus there was a unified response by the dominant fractions of the comprador and indigenous capitalist class, both expressing concern over possible restrictions on the free movement of capital. They were concerned, in fact, that even the *appearance* of restriction would inhibit foreign investment. The state elites, however, were fully aware of the ideological value of such a review process and, in a minority government situation with pressure from the New Democratic Party, appeared to be following the interests of the Canadian Federation of Independent Business which represents small Canadian capitalists – that is, those threatened by foreign takeovers and manipulated by the two dominant fractions of the capitalist class in Canada. It would not be correct to argue in this case that the state acted against the interests of the dominant fractions of the capitalist class; the state was simply looking after the 'common affairs' of the dominant class. It is not that the dominant capitalists are concerned about state intervention; they have frequently encouraged such interventions. Rather, they were concerned how the controls would be used and by whom.

It is always important to look beyond the level of state policy to that of actual practice, and here the record of the FIRB speaks for itself. As of mid-1976, it had approved 84 per cent of all the applications for takeovers and 94 per cent of new foreign businesses. Rather than a 'screen,' it has become a 'funnel' for foreign direct investment by steering this capital towards particular activities. There is an appearance of action, but the FIRB is a lion without teeth, a giant public relations exercise to 'cool out' nationalist sentiment. Neither its purpose nor its practice is to prevent foreign control over the Canadian economy. This could be accomplished much more simply and effectively.

In areas where Canadian capitalists are strong, particularly in banking, life insurance, trust companies, transportation, utilities, and the mass media, the state has provided strong protection against foreign control. In these areas, legislation prohibits foreign capitalists from owning sufficient stock to control or take over companies thus protecting the 'turf' of Canadian capitalists. But legislation (as in the FIRB) to 'protect' other areas such as retail trade, manufacturing, and resources, although recommended on several occasions, has only recently been enacted. Moreover, the Foreign Investment Review Act simply reviews or examines proposed takeovers of Canadian companies in these sectors by foreign capitalists, and there are no across-the-board prohibitions (as in the other areas) or any effect on the many companies which already exist. This difference between various sectors of the economy reflects in legislation the historical development of these sectors under the command of either indigenous or foreign-controlled capitalists; that is, the law is a mirror of the economic power structure of Canadian society.

In terms of who is administering the act, the dominant fractions of the capitalist class have little to be concerned about. Head of the FIRB since

1974 has been James Richard Murray, educated in McGill's undergraduate and law programs. His father is James Richard Murray, former chairman of the Canadian Wheat Board (and thus part of the bureaucratic elite) and director of such companies as Federal Grain and Buckerfields. The son was with the Foreign Service Office, Department of External Affairs, Canadian Embassy in Washington from 1945 to 1950. He then joined the Hudson's Bay Company and became its managing director as well as a vice-chairman of the US-controlled Hudson's Bay Gas and Oil Company, and a director of the Canadian-controlled Royal Trust. He dropped these directorships and his other directorships on Air Canada and *Time* Canada before becoming head of the government's screening agency. He will have plenty of opportunity to discuss state policy with his corporate elite colleagues in the club rooms of such exclusive men's clubs as the Vancouver and Mount Royal clubs. He represents one of the few cases of movement from the economic elite to the bureaucratic elite in recent times, but presumably his job, like that of Jean-Luc Pepin who was also recalled from the corporate world to head the Anti-Inflation Board, warranted someone perceived as 'safe' by both the state and corporate elite and experience in both. Pepin, as would be expected, turned out to be the right choice – for the corporate world at least. The record of the AIB illustrates its propinquity to control wages while in the long run profits have only been enhanced.[20]

Another area related to state regulation is that of government investigations. The most recent example which some may perceive as a threat to dominant capitalists is the Royal Commission on Corporate Concentration. Once again, such a perception would be misplaced, ignoring the ideological value of such ventures and the adaptability of dominant capitalists to such situations. Why was this royal commission called? Prime Minister Trudeau's official reason, in his press release announcing it on 22 April 1975, said: 'With current activities suggesting that further large-scale concentration of corporate power in Canada may be taking place, particularly in relation to conglomerate enterprises, the Government has decided that it is necessary at this time to inquire into whether and to what extent such concentrations of corporate power confer sufficient social and economic benefit to Canadian society as to be in the public interest.' But this is no more than 'motherhood' – political rhetoric for public consumption. A more revealing reason appears in another not so well prepared comment by Trudeau in *Hansard* on the same day: 'I would certainly agree that in a constitutional sense the government has the power to act [to curb corporations]. I do not agree that in a legal sense we have made laws which permit us to interfere with the rules of the game as they are now played legally by the corporate players.' What does this more candid statement mean? It means that Trudeau and the other Liberals have been unable to have as much impact on Canada's economy – its inflation rates and unemployment, both volatile political issues – through the traditional fiscal mechanisms of the state as they would like, and they have decided to turn attention towards the real economy, the private economy, that directs this country. It has been decided that some of the political heat, particularly stimulated by the Power Corporation's attempt to take over Argus Corporation, will be shoved off onto the nebulous 'business community' and buried in a royal commission. In other words, the focus will be off the Liberal government, at least for a while, leaving a public impression that 'something is being done.'

What does this mean? It does not mean, as Peter Newman has suggested, a 'show-down' between business and government.[21] If that were the case, the commission members would be radically different from the ones Trudeau selected. Newman should have investigated who runs the commission and what interests are served – the interests of big business and giant corporations: the very institutions that are supposed to be investigated. Robert Bryce, head of the commission, was himself one of the most powerful civil servants during most of the 1960s when, as Trudeau said, the laws were *not* made to interfere with the 'rules of the game' of the 'corporate players.' Bryce's father was a member of the economic elite, as is another commissioner, Pierre Nadeau, currently president of Petrofina and a director of the Royal Bank. The third commissioner and the chief research director have both made their careers servicing corporate giants.[22] Not a likely lot for a 'show-down.'

What then will the conclusions of the commission most likely be?[23] Even before the commission got underway the research director, Donald Thompson, already gave a strong indication. 'Big, big business is beautiful,' according to a *Globe and Mail* profile which quotes Thompson as saying: 'I hope the organization will tell us about the positive side of the social implications of large size. It could be that we will conclude, not that there's too much corporate concentration but that there's too little.'[24] As if dominant corporations and the capitalists needed an invitation!

Following Mr Thompson's obviously unbiased perspective, it is likely that the commission will find that what Canada needs is to develop some score of giant multinational companies that will be able to operate on a world scale to help strengthen Canada's economic position. This seems to be the theme hummed by the dominant capitalists and their spokesmen in the state system. Ontario treasurer, Darcy McKeough, said before the Bryce Commission that 'the size of the postal workers union is more of a problem than the size of Massey-Ferguson or Argus Corporation.' That depends upon whose 'problems' McKeough is talking about. His are quite obviously seen from a corporate perspective, as the following statement attributed to him also suggests: 'Judged by international standards, many of our firms are of sub-optimal size.'[25] A similar theme is again taken up by Don McGilivray in the *Monetary Times* (9 May 1976), when he asks: 'Are Canadian corporations becoming giants at home but pygmies abroad?' Although cast in more technocratic language, Robert Bryce's answer to this question indicates his internalization of the perspective of big business. He is reported to have said: 'There are a lot of these oligopolies in Canada which aren't against the law and which, in fact, reflect the situation that we have a limited number of big companies that are able to compete internationally working in a reasonably moderate sized market in Canada.'[26]

In addition to this major conclusion, or justification, the commission is likely to recommend some type of greater disclosure of information by corporations to the state (long overdue in Canada) and, along with this, a hope that corporations will work more closely with the state in determining economic policy. It clearly will not touch the fundamentals of the private exercise of power and the private advantages accruing from this power. It will hardly find any necessity for corporations to become accountable to their workers or to consumers or for any real democratization or decentralization of the economy. But what about the 'social benefits' mentioned in the mandate? It is unlikely that the commission will ever even come to a real understanding of what this means. Here is what the research director has already said: ' "That word, 'social,' has troubled everyone who's read it" [Thompson] says. Most of the work on the social implications of large scale size has been done by sociologists rather than economists, and Mr. Thompson feels that sociological research is "soft" and unreliable.'[27] Research is 'unreliable,' presumably, when its conclusions do not match the predisposition of the commissioners. The dice have been loaded well in advance to determine the outcome of such an inquiry.

All this aside, what does the government do with the massive reports it commissions? In other words, what differences do such inquiries really make (aside from their obvious ideological value)? The most recent example of a similar study is the *Senate Report on the Mass Media*, an impressive document in terms of its data if not in its conclusions. In spite of its shortcomings, the *Report* resulted in an anti-trust action against the Irving media interests in New Brunswick, a commendable undertaking and the first of its kind in the highly concentrated media world. But, after some delay, the Irving interests had the court ruling overturned (both in New Brunswick and in the Supreme Court of Canada) and today roll happily along as before.

What has changed in the media since the *Report* was filed? Quite a bit. The *Report* found there to be enormous concentration within the media that was detrimental to everyone's interests except, of course, those few who controlled the media. It identified the largest media complexes in the country in 1970 but since then some interesting changes have been occurring. Telemedia Quebec, one of the largest fifteen, was acquired by Montreal Trust, itself a subsidiary of Power Corporation, adding to Power's already extensive newspaper holdings in Quebec which put it among one of the original fifteen largest. Then Standard Broadcasting, itself a subsidiary of Argus Corporation, took over Bushnell Communications, another of the fifteen largest.[28] This takeover was accomplished with the approval of the Canadian Radio-television and Telecommunications Commission (CRTC) which provided Standard with a telegram to that effect. Since the Senate *Report*, in addition to a multitude of smaller newspapers being bought out by the largest chains, *four* of the *fifteen* largest entire complexes have been reduced to two, and, if the Power-Argus deal eventually works out, these four would be reduced to *one*.[29]

But does this ownership of the media – or any economic corporation for that matter – make any difference? There is some strong evidence that it does. In a *New York Times* article of 6 April 1975 entitled 'Paul Desmarais, An Aggressive French-Canadian' the following is reported: 'Three years ago, his largest newspaper, *La Presse* in Montreal, was closed by a long and bitter strike, with the employees seeking a greater measure of control. "Nobody is going to control this paper," Mr. Desmarais said. "It's my newspaper. If they want control, let them start their own newspaper." That strike represented a showdown with the Quebec separatists among editors and reporters. Mr. Desmarais won the battle.'

It does matter who owns and controls media complexes and economic corporations, but the history of government investigations into such matters is one of inaction and inadequate response to the conditions uncovered. Only recommendations the government is predisposed towards are carried out, and the investigators themselves are carefully selected to work within the framework of capitalism for their solutions.

POLITICAL PARTY FINANCING

Political party financing has long been an obvious source of corporate influence on politicians. Even in a non-election year, the two major parties use about $2 million annually to keep their political machines lubricated. The grease is supplied by the dominant corporations, as Geoffrey Stevens has pointed out: 'The two major parties are heavily dependent on contributions from the corporate sector. The chartered banks are their ranking angels. In fiscal 1974-75, the Bank of Montreal gave the Liberals $25,000, plus another $25,000 in prepayment of its 1975-76 contribution; it gave the Conservatives one payment of $50,000. The Canadian Imperial Bank of Commerce donated $26,233.20 to the Liberals and $26,000 to the Tories. For the Royal Bank, it was $25,360 to the Grits and $25,100 to the Tories. For the Toronto-Dominion Bank, $20,261.60 to the Liberals and $20,800 to the Conservatives, and for the Bank of Nova Scotia, $20,180 to the Liberals and $21,000 to the Tories.'

Thus, between them, Canada's five dominant banks supplied $285,000 in contributions to the two dominant parties in one non-election year. They were not alone, however: 'Alberta Gas Trunk Line Co. Ltd., a member of the Foothills group which is seeking to build an all-Canadian gas pipeline up the Mackenzie River, contributed $15,270 to the Liberals then covered its bet with $15,000 to the Conservatives ... Following is a partial list of some of the larger contributions to the Liberal Party, with their donations to the Tories in parenthesis. British Columbia Forest Products, $10,000 ($10,000); Crown Zellerbach, $5,000 ($5,000); Falconbridge Nickel, $4,000 ($4,000); International Nickel, $25,700 ($25,800); Noranda Mines, $15,000 ($15,983); Gulf Oil, $21,449.60 ($21,703); Southam Press, $10,000 ($10,000); London Life, $6,000 ($6,000); Dow Chemical, $10,840 ($10,109.80); Dominion Foundries and Steel, $25,000 ($25,183); IBM, $5,880 ($6,183); Moore Corp., $5,000 ($5,000); Molson Companies, $8,200 ($8,373.20); Weyerhaeuser Canada Ltd., $5,000 ($5,000). Even Denison Mines, whose chairman, Stephen Roman, ran unsuccessfully for the Tories in the 1974 election, proved even-handed in its 1974-75 donations – $25,000 to the Liberals and $26,000 to the Conservatives ... On the other side of the coin, department stores seem to prefer Conservatives. Eaton's of Canada gave the Tories $26,368 and the Liberals $15,000; for Simpsons-Sears, it was Conservatives $13,330, Liberals $700.'[30]

Twenty-five of the top corporations operating in Canada gave nearly $400,000 to each of the two dominant parties in 1975. There is little difference in party choice for foreign-controlled firms or those firms that are consortia of Canadian and US capital; in fact, if there is any difference, it is a slight preference for the Conservatives who received an average of $11,618 from the ten foreign-controlled or related firms examined, compared to an average of $10,384 for the Liberals.

This type of reliance for party funding will ultimately be expressed in the type of approach the state takes towards the corporate world. In his comprehensive analysis of this question, K.Z. Paltiel was led to conclude that 'overdependence of parties on any single source or socio-economic group inevitably narrows the freedom of action of political decision-makers. Such parties tend to become the spokesmen of narrow social interests losing the aggregative function attributed to parties in liberal-democratic thought.'[31] Even within the capitalist class there are few corporations like the Bank of Montreal that could manage to give the two major parties $100,000 between them without feeling the pinch.

The fact that Canada's top corporations give, and the two major political parties receive, such large donations reflects the ideological affinity between them. For the corporations they are a form of 'insurance' and leverage enabling them to keep avenues of access open. For political parties and politicians, they defray the costs of campaigning. To 'bite the hand that feeds them' would certainly jeopardize their ability to be re-elected. Nevertheless, this must be perceived in the broadest sense. Specific corporations and specific capitalists may be rejected by state actions because their particular interests are in conflict with the general interest of the capitalist class and the state. Very seldom, however, are the general interests of labour taken into account at the expense of capital. The bias of the Canadian state is in favour of capital over labour and big capital (whether Canadian or foreign) over small capital.

While the relationship between capitalists and the Canadian state cannot be fully revealed by examining the personal ties, state decision-making bodies, and political party financing, the exploration of these areas in this paper does at least serve to indicate the general affinity between the dominant class and the state. This general affinity means that the state in Canada is predisposed to ensure the general interests of capitalists and assure capitalists that the conditions necessary for the orderly extraction of economic surplus into their hands are provided. To understand the peculiarities of each individual transaction between the Canadian state and capitalists would require detailed case studies, but generally this type of information is carefully guarded. John Turner, former Liberal finance minister, summarized the problem of access to information when speaking to the Canadian Bar Association: '[In politics] there is a vested interest in presenting any policy or any decision in the most favorable light. This sometimes means selecting facts. It often means managing or manipulating information. It often involves orchestrating and timing. Full and immediate revelation of all the facts can be embarrassing. I know. I've been there.'[32] Only after several decades does this type of detailed information emerge in Canada's archives.

Nevertheless, the various kinds of information presented here serve to substantiate the thesis that Canada's capitalists have enjoyed a close relationship with their state. The state has served both as an important recruiting ground for many members of the corporate elite, and in return many appointed positions within the state that are investigatory, regulatory, advisory, and policy-setting have a very high proportion of members from the Canadian corporate elite, the most powerful fraction of the capitalist class.

As was suggested, to understand the full implications of such an intimate relationship would require detailed case studies. This evidence, however, should make the reader examine closely state policies which *appear* to contradict the wishes of capital. For example, a policy such as the recent creation of PetroCanada, a Crown corporation now operating in the oil industry, should be seen for what it is – a move by the Canadian state to look after the general interests of Canadian capitalists, not Canadians in general. As Maurice Strong, chairman and president of PetroCanada has candidly admitted: 'The time will come when it will be recognized that the private petroleum industry's survival in a large measure has been ensured by PetroCanada's existence ... For one thing our presence relieves the pressure for the nationalization of the whole industry.'[33] As the former vice-president of Dome Petroleum and president of Power Corporation knows well, Petro-Canada is mainly oriented towards exploration and is not intended to compete with the international oil cartels. Its task will be to socialize oil companies' risks, not their profits.

While the oil industry is not alone in its ability to pass its risks onto the state, Larry Pratt's analysis of Syncrude in *The Tar Sands* serves as an important illustration. By a capital strike, Syncrude threatened to withdraw from an oil sands project and brought the federal, Alberta, and Ontario governments to their knees. As Pratt summarizes the Syncrude situation: 'The companies' conditions for development of the tar sands include much higher prices and returns, but they also want to transfer much of the risk and the heaviest costs involved to the public sector. Thus government must shoulder the enormous financial burden of building the massive infrastructure required to service and supply these remote projects, provide equity and debt financing, royalty holidays, guaranteed returns and prices, ensure labour stability, train a work force, underwrite environmental studies and costs – all of which carries a price tag in the billions.'[34] The power of the Syncrude partners in forcing such a 'sweet deal' cannot be reduced to personal ties with the Canadian state (although there are enough of these). It must be seen in terms of the tremendous resources, technology, capital, and market access they control. It is this power that gives them such enormous leverage in dealing with the Canadian state. It is power like this which explains ties between capitalists in Canada and the state.[35]

In the oil industry, it is the dominant comprador elite within Canada, supported by foreign-based capitalists controlling the multinational headquarters of these companies, who have determined Canada's oil policy. To a large extent this has been the case in all areas related to resource and manufacturing based companies, with the notable exceptions of the steel industry, food and beverages, and the pulp and paper industry where dominant indigenous Canadian capitalists have had much more impact. On the other hand, state policy associated with most financial institutions, transportation, utilities, and mass media has acted to support dominant indigenous capitalists. This pattern suggests that there is not a basic conflict of interest between foreign-controlled capitalists who control the major productive sectors of the Canadian economy and the dominant indigenous Canadian capitalists who thrive in the areas of circulation and service.

As is stressed in several articles in this collection, the Canadian state is a fragmentary one consisting of a federal government, two territories, and ten provinces. At the provincial level the state is often forced to reconcile conflicting demands from foreign capital attracted to provide manufacturing capacity or resource extraction and from the dependent class of small service capitalists which emerges in conjunction with this foreign-led activity. This service capitalist class, in turn, particularly because it is vulnerable, turns to the provincial state.[36] The fact that both the foreign and Canadian-based fractions of the economic elite have enjoyed such a close relationship with various branches of the Canadian state serves to reinforce their respective bases of power. Outside these two dominant fractions of the capitalist class, small capitalists and members of other classes do not have nearly as great an impact in determining federal state policy.

As long as the various branches of the Canadian state continue to be controlled by the two major political parties, there is little hope that the state will be used to alleviate problems associated with foreign control because it is not in the general interest of Canada's own leading capitalists to promote such a policy.[37] As long as Canadian society continues to be shaped by the capitalist mode of production, the most powerful class will be the capitalist class. As long as capitalists control the means of production and circulation they will use their power to ensure that the Canadian state will be used to their best advantage. And their best advantage does not represent the common interest of most Canadians.

NOTES

1 This paper focuses on only a limited aspect of the relationship between the state and capitalists in Canada; it is meant to be read alongside other papers in this collection, particularly those by Leo Panitch, David Wolfe, Rianne Mahon, and Dennis Olsen.
2 (London 1869), 561
3 Marx and Friedrich Engels, *The German Ideology* (New York 1970), 80, 106
4 *Democratic Theory: Essays in Retrieval* (London 1973), 47.
5 See the views presented by nine of Canada's top capitalists in *A Case for the Enterprise System*, assembled by the Investors Group and published in Sept. 1975. It was serialized in Canada's largest newspapers during this period in full-page advertisements.
6 *Globe and Mail*, Toronto, 5 April 1976
7 The following sketches are based in part on David Nock, 'The Intimate Connection: Links between the Political and Economic Systems in Canadian Federal Politics,' unpublished PH D thesis, University of Alberta, 1976, chap. 4. Earlier prime ministers also had extensive business careers; see, for example, J.K. Johnson's 'John A. Macdonald and the Kingston Business Community,' in *To Preserve and Defend,* ed. Gerald Tulchinsky (Montreal 1976).
8 For the criteria used to select the 113 dominant corporations, see Wallace Clement, *The Canadian Corporate Elite: An Analysis of Economic Power* (Toronto 1975) 125-32.
9 For a detailed review of King's early career, see Henry S. Ferns and Bernard Ostry, *The Age of Mackenzie King: The Rise of the Leader* (1955, Toronto 1976).
10 Nock, 'Intimate Connection,' 227-8, 244
11 For a detailed listing of 'elite switchers,' see Clement, *Canadian Corporate Elite,* 260-5.
12 *Toronto Star,* 19 June 1976; also the *Financial Post,* 19 June 1976
13 F.A. Kunz, *The Modern Senate of Canada, 1925-1963* (Toronto 1967), 66
14 *Gazette,* Montreal, 21 April 1976
15 *The Canadian Establishment* (Toronto 1975), 316
16 *Financial Post,* 19 June 1976
17 Health and Welfare Canada, *News Release,* 5 May 1976
18 *Globe and Mail,* 31 Dec. 1975. As will be shown, it is doubtful whether the Canadian Radio-television and Telecommunications Commission acts contrary to the benefit of dominant media complexes; indeed, it gives state-sanctioned media monopolies to a privileged few.
19 Michael J. Trebilcock, 'Winners and Losers in the Modern Regulatory State,' University of Toronto, Faculty of Law, 1975, pp. 13, 14

20 See Leo Panitch, 'Controls for Whom?' *This Magazine,* x (Feb.-March 1976).
21 *Canadian Establishment,* 390
22 See James Lorimer, 'Big Business Probe of Big Business,' *Globe and Mail,* 5 Nov. 1975.
23 This is written in the midst of the Bryce Commission hearings and no official reports have been issued.
24 *Globe and Mail,* 4 Oct. 1975
25 *Ibid.,* 4 June 1976
26 *Ibid.,* 24 April 1976
27 *Ibid.,* 4 Oct. 1975
28 *Ottawa Journal,* 29 April 1975
29 As of June 1976 Power Corporation held 428,082 common (25.3 per cent) and 4,053,038 class c participating non-voting shares (59.9 per cent) in Argus Corporation. However, 61 per cent of Argus voting shares are held by Ravelston Corporation which is controlled by John A. McDougald. *Globe and Mail,* 9 June 1976
30 *Globe and Mail,* 11 Feb. 1976
31 *Political Party Financing in Canada* (Toronto 1970), 161
32 *Globe and Mail,* 1 Sept. 1976
33 *Ibid.,* 21 Jan. 1976
34 *The Tar Sands: Syncrude and the Politics of Oil* (Edmonton 1976), 95
35 A further example where the state has facilitated private interests in the oil and gas industry is provided by Edgar Dosman, *The National Interest: The Politics of Northern Development, 1968-1975* (Toronto 1975). Dosman analyses relations between the state and North America's largest energy companies in their exploitation of the North, particularly the supportive role palyed by the state.
36 For a detailed discussion of emerging classes in Alberta, see Larry Pratt's article in this volume, and for a broader view see Garth Stevenson's article; also see Pierre Fournier's *The Quebec Establishment* (Montreal 1976).
37 See Wallace Clement, *Continental Corporate Power: Economic Elite Links between Canada and the United States* (Toronto 1977), especially chap. 10.

PART IV
THE STATE IN ACTION: ECONOMIC AND
SOCIAL POLICY

9

The state and economic policy in Canada, 1968-75

DAVID WOLFE

In recent years the responsibility for the management of the economy has proved an increasingly burdensome task for the governments of many advanced capitalist countries. This recent experience stands in sharp contrast to that of the first two post-war decades when many commentators hailed the intervention of governments in the economy as the agents responsible for the conversion of 'capitalism from the cataclysmic failure which it appeared to be in the 1930's into the great engine of prosperity of the postwar Western world.'[1] Although there has been much bemoaning the recent ineffectiveness of governments in their assumed task of economic management, there have been very few attempts to analyse the reasons for this dramatic reversal of events. What has been lacking is an attempt to explain the developments in economic policy of recent years within the framework of an overall analysis of the development of advanced capitalist society.

This paper[2] attempts to employ some of the concepts of the Polish economist, Michal Kalecki, and the German political scientist, Claus Offe, to develop an analytical framework within which the current problems of economic policy can be examined. The framework which is presented focuses on the relations between the state and the economy in advanced capitalist society. It explains the growing economic responsibilities of the state in terms of the dual functions of accumulation and legitimation. These functions are applied to analyse the contradictory nature of the tasks which the state must perform in order to manage the economy successfully. This framework is then used to analyse the problems which confronted Canadian economic policy-makers in the period between 1968 and 1975 and the policies to which they resorted in order to solve these problems. The conclusion which is reached suggests that, to a large degree, the problems which confronted the government in the area of economic policy are similar to those which are currently being faced by the governments of other advanced capitalist countries as well. The problems of economic policy are the outcome of deeply rooted conflicts in advanced capitalist society, conflicts which are mirrored in the accumulation and legitimation functions of the state. The contradictory nature of these functions has led to attempts by the state to implement policies of conflict management, such as incomes policies, rather than to attempt to resolve the underlying conflicts themselves. In light of the analysis here, there seems little likelihood that current efforts by the state in Canada to resolve its economic problems will be successful.

II

One of the key features of advanced capitalist society is the qualitatively expanded role which the state has assumed in the direction of the economy. This qualitative difference in the role of the state distinguishes advanced capitalist society from the earlier stage of liberal or competitive capitalism. The two most important events which brought about this transformation were the Great Depression of the 1930s and the massive economic mobilizations undertaken by various nation-states during the Second World War. The breakdown of competitive markets on an international scale during the 1930s created demands on the part of both business and labour for the state to assume a larger role in the direction and stimulation of national economies. The unprecedented scale and success of the economic mobilizations for the Second World War had great heuristic value in demonstrating the ability of the state to manage the economy. The implications of this experience were clearly understood by large segments of the business community, which had enjoyed a wave of prosperity resulting from the stimulus created by wartime investments, and by labour which saw the liberal myth of nonintervention shattered by the high degree of control the state exerted over the direction of the war effort.

The value of this lesson was not lost on the governments of the major advanced capitalist countries. Under strong pressure from labour movements, and in some cases under the leadership of social-democratic parties, many of them adopted for peacetime purposes after the war some of the policies of national economic planning which they had employed during it. Although the actual policies adopted differed from country to country, in general they were based on the Keynesian view that the general level of activity in the economy was governed by the level of investment and the level of effective demand. They accepted the fact that it was the government's responsibility to maintain a high level of effective demand to improve private firms' expectations about the future rate of return on their potential investment projects, and thereby to guarantee a high and stable level of employment and income for the whole economy.

The major element of economic policy has been the application by governments of discretionary fiscal policies whereby the deficits and surpluses of government budgeting have been regulated so as to provide the maximum contribution to the maintenance of a steady rate of economic growth. Discretionary fiscal policies have not been uniformly applied by all the governments, and the timing and magnitude of the discretionary changes in taxing and spending have not always been such as to have the optimum effect on economic stability. Nevertheless, the use of such policy tools has largely been responsible for the avoidance of major recessions in the post-war period and for the limiting of those downturns which occurred to a much shorter duration and lower intensity than previous ones. The adoption by most governments of complex social welfare programs involving income transfers to low-income earners and the unemployed has also contributed significantly to maintaining high levels of effective demand throughout the post-war period and thus to the general level of economic buoyancy. The stabilizing effects of income transfer programs are even greater when employment begins to fall because of the automatic rise in spending on programs such as unemployment insurance. Fiscal policy has also been complemented by the adoption of a series of tax incentives designed to reduce the effective cost of capital to corporations and thus increase their inducement to invest. The various devices employed, such as accelerated depreciation allowances, investment allowances, lower corporate tax rates, and tax incentives for research and development, have all had the effect of reducing the level of effective taxation on those corporations willing to undertake research or investment projects at the time and of the magnitude desired by their respective governments. In periods of growing pressure on corporate profit rates, tax policy has been used consistently to maintain a stable level of post-tax profit rates. Corporate tax policies have thus played a central role in the maintenance of profitable accumulation in advanced capitalist economies. These policies have been complemented as well by a series of others, such as selective nationalizations of less profitable industries, provision of subsidized sources of credit, improved regulation of international financial and monetary relations, and the reduction of international barriers to trade through successive rounds of the General Agreement on Tariffs and Trade. All of the measures have expanded the role played by the state in the economies of advanced capitalism and have helped to maintain the conditions for profitable capital accumulation.[3]

The basic consequence of increased state intervention in the economies of the advanced capitalist countries has been to reduce the risks and consequences of the unimpeded operation of the market for both capital and labour.[4] By partially subsidizing the costs of capital and by guaranteeing high levels of demand, the state has helped to reduce the uncertainty which large oligopolistic corporations face in the market. Furthermore, through policies designed to ensure full employment and to compensate those members of the labour force who suffer the ill effects of unemployment, the state has reduced the private costs previously borne by individual workers. As a result of this dual role which the state has come to play in the advanced capitalist economy, Claus Offe and James O'Connor have defined two of the basic functions of the state in advanced capitalist society as the accumulation and the legitimation functions.[5] As O'Connor has pointed out, many economic policies of the state have a twofold character corresponding to these two functions of the state in advanced capitalist society. The most basic of these economic policies, of course, is the classical Keynesian policy of maintaining full employment. Full employment policy is an essential aspect of the accumulation function of the state because it ensures the high and stable level of demand which is the necessary incentive for sustained investment by private firms. At the same time, full employment policy is an essential aspect of the legitimation function of the state because it removes the most destructive consequences of the market economy for members of the working class, the fear of unemployment, and thus helps ensure their loyalty to the system. Paradoxically enough, it is the success of the state in advanced capitalism in implementing full employment policies which seem to plant the seeds of its most unresolvable problem.

The political implications of Keynesian full employment policies were pointed out in a somewhat prophetic article written by Michal Kalecki in 1943. Kalecki predicted that in such a situation capitalists would recognize that the disciplinary role played by the unemployed in the labour market would lose its impact. Loss of the fear of unemployment would prompt workers and trade unions to adopt a more militant and intransigent attitude in their wage negotiations with the capitalists. Although the capitalists would recognize that full employment was beneficial in terms of providing them with continuously profitable investment prospects, they were more appreciative of the importance of 'discipline in the factories' and 'political stability.' 'Their class instinct tells them that lasting full employment is unsound from their point of view and that unemployment is an integral part of the normal capitalist system.'[6] On the other hand, Kalecki also foresaw that in slump conditions the pressure of the masses would likely force the government to undertake public investment schemes financed through borrowing. This is what has occurred. Throughout the post-war period governments have been subjected to conflicting pressures from capital and labour to utilize fiscal policy for the maximum benefit of each. In all the advanced capitalist countries, prolonged periods of high unemployment have become politically unacceptable due to the refusal of the labour movement and other wage earners to tolerate a government that will not do all it can to maintain a high level of employment. The political power of labour to offset the traditional power of capital has resulted in a situation in which the threat of unemployment as a bargaining tool on the side of capital has been seriously reduced. Thus, the experience of relatively high employment levels throughout the post-war period has substantially improved the bargaining position of labour and the trade unions. The combined effect of the implementation of full employment policies and more comprehensive social welfare schemes, such as unemployment insurance, has been to create a situation in which the bargaining power (both politically and economically) of labour movements throughout the advanced capitalist countries has been substantially increased. The emergence of inflation as the primary economic problem of the advanced capitalist countries since the mid-1960s has resulted from the increased efforts of trade unions to use this bargaining power to increase their money-wage levels. The ability of trade unions to redistribute income towards wages is seriously limited by the ability of firms to raise their prices in order to maintain their profit margins. Thus both firms and unions possess a certain ability to limit each others' efforts to substantially redistribute real income towards profits or wages.[7]

The result of increased state intervention in the economy, principally through the adoption of Keynesian full employment and other social welfare policies, has been to alter dramatically the nature of the historical confrontation between capital and labour. By assuming responsibility both for establishing a profitable basis for the accumulation process and for guaranteeing the wage and income security of the whole labour force, or, in other words, by attempting to reduce the historical costs of the market to both capital and labour, the state has transferred the sphere of class conflict from the economic order to the political order. Class conflict over the surplus of the production process is no longer fought out in the universalistic terms of economic liberalism (fair returns to factors of production), but is now fought out in the political terms of the division of the national income between wages and profits. To the extent that labour is successful in increasing its share of income, the government is then compelled further to subsidize capital in order to guarantee that it continues to invest and accumulate at a profitable rate. To the extent that the government attempts to discourage labour in its attempt to gain a higher share for wages, it runs either the risk of a potential legitimation problem in the form of massive labour alienation or the immediate risk (given the formally democratic nature of the political process) of being repudiated at the next election. ' ... the actual fact of unemployment changes its social definition wherever it appears; it is no longer perceived as a periodic event in a blindly operating economic cycle but as a "culpable" and therefore "actionable" failure on the part of political-administrative direction ... As a result of this "re-definition" of unemployment a situation arises in which it is not that "social peace" is more reliably safeguarded but that the conditions for its continuance have become more severe.'[8]

The realities of what Kalecki termed the 'political business cycle' highlight, in rather dramatic form, the contradictory nature of the state's accumulation and legitimation functions. In order to perform its accumulation function successfully, the state must be prepared to counter persistent inflationary wage demands with counter-cyclical budgetary policies designed to relieve the upward pressure on corporate profits. In other words, to perform adequately the accumulation function the state is required to manipulate the political business cycle in such a way as to make a maximum contribution to the maintenance of high profit levels. Yet, at the same time, in order to perform its legitimation function adequately, the state must ensure a high and stable level of employment and income.

The recognition by many governments in the mid-1960s of the inadequacy of classical Keynesian demand management policies as a tool for simultaneously fulfilling both the accumulation and legitimation functions of the state prompted the search for a wages and prices policy as a more reliable alternative, one that might also deal with the tendency for each new cycle to begin at successively higher levels of price inflation and of unemployment than the previous one. However, in almost all cases in which it has been tried, an incomes policy has failed to bring about more than a temporary solution to the problem. The usual result has been that the governments have failed in their efforts to impose wage restraint and have merely succeeded in politicizing the conflict over the division of the national income. ' ... when the state seeks, through a statutory incomes policy or through direct legal controls over unions, to restrict the implementation of workers' calculations *vis-à-vis* the wage contract, it runs the risk of directly connecting the state with the maintenance of that socio-economic inequality which otherwise seems to emerge as the ineluctable product of free individuals engaging in a free market. This tends to identify the state rather than the market as the fulcrum of society and thus brings out the inconsistency between legal and political equality guaranteed by the state and socio-economic inequality protected and maintained by the state.'[9]

One important additional factor which further complicates the struggle over the division of the national income is the effect of the international economy and of foreign competition on the profitability of domestic firms. The extent to which the struggle results in either spiralling inflation or in a serious squeeze on the profitability of domestic firms depends to a large degree on the strength of each national economy in comparison with its major economic rivals. Those national economies with the highest rate of growth and the strongest balance of payments position are generally better able to reconcile the competing claims being made on the national income.[10] International competition plays a crucial role in setting limits on the ability of domestic firms to raise their prices whenever their costs go up. If firms competing with foreign rivals cannot raise their prices when their costs go up, the result is that their profit margins are squeezed; consequently the relative share of wages in the national income is increased. In a capitalist economy, declining profitability may lead to lower levels of investment, lower levels of economic growth, and eventually to economic stagnation. As the economic decline spreads, the share of wages may be increasing, but both real and money wages may fall. In the context of an increasingly competitive international capitalist economy, the success or failure of a national economy can have drastic consequences not only for the division of the national income but for the rise or fall in standards of living as well.

An essential element in determining the relative strength or weakness of a national economy is the position of its multinational firms, which have come to play an ever more predominant role in the economies of the advanced capitalist countries. In many respects, this predominance is the direct consequence of deliberate policies adopted by many of the countries involved.[11] Despite the spread of multinational firms across national boundaries, the extent to which they are still primarily responsive to the demands of their parent countries has been vastly underplayed. The parent government retains its primary claim on the loyalty of its multinationals because of three factors: the headquarters of the company is under its legal jurisdiction; there is normally a close tie between the managers of the parent company and the government in the parent country; and, finally, the largest portion of the company's assets is normally located in the parent country. These factors give the state in the parent country the power to influence the actions of its multinational enterprises in the directions it desires through its ability to alter financial flows, change trade patterns, alter competitive relations, control the flow of technology, and affect the pattern of intercompany pricing of the multinational enterprises.[12]

As the international rivalry between American, European, and Japanese multinational firms increases, the state in the respective parent countries is likely to intervene more vigorously on behalf of its corporations in an attempt to manipulate this modern form of international economic rivalry for the maximum advantage of the domestic economy. Thus the success of multinational firms in capturing new markets and sources of supply, and in retaining existing ones, will depend increasingly on the international mobilization of their parent states on their behalf. Those corporations whose states enjoy significant advantages in international relations would similarly be expected to benefit from these advantages. The prospect, therefore, is for an increasing degree of 'inter-imperialist rivalry' between the states of the leading advanced capitalist countries on behalf of their multinational firms.[13] And the prospects for those nation-states who fail in this new form of international rivalry is an increasing degree of domestic conflict over the division of the national income, as their leading firms prove less able to compete internationally and the economy suffers the inevitable consequences of a profit squeeze. It should also be evident that those nation-states with few domestically based multinational firms are placed at a serious competitive disadvantage in this new form of international competition and thus tend to be placed in a more dependent position.

III

The end of the Second World War in Canada was marked by the adoption of Keynesian full employment and a host of new social welfare policies by the government.[14] The adoption of these policies in Canada at the end of the war was thus part of the 'post-war settlement' between capital and labour which occurred in all the advanced capitalist countries.[15] As Leo Panitch has suggested in his article in this volume, this 'settlement' in the Canadian case was less oriented towards the legitimation function than in Europe, and this was reflected in the post-war period in the more restrictive labour legislation in Canada, the generally lower level of social security spending as a percentage of gross national product, and the higher level of unemployment that has been taken as the norm in this country as compared to other advanced capitalist countries. Nevertheless, the trend in Canada was the same as elsewhere, as was the *dynamic* governing economic policy in terms of the necessity of striking a balance between accumulation and legitimation. Economic growth was rapid during the years after the war, with

259 David Wolfe

Table 1
Economic indicators, 1960-75 (percentages)

(1971 dollars)	Change in G.N.E.[a]	G.N.E. implicit price index	Annual changes in CPI	Unemployment rate
1960	2.9	1.2	1.2	7.0
1961	2.8	0.5	0.9	7.1
1962	6.8	1.4	1.2	5.9
1963	5.2	1.9	1.8	5.5
1964	6.7	2.5	1.8	4.7
1965	6.7	3.2	2.4	3.9
1966	6.9	4.4	3.7	3.6
1967	3.3	3.9	3.6	4.1
1968	5.8	3.3	4.0	4.8
1969	5.3	4.4	4.6	4.7
1970	2.5	4.7	3.3	5.9
1971	5.7	3.2	2.9	6.4
1972	6.0	4.9	4.8	6.3
1973	6.9	8.4	7.6	5.6
1974	2.8	13.8	10.8	5.4
1975	0.2	9.7	10.8	7.1

[a] Gross national expenditure is identical in amount to gross national product: GNE is the sum of all final outputs; GNP is the sum of all factor earnings.
Source: Canada, Department of Finance, *Economic Review* (April 1976), Reference Tables 5, 45, 47, and 34

a special upsurge in the level of economic activity during the Korean War because of the high level of demand for Canada's raw material exports. The strong state of the economy continued with some minor ups and downs until the recession of 1958 when the strong downturn in the American economy produced a similar effect on Canada. The slack state of the economy lasted through until 1962 as a result of a combination of inadequate management of the economy by the Conservatives under John Diefenbaker and a decline in international demand for the products of Canada's resource industries.[16] By 1962, however, the pace of economic activity had begun to pick up once again, and with the return to power of the Liberals in 1963 economic policy became more expansionary. The publication of the Economic Council of Canada's *First Annual Review* in 1965 provided justification for the continuation of a policy of sustained economic expansion.[17] The government's general acceptance of this position is reflected in the budgets of the mid-1960s which sought to achieve sustained economic growth and a high level of employment. The success of this policy can be seen in the suc-

Table 2
Shares of the national income, 1960-75

	Wages and salaries[a]		Corporation profits before taxes		Interest and investment income		Farm and small business income		Total[b]	
	$ millions	%	$ millions	%	$ millions	%	$ millions	%	$ millions	%
1960	20,141	68.6	3,870	13.2	1,129	3.8	4,218	14.4	29,358	100
1961	21,009	69.0	4,066	13.4	1,284	4.2	4,087	13.4	30,446	100
1962	22,468	67.9	4,450	13.4	1,416	4.3	4,757	14.4	33,091	100
1963	23,932	67.3	4,932	13.9	1,563	4.4	5,138	14.4	35,565	100
1964	26,034	67.4	5,841	15.1	1,724	4.5	5,012	13.0	38,611	100
1965	28,878	68.1	6,318	14.9	1,891	4.5	5,282	12.5	42,369	100
1966	32,629	68.7	6,714	14.1	2,070	4.4	6,066	12.8	47,479	100
1967	36,160	71.0	6,823	13.4	2,362	4.6	5,594	11.0	50,939	100
1968	39,318	70.5	7,742	13.9	2,623	4.7	6,099	10.9	55,782	100
1969	43,949	70.9	8,294	13.4	3,082	5.0	6,622	10.7	61,947	100
1970	47,620	72.8	7,699	11.8	3,428	5.2	6,635	10.2	65,382	100
1971	52,299	72.4	8,681	12.0	3,778	5.2	7,525	10.4	72,283	100
1972	58,256	71.7	10,704	13.2	4,327	5.3	7,940	9.8	81,227	100
1973	66,053	69.0	14,386	15.0	5,270	5.5	10,044	10.5	95,753	100
1974	77,155	67.9	18,303	16.1	7,014	6.2	11,079	9.8	113,551	100
1975	87,949	70.3	17,768	14.2	7,674	6.1	11,776	9.4	125,167	100

[a] Includes military pay
[b] National income at factor cost before adjustment
Source: *Economic Review* (April 1976), Reference Table 8

cession of large annual increases in the gross national product which Canada experienced in the mid-1960s and in the relatively low levels of unemployment as well (see Table 1). This cycle of economic growth was marked by the rise and fall in relative shares of the national income which usually occur in the different stages of the business cycle. In the upswing of the cycle from 1962 to 1965, profits rose at a faster rate than wages and salaries. The relative increase of profits and of interest as a proportion of the national income can be seen in Table 2. However, after the early part of the cycle, wages began to catch up and regain the share of the national income which they had held previously. This new development provided the focus for economic policy in the late 1960s and set the stage for what have proved to be the policy concerns of the recent period.

In 1966 the sharp rise in the number of strikes and the number of contracts rejected by the rank and file of union members drew national atten-

Table 3
Union membership in Canada, 1960-75

	Union membership (000)	Total non-agricultural paid workers (000)	Union membership as percentage of non-agricultural paid workers
1960	1,459	4,522	32.3
1961	1,447	4,578	31.6
1962	1,423	4,705	30.2
1963	1,449	4,867	29.8
1964	1,493	5,074	29.4
1965	1,589	5,343	29.7
1966	1,736	5,658	30.7
1967	1,921	5,953	32.3
1968	2,010	6,068	33.1
1969	2,075	6,380	32.5
1970	2,173	6,465	33.6
1971	2,231	6,637	33.6
1972	2,371	6,893	34.4
1973	2,610	7,181	36.3
1974	2,726	7,637	35.7
1975	2,875	7,817	36.8

Source: Canada, Department of Labour, *Labour Organizations in Canada* (1974-5),
Table I, p. xix

tion to the increased urgency with which labour's wage demands were being put forward.[18] Membership growth in the trade union movement in Canada had been relatively static from the mid-1950s to 1964. However, between 1964 and 1968 membership grew by more than 500,000 (Table 3). The increased sense of strength which the labour movement drew from this growth was combined with the strongly expansionary state of the economy to lay the basis for a marked growth in labour income and a significant shift in the share of national income going to wages and salaries. The increased determination with which the unions bargained in the latter part of the decade is reflected both in the significant wage gains which they made and in the record number of man-days lost due to strikes in 1966 and again in 1969 (Table 4). The labour movement demonstrated throughout this cycle of economic growth that it was prepared to press the claims of its members for a significant share of the country's increased economic prosperity. This pattern of behaviour on the part of the organized labour movement appeared to represent an important new factor in the Canadian economy. It provided

Table 4
Strikes and lockouts in Canada, 1960-75

	Number	Workers involved	Man-days duration	Percentage of estimated working time
1960	274	49,408	738,700	.06
1961	287	97,959	1,335,080	.11
1962	311	74,332	1,417,900	.11
1963	332	83,428	917,140	.07
1964	343	100,535	1,580,550	.11
1965	501	171,870	2,349,870	.17
1966	617	411,459	5,178,170	.34
1967	522	252,018	3,974,760	.25
1968	582	223,562	5,082,732	.32
1969	595	306,799	7,751,880	.46
1970	542	261,706	6,539,560	.39
1971	569	239,631	2,866,590	.16
1972	598	706,474	7,753,530	.43
1973	724	348,470	5,776,080	.30
1974	1218	580,912	9,221,890	.46
1975	1171	506,443	10,908,810	.53

Source: Canada, Department of Labour, *Strikes and Lockouts in Canada* (1975), Table I, p. 6

the first serious indication of the understanding which the labour movement had of its heightened bargaining power under conditions of relative full employment. This new-found militancy of organized labour in its approach to bargaining certainly had a profound influence on government thinking with respect to the goals of economic policy.

Labour's new aggressiveness in pressing its wage demands was regarded with some discomfort by government policy-makers charged with the responsibility for ensuring that economic growth was achieved with a moderate rate of price increases. From the government's perspective the Canadian economy had reached what could be called a state of 'virtual' full employment in 1965. As economic growth continued at a fairly strong pace in the next few years, the increasing rate of inflation, from 1.8 percent in 1964 to 4.0 in 1968 (Table 1), became a source of growing concern to the government. Accordingly, the government attempted to cut back slightly in the overall level of demand by employing a more restrictive fiscal and monetary policy in 1966 and 1967. However, by late 1967 it was clear that these accepted tools of economic policy were no longer operating with the desired results. Despite a sharp drop in the growth of the GNP and a rise in the rate of unemployment, prices continued to increase. In order to explain this unexpected development, the government adopted the view that Canada was no longer experiencing an inflation of the normal demand-pull variety, but was undergoing a new type of cost-push inflation. In the opinion of R.B. Bryce, the deputy minister of finance during this period, this new type of inflation would not respond to the normal tools of economic policy because ' ... there has also been a structural element in the persistence of this particular price and cost inflation, engendered by the expectation that the business cycle has been cured at last, by the increased size and importance of the government sector, by the belief that governments are committed to maintaining or restoring full employment and by other factors, such as the continued world-wide prosperity ... the widespread belief that inflation will continue finds its expression and effect in demands for large wage increases by workers, and for high interest rates by lenders, and in a willingness on the part of business to pay both. This last result has substantially reduced the effectiveness of fiscal and monetary policy in checking wage and price increases.'[19]

This view of the source of inflation in the late 1960s and the limitations of traditional policy tools for dealing with it led the government to search for a new policy option to deal effectively with the problem of cost-push inflation. The government's policy-makers were concerned especially with finding a way of limiting wage and cost increases in the economy without the high economic and social costs that a prolonged period of unemployment would impose on the whole society. This concern led them to view the much-used European option of an incomes policy as an increasingly attractive alternative. The new policy was formally announced with the publication of the government's white paper entitled *Policies for Price Stability* in December 1968. The white paper stressed the government's belief that the present policy tools available to it were not adequate to resolve the existing conflict between achieving the dual objectives of maintaining a high level of employment and restoring price stability. For these reasons the government announced the formation of the Prices and Incomes Commission (PIC) to be 'charged with the responsibility for conducting studies of price and income developments in Canada, and for producing regular reports on its findings. The purpose of the Commission [was to be] to *discover* the facts, *analyze* the causes, processes and consequences of inflation, and to *inform* both the public and the government on how price stability may be achieved.'[20] The government emphasized the point that the underlying feature of its approach to an incomes policy was to be its voluntary nature.

Beginning in June 1969 the commission undertook a series of discussions with the leading economic interest groups in the country to lay the basis for a voluntary program of price and wage restraint. The commission's efforts to reach some kind of consensus were dealt a critical blow on 17 October 1969 when the Canadian Labour Congress and the Confederation of National Trade Unions, the two largest labour organizations in Canada, issued a joint news release formally rejecting the commission's attempts to implement a voluntary restraint program. The trade union organizations stated: 'We believe that the time has arrived for governments to impose, over the next year or two, a freeze on all prices ... We reject outright the idea that voluntary guidelines can cope effectively with the current inflation. This is a highly oversimplified approach to a very complicated problem ... For guidelines, or an incomes policy, to be at all fair it would require all non-wage and salary forms of income, including profits, rents, interest, professional fees, unincorporated business income, speculation in real estate prices, and so on, to be effectively restrained. We do not believe that it is at all possible to bring many of these forms of income under a meaningful policy of voluntary restraint.'[21]

The rejection by the labour movement of the PIC's efforts to achieve any kind of consensus on the control of inflation meant that the commission had failed. However, the rejection is significant from another perspective as well. It signified that the new level of economic rationality which the labour movement had displayed in its more militant approach to bargaining was not an isolated phenomenon but extended to the political sphere as well. The labour movement was not prepared to sacrifice politically the important economic gains which its members had won at the bargaining table.

The commission's response to this development was to turn its efforts towards organizing a price restraint program in order to demonstrate to the labour movement that such a program could be made to work. After several preliminary meetings with the representatives of various business organizations, the commission decided that the potential basis existed to implement such a program and decided to convene a National Conference on Price Stability in early February 1970. The conference was attended by 250 leading business representatives who agreed upon a program to restrain price increases over the course of the year. With the agreement on the price restraint program worked out, the PIC immediately proceeded to establish a Price Review Division and staffed it with employees of several government departments and several large companies. By late spring 1970 the PIC once again felt that the time was ripe to attempt to implement an agreement on wage restraint as well. After several more discussions were held with representatives of the trade union movement with no results, the PIC went ahead on its own to propose a set of guidelines for limiting wage increases, including fringe benefits. Predictably, the response of the labour movement was totally negative. From this point on, the wage restraint program became largely an exercise in wishful thinking on the part of the commission, with only the federal and provincial governments making any effort to follow the guidelines. For the second time within the space of a year, the trade unions proved to be the major stumbling block to the successful establishment of an incomes policy.

Although there had been, in fact, a certain abatement in the rate of increase in the Consumer Price Index (CPI) for 1970, this improvement had been brought about largely as a consequence of the squeezing of corporate profit margins. The share of the national income going to labour, which had been climbing steadily since 1963, continued to do so, and hit a high in 1970 of 72.8 per cent (Table 2). This was in spite of the best efforts of the Prices and Incomes Commission. On the other hand, corporate profits, which had been falling steadily as a share of the national income since 1964, continued to do so and hit a low of 11.8 per cent in 1970 (Table 2). These developments were undoubtedly due, at least in part, to the low rate of growth in the economy in 1970. However, many business leaders felt that the price restraint program had operated largely to the detriment of business and the PIC had had little or no effect on wage-push inflation. Consequently, on 1 December 1970 the PIC issued a formal statement announcing that the price restraint program would be terminated at the end of the year.

There are many lessons to be drawn from the experience of the Prices and Incomes Commission. In the eyes of the commission itself the programs which it had carried out had been instrumental in helping to lower the rate of increase in the CPI: 'While other influences were of course also at work, the price restraint programme helped to reduce the year-to-year increase in the consumer price index in Canada from 4.5 per cent during 1969 to 3.3 per cent during 1970, and still further to 2.9 per cent during 1971.'[22] The commission also came to the conclusion that the major shortcoming in its efforts was the result of the voluntary nature of the program it had been instructed to initiate. After a general review of the sources of inflation and the possible remedies for it, the commission argued strongly for the use of compulsory wage and price controls in any future efforts to deal with inflation.[23] In their opposition to the PIC, the trade unions demonstrated their unwillingness to be co-opted into public policies which were clearly designed to retard the relative growth of wages in the national income. The failure on the part of the government and the PIC to obtain union co-opera-

266 The state and economic policy

Table 5
Budgetary forecasts, 1968-76 ($ millions)

Budget speech	Fiscal year	Budgetary surplus or deficit	National accounts surplus or deficit	Non-budgetary requirement	Cash requirement
22 Oct. 1968	1968-9	−675	−435	−600	−1,275
	1969-70	5	250	−650	−400
3 June 1969	1969-70	375	575	−775	−525
12 March 1970	1970-1	250	130		
3 Dec. 1970	1970-1	−320	−570	−1,250	−1,570
18 June 1971	1971-2	−750	−650	−1,680	−2,430
14 Oct. 1971	1971-2	−1,000		−1,600	−2,600
8 May 1972	1972-3	−450	−800	−1,550	−2,000
19 Feb. 1973	1973-4	−975	−640	−1,025	−2,000
2 Aug. 1973	1973-4	−600		−900	−1,500
18 Nov. 1974	1974-5	250	275	−1,250	−1,000
	1975-6	−1,000	−1,550	−2,000	−3,000
23 June 1975	1975-6	−3,175	−3,675	−2,125	−5,300

Source: Canadian Tax Foundation, *The National Finances,* 1968-76, annually

tion revealed the relatively low level of support which the Canadian state enjoys from the trade union movement, at least in comparison to other countries where the trade unions have been willing to participate in incomes policies for short periods of time. It also served as an indication that future attempts by the government at constructing a voluntary policy were not likely to be well received by the unions.

In turning to incomes policy to cope with its economic difficulties, the government did not abandon the use of traditional tools, but rather combined them, as insurance, with the new policy thrust. Emphasizing the 'fight against inflation,' Finance Minister Edgar J. Benson introduced budgets in 1968, 1969, and 1970 which were highly restrictive.[24] They not only attempted to reduce the budgetary deficit through increasing taxes and restricting growth in public expenditure, but also consistently 'erred' on the conservative side in forecasting deficits. The result was that the budgets were more restrictive on the level of demand in the economy than the stated intention at the time of their introduction (see Tables 5 and 6). Throughout most of the period from late 1968 to mid-1970, monetary policy was tied fairly closely to the goals of fiscal policy and to the goals of the Prices and Incomes Commission. Monetary policy followed a moderately expansionary course throughout most of 1968 and into 1969. This reflected a certain amount of uncertainty on the part of the government as to the actual

Table 6
Fiscal and monetary policy, 1960-75 ($ millions)

	Federal government, surpluses and deficits			Growth of money supply Currency and demand deposits – annual rate (percentages)
	National accounts	Budgetary accounts[a]	Total cash requirements[a]	
1960	−229	−413	−376	1.2
1961	−410	−340	−294	5.2
1962	−507	−791	−478	3.3
1963	−286	−692	−1,464	5.9
1964	345	−619	−283	4.9
1965	544	−38	−379	6.4
1966	231	−39	−160	6.9
1967	−84	−422	−532	9.7
1968	−11	−794	−589	4.4
1969	1,021	−576	−1,937	7.4
1970	266	393	−244	2.3
1971	−145	−379	−2,188	12.8
1972	−600	−614	−1,727	14.0
1973	222	481	−1,388	14.4
1974	593	−673	−1,319	9.7
1975	−4,504	−1,146	−1,507	13.8

[a]Fiscal year ending 31 March
Source: *Economic Review* (April 1976), Reference Table 55; *The National Finances*, 1975-6, Table 3-8, p. 36, Table 17-2, p. 228; Canada, *Bank of Canada Review* (Feb. 1976), Table I and previous issues

strength of the economy and the potential for an economic downturn. However, by early 1969 it was apparent to both the fiscal and monetary authorities that the underlying current of demand in the economy was quite strong and, as a consequence, the growth of the money supply was curtailed more sharply in the latter half of 1969 and the first half of 1970 (Table 6).

This contraction in the rate of growth of the money supply undoubtedly combined with the severely restrictive fiscal policy of the minister of finance to produce the economic slowdown that became quite marked by early 1970. At the same time, the increased demand for money in Canada created by the contraction of the money supply led to large capital inflows into the country and consequently a significant increase in the size of the country's international reserves. In response to this growth in the level of reserves, the Bank of Canada was forced to unpeg the exchange value of the Canadian dollar which had been fixed at $.925 (US) since 1962.[25] The floating of the dollar at this crucial point had important consequences for the government's campaign against inflation. The exchange rate quickly rose in value to a level near parity with the US dollar. This had the effect of lowering the cost of imports from the United States and thus obviously helped to bring down the rate of inflation. At the same time, however, it also served to raise the cost of Canadian exports and thus contributed to a reduction in the demand for Canadian products and indirectly contributed to the rising level of unemployment in Canada and the slowdown in the growth of the economy.[26] Thus it can be seen that developments in the sphere of monetary policy in 1969-70 were closely tied to the goals of the government's anti-inflationary policy. The significant reduction in the rate of increase in the Consumer Price Index that was achieved in 1970 was done not merely as a result of the price restraint program of the Prices and Incomes Commission but rather by the use of all the policy tools available to the government. However, it was achieved only at the expense of a significant rise in the rate of unemployment and a drop in the rate of economic growth (Table 1).

The question is whether the government felt that the costs had been worthwhile or whether, in fact, they had been too high. The answer to this important question has been provided by Mr Bryce: 'We have to demonstrate ... to the strongly organized unions and to the strong business firms that they cannot count on public policy giving a continuing preference to full employment over price stability – that they cannot, in the jargon, "look across the valley" and count on their current inflationary actions being vindicated by the weakness of public policy in relaxing restraint before the pattern of price and wage behaviour has been changed. If this is the situation, as I contend a realistic up-to-date appraisal of the behaviour of our institutions and markets now indicates, then the future duration of the benefits of our policy of restraint should be considerably greater than the period over which we must suffer the cost of restraint. Indeed what seems to me to be at stake is whether the basic full employment policy that evolved after the Depression and the War can be made to work without exploding, in the economic environment of the latter third of this century in which powerful organized interests contend with each other in highly developed and sophisticated markets in most of the developed industrial world. It is in these terms, I suggest, that one can and does find the justification for the economic and social costs of the restraint program.'[27]

It would appear obvious from this statement that the economic costs of its policies were felt by the government to be vindicated by the nature of the circumstances in which they were undertaken. Mr Bryce, however, failed to consider whether the political costs of these policies were also justified. By the middle of 1970 it was becoming apparent to Mr Benson and to his cabinet colleagues that the political costs of their current course of action might be much higher than they were willing to pay. As is usual in such a situation, the pendulum had begun to swing back the other way and as the government became aware of the effect that its restraint policies were having on public opinion, a change of course began to seem more desirable. During 1970 budgetary expenditures grew due to an increase in equalization payments to the provinces, increased capital expenditure, manpower training projects, and a summer employment program for students.[28] The combination of these additional expenditures and the shortfall in revenue resulting from the drop in the rate of economic growth in 1970 necessitated the presentation of a supplementary budget on 3 December 1970. In his budgetary statement the minister of finance changed his stand dramatically from the one which he had taken in March. He placed a great deal of emphasis on the seriousness with which the government viewed the current levels of unemployment. He also pointed out that since the late spring the government had been following a more expansionary monetary policy. The minister then proceeded to announce several expenditure and tax changes that would result in a smaller budgetary deficit for 1970-1. This new direction for economic policy was continued in the next full budget of 18 June 1971 and went even further in a supplementary budget statement on 14 October 1971. Reductions in tax rates on the lowest brackets and temporary employment programs yielded an expected budgetary deficit for 1971-2 of $1000 million.

Part of this package was a direct response to the New Economic Policy announced by US President Nixon in August 1971. But it also was evidence of the government's strong concern with the upcoming election in 1972 and the reaction it might expect from the electorate to the high rate of unemployment in the economy. The pattern of behaviour revealed in the government's fiscal policy over this period represents something more than what would be expected from the normal operation of counter-cyclical budgetary policy. Rather, the sudden and dramatic swings in fiscal policy appear to have been determined by the changing sensitivity of the government to the competing pressures on it from business and labour. Given that one of the major avenues of labour pressure is through the electoral process, it is not surprising to find that the government became much more concerned with the problems of unemployment and economic growth as the next federal election approached. The government's alternating imposition of restrictive and expansionary fiscal policies on the economy reflected its unsuccessful attempt to balance the simultaneous requirements of the accumulation and legitimation functions.

IV

The year 1972 brought a host of changes in Canadian economic policy. In addition to a new minister of finance, and a federal election, it also witnessed the emergence of a serious new concern at the centre of economic policy. As was pointed out earlier, the multinational corporation poses a special kind of problem for those charged with the control of economic policy in the advanced capitalist states. The point was brought home to Canada rather dramatically when the United States undertook a co-ordinated series of new policies in August 1971, designed to promote greater investment by US multinationals in the United States and to encourage the multinationals to relocate some of their manufacturing enterprises within the country and supply their foreign markets through increased exports. This was seen as one way of helping to reduce the US balance of payments deficit. The measures that composed this part of the package included a special investment credit for firms undertaking new investment in the United States, proposals for an accelerated depreciation range that would enable firms to derive greater tax benefits from new investments in the United States, and the Domestic International Sales Corporation proposal which was designed to provide for the deferral of corporate income taxes on profits earned by American corporations from exports. The US government believed that the DISC proposal was necessary to counteract the provision in the US tax laws which permitted American overseas subsidiaries to defer payment of income tax on profits earned abroad until they were repatriated. It was felt that this tax provision gave firms an undue incentive to locate plants overseas to supply foreign markets rather than produce the goods domestically and export them.[29] It was the DISC proposal which gave rise to the greatest concern among Canadian policy-makers. In the words of one interdepartmental committee of the Canadian government: 'The DISC legislation posed three potential threats to the Canadian economy – increased competition from US exporters in Canadian markets, increased competition in third country markets and increased incentives for new capital investment and the accompanying new employment opportunities to be located in the United States rather than in Canada.'[30] The vulnerability of the Canadian economy because of its heavy dependence on foreign ownership of industry in the manufacturing and resource sectors of the economy was evident. The government and its new minister of finance, John Turner, wasted no time, however, in demonstrating that they were not prepared to be out-bid by the US government for the loyalty of US multinational firms.

Mr Turner's first budget, brought down on 8 May 1972, continued in the strongly expansionary direction that had been established by his predecessor. It focused much more clearly, however, on the twin themes of industrial expansion and employment and the manner in which these two problems were interrelated: 'Mr. Speaker, my first words to this House as Minister of Finance last February were that my most urgent priority was jobs. This remains my first priority ... The main thrust of this budget is to deal with this problem: to buttress the Canadian economy – to provide incentives for Canadian industry to grow and compete and provide jobs ... Multinational corporate giants have come to assume an increasingly dominant role on the world economic stage and in the Canadian economy. I fear that the world is in the process of being transformed into massive trading blocs, which in itself is of immense significance to Canada as a major trading nation ... What I shall strive to do tonight is to set the stage for Canadian industry to be competitive in world markets. Our ability to gain access to world markets is a prerequisite to the success of any industrial policy that focuses on growth and jobs.'

Mr Turner immediately followed up this 'bold' pronouncement with an equally 'bold' policy initiative. He announced a new two-year write-off of the cost of all machinery and equipment purchased after 8 May 1972 for use in the manufacturing and processing of goods in Canada. To this most generous incentive to the manufacturing industries, he also added a reduction in the top rate of corporate income tax applicable to manufacturing and processing profits earned in Canada after 1 January 1973, from 49 to 40 per cent. There can be little doubt that the stimulus provided to increased corporate investment by the combined effects of the two-year write-off and the corporate tax cut was substantial indeed. Faced with the prospect of a loss of domestic employment due to the actions of foreign governments and multinational corporations, the Canadian government reacted in what could only be called a textbook fashion. It immediately attempted to regain the allegiance of the US-based multinationals by outbidding the US authorities in a battle of tax incentives. There can also be little doubt that the Canadian government was determined not to lose such a contest. The generosity of the Turner corporate tax cuts is ample proof of that fact. An independent econometric study of the relative effects of the Canadian and American measures to induce greater investment in their domestic economies concluded that the degree of stimulation provided by the Canadian policy was much greater.[31] It seems clear that the potential threat posed by the DISC legislation was used by the minister of finance as an elaborate rationalization to implement an expansionary fiscal policy that concentrated on greater benefits to producers and the owners of capital rather than on greater benefits to consumers and wage earners. The effects of such a policy choice on the redistribution of income in Canada are not insignificant; just as the temporary employment programs introduced in the fall of 1971 were a response to labour pressure over the rate of unemployment, the corporate tax cuts introduced by John Turner were partly a response to business pressure over the fall in profits which resulted from the failure of the PIC. Federal fiscal policy in late 1971 and early 1972 can thus be seen as a further attempt to balance the simultaneous requirements of the accumulation and legitimation functions.

It did not take long for the political consequences of the government's policy action to be felt. The year 1972 was one of many changes and surprises in Canada, and not the least of them was the near-defeat of the Liberal government in the federal election of that year. There were undoubtedly many causes of that electoral disaster for the Liberals and this is certainly not the place to undertake an extensive analysis of the electoral behaviour involved. None the less, it is readily apparent that economic issues did play an important part in the outcome of the election. There was obviously a strong element of lingering dissatisfaction on the part of the electorate with the Liberal government's deliberate policy of halting inflation on the backs of the unemployed in 1969 and 1970. Several opinion studies taken during the election revealed that the issues of unemployment, inflation, and the economy were uppermost in the voters' minds.[32] What was even more interesting about the 1972 federal election was the degree of success which the NDP enjoyed as a result of its election campaign which had focused almost exclusively on the issue of the corporate tax cuts and the inequities of the corporate and personal income tax.

As a consequence of the outcome of the 1972 election, the first budget brought down by the minority Liberal government on 19 February 1973 was a strange mixture of competing policy alternatives. Because Parliament had been adjourned before the corporate tax cuts had been passed into law, the government was compelled to reintroduce them in the 1973 budget in order to get them enacted. Finance Minister Turner was determined to see them passed. In order to do so, however, he had to gain the support of the NDP, which held the balance of power in the new Parliament, for his budget proposals. At the same time, there was a strong feeling on the part of some members of the cabinet that the restrictive economic policy which the government had followed in the period from 1968 to 1970 had cost them dearly in the past election. According to one report, they were determined not to be placed in the same position if a snap election were forced by the NDP. The prime minister, in particular, felt quite strongly on this point.[33] For these reasons, the budget which was introduced by Mr Turner on 19 February was a strongly expansionary one in spite of the warnings of the Department of Finance that the economy was already well on the way to a strong upswing on its own. In addition to the corporate tax cuts the budget contained several other expansionary measures, including a personal income tax cut of 5 per cent and a provision to index the basic personal exemption to the annual increase in the CPI. The stimulus it provided, combined with the natural impetus of an expanding economy and strong international demand, resulted in the largest annual increase in the GNP since 1966, a moderate fall in the rate of unemployment, and a significant rise in the CPI (Table 1). Reliance was not placed only on fiscal policy in this period to provide the stimulus which the economy needed. After the extremely tight control which the Bank of Canada had exercised over the growth of the money supply in 1969 and 1970, the bank undertook an almost complete reversal of policy in the next three years. Between 1971 and 1973 the narrowly defined money supply (consisting of currency and demand deposits) grew at annual rates of between 12.8 and 14.4 per cent (Table 6), which undoubtedly contributed significantly to the strong degree of demand in the economy. This policy was designed to avoid the further appreciation of the Canadian dollar relative to the value of the US dollar.[34]

The next budget was introduced by the government on 6 May 1974. This budget was intended to be neutral in its fiscal impact as it read the economy as expanding quite steadily under the influence of the previous year's budget. In a rather controversial move, however, it did propose a further extension of the corporate tax-cut scheme. This suggestion proved to be unacceptable to the NDP, and as a consequence the government was defeated on the issue of the budget. The Liberals were returned with a new majority in the ensuing election and this fact gives rise to further speculation about the nature of the electorate's behaviour. As was stated previously, the issues which determine the outcome of an election are many and varied, but one which undoubtedly played an important role in the 1974 election was the generally more buoyant economic conditions of 1973 and 1974 which inspired greater confidence in the Liberals.

By the time the government reintroduced its budget in November 1974, economic conditions had changed dramatically. The American recession was under way and its effects had already made themselves felt in Canada. Under these circumstances Mr Turner deemed it advisable to bring down a more expansionary budget than the one which had been defeated in the spring. He also, however, insisted on including for a fourth time the by-now infamous corporate tax cuts, this time with no specific time limit. The budget of 18 November 1974 began on a note of pessimism. It now seemed to the minister of finance that a structural change had occurred in the operation of the Canadian economy, for it appeared to reach a stage of relative scarcity and tightness in the labour markets at a much higher level of unemployment than it had previously, which raised serious problems for the government's goals of maintaining high levels of employment and output simultaneously with relative price stability. At the same time, Mr Turner was becoming more concerned with what he saw as an increasingly competitive struggle over the division of the national income under conditions of accelerating inflation: 'Given the inflation which has occurred, no group is willing to exercise restraint unless it knows that others will also exercise restraint ... The hard truth remains, however, that in this struggle the sum total of all the claims on the nation's resources – however justified they may seem to be – clearly exceeds what in fact is available to be shared. No group is likely to succeed in getting the full share of the real national pie to which it feels entitled ... We have to find a better way of reconciling the competing interests of the various groups which make up our society ... This is why we need a national consensus about what the various groups can safely take from the economy over the next few years.'

A scant four years after the abortive attempt at a prices and incomes policy had been abandoned, the Liberals found themselves faced with an almost identical problem. The sharp turn away from a restrictive fiscal policy which the Liberal government had undertaken in mid-1970 had had its effect on the economy. It had combined with the sharp upswing in the American economy and the international commodities boom of 1973-4 to produce an exceptionally strong rate of growth in the Canadian economy. It also had led to a strong resurgence of inflationary price increases in 1973 and 1974 as can be seen from the rate of increase in the CPI (Table 1). As is usual in the upswing of the business cycle, wages dropped dramatically from the high share of the national income which they had held in 1970, 72.8 per cent, to a low of 67.9 per cent in 1974. In the same period, the share going to corporate profits rose just as dramatically from 11.8 to a high of 16.1 per cent (Table 2). This sharp reversal in the fortunes of wage and salary earners was not accepted passively, for the rise in the level of strike activity in 1974 is evidence of the increased determination of the labour movement to recover some of the benefits which it had lost (Table 4). It was in response to this growing pressure from the trade unions that Mr Turner issued his dire pronouncements in the 1974 budget concerning the inadequacy of the economic pie to meet the demands of competing economic interest groups.

What many of the economic policy-makers in this country appear to have overlooked is the fact that over the course of the last fifteen years there has been yet another shift going on as well, a shift in the revenue base of the government to the personal income tax as the dominant source of income. The share of revenue for all levels of government derived from the personal income tax rose from a low of 25.5 in 1962 to a high of 38.5 per cent in 1975; at the same time, the share of all government revenue derived from the corporate income tax fell steadily from a high of 14.8 in 1960 to a low of 9.5 per cent in 1971 and returned to 10.7 per cent in 1975 (Table 7). It should be noted that the growth in the share of revenue derived from the corporate income tax reflects the tremendous growth in corporate profits since 1971 (Table 2), rather than a significant increase in the rate of taxation on corporations in the same period (Table 9). The same trends are evident in the shifting of the bases of revenue for the federal government as well. Personal income taxes as a source of federal government revenue grew steadily from a low of 37.3 per cent in 1962 to a record post-war high of 49.6 in 1975; at the same time, corporate profit taxes as a source of federal government revenue fell from a high of 20.1 per cent in 1960 to a low of 14.4 in 1971 and recovered slightly to 15.3 per cent in 1975 (Table 8). It is equally obvious from Table 2 that these trends do not mirror any similar trend in the distribution of the national income between wages and salaries on the one hand and corporate profits on the other. They reflect rather a steady rise in the level of effective taxation on personal income at both the federal and provincial levels of government and a not quite so steady but still noticeable fall in the effective rate of taxation on corporate profits (Tables 9 and 10). This shift represents an essential element of the state's strategy to support and promote the conditions for the profitable accumulation of capital in Canada. The most dramatic declines in the effective rate of taxation on corporate profits in both the mid-1960s and in the early 1970s have been associated with the introduction of very generous packages of tax incentives by the federal government to promote greater capital investment by corporations. While this factor cannot account for all of the observed shift, it does provide an important insight into the reasons for its occurrence.

The shifting of the tax base has not been without its implications for the other important role of the state in advanced capitalist society, the performance of its legitimation function. There is a growing body of economic literature which suggests that the increasing burden of taxation borne by the

Table 7
Total government revenues, 1960-75 (distribution by source)

	Direct taxes persons[a]		Direct taxes corporations		Indirect taxes		Other revenue		Total	
	$ millions	%	$ millions	%	$ millions	%	$ millions	%	$ millions	%
1960	2,794	26.1	1,588	14.8	4,901	45.8	1,427	13.3	10,710	100
1961	2,944	25.9	1,649	14.5	5,159	45.4	1,613	14.2	11,365	100
1962	3,180	25.5	1,753	14.0	5,807	46.5	1,751	14.0	12,491	100
1963	3,387	25.5	1,891	14.2	6,115	45.9	1,915	14.4	13,308	100
1964	3,917	26.1	2,100	14.0	6,877	45.8	2,110	14.1	15,004	100
1965	4,431	26.4	2,197	13.1	7,741	46.2	2,392	14.3	16,761	100
1966	5,792	29.7	2,355	12.0	8,669	44.4	2,710	13.9	19,526	100
1967	7,009	31.9	2,396	10.9	9,489	43.2	3,082	14.0	21,976	100
1968	8,244	33.0	2,852	11.4	10,303	41.3	3,575	14.3	24,974	100
1969	10,055	34.5	3,221	11.1	11,423	39.2	4,442	15.2	29,141	100
1970	11,547	36.2	3,070	9.6	12,055	37.7	5,282	16.5	31,954	100
1971	13,042	36.9	3,346	9.5	13,048	36.9	5,880	16.7	35,316	100
1972	14,656	36.9	3,877	9.8	14,697	37.0	6,488	16.3	39,718	100
1973	17,064	37.3	4,747	10.4	16,500	36.0	7,448	16.3	45,759	100
1974	21,022	36.9	6,468	11.3	20,541	36.1	8,940	15.7	56,971	100
1975	23,650	38.5	6,595	10.7	20,826	33.9	10,390	16.9	61,461	100

[a]After 1966 includes Canada Pension Plan and Quebec Pension Plan
Source: *Economic Review* (April 1976), Reference Table 52

wage and salary earners has at least been partly responsible for the acceleration of inflation in this country. The evidence from recent studies suggests that there is an increasing tendency on the part of well-organized workers to attempt to recoup the real wages lost through higher taxation by pushing up the level of their money wages.[35] This suggests that the most pressing problem which the government has faced in economic policy may in fact be a problem largely of its own making. In attempting to foster the conditions for profitable capital accumulation by reducing the burden of taxation on corporate profits, the government has shifted the growing burden of this taxation to wage and salary earners. A more logical solution to this dilemma might have been to reduce the level of government expenditures and thereby reduce the necessity for increased taxation. To do so by reducing its commitment to the package of social services legislation which has come to be associated with the welfare state would exacerbate the legitimation problems which the government faces.[36] Thus, raising the effective level of taxa-

Table 8
Federal government revenues, 1960-75 (distribution by source)

	Direct taxes persons		Direct taxes corporations		Indirect taxes		Other revenue		Total	
	$ millions	%	$ millions	%	$ millions	%	$ millions	%	$ millions	%
1960	2,503	38.4	1,308	20.1	2,177	33.4	529	8.1	6,517	100
1961	2,629	38.8	1,345	19.8	2,188	32.3	617	9.1	6,779	100
1962	2,605	37.3	1,314	18.8	2,400	34.4	660	9.5	6,979	100
1963	2,730	37.3	1,412	19.3	2,449	33.4	732	10.0	7,323	100
1964	3,129	37.5	1,575	18.8	2,845	34.1	806	9.6	8.355	100
1965	3,332	36.6	1,652	18.2	3,245	35.7	866	9.5	9,095	100
1966	3,634	36.4	1,774	17.8	3,570	35.7	1,006	10.1	9,984	100
1967	4,305	39.5	1,758	16.1	3,705	34.0	1,138	10.4	10,906	100
1968	5,125	42.0	2,107	17.2	3,761	30.8	1,225	10.0	12,218	100
1969	6,503	44.9	2,402	16.6	4,028	27.8	1,557	10.7	14,490	100
1970	7,436	47.9	2,276	14.6	4,034	26.0	1,782	11.5	15,528	100
1971	8,299	48.1	2,476	14.4	4,480	26.0	1,985	11.5	17,240	100
1972	9,310	47.7	2,841	14.6	5,121	26.2	2,246	11.5	19,518	100
1973	10,889	48.1	3,455	15.3	5,837	25.8	2,457	10.8	22,638	100
1974	13,507	46.0	4,618	15.7	8,495	28.0	2,733	9.3	29,353	100
1975	15,243	49.6	4,718	15.3	7,888	25.7	2,902	9.4	30,751	100

Source: *Economic Review* (April 1976), Reference Table 54

tion on personal income remained the most viable alternative. However, by indirectly contributing to the inflationary spiral this policy merely added to the state's other problems and proved to be no solution in fact. The conflicting demands of the accumulation and legitimation functions constantly place the state in the position of having to trade off irreconcilable policy goals. The refined art of 'fine tuning' tends to become more one of crisis management.

This was essentially the situation that the government faced early in 1975 as the downturn in the economy accelerated, and as pressure for wages to catch up to cost increases led to a shift in the national income from corporate profits to wages and salaries. The situation in the economy in late 1974 and early 1975 bore a remarkable resemblance to that of 1968-9 (Table 2). In a special publication on wage developments in Canada in March 1975, the business-oriented C.D. Howe Research Institute of Montreal observed that there was nothing particularly unusual about this development: 'The erosion in real earnings – that is, earnings adjusted to eliminate the effects of higher prices – that the average worker experienced between 1972 and

Table 9
Direct taxes as a percentage of income, all levels of government, 1960-75

	Personal income	Direct taxes persons		Corporation profits	Direct taxes corporations	
	$ millions	$ millions	%	$ millions	$ millions	%
1960	29,595	2,794	9.4	3,870	1,588	41.0
1961	30,104	2,944	9.8	4,066	1,649	40.6
1962	32,788	3,180	9.7	4,450	1,753	39.4
1963	34,829	3,387	9.7	4,932	1,891	38.3
1964	37,282	3,917	10.5	5,841	2,100	36.0
1965	41,071	4,431	10.8	6,318	2,197	34.8
1966	46,094	5,792	12.6	6,714	2,355	35.1
1967	50,579	7,009	13.9	6,823	2,396	35.1
1968	55,677	8,244	14.8	7,742	2,852	36.8
1969	61,804	10,055	16.3	8,294	3,221	38.8
1970	66,633	11,547	17.3	7,699	3,070	39.9
1971	73,876	13,042	17.7	8,681	3,346	38.5
1972	83,189	14,656	17.6	10,704	3,877	36.2
1973	95,487	17,064	17.9	14,386	4,747	33.0
1974	111,469	21,022	18.9	18,303	6,468	35.3
1975	127,886	23,650	18.5	17,768	6,595	37.1

Source: *Economic Review* (April 1976), Reference Tables 12, 52, 8, 52

1974 reflects both an unusually rapid rate of inflation over this period and the normal kind of wage patterns that occur during the latter stages of a business cycle expansion. Workers are now seeking to catch up for inflation and to obtain their traditional share of increased economic output, even though the Canadian economy has now entered the contraction phase of the business cycle.'[37]

The government, however, was not prepared to regard the mounting pressure of wage demands and the shift to a greater share of wages in the national income as the normal patterns which occur during the latter stages of the business cycle expansion. Finance Minister Turner, in particular, appeared quite unwilling to see the gains for corporate profits, for which he had fought so hard with his corporate tax incentives, evaporate under increased pressure from wage demands. It was in this atmosphere that he launched his efforts of May and June 1975 to formulate a consensus between business and labour on wage and price increases. The whole undertaking bore a striking resemblance to the activities of John Young as chair-

Table 10
Direct taxes as a percentage of income, federal government, 1960-75

	Personal income	Direct taxes persons		Corporation profits	Direct taxes corporations	
	$ millions	$ millions	%	$ millions	$ millions	%
1960	29,595	2,503	8.5	3,870	1,308	33.8
1961	30,104	2,629	8.7	4,066	1,345	33.1
1962	32,788	2,605	7.9	4,450	1,314	29.5
1963	34,829	2,730	7.8	4,932	1,412	28.6
1964	37,282	3,129	8.4	5,841	1,575	27.0
1965	41,071	3,332	8.1	6,318	1,652	26.1
1966	46,094	3,634	7.9	6,714	1,774	26.4
1967	50,579	4,305	8.5	6,823	1,758	25.8
1968	55,677	5,125	9.2	7,742	2,107	27.2
1969	61,804	6,503	10.5	8,294	2,402	29.0
1970	66,633	7,436	11.2	7,699	2,276	29.6
1971	73,876	8,299	11.2	8,681	2,476	28.5
1972	83,189	9,310	11.3	10,704	2,841	26.5
1973	95,487	10,889	11.4	14,386	3,455	24.0
1974	111,469	13,507	12.1	18,303	4,618	25.2
1975	127,886	15,243	11.9	17,768	4,718	26.6

Note: In both Tables 9 and 10 the corporate profits and the corporate tax columns are not directly comparable because the latter includes the taxes on government business enterprises while the former does not.
Sources: *Economic Review* (April 1976), Reference Tables 12, 54, 8, 54

man of the Prices and Incomes Commission in 1969. The difference was that behind Mr Turner's gloved hand of consensus lay a mailed fist of more forceful measures. In a speech to the Investment Dealers Association of Canada, which proved less prophetic than premonitory, Mr Turner warned that huge wage demands by labour, which would damage Canada's competitive position as an exporting nation, would lead to government action. He said that the recent increases in wages and salaries in Canada, which were substantially higher than wage increases in the United States, posed a serious danger to Canada's international competitive position and their effects were already being reflected in Canada's large and growing balance of trade deficit. He estimated that Canada's capital expenditure requirements for the next decade could amount to $500 million in 1974 dollars. In order to generate this amount of capital for investment, he reminded his audience that there must be an awareness of the 'importance of maintaining corporate profits at an adequate level to attract new funds from outside and generating funds internally through retained earnings with which to finance expanded capital investment.'[38]

In the context of this debate over the sources of Canada's capital investment funds for the next decade and the potential threats posed by labour's militancy, it is revealing to examine a related development which apparently was overlooked by Mr Turner in his speech, namely, the contribution of US direct investment in meeting these needs. In the decade of the 1950s the net contribution of US direct investment to Canada's capital needs amounted to $1208 million. However, in the next eight years, from 1960 to 1967, this surplus became a deficit of $1744 million.[39] In the period under examination this trend not only continued but accelerated as well. From 1968 to 1975 the net difference between income remitted to US parent corporations and new capital inflow to Canada increased more than threefold to $6588 million.[40] The high degree of dependence in the Canadian economy on foreign-based multinationals and the lack of domestic-based ones has meant that, for Canada, the intensified rivalry between large oligopolistic corporations in the international economy has produced a net outflow of capital at an accelerating rate. And, as might be expected, this net outflow of capital has contributed its share to the growing conflict between labour and capital over the division of the national income.

It was in an environment of rising unemployment, accelerating inflation, a strong shift in the distribution of the national income in favour of wages and salaries, and a growing concern with Canada's deteriorating international competitive position that John Turner brought down his final budget of 23 June 1975. By that date, his talks on a wage-price consensus with representatives of business and labour had failed, and it was generally believed that he would introduce some form of mandatory wage and price restraints. To the surprise of all and for reasons that are not totally clear, Mr Turner chose not to follow this course of action. He echoed in the budget many of the same concerns which he had expressed in his speech to the Investment Dealers Association. He felt that the country was caught in a real dilemma with the possibilities of either increased inflation or increased unemployment facing it. Given this dilemma, he did not appear to have a great deal of difficulty in deciding which was the worse alternative. He reiterated his concern with the size of the cost increases that were being built into the economy through large wage gains and once again voiced his fears that these cost increases were seriously damaging Canada's ability to compete internationally. Thus the major focus of the budget was on an attempt to deal with these inflationary cost increases without adversely affecting the country's employment prospects. The methods chosen to accomplish this objective consisted largely of exercising greater restraint in the area of government expenditure and, in particular, exercising a tougher wage and salary policy in the federal government. This was to be achieved by cutting the growth of government expenditures by one billion dollars in the current fiscal year, by renegotiating its contribution to hospital insurance programs with the provinces, by placing a ceiling on its contributions under the Medical Care Act, and by instituting changes in the Unemployment Insurance Act that would reduce the amount of the cost borne by the government and increase the amount borne by employers and employees. Taken as a whole, the discretionary effect of the budget was intended to be decidedly restrictive in spite of the sizeable deficits which were forecast. It must be kept in mind that much of the projected deficit was a passive one, resulting from the sharp downturn in the level of economic activity, and that the changes introduced in the budget all had a restrictive intent.[41] Thus it appears that when Mr Turner was faced with the dilemma of simultaneous inflation and unemployment, he responded in the same fashion as his predecessor had six years earlier.

Clear though the intentions of this budget may have been, it was felt by many economic commentators to have avoided the main issue. Over the course of the summer, the government and Mr Turner came under increasing pressure to take more direct actions to deal with inflation, which showed little sign of abating. It appears that the pressure finally got to the minister of finance and in September he tendered his resignation. The prime minister quickly appointed Donald S. Macdonald to take his place, and in a rapid move to counter what was feared to be a dramatic loss of business confidence in the government he introduced a selective program of wage and price restraints in a nation-wide television broadcast on 13 October 1975. The government's program, tabled in the House of Commons the next day and entitled *Attack on Inflation*, consisted of four main policy elements: fiscal and monetary policies aimed at increasing total demand at a rate consistent with a falling rate of inflation; government expenditure policies aimed at limiting the growth of public expenditures; structural policies to deal with the special problems of energy, food, and housing; and a prices and incomes policy which established guidelines for determining prices and the incomes of groups.

Similar developments in the field of monetary policy also indicated that the government intended to pursue its anti-inflationary policy with all vigour. In September 1975 the Bank of Canada raised its lending rate to the chartered banks from 8¼ to 9 per cent in a move designed to contain inflation. At the time the anti-inflation program was introduced in October, the governor, Gerald Bouey, made it known that he considered the bank's past actions in allowing the money supply to expand too rapidly to be at least partially responsible for the country's inflationary dilemma. He committed the Bank of Canada to a steadier and slower approach to monetary growth in order to ensure the success of the government's anti-inflation policy.[42] To support this point, the bank again announced an increase in its lending rate from 9 to 9½ per cent in March 1976, at a time when many financial analysts were expecting a drop in interest rates because of the rapidly appreciating value of the Canadian dollar.[43] Thus it appears that in 1975-6 the government turned the direction of the major economic policy tools at its disposal – discretionary fiscal policy, monetary policy, and mandatory wage and price controls – sharply towards the curtailment of the major economic problems of inflation and spiralling wage increases.

The similarity between the government's policies in this period and its policies in 1969-70 are too striking to go unnoticed. On the basis of the analysis presented here, there seems little reason to believe that the outcome will be any different. The only question of major significance which remains unanswered is whether the mandatory wage and price controls imposed in October 1975 will have an even more alienating effect on the organized labour movement than did the voluntary Prices and Incomes Commission in 1970 and thus create greater legitimation problems for the Canadian state in the future.

In the middle of 1977 it is still too early to answer the above question unequivocally; however, some preliminary observations are possible. Over the eighteen months since its inauguration, the reaction to the government's anti-inflation program has been mixed. This is especially true of the trade union reaction to the program. On the one hand, the labour movement, as represented by the CLC, has expressed strong and militant opposition to the wage and price control program. This opposition was in evidence at the CLC's demonstration in Ottawa in March 1976 and again at its National Day of Protest on 14 October when over one million of its members went on strike. Yet the CLC introduced Labour's Manifesto for Canada at its national convention in May 1976, a tremendously ambiguous document which has made the extent of the CLC's opposition to the anti-inflation program appear quite inconsistent. By involving the CLC in a series of discussions with the government on tripartism, the manifesto has detracted from and weakened the labour movement's struggle against wage and price con-

283 **David Wolfe**

trols. Moreover, through its involvement with the government in the discussions on post-controls society, the CLC has demonstrated its failure to recognize that the government is primarily interested in tripartism as a means to secure wage restraint. The one factor which will likely save the labour movement from compromising its own position is the inability of the government to offer the CLC a strong enough inducement to actually co-opt it into a tripartite arrangement. Certainly there appears to be little likelihood at present that an effective corporatist solution to the country's current economic problems will emerge.[44]

The anti-inflation program has enjoyed only limited success in realizing its economic goals. While the rate of increase in the CPI dropped significantly in 1976, it was questionable whether this was primarily the result of the Anti-Inflation Board's activities or the result of other economic factors such as a substantial drop in the rate of food price increases. This success in the area of price moderation was not achieved without the sacrifice of other economic goals, as was the case with the fiscal restraint program of 1970-1. Economic growth in 1976 improved somewhat over the performance of 1975, yet it was lower than had been expected and the difference was attributed to the restraint program. Unemployment levels remained extremely high at more than 7 per cent throughout 1976. But the most significant result of all was the low level of increase in capital spending by business in 1976 and the projections for continued hesitancy on the part of business to invest in the next few years. In spite of the worsening economic situation, the government has refused to undertake any major initiatives to correct the problem. Apart from a reduction in the Bank of Canada's interest rate, which was determined primarily in response to the rate of growth of the money supply, and some half-hearted measures aimed at job creation, the government's economic policy for 1977, as articulated in the spring budget of 31 March, was decidedly restrictive. Furthermore, the minister of finance gave no indication that the government was prepared to end its wage and price control program or reverse its fiscal policies as unemployment mounted steadily through the middle of 1977.

In both 1969 and 1975 the government initiated a concerted effort using a combination of restrictive fiscal and monetary policies, a curb on the growth of government expenditures, and a form of incomes policy in order to slow inflation and the rate of wage increases. In each instance the government was able to achieve a temporary reduction in the rate of increase in inflation and wages but only at the expense of a substantial reduction in the rate of growth of employment and the size of the economy. In neither instance did the government's policy initiatives recognize the growing contradiction between the accumulation and legitimation functions of the state or attempt to come to grips with the underlying class conflicts in Canadian society . The probable outcome of the government's most recent restraint program will be a further intensification of the struggle over the division of the national income after controls are removed. It can be expected that the trade unions and other wage earners will waste little time in attempting to recover whatever losses in real income they have suffered as a result of the government's restrictive economic policies. This, in turn, will probably result in a further worsening of the trade-off between inflation and unemployment. The long-term prospects for economic policy in Canada would tend towards further difficulty on the part of the government in achieving the desired goals of steady economic growth with full employment and relative price stability. This lack of success will reflect the growing inability of the state to perform both its accumulation and legitimation functions simultaneously.

NOTES

1 Andrew Shonfield, *Modern Capitalism: The Changing Balance of Public and Private Power* (London 1969), 3
2 This is a revised version of a paper presented to the annual meetings of the Canadian Political Science Association in Quebec City on 31 May 1976. I have benefited greatly from the many discussions which I have had with John Keane, Bob Baldwin, Peter Warrian, Irwin Gillespie, Leo Panitch, and Don Swartz. Needless to say, the responsibility for the final product is entirely my own. I would also like to extend a special thanks to Marlys Edwardh, Chuck Rachlis, and David Rayside for general support and encouragement throughout the project. The research for this paper was undertaken with the financial support of a Canada Council Fellowship, which is gratefully acknowledged.
3 Angus Maddison, *Economic Growth in the West: Comparative Experience in Europe and North America* (New York 1964), 106; Shonfield, *Modern Capitalism*, 6; Organization for Economic Co-operation and Development, *The Aims and Instruments of Industrial Policy: A Comparative Study* (Paris 1975), 39-41; Mervyn A. King, 'The United Kingdom Profits Crisis: Myth or Reality,' *Economic Journal*, LXXXV, 337 (March 1975), 45
4 The concepts of 'capital' and 'labour' are used here and throughout this paper in both their economic and sociological senses. In their economic sense, the concepts refer to the two major inputs in the productive process and to the two major factors of production between which the product of production is distributed. In their sociological sense, the concepts refer to the two major

classes of advanced capitalist society, the capitalist class and the working class. While the terms 'labour' and 'labour movement' are substituted for the term 'working class' throughout this paper, it should be noted that the two are not co-extensive. The present analysis assumes that the organized labour movement represents the most advanced and politically conscious elements of the working class in advanced capitalist society and, consequently, the most politically relevant segment of the working class. However, by no means are the interests of the labour movement always assumed to be identical with the interests of the working class as a whole.

5 O'Connor, *The Fiscal Crisis of the State* (New York 1973); Offe, 'Political Authority and Class Structures – An Analysis of Late Capitalist Societies,' *International Journal of Sociology*, II (1972); Offe, 'The Abolition of Market Control and the Problem of Legitimacy (I),' *Kapitalistate*, 1 (1973); cf. Jurgen Habermas, *Legitimation Crisis* (Boston 1975), Part II. The question of legitimation problems in advanced capitalism is treated in a much narrower context in this paper than it is by Offe and Habermas or even by O'Connor.

6 *Selected Essays on the Dynamics of the Capitalist Economy, 1933-1970* (Cambridge 1971), 141

7 Ian Gough, 'State Expenditure in Advanced Capitalism,' *New Left Review*, 92 (July-Aug. 1975), 70; cf. Aubrey Jones, *The New Inflation: The Politics of Prices and Incomes* (Harmondsworth 1973), 44-5, 120; Joan Robinson and John Eatwell, *An Introduction to Modern Economics* (London 1973), 190. This is by no means the only cause of inflation in contemporary capitalist economies, but most certainly the prime cause. For a fuller discussion of the problems, cf. Dudley Jackson, H.A. Turner, and Frank Wilkinson, *Do Trade Unions Cause Inflation?* (Cambridge 1975). It is also important to note, with regard to the measurement of the distribution of income between capital and labour, that the wages and salaries category in the national income accounts includes many income earners who are not properly part of the working class. Thus the national income figures used in this paper should be taken as an indication of the distribution of the social product between capital and labour rather than an accurate account of it.

8 Claus Offe, 'Structural Problems of the Capitalist State: Class Rule and the Political System. On the Selectiveness of Political Institutions,' in Klaus von Beyme, ed., *German Political Studies* (London 1974), 1, 50-1

9 Leo Panitch, *Social Democracy and Industrial Militancy: The Labour Party, the Trade Unions and Incomes Policy, 1945-1974* (Cambridge 1976), 249

10 Gough, 'State Expenditure,' 87-8

11 Bill Warren, 'The Internationalization of Capital and the Nation State: A Comment,' *New Left Review*, 68 (July-Aug. 1971), 85

12 Jack N. Behrman, 'The Multinational Firm and the Nation State: Another View,' in Gilles Paquet, ed., *The Multinational Firm and the Nation State* (Toronto 1972), 135

13 Bob Rowthorn, 'Imperialism in the Seventies – Unity or Rivalry?' *New Left Review*, 69 (Sept.-Oct. 1971), 48-50

14 Throughout the remainder of this paper, the analysis will focus on the federal level of government. Although Donald Smiley in *Canada in Question: Federalism in the Seventies* (Toronto 1972), 114-20, has raised the question of the impact of the provincial governments on economic policy, recent evidence suggests that the federal government still plays the predominant role in this field due to its control over the major instruments of fiscal and monetary policy; cf. M.A. Sheikh and S.L. Winer, 'Stabilization and Nonfederal Behaviour in an Open Federal State,' Economic Council of Canada, Discussion Paper no. 58, July 1976.

15 Other articles in this volume deal with the social forces at work in Canada in producing the post-war settlement, but cf. Donald Creighton, *The Forked Road: Canada, 1939-1957* (Toronto 1976), 77-82. For a detailed account of the planning of Canada's post-war welfare state, see J.L. Granatstein, *Canada's War: The Politics of the Mackenzie King Government, 1939-1945* (Toronto 1975), chap. 7. The goals and intentions of the government regarding fiscal policy in the post-war economy were summarized in Department of Reconstruction, *Employment and Income with Special Reference to the Initial Period of Reconstruction* (Ottawa 1945), which was presented to Parliament by the minister of reconstruction in April 1945. A personal account of the origins of the *White Paper on Employment and Income* can be found in W.A. Mackintosh, 'The *White Paper on Employment and Income* in Its 1945 Setting,' in S.F. Kaliski, ed., *Canadian Economic Policy since the War* (Montreal 1966).

16 Robert M. Will, *Canadian Fiscal Policy, 1945-63*, Studies of the Royal Commission on Taxation, no. 17 (Ottawa 1966), 61-2

17 The formation of the Economic Council itself in 1963 was the combined result of a concern over the prolonged inability of the economy to pull out of the 1958-62 recession and a growing feeling that there was a need for a consensus-creating body, similar to the ones established in France and Britain, to chart a course for the economy, that could be agreed upon by all relevant parties. H.E. English, 'Economic Planning in Canada,' in T.N. Brewis *et al., Canadian Economic Policy* (rev. ed., Toronto 1965), 359-61, and Gilles Paquet, 'The Economic Council as Phoenix,' in Trevor Lloyd and Jack McLeod, *Agenda 1970: Proposals for a Creative Politics* (Toronto 1968), 138

18 Stuart Jamieson, *Industrial Relations in Canada* (Toronto 1973), 96-101. It should be noted that this new wave of labour militancy was not distributed

evenly across all sectors of the economy but was largely concentrated in a few
principal sectors, such as the construction industry, railways, and other segments of the transportation sector and part of the public sector (which had just
been granted collective bargaining rights).

19 'Government Policy and Recent Inflation in Canada,' in N. Swan and D. Wilson, eds., *Inflation and the Canadian Experience* (Kingston 1971), 230
20 Canada, Department of Consumer and Corporate Affairs, *Policies for Price
Stability* (Ottawa 1968), 28
21 G.A. Berger, *Canada's Experience with Incomes Policy, 1969-1970*, Prices and Incomes Commission (Ottawa 1973), 10
22 George Haythorne, 'Prices and Incomes Policy: The Canadian Experience,
1969-1972,' *International Labour Review*, CVIII (1973), 496
23 PIC, *Inflation, Unemployment and Incomes Policy, Summary Report* (Ottawa
1972), 47-8
24 *Can. H. of C. Debates*, 22 Oct. 1968, p. 1683; 3 June 1969, pp. 9414-23; 12
March 1970, p. 4740
25 Thomas J. Courchene, 'Stabilization Policy: A Monetarist Interpretation,' in
L.H. Officer and L.B. Smith, eds., *Issues in Canadian Economics* (Toronto 1974),
52
26 Officer and Smith, 'Trade-Offs in Stabilization Policy,' in *ibid.*, 23
27 'Government Policy and Recent Inflation,' 241
28 W.I. Gillespie, 'The Federal Budget as Plan, 1968-1972,' *Canadian Tax Journal*,
XXI, 1 (1973), 715
29 Bruce Wilkinson, 'Recent American Tax Concessions to Industry and Canadian Economic Policy,' *Canadian Tax Journal*, XX, 1 (1972), 2-3
30 Canada, Tax Measures Review Committee, *Corporate Tax Measures Review: Final Report to Parliament* (Ottawa 1975), 12
31 John Helliwell and John Lester, 'Reviewing the Latest DISC: Simulations of Its
Aggregate Impact on Canada,' *Canadian Tax Journal*, XX, 4 (1972), 297
32 John Meisel, *Working Papers on Canadian Politics* (enlarged ed., Montreal
1973), 220
33 Wayne Cheveldayoff, 'Control of Money Supply Called Ottawa Plan Key,'
Globe and Mail, Toronto, Report on Business, 28 Oct. 1975
34 Courchene, 'Stabilization Policy,' 53. In his recent study, *Money, Inflation and
the Bank of Canada: An Analysis of Canadian Monetary Policy from 1970 to Early
1975* (Montreal 1976), Courchene has presented a more detailed analysis of
monetary policy in this period from a monetarist perspective.
35 Jackson *et al.*, *Do Trade Unions Cause Inflation?* 63-103, present this argument
with respect to the United Kingdom. Several studies of the Canadian experience
have reached similar conclusions: cf. D.A.L. Auld, 'The Impact of Taxes on

Wages and Prices,' *National Tax Journal*, XXVII, 1 (1974); C.J. Bruce, 'The Wage-Tax Spiral: Canada 1953-1970,' *Economic Journal*, CXXXV, 338 (1975); T.A. Wilson, 'Taxes and Inflation,' *Report of the Proceedings of the Twenty-fifth Tax Conference*, Canadian Tax Foundation (Toronto 1972).

36 It should be noted that this solution is being attempted by some provincial governments and is being met by resistance on the part of those most dependent on this form of state assistance. It remains to be seen how far the governments will go in implementing this strategy and how seriously it will contribute to the legitimation problems of the state.

37 Barbara Goldman and Judith Maxwell, *Wage Developments in Canada: The Pressure to Catch Up* (Montreal 1975), i

38 *Globe and Mail*, 7 June 1975

39 Kari Levitt, *Silent Surrender: The Multinational Corporation in Canada* (Toronto 1970), 168

40 United States, Department of Commerce, 'US Direct Investment Abroad in 1974,' and 'US Direct Investment Abroad in 1975,' *Survey of Current Business* (Nov. 1975 and Aug. 1976). Remitted income includes profits remitted to the US parent corporation plus royalties and licence fees.

41 W.I. Gillespie, 'The June 1975 Budget: Stabilization and Distribution Effects,' *Canadian Public Policy*, I, 4 (1975), 549

42 Cheveldayoff, 'Control of Money Supply'

43 'Large Money Supply Rejected as Way to Cut Interest Rates,' *Globe and Mail*, 19 March 1976

44 Leo Panitch, 'Labour's Manifesto,' *This Magazine*, X, 5 and 6 (Nov.-Dec. 1976), 11

10

The labour force and state workers in Canada

HUGH ARMSTRONG

During Pierre Elliott Trudeau's triumphant rise to political power in the late 1960s, one of his more memorable promises was to 'get the state out of the nation's bedrooms.' This catchy phrase no doubt played its part in building the attractive image of a swinging reformer as Canada's prime minister. However, if the state has relaxed somewhat its vigilant concern for sexual morality, the same cannot be said for its attention to other affairs. The state may be withdrawing gracefully from the bedroom, but it is moving in with increased determination almost everywhere else. From egg marketing board to day-care centre, from the nationality of rock groups on the radio to the language of work in the plant, from beer advertising to oil drilling, state intervention is on the rise.

The hostile reception accorded Trudeau's more recent musings on the decline and fall of the 'free enterprise' system notwithstanding, this increased intervention is not the result of a personality quirk or of closet socialism on his part. Canada shares with all the other advanced capitalist countries the experience of greatly increased state intervention during recent years, however laissez-faire their dominant ideologies might be. There is, of course, an ambiguity in the term 'state intervention' with regard to the distinction between the state's influence on the management of the economic system as a whole and the state's direct determination of a large segment of the economy through state spending. In other words, without implying a position of state neutrality or of a freely competitive economy, the state as umpire should be distinguished from the state as one of the players. With the imposition in 1975 of wage and price controls, much of the current debate in Canada is directed towards the issue of intensified state regulatory activities. And of course Canada has not been alone in trying to cope with inflation through state regulation. Yet it is more rewarding in theoretical terms, as well as more feasible in quantitative terms, to compare Canada with the others on the longer-run question of the state's growing direct share of the economy. On this score, neither its current level of state spending nor its growth rate sets Canada apart from, say, the other members of the so-called 'Group of Ten.'[1]

The broad purpose of this article is to examine aspects of the post-war growth of the Canadian state sector through a documentation of the substantial growth in the number of state workers in the context of the persistence of the problem of unemployment in this period. Making use of the theoretical contribution of James O'Connor,[2] the paper demonstrates that the state's policy commitment to full employment since 1945 has entailed a large direct role for the state in job creation in the face of the inability of the 'private' sector to provide sufficient new jobs for the labour force. This perspective provides an important background for understanding the contradictions which capitalism in Canada, as elsewhere, has come to face since the 1960s – particularly evident in the increased militancy of state workers[3] and the deterioration of many state services – as the state's role as guarantor of high employment and provider of social services increasingly has come into conflict with the requisites of private capital accumulation.

THE 1945 WHITE PAPER ON EMPLOYMENT AND INCOME

'What would happen when the boys and girls came home and war production ceased? There were misgivings and fears. Memories of the depressed thirties were in everybody's mind.'[4] Thus did C.D. Howe recall in 1954 the grave concern felt by the federal government near the close of the Second World War that Canada was headed for a return to the pre-war conditions of unemployment and social unrest. To avoid such a haunting spectre, it was estimated that about a million new jobs would have to be created during the period of transition from the conditions of war to those of peace. The estimate was contained in the April 1945 *White Paper on Employment and Income*, which announced that the government would be prepared 'in periods when unemployment threatens to incur the deficits resulting from its employment and income policy, whether the policy is best applied through increased expenditures or reduced taxation. In periods of buoyant employment and income, budget plans will call for surpluses.'[5] Because of this seemingly radical departure from pre-war fiscal thought and practice, the white paper has been described by T.N. Brewis[6] as a 'revolutionary' document which 'set the stage for post-war Canadian policy.' There can be no doubt as to the influence of Keynesian thought in official Ottawa during and after the war. Prime Minister William Lyon Mackenzie King, for one, was certainly persuaded of its political as well as its economic value. The Brewis view of the white paper as a 'revolutionary' document, however, is implicitly disputed by W.A. Mackintosh who, as a senior wartime official in Howe's Department of Reconstruction and Supply, was its principal author. In a lecture series organized to commemorate the twentieth anniversary of the publication of the white paper, Mackintosh recalled having had 'no conscious intention to sell the Government of the day a revolutionary or even novel approach to postwar policy.' At issue was neither a theoretical breakthrough nor a departure from wartime experience. The innovation was that the state (at least at the federal level) made a clear, full, open, and long-term *commitment*, as a primary object of policy, to maintain a high and stable level of employment and income.[7] Therein lies the document's significance. It was an exercise in reassurance, not revolution. Hoping to 'produce a substantial consensus on the magnitude of the task and the direction in which to move and some measure of its feasibility,' Mackintosh wrote 'a single coherent statement, in simple language for laymen, of what had already been done and what could be expected of postwar conditions.'[8]

In simple, comprehensive terms, then, the federal government set out in the white paper its approach to the creation of a million new jobs. The use of state spending on current goods and services was ruled out as an instrument of employment policy because it could not 'to any large degree be determined with reference to the needs of employment, except in terms of reasonable stability.' And the federal government acknowledged that it and like governments had very little experience in 'the deliberate use of public investment expenditures as a permanent instrument in employment policy,' and would thus have to proceed cautiously in this direction. Such a line of reasoning was consistent with the government's belief that it was neither desirable nor practicable 'to look to the expansion of government enterprise to provide, to any large degree, the additional employment required' and was also consistent with its proclamation that 'a major and early task of reconstruction is to facilitate and encourage an expansion of private industry, including primary with other industries.' It attached higher importance to boosting exports, private investments, and consumption than to using public investment. Even where 'genuine public investment' was deemed appropriate in the field of the development and conservation of natural resources, its goal was to be to 'induce more private investment and not supplant it.'[9]

In the white paper, then, the diagnosis was that the danger of a severe unemployment problem with its attendant social unrest loomed large during the transition period from wartime to peacetime conditions. The prescription was to commit the state openly to a full employment policy, a policy to be implemented primarily by stimulating job creation in the 'private' sector.

It is now possible to assess over a reasonably long term developments in the labour force against the government's diagnosis and prescription, as articulated in April 1945. As will be shown below, unemployment has turned out to be more a structural than a transitional problem, the state has failed to honour its commitment to full employment, and the new jobs that have been created have not been predominantly in the 'private' sector. Before presenting the evidence showing how far off the mark the white paper was, however, it is in order to outline briefly O'Connor's argument concerning growth and its consequences for the advanced capitalist state, an argument which seems to fit the post-war Canadian experience of structural unemployment and direct state job creation more closely than does the analysis set out in the white paper.

THE O'CONNOR ARGUMENT

O'Connor starts his book with two premises concerning the advanced capitalist state: first, the state 'must try to fulfill two basic and often mutually contradictory functions – *accumulation* and *legitimation*'; second, 'the fiscal crisis of the state can be understood only in terms of the basic Marxist economic categories,' as state spending has a twofold character corresponding to these functions, with social capital expenditures and social expenses fulfilling the accumulation and legitimization functions respectively. The social capital expenditures are further subdivided into social investment expenditures on physical and 'human' capital and social consumption expenditures, notably for urban-suburban development and for social insurance.[10]

O'Connor then puts forward two theses: first, the 'the growth of the state is both a cause and an effect of the expansion of monopoly capital' and, second, that the growth of state expenditures and state expenses results in a fiscal crisis, or structural gap, between state spending and state revenues, a crisis exacerbated by the successful yet wasteful and even contradictory claims made on the state by a host of special interests, including organized labour and the poor. In arguing for these theses, O'Connor divides the economy into three sectors: competitive, monopoly, and state. The competitive sector is something of a residual category both in terms of his argument, with economic growth being seen as the result of the 'single process' of monopoly and state sector growth, and in terms of its role, with much of the 'surplus working population' as well as most of the 'surplus capitalists' being relegated to it. Unlike the competitive sector, the monopoly sector is capital-intensive, with high productivity (the growth of which is responsible for most of the sector's production growth), with large-scale stable production for national and international markets, with strong unions, and with relatively well-paid jobs, almost all of which are full-time and year-round and many of which are white collar. In the state sector, which includes the production of goods and services on contract to the state, productivity is low, demand for labour is quite stable, and unions, once weak, have become stronger than those in the competitive sector.

Most of O'Connor's attention is focused on the interplay of the monopoly and state sectors as it affects the state sector. Social investment expenditures by the state are seen to result from the increased scale, complexity, 'indivisibility,' and interdependence of physical capital projects in the monopoly capitalist era, as well as from the increased need to upgrade labour skills. Social consumption expenditures provide monopoly sector workers in particular with state-subsidized suburbs and social security, albeit in a wasteful fashion. State social expenses are mainly devoted to increased warfare and welfare spending to keep under control the growing 'surplus population' which is increasingly excluded from monopoly sector jobs where productivity hikes are insistently sought and achieved.[11]

Given the emphasis in this article on structural unemployment and state job creation, some elaboration of the factors pushing up social expenses on welfare, as seen by O'Connor, is appropriate. While the unbalanced development of regions and industries and the unequal class distribution of wealth and income are inherent to capitalism, they take on new significance in the monopoly capitalist phase. The internationalization of capital means that regions and industries rise and fall on a massive scale. Only the state has the resources with which to attempt to cope with these momentous changes. State intervention also has the effect of protecting inefficient industries by helping them avoid bankruptcy, especially during recessions. And during recessions giant firms lay off workers rather than lower prices. Finally, underdevelopment, industrial bankruptcy, and unemployment are no longer perceived, under monopoly capitalism, to be the products of the impersonal operation of free markets. They are instead attributed to the policies consciously adopted by giant firms, by unions, and by the state. The state in particular comes under increased pressure, then, to prevent them.

Although the white paper's emphasis on social unrest stemming from unemployment is shared by O'Connor, the two positions are, of course, very different. Not surprisingly, the language of the white paper clearly indicated acceptance of capitalist investment criteria, and indeed it stated explicitly a preference for private investment, while O'Connor is equally explicit in his choice of Marxist explanatory categories and politics. The unemployment problem was seen in the former to be transitional, with those engaged in the war effort having to find peacetime jobs, but it is seen by the latter to be structural, with monopoly sector growth generating a surplus population. Finally, while the authors of the white paper placed considerable faith in the capacity of the 'private' sector to create jobs, O'Connor directs our attention to the reasons for the heavy and direct job creation by the state. In the following two sections, Canadian evidence is marshalled to show that unemployment is much more than a transitional problem, and that the 'private' sector has failed to create the jobs required by Canadians since the Second World War. The evidence thus runs counter to the diagnosis and the prescription of the white paper while providing partial support for the O'Connor position.

THE UNEMPLOYMENT RECORD

There has been substantial fluctuation in the annual average unemployment rate in Canada since the Second World War,[12] and most of the peaks and troughs show up in Table 1. Thus the 1951 rate was the lowest from 1949 on, the 1966 rate was the lowest of the 1960s and 1970s, and the 1974 rate has been the lowest of the 1970s. Meanwhile the 1961 rate was the highest of the post-war period, until matched in 1976.[13] Beyond the fluctuation, however, a gradual if irregular upward trend can be discerned. Before 1958, the post-war rate was by Canadian standards relatively low, never reaching 5.0 per cent. In the nineteen years from 1958 to 1976 inclusive, it was above 5.0 per cent thirteen times, at or above 6.0 per cent eight times, and at or above 7.0 per cent five times.

It would be useful to look as well at the labour force participation rate because its increase is sometimes blamed for higher unemployment. The participation rate is the percentage of the civilian population fourteen years of age and over[14] (excepting residents of the Yukon and Northwest Territories, Indian reservations, prisons, and mental institutions) that is in the labour force. In order to assess the relationship of the participation rate to unemployment, it might help to compare it in Table 1 with what can be called the employment rate, or the percentage of the same population that is employed. What is striking is that the participation rate did not again reach its

295 **Hugh Armstrong**

Table 1
The Canadian labour force, 1946-76

	Labour force (000)	Participation rate (%)	Unemployment rate (%)	Employment rate[a] (%)
1946	4,829	55.0	3.4	53.1
1951	5,223	53.6	2.4	52.4
1956	5,782	53.5	3.4	51.7
1961	6,521	54.1	7.1	50.2
1966	7,420	55.1	3.6	53.1
1971	8,631	56.1	6.4	52.5
1974	9,662	58.3	5.4	55.2
1976[b]	10,308	61.1	7.1	56.7

[a]This concept is defined in the text.
[b]For methodological reasons, these data are not directly comparable to those for earlier years; see note 15.
Source: calculated from Statistics Canada, *The Labour Force,* various issues

1946 level of 55.0 per cent until 1966, after a post-war low of 52.9 per cent in 1954 and 1955.[15] Furthermore, if yearly changes in the participation and unemployment rates are compared, it is discovered that the two rates moved in the same direction ten times while moving in the opposite direction sixteen times (there was no yearly change in the participation rate the other four times). It is therefore questionable to attribute rising unemployment to rising participation, either over the long term or year by year. Indeed, the 1946 proportion of the adult population with jobs was not surpassed until 1973, a fact that is obscured by all the attention focused on participation rates in official Ottawa in the face of consistently high unemployment.

Against this backdrop of rising structural unemployment and the absence of an increase in the proportion of Canadian adults with jobs during the quarter-century after the second World War, the question of the rapid growth in the numbers of state workers can now be fruitfully examined.

THE GROWING NUMBERS OF STATE WORKERS

As is well known, the absolute number of state workers in Canadian government agencies, educational institutions, and hospitals has increased dramatically.[16] To be specific, between 1946 and 1974 their ranks grew from at least 417,430 to at least 1,939,720 or by 365 per cent. More significantly, the proportion of all Canadian workers employed by the state more than doubled from at least 8.9 per cent in 1946 to at least 21.2 per cent in 1974. Over a third of all new jobs were created directly by the state during this period, notwithstanding the heavy white paper emphasis on job creation in the 'private' sector.

State workers can conveniently be divided into three categories: government workers, education workers, and hospital workers. (The data on the first two categories are drawn from the *Taxation Statistics* series published annually by the Department of National Revenue for each tax year from 1946 on; the data on hospital workers are drawn from the *Hospital Statistics* series published by Statistics Canada.[17]) The category 'government workers' is not limited to civil servants: municipal government workers are included although they are not civil servants; and the employees of some but not all government enterprises are also included in this category. The criterion used by the Department of National Revenue seems to be the form of management of the enterprise concerned, as reflected in its name. Most of the clearly proprietary enterprises are excluded, even if they receive substantial state subsidies (for example, the Canadian Broadcasting Corporation). On the other hand, if a board or commission heads the enterprise, it is included. Hence, the National Film Board, the Hydro-Electric Power Commission of Ontario, and the Toronto Transit Commission, for example, are classified under the relevant level of government. Members of the armed forces are excluded, but civilian members of the Department of National Defence and members of the RCMP and other police forces are included. Employees of non-profit institutions are excluded, even if the institution concerned (for example, Children's Aid Societies) is largely or fully financed by a government, unless the employee's T4 tax slip is 'raised' or filled in by that government. Such are the major limitations imposed by the available data on government workers.[18]

Little comment is needed on Table 2. The most striking feature of the enormous growth in the numbers of government workers is its unevenness by level of government. In 1946 the federal total was greater than the combined provincial and municipal total, but it was smaller than either of the other two by 1971.[19] For all the ire directed from certain quarters at an Ottawa bureaucracy mushrooming out of control, the growth in the number of federal workers was only 138.9 per cent during the entire 1946-74 period, as against a figure of 533.5 per cent for provincial and municipal workers taken together.

The last column in Table 2 indicates that the proportion of those with work who were employed by government at all levels grew from 6.0 per cent in 1946 to 13.0 per cent in 1974. By looking at Table 3, we can compare the

297 Hugh Armstrong

Table 2
Government workers, by level of government, 1946-74 (selected years)

	Federal	Provincial[a]	Municipal	Total	Government workers as percentage of all workers
1946	146,257	64,991	67,120	278,368	6.0
1951	145,720	102,050	87,070	334,840	7.2
1956	185,885	138,239	118,278	442,402	7.9
1961	231,136	200,343	181,521	613,000	10.1
1966	258,281	299,047	256,716	814,044	11.4
1971	321,050	394,431	361,726	1,077,207	13.3
1974	349,340	449,825	386,902	1,186,067	13.0
1946-74:					
Increase	203,083	384,834	319,782	907,699	
Percentage increase	138.9	592.1	476.4	326.1	

[a]Includes territorial governments
Sources: calculated from Department of National Revenue, *Taxation Statistics* (Ottawa, various years) and from Table 1

Table 3
New government workers, 1946-74 (selected periods)

	Total new workers	New government workers	As percentage of all new workers
1946-51	431,000	56,472	13.1
1951-6	488,000	107,562	22.0
1956-61	470,000	170,598	36.3
1961-6	1,097,000	201,044	18.3
1966-71	927,000	263,163	28.4
1971-4	1,058,000	108,860	10.3
1946-74	4,471,000	907,699	20.3

Source: calculated from Tables 1 and 2

growth in government employment to that in the Canadian economy as a whole during specific post-war periods. While government has been directly responsible for creating an increased number of jobs during each five-year period (the final period being only three years long), the proportions of all new jobs going to government workers have fluctuated considerably. It will be recalled that during the 1956-61 and 1966-71 periods, unemployment rose sharply. It was during these two periods that the government shares of new jobs were particularly high.[20] On the other hand, before 1958 post-war unemployment was relatively low, and between 1961 and 1966 it dropped sharply. As a result, while the numbers of new government jobs and the proportions working for government certainly increased during each of the 1946-51, 1951-6, and 1961-6 periods, the government shares of new jobs were relatively low during these periods of low or dropping unemployment.

The 1971-4 period was also one of falling unemployment, but this cannot alone account for the sharp drop in the government share of new jobs, a drop that for the first time resulted in a decline in the government share of all jobs. One factor is that, for reasons of data availability, the most recent period is shorter than the others, making comparisons between it and them more vulnerable to short-term fluctuations. Indeed, using a different data source,[21] it can be estimated that government was directly responsible for an incredible 87 per cent of the few jobs created the following year, 1975, when the unemployment rate rose sharply again. And the rate continued to rise, although less markedly, in 1976.

Another, more significant, factor appears to be the concerted efforts by all governments in the 1970s to curb the growth of government jobs. Although the resulting 'cutbacks' have been politically most visible in the education and hospital categories discussed below, these efforts have no doubt been largely responsible for checking government job growth as well. They have been prominently billed as a central government contribution to the fight against inflation, and have been accompanied by an ideological offensive to persuade Canadians to tolerate higher 'normal' unemployment rates.[22] The extent to which they have also been accompanied by farming out more government work (and thus workers) to the 'private' sector is probably substantial, but difficult to measure.[23] In any event, during the entire 1946-74 period, government was directly responsible for the creation of 20.3 per cent of all new jobs, making the government share of all jobs rise from 6.0 per cent to 13.0 per cent.

As might be expected, Table 4 shows that the growth in the education work force has been immense, both in absolute and in relative terms. (The same data source has been used for education workers as for government workers, the *Taxation Statistics* series.[24]) The 1974 figure represents an increase of 342,205 workers, or 483.1 per cent over the 1946 figure. The number of education workers has thus been growing at an even faster rate than has the number of government workers, whose comparable rate was seen in Table 2 to be 326.1 per cent. (The rate of job growth in the economy as a

Table 4
Education workers, 1946-74 (selected years and periods)

	Total education workers		New education workers	
	Number	As percentage of all workers	Number	As percentage of all new workers
1946	70,840	1.5		
1951	93,563	1.8		
1946-51			22,723	5.3
1956	130,286	2.3		
1951-6			36,723	7.5
1961	179,171	2.9		
1956-61			48,885	10.4
1966	286,764	4.0		
1961-6			107,593	9.8
1971	390,960	4.8		
1966-71			104,196	11.2
1974	413,045	4.5		
1971-4			22,085	2.1
1946-74			342,205	7.7

Sources: *Taxation Statistics* and Table 1

whole from 1946 to 1974 can be calculated from Table 1 as 100.1 per cent.) Table 4 also provides some data on the pace of growth in the education work force, in absolute terms and relative to the creation of new jobs in the economy as a whole. While it grew at a faster rate than did the government work force in the 1946-74 period, the education share of all new jobs was smaller than the government share (7.7 per cent compared to 20.3 per cent). Still, the education share was substantial, and it would have been depicted as being higher had it not been for classification changes for non-teaching education workers (see note 24).

The remarkable stability in the education share of new jobs between 1956 and 1971 indicates that cyclical unemployment was not combatted by expanding the number of education workers. In fact, the period of their greatest absolute growth, 1961-6, was also a period of declining unemployment. Instead, of course, changes in the education work force reflect above all changes in the size and level (that is, primary, secondary, post-secondary) of enrolment. And enrolment changes are themselves the result of the combined effect of changes in the school age population and in the enrol-

Table 5
Hospital workers, 1946-71 (selected years and periods)

	Total hospital workers[a]		New hospital workers[a]	
	Number	As percentage of all workers	Number	As percentage of all new workers
1946	68,222	1.5		
1951	93,725	1.8		
1946-51			25,503	5.9
1956	134,320	2.4		
1951-6			40,595	8.3
1961	192,391	3.2		
1956-61			58,071	12.4
1966	266,930	3.7		
1961-6			74,539	6.8
1971	313,005	3.9		
1966-71			46,075	5.0
1974	340,608	3.7		
1971-4			27,603	2.6
1946-71			272,603	6.1

[a]Includes federal and all other public hospitals but not private hospitals
Sources: calculated from Statistics Canada, *Hospital Statistics – Personnel* (currently cat. no. 83-227), and from Table 1

ment ratio, or the percentage of this population in school. Both the birth rate and the faith in education as an economic investment have declined appreciably in Canada during the last decade or so, stabilizing thereby the school age population[25] and the enrolment ratio.[26] Hence the abrupt end to the growth in the numbers of education workers.

As with other categories of state workers, the number of hospital workers has grown very substantially.(As hospital workers cannot be separated from other 'institutional' workers in the *Taxation Statistics* series, another data source, the *Hospital Statistics* series, has been used.) Table 5 shows the total number of service personnel, including medical staffs involved in formally organized educational programs, employed in federal and public hospitals at 31 December of the year in question.[27] All of this growth occurred, by the way, in the public hospitals, as the number of workers in federal hospitals probably declined slightly from an estimated 13,000 in 1946 to a relatively insignificant 8494 in 1974. As with the other state categories, the hospital share of new workers fell off dramatically during the brief 1971-4 period. Here too the impact of the 'cutback' measures was felt. The overall increase in the state hospital field during the entire period was 399.3 per cent, making the growth rate in the hospital work force higher than that in the government work force but lower than that in the education work force.

The enormous growth, both absolute and relative, in state employment as a whole is driven home by Table 6. While the civilian population fourteen and over grew by 88.7 per cent and the number of workers grew by 95.8 per cent between 1946 and 1974, the number of state workers grew by 364.7 per cent. Among state workers, as has already been noted, the number of government workers grew most slowly, 326.1 per cent, and the number of education workers most quickly, 483.1 per cent, while the number of hospital workers grew by 399.3 per cent. Where fewer than one in ten workers had been a state worker in 1946, more than one in five was by 1974, as the percentage working for the state increased steadily throughout the post-war period until 1971.

Not only has the total number of state workers grown rapidly and continually but, as Table 6 also demonstrates, so has the number of new state workers during each five-year period. This was not true of the total number of new workers, which actually fell off slightly during periods when unemployment was rising. New state workers thus made up particularly large portions of all new workers in the 1956-61 and 1966-71 periods. Growth in education and hospital employment does not appear to have been sensitive to changes in the unemployment rate. The rate of direct job creation by government, however, has been strongly affected by the unemployment rate, at least until 1971.

More generally, over a third of all the new workers of the 1946-74 period were hired directly by the state. Furthermore, while there have been fluctuations during periods of rising and falling unemployment in the share of new workers who were state workers, it is clear that until 1971 the long-term trends were not only towards larger percentages of all workers being employed by the state but also towards larger percentages of new workers being new state workers. These long-term trends indicate a 'ratchet effect' rather than a 'pendulum effect'[28] as the cyclical trend was combined with a secular trend. During the short period since 1971, state hiring freezes and 'cutbacks' appear to have been widespread. The significance of this apparent fundamental change in the state role in direct job creation is briefly addressed in the concluding remarks below. In any event, were it not for the rapid growth in state employment throughout the post-war years, the gradual long-term rise in unemployment would have been much more marked.

Table 6
State workers, 1946-74 (selected years and periods)

	Total state workers		New state workers	
	Number	As percentage of all workers	Number	As percentage of all new workers
1946	417,430	8.9		
1951	553,897	10.9		
1946-51			136,467	31.7
1956	707,008	12.6		
1951-6			153,111	31.4
1961	984,562	16.3		
1956-61			277,554	59.0
1966	1,367,738	19.1		
1961-6			383,176	34.9
1971	1,781,172	22.1		
1966-71			413,434	44.6
1974	1,939,720	21.2		
1971-4			158,548	15.0
1946-74			1,522,290	34.0

Source: Tables 1-5

Before proceeding, it must also be pointed out that the data just presented summarizing the growth in the numbers of state workers do not take into account another important component of the state's overall impact on job creation. In addition to state workers, the state also employs indirectly many more workers through its purchase of goods and services from the 'private' sector. Unfortunately, there do not seem to be any very rigorous or comprehensive studies which estimate the employment effects of these purchases. Nor is it possible to try and generate such an estimate here.[29] Some indication of the magnitude of the effects, however, can be grasped by translating an estimate made by the president of the Canadian International Development Agency of the job impact of CIDA purchases in fiscal 1970-1. Given the absence of any foreign aid program in 1946, the 34,000 jobs cited by Paul Gérin-Lajoie for this small part of total state purchases alone represents almost one per cent of all new jobs created between 1946 and 1971.[30] To repeat, the summary figures appearing above in Table 6 *exclude* the many workers who are indirectly employed by the state, as garbage collectors, doctors in 'private' practice, school book binders, computer salespersons, security guards, office building cleaners, dairy farmers, con-

struction workers, paper clip makers, and so on and so on. Also excluded
are the military, most workers in proprietary state enterprises, and almost
all workers in ostensibly private or voluntary organizations supported in
whole or in large part by state funds.

Despite these significant exclusions, the post-war evidence contradicts
the diagnosis and prescription presented in the 1945 *White Paper on Employment and Income*. Instead, it lends at first glance considerable support to
one of O'Connor's theses: that the growth of the state is both a cause and
an effect of the expansion of monopoly capital.[31] The unemployment rate,
which has gradually if irregularly risen in Canada at least since the Korean
War, indicates not a transitional or even a cyclical problem but a structural
one. More significantly for present purposes, the rate has been as 'low' as it
has in the years since the Second World War only because of the massive
growth in the numbers of state workers. Of the 4,471,000 jobs created in
Canada between 1946 and 1974, over a third went directly to state workers.
Despite the most generous of state efforts at all levels to stimulate job creation in the 'private' sector, the state has had to assume the central role of
employer of last resort.

If the white paper offered no hint of the coming centrality of this role,
O'Connor, with his analysis of the surplus population generated by monopoly sector growth and of the attendant social expenses incurred by the advanced capitalist state, does provide a suggestive framework for understanding its centrality. As employer of last resort, the state is attempting in
his terms to fulfil in part its legitimization function. This is, however, only
one of the two functions assigned by O'Connor to the state. In carrying out
its second, accumulation function, the state mounts and expands a multitude of programs which directly and indirectly subsidize the 'private' sector.
Large numbers of state workers are hired to run many of these programs.
Among the more obvious of them, in no particular order, are regional expansion grants, roads to resources, municipal industrial parks, manpower
retraining, research and development, export credits, fast depreciation allowances, and the operation of airports.

To conclude, O'Connor argues that under the conditions of advanced
capitalism both state functions are elevated to new importance, and thus
that the ranks of state workers grow immensely. The overall evidence presented here, supporting his argument and countering the expectations on
unemployment and job creation found in the 1945 white paper, suggests
then that the O'Connor analysis can be fruitfully used in the abundance of
further work that needs to be done on the state. It is important to note in

this respect, however, that it will also be necessary to go beyond O'Connor's work, particularly in the area of class analysis which is uneasily situated in his approach. The advanced capitalist state cannot be understood without a much more profound class analysis of concrete social formations than we have so far been able to muster, not least in dealing with the class position of state workers themselves. Functional analyses of the state are themselves inadequate in so far as they are not situated in analyses of the balance of class forces. If any lesson can be learned from the most recent, short period of Canadian job creation and unemployment, it is that the growth in the numbers of state workers is not the inevitable response to structural unemployment. As this is written in the winter of 1977, the officially counted jobless in Canada number well over 900,000, or 9.1 per cent of the labour force in actual terms. In the absence of heightened class struggle, in a political climate in which 'nobody really cares about unemployment,' a growing surplus population will apparently just have to lump it. Thoroughgoing examinations of the class forces at work, both inside and outside the state system, will not be irrelevant to the political outcome.

NOTES

1 Total state spending was equivalent to 31.6 per cent of Canada's gross national product in 1946, before the transition to a peacetime economy was completed. By 1951 it had dropped to 24.4 per cent, and it then rose erratically but considerably to 39.1 per cent in 1974. State spending on goods and services alone, the so-called 'exhaustive' state spending, was 14.8 per cent of the GNP in 1946, and thereafter rose to 23.2 per cent in 1974. These date are taken from Canadian Tax Foundation, *The National Finances, 1972-73* and *1975-76* (Toronto 1972 and 1976), Tables 2-10 and 2-12. Using United Nations data, David B. Perry reported in a 1972 article – 'The Importance of Government in the Economy: An International Comparison,' *Canadian Tax Journal*, xx (1972), 534-7 – that Canada in 1969 ranked fifteenth of twenty-nine capitalist countries surveyed, including all the most important ones, such as those in the Organization for Economic Co-operation and Development (OECD), in terms of current state expenditures as a percentage of gross domestic product (GDP).

2 *The Fiscal Crisis of the State* (New York 1973)

3 Militancy can be measured in terms of unionization and strike action. In 1971 the Canadian Union of Public Employees became the largest union in Canada, the Public Service Alliance remained the third largest, and the Quebec Teachers' Corporation took over fifth spot, as reported by Statistics Canada, *Corporations and Labour Union Returns Act (CALURA) Report for 1971, Part II – Labour Unions* (Ottawa 1973), 36. In 1972 the Common Front of Quebec state

workers staged what was almost certainly the largest strike ever in North America.

4 As quoted by W.A. Mackintosh, 'The *White Paper on Employment and Income* in Its 1945 Setting,' in S.F. Kaliski, ed., *Canadian Economic Policy since the War* (Montreal 1966), 13

5 Minister of Reconstruction, *White Paper on Employment and Income* (Ottawa 1945), 21

6 'Economic Growth: Concepts and Objectives,' in Brewis, ed., *Growth and the Canadian Economy* (Toronto 1968), 16

7 Mackintosh indicates that he went to considerable pains to ensure that the federal government fully realized and backed just what its commitment entailed. The battle over Keynesianism may have been pretty well conceded, and the state may have stumbled without full awareness under hectic wartime conditions into assuming responsibility for employment. The principal author of the white paper made certain, by his own account, that the state clearly understood and publicly recognized its policy and responsibility over the longer haul of peacetime conditions.

8 'The *White Paper*,' 15

9 *White Paper*, 3-4, 16

10 *Fiscal Crisis of the State*, 6 ff. O'Connor argues that in Marxian language social investment and social consumption expenditures can be termed 'social constant capital' and 'social variable capital' respectively. It should be made clear that this discussion is based on *The Fiscal Crisis of the State* and does not take into account O'Connor's new book, *Class Struggles: Studies in the Marxist Theory of Capitalism and Socialism* (forthcoming), of which only what is apparently a synopsis entitled 'On the Theory of Declining Capitalism and Primitive Socialism,' *Benchmarx*, II (July 1975) from the Institute for Policy Studies in Washington, and what is apparently a chapter entitled 'Productive and Unproductive Labor,' *Politics & Society*, V, 3 (1975), 297-336, were available at the time of writing.

11 *Ibid*, chaps. 4-6. This part of the O'Connor argument runs parallel to that developed by William J. Baumol; see, for instance, his 'Macroeconomics of Unbalanced Growth: The Anatomy of Urban Crisis,' *American Economic Review*, LVII, 3 (June 1967), 416-26. It also shares features with the 'dual market theory'; see, for example, G. Cain, 'The Challenge of the Dual and Radical Theories of the Labour Market to Orthodox Theories,' American Economic Association, *Papers and Proceedings* (May 1975).

12 As the data set out here are drawn from the monthly Labour Force Survey of Statistics Canada, they vary slightly from census data, especially concerning unpaid farm workers on farms and in other family businesses. More significantly,

the ways in which these official data understate unemployment should be mentioned. To be fair, the exclusion of the military from the labour force and thus from the employed labour force has the effect of artificially raising the unemployment rate, but this definitional provision is more than offset by the exclusion of several other groups with high unemployment levels. There are usually almost as many Canadians in various manpower retraining programs as there are in the military, and of course they are in such programs precisely because they are unemployed. For one reason or another, residents of the Yukon and Northwest Territories, all Indians on reserves, and all inmates of penal and health institutions are excluded from the labour force, their high unemployment rates notwithstanding. And two more groups with presumably high rates, itinerants and illegal immigrants, are probably underrepresented in the Labour Force Survey as in other surveys. Another factor to be considered is that workers are defined as being employed even if during the week surveyed they secured work for only an hour while seeking full-time work. Finally, and most importantly, there is the elusive question of the voluntarily idle or retired or, more precisely, of the large group that is not in the labour force because of the judgment that to seek work is hopeless. Some who have lost hope are counted among the unemployed, many more are not. Among the voluntarily idle or retired there are, of course, the elderly who are legitimately retired. But many more in this group are of working age. Indeed, it has been suggested by the Committee on Youth of the federal Department of the Secretary of State in its report, *It's Your Turn ...* (Ottawa 1971), 15-29, that the hidden unemployment of the voluntarily idle or retired is found particularly among the young. While no attempt is made here to estimate how many make up the hidden unemployed, an indirect indicator might be mentioned. Labour force participation rates are highest where unemployment rates are lowest (especially Alberta and Ontario), and vice versa. Thus, where unemployment is high (the Atlantic provinces, Quebec, and to a lesser extent British Columbia), hopes and the participation rate are low. See N.H.W. Davis, *Cycles and Trends in Labour Force Participation* (Ottawa 1971, Statistics Canada cat. no. 71-517), 72, on the importance of the 'discouraged worker effect.'

13 Using 1961 criteria, the 1976 unemployment rate would have been even slightly higher than the 1961 rate. In 1975 the Labour Force Survey was altered somewhat, with the result that unemployment was reduced by 0.2 percentage points. The impact of the change was more substantial on the participation and employment rates set out in Table 1. By asking different questions and coding the responses differently, Statistics Canada raised the participation rate by 2.3 percentage points and the employment rate by 2.1 percentage points, despite the fact that even fewer so-called 'discouraged workers' who had given up looking

for work were now included in the labour force. Differences between regions
have been made less pronounced with the new survey, as have those between
the sexes. Indeed, because married wormen are now asked additional questions
about labour force activities, their participation has been boosted some more.
Women for the first time are considered to have a higher unemployment rate
than men. See also note 15.

14 From 1975 on, fifteen years of age and over

15 The gradual rise in the participation rate since the mid-1950s can be more than
accounted for by the rise in the female rate, as the male rate has actually been
slowly but steadily dropping. Where there were well over three male workers for
every female worker in 1946, there were fewer than two in 1976. The stability in
the participation rate depicted in Table 1 thus masks a dramatic rise in the female rate, and more precisely in the married female rate. I have discussed why
more and more married women are joining the labour force, despite the inferior
and segregated conditions they encounter, in an article with Pat Armstrong,
'The Segregated Participation of Women in the Canadian Labour Force, 1941-
71,' *Canadian Review of Sociology and Anthropology*, XII, 4 (Nov. 1975), 370-84.

16 The approach to counting state workers, and the data up to and including those
for 1971, are drawn from my MA thesis, 'The Patron State of Canada: An Exploratory Essay on the State and Job Creation in Canada since World War II,'
Carleton University, Ottawa, 1974. While some information on data sources
and assumptions is provided here in succeeding notes, full details are to be
found in the thesis. Where it was necessary to make estimates in using official
statistics, the effort was consistently made to be conservative regarding state
workers. The numbers of state workers presented here are therefore almost certainly understated.

17 As J.E. Hodgetts and O.P. Dwivedi indicated in 'The Growth of Government
Employment in Canada,' which appeared in Frederick Vaughan *et al.*, eds.,
Contemporary Issues in Canadian Politics (Scarborough 1970), *Taxation
Statistics* provides the most consistent data available on government workers.
Contrary to what they stated, this series also provides some data on education,
although a significant inconsistency discussed in notes 20 and 24 affects the
treatment of both education and government workers. Unfortunately, it is impossible from this source to separate out hospital workers from other institutional employees, necessitating use of the Statistics Canada *Hospital Statistics*
series.

18 The figures in Table 2 are somewhat higher for the years 1946 to 1966 than are
the comparable figures in Hodgetts and Dwivedi, *ibid.*, 215, because I have included those government workers who filed non-taxable returns. Although their
approach is in general quite useful, they do not explain their exclusion of those

filing non-taxable returns. The low incomes or high deductions and exemptions of these workers do not *per se* justify exclusion, at least in the context of this article. While in many cases the low incomes are themselves the result of part-time work, it should be kept in mind that part-time workers are included in the labour force and hence should be included here for comparative purposes. Because National Revenue classifies workers according to their largest *single* sources of income, there is no danger of double-counting those with two or more jobs, whether full- or part-time. Significant changes in the numbers of non-taxable returns, such as occurred between the 1970 and 1971 tax years, appear to have been caused primarily by changes in the tax rate. While one effect of including those filing non-taxable returns is, of course, to increase the share of all jobs filled by government workers, their inclusion also reduces their overall rate of increase.

19 The federal total was passed by the provincial total in 1964 and by the municipal total in 1967.

20 Because of a classification change by National Revenue, the number of municipal government workers has been artificially increased since 1960 through the inclusion of most non-teaching education workers. The growth rate for the 1956-61 period has thus been particularly affected. On the other hand, the number and growth rate for education workers have been artificially decreased to an equal extent since 1960.

21 The fourth quarter, 1975, issues of the following Statistics Canada publications: *Federal Government Employment* (cat. no. 72-004), *Provincial Government Employment* (cat. no. 72-007), and *Municipal Government Employment* (cat. no. 72-009). For what it is worth, if the additional 4300 full-time teachers estimated by Statistics Canada (in *Education in Canada, 1975*, cat. no. 81-229) to have been hired in 1974-5 are added, almost exactly 100 per cent of the new jobs that year are accounted for, without looking at hospital workers. 'Private' sector employment thus actually shrank in absolute terms in 1975, as it is almost certainly doing again in 1977 – expected on all sides to have the highest post-war unemployment rate.

22 Cf. Economic Council of Canada, *People and Jobs* (Ottawa 1976), especially chaps. 8 and 10. The theme has been picked up by *Maclean's* in Ian Urquhart's 'Unemployment: Does Anybody Really Care?' 24 Jan. 1977.

23 I have in mind, for example, the rental of office space, the hiring of consulting and security firms, and contracts for garbage collection.

24 Once again, workers filing non-taxable returns are included, increasing their percentage of new jobs but reducing their growth rate. The non-teaching employees of school boards and of non-university post-secondary institutions are excluded, while those of universities are included, as are teachers in 'private,' non-profit schools. The overall effect is to understate the numbers of education

workers. With the method used here, the 1968 estimate for education workers would be 342,261, a conservative figure when compared with the 1968 figure from a DBS (now Statistics Canada) paper of 515,000 for all education workers (including all those in private schools), and the 1968 figure from an Economic Council of Canada study of 477,000 (excluding all those in 'private' and 'other' schools). See Miles Wisenthal, 'Developments in Education Statistics for Economic Planning,' in *Some Recent Developments in the Dominion Bureau of Statistics* (papers prepared for the 1970 Annual Meetings of the Canadian Economics Association), 48; and J. Cousin *et al.*, *Some Economic Aspects of Provincial Education Systems* (Ottawa 1971), 9.

25 In 1971 the Canadian population aged 0-14 was a scant 188,978 or 3.1 per cent more than it had been in 1961. The overall population grew by 18.6 per cent during the decade; calculated from *Canada Year Book* (1975), 166.

26 The disenchantment of potential students and their parents has been matched by that of most provincial govrnments, which, led by Ontario, have as a result altered the education system to make it more consumption- and less investment-oriented. Along with the plunge in the stock of schools has gone a wistful harking back to the halcyon days of the 1960s among school administrators, especially at the university level. Consult any current issue of the management journal, *University Affairs*. On the sudden demise of human capital theory and the related significance of the Hall-Dennis and Wright reports in Ontario and beyond, see Alexander Lockhart, 'Educational Policy Development in Canada: A Critique of the Past and a Case for the Future,' in Richard A. Carlton *et al.*, eds., *Education, Change, and Society: A Sociology of Canadian Education* (Toronto 1977).

27 Unfortunately, it has not been possible to include only those full- and part-time workers for whom hospital jobs were the largest single sources of income. This results in a slight overstatement, but one which is more than balanced by the exclusion of workers in 'private' hospitals, which invariably receive state support in one form or another. Also excluded are those who worked for privately operated cafeterias, laundries, laboratories, security agencies, etc., in hospitals, and those who worked in the 'private' sector outside hospitals supplying them with goods and services.

28 These terms are borrowed from R.A. Lockhart, who uses them in a similar context in his MA thesis, 'The Effects of Recent Techno-Economic Changes on the Mobility Patterns and Opportunities of the American Middle-Class,' Simon Fraser University, Burnaby, 1970.

29 An estimate was made in my thesis, 'The Patron State,' 141-7, of indirect state employment in one industry which is particularly associated with efforts to combat unemployment – the construction industry. Surprisingly, between 1951

and 1971 the proportion of all new jobs going to 'private' sector construction
workers employed on state projects other than housing was only 1.9 per cent.
The percentage was this low despite the facts that, principally in carrying out its
accumulation function, the state increased during the 1951-71 period both its
share of all construction (whether done by state workers or let to 'private' firms)
and the share of all state construction let to these firms. State involvement in
housing, whether achieved through direct spending or through the manipulation
of mortgage rates, has apparently proven to be a much more responsive
counter-cyclical instrument than has state involvement in public works in general.

30 'The Economic Impact of Canada's Foreign Aid Program on the Canadian
Economy,' an address to the Montreal Board of Trade, 12 March 1973, p. 13.
Between 1970-1 and 1975-6 non-loan 'aid to developing countries' more than
doubled. Yet despite its undoubted indirect job creation impact, it still accounted for only about 2 per cent of federal spending in 1975-6.

31 His second, fiscal crisis thesis is not addressed by the evidence presented here,
although at a common sense level it would appear ever more difficult for the
state to match its revenue to its spending if relatively fewer and fewer 'private'
sector taxpayers are paying the wages of relatively more and more state workers. This view would be reinforced by the fact that – as Rick Deaton shows in
'The Fiscal Crisis and the Revolt of the Public Employee,' *Our Generation*, VIII,
4 (Oct. 1972), 32-3 – corporate income taxation has since the mid-1960s accounted for less and less revenue and individual income taxation for more and
more. Indeed, as Ian Gough points out in 'State Expenditure in Advanced
Capitalism,' *New Left Review*, 92 (July-Aug. 1975), 61, this is the case for all the
advanced capitalist states in the OECD. However, the fiscal crisis thesis requires
the demonstration that growth in the monopoly sector has stopped or at least
decelerated appreciably (whatever the number of workers left in this sector),
thus both raising the accumulation and stabilization demands made on the state
while simultaneously diminishing its capacity to meet them. O'Connor is apparently now working on this question; see 'On the Theory of Declining Capitalism
and Primitive Socialism.'

11

The politics of reform: conflict and accommodation in Canadian health policy

DONALD SWARTZ

'The architects of the modern welfare state tried to reform neither the worker nor the economic system in which he made his living. Rather they required him by law to provide for himself and his family so that he could better withstand the vagaries of Capitalism.'

The history of capitalist societies reveals many paradoxes, not the least of which is the continuous growth of the involvement of the state in economic and social affairs despite the official ideology of 'free' enterprise and self-reliance. Almost invariably, this growth in state activity has been undertaken in the name of progress, reform, and the betterment of mankind. Yet the results are, to put it charitably, ambiguous. Activities designed to 'regulate' corporations have been viewed (for different reasons) as ineffectual at best, and often as primarily benefiting the regulated. Similarly, several independent studies have revealed that despite the rise of the 'welfare state' since the Second World War the distribution of income has not changed, and that this rise has been financed through a taxation system which, in total, is sharply regressive. None the less, the situation of the unemployed, retired, and incapacitated is not so desperate as it was in the 1930s. Data on income distribution do not include the impact of government expenditures on goods and services and a recent study suggests that the overall effect of the growth of state activity has been to provide at least some redistribution of consumption.[1]

In the last decade theorists writing from a Marxist perspective have begun to analyse systematically the role and nature of the state in capitalist societies. It is the intent of this paper to further this development by examining the role of the Canadian state in the provision of health care. Following some general theoretical considerations, an historical analysis of state involvement in this area will be presented. In so doing we shall seek to understand the forces giving rise to state involvement and the nature of that involvement, and to draw some conclusions about the limits of reform in a capitalist society.

Marxist theories of the state in capitalist societies rest upon two basic and interrelated assumptions. The first is that such societies are characterized by a fundamental conflict between the working class whose labour produces the goods and services and the capitalist class that controls that production and appropriates the surplus value created. It is also assumed that the state in such societies is a particular complex of institutions, 'whose main purpose is to defend the predominace in society of a particular class,'[2] namely, the capitalist class. The predominance of the capitalist class lies precisely in its control of the means of production, a control which ultimately enables it to create economic and social havoc by suspending production. At the same time, private control of the means of production defines a basic characteristic of the state in that it is relegated to an indirect role in the sphere of production. Consequently, the state is made dependent upon the capitalist class, for short of challenging that class's fundamental power, the serviceability of any state policy depends upon the consent of the capitalist class to continue production.

These assumptions, while indispensable to understanding the nature of the state, do not provide much guidance for an historical analysis of the growth of the state's role in civil society. An important advance in this respect has been made by James O'Connor in *The Fiscal Crisis of the State*, which focuses primarily on the growth of state expenditures and must be considered as a point of orientation for Marxist studies of this phenomenon. O'Connor begins his analysis by identifying two basic categories of state expenditures. (1) *Social capital expenditures:* such expenditures are required for profitable private capital accumulation; they encompass two subcategories: one consists of 'social constant capital' and increases the productivity of labour power (infrastructure, research and development financing, etc.), while the second is 'social variable capital' and lowers the reproduction costs of labour (health care, education, etc.). (2) *Social expenses expenditures:* these are non-productive expenditures, such as on welfare, designed to foster social harmony and secure the legitimacy of the system.

In general, O'Connor sees state expenditures as both a cause and a result of economic development. To foster private accumulation the state undertakes social capital expenditures which largely benefit the monopolistic sector of the economy. In these industries productivity increases, associated with advances in technology in combination with corresponding reduction in employment, result in output exceeding the growth in purchasing power in the economy as a whole. This in turn requires the state to undertake increased social expenses (welfare and warfare) to augment purchasing power without increasing productivity. The result of this dynamic is a fiscal crisis which arises as state expenditures come to outstrip revenues. Within this general model O'Connor's analysis stresses the fact that social security expenditures are designed to promote capital accumulation. He notes that, while these expenditures provide benefits to non-workers (unemployed, retired, sick or injured), their real purpose is to create a sense of security amongst employed workers, raising morale, smoothing 'labour relations,' and thus facilitating exploitation. Consequently, 'the fundamental intent and effect of social security is to expand productivity, production, and profits.' Given the fact that capitalist economic development is a disruptive process, replacing living labour with 'dead' labour and old skills with new ones, in an anarchic fashion which circumscribes planned re-employment, the expansion of social security is seen to be a 'direct effect of technological, cyclical, and other forms of unemployment that accompany capitalist economic development.'[3]

While these few remarks in no sense do justice to the scope of O'Connor's work, and the many insights it contains, they do enable us to grasp its essence. In brief, the state is seen as an essentially reactive institution which expands in direct response to the obstacles the capitalist class encounters in its relentless drive to accumulate. This analysis comes uncomfortably close to the 'necessity thesis' argued by Polyani and other non-Marxists, who tend to explain the expanded role of the state as an unavoidable result of the unworkable nature of laissez-faire capitalism.[4] More importantly, however, this thesis tends to abstract reforms from their origins in the class struggle both at the level of production and in the sphere of politics. Most social security programs are state-run versions of benefits workers won from particular employers through collective bargaining (formal or informal). If they advanced productivity and profits so much, why did employers resist them so strongly, and find it necessary to turn to state legislation to implement them? Secondly, this thesis is not particularly helpful in explaining either the historical specificity of various reforms or their varying completeness and forms of operation. Regarding the latter, for example, it is apparent that the extent of social security is not greatest where unemployment is greatest and, indeed, the reverse is more likely to be the case. Moreover, the level of unemployment itself is not determined independently of political considerations. Social security legislation, as D. Wedderburn notes: 'represents a compromise between the market and laissez-faire on one hand, and planned egalitarianism on the other. How near to either extreme a particular piece of legislation falls depends both upon the balance of political forces and upon the awareness of reformers of the difficulties and dangers ... because a social reform won at a particular point of time can become adapted, modified, less effective as a result of market forces acting upon it.'[5] The case of the United States, for example, with its limited social security programs, especially as regards health care where the state's medicaid program provides lucrative returns to its purveyors and little to its recipients, cannot be understood without considering the pitiful force (industrially and politically) that the American labour movement presently represents.

At a more general theoretical level O'Connor's thesis reveals several weaknesses as well, central to which is an undialectical conception of the relationship of the state to civil society in general, and to the ongoing class struggle in particular. In an extremely penetrating and constructive critique of O'Connor's work, Ian Gough argues that his thesis is based upon 'a false polarization of the economy and the superstructure. The former is seen as an autonomous "factor" leading, if unchecked, to some form of breakdown, whereas the latter is interpreted as a passive instrument in the hands of the bourgeoisie whose *functions are determined* by the offsetting action required in order to avoid or check the tendencies to breakdown.'[6] Against this view Gough counterposes two general and interrelated considerations in the Marxist theory of the state. Firstly, the state must be understood as having a structurally determined 'relative autonomy' from the capitalist class, not only in order to represent that class's interest as the 'national interest' but also because of the capitalist class's inability to achieve political unity, given the conflicting economic interests of various class fractions and the narrow views of many of its individual members. If this point has escaped some Marxists, it has been well appreciated by Canadian politicians. In the words of Mitchell Sharp: 'Businessmen are not very sophisticated, and seldom have a unified viewpoint on specific government policies.'[7]

The second consideration emphasized by Gough is that political analysis must 'situate the class struggle at its heart.' The expansion of the state should be understood as developing both in response to and in anticipation of class conflict. In order to realize the broad political interests of the capitalist class the state must perform what Gough refers to as a dual role: 'The capitalist state simultaneously acts to organize the dominant classes as a political force and to politically disorganize the dominated classes.'[8] On the one hand, the state undertakes various activities to expand and regulate production and consequently to expand the hegemony of the capitalist class. In so doing it acts both to save the bourgeoisie from its own greed and to cloak its pursuit of self-interest in the robes of public responsibility and control. The myriad boards, commissions, and regulatory agencies established by the state reflect such efforts. On the other hand, the state seeks to neutralize the counter-ideology which develops within the working class as a result of its experiences, one which is vague in form but none the less expresses both economic and political discontent. It becomes a primary task of the state to absorb and reconstruct this ideology into a substantial form which is consistent with capitalism, and to enhance the status of reformist working-class leaders who are then able to show that 'limited reformist pressures from secure organizational bases bring evident returns.'[9] Central to doing so is the separation of the economic as opposed to the political demands of the working class, and the development of reforms designed to actually palliate the former without interfering with the basis of capitalist power. In order to do this the state may find it necessary to act in a fashion contrary to the short-run economic interests of the capitalist class, or even the long-run interests of certain fractions of it. How great these concessions will be and, consequently, the degree of autonomy from the bourgeoisie that the state exhibits, are determined by the strength of the working class, as well as by the economic condition of capital at a given time.

All of this does not of course rule out the use of coercion by the state to deal with class conflict, especially if the material conditions for legitimating concessions are absent, but also if, in combination with such concessions, coercion is necessary to convince the bourgeoisie that lasting, political benefits are a likely result. This latter point was well understood by Kaiser Wilhelm I, the 'grandfather' of the idea of health insurance as a reform, who observed that 'The cure of social ills must be sought not exclusively in the repression of social democratic excesses, but simultaneously in the positive advancement of the welfare of the working classes.'[10] This does not mean that such reforms do not contribute to capital accumulation. Ultimately, any state action which undermines the formation of revolutionary consciousness within the working class serves this end. More concretely, it may well be the case that the bourgeoisie will be able to recoup these concessions or otherwise distort their implementation so as to be the prime beneficiary, for the fruits of struggle in the absence of continued struggle may be lost to the working class.

THE GROWTH OF STATE INVOLVEMENT IN HEALTH CARE

The Canadian state is involved in a myriad of activities ostensibly designed to advance the health status of Canadians in all areas from sanitation to medical research. Among these, state financing of medical services through hospital and medical insurance stand out. These services are personal health services – that is, they are consumed by individuals. Together, as of 1973, they comprised 89 per cent of all health expenditures, and most of these were financed through state insurance plans.[11] State involvement in the financing of personal health care came late in Canada relative to most capitalist countries; hospital insurance was not enacted until 1958 and medical insurance a decade later still. As a result, government health expenditures were negligible prior to 1960. Just how negligible can be seen in Table 1.

The nature and history of these reforms is poorly understood in Canada, primarily because they are generally associated with the Saskatchewan CCF-NDP's introduction of medical insurance in 1961, occasioned as it was by the infamous 'doctors' strike.'[12] Consequently, the development of health insurance tends to be seen not only as a struggle between progressive government desiring to introduce 'popular' legislation in opposition to a vocal and organized pressure group (the medical profession), but as legislation which has something to do with the state becoming socialist. The actual history and the reality of health insurance are quite different from this image.

In Canada, as in other capitalist countries, the idea of health insurance grew out of the problems industrial workers experienced in gaining access to medical care. Unions or friendly societies either set up insurance funds for their members themselves, or did so through an arrangement with employers; in some cases employers themselves made payments into such funds as a 'fringe-benefit.' More typically, employers set up welfare provisions of their own, and in doing so were motivated by two main considerations. Many, especially those who had difficulty recruiting and maintaining a labour force (owing to the remoteness of the work location or the hazards of the jobs involved), saw health insurance as a way of increasing the efficiency of labour. Sir Henry Thornton, president of the CNR, explained this reasoning to the British Columbia Royal Commission on State Health Insurance and Maternal Benefits in a remarkably candid moment: 'We creosote ties ... They are materials. We conserve them; the successful business is the one that does the same thing for its men.'[13] Others saw political benefits in health insurance, because of their realization that 'distress breeds a dangerous temper.'[14]

Table 1
Government health expenditures in Canada (1949 dollars)

	Federal government		Provincial governments	
	Percentage of GNP	Dollars per capita	Percentage of GNP	Dollars per capita
1937	.02	.15	.5	4.01
1945	.04	.51	.4	4.32
1955	.2	2.69	.9	11.65

Source: R. Bird, *The Growth in Government Expenditures in Canada,* Canadian Tax Foundation (Toronto 1970), Appendix C, Tables 13, 14, 17, and 18

These local *ad hoc* arrangements, however, faced serious limitations in that they were based on the factory as the unit of organization. Firstly, insurance schemes were generally initiated by workers where sickness and accidents were relatively concentrated, but precisely because of the extensiveness of health problems these units were financially unable to cover the costs of treatment and support those stricken for the duration of the disease. Employer-sponsored plans may not have had the same financial limitations but were no more adequate. One major problem stemmed from the competitive nature of capitalism itself. In the short run, paternalistic welfare plans added some cost to the price of a firm's products. In competitive industries, an employer instituting such plans ran the risk that the competition would undercut his price, gaining an advantage which could preclude surviving long enough to realize the expected long-run benefits. Just as limiting, perhaps more so, was the nature of these employer-sponsored plans themselves. Since they were controlled by the employer, access to benefits was determined by him. They were, in short, paternalistic programs, designed to combat employee discontent by offering benefits to 'loyal' employees, and so blunt the tendencies of workers to unionize and/or turn to socialism in an effort to realize their own interests. As such, their success was limited to less militant sectors of the working class and, indeed, in some instances provoked distrust and militancy.[15] The conclusion to be drawn here is not that because of these limitations state action regarding health insurance was inevitable. Rather, it is the industrial and political militancy of the working class which reveals the limitations of these *ad hoc* arrangements. Where workers reject paternalism, where industrial unrest is widespread, and where socialist ideology threatens to take broad root among workers, the need for state reform becomes apparent.

Given these considerations it is not surprising that it was in British Columbia that state action was first and most often considered. With a long history of industrial militancy, and a degree of communist and socialist strength in the labour movement unmatched in any other province,[16] British Columbia had no less than *two* provincial royal commissions on the issue by 1928. The interim report of the second, based upon an examination of the two major precedents of state action in this field (Germany in 1883 and Britain in 1911), expressed the view that such action was undertaken basically to pacify the working class, and that a state-run insurance scheme was the appropriate form of response. The rationale for an insurance scheme had been clearly expressed almost a decade earlier by perhaps Canada's most astute and class-conscious politician, W.L. Mackenzie King, who wrote: 'Social insurance, which in reality is health insurance in one form or another, is a means employed in most industrial countries to bring about a wider measure of social justice, without, on the one hand, disturbing the institution of private property and its advantages to the Community, or, on the other, imperilling the thrift and industry of individuals.'[17] It is perhaps not surprising, then, that in 1935, faced with a radical CCF opposition representing almost a third of the electorate, and amidst a growing political radicalization among the unemployed in British Columbia, the Pattullo government introduced legislation to establish health insurance.

Although passed by the legislature, and supported in a provincial referendum on the subject, the legislation was never promulgated. It was in any case already substantially watered down.[18] Whereas the first draft proposed to cover both the unemployed and employed workers earning less than $2400 annually, the legislation covered only employed workers earning less than $1800 annually. These revisions were undertaken in a futile effort to meet the opposition of the medical profession and the business communities. The medical profession, like its counterparts in other provinces,[19] favoured some form of health insurance because the depression had hurt doctors economically. But the profession wanted the state only to cover the health bills of the unemployed and very poor employed workers, that is, those who could not afford anything for medical care. Businessmen, on the other hand, had several concerns, despite the fact that the survey of major employers done by the second royal commission revealed that only a small minority opposed state health insurance and, indeed, that perhaps a majority actually favoured it. Because of the province's shaky financial position, they were opposed to both additional provincial and municipal debt which might result in defaults on loans they held and additional taxes which would further diminish the markets for their products. Consequently, they opposed the scheme favoured by the medical profession. This led the government to revise the initial legislation and exclude the unemployed, which ensured the opposition of the medical profession but was still insufficient to pacify the employers who feared they would be at a disadvantage relative to their competitors in other provinces who, without the costs of health insurance, would be able to undercut their price. This objection, which suggests that most businessmen viewed health insurance as a *political* reform, that is, lacking economic advantage for them, ultimately forced the Pattullo government to capitulate.

The obvious conclusion from the BC experience – that federal action was necessary – was not missed by the proponents of social reform. The case for health insurance and the necessity of a federal program was clearly expressed by A. Grauer in his study for the Royal Commission on Dominion-Provincial Relations (the Rowell-Sirois Commission).[20] More important, at least initially, were the efforts of Ian Mackenzie, a BC Liberal philosophically close to Mackenzie King. As a result of his experiences in British Columbia, Mackenzie became committed to health insurance, and as soon as he joined the King cabinet in 1939 he began to push King to effect a program. King, who viewed social security as the key to his life's work, was attracted to the idea, regarding health insurance as perhaps the crowning touch.[21] Indeed, for both King and the Liberal party the idea of health insurance was an old one. At the party convention in 1919, when King was first elected leader, health insurance was endorsed as Liberal party policy. But as Leo Panitch has aptly put it, in his article in this volume, '... ideas, if they are socially disembodied in the sense of not correlating with the nature and balance of class forces in a society, can themselves have little impact.' He points out that, to this point, a large proportion of the population was composed of rural independent commodity producers. This did not mean, as seems to be implied, that there was no need for government action, at least with respect to health care. In Saskatchewan and Alberta an extensive municipal doctor plan was developed at the instigation of the rural population whereby a municipality paid a doctor a retainer which, when added to his fee for service collections from individuals requiring care, was sufficient to attract a physician to rural practice.[22] Rather, the case is that, in the context of a capitalist economy, health insurance is the method of action acceptable to the state and a rural economy poses administrative problems. This was clearly expressed by Brooke Claxton in advancing the federal proposals to the 1945 Dominion-Provincial Conference: 'Contributory insurance plans operate in industrialized countries. Other countries whose economies are chiefly rural find greater difficulty in embarking upon a system of outright insurance that depends upon systematic, periodic contributions, since no easy method of deducting contributions from wages can be devised for the agricultural population.'[23]

Ian Mackenzie's passion for health insurance struck a responsive chord in King precisely because King, ever the astute politician, perceived the balance of class forces to be changing, and that the militancy and radicalism of the working class was extending well beyond British Columbia. Between 1941 and 1943 there were a number of strikes in manufacturing industries, many of which resulted in settlements that exceeded the terms of wartime wage controls.[24] The forces producing industrial militancy also found a certain political expression. In August 1943 the CCF won 32 per cent of the vote in Ontario and thirty-four seats. In the federal by-elections in the same month three out of four seats went to parties of the 'left.' The feeling that a political response by the state to these developments was necessary was not confined to certain sections of the Liberal party. J.M. Macdonnell, president of National Trust and architect of the Conservative's 'progressive' platform, in September 1943 expressed the current reality to the Toronto Conservative Businessmen's Club: 'Would you rather adopt a policy which will retain the largest amount possible of free enterprise or – hand over to the C.C.F.?'[25] King's reaction to these developments was conditioned by the commonly held belief that with the end of the war a severe recession would ensue. Under these conditions a repeat of the 1919 Winnipeg General Strike, on a wider scale, was not, in his mind, a remote possibility.

Extensive planning for a program of social reform was initiated in 1941, beginning with the re-establishment of a committee of senior civil servants chaired by Dr J. Heagerty, deputy minister of health, to develop a health insurance plan. By 1943 this committee, working in close co-operation with a parallel committee from the Canadian Medical Association, and spurred on by Ian Mackenzie, not only decided in favour of health insurance but framed its recommendations in the form of a model bill, which, given the facts that the provinces had jurisdiction over health care and a constitutional amendment was unlikely, would pave the way for the basic uniformity needed to justify federal financial support.[26] Two features of this draft bill deserve mention in this context. Firstly, it embodied a broad attempt to improve health levels beyond simply expanding access to physicians. The 'model bill' proposed not only a more extensive insurance scheme than is extant in any province today but also included an emphasis on public health/disease prevention which no province has yet approximated. Secondly, it reflected what has become the pattern of much Canadian social reform legislation which, despite being proposed to deal with working-class dissent, has been designed to provide universal benefits independent of class position (viz. family allowances).[27]

Despite this auspicious beginning, neither this bold plan nor any segment of it was to be realized in the 1940s. Existing accounts[28] would seem to imply that the King government favoured health insurance, but that federal-provincial jurisdictional problems scuttled the policy. An offer to share costs with any province which adopted a plan acceptable to the federal government was included among proposals made to the 1945 Dominion-Provincial Conference on post-war reconstruction. The failure of the conference to agree on tax sharing, combined with Ontario's rejection of federal 'encroachment' into provincial jurisdiction, as the health insurance proposals were alleged to do, are the basis of these interpretations. That George Drew, the Ontario premier, rejected the federal proposal for health insurance is clear, but the federal-provincial jurisdictional problem was unlikely to have been the cause. If it was, then one could have expected Ontario to have utilized the Ontario Municipal Health Services Act, passed in 1944. In fact, no services were ever provided under the legislation. A much more likely explanation of Drew's stance is that it reflected the sentiments of that segment of the capitalist class which opposed any additional concessions to the working class, and also reflected, perhaps, an astute reading of the working-class threat implied in the 1943 CCF vote, which, based upon the 1945 elections, turned out to be more apparent than real, at least in Ontario.[29]

However, there is reason to believe that for the federal government, at least with respect to health insurance, the 1945 conference was anti-climactic. To begin with, as J.L. Granatstein notes, King himself was unsettled by the cost of the health insurance proposal, perhaps as a result of the vociferous opposition by some cabinet ministers and key civil servants in the Department of Finance. The full program carried a price tag of $250 million, and it was suggested by the *Financial Post* at the time (20 May 1944) that the estimated costs were 30 per cent too high, because of unnecessary generosity in estimating the cost of physicians' services. This is not unlikely and was probably the price of gaining the support, in principle, of the medical profession. More importantly, however, it would appear that business was unsettled by the degree of reform already undertaken. Businessmen's concern during this time, that the government was going too far with its reforms, reflected the attitudes of the various 'business' members of King's cabinet (Howe, Ilsley, Ralston, Crerar), all of whom favoured some reforms, but not all of those being considered.[30] On 3 June 1944 the *Financial Post,* which had closely followed the health insurance issue without editorializing, now described it as 'a vast, unwieldly and very costly piece of legislation.' By this time the King government had already in their view enacted a substantial program of reform: unemployment insurance (1940), family allowances (1944), and collective bargaining legislation (1944); and, in short, as one participant in this period remarked, 'Business didn't want any more.'[31]

King's realization that his government was straining its relationship with business culminated in its 1945 *White Paper on Employment and Income,* which was explicitly intended to reassure the business community and regain its confidence. While affirming the government's commitment to policies designed to offset the expected post-war recession, this document firmly stated that these policies would be primarily designed to develop production and employment in the private sector. Health insurance fit poorly into this strategy, for unlike family allowances and unemployment insurance it would not augment generalized purchasing power, but rather would commit a large chunk of government money to the purchase of health services and the growth of employment in the (quasi) public sector. These considerations lead us to interpret King's strategy regarding health insurance prior to the 1945 conference on reconstruction as one designed to preclude its enactment at that time. First of all, he had decided when preparing the 1944 throne speech not to introduce legislation directly, but to proceed by first getting provincial agreement to the proposal. Secondly, a close examination of the proposal reveals that it contained an interesting contradiction. While the Dominion's proposals indicated the share of costs it would absorb, and that actual payments to provinces would not be the Dominion's share of estimated costs but actual costs, they also limited the maximum Dominion contribution to $12.96 per capita. Over time, that maximum would have reduced the Dominion's share to a negligible proportion (in 1971 per capita health expenditure on medical and hospital insurance was $306), leaving the 'fool's' share to the provinces. Not until many years later was anyone to admit that such a 'ceiling' existed in the Dominion's offer.[32]

For the next decade health insurance was to be virtually a non-issue for the federal government despite the fact that the minister of health, Paul Martin, was intensely committed to it.[33] In general, the earlier reforms, post-war economic recovery, and the anti-communism of the 'cold war' were sufficient to contain and, in some measure, beat back the progressive forces unleashed by the depression and the war effort. The single exception (whether to appease Martin or to stimulate the construction industry) was a scheme of federal health grants to the provinces, begun in 1948, largely to promote hospital construction. However, in the provinces of British Columbia and Saskatchewan, where the CCF largely sustained its wartime electoral promise, the health insurance initiative was maintained. A weak program of hospital insurance which never did operate properly was introduced in British Columbia in 1949 at the instigation of the Liberal half of the Liberal-Tory coalition government in an abortive attempt to free the province from the 'spectre of socialism.'[34] In Saskatchewan, the CCF's electoral victory in 1944 laid the basis for the first effective state health insurance program in North America. Yet even this victory was a distinctly limited one. Although the CCF leaders saw 'socialized medicine' as their most important reform (which they conceived to be a system of salaried physicians under the control of the government), in the face of opposition from the doctors they backed down. Instead they introduced a hospital insurance scheme for everyone (1947), and medical insurance for pensioners (1950), administered by a doctor-controlled commission which, as S.M. Lipset has clearly shown, removed from the government effective control over the production, distribution, and price of health services.[35]

Health insurance reappeared abruptly as a federal issue at the 1955 Federal-Provincial Conference, when Leslie Frost, premier of Ontario, suddenly announced that Ontario wanted hospital insurance, a demand which left Prime Minister Louis St Laurent speechless. There is no evidence that Frost was motivated by a sudden concern for the health of the people of Ontario. Indeed, despite his request, Frost personally opposed hospital insurance, fearing that the taxes required would undermine Canada's international competitiveness and reduce the home market for commodities. Writing to St Laurent to explain his request, Frost stated that he was under 'tremendous pressure' from the unions, and health insurance (in whole or part) was in any case inevitable sooner or later.[36] By 1955 it was clear that the TLC and CCL were about to merge, an event motivated by the stagnation both numerically and politically of the labour movement in Canada, as well as the AFL-CIO merger in the United States, and it seems that the pressure on Frost was part of the political strategy underlying the merger. Claude Jodoin, the first president of the CLC, stated in November 1955 that 'The establishment of a government subsidized national health scheme will be the No. 1 aim of the new Canadian Labour Congress when the TLC and CCL unite next year.'[37] A further consideration, which explains why the Frost government was only interested in hospital insurance, was the financial burden on the province of the hospital network. Since 1948, pushed by the availability of federal grants, all provinces had helped finance hospital construction. Yet with less than 50 per cent of the population having any hospital insurance, many hospitals incurred deficits, putting pressure on the province to keep them solvent.[38]

With Ontario's voice added to those of Saskatchewan and British Columbia where there were hospital insurance programs in effect, the pressure on the federal Liberals was intense. Martin argued that they should move boldly and introduce medical insurance as well, to keep the Liberal party's reform image clear. Despite the looming threat of electoral defeat at the hands of John Diefenbaker, the cabinet was unmoved, and a reluctant Liberal party moved in 1957 to introduce the Hospital Insurance and Diagnostic Services Bill.[39] In essence, the legislation empowered the federal government to share the costs of acute hospital care and diagnostic services with any province establishing an insurance program for which all residents were eligible, with the scheme becoming operative only when six provinces agreed to participate (further details will be considered later after the analysis of the introduction of medical insurance). Clearly the Liberals were vying for popular support while simultaneously trying to respond to the 1956 recession in terms acceptable to business, but it did not prevent their defeat. This defeat itself set in motion the forces which, ten years later, would result in medical insurance.

After the 1958 débâcle, the Liberal party, used to seeing itself as the 'Government party,' was disorganized and demoralized. In an effort to generate some direction, Lester Pearson called on Mitchell Sharp to organize a private conference in 1960 to re-evaluate policy for the floundering Liberals. The case for social security at this conference (known as the Kingston Conference) was made by Tom Kent who, in light of Russian economic and technical progress (remember Sputnik in 1959), saw a new role for social security. Arguing that social security legislation was a response to social unrest in the 1930s and 1940s and with it the rise of the CCF, he pointed out that this early legislation had effectively vanquished the threat of socialism. However, he suggested that this success had not eliminated the need for additions to the social security system. Kent argued that the Russian advance had resulted in an almost hysterical reaction which eulogized the free market and saw social security as socialism. In his view, this thinking was wrong on both counts: 'The sort of peace of mind, of freedom from fear, that social security promotes is civilizing and energizing rather than destructive.'[40] Kent's views were well received by Pearson and the left-of-centre Liberals – who by 1962 were committed to health insurance (and to Tom Kent, given his subsequent career). However, the party's right wing took longer to be convinced, and it was not until 1965 that the Liberal party was solidly behind medical insurance.[41]

Several factors lay behind the emergence of this consensus, factors that distinguish the impetus to reforms from their conservative objectives which

Kent understood so well. To begin with, the labour movement, particularly in Ontario and Quebec, began to emerge from the somnolence of the 1950s, and with the reduction in unemployment following the 1961 recession found their bargaining position strengthened. An unprecedented wave of rank-and-file rejections of settlements negotiated by union leaders commenced and strikes increased sharply, as did defiance of court orders regarding pickets.[42] The situation was particularly acute in Quebec, where the so-called Quiet Revolution was giving way to separatist demonstrations and militant unionism, and where the Liberal party itself was confronted with a crisis brought about by a series of scandals involving its Quebec lieutenants, Dupuis, Rivard, and Favreau.

In rebuilding the Quebec wing of the party, the federal Liberals turned to the 'Three Wise Men,' Marchand, Pelletier, and Trudeau, whose experiences in Quebec made them well aware of the radicalization underway among both members of the working class and younger intellectuals, and whose ideology predisposed them towards meeting this development with social reforms rather than repression. Whether their entry into federal politics is seen as a strategic move against separatism *per se,* or a shift to a level of government capable of providing these reforms (or both), the result was a marked shift in the balance of the party leadership, and the Pearson Liberals declared in favour of medical insurance. Substantial opposition within the business community[43] and the medical profession persisted, but in responding to this the Pearson government had a powerful ally in the form of the recent report from the Royal Commission on Health Services (the Hall Commission). This commission was formed at the request of the Canadian Medical Association, following the introduction of medical insurance by the CCF in Saskatchewan in 1961, in the hope of vindicating current medical care in Canada and preventing any other province from following Saskatchewan's example. Much to the CMA's dismay, the report declared in favour of universal medical insurance, and Pearson used this well. Following the tabling of the report, Emmett Hall and the other commissioners actually toured the country proselytizing on its behalf.

The Pearson government introduced the Medicare Act (C-227) in July 1966. In essence it was identical to the earlier hospital insurance bill. The federal government offered to split the costs of physicians' services with any province adopting an acceptable plan. Such a plan would have to be universal, portable from province to province, cover all physicians' services, with the insurance fund administered on a non-profit basis. As such, it drew public opposition from doctors and insurance companies. The doctors realized that if the plan was universal, their fee schedule would have to be set in negotiation with the provinces, and physicians, in theory, would be accountable to the state for billings. Given provincial responsibility for health services, the impact on physicians was determined at that level (discussion of this will be taken up below). The terms of the federal proposal, however, did pre-empt the insurance companies from this market.[44] In justifying this action the Liberals emphasized that the reason for doing so was efficiency. Public administration of the insurance fund, as the Saskatchewan experience revealed, operated with an overhead cost of 5 per cent as opposed to an average of 27 per cent for private (profit or non-profit) plans.[45] However much they disliked it on grounds of principle, this action did not seriously affect the insurance companies as their share of the medical insurance market was a small one, and this share in turn was a small fraction of their overall premium volume.

In any event, the insurance companies *per se* were not the major problem faced by the Liberals. Their real task was to get the reluctant provinces, primarily Ontario and Quebec, to join the plan. This reluctance was no doubt a reflection of pressure from the provincial medical associations and insurance companies, but also from their governments' commitment to keeping their provinces attractive (that is, cheap) to manufacturing industries. The federal government responded by reaching back to the model bill developed by Heagerty in 1943, and Finance Minister Edgar Benson, in the 1968 budget, announced a social development tax of 2 per cent which, despite official denials, was essentially a medicare tax. For Ontario and Quebec this meant they were going to contribute to medicare whether they got any federal monies back or not.[46] Capitulation was not long in coming.

THE CONTRADICTIONS OF REFORM

After a struggle lasting over fifty years the Canadian working class had achieved a real victory. Its members could now receive medical services (with some exclusions such as drugs) independently of their current financial position. The horror of denying themselves or their families medical services, or the humiliation of seeking services for which they could not pay, was gone. These realities are no doubt reflected in the fact that health services were considered the 'best value' of all government expenditures in a recent public opinion poll.[47] But what kind of victory was it? What social change did it bring about with regard to the production and distribution of health services? To answer these questions it is necessary first to understand the structure and development of the health care system (that is, the institutional mechanisms through which medical and hospital services were produced and distributed) prior to health insurance.

Despite the large role played by the state in the early development of Canada, the health system was overwhelmingly a creation of private interest and initiative. The original medical practitioners were petit-bourgeois independent commodity producers, selling their services on a fee per service basis at the prevailing price. The medical practitioners were a heterogeneous lot, ranging from physicians (practitioners with a university education), to midwives with years of experience, to patent medicine peddlars. The market was highly competitive and not particularly lucrative, which gave rise to efforts, primarily on the part of the physicians, to restrict entry to it. One physician expressed the problem in a letter to his local newspaper: 'Believe me Mr. Editor, you or your city compeers can form no conception of our position ... Under my nose, lives neighbour B who bleeds and extracts teeth at exactly half the professional charge.'[48] What the physicians sought was a licensing monopoly from the state which would at one and the same time remove competing practitioners from the market as well as enable them to control the supply of physicians.[49] In 1865 the Parker Act culminated a seventy-five year struggle and realized both of these objectives for physicians in Upper Canada. Similar legislation quickly emerged in all provinces in the immediate post-Confederation years.

An examination of why the state was interested in granting such a monopoly is beyond the scope of this paper. However, the existence of such a monopoly had an important impact on the subsequent development of the class position of the medical profession and, consequently, on the nature of the health system. The class position of professionals in general has been a contentious one for Marxist theory. Traditionally, they have been viewed as a component of the 'forever being proletarianized' middle class. However much this may apply to many occupational groups which have sought sanctuary under the rubric of professionalism, it does not apply to the medical profession.[50] In gaining its monopoly the medical profession acquired full control over the definition of disease, as well as how, when, and where to treat it. In short, they were given *de facto* control over the production process. This becomes particularly important when the development of the hospital is considered.

Hospitals in Canada, as elsewhere, were initially formed as places for the sick poor to be taken to die. Mostly they were founded by church orders and/or charitable organizations. Patients were often tended by medical practitioners unable to earn a living in private practice, but also by physicians of good repute (sometimes from humanitarian motives, and sometimes because indigents were the sole source of 'volunteers' for medical research and teaching). With the development of medical science in the last quarter of the nineteenth century, however, hospitals were transformed into places for the treatment and cure of those who could afford these services. Their subsequent growth can be understood best as a process in which the dominant classes in particular locations, including socially prominent physicians, pooled some of their resources to build a private non-profit organization, filled with the latest equipment and trained labour, hoping to attract trained physicians who wished to establish themselves in private practice. However, due to the fact of their medical monopoly, physicians perforce assumed *de facto* control over the operation of the hospital, a control formalized in the provincial hospital acts. In Ontario, which is representative of the situation generally in Canada (and the United States), the physicians of a given hospital must be organized into a self-governing body. These physicians annually recommend to the board of directors (on which physicians hold by law at least five seats if there are a hundred beds or more) which physicians shall have the 'privilege' of admitting and treating their patients (that is, be able to use the hospital without charge to earn fees from medical practice). The board may reject the physicians' recommendations but cannot appoint physicians directly. These self-selected physicians thus effectively control the hospital since they alone can admit and specify care to patients and hence determine the hospital's revenues and expenditures. This does not reduce the board to a purely honorific function and make it simply a source of prestige to its members. Its tasks are important but largely external – fund-raising, political negotiations, and the like – although it is also ultimately responsible for ensuring that the bottom line of the balance sheet is not regularly coloured in red. The odd case of conflict between physicians and hospital directors should not obscure the essentially complementary nature of their respective interests. Typically employers, corporate executives, or their spouses,[51] hospital directors can be counted on to view wage demands by hospital workers as counter to the public interest, but expansion, purchase of equipment, supplies, etc. from the private sector as just the opposite. Seeing as such purchases create opportunities for physicians to expand services and hence increase their incomes, the two controlling groups are thus united in favour of low wages and efficient use of labour to maximize the resources available for hospital expansion.

Government-sponsored health insurance in no way altered this structure of power. Despite a warning from the federal Director of Health Insurance Studies that 'if we have no control over the doctor under a prepaid hospitalization plan, we have no control over unnecessary use of hospital beds,'[52] hospital insurance brought no alteration to the basic control the physicians have over hospital expenditures, save a guarantee that all bills would be

paid by the state. Some change could have been generated by democratiz-
ing the governance of the hospitals, that is, by challenging the self-perpetu-
ating nature of the boards or by a state takeover of direct administrative
control, enabling it to force some economies through strict budgeting. This
was, however, never seriously considered. As Health Minister Paul Martin
stated: 'In Canada I do not think anyone seriously proposed that the title to
our hospitals should be transferred from religious or private bodies to the
state.'[53]

When we turn to medical insurance, where the issue of controlling physicians is again directly raised, a brief examination of the programs established by the provinces reveals that, with one small exception, the control
by physicians of the production, distribution, and price of health services
was untouched. Of course, the provincial medical associations had to bargain for the fees that would be paid for specific services, and some mechanism had to be set up to ascertain whether monies spent on physician services were justifiable. However, to recognize this is not to conclude that the
bargaining over fee levels restricts costs and physicians' incomes, or that the
auditing procedures give the state any control over the delivery of medical
care. Since the development of private medical insurance plans, physicians
have tended to charge according to a fee schedule (price per service) set by
their provincial associations. Designed to prevent price competition, the fee
schedule was really a 'floor' price, with physicians accepting the fact that
bills sent to those daring enough to have sought services they could not
afford would go unpaid in whole or in part. The first thing that medical insurance did was to guarantee physicians payment for all services rendered
at the percentage of the profession's fee schedule the government agreed to
pay (usually 90 per cent). However, the real issue was whether or not physicians could charge the patient the full fee or more, without forfeiting eligibility to the money the plan guaranteed (that is, without the patient having
to pay the total cost out of pocket). In all provinces except Quebec, physicians are able to do this, which is termed the right to 'opt out.' (Initially, the
newly elected Bourassa government proposed to allow 3 per cent of physicians, in any speciality or region, to opt out. This was rejected as too restrictive by the physicians and too liberal by the unions which began mobilizing
support for socialized medicine, a nationalized pharmaceutical industry,
broader coverage, and financing based on a progressive income tax. The
government in part gave in to the unions and, in a subsequent revision, the
opportunity for 3 per cent to opt out was removed. The Bourassa government stood by this in spite of a 'strike' by the specialists.[54]) As regards auditing procedures, the systems designed to control 'abuses' have presup-

posed that the individual physician will be responsible for the care of his or her patients, answerable only (if at all) to the medical profession. All that is possible for the state to do under such circumstances is to monitor the billing patterns of similarly qualified physicians, to identify individual physicians who appear to deviate from the group norm, and then ask the medical profession to investigate the exceptions. For all intents and purposes this investigation becomes simply an issue of fraudulent business practice, that is, determining whether or not false billings have occurred.[55]

In short, state hospital and medical insurance effected no change in the nature of the health care system. Its control remained firmly in private hands, held by physicians and the drug and medical supply corporations. What health insurance amounted to was an unlimited subsidy to these fractions of the bourgeoisie in the form of a guarantee by the state of payment for any services and goods physicians mandated. Such a policy cannot fail, however, to have certain distributive consequences. The most obvious distributive effect is that the costs of health care have grown astronomically as a percentage of gross national product (see Table 2), and by 1973 personal health expenditures amounted to $371.54 per capita.[56]

When the effects of this growth on the pattern of consumption are examined, changes are much less evident. Studies on regional differences, which have focused on the relative availability of services both among provinces and between rural and urban areas within provinces, reveal little evidence of an equalizing trend. The reason, in the words of a recent study, lies in the basic nature of the legislation itself: 'While universal coverage gives the underdoctored areas more money to spend on health services, it provides the same benefit to overdoctored areas.'[57] These authors point out that some provinces have developed policies to encourage internal redistribution of physicians but these have been weak and ineffective, and in one case, British Columbia, where the policy applied only to immigrant physicians, it has been challenged as discriminatory.

The effects of health insurance on income class differences in health services consumption is more complex. Studies using rather crude measures show that lower income classes have had a marked increase in use, with no change by the upper income classes. But R. Beck's more extensive study[58] (using the largest population base, and measuring the trend in consumption of various services by income class) shows that, while lower income classes have increased their consumption of general practitioner services, both absolutely and relatively, their level of consumption is still less than upper income classes. The latter seemed to actually reduce their consumption of these services, shifting to specialist services, so much so that income class

331 Donald Swartz

Table 2
Total personal health care[a] expenditures as a percentage of GNP

1946	2.88	1972	6.4
1956	3.36	1973	6.1
1960	4.71	1974	5.9
1965	5.2	1975	6.6
1970	6.2	1976	6.6
1971	6.5		

[a]These figures include government and private expenditures, but exclude public health, education, and construction expenditures.
Sources: 1946-56: Royal Commission on Health Services – figures are actually the percentage of GNE; 1960-73: Health and Welfare Canada, *National Health Expenditures in Canada, 1960-73*, Table 5; 1974-6: preliminary estimate provided by Health and Welfare Canada

differences in the use of specialists and their services seems to have widened. The explanation for these results lies in the fundamental inequalities inherent in capitalist societies. As indicated above, the development of hospitals reflects the historic distribution of wealth in Canada, and specialists are drawn to better hospitals. At the same time affluent and educated classes are more aware both of disease symptoms and the formal status of different physicians.[59] Similarly, access to medical care is more difficult for workers, as it may mean loss of work time, and hence income, which cannot be afforded. Finally, as Beck notes with all the appropriate caution, it appears as if general practitioners base their decisions to refer patients to more intensive and expensive care, in part at least, on the social class of the patient.

The evidence that health insurance has had a rather limited effect on increasing access to health care, combined with the enormous increase in costs of that care, suggests that most of the benefits from these expenditures were appropriated as increases in income by those working within the health system itself. This seems to be the conclusion drawn by bourgeois politicians and the mass media as well. However, in doing so they have focused attention on the growth in hospital costs, which, being a labour intensive operation, has meant criticism of the wage increases won by hospital workers. While this is understandable, it is also specious. The place to begin an analysis is with an examination of the increases in income within the health care delivery system. Table 3 shows the income increases for the three main categories of participants: physicians, hospital administrators, and hospital workers.

Table 3
Income trends within the health care sector, 1962-72

	Income			Income increase	
	1962	1966	1972	1962-72	1966-72
Selected hospital workers[a]					
Registered nurse	$3744/yr	4668	7656	104%	64%
Nursing auxiliary	2592	3312	5760	122	74
X-ray technician (male)	4092	4728	7644	87	62
Maid	1932	2628	4560	130	74
Hospital executives[b]					
Chief executive officer		$13,500/yr	$24,000/yr		69%
Assistant to CEO		10,250	15,000		54
Chief financial officer		9750	14,000		47
Chief nursing		9000	14,000		58
Physicians[c]					
All fee-practice MD	$16,966/yr	$23,262	$39,977	136%	72%

[a]Computed from monthly salary data, assuming 12 months employment. Nurses were selected because they are the largest group of hospital workers, and maids because they won the largest pay increases among hospital workers. X-ray technicians pay increases were typical of those won by technical support staff. Source: Health and Welfare Canada, *Salaries and Wages in Canadian Hospitals, 1962-1970* and *1969-73*
[b]These figures consist of an unweighted average of the annual salaries of these executives in hospitals of 500+ beds and 100-199 beds. Both salaries and changes in salary varied widely by hospital size but these figures provide a good illustration for comparative purposes. Data are not available for 1962. Source: as above
[c]Source: published and unpublished statistics provided by Health and Welfare Canada. The figures reflect net income from medical services, where net income is income after office/practice expenses but before taxes. As with all businessmen, some percentage of deductions from gross income are recovered in the future (sale of equipment, goodwill) and so the actual figures are underestimates. This discrepancy has apparently grown over time as physicians have increasingly utilized accountants, management consultants, etc.

The data show clearly that the major beneficiaries of health insurance have been physicians whose percentage increase in income between 1962 and 1972 (136 per cent) exceeded even that of hospital maids whose income increased most among hospital workers. In dollar terms the gap between maids' income and physicians' incomes increased from about $14,000 to $35,000. The increase in physicians' incomes, which raised this component of health costs from 16.9 to 18.7 per cent between 1965 and 1971, moved their income from 4.8 times the average industrial wage in 1961 to 6.5 times the average industrial wage in 1971.[60] Compared to management personnel, hospital workers made some relative gains, although in dollar terms the gap widened markedly. Yet in certain respects these are overstated. Firstly, management has available various non-salary benefits (cars, expense accounts) and secondly, hospital workers have virtually no promotion possibilities whereas managerial personnel do. None the less, relative to all workers, hospital workers have been poorly paid and over this period little happened to rectify the balance.[61]

The tremendous increase in physicians' incomes provides the basis for understanding the mechanism through which health insurance generates spiralling health costs. Based upon a detailed examination of expenditures on physicians' services from 1957 to 1971, R. Evans observed that the growth in these expenditures is not primarily due to increases in fees, hours of work (they seem to have declined), or patients seen, but rather that 'physicians reorganized their practices and generated more income from a given number of initial patient contacts.'[62] This is accomplished by expanding hospital-based services, giving more extensive services (diagnostic and curative), and physician 'upgrading' (from general practitioner to specialist status) so that higher fees can be charged. No doubt the care-seeking actions of Canadians play some role here, but the fact remains that beyond the initial office visit to a physician which is patient-controlled, all subsequent services are ordered by physicians. Similarly, advances in medical technology over the last eighty years, in theory at least, justify more extensive treatment in some instances but the increased services must be understood as primarily designed to increase physician income. This has a long and recognized history within the medical profession as the following quotation by Dr McPhedrox, president of the Canadian Medical Association, in 1945 reveals: 'As long as practitioners are forced to resort to surgical procedures to make "the difference between a bare living and a decent income" just so long will the scales be weighted against any patient who presents himself for examination.'[63] Despite the increase in physicians' incomes, judging by their claims of 'poverty' filling the newspapers a decent income has not yet been achieved. We should not be surprised when independent investigations discover that between 25 and 40 per cent of surgical procedures are 'medically' unjustified.[64]

At the same time as practice reorganizations generate physician income, they reverberate throughout the health system, causing a mushroom growth of private laboratories to do testing and an expansion of the hospital labour force especially in the relatively higher cost categories of nursing, diagnostic/therapeutic, and general administration.[65] At the same time, intensive care wings, overflowing with modern technological apparatus, expand, in effect replacing cheaper basic care beds with more costly ones, and driving up daily patient costs.

Both the federal and provincial governments were well aware that the health insurance programs were bound to result in a dramatic escalation of health care expenditures. For example, coincident with the announcement of medical insurance, the federal government established a task force to study ways of controlling costs. Much attention was given to the idea of developing community health centres which would employ salaried physicians, in the hope of reducing the rate of hospitalization, and the idea of using para-professionals to do much of the routine work done by physicians,[66] with federal and provincial funds being expended on various demonstration projects. These tentative steps towards reform aroused the intense opposition of the medical profession as it saw them as undermining the profession's control over the delivery of health care. But it was assuaged by the fact that the projects were confined to areas physicians themselves were unwilling to service, that is, the North and impoverished inner city areas.

The economic recession in the 1970s brought an end to even these mild attempts to reform the health system and improve access to it for the poor. The demands of the bourgeoisie for increased profits in the context of a stagnant economy meant that state expenditures for services to the working class had to be redirected into profits.[67] The provinces began a well-publicized campaign to close down hospitals and parts thereof (a euphemism for laying off hospital workers), and both levels of government ended or curtailed various demonstration projects begun during the last few years. The strategy of contraction was the mirror image of the policy of expansion, in this case a reduction of the market subsidy without any change in the structure of power and privilege within the health system. Just as the poor benefited least from the subsidy, they will be hurt most by its withdrawal. For example, immigrant physicians comprise a disproportionate share of physicians working in underserviced areas in the north, rural areas, and the outpatient clinics of the cities where the poor, working poor, and immigrant populations predominate.[68] But the federal government in 1975, bowing to pressure from the Canadian Medical Association, announced curbs on the immigration of foreign doctors into Canada, projecting a saving of $250,000 annually for each doctor kept out. In so doing, the government claimed that this would not adversely affect health levels by pointing to the relatively high doctor/population ratio (ignoring the maldistribution), and suggesting that more physicians would only result in more unnecessary care as physicians sought to sustain per capita annual incomes. A clearer recognition of medical monopoly power combined with refusal to challenge that power by the state could not be found.

This article has tried to show that the state viewed health insurance as an economic concession to the working class in order to realize better the long-run political and economic interests of the capitalist class. In so doing, however, health insurance was adapted to the existing structure of power and privilege within the health system, which not only precluded any significant shifts in the distribution of health services but also ensured that what Miliband has termed the 'bias of the system' would operate so that the major beneficiaries would be the dominant classes themselves. Beyond this, however, it must be emphasized that the idea of health insurance itself reveals even more basic limitations of reform by capitalist states. This idea presupposes that health is something to be bought and sold like any other commodity, that the social problem is its cost to individuals lacking health, or, in other words, that health is a problem located in the sphere of personal consumption in general, and more specifically limited to the consumption of physicians' services. The problem with this is that, like much of bourgeois ideology, it individualizes what are social problems.

It is now widely recognized that roughly 50 per cent of those seeking health care in Western capitalist societies are suffering from non-organic disease – stress, nervous tension, psychosomatic disorders – which are rooted in social conditions, and that many other diseases (heart disease, alcoholism) and deaths (suicides, infant mortality) have similar roots. These social conditions are precisely those which characterize the living and working conditions of the working class, and this accounts for the strong relationship between class and these diseases.[69] At the same time, the very development of capitalism has produced, both through its products (nutritionless, chemically laced foodstuffs) and its processes (industrial poisonings), a horrifying growth of chronic degenerative diseases (that is, cancers). For most of these diseases modern medicine can provide no cure, and medical treatment largely consists of ever more costly care, care that is seldom more effective and often less humane.[70] This is not to deny that medical science has made important contributions to treating disease, but to recognize that this applies only to certain diseases, and that here too advances in diagnosis and the management of suffering have to be separated from restoration to health. Consequently, it is not surprising that contemporary research suggests that reductions in infant mortality, the best predictor of life expectancy, are most closely associated with improvements in living conditions and with larger expenditures on public health and on nurses, and that larger expenditures on physicians are associated with relatively higher rates of infant mortality.[71] An awareness of the limits of personal health care is not just a recent phenomenon. In presenting his committee's recommendations for health insurance and a public health program to Parliament in 1943, Dr Heagerty pointed out, in reference to Britain, that while health insurance, as intended, had countered socialist tendencies within the British working class, it had done little to advance their actual health, for which *preventive medicine* was required. Yet it is precisely such a policy, one which would place collective consumption above personal consumption, that would subordinate economic development to human development, that the state in any capitalist society is incapable of effecting. Its very inability to do this in turn ensures that there is an unending supply of candidates for the ministrations of physicians, and an unending drain on the resources of the working class. To this, reform is no solution.

NOTES

The assistance of Patricia Pepall in researching material for this paper is warmly acknowledged as is the financial support which the School of Graduate Studies of Carleton University provided. Thanks are also due to Leo Panitch whose editorial skill, evident only to those who read the original draft, was much appreciated. The introductory quotation is from B. Gilbert, *The Evolution of National Insurance in Great Britain: The Origins of the Welfare State* (London 1966), 452.

1   W.I. Gillespie, 'On the Redistribution of Income in Canada,' *Canadian Tax Journal* (July-Aug. 1976), 419-50. A more detailed analysis of income distribution since the Second World War can be found in L. Johnson, *Poverty in Wealth* (Toronto 1974).

2   R. Miliband, *The State in Capitalist Society* (London 1969), 3

3   *The Fiscal Crisis of the State* (New York 1973), 138. Perhaps the most extreme statement by a Marxist in this regard is by Claus Offe. Discussing the welfare state in general, he notes: ' ... some authors have recently raised the question of whether politics is relevant at all ... It is exactly this situation that best describes the development of the welfare state ... Far more important policy determinants are economic and social variables such as the growth of productivity, the extent of social mobility, the technological level of basic industries, the size and composition of the workforce, the age structure of the population, and other macroeconomic and macrosociological indicators.' 'Advanced Capitalism and the Welfare State,' *Politics and Society* (Summer 1972), 484

4   A good review of this thesis and other explanations of the welfare state is found
    in D. Wedderburn, 'Facts and Theories of the Welfare State,' in R. Miliband
    and J. Saville, eds., *The Socialist Register 1965* (New York 1965), 127-46.
5   *Ibid.,* 143
6   'State Expenditure in Advanced Capitalism,' *New Left Review,* 92 (July-Aug.
    1975), 56 (emphasis added)
7   Sharp is a former Liberal cabinet minister and federal bureaucrat; interview
    with the author at the House of Commons, Aug. 1976.
8   'State Expenditure,' 65
9   E.P. Thompson, 'The Peculiarities of the English,' *Socialist Register 1965,* 344.
    For a discussion of the coincidence between the development of the working
    class as a political force in Canada and the growth of interest in theories about
    the extension of state functions, see Elisabeth Wallace, 'The Origin of the Social
    Welfare State in Canada, 1867-1900,' *Canadian Journal of Economics and Politi-
    cal Science,* XVI, 3 (Aug. 1950), 383.
10 Quoted in Canada, *Report of the Advisory Committee on Health Insurance* (16
    March 1943), 57 – also known as the *Heagerty Report*
11 Canada, Health and Welfare Canada, *National Health Expenditures in Canada,
    1960-73* (April 1975), 3
12 See R. Badgley and S. Wolfe, *Doctors' Strike* (Toronto 1967).
13 Quoted in British Columbia, *Interim Report of the British Columbia Royal Com-
    mission on State Health Insurance and Maternity Benefits* (1928), 23
14 *Advisory Committee on Health Insurance,* 50
15 These points are emphasized in *ibid.,* 50. For an excellent analysis of the idea of
    welfare paternalism, see K. Stone, 'Origins of Job Hierarchies in the Steel
    Industry,' *Review of Radical Political Economics,* VI (1974), 113-73.
16 An overview of the relatively high level of political and industrial militancy in
    British Columbia can be found in S. Jamieson, *Industrial Relations in Canada*
    (Toronto 1973); the subject is dealt with in detail in M. Robin, *Radical Politics
    and Canadian Labour, 1880-1930* (Kingston 1968).
17 *Industry and Humanity* (1918, Toronto 1973), 222
18 Partial accounts can be found in M. Robin, 'The Politics of Class Conflict,' in
    Robin, ed., *Canadian Provincial Politics* (Scarborough 1972); M. Ormsby, 'T.
    Dufferin Pattullo and the Little New Deal,' *Canadian Historical Review,* XLIII, 4
    (Dec. 1962), 277-97; and H. Angus, 'Health Insurance in B.C.,' *Canadian Forum,*
    XVII (1937), 12-14.
19 At least Ontario and Manitoba set up special programs during the depression
    which made health care available to those on the welfare rolls. In Ontario a per
    capita fee was paid to physicians for each welfare recipient who registered as a
    patient, the allocation of money to specific physicians being done entirely by

the medical profession itself. It appears that this program was set up at the instigation of the medical profession and is best understood as a program of relief for fee-for-service physicians; see the *Ontario Medical Association Bulletin* (Feb. 1935).

20 'Social Insurance, Part II, A Background Study for the Royal Commission on Dominion-Provincial Relations,' mimeo. (Ottawa 1938), 22

21 PAC, King Diary, 27 Jan. 1943

22 See Badgley and Wolfe, *Doctors' Strike,* chap. 1. None the less, it would appear that in general the need for the benefits of 'welfare state' programs is less among the petite bourgeoisie.

23 PAC, *Dominion Proposals to the Dominion-Provincial Conference, 1945,* p. 64. Initially health insurance schemes were viewed as contributory insurance, made compulsory by law by the State but without any financing from general state revenues. The reason for this was largely ideological, maintaining the idea that benefits were earned and not a right based on need. Once established, however, other forms of financing tend to develop in order to reduce or contain administrative costs. It should be noted that where working-class pressure was *strong enough,* the rural population *was simply excluded from the program* (for example, Britain in 1911 and Germany in 1883) rather than used as the grounds for not introducing a program at all.

24 See Jamieson, *Industrial Relations,* chap. 3.

25 Quoted in J.L. Granatstein, *Canada's War: The Politics of the Mackenzie King Government, 1939-1945* (Toronto 1975), 251

26 See *Advisory Committee on Health Insurance.* In general, the report was consistent with the position of the CMA. Given the experience of the depression, many physicians favoured health insurance. The CMA or, more precisely, its provincial components, had in several cases, as noted, good experiences with provincial programs; the CMA itself was on record as favouring health insurance – see B. Blishen, *Doctors and Doctrines* (Toronto 1969), app. I and II – and the voluntary physician-sponsored insurance plans were just beginning. The major difference was that the CMA did not accept the principle of universal coverage which the draft bill embodied. As well, while the bill stated that the payment of physicians should be determined by a method acceptable to a given province and the provincial medical association, the CMA position was that only fee-for-service, with the fee set unilaterally by the profession, was acceptable; see its 'Brief to the House of Commons Special Committee on Health Insurance, 1943' (PAC).

27 Although the family allowance measure was designed within the general context of the King government's commitment to Keynesian policies, this should not obscure the specific impact of working-class pressures. Family allowances were conceived in the context of labour's strength in opposing wartime wage con-

trols. 'Probably ¾ of labour's real grievances on the score of wages could be removed by the immediate establishment of children's allowances paid by the State ...' J. Pickersgill to King, quoted in Pickersgill, *The Liberal Party* (Toronto 1962), 32

28 See, for example, M. Taylor, 'The Canadian Health Insurance Program,' *Public Administration Review,* XXXIII (Jan.-Feb. 1973), 31-9; and I. Goffman, 'The Political History of National Hospital Insurance in Canada,' *Journal of Commonwealth Studies,* III (1965), 136-47.

29 Concrete information is not available but it is likely that Drew's stance was largely a part of the 'GET KING' strategy advanced by a group of Toronto Conservatives and ex-Liberals known as the Committee for Total War, which opposed King's vacillation on the conscription issue. See, for example, Granatstein, *Canada's War,* chap. 7. In addition, it is probable that Drew, like his Liberal predecessor Mitchell Hepburn, was 'partial' to the Ontario mining interests who were prepared to go to any lengths to keep the unions out of northern Ontario. (I am indebted to Reg Whitaker for bringing this point to my attention.) On the failure of the Ontario government to use the Municipal Health Services Act, see H. Shillington, *The Road to Medicare* (Toronto 1972), 37.

30 See Granatstein, *ibid.,* especially 262-78.

31 Mitchell Sharp, interview with the author

32 The admission was made by Paul Martin in the debates over hospital insurance. *Can. H. of C. Debates,* 25 March 1957, p. 2677

33 This commitment is evident in various statements and documents scattered throughout Martin's papers, and was confirmed by Mitchell Sharp in my interview with him.

34 Robin, 'Politics of Class Conflict,' 51

35 *Agrarian Socialism* (rev. ed., New York 1968), especially chaps. 7 and 11

36 Frost to St Laurent, 27 Sept. 1955, PAC, Martin Papers, v. 6. Initially, Frost argued for a plan which would be inferior to existing private plans and/or subsidize those unable to afford such plans. He was dissuaded from this by his own advisers as well as federal people on the grounds that this would ultimately be more costly and raise the problem of accountability for government expenditures. See memo from G. Davidson, deputy minister of health, to Martin, 5 Aug. 1955, *ibid.,* v. 15.

37 *Montreal Star,* 3 Nov. 1955

38 According to a confidential report from the insurance companies to the federal government, in 1953 only 46 per cent of Canadians had any hospital insurance. This insurance in turn covered at best 35 per cent of hospital costs. Consequently, by 1955 Group A hospitals in Ontario reported operating deficits of $13 million. J. Willard to Martin, Feb. 1955, Martin Papers, v. 28

39 Summary of cabinet meeting, 20 Jan. 1956, *ibid.,* v. 6

40 Kent, 'Social Security,' Proceedings of the Kingston Conference, mimeo., n.d., p. 25

41 This account of the background to the Kingston Conference and its impact on the Liberal party is based on my interview with Mr Sharp.

42 Jamieson, *Industrial Relations*, 94-9

43 There was opposition from the financial community which, according to Sharp, felt the Canadian government was not being financially responsible. Mr Sharp stated in the interview that, in an attempt to attenuate their fears and regain the illusive but necessary 'business confidence' the implementation of the program was delayed one year.

44 Because the basic policy would have to be identical for all insurers and operated on a non-profit basis, the private carriers would have had to set up a common carrier to average out risks, making it very cumbersome. The only advantage would be that this arrangement could be useful to individual carriers to peddle supplementary insurance (that is, on drugs). Ontario tried such an arrangement but the cost forced its abandonment.

45 Figures are from a speech by Emmett Hall to the Community Welfare Planning Council, 4 Jan. 1965, PAC, Royal Commission on Health Services, 56.

46 A. Jones, 'Federal Financing of Medical Care in Canada,' unpublished course paper, School of Social Work, Carleton University, April 1976. Jones also shows the regressive nature of this tax, which had a ceiling of $120. Viewed from the point of taxes paid, the percentage increase is regressive over the whole income range.

47 CIPO poll, reported in the *Citizen*, Ottawa, 23 Oct. 1976

48 H.E. MacDermot, *History of the Canadian Medical Association* (Toronto 1935), 2

49 There are two central aspects of this monopoly. First of all, it is an economic monopoly. As Section 51 of the Ontario Medical Act states: 'No person not registered shall practise medicine, surgery, or midwifery for hire, gain or hope of reward.' Secondly, the right to register a would-be physician is the responsibility of the College of Physicians and Surgeons of Ontario, which, composed of all registered doctors in the province plus representatives from the medical schools, determines the conditions of eligibility for registration, a right which gives the profession a tremendous amount of control over the supply of physicians. Contrary to popular belief, the college has little to do with the competence of practising physicians and as late as 1964 denied any responsibility in this area. On this point and the intentions of physicians seeking a monopoly in general, see E. McNabb, *A Legal History of the Health Professions in Ontario: A Study for the Committee on the Healing Arts* (Toronto 1970). It should be noted that there is no evidence to suggest that the physicians could justify this monopoly on the basis of the superiority of their type of medical practice.

50 This traditional view is followed by Leo Johnson, for example. Johnson uses two basic indicators of proletarianization: (a) the percentage of an occupation paid on a salaried basis and (b) relative income gains. Yet his data on the medical profession provide no support for his argument. See Johnson, 'The Development of Class in Canada in the Twentieth Century,' in G. Teeple, ed., *Capitalism and the National Question in Canada* (Toronto 1972).

51 Little research on hospital boards has been done in Canada. For some evidence that corporate leaders sit on such boards, see W. Clement, *The Canadian Corporate Elite* (Toronto 1975), 251-3. A recent study of hospital directors in the United States found over 50 per cent to be businessmen, bankers, financiers, and lawyers. *Health PAC Bulletin* (Jan.-Feb. 1977)

52 Memo to the deputy minister of health, 21 Feb. 1952, Martin Papers, v. 28

53 *Can. H. of C. Debates,* 26 July 1956, p. 6519

54 See M. Taylor, 'Quebec Medicare: Policy Formulation in Conflict and Crisis,' *Canadian Public Administration* (Summer 1972), 211-50. Besides labour's opposition to further concessions to the doctors, Taylor notes that many doctors were French-speaking and could not easily emigrate from Quebec, a fact which undermined their position.

55 For an overview of these 'control' systems, see an article by R. Després, R. Murray, A Titus, and N. Yourechuck, written under the editorship of A. Ruderman, 'Control Measures for Physicians' Fee Payments under Provincial Health Insurance Schemes,' *Canadian Journal of Public Health,* LXII (July-Aug. 1971), 271-84.

56 *National Health Expenditures in Canada, 1960-73,* Table 3

57 N. Roos *et al.,* 'The Impact of the Physician Surplus on the Distribution of Physicians across Canada,' *Canadian Public Policy,* II, 2 (1976), 189. Their research also suggests that, as regards specialists, the geographic maldistribution may actually have been exacerbated.

58 'Economic Class and Access to Physician Services under Public Medical Care Insurance,' *International Journal of Health Services,* III (1973), 341-55. See also P. Enterline *et al.,* 'The Distribution of Medical Services before and after Free Medical Care,' *New England Journal of Medicine,* 289,22 (1973); and R. Badgley *et al.,* 'The Impact of Medicare in Wheatville, Sask., 1960-65,' *Canadian Journal of Public Health,* LVIII, 3 (March 1967).

59 On the relationship between social class and knowledge of disease symptoms, see Blishen, *Doctors and Doctrines,* 19.

60 On the increase in the percentage of health costs accounted for by physician fees, see 'Science for Health Services,' *Science Council of Canada Report no. 22* (Ottawa 1974), Table II. 2, p. 48. On the relative growth in physician earnings,

see A. Ruderman, 'The Economic Position of Ontario Physicians and the Relation between the Schedule of Fees and Actual Income from Fee Practice,' in E. Pickering, *Report of the Special Study regarding the Medical Profession in Ontario,* submitted to the Ontario Medical Association, 1973.

61 Lack of comparability and weaknesses in the data forced the comparison of wage gains to end in 1972. In 1974 hospital workers launched a big 'catch-up' campaign which may account for the rise in health expenditures in 1974 and 1975 (see Table 2). However, those categories of workers receiving the largest increases also suffered job losses due to lay-offs. As for physician incomes, the recent period is complicated by changes in the Income Tax Act and a growth in the number of physicians receiving some salary from hospitals, which resulted in a delay in the publication of 1974 physician earnings.

62 'Beyond the Medical Marketplace,' in S. Andrepoulos, ed., *National Health Insurance: Can We Learn from Canada?* (Toronto 1975), 162

63 Quoted in the Health Study Bureau's 'Review of Canada's Health Needs and Health Insurance Proposals' (Toronto 1946), 39

64 See, for example, K. Clute, *The General Practitioner* (Toronto 1963). A more recent study by Dr F. Dyck, in 1974, found roughly 40 per cent of all hysterectomies done in Saskatchewan were medically unjustified. 'Report of the Committee on Hysterectomies,' Saskatchewan College of Physicians and Surgeons (Saskatoon 1974)

65 For example, in Ontario between 1970 and 1974 the number of paid hours per patient day of diagnostic and therapeutic personnel increased 33 per cent, and that of administrative personnel by 18 per cent. Statistics Canada, *Hospital Statistics Annual Report* 83:212 (Ottawa, selected years). Evans, it should be noted, while recognizing that available data preclude a precise determination, argues that wage increases *were* a significant factor in the increase of hospital costs. While wage increases undoubtedly played some role, Evans' estimate suffers from the fact (inexplicable to me) that he seriously *underestimates* the proportion of graduate nurses among hospital workers – he estimates 9 per cent while the data I have seen suggest 25 per cent (see, for example, *Hospital Statistics,* I, 83:227, p. 35 and Table 39, p. 230). As the wage increases of nurses were relatively low this implies his index of wage cost increases is an overestimate.

66 See, for example, the multi-volume report on community health centres by Dr J. Hastings (1973), and the *Report of the National Conference on Assistants to the Physician* (April 1971), Health and Welfare Canada. Extensive evidence was accumulated which showed that physicians on salary performed fewer operations.

67 See David Wolfe's article in this volume.

68 See Roos *et al.,* 'Impact of the Physician Surplus.'

69 On the relationship between class and disease, see J. Siemiatycki, 'The Distribu-
    tion of Disease,' *Canadian Dimension* (June 1974). Data on the diseases physi-
    cians encounter are in H. Dreitzel, ed., *The Social Organization of Health* (New
    York 1971), viii. The relationship between social conditions, especially unem-
    ployment, and heart disease, suicides, and infant mortality has been well docu-
    mented by H. Brenner in his 'Fetal, Infant, and Maternal Mortality during Peri-
    ods of Economic Instability,' *International Journal of Health Services*, III (1973),
    145-59. A brief report on his more recent work can be found in the *Globe and
    Mail*, Toronto, 1 Nov. 1976.

70 The distinction between care and cure is made in V. Navarro, 'The Industriali-
    zation of Fetishism or the Fetishism of Industrialization: A Critique of Ivan
    Illich,' *International Journal of Health Services*, v (1975), 351-71. A good review
    of the limits of modern medicine can be found in M. Renaud, 'On the Structural
    Constraints to State Intervention in Health,' *ibid.*, 559-72.

71 R. Fraser, 'An International Study of Health and General Systems of Financing
    Health Care,' *ibid.*, III, 369-90

12

Origins of the welfare state in Canada

ALVIN FINKEL

Social democrats have argued that the movement since the 1930s towards greater state provision of social security for citizens is evidence that capitalism can be controlled and that the political power of the bourgeoisie can be reduced without fundamental changes occurring in the structure of ownership and control of industry. The CCF-NDP threat; the influence of middle-class professionals; the bleeding hearts of depression and wartime politicians; and the collective national spirit that characterized the war and post-war reconstruction period: all are invoked to explain the expansion of the state's role in providing social security. The major survivors of the League for Social Reconstruction, founded during the depression as the intellectual brain trust of the nascent CCF, recalled forty years later: 'What is difficult for us to grasp today is that the social planning which was prescribed by the LSR in the thirties was a major heresy for those in government and in the business community. Government had its role and business had its role and the two roles had to be kept separate. Government's 'interference' in business was restricted to the enactment and enforcement of safety and health standards in factories and mines, subsistence minimum wages, and regulations for the adjudication of industrial disputes – at best a guardian and umpire role. But for the government to intervene in the self-regulating economic system for the purpose of setting social goals that might inhibit the full play of the profit motive was regarded as a cardinal sin. To suggest further that government should plan the nation's economic life in the interests of the good of the majority of its people was to challenge the foundations of the faith.'[1]

The problem with the LSR analysis is that it totally ignores the class nature of the state. It is assumed that where government planning exists and where a number of welfare programs exist – although Canada's welfare state is generally conceded to be incomplete – that the direction of economic planning is 'in the interests of the majority of the people.' What is to be argued here, however, is that the 'welfare state,' while it places a floor on the standard of living of working people, was not constituted, even in its incomplete Canadian form, to reduce the economic and political power of the business leaders.[2] Indeed, the opposite is the case. It was devised by governments that wished to preserve the power of the ruling class but saw that power threatened by working-class militancy directed against an economic system that seemed unable to provide jobs or security. The upsurge of radicalism in the working class first in the Great Depression and then during the war forced an important section of the bourgeoisie to rethink its strategies with regard to the role of the state. The Canadian state had financed much of the infrastructure for Canadian industry and had intervened, when necessary, to defeat working-class attempts to improve wages and living standards through the formation of unions and the waging of strikes. Now, however, the provision of police and railroads alone could not create sufficient economic stability to fend off the working-class attack. The result was a rethinking among many businessmen of the proper relations between the state, industry, and the people.

In the first place, however, it is important to question whether the term 'welfare state' does not conceal more about Canada than it reveals. It is true of course that welfare programs place a floor on income and to that extent the winning of such programs has been a victory for the Canadian working class. Nevertheless, the Economic Council of Canada reported in 1972 that at least 27 per cent of Canadians must be said to be living in poverty if poverty were defined as 'an insufficient access to certain goods, services, and conditions of life which are available to everyone else and have come to be accepted as basic to a decent, minimum standard of living.'[3] A study prepared for the council indicated that governments, while establishing programs that transferred wealth to the lowest income group, used methods of taxation that involved 'extreme regressivity ... at the lower end of the income scale and the lack of any significant progressivity over the remainder of the income range.'[4] Statistics Canada data indicate that negligible redistribution of wealth has occurred in Canada since 1950.[5] Moreover human 'welfare' is not an easily quantifiable economic proposition. Ecological destruction, the destruction of health in many factory and mine jobs, and the psychological problems created for people who do seemingly mindless work over which they have no control are less quantifiable but no less important measures of human welfare.

What is to be examined here are the origins of the 'welfare state' in Canada. The period studied covers the years 1930 through to 1945, that is, from the onset of the Great Depression to the end of the war that terminated the depression. It was during this period that the dictates of political economy created the debate on the 'welfare state' and finally the establishment of certain policies that provided the framework of the Canadian 'welfare state.' Of course, there were further programs added after 1945 that are not dealt with here. Nor are all the programs introduced by 1945 examined in detail. But the motivations behind welfarist policies as a whole are suggested by the debate on the particular policies discussed here. In short, by focusing on a few policies at a particular period, an attempt is made to reconstruct the motivations of the Canadian state in introducing welfarist policies. In particular, the question of the class nature of Canadian government is examined against the background of policies that certain critics, as above noted, thought to be of necessity directed against the bourgeoisie and in favour of the working class.

II

Social legislation in Canada before the Great Depression was minimal. The working class had not long been the majority group in the country and the agricultural class, over-represented in voting by rurally weighted electoral boundaries both at the federal and provincial levels, had little understanding of urban society and largely supported the capitalist class in its resistance to social legislation. The trade union movement, while it pressed for legislative changes, was weak and politically unimportant. Before the First World War the only victories it could claim were the winning of free public education and a number of public health services – though, in the case of Montreal and probably other cities, even these victories had not really been won by 1914. The public education debate, it might be noted, centred in part on the need for a partially literate work force for industry.[6]

Additional social legislation came slowly. Workmen's compensation had been introduced by all provinces except Prince Edward Island by 1920. An American study of the introduction of compensation indicates that this measure was desired by large corporate interests as a means of fending off the more radical employer-liability type of legislation which made employers legally responsible for employees injured at work. A state-wide program would remove the onus on individual businessmen and thus remove the need for shorter working hours and costly safety measures. A recent study of the origins of workmen's compensation in Ontario suggests that Canadian employers thought along the same lines. While the Canadian

Manufacturers' Association and its provincial branches often opposed specific features of proposed compensation legislation, they did not sway from their support of the principle itself. Before the introduction of workmen's compensation in Ontario in 1915, many employers taken to court by employees under the province's employer-liability legislation had been found negligent and therefore liable by juries sympathetic to the injured employees. Jury awards to injured employees for compensation by the employers were common enough and generous enough that many companies found themselves unable to find insurance companies that would provide them with insurance against liability.[7]

The high rate of unemployment before the First World War and the expected return to high unemployment at the war's end prompted the Ontario government to name a Royal Commission on Unemployment in 1916. The commission discussed and rejected the idea of a government-run unemployment insurance scheme, though it urged the province to aid financially company and trade union private programs for unemployment benefits.[8] The end of the war did bring some social legislation in the form of federal pensions for war widows and legislation in most provinces for mothers' allowances. Throughout the 1920s, however, the Trades and Labour Congress pressed unsuccessfully for universal old age pensions, unemployment insurance, sickness insurance, and disability insurance. And the only program passed by the federal government was a pension scheme for the needy poor. The scheme, which provided only twenty dollars a month and was available only from age seventy, was a concession won by the small Labour group in the House of Commons, under the leadership of J.S. Woodsworth, for support of King's precarious minority Liberal government of 1925.[9]

Few would have thought that the Conservative government of R.B. Bennett, elected in 1930 on a campaign of high tariffs for Canadian manufacturers and primary producers, would have been interested in introducing new programs for social security. Bennett was one of Canada's leading capitalists and had important holdings in almost all sectors of the economy. He had been a partner with Lord Beaverbrook in the financial manœuvrings that had created such concerns as the monopolistic Canada Cement Company; he was the majority shareholder in the Eddy Match monopoly and in the E.B. Eddy Newsprint Company and had some say in Eddy policies even as prime minister; he had been western solicitor for the Canadian Pacific Railway; he was the second largest individual shareholder in the Royal Bank; he had been president of the Turner Valley operations of Imperial Oil as well as Imperial's chief lawyer, and held thousands of shares in metal-mining companies; he was a past vice-president of Alberta Pacific

Grain Elevators and a past director of such oligopolies as Imperial Tobacco and Canada Packers; at his death in 1947 he was worth forty million dollars.[10] Truly, here was a man who might claim to represent the big bourgeoisie as a whole and use the power of the state to achieve compromises among its different – though partly interlocked – sectors. Bennett's cabinet included many other men who had ties with big corporations, and the government's appointment of top civil servants and members of royal commissions reflected a belief that success in private business was a chief qualification for government service.[11] The tenor of Bennett's government might be thought to be best encapsulated by his oft-quoted statement that the 'iron heel of repression' was to be applied to those who rebelled against the existing order. Trade union organizing attempts were suppressed with state aid, Communists were imprisoned, militants of foreign birth were deported, and unemployed young men were put in remote camps where they received no wages and were fired upon when they tried to come to Ottawa to seek redress.[12] Yet it was this clearly anti-labour government that introduced unemployment insurance, a federal manpower agency, government mortgage-lending, and a variety of marketing boards. It also promised in 1935, if re-elected, to introduce a universal pension program and health insurance. Why? A.E. Grauer, writing for the Royal Commission on Dominion-Provincial Relations in 1939, summed up the type of philosophy that began to make certain social reforms acceptable to conservatives not only in Canada but in many industrialized nations: 'Since the Great War, the Great Depression has been the chief stimulus to labour legislation and social insurance. The note sounded has not been so much the ideal of social justice as political and economic financial expediency. For instance, the shorter working week was favoured in unexpected quarters not because it would give the workers more leisure and possibilities for a fuller life but because it would spread work; and the current singling out of unemployment insurance for governmental attention in many countries is dictated by the appalling costs of direct relief and the hope that unemployment insurance benefits will give some protection to public treasuries in future depressions and will, by sustaining purchasing power, tend to mitigate these depressions.'[13]

Social insurance, then, from this particular depression point of view, was intended to stabilize destabilized economies and not necessarily to redistribute wealth. That later studies should indicate that wealth had not been redistributed would only validate the view of conservatives who believed certain social reforms, if carried out in a certain way, would reinforce rather than disturb the status quo.

Sir Charles Gordon, president of Canada's then-leading bank, the Bank of Montreal, and president of Dominion Textiles, the country's leading textiles firm, was one conservative who argued that unemployment and old age insurance programs were necessary to stabilize the economy. Accepting that structural unemployment was inevitable, Gordon told the Bank of Montreal annual meeting that an organized national system of social security was cheaper and more efficient than the haphazard municipal systems of relief that were in effect during the depression. The British experience was cited as proof that a country could weather better an economic recession if it collected funds in boom times to be released to the unemployed when the economy faltered.[14]

Gordon, who was second only to Sir Herbert Holt in assets over which he had trusteeship, was especially concerned that unemployment insurance be introduced. Reflecting the views of the bankers, Gordon wrote Bennett in January 1934 to urge unemployment insurance as an alternative to direct relief. The result of direct relief was that many municipalities and even provinces were in so much debt that they were '... threatening to strangle their general credit to the point where it would be difficult if not impossible to carry through refunding operations for any maturing issues, letting alone the finding of money for any new capital undertaking.'

The need to prevent future recourse to extensive direct relief convinced Gordon of 'the urgent desirability of invoking some system of unemployment insurance.' The British Parliament's recently reorganized unemployment insurance scheme was presented as a model, especially since it covered four-fifths of all working people. Concluded Gordon: 'May I suggest to you that *for our general self-preservation* some such arrangement will have to be worked out in Canada and that if it can be done soon so much the better.'[15]

The Bank of Nova Scotia's executives cautioned against expectations that unemployment insurance would completely obviate the necessity for direct relief. But they endorsed the principle as going at least part way in decreasing the burden of relief on national and local budgets. Like many advocates of insurance, the bank advised that a workable insurance scheme must be tied to a better-developed and nationally co-ordinated system of unemployment bureaus such as existed in Great Britain. Only in this way could unemployment insurance become a scheme for re-employing the unemployed rather than a fund for 'malingerers.'[16]

The municipalities' supposed profligacy with relief was not the result of control of the lower levels of government by benevolent individuals glad to open up the public purse to those experiencing hard times. Rather it was the result of well-organized and generally Communist-led campaigns of the unemployed workers in the major municipalities. Supported by trade unionists, the massed unemployed presented the spectre of a revolt of the workers to the frightened pillars of communities in charge of municipal councils. The councils were forced to grant more relief, often at the price of defaulting on the cities' debts. As a result, both the municipal leaders and their banker-creditors looked to the federal government to provide programs that would calm the militancy of the unemployed and preserve the credit of the municipalities.[17]

Unemployment insurance was seen as the first plank of a program of social security that would take care of those out of work and reduce the number of people seeking jobs. A.O. Dawson, 1934-5 president of the Canadian Chamber of Commerce, president of Canadian Cottons, and director of many firms, was, like his fellow textile executive, Sir Charles Gordon, interested in copying the British example for social security programs. Speaking on employer-employee relations to the Canadian Chamber of Commerce in September 1934, Dawson urged the government to establish a fund for sickness, unemployment, and old age. It would be financed through a compulsory contribution of 5 per cent of every employee's wages with contributions of an equivalent amount also to be made by the employers and the government. A reasonable pension for workers retiring at the age of sixty-five would be one of the benefits from this program, argued Dawson, who was concerned that technological changes would prevent the employment of all available hands even after the depression was over. (Canadian Cottons had endured a bitter strike in 1929 in its Hamilton plant where lay-offs accompanied the introduction of assembly-line techniques.[18]) Insurance programs would reduce the total labour force by retiring its oldest members and giving sustenance to younger workers laid off while they sought new jobs. The result would be that individual employers would not need to fear the consequences of labour-saving machinery and of speed-up techniques meant to reduce total labour requirements; responsibility for the unemployed and the aged would be socialized. Like Dawson, *Pulp and Paper of Canada*, the organ of the newsprint industry in Canada, saw a comprehensive insurance scheme as necessary to control working-class discontent. Pensions would be useful because they would vacate jobs for younger workers. The journal observed that keeping young people idle between the leaving of school and the time of finding a job 'breeds shiftlessness, discontent and ultimately disorder.'[19] Just as the militancy of the unemployed had forced increases in relief payments, it also forced a debate among businessmen on the question of social insurance as a means of preventing recurrences of such militancy during times of unemployment, whether caused by cyclical or structural factors.

Bennett largely shared the sentiments of people like Gordon and Dawson and the pulp and paper executives. Promising a universal old age pension scheme in the 1935 election as an extension of the social security program that had been begun earlier that year with the introduction of unemployment insurance, Bennett vowed to reduce the age of retirement to sixty. 'Labour-saving machinery, elimination of duplication and growing concentration of business make it impossible to ever supply again work for all the people,' commented Bennett. On the other hand, these advances meant increased production and, if the state had some role in the distribution of the benefits of this increase in national income, more and more people could legitimately be removed from the labour force and provided for by the state.[20] Bennett, like Dawson, believed that unemployment insurance would head off the militancy that resulted from cyclical unemployment and that might also result from structural unemployment as it had in the case of Canadian Cottons.

'Iron-Heel' Bennett also recognized that repression alone might not be sufficient to preserve the existing system against the threat of socialism. As he wrote a New Brunswick publisher: '... Tim Buck has today a very strong position in the province of Ontario and he openly demands the abolition of the capitalist system. A good deal of pruning is sometimes necessary to save a tree and it would be well for us in Canada to remember that there is considerable pruning to be done if we are to preserve the fabric of the capitalist system.'[21]

Unemployment insurance was introduced as part of a 'reform' package in the parliamentary session of 1935, a package generally referred to as the 'Bennett New Deal.' The New Deal legislation, presented on the eve of a general election, was designed to reinvigorate a discredited Conservative government through a program of construction, social insurance, government mortgage-lending, and producers' marketing boards, which it was hoped would pacify demands of workers and farmers and restore investors' confidence. Unemployment insurance was introduced with a promise that health and old age insurance would follow; a national minimum wage-maximum hours law was passed; the public works program was expanded and the government entered the second mortgage-lending field in order to spur home construction; a producers' marketing boards program introduced the previous year was also expanded.[22]

Workers and farmers were not impressed by the apparent death-bed conversion of the Bennett government. But it has been wrongly argued that the general reaction of the business community was negative. It is true that CPR president Edward Beatty and the Montreal *Gazette*, among others, were, as the *Gazette* put it, 'shocked and startled.'[23] But the response of the manufacturing and financial sectors which traditionally supported the Conservative party was generally one of positive support. The Conservatives, unable in the two years before the New Deal to collect corporate contributions, appeared to have been revived.[24] While the New Deal may not have been the major reason for this resurgence in party finances, it did not seem to hinder Tory fund-raising.

A veritable 'who's who' of Canadian manufacturing and finance wrote Bennett to pledge their support for the New Deal effort. Included were such luminaries of Canadian business as: A.O. Dawson, president of the Canadian Chamber of Commerce and president of Canadian Cottons; H.B. Henwood, president of the Bank of Toronto; C.H. Carlisle, president of Goodyear Tire and later also of the Dominion Bank of Canada; Colonel the Hon. H. Cockshutt, president of Cockshutt Plough; Thomas Bradshaw, president of North American Life; J.D. Johnson, president of Canada Cement; Ward Pitfield, president of Ward Pitfield Investments; W.W. Butler, president of Canadian Car and Foundry; J.W. McConnell, president of St Lawrence Sugar Refining and the *Montreal Star*; C.J. Ballantyne, president of Sherwin-Williams Paints; James McGroary, chairman of George Weston Bread; Arthur Purvis, president of CIL and Dupont; and F.N. Southam, president of Southam Publications.[25] Conspicuous by its absence was support from industrialists in the primary sectors.

There were business opponents of the New Deal. It is difficult to divorce business views on social welfare from their views on other subjects. For example, the leading department store officials, having been roasted before the Stevens Royal Commission on Price Spreads, had no good words for any Tory policies even though Stevens had been forced to resign both from the chairmanship of the commission and from the cabinet. The department stores, as importers, were also opposed to the super-protective tariffs that were fundamental to the manufacturers' support of the Conservative party. Nevertheless, Sir Joseph Flavelle, chairman of the Canadian Bank of Commerce and former president of Simpson's as well as Canada Packers, had been a life-long Conservative. It is difficult to determine whether his denunciation by Stevens or his generally reactionary views or both caused him to turn against that party and support the King Liberals in 1935. Similarly, CPR president Edward Beatty, another Liberal convert, was also a thorough-going reactionary who might have switched allegiances even had the New Deal not been introduced. Beatty had attempted for five years to convince his friend Bennett, former chief western solicitor for the railroad, to hand over the publicly owned Canadian National Railways to the CPR. While Bennett introduced the policy of non-competition between the two railway systems, it was politically impossible for him to bequeath the CN to the CP. Beatty, obsessed with the idea of gobbling the CN, felt betrayed.[26]

The existence of these opponents of reform is hardly surprising. Bennett, after all, was himself a newcomer to the idea that these reforms were necessary to stabilize and legitimize the existing political and economic arrangements. The onset of an election no doubt played an important role in persuading Bennett to act. But one must remember that Bennett, as the head of the capitalist state, could not afford to wait until every capitalist was convinced that change was necessary. 'To save the fabric of the capitalist system' was his aim and while certain individual capitalists and even capitalist sectors as a whole might disagree with his solutions, sufficient overall support and encouragement existed in the ruling class to allow him to act. Nor had Bennett completely rejected the 'iron-heel' approach to class conflict. The repression of the on-to-Ottawa trek of relief camp inmates, after all, occurred after the New Deal session of Parliament. But Bennett had realized that the stick alone, while it could play some role in intimidating the working class, had proved an insufficient instrument for mediating class conflict in favour of the bourgeoisie. The carrot was also necessary.

Bennett lacked neither traditional Conservative business support nor newspaper support for his New Deal: the defeat of his government was less the rejection of the New Deal than of a government that had waited five years to act upon problems already obvious when it took power. Bennett had not launched the 'legislative assault on the corporate elite' which Richard Wilbur attributed to him and he was defeated not by the corporate elite but by the working people and farmers.[27]

Insurance and other programs, while meant to counter the communist threat, were not meant to redistribute wealth. Bennett made this clear in the debates on unemployment insurance in the House of Commons. In one debate, A.A. Heaps and the small Labour caucus argued for a non-contributory plan financed by a steeply graded income tax. A communist campaign among organizations of the unemployed, trade union locals, and labour councils called for a similar plan. Bennett attacked such a plan and said that 'insurance involves premiums and premiums should be paid by the joint action alike of the insurer and the insured themselves and with the assistance of the state.'[28] Insurance programs then were seen as a kind of forced savings by workers for times of unemployment, old age, or infirmity rather than as a means of increasing the relative overall income for workers.

As the *Financial Times*, speaking for St James Street, commented on 5 August 1932, workers did not have the foresight that corporations had, to build reserves 'against distress in the event of future unemployment.' Indeed, whatever redistribution might take place as a result of the contributions of the employers and the state was to be taken away by increasing the income tax collected from working people.

In 1930 only 3 or 4 per cent of working-age Canadians earned the $3000 per annum above which income tax was paid. Bennett believed these men were treated unfairly since they also paid taxes on dividends, and the money from which dividends was received was, in turn, subject to corporation tax.[29] Bennett reduced the personal tax exemption to $2000 and though inflation in the war and post-war period devalued the dollar time and again, governments did not raise the exemption. Workers who before the 1930s paid no direct taxes were faced then with both income taxes and insurance premiums to be deducted from their wages. Income that the worker once received to dispose of as he saw fit has been deducted from workers' wages for specific state 'welfare' programs. Such deductions from wages – as opposed to the stiff taxes on profits and salaries called for by the left – provide the state with an income for social programs without necessitating a redistribution of wealth. While the left wanted to rob Peter to pay Paul, the state saw fit to rob Paul to pay Paul. The worker would simply have his wages rationalized so that a large portion went, through taxes and premiums, to pay for services that he previously had to set aside money for on his own.[30]

The Mackenzie King Liberals, resurrected in 1935, were rooted in this period mainly in the primary industries – metal-mining companies, the Winnipeg Grain Exchange, the lumber industry – and supported by importers and exporters, in general. The export sector, while interested in achieving class harmony, thought the Bennett programs exacted too high a price. While the banks and the largely domestic-oriented manufacturing industries saw these programs as leading to a greater stability in the domestic market, the export-oriented sectors feared their result would be higher costs of operation.[31] The compromise that was worked out over time by the Liberals involved the granting of exemptions from various taxes to the exporters, particularly the mines, as compensation for the burden of insurance programs. Low taxes for these exporters has meant higher taxes on income for working Canadians.

The control of the export sectors and particularly the mines over the provincial governments in whose spheres they largely operated was a constant complaint of Mackenzie King.[32] Ontario and Quebec, in particular, resisted King's attempts to reintroduce a federal unemployment insurance scheme after the Bennett scheme was judged unconstitutional by the Judicial Committee of the Privy Council in 1937.[33] King, leading a federal party that traditionally emphasized provincial rights and which depended for much of its finances upon the same 'provincial' interest groups that dominated the junior governments,[34] was wary about reintroducing the Bennett schemes and rejected the requests of what he told his diary were 'Tory' big business interests who sought to impose expensive self-interested legislation without regard to the provisions of the constitution. For the most part, King, at this point, quite opposite to Bennett, still rejected the idea that manufacturing was decisive in the Canadian economy or that the purchasing power of the urban workers was the crucial factor in the home market. In a revealing diary entry on 8 November 1937, King tells of his tariff discussions with American secretary of state Cordell Hull and indicates a hewers-of-wood, drawers-of-water conception of the Canadian economy: '... I spoke of the home market argument, pointing out that the home market in Canada was the purchasing power in the hands of our agriculturists for manufacturers while the home market in the United States was the purchasing power in the hands of the manufacturers and those employed in industries for the purpose of agricultural products. This, the result of Canada being an exporter chiefly in natural products; the United States an exporter wholly of manufactured products.'

The overall conversion of the 'national' business community to social insurance measures was indicated by the hostile reaction to the ruling of the Judicial Committee in 1937 that federal unemployment insurance was unconstitutional. The Ontario Associated Boards of Trade and Chambers of Commerce, representing all the boards in the province, congratulated King on his efforts to join with the provinces in securing an amendment to the British North America Act to permit unemployment insurance and labour agencies under federal authority.[35] In December 1937 *Canadian Business*, house organ of the Canadian Chamber of Commerce, attacked the 'constitutional fetish' of the three provinces – Quebec, Ontario, and New Brunswick – that were opposing federal insurance, largely, in the case of the first two provinces, at the behest of the mining companies.

The Royal Commission on Dominion-Provincial Relations, which was not empowered to deal with the merits of social insurance, nevertheless heard calls for such legislation from such groups as the Retail Merchants' Association, the Ontario Association of Real Estate Boards, and the Canadian Manufacturers' Association. The merchants argued for contributory unemployment insurance as a means of increasing purchasing power when recessions struck. The real estate men added that unemployment insurance was a proper substitute for relief which was paid by municipal property taxation; reduction in such taxation was necessary if the housing industry was to be revived and unemployment insurance was the means to this end. The CMA, using the familiar forced-savings argument, called, as it had in the past, for a universal contributory pensions plan to replace the selective deserving-poor program.[36]

The major attempt to place a program of social insurance in the context of an overall program for economic stability was that of the National Employment Commission, which reported in 1938. Its chairman, Arthur Purvis, was one of Canada's most influential businessmen. He was president of the Canadian branches of CIL and Dupont Rubber and a director of a large number of firms. Purvis, like Bennett, advocated a conservative form of state planning to ensure the existing property and power relations among the various social classes in Canada. His vice-chairman on the commission was the veteran Trades and Labour Congress president Tom Moore and the general concurrence of the two men on the best means to attack unemployment reflected the conservative ideology of the American-dominated crafts unions which predominated in the TLC.[37] Purvis believed that insurance and other spending programs could serve the purpose of lifting the economy when it began to sag and could also provide other benefits for industry. His report called for a 'coordinated attack' on unemployment. This would include unemployment insurance and perhaps other insurance programs, a national network of labour exchanges, expanded federal vocational education programs, and a comprehensive housing policy including subsidized rental housing for the poor and state loans to persons seeking home improvements. The emphasis was on a strengthening of the role of the central government in dealing with unemployment. For reasons of efficiency, the wasteful and unco-ordinated municipal relief programs had to be eliminated and replaced by a program of federal planning that would make the central government a major source of investment in the market-place when the private investors, for whatever reasons, were not sufficiently carrying on the process of capital accumulation to maintain employment and hence demand at reasonable levels.

The Purvis report was rejected as 'Tory' by Mackenzie King. He was horrified by the commission's disregard for provincial rights and described Purvis' report contradictorily as an 'academic treatise' and a Tory big business report.[38] Purvis had been suggested as chairman to King by Charles Dunning, minister of finance. King had appointed Dunning minister of finance because of his direct connections with Montreal capital and yet distrusted him and his appointees for these connections. Ironically, King, who always felt business exercised too great an influence over governments, both Liberal and Conservative, was to the right of many of the businessmen and rejected as 'Tory' certain social measures they proposed despite the fact that they went no further than his prescriptions twenty years earlier in *Industry and Humanity*.

The Purvis report reflected the attitudes of those businessmen who were most keen to use the state to prevent the repeated crises from which capitalism, through the market-place alone, could find no protection. The 'national' business community, led by the Canadian Chamber of Commerce, gave support to the Purvis proposals and urged the federal government to alter the constitution so as to make possible its implementation. The Montreal Board of Trade told the Royal Commission on Dominion-Provincial Relations: '... taxation for the purpose of social services transfers purchasing power from the richer to the poorer classes, raises the standard of living of the poor, increases their demand for commodities and thereby tends towards industrial stability and prosperity. Furthermore, in a period of economic depression, heavier government expenditures, whether paid for by taxes or by loans, are justified and necessary in order to fill the gap resulting from the fear and inactivity which paralyze private enterprise.'[39]

Indeed, the perspective of virtually all the business presentations before the Rowell-Sirois Commission was for increased federal government control over areas traditionally within the provincial sphere and for the weakening of the provincial governments. But the resource industries, who had fattened the most from provincial troughs, were as absent from the long roll call of companies and business organizations making their views known to the commission as they were from the similar list of industrialists praising R.B. Bennett's New Deal.[40]

The combined urgings of 'Tory' businessmen and the depression militancy of farmers, workers, and the unemployed were insufficient to push cautious Mackenzie King to the point his Conservative predecessor had reached by 1935. But the onset of war strengthened the position of the working class and made it apparent that Bennett had been correct in his prognostication that capitalism was threatened by a working-class uprising if reforms were not forthcoming. During the 1930s, despite the general militancy of both workers and the unemployed, the state machinery had been used effectively to hold back attempts at unionization. The repression of Communists and the CIO, while it defeated neither group, held trade unionists in 1939 to a number not substantially greater than the 1930 figure. By the end of six years of war, however, the trade union movement had more than doubled in membership, the result largely of the successful organization of mass-production industries.[41] Government labour policies during the war were extremely repressive. But it proved impossible to prevent unionization under wartime conditions of full employment and even labour shortages. As a result, by war's end King had turned his attention not to the question of whether there would be unions but what kind of unions there would be.[42]

The militancy of the trade union movement had its counterpart in the rising popularity of left-wing political parties and especially the CCF.[43] The Conservative party, in the face of working-class agitation and the CCF threat, began to reassert its New Deal programs. Arthur Meighen, briefly resuscitated as party leader in late 1941, lost to a CCF candidate in a by-election in February 1942 in York South, a supposedly safe working-class Tory seat in Toronto. Meighen had made conscription and the war effort the issue; the CCF had successfully argued that the real issue was reconstruction after the war and what working people should expect from governments after having sacrificed so much to defeat fascism.[44] Meighen, an admirer of the Roosevelt New Deal in the 1930s and a supporter of the Bennett reforms had moved far to the right by the 1940s.[45]

Indeed, the oscillations of Meighen, like those of Bennett and King, between the use of repression and the use of social programs to diminish class conflict, indicates the extent to which the latter was regarded as tactical. Meighen, after all, had sent in troops to break the Winnipeg General Strike and had, as minister of justice, composed the infamous Section 98 which outlawed all activities that might be construed as falling within the rubric of a vaguely defined 'sedition.' Yet, faced in the 1930s with a widening gulf between the workers and capitalists, he had decided it was tactically correct to introduce social programs to pacify the workers and became the Tory spokesman in the Senate for the Bennett New Deal programs. Later he turned against such programs, believing that the war effort might be used to unite the 'nation' and obscure class conflicts.

But other Conservative party leaders, and especially J.M. Macdonnell, recognized that more than ever it was tactically necessary to use the state machinery to initiate reforms that would blunt the working-class offensive of the war years. Macdonnell, president of National Trust, had thought even before the war years that it was dangerous to wait for private economic forces to correct the depression. He told a Conservative party conference in 1933 that government had a role to play in stimulating demand during recessions. In an earlier address in the same year, Macdonnell had made his position clear: what was necessary was to '... remove the grit from the individualist machine and make it run smoothly – meanwhile allowing the process of the last century to continue viz. the gradual socialization of those things which the sense of the community agrees should be socialized.' In September 1942 Macdonnell organized an unofficial conference of Conservatives in Port Hope, Ontario, to draw up a possible program for the party to deal with 'modern needs' and to prevent Canada from being engulfed by 'totalitarianism' of either left or right. The full range of reforms in the New Deal were reasserted and, reflecting the new political realities, other reforms were added. Not only would the workers have a variety of social insurance programs for home-buying to protect them from the hazards of the market-place, but they would have guaranteed rights to trade unions and collective bargaining.[46] Bennett, in 1935, had angrily rejected a CCF suggestion that blacklisting of trade unionists by employers be made illegal.[47] But, in 1942, with the trade union movement having established itself in many mass-production industries despite repressive state policies, the Conservatives accepted the inevitable.

Though the Montreal *Gazette* and other elements in the Conservative party were still unconvinced that their party should commit itself to the welfare state, the party convention in December 1942 chose Macdonnell's candidate, John Bracken, the premier of Manitoba, as its new leader, and adopted substantially the Port Hope policies as the party platform.[48] The 'duty of the state,' said the platform, was to maintain both a 'high level' of income for the individual and 'the principle of private initiative and enterprise.'[49]

Mackenzie King was finally being forced to act in this period. His earlier objections to the Purvis report's disregard for provincial rights were lessened by the report of the Rowell-Sirois Commission in 1940 that a strengthened federal government and correspondingly weaker provincial governments were necessary to equalize living standards across the country and to revive investor confidence shaken by the bankruptcies of many junior levels of government. Social insurance programs, for example, it recommended, should be under federal jurisdiction. Shortly after the report was tabled, King, taking advantage of Maurice Duplessis' defeat by Adelard Godbout's Liberals in Quebec (largely thanks to the aid of federal ministers) and Ontario premier Mitch Hepburn's temporary willingness to make concessions for the war effort, was able to secure a constitutional amendment allowing the federal government to reintroduce the unemployment insurance bill.[50]

The unemployment insurance bill, however, was not followed by further reform legislation until 1944. In the interim, the King government had actually considered discontinuing the programs of government mortgage-lending begun by Bennett in 1935 with the Dominion Housing Act and extended slightly by the Liberals in 1937 in the National Housing Act. The life insurance companies, mortgage companies, construction industry, and timber industry had all been active in convincing Bennett to include this legislation in the New Deal.[51] Now these business sectors all joined labour in opposing its removal; the legislation was left in place.[52]

But King, who had bowed to the most conservative elements of the business community before the war, was now faced with the certainty of political deféat if he did not act to create some or all of the programs that the other two major parties were advocating and which King had also supposedly supported since the First World War. The Liberal administration in Ontario had been badly defeated in the provincial election of 1943 and several federal Liberal seats had been lost in by-elections. A poll in September 1943 gave the CCF the support of 29 per cent of the electorate; the Liberals and Tories each had 28 per cent.[53] King had made, in a sense, his life's work the harmonizing of class relations in Canada and, during his years of employment with the Rockefellers, the United States. As deputy minister of labour, minister of labour, and finally prime minister, he had sought to devise means of ensuring labour peace and the unity of labour and capital 'under the ideal of social service.' In his 1918 book, *Industry and Humanity*, to which he would make endless references in the future, King, with the aid of confusing and semi-mystical charts, argued that public opinion was the major means of forcing the parties within industry to co-operate.[54] In practice, King's labour policies had been designed to maintain the status quo of social relations.[55] *Industry and Humanity* also spoke favourably of the British Labour party's idea of a National Minimum standard of living, which would be collectively guaranteed by society as a whole through state action. Minimum wages, maximum hours, and programs of social insurance were to be part of the state program to achieve the National Minimum. But again, in practice, King had been in office for many years without introducing such programs. Now, however, he was finally acting in order to introduce 'a wholly new conception of industry as being in the nature of social service for the benefit of all, not as something existing only for the benefit of a favoured few.'[56] A shift in class forces had occurred and made impossible the continuation of a do-nothing approach. King could at last dare to defy the more reactionary wing of the bourgeoisie and his party.

King, it might be emphasized, was not a businessman and did not pretend to act as a spokesman for business. His general views were compatible with business views but he always felt that businessmen were, at heart, Tories. He feared both the political and economic consequences of offending the business community. Thus it is not surprising that programs to which King was committed twenty-five years earlier were not introduced until the mid-1940s. Given the Liberal party's need of business support and King's commitment to keeping the business community happy enough that new private investment in the Canadian economy would not be reduced, it is hardly surprising that little social legislation was introduced in the 1920s, a period when the trade union movement was in retreat after its victories of the war period. Industry was hostile to social legislation at that time and there seemed to be no pressing need to act. While a shift in business thinking occurred in the 1930s as a result of the militancy of workers and the unemployed, such a shift was, as observed, less pronounced among Liberal businessmen than among traditionally Tory sectors of business. King could still not afford to go too far without committing political suicide. By 1944, however, he could argue that class conflict had reached such a point that social legislation was the only alternative to socialism. While some members of the ruling class remained unconvinced, and even actively opposed such legislation, the class as a whole was won over.

Jack Granatstein, in an excellent account of the wartime debate within government on the question of social security legislation, argues correctly that at the root of the social reform programs of 1944 and 1945 – family allowances, mortgage-lending programs, spending programs for reconversion of the wartime economy to a peacetime economy – 'was the fear of postwar unemployment, depression and possible disorder.' He notes that these programs were balanced by various programs of assistance to industry as part of 'an attractive – and expensive – package' to pacify the business community.[57] The 'package' approach to various state programs meant to produce stability of class relations was not new. The Bennett New Deal, the Purvis report, the Montreal Board of Trade report to the Rowell-Sirois Commission, the Conservative Port Hope platform, all similarly integrated programs such as housing construction, social insurance, marketing boards, bonuses to business, etc., in an attempt to devise a system that would use the state to smooth out certain contradictions within capitalism and thereby calm the restiveness of the working people. Interestingly, while the *Report on Social Security for Canada*, prepared by Professor Leonard Marsh for the Committee on Reconstruction set up by the cabinet, received a great deal of government attention, the actual legislation fell far short of its recommendations, particularly in the ignoring of the recommendation for health insurance.[58] Clearly, 'welfare state' measures in Canada were not to be introduced all at once.

III

The government *White Paper on Employment and Income* of 12 April 1945 was a further attempt to make clear that the state was to play a large role in stabilizing the economy in order to legitimize the private-enterprise system. So as to maintain a 'high and stable level of employment and income,' the government would seek to keep its revenues and expenditures in balance not one year at a time but over longer – though unspecified – periods. This would allow the government to budget for surpluses when the economy was in a buoyant stage of the business cycle. When the cycle turned downward and unemployment threatened, the government would 'incur defecits and increases in the national debt resulting from its employment and income policy, whether that policy in the circumstances is best applied through increased expenditures or reduced taxation.'

While such crypto-Keynesianism was not a common demand of the business community, Granatstein exaggerates in commenting that 'before the war, budget deficits had been akin to sin; in 1945 they were simply an economic tool.'[59] It would be fairer to say that before the war proponents of greater government expenditure largely evaded the question of where the money for increased spending would be found. The Montreal Board of Trade, quoted above, seemed to regard financing by debt or taxation as equally acceptable measures, providing in both cases that the levels discussed were within reason.

The 'welfare state' from the beginning was regarded as a contradictory blessing by the governments and businessmen who felt obliged to support it. Michal Kalecki, arguing in 1943 that businessmen still largely opposed government measures for stimulating employment and particularly measures which would subsidize consumption, believed that even if mass pressure converted them to the opposite view they would soon be in the opposition camp once again. The 'maintenance of full employment,' he argued, would remove from the bosses the threat of unemployment as a disciplinary measure. Working-class militancy would be increased and demands for wage increases and better working conditions would result in large numbers of strikes. This proved to be the case in the war years. And, as Kalecki noted, even the fact of increasing profits does not compensate capitalists for what appears to be a threat to their control over their factories. In this context, the attack against social insurance and government spending by the business community in recent years is a call for a return to the 'individualism' of a former day when a job or relief from the state was a privilege and not perceived as a right.[60]

How far, then, will the capitalist class go to undo the measures that they were willing to concede in an earlier day in order to pacify working-class militancy and stabilize the economic system? No easy answer can be given to this question. What has been suggested is that the radicalism of the depression years and the fears that such radicalism engendered brought the first abortive attempt in 1935 to introduce state policies for stabilization. The even greater working-class militancy of the war years forced even the cautious members of the ruling class to give way at the war's end. It can be assumed that the curbing of working class militancy remains an aim of Canadian businessmen and, to some degree, the welfare state that was meant to pacify workers now appears, as Kalecki argued, to encourage their militancy. On the other hand, from the beginning, capitalists who supported 'welfare state' measures recognized the compensatory stimulus to consumption that these spending programs provided and their role in smoothing out the business cycle. It may be true, nevertheless, that the capitalist class as a whole would be willing to endure a steeper business cycle *if* this is the price of forcing the working class to be more insecure and less demanding. In this context, the extent to which workers resist cuts in state spending will play a crucial role, just as, at the present time, the future of wage controls appears dim because of the non-support of the working class.

The capitalist state's continued willingness and ability to maintain a high level of social expenditures is affected by still another factor – although more than a cursory discussion of this is beyond the scope of this essay – and that is the growth of the economy. From the beginning, ruling-class supporters of the welfare state believed that continuous economic growth was inevitable and that with the growth of the economic pie an analogous growth in social benefits could be allowed. Questions of what was produced and the question of relative distribution of wealth could be ignored as long as overall wealth increased and the share of income of various classes increased proportionately owing to state measures that put a floor on the income of the working class. But economic growth has slowed down, and state spending, involving spheres of activity that have little tendency to show increasing rates of productivity, has tended to increase at rates faster than the rates of economic growth.[61] It is clear that capitalists cannot continue to expect to get away with an availability of cheap resources, a continued neglect of environmental factors and the safety of workers, and the continued availability of an exploitable Third World from which superprofits can be extracted.

In these conditions, bourgeois politicians find themselves in the unpalatable role of having not only to justify temporary cutbacks in minimal social service programs, but more generally to 'resocialize' a populace weaned on the ideology of permanent capitalist affluence. As Pierre Trudeau himself recently put it: ' ... a large part of my message as a politician is to say: we have to put an end to rising expectations. We have to explain to people that we may even have to put an end to our love for our parents or old people in society, even our desire to give more for education and medical research.'[62]

Of course the capitalist state, acting on behalf of the interests of the capitalist class as a whole, can afford to ignore reactionary demands from particular individuals or even particular sectors of the ruling class. Trudeau's recently acquired illiberalism with respect to social legislation reflects the growing sense of crisis amongst the capitalist class as a whole. It is not that Trudeau opposes in principle social legislation or even that he is a direct representative of the big bourgeoisie. Rather it is simply that, like Mackenzie King, Trudeau takes existing class relations as a given and determines policies within limits set by these class relations. In part, these limits can be understood in terms of the class origins of these politicians and the class composition of the bourgeois parties. But there are other, more directly economic, limits that the politicians dedicated to the existing class relations must labour under. These are perhaps best outlined in a speech by Liberal finance minister, Charles Dunning, in 1938: 'We must follow policies which will enable it [private enterprise] to work in accordance with its essential principles. The most important of these principles is that decisions as to whether the individual shall spend and consume or shall save and invest or shall save and hoard are left to the individual's own initiative. If therefore the answers to the questions as to whether plants are to be built or extended, new houses are to be created and industry is going to expand or to stagnate, depend upon the decisions of tens of thousands of individuals who are free agents and not regimented sheep, it follows that governments must pursue policies which create confidence rather than fear and uncertainty, which give leadership and guidance and encouragement rather than stifle initiative and paralyze new enterprise.'[63]

In short, then, the 'welfare state' changes nothing that is fundamental about capitalism. While it places a floor on workers' incomes, it leaves unaltered the control of means of production. Production for profit and not for use and the reduction of labour to an extension of the machines it operates for the benefit of capital remain the goals of the economic system. Indeed, the oscillations in support for state social spending among the ruling class result from disagreements in particular circumstances as to how useful that expenditure is towards these goals. It is clear that the working class must defend every 'welfare state' gain that it has won. On the other hand, there can be little doubt that government social programs do serve the function of legitimizing the system by making it appear that the worst aspects of laissez-faire have been compensated. At the present time, though, the ruling-class pendulum seems to have swung away from these programs and back towards the idea of a large dose of unemployment as a means of teaching the working class respect for its betters. It is dangerous to hazard a guess as to how serious the current *economic* crisis of capitalism really is – it has recovered from crises before – but there can be little doubt that the *legitimization* crisis of capitalism will increase as it attempts to force workers to accept both lower wages and fewer state benefits. But one should be careful not to assume the stupidity of one's enemy: the class struggle has forced the ruling class to concede various reforms in the past and, in the Canadian case, part of the ruling class was willing to make these concessions before it was absolutely necessary. It would be wrong to assume blithely that, given a strong working-class reaction against government cut-backs, the capitalist class will not relent again. While cut-backs must be opposed, such opposition must be placed within the context of an attack on the capitalist system as a whole or, like wage struggles, it may prove episodic and leave unchanged the relative force of bourgeois ideology in the working class.

NOTES

1 Research Committee of the League for Social Reconstruction, *Social Planning for Canada* (1935, Toronto 1975), xix
2 Hugh G.J. Aitken, for example, says that the theory that the state acted merely as an agent for private economic interests in the nation-building period 'could probably be supported' and that the distinction between 'the state' and 'private enterprise' in Canada 'often seems artificial.' 'Defensive Expansionism: The State and Economic Growth in Canada,' in Aitken, ed., *The State and Economic Growth* (New York 1959), 79-114. From a more radical perspective, H. Viv Nelles details the virtually complete power that resource companies had in dictating provincial 'regulatory' policies dealing with the resource industries. *The Politics of Development: Forests, Mines & Hydro-Electric Power in Ontario, 1849-1941* (Toronto 1974)
3 *Canada Year Book* (1972), 1218-19
4 Allan M. Maslove, *The Pattern of Taxation in Canada* (Ottawa 1972), 64
5 *Income Distribution by Size in Canada, Selected Years: Distribution of Family Incomes in Canada* (Ottawa 1972), reported the following after-tax comparisons for quintiles of the population for 1951 and 1972:

	1951	1972
Top 20%	41.1%	39.1%
2nd 20	22.4	23.7
3rd 20	17.4	18.3
4th 20	12.9	12.9
5th 20	6.1	5.9

6 See R.B. Splane, *Social Welfare in Ontario, 1791-1893: A Study of Public Welfare Administration* (Toronto 1965); Dennis Trevor Guest, 'The Development of Income Maintenance Programmes in Canada, 1945-1967,' unpublished PH D dissertation, University of London, 1968; Elisabeth Wallace, 'The Origin of the Social Welfare State in Canada, 1867-1900,' *Canadian Journal of Economics and Political Science*, XVI, 4 (Aug. 1950), 383-93. On Montreal, see Terry Copp, *The Anatomy of Poverty: The Condition of the Working Class in Montreal, 1897-1929* (Toronto 1974). On the education question, see Greg Kealey, ed., *Canada Investigates Industrialism: The Royal Commission on the Relations of Labor and Capital, 1889* (Toronto 1973), xix, 15-16, 22, 39-40.

7 James Weinstein, *The Corporate Ideal in the Liberal State, 1900-1918* (Boston 1969); Michael Bliss, *A Living Profit* (Toronto 1974), 142; Michael Piva, 'Workmen's Compensation Movement in Ontario,' *Ontario History* (March 1975), 39-56

8 Public Archives of Ontario, *Report of the Ontario Commission on Unemployment* (1916), 82-3

9 Kenneth McNaught, *A Prophet in Politics: A Biography of J.S. Woodsworth* (Toronto 1959), 218-20

10 A complete list of Bennett holdings is found in Public Archives of Canada (PAC), R.B. Bennett Papers, v. 901, pp. 563867-3900; Bennett's partnership with Beaverbrook is discussed in A.J.P. Taylor, *Beaverbrook* (London 1972), 15, 34, 36-7, 86; Bennett's involvement with Eddy is detailed in Bennett Papers, v. 915, 916, and 917; the labelling of Canada Packers and Imperial Tobacco as oligopolies appears in *Report of the Royal Commission on Price Spreads and Mass Buying* (Ottawa 1935), 53, 59.

11 For example, C.H. Cahan, Bennett's only secretary of state, was a leading Montreal corporation attorney and industrialist and, like Bennett, a past Beaverbrook protégé. Cahan had been, on behalf of the Bank of Montreal, legal adviser and executive head of a vast array of tramway, electric light, and hydroelectric enterprises in South America, Trinidad, and Mexico. National revenue minister E.B. Ryckman was past president of Dunlop Tire and director of Gurney Foundry, IBM, Addressograph Company, Russell Motor Company, and others. When illness forced his retirement, he was replaced by millionaire investment banker, R.C. Matthews, later a president of the Canadian Chamber of

Commerce. Finance minister E.N. Rhodes was past president of the British
America Nickel Corporation, later purchased by International Nickel. See
Canadian Parliamentary Guide (1930-5). Links between politicians as well as
leading civil servants and the corporations are traced in Libby C. and Frank W.
Park, *Anatomy of Big Business* (Toronto 1962); John Porter, *The Vertical Mosaic*
(Toronto 1965); Wallace Clement, *The Canadian Corporate Elite* (Toronto
1975).

12 See Ronald Liversedge, *Recollections of the On-to-Ottawa Trek*, ed. Victor Hoar
(Toronto 1973).

13 *Labour Legislation: A Study Prepared for the Royal Commission on Dominion-
Provincial Relations* (Ottawa 1939), 5-6

14 *Report of the Annual Meeting of the Bank of Montreal* (3 Dec. 1934)

15 Gordon to Bennett, 6 Jan. 1934, Bennett Papers, v. 811, p. 503059 (emphasis
added)

16 *Monthly Review of the Bank of Nova Scotia* (Aug. 1934), 4

17 See Oscar Ryan, *Tim Buck: A Conscience for Canada* (Toronto 1975), 128-9;
A.B. McKillop, 'The Communist as Conscience: Jacob Penner and Winnipeg
Civic Politics, 1934-1935,' A.R. McCormack and Ian Macpherson, *Cities in the
West* (Ottawa 1974),181-209; Liversedge, *Recollections*, 15-34; 'Some General
Observations on the Administration of Unemployment Relief in Western Cana-
da: Report for the Prime Minister's Office, 1932,' Michiel Horn, ed., *The Dirty
Thirties* (Toronto 1972), 272-6.

18 *Financial Times*, 21 Sept. 1934; Dorothy Kidd, 'Women's Organization: Learning from Yesterday,' in *Women at Work: Ontario, 1850-1930* (Toronto 1974),
351-7

19 (June 1935), 302

20 *Winnipeg Free Press*, 10 and 19 Sept. 1935. There were, of course, businessmen
who opposed unemployment insurance and indeed businessmen who opposed
all of the Bennett reforms. Business opponents of unemployment insurance argued that it would add to the cost of doing business and hurt Canada's export
position. It would encourage sloth and remove the insecurity of employees
which allowed employers to impose labour discipline. Further, it would hit all
industries equally regardless of the incidence of unemployment in a given industry. Prominent opponents of unemployment insurance included CPR president Edward Beatty, Canadian Bank of Commerce vice-president Sir Thomas
White, and the Montreal *Gazette*, among others.

21 Bennett to Howard Robinson, 11 June 1935, Bennett Papers, v. 715

22 The philosophy and programs of the 'New Deal' were introduced in a series of
radio speeches, which are reprinted in large part in Ernest Watkins, *R.B. Bennett: A Biography* (Toronto 1963), 253-63.

23 J.R.H. Wilbur, *The Bennett Administration, 1930-1935* , CHA Booklet no. 24 (Ottawa 1969), 14
24 The party's poor financial position in the period before the New Deal is discussed in J.R.H.Wilbur, 'H.H. Stevens and the Reconstruction Party,' *Canadian Historical Review*, XLV, 1 (March 1964), 6.
25 Bennett Papers, v. 713, 714, 715, 718, 949
26 On Flavelle, see Michael Bliss, 'A Canadian Businessman and War: The Case of Joseph Flavelle,' in J.L. Granatstein and Robert Cuff, eds., *War and Society in North America* (Toronto 1971), 20-36; on Beatty, see D.H. Miller-Barstow, *Beatty of the CPR* (Toronto 1950).
27 The *Gazette*'s defection must be balanced against the continued support in Montreal of the *Montreal Star*, presided over by financier Lord Atholstan and St Lawrence Sugar president J.W. McConnell. The Toronto *Evening Telegram* and the *Mail and Empire* gave enthusiastic support. Most importantly, F.N. Southam told Senator C.J. Ballantyne that he had directed his usually Liberal chain of newspapers to give positive support to Bennett and the New Deal. See Bennett Papers, v. 715 and 949. A detailed discussion of reaction to the New Deal is found in Alvin Finkel, 'Canadian Business and the "Reform" Process in Canada in the 1930's,' unpublished PH D thesis, University of Toronto, 1976, pp. 125-8; and in Wilbur, *The Bennett Administration*, 20.
28 *Can. H. of C. Debates*, 28 April 1931, p. 1077; 29 April 1931, p. 1104
29 *Ibid.*, 6 May 1930, p. 1831
30 See Leo Johnson, *Poverty in Wealth* (Toronto 1974), 24-6.
31 *Financial Post*, 1 June 1935
32 Mitch Hepburn, the premier of Ontario, for example, was seen by King as 'in the hands of McCullagh of the *Globe* and the *Globe* and McCullagh in the hands of financial mining interests.' PAC, King Diary, 13 April 1937. In general, King, in his diaries, regarded many Canadian politicians, both Liberal and Conservative, as 'in the hands' of various business interest groups.
33 See Richard M.H. Alway, 'Hepburn, King, and the Rowell-Sirois Commission,' *Canadian Historical Review*, XLVIII, 2 (June 1967), 113-41.
34 King's desire to maintain the support of the mining companies is indicated, for example, by his opposition in 1934 to the Conservative government's 10 per cent tax on the windfall profits gained by gold-mining companies when the price of gold increased from $21 to $35. He wrote an opponent of the tax: 'The present Government has made many blunders, but I think this one with respect to the ten per cent tax on the production of gold is perhaps the worst of the lot, considering, as you say, that it formed the major feature of this year's budget ... I hope that some of those who have suffered as a result of the Government's policies will lend us a hand when the time comes to put the present Administration out of office.' King to James E. Day, barrister, 5 May 1934, PAC, King Papers, v. 199, pp. 170306-7

35 12 Nov. 1937, *ibid.*, v. 238, p. 204650

36 Royal Commission on Dominion-Provincial Relations, *Report of Hearings*, 31 May, p. 9691 (merchants); 19 Jan., p. 2739 (real estate); 17 Jan. 1938, p. 2375 (CMA)

37 The Canadian sections of CIO unions were, until 1939, still in the TLC. But they were clearly a minority within the organization and indeed only began to rival the crafts unions in their membership during the war period after their ouster from the TLC and the formation of their own federation, the Canadian Congress of Labour. See Irving M. Abella, *Nationalism, Communism, and Canadian Labour* (Toronto 1973).

38 King Diary, 4 April 1938. After calling the report an 'academic treatise,' King said: 'It was a mistake having Purvis as chairman, he being a big businessman and a Tory at heart, not understanding methods of politics ... '

39 Royal Commission on Dominion-Provincial Relations, *Report of Hearings*, pp. 524-5 (Chamber of Commerce); p. 8153 (Board of Trade)

40 See Finkel, 'Canadian Business,' 352-89.

41 Estimated trade union membership in Canada, according to the Dominion Department of Labour annual reports, was 310,534 in 1931 and 315,073 in 1939. Grauer, *Labour Legislation*, 68. There were 711,117 trade unionists in 1945. Canada, Department of Labour, *Labour Organizations in Canada* (1963)

42 'Orders-in-council were passed freezing wage levels, facilitating the use of troops in labour disputes, and limiting the right to strike. The government also refused to force employers to negotiate with their workers and continued to appoint men whom the Congress [of Canadian Labour] considered 'anti-labour' to government boards.' See Abella, *Nationalism, Communism*, 72; see also Stuart Jamieson, *Times of Trouble: Labour Unrest and Industrial Conflict in Canada, 1900-66* (Ottawa 1968).

43 See Jack Granatstein, *Canada's War: The Politics of the Mackenzie King Government, 1939-1945* (Toronto 1975), 264-5.

44 Jack Granatstein, *The Politics of Survival: The Conservative Party of Canada, 1939-1945* (Toronto 1967), 110

45 Roger Graham, *Arthur Meighen: No Surrender* (Toronto 1965), III, 67, 117

46 Queen's University Archives, Macdonnell Papers, v. 52, 'Remarks on the History of Inflation: An Address Given to the Liberal-Conservative Summer School at Newmarket, September, 1933.' and 'The Canadian Institute on Economics and Politics: Reports of Two of the Addresses.' The Port Hope conference is discussed in Granatstein, *Politics of Survival*, 125-50 and 207-10, and John R. Williams, *The Conservative Party of Canada, 1920-1949* (Durham, NC 1956), 72.

47 *Can. H. of C. Debates*, 18 Feb. 1935, pp. 949-52

48 Williams, *Conservative Party*, 70. Bracken, like Macdonnell, was no recent convert to the Port Hope philosophies. In a statement to Canadian Press in 1933 he had praised the Roosevelt New Deal and concluded that 'controlled inflation combined with new public works by the federal government would seem to be inevitable if the problems of the unemployed and the debtors in all classes are to be met in a constructive way.' *Winnipeg Free Press*, 10 Aug. 1933

49 Granatstein, *Politics of Survival*, 213

50 Canada, *Report of the Royal Commission on Dominion-Provincial Relations*, Book Two: *Recommendations* (Ottawa 1940), 151, 157, 270-4; J.W. Pickersgill, ed., *The Mackenzie King Record* (Toronto 1960), I, 60-1

51 The Canadian Construction Association, in particular, took credit for the legislation. *Monetary Times*, 11 Jan. 1936. The position of the mortgage companies was outlined by T. Darcy Leonard, solicitor of the Dominion Mortgages and Investments Association, in *Journal of the Canadian Bankers' Association* (April 1936), 297-303. See also *Canadian Lumberman*, 1 July 1934; and *Can. H. of C. Debates*, 25 June 1935, p. 3948.

52 See PAC, Department of Finance Papers, 1942, v. 704-6.

53 Granatstein, *Canada's War*, 264-5

54 (1918, Toronto 1973), 336

55 An especially trenchant evaluation of King's labour policies is provided by Jamieson in *Times of Trouble*, 128-32, 276-94. Jamieson's conclusions are substantially the same as those of the stridently anti-King study, H.S. Ferns and B. Ostry, *The Age of Mackenzie King: The Rise of the Leader* (1955, Toronto 1976).

56 *Can. H. of C. Debates*, 28 July 1944, p. 5535

57 *Canada's War*, 276, 278

58 (Ottawa 1943, Toronto 1975)

59 *Canada's War*, 277, 278

60 'Political Aspects of Full Employment,' reprinted in E.K. Hunt and Jesse Schwartz, *A Critique of Economic Theory* (Middlesex 1972), 426-9. I would disagree with Kalecki that, by 1943, the pressure of the masses had yet to make itself felt in the viewpoints adopted by big business, at least in Canada.

61 The contradictions that confront the 'welfare state' are discussed in James O'Connor, *The Fiscal Crisis of the State* (New York 1973); and Rick Deaton, 'The Fiscal Crisis of the State in Canada,' in Dimitrios Roussopoulos, ed., *The Political Economy of the State* (Montreal 1973), 18-56.

62 *Maclean's*, 10 Jan. 1977, p. 8

63 Quoted in *Canadian Business* (July 1938), 12

PART V
THE STATE IN ACTION: IDEOLOGY AND SOCIAL CONTROL

13

Capitalism, class, and educational reform in Canada

STEPHEN SCHECTER

Writing to urge Draper not to give up the assessment clause, 'above all others ... the poor man's clause, and at the very foundation of a system of public education,' Ryerson complained of objections 'by precisely the class of persons – or rather by the individuals that I expected. I have heard one rich *man* objecting to it – a Methodist – a magistrate – a man who educated his own children at College and in Ladies' Seminaries – but who looks not beyond his own family. He says, I am told, "he does not wish to educate *all the brats* in the neighbourhood." Now to educate "all the brats" in every neighbourhood is the very object of this clause of the bill; and in order to do so, it is proposed to *compel* selfish rich men to do what they ought to do, but what they will not do voluntarily.'

So wrote Egerton Ryerson, chief superintendent of education for Upper Canada (Canada West), to the leader of the legislative assembly in 1846, justifying the introduction of a compulsory assessment on all property to finance a system of public education.[1] For Ryerson and his colleagues the establishment of such a system was the means by which the state would save the bourgeoisie from itself. Its purpose was the social control of a potentially dangerous Irish Catholic labouring class, for whom 'poverty and ethnicity coalesced in a way that heightened the potential for social conflict and animosity.'[2] The heavy influx of famine Irish in 1847 which, as in an earlier period, provided the unskilled labour force for the construction of canals and railroads, led Ryerson to warn Upper Canadians that 'the physical disease and death which have accompanied their influx among us may be the precursor of the worse pestilence of social insubordination and disorder.'[3]

To the Canadian bourgeoisie, however, it was far from clear that the state ought to be educating all the brats in the neighbourhood. Instead, the

Canadian upper class used the state's money to finance investment in the railways on which their profits and power were built. The overinvestment in railways brought on successive financial crises which only reduced further their willingness to direct scarce funds to projects like a public school system. In 1841 the Act of Union had been needed to bail the Canadian financial bourgeoisie out of bankruptcy, and by 1859 overinvestment in railroads had cost the public 'over 4 million pounds, accounting for nearly one half of the total debt of the province.' The dominance of this commercial bourgeoisie reflected and reinforced the mercantile-agrarian base of the economy, which meant that 'the factory system was virtually absent.'[4] Under such conditions it is not surprising that the Canadian bourgeoisie had trouble understanding the need for an educational system which, Ryerson assured the manufacturing employers, would instil in the working class precisely those habits of 'discipline, punctuality and good conduct' that industrial capitalism required.[5] The bourgeoisie's perception that a common school system was not necessarily a worthwhile investment seemed accurate in that school attendance did not markedly increase in the decade following the establishment of common schools; and this was especially so for the working-class children the schools were designed to socialize, though the process was uneven in different cities. To a large extent this was the result not only of poor facilities and transportation but also of the transience of urban life that was the hallmark of Irish Catholic labourers in a society still more commercial than industrial.[6]

The situation was replete with historical irony. The colonial dependence of the Canadian economy, and the dominant financial bourgeoisie that it generated, meant that the upper class was quite willing to use the state to further its own interests but that its perception of these interests was limited to the accumulation of capital within the confines of that mercantile-agrarian economy. Because that economy did not generate a strong industrial impulse and therefore a strong working class, the upper class could not see the value of using the state for legitimation purposes. The professional clerisy of mid-nineteenth-century British North America could see the value, however, precisely because capitalism was already an international system, and most certainly on an ideological level. If industrial capitalism was not yet a strong force in Canada, it was elsewhere; and elsewhere it was realized that education could be an effective means to subordinate the working class.

These lessons were not lost on Canadian educational reformers who were in close contact with each other, and with educators in Europe and the United States.[7] What the reformers saw in these countries was the future, a future they espoused for their own, less industrialized, society, but a future that was none the less worrisome because it was marked not only by progress but also by the inevitable contradictions of capitalism: class conflict and social misery. What they learned was that in British North America 'education could replace much of the coercion of English labour to strict factory rules and internalized self-discipline' by helping 'to break pre-industrial work habits, to "Canadianize" the immigrant worker, removing him from his traditional origins and practices.'[8] As Alexander Forrester, superintendent of education for Nova Scotia in the late 1850s, concluded, it was 'far more the duty and interest of the State, as such, to countenance and make provision for a national system of education than it is to support a police or constabulary establishment.'[9]

In suggesting that a common school system precede industrialization, Ryerson and his colleagues were acting as the avant-garde of the Canadian bourgeoisie. It therefore took considerable time, much debate, and several reversals before the bourgeoisie would implement their reforms. In the years between 1836 and 1851 in Upper Canada several attempts at school reform were made and blocked by both Tory and Reform administrations.[10] However much the questions of property tax and local control surfaced in the long debate, the key to early school reform lay in persuading the bourgeoisie as a class that investment in schools was as worthwhile as investment in railroads. It is true that Toronto city councillors voted to close the schools in 1848 rather than comply with the 1847 Free School Act and levy taxes, but by the time the dust had settled Ryerson had compromised by allowing municipalities the option of property assessment or rate-bills and providing for the election of trustees; and the Toronto City Council responded by voluntarily imposing property assessment in 1852 to cover the expansion of the public school system. Essential to the resolution of this conflict was the fact that the Toronto Reform element of the Canadian upper class had finally got the message, as the *Globe*'s statement of 11 December 1851 would seem to indicate: 'Educate the people and your gaols will be abandoned and your police may be disbanded.'[11]

To get that message across was a considerable uphill battle, as a committee of the Nova Scotia legislature pointed out in 1838: 'a people whose whole revenues are raised by duties on imports, must have their feelings deeply interested, and be firmly convinced of the necessity of direct taxation ... or else they will resist and defeat a measure, however wisely and accurately framed.'[12] What followed was a long and concerted campaign by the educational reformers, who formed part of the political elite of British North America, as either ideologues or politicians or both. Those who were members of assemblies used their positions to lobby for educational reform. Committees were set up and the reports issued became important instruments of propaganda. Journals, newspapers, the publication of pamphlets and letters, and the conduct of speaking tours were all ways in which the ideology of school reform was propagated and converts won.[13]

The reformers were also aided by the social transformations in British North America which made their warnings pertinent. In New Brunswick immigration increased between 1814 and 1849 with the growth of the timber trade. Irish immigrants formed 70 per cent of the total influx and 15 per cent of the population by 1851.[14] In the same year in Hamilton, the labourers building the Great Western Railway at Dundas went out on strike. The city's elite which called out the troops to protect their overinvested funds 'promoted education as well as railroads ... and supplied the leadership in the modernization of the schools which took place in the 1850s.'[15] Yet in the course of their campaign the educational reformers did not limit their addresses to the upper class and its political representatives, but took pains to spread the gospel among the literate and voting classes who formed the political community of British North America and the social support of that system upon which the power of the Canadian upper class rested.

In addressing themselves to the petite bourgeoisie, however, they added new elements to their ideology, based on the fear and hope which characterized the reformers' own attitudes to the coming industrial capitalism. The basis of their appeal to the petite bourgeoisie shifted from social control of the working class to upward mobility and the training of a law-abiding citizenry. Forrester's address to the people of Nova Scotia around 1860 best exemplified the way in which they skilfully wove these themes together: 'The veriest tyro in political economy knows that the real advancement of any country, depends on the intelligence, the skill, the industrial and moral habits of its inhabitants ... Or, to speak without a figure, pauperism, and vice, and crime will, to the extent to which these qualities are diffused, be comparatively unknown ... And the result of all this ... will be the increased and the ever increasing value of property. It signifies little as to the nature of that property ... for all will be benefited, – the labourer, the tradesman, the farmer, the manufacturer, the rich and the poor, the learned and the unlearned. And what is the instrumentality or agency by which a population possessed of these qualities shall be reared and perpetuated and extended? It is education, and education alone ... such ... as will consist not merely in the imparting of knowledge, but in the training up of the young in the way they should go.'[16]

In developing this ideology the educational reformers clearly knew their audience, for the precarious nature of the Canadian economy, together with its slow transformation to industrial capitalism, was undermining the position of the petite bourgeoisie. This petite bourgeoisie consisted of subordinate elements of the entrepreneurial class and certain segments of the propertied artisan class. In Hamilton, for example, many members of the entrepreneurial class were not in the local elite; and many suffered considerable reversals of fortune, hooked in as they were to the Montreal and Toronto merchant houses and banks and dependent through them on English and Scottish banks and the vagaries of British capitalism. To many of them free schools could only have meant government taxation of badly needed capital, a need which, ironically enough, often derived from their attempts to cash in on the railroad boom, itself based precariously on the adventures of British and Canadian finance capital. At the same time these adventures led to considerable setbacks, which in many cases were accentuated by the transformation of Canadian society to a more industrial capitalist base. For artisans and craftsmen this latter change was registered in the decline in occupational inheritance in the decade 1851-61. These pressures led certain segments of the propertied artisan class and those 'merchants, higher master artisans and manufacturers who composed a stratum united by aspiration and anxiety' to look to the schools for upward social mobility. It was this same coalescence of forces that led Ryerson and his colleagues to link fear and hope in their proposals for school reform. In linking education to the absence of crime, vice, and pauperism, they fed the fears of many people for whom the advent of industrial society represented general upheaval and, in many cases, considerable personal upheaval: 'The fear of failure – if not for oneself, then for one's children – permeates nineteenth century writing, expressing itself most concretely in the reforming of schools, which assumed increasing importance as agencies of middle-class social advancement.[17]

In actual fact, however, school reform, then as now, had less to do with providing avenues of upward mobility and more to do with legitimating a changing class structure. The absence of a publicly financed common school system prior to the 1840s did not mean the absence of schooling. Literacy was quite widespread; and, though illiteracy was more prevalent among the poor, some illiterates were quite wealthy, reflecting the fact that literacy skills were far from indispensable to economic success. The importance of the social mobility theme in the early school reformers' campaign lay in its ideological force. In gaining converts to their proposals, the reformers developed a whole ideology of school reform the claims of which in reality could not be met. Education never has been essential to national prosperity or upward mobility in the sense that reformers have claimed, but the idea has been effective in legitimating social inequality and providing the ideological framework within which educational reform has been argued.[18]

What is so striking about Canadian early school reform is the frankness with which the reformers acknowledged that its basic purpose was the social control of an emerging working class. In practice this meant the establishment of a state-controlled system based on the principles of centralization and uniformity – standardized textbooks, the development of a Normal School, the establishment of an effective inspectorate. All these reforms interlocked. Uniform textbooks were necessary if the education people were to receive was to be 'in harmony with the views and feelings of the great body of the people, especially of the better educated classes.'[19] Uniform texts, however, were useless without a provincial board to provide them and ensure that only they were used. They were also useless without teachers trained in their proper use; but a Normal School required financing. In short, 'the only way in which a State, or National, System of Schools can be established and maintained in connection with local popular institutions, is, by the Executive authority making the General Regulations, and being able to secure their observance by means of the distribution, and a veto power in the application of the Legislature School Grant, or State Fund, in aid of Schools.'[20]

The practices which flowed from a state system of schools included graded schools, internal promotion and classification, a varied but uniform curriculum catering to different classes, age- and sex-segregated classrooms, the elaboration and enforcement of codes of discipline, and hierarchical authority relations which placed both children and parents subordinate to the teacher.[21] These practices covered the hidden as much as the overt curriculum of schooling, both of which were as indispensable then as they are now to the effective subordination of the working class. As with the establishment of uniform textbooks, these practices required both money to make them available and people to carry them out. In this respect state funding and a state bureaucracy were integral elements of the early school reform. One without the other was useless, and both had to be directed to a common purpose of social control. In Ontario, for example, in the 1850s, judicious use was made of provincial grants for education 'to stimulate local governments to adopt certain policies or practices – the first a greater concern for attendance (it was not yet compulsory) and the second the employment of more highly qualified teachers.'[22] In Toronto increased funds led to the construction of six new and bigger schools which 'enabled the principles of centralization and classification to come at once into practical effect.'[23] Within the school system more and more teachers and superintendents came to understand that *'patient silence and respectful attention are perhaps the most valuable lessons which a child can learn in school.'*[24]

The history of early school reform in Canada raises a number of interesting points. It has been suggested that educational reform comes about in stages as the result of the contradiction between the changes in the wage labour system (brought about by a continuously developing capitalist economy) and the conservatism of an education system (reproducing an earlier period's social relations of production).[25] Analysis of the Canadian experience would indicate that changes in the education system may also presage changes in the economy, and that over a long period there is a more ongoing dialectic between educational reform and the transformations of capitalism. Precisely because school reform preceded industrialization in Canada, the educational reformers were so central and the reforms themselves so prescient. Yet that reform would have been impossible had capitalism not already been an international system. The practice and ideology of that reform movement was as much a response to the social transformations of capitalism elsewhere as it was to the social reality of British North America. Ironically, the hinterland status of Canada economically was not reproduced ideologically; and, to the extent that educational reform helped save the bourgeoisie from itself, it could be said that the Canadian bourgeoisie was saved not only in spite of but also because of the uneven development of capitalism.

Early school reform in Canada was not, however, suspended in an ideological ether, but underpinned by a changing social reality, even though the nature of the Canadian economy and its class structure made the transition to industrial capitalism slower than elsewhere. It was to the containment of the social contradictions raised by that transition that the early school reformers addressed themselves. The social control functions of schooling were twofold. On a specific level the reforms were designed to discipline the nascent labour force for industrial capitalism. On a general level they were designed to legitimate that social order in such a way that the upheaval it brought could be dealt with without questioning the social order itself. That upheaval did not affect only labourers. It meant downward mobility for part of the petite bourgeoisie and fear of downward mobility for others; while for all those classes with a stake in property it bred the 'fear of a motley of Americanism, civil disorder, ignorance and the lower classes generally.'[26] This general disorder was not only a threat to property; it was also a threat to the sense people made of their lives.[27] People's embrace of the emerging capitalist society was highly ambiguous. Even the dominant classes experienced considerable unease over a social structure that offered at once such wealth, such misery, and such conflict. Yet capital takes care of its own, and in this case threw up, in the ideology of school reform, the ideological counterpart to its own material contradictions.

On one level the reformers' ambiguity reflected the ambiguity of those very classes whose interests they were trying to defend. On another level the reformers were more perspicacious, in that they saw that systemized schooling could be an effective antidote to the disagreeable aspects of social life that seemed to be the price of capitalist progress. They played on that generalized fear in order to win support. Yet on a third level the reformers practised self-deception, first in thinking that capitalist progress was possible without the attendant dislocation and exploitation; second, in claiming that education would make this prospect possible. In that sense they were both the avant-garde of the bourgeoisie and the prisoners of a class structure which insisted that the solution to the bourgeoisie's problems be found within the limits of that class structure. That is why the response they came up with was both true and false. Schools after the reform did not promote social mobility, though they did reflect the changing class structure of the wider society. In the Central School in Hamilton, for example, there were proportionately more upper-class students in 1861 than in 1853, and upper-class students dominated the upper levels of the school. The sex-age distribution only underlined the class use of schools, for it was the sons of professionals and proprietors who continued on at school, while it was the daughters of artisans who did so.[28] Yet schooling as the means of social mobility has remained an effective legitimizing myth to this very day. Its force has derived not only from the class use of schools, which has also continued to this day, but also from the power the dominant classes hold to make their version of reality the accepted one.

The system which arose from the early school reform was therefore essential to making its proponents' ideological claims socially self-evident. It was essential because it generated its own logic, a logic that seemed to derive from the nature of the system itself and that operated under the guise of a neutral ideology, even if its basic thrust was the subordination of the Canadian working class and its basic impulse the harmonizing of the contradictions of the burgeoning capitalist economy. The compromise allowing for the election of trustees, for example, in no way imperilled the efficiency of Ryerson's reform. On the contrary, Toronto's new trustees were heavily biased in favour of the upper class. The fact of their election shielded the system even further from the revelation of its class bias, though behind the criterion of economy in the location of the new schools the trustees voted to construct lay the aim of bringing working-class children into the schools. In fact, the early school reforms led to no appreciable improvement in the patterns of school attendance among children of the labouring classes, which suggests that the new system's most important initial accomplishment was, as in Hamilton, that it 'effectively destroyed the city's educational alternatives.'[29] This monopoly position was important if a system was to be established that would effectively carry out the functions of social control. Hence Ryerson's original hostility to separate schools, and his acquiescence to the fact when he realized that the Catholic clergy was just as intent on inculcating the proper degree of subordination in its pupils. Hence the need to understand the expansion of school facilities in Toronto, in spite of the poor attendance figures, in terms of its long-term rationale, so that by the time 'the labouring classes were finally able to afford, in every sense of that term, to send their children to school ... [they] had no choice but to accept an educational environment that they had not created and over which they exerted little, if any, control.'[30]

The early school reform was instrumental in creating that environment, for it established an educational bureaucracy with an educational ideology and a set of organizing principles and practices which would see to it that future responses would develop within the context of what had already been laid out. As Ryerson understood only too well, herein lay the importance of centralized control of the teaching profession. He was well rewarded when the Toronto superintendent of schools, G.A. Barber, made clear in his report of 1857 that the schools were not catching those children for whom they were designed. After explaining to the board of trustees that they had two options – a reintroduction of the rate-bill system or the introduction of compulsory schooling – Barber came down firmly in favour of the latter.[31] The debate over compulsory schooling is especially revealing of the system's importance and operation. Yet it also shows how future educational reforms emanated from not only the system's logic but also its contradictions, contradictions that are also those of the wider capitalist society. The history of schooling must therefore be seen as an ongoing dialectic between educational reform and the transformations of capitalism, of which the relative autonomy of the school system is an important part. Educational history is not easily divisible into discrete periods in which a conservative education system is wrenched into line, following the lead given by underlying economic transformations. As the Canadian experience shows, educational reform has its own dynamic which flows from the education system's own relative autonomy, even if 'l'autonomie relative du système d'enseignement est toujours la contrepartie d'une dépendance plus ou moins complètement cachée par la spécificité des pratiques et de l'idéologie qu'autorise cette autonomie.'[32] What the school reforms of the 1850s and 1860s in Canada did was to create the systems which allowed this relative autonomy to operate on a national level.

I I

Every boy is born a communist. He believes instinctively in the great brotherhood of man. He unhesitatingly subscribes to the doctrines of Fraternity, Equality and Liberty. It follows naturally that he firmly believes everything to be his which is not beyond his reach. It is only by good training that he arrives at the distinction between *meum* and *tuum* – that it is wrong to consider 'all things common.' (Principal Millar, Dartmouth High School, 1885)[33]

To the consternation of liberal educators, the early school reforms did not lead to the mass invasion of schools by the children of the labouring classes. The absence of working-class students was in part the result of the working and living conditions of the labouring classes. It was also, however, a form of working-class resistance to an attempt by upper-class trustees and school experts to impose upon them an institution whose main function was to legitimate their own oppression.

The working classes were not unaware of the class bias of this new school system. The education the labour press had in mind in the 1880s was 'a combination of work and study, four hours of each per day, certainly not the common school education of Ryerson.'[34] If workmen desired education because it was character-building, they gave the latter a definition quite different from Ryerson's. Education became a means to the respect which capitalism denied workers, though the hidden uses of education for class control produced the same tensions then as it does now, including a suspicion that education is not all that deserving of respect. This attitude runs through the working-class response to educational reforms imposed from above. In testimony to the 1913 Royal Commission on Industrial Training and Technical Education, the president of the Canadian Mine Workers, District no. 96, Mr McDougall, expressed much the same view: 'The mining schools have helped the men to higher positions because they cannot get them unless they study for them, and pass the examinations, although there are a lot of practical men today working in the mines that could teach some of those fellows that went to those schools some things they never knew.' At the same time he argued that education was important in so far as it provided effective training that would help to avoid accidents.[35]

Although this working-class response generally remained within the limits of the dominant value system, there were times when it went further: 'Education could lead to a rather different direction as the Palladium saw it: "Educate first, agitate afterwards. Ignorance, superstition and timerity are the weapons which our oppressors have used most effectively against us in the past. Secure an education at any cost, put the ballot to its proper use, and then the fall of the venerable structure of legal robbery, alias monopoly, will shake to its centre ..." '[36] By the time the question of technical education arose, certain sections of the working class had become considerably more class conscious. While James Simpson, a member of the Socialist Party of Canada and labour's representative on the Royal Commission on Technical Education, 'was preparing his report for presentation to the federal government, Local No. 24 put itself on record as opposed to technical education as a capitalist device to increase the efficiency of the capitalist system, and therefore postpone the final hour.'[37]

Even when working-class resistance to educational reform was not as radical as this, it still went on, forming part of a long tradition going back at least to the *guerre des éteignoirs*, the resistance to the 1846 act in Lower Canada by the habitant who 'saw, in the central power and in the organizations which it established, a thinly veiled device for raising taxes and keeping the people in line.'[38] The history of educational reform must be viewed as Bowles and Gintis see it, as the product of 'class conflict, not class domination.'[39] It is only because of class conflict that the relative autonomy of schools develops. For just as early school reform was a response to rising class conflict outside the schools, the reform itself generated class conflict inside; and the latter in turn generated another reform within the schools in the form of demands for compulsory schooling.

This kind of dialectic is crucial to understanding the history of school reform in Canada. Yet this dialectic operates at both a material and ideological level, and produces at each level contradictions which fuel further developments. Compulsory education, for example, legislated in Ontario in 1871, was not immediately effective in getting children to attend, as the 1889 Report of the Royal Commission on the Relations of Capital and Labour testified. Quebec did not pass a compulsory education law until 1943, yet it had the highest daily attendance rate of all the provinces. Quebec claimed that its success was due to legislation forbidding child labour, but testimony of royal commissions indicated that such laws were not strictly enforced. More fundamental changes in the economy resulting in new work patterns, family structure, and urban amenities better explain the increased use of schools by all classes.[40] Compulsory education did, however, increase the school's powers to act as an effective agent of social control, not only by adding one more weapon to its arsenal but also by doing it in such a way that the class bias of the system receded behind its own seemingly incontrovertible logic. Eventually everyone would understand that obligatory attendance at schools was only natural.[41] At the same time, working-class resistance to early school reform was turned against the working class itself. Proponents of compulsory education could thus delude themselves that what they were doing was really in the best interests of the working class; and the arguments invoked became new elements in the legitimizing myths of schools: 'If, then, from the poverty, the cupidity, or the apathy of parents, the education of their children be neglected, it is surely the duty of the State to interpose its authority in their behalf, by means of a compulsory law.'[42]

Reforms like compulsory education thereby made the school system relatively more autonomous; and without that relative autonomy the reforms' legitimating power would be severely limited. On the other hand, the reforms also emerged out of that relative autonomy, both materially and ideologically. Materially, 'The need for compulsory attendance was rendered imperative as grading and class teaching replaced the gradeless one-room schoolhouse.'[43] Ideologically, it was rendered imperative by the very fiction of the early school reformers' claims. The establishment of a public education system thus made it possible for the solution to its own contradictions to seem to flow from the structure of the system itself. The self-evident nature of these reforms was important not only for the effective subordination of the working class but also for the effective integration of the teachers, superintendants, and trustees who formed the educational bureaucracy upon which the reproduction of the school system depended. The growth of a school bureaucracy in the form of provincial teachers' associations, national educational associations, etc., made possible by the early school reforms, provided the network whereby the ideology of school reform became institutionalized. The debates on compulsory education and reform schools were both carried on extensively within provincial teachers' associations, with the teachers themselves supplying the rationales.[44]

The importance of the educational bureaucracy derived also from the very nature of its position, which forced it to face what capitalism threw up in the area of reproduction. The debate over compulsory education revealed how that reform was also an ideological counterpart to the social contradictions of the emerging capitalism outside the workplace. It was as though the presence of street urchins became a metaphor for the seamy side of capitalist society, reminding the dominant and respectable classes 'that the social condition of the body corporate of which they form a part, cannot be of the highest order.'[45] Vagrancy and idleness became fused with crime in the literate and popular imaginations; and the response of progressive schoolmen, where compulsory education failed, was the establishment of reform schools. The same Principal Millar who understood that 'every boy is born a communist' understood too that the compulsory school law, though good, 'does not quite go far enough ... What we require is a place – not a jail – where our incorrigibles will be taught the subjects of a common school course; where they will, in addition, be trained to habits of obedience, self-restraint, industry; where they will be taught to use the ordinary tools of mechanical pursuits; and, in short, where they will be given a chance to develop into useful, respectable citizens.'[46]

One of the consequences of the debate over vagrancy and school reform was the image of the hapless child which opened up the 'belief in the capacity as well as the necessity for education and training [that] sustained the reform impulse.'[47] In reality vagrant children were no less the consequence of capitalist business cycles and exploitation than the 'factory apprentices ... imprisoned in a "black hole" for hours at a time' in a Montreal cigar factory.[48] Educators, however, seized on the child itself as victim and menace and transformed that image into a rationale for a series of reforms imposed over and against the working class, yet justified as being for its sake. Such was the impulse behind many of J.L. Hughes' reforms in the Toronto schools. The introduction of kindergartens, child study, learning by doing, manual training, were all advocated as part of the new pedagogy developed by Froebel and others which held that 'educating the child through his activities is the true solution for the waywardness of youth.'[49] Character formation remained the basic aim of the reforms, as one of the manual training teachers explained to the Dominion Education Association of 1901: 'Again, I said just now that the will power, the power of inhibition, is largely developed by Manual Training. The man who has not learned to control himself in small actions, cannot effectively control his passions and desires.'[50]

The cult of domesticity which fueled much of the rural consolidation and urban reform movements similarly derived its ideological rationale from the presence of 'street arabs' with their 'undisciplined irregular habits' that exemplified the sensuality which 'represented in the lexicon of middle-class morality "the grave of all social progress." '[51] As early as 1851 Walter Eales had praised the ideal family with its sexist division of labour,[52] an ideal that worked its way through to teachers like Mrs Holiwell speaking in 1865 of the appropriateness of the school to develop 'the attributes of the true lady' – 'a perfect control of temper ... a modest estimate of self,' etc.; and to the subordination of teachers within the profession as advocated by Forrester: 'It is sufficient for us to know that, ... there is a position of subordination and of dependence assigned to the former [women] ... and, accordingly, it is generally admitted, that the infant and primary departments are best fitted for the female.'[53] By 1915, 82 per cent of elementary school teachers were women. Attachment to this role of women informed much of further reform in both urban and rural schools, even as the need for these reforms emerged out of the decline of rural life and the integration of women into the wage labour system. Middle-class moralizing permeated the demands of middle-class women for more educational provisions for wage-earning women as well as the aims of the public health movement from 1890 to 1914.[54] There, too, though the working class through its Trades and Labour Councils were among the first to support the movement, no effort was made on the part of professionals to involve working-class communities, so that ultimately school health programs took on an aspect of coercion against supposedly indifferent parents, the product of working-class life. Urban school reform thus formed part of the wider urban reform movement at the time which 'sought to reform urban-industrial society through the child and through the school.'[55]

Educational reform, then, is always a response to the contradictions of capitalism, even if the correspondence between the two is not always direct. The contradictions may very well surface at the level of ideology, but ultimately they derive from transformations in the economy. This was true not only of schools but also of other areas of reproduction; and it was their common origin which lent a similarity to the changes in each of these areas of social life. Beneath the cult of domesticity, for example, rippled incidences of hysteria and other nervous disorders described as 'common afflictions among more affluent young women in the latter nineteenth century.' This hysteria may have been the result of a reduction in the period of autonomy from family that young people had previously enjoyed, brought on by changes in the work and family structure in nineteenth-century Canada. Behind these changes lay 'the erosion of apprenticeship during the first half of the nineteenth century' which created 'a crisis of youth' to which the 'lodger evil,' the cult of domesticity, and school reform became an interlinked response; and behind the decline of apprenticeship and the crisis of youth lay the rise of industrial capitalism which provided the material backdrop for the school reforms of the progressive era.[56]

Changes in the Canadian economic structure – principally the 'wheat boom' and the rise of corporate capitalism – were also the motor forces behind the consolidation of rural schools and the implementation of technical education. Itself a response to changes in international capitalism – the end of the land frontier in the United States, rising demand for food, agricultural innovation – the wheat boom led to economic growth in Canada and the mass settlement of the prairies. It also led, however, through a federal government policy of land and revenue concessions to eastern monopolies, high tariffs and interest rates, poor credit facilities, etc., to intense resentment among this new population in the West. Out of this resentment emerged that era of both rural and urban radicalism for which the region became famous, with an intensity of class conflict which was exacerbated by the tension arising from the role which different ethnic groups played in those struggles.[57]

Massive immigration and internal shifts of population in Canada represented not only western settlement but also the integration of new social strata into the wage labour system consequent upon the 'expansion of capital and transformation to a capitalist mode of production [which] accelerated rapidly during the 1890-1914 period.' The emergence of large-scale manufacturing entailed the growth of a stratum of supervisory personnel to execute corporate policy within this new organization of work. This is reflected in the growth of the white-collar sector, and especially its proprietory and managerial component between 1901 and 1921. There was also a marked growth in the clerical component of the white-collar sector, especially among female workers.[58]

As before, educational reforms served a double purpose of social control, providing a disciplined and stratified labour force in line with the new requirements of Canadian capitalism and containing the class conflict that emerged in the forms of ethnic and labour unrest, petit-bourgeois radicalism, and general social upheaval. The guidelines laid down by the federal Department of Labour for administering the Technical Education Act were indicative of the general control functions behind the reform. Officials were directed to draw 'the attention of the provinces to the importance of training for citizenship as well as for employment' and 'to secure through every possible agency the continued sympathy and cooperation of our industrial labour organizations.'[59] As for the workplace, the report of the Royal Commission on Industrial Training and Technical Education was equally clear about the socialization tasks that underlay the new reforms: 'The full results of Industrial Training and Technical Education are to be sought through, – 1. The discipline which comes from interest in work ... 4. The preservation and strengthening of a spirit of willingness to accept and fill one's place in organised society which implies relative positions and relative degrees of authority.'[60] Both rural consolidation and technical education brought about changes in the financing, structure, and hidden curriculum of schools that made it possible for the schools to carry out these tasks effectively.

Rural consolidation, for example, made it financially possible for the schools to Canadianize the immigrant population; and, given the context, this was the process whereby 'the pure gold of Canadian citizenship' would emerge from the educational melting pot with a definite class bias. Furthermore, only the common school could perform that task since 'the Church, the only other great socializing agency stands divided' while the common school had the advantage of exerting 'influence over youthful minds at their most impressionable stage of development.' It is in this light that the Manitoba schools question must be understood. If the schools were to be left in the hands of local religious communities they would be unable to carry out effectively their socialization tasks, especially given the financial constraints on the government. The Manitoba government made that clear in its response to the Dominion government.[61] Religious differences in and of themselves would never have generated the controversy they did had they not been fused with ethnic and class differences as well.

The introduction of technical education meant that the secondary school curriculum could be diversified, more secondary school teachers trained, and secondary education extended to greater numbers. These reforms were important not for the skills they provided but for the character formation they permitted. As the Royal Commission on Technical Education grasped, 'the working mechanic and also the foremen, in the workshop or factory, receive their education at the continuation schools. Only those who are to become foremost leaders and directors of industry in a large way, and those who are to teach, take the full course in a technical college.' The education the working mechanic and foreman received would ensure that they possessed the dispositions and attitudes necessary, from capital's viewpoint, to hold subordinate but supervisory positions in the new occupational hierarchy. As the superintendent of No. 1 Mining District in Nova Scotia told the commission, someone who takes the time to study at night 'does not form dissipated habits, but keeps his mind occupied, which would not be the case if he was running around free, as they did in former years.' Much the same process was at work in the rural school reform. According to the commission rural high schools would provide adolescents with the required 'education, acceptable and capable leadership' that emerged from the agricutural colleges. For 'the practical working farmer' more subordinate levels of schooling would suffice.[62] The internal slotting made possible by the consolidated and therefore expanded rural school system would reproduce the class, regional, and occupational divisions produced by the changing nature of Canadian capitalism.

At the same time, the extension of secondary schooling reinforced educators' claims about the egalitarian effects of schooling. Schooling seemed to offer an avenue of upward mobility and an explanation for the unequal reward structure of the workplace. To be socially effective, however, the claims had to be justified in the language of school reform. The extension of secondary schooling was therefore justified by a redefined status of youth, which could not entirely evade acknowledging the social control functions behind the reforms: 'If the child's schooling closes at the end of the elementary school period, the chief opportunity for character formation is lost to the school, because the significant aims and purposes of life do not begin to take shape until the youth enters upon the period of adolescence.'[63] The autonomy of the schools on which the reforms' success hinged was relative indeed.

Like capitalism itself, the relative autonomy of schools is marked by both contradiction and a logic ironic but indispensable. Not only do pressures from the economy and the school system converge, seemingly independently, to create the demand for new reforms, but each element within the reforms reinforces the others, adding to the reformers' progressive claims the aura of inevitability. Even the conservative response to the social and economic transformations of Canadian capitalism stimulated this process. The idealization of rural life, which formed part of this response, led to the introduction of 'new subjects and experiences – Agriculture, Nature Study, School Gardens – which it was believed, would make the schools more relevant to country life.' Yet the introduction of new subjects required more qualified teachers and increased costs which added to the pressures for the consolidation of rural schools.

The reformers claimed the progressive label for their measures because they would provide more relevant education and equal facilities. Conservative criticism of the new pedagogy, however, unwittingly revealed the reformers' underlying class bias, which overlapped with a central Canadian imperialism on the ideological level. In an address to the Dominion Educational Association of 1904, Agnes Cameron pointed out how the top levels in the BC educational bureaucracy pushed agriculture into the schools, 'but, alas, the books had been compiled for Ontario, and they told of Ontario soils and warned against Ontario weeds, and somehow neither teacher nor farmer seemed to be able to adjust them to the longitude of British Columbia.' If the books were of little value for their technical information, they were important for their latent socialization message. A conservative account of a Nova Scotian rural schoolhouse in 1925-6 indicates how the class bias of schools operated through the instruction of grammar: while the school attempts to inculcate proper grammar into the pupils, the community 'prefers a dialect terse, racy ... and picturesquely ungrammatical figuratively, though not far from correct English in essential structure.'[64] Yet if the progressive reforms won out over conservative pleas for 'tradition,' it was because they were more in tune with the underlying societal changes that required new forms of social control. As with all progress under capitalism, progressive education had a double-edged nature. While it offered the promise of equalized resources, enriched curriculum, and child-centred study, in practice it subverted these promises by transforming these reforms into more refined techniques of social control. Curriculum enrichment led to streaming; child development led to testing and tracking – reforms which, like those of the late nineteenth century, functioned so as to bring the working-class child to acquiesce in his own subordination.

The conservative critique did have an ambiguously progressive side, for in exposing the absurdities and contradictions of progressive education it undermined the legitimacy of those reforms. In their lament for the world they had lost, conservatives were keeping alive principles which capitalism had rendered obsolete and which only the socialist transformation of capitalism could reinstate. In the case of the early school reform, for example, the price the bourgeoisie had to pay for the increased class use of schools was the loss of local control. Of course local control in that previous era meant more informal control by a less professionalized dominant class, but, given a different class content, local control could become, as it has today, a rallying cry for radical school reform.[65] Yet the radical edge of the conservative critique remains implicit, and the overt terms of the debate between conservative and progressive educators, which has continued to this day and marks one more sign of the school's relative autonomy, have only served to obfuscate the class nature of schooling; while with each successive reform the role and power of the educational bureaucracy becomes augmented and refined.

III

The Report will probably stand next in importance to the establishment of the National Policy. The National Policy provided the broad highway to industrial prosperity; the Commission has, at least, indicated how it should be travelled. (Reaction of the Canadian Manufacturers' Association to the Report of the Royal Commission on Technical Education, 1913)

The TLC declared itself in complete sympathy with a 'most voluminous, comprehensive and impressive report.' (Reaction of the Trades and Labour Congress to the same report)

We know that we are wage slaves pure and simple. Our masters are the capitalist class, and we are forming a party to fight this class. When members of the bourgeoisie come down below their own level we know they come down for their own benefit. (Delegate Lewis of the Machinists' Union at the founding convention of the Canadian Labour Party in Toronto, 1918)[66]

The technical education campaign was revealing of the way in which not only the relative autonomy of the school operated in the Canadian setting but also of the way capital and labour behaved. In the case of technical education, and rural school reform, the educational bureaucracy again played a key role. The MacDonald Education Movement funded initial experiments – rural school gardens, consolidated rural schools, manual training centres – but even this limited corporate involvement came at the behest of Dominion Agriculture and Dairying Commissioner J.W. Robertson, a leading educational reformer who subsequently chaired the Royal Commission on Technical Education and provided a key link between the corporate and educational elites. Only the federal government had the means to fund these projects on a massive scale, but it did not enter the picture until 1913 with passage of the Agricultural Instruction Act. As for technical education, the lobbying of the Canadian Manufacturers' Association, the Trades and Labour Congress, and the Dominion Educational Association notwithstanding, the federal government did not implement the recommendations of the royal commission until 1919, and even then it provided only $10 million instead of the recommended $30 million.[67]

The slowness of the state to act and the leading role of the educational reformers had a common source in the relative underdevelopment of the Canadian economy, which made educational reform seem less urgent. Despite the CMA insistence on technical education as 'the domestic side of the tariff,' the shortage of skilled labour had little to do with the absence of technical education and much to do with the fluctuating and dependent nature of the Canadian economy. In fact, the National Policy only increased Canada's technological dependence, which, in the educational sphere, showed up in the state's refusal to finance the expansion of the University of Toronto during the 1890s, in spite of the fact that educators stressed its importance for national development, and in 'the slow rate of growth in higher education' in general. The CMA's endorsement of technical education was less an example of the industrializing impulse of an indigenous bourgeoisie than a smoke screen for the dominance of a financial bourgeoisie whose role was critical in keeping the Canadian economy relatively underdeveloped and dependent on foreign capital and technology.[68] The tactic had been used before. When the director of the Ontario Bureau of Mines castigated Canadian bankers in the mid-1890s for abandoning investment to international capital, 'the *Monetary Times* proffered the usual excuses and explanations for Canadian reticence, but placed its faith in education.' Evidence to a House of Commons committee in 1910, however, indicated that Canada had its own share of technical expertise, at least sufficient to make 'the operation of a nickel refinery within Canada ... both possible and profitable.'[69]

The royal commission also helped to cloud the issue by justifying technical education in terms of its contribution to skilled labour and national wealth, even though individual testimony from managers and employers questioned these claims. The manager of the Dominion Iron and Steel Company, for example, after suggesting that graduates of technical colleges have 'a notable deficiency in the ability to write a letter,' went on to say: 'I do not think the manipulation of machines and things in laboratories is at all equivalent to that sort of work in factories.' He may learn to make a bolt in technical college, 'but the thing he has not learned is that he must make that bolt accurately, properly, drilling and turning it out at a price that will enable his employer to live and make a profit.' As the CMA put it, 'The greatest difficulty manufacturers have to face is the securing of competent, well-trained mechanical experts to act as foremen, superintendents, managers, etc.'[70] What the educational bureaucracy and the CMA did, through the royal commission's report,[71] was to provide a wider legitimizing base for reforms that were needed for purposes of social control. The schools could not act as efficient disciplinarians of the new working class if the educational system's structure and practice were not reoriented to the changed industrial capitalism that was emerging. As such, the CMA's advocacy of technical education for social control reflected the concerns of the entire Canadian upper class. Members of the financial bourgeoisie, who by 1910 wielded a disproportionate influence among the Canadian industrial elite,[72] were no less aware of the need for social control. As the general manager of the Bank of Commerce explained to the Canadian Club of Halifax in 1908, the flow of capital 'was threatened ... by the spread of "democratic sentiment" and concomitant "hatred of success," as well as by labour strife.'[73]

When the state finally did act, it too did so out of a similar concern. When the Borden government at last introduced technical education, it was 'in the context of an unemployment problem resulting from the phasing out of the munitions industry.'[74] The federal government's previous reluctance to fund technical education indicated therefore an awareness that its importance to the National Policy was minimal. Rather the timing of the Technical Education Act reflects once again how educational reform was an outcome of class conflict and not simply class domination, and of class conflict on a scale wider than the workplace itself. The vocational education movement thus formed part of a response to not only the new occupational requirements of corporate capitalism but also the class conflict it provoked.[75] Working-class discontent and organization were on the rise, as delegate Lewis' remark made clear. Between 1915 and 1919 'total union membership in Canada almost trebled ... to 378,000 ... Strikes and other manifestations of unrest and conflict likewise mounted sharply ... reaching a dramatic climax in the Winnipeg General Strike of 1919.' In 1917 the TLC convention endorsed the formation of a national labour party. In the West working-class militancy took an even more radical form. The BC Federation of Labour went beyond electoral politics to advocate direct action and the general strike, culminating in its endorsement of the One Big Union.[76]

The federal government's response to growing class conflict was twofold: repression and integration. This response had a long and dishonourable history, and, viewed in this larger perspective, technical education was part of the attempt by the political representatives of the bourgeoisie to integrate the working class into capitalism without having to resort to outright coercion. There was a structural bias to this attempt. In general, the federal government's efforts at integration were directed at the central executive of the TLC, not because they were eastern Canadian or national officers but because they were moderate. The technical education lobby itself was an alliance of educators, industrialists, and labour leaders rooted especially in Ontario. Thus, in the same year that the federal government forcibly suppressed the Winnipeg General Strike it also introduced technical education. The instrumental role of W.L. Mackenzie King in pushing technical education onto a reluctant government gives this interpretation added weight in view of King's historic role in pushing for greater use of non-coercive measures to contain the Canadian working class – though he had also served as secretary to the 1903 royal commission which advocated outlawing radical socialistic unions such as the United Brotherhood of Railway Employees and the Western Federation of Miners. Indeed, the legitimation aspect of technical education assumed greater importance 'as leadership in the movement for federal support shifted away from the CMA and into the hands of the two important labour ministers.'[77]

It is interesting, in this respect, that technical education, as a legitimizing weapon, assumed its greatest importance in Ontario where the labour leadership was itself highly reformist. Ontario had already passed its own Industrial Education Act in 1911 and was the only province to use its entire federal allotment within the initial ten-year period.[78] In part this reflects the relatively more extensive development of industrial capitalism in Ontario, but it also indicates how legitimizing strategies like technical education, to be effective, are dependent on a reformist labour leadership. The situation was similar to the public power movement in Ontario where,'Unlike their American counterparts who had to keep glancing nervously over their shoulders at the stirring masses, the Canadian businessmen reformers could take dead aim on their objective without the disquieting suspicion that their rhetoric might be turned against them.' They did not have to fear that their call for public ownership of the utilities would be translated by socialists into a call for nationalization of the means of production precisely because 'In Canada, labour was relatively weaker, and in the east more conservative.'[79] In a similar vein industrialists and middle-class educational reformers could win labour support for technical education even as they dominated the movement, and justify it in terms that denigrated the working class even as they pointed out its benefits. Apropos the value of continuation schools in Nova Scotia, for example, the commissioners accepted the view that '... if a marble palace were placed in every community and trades were taught in toto, giving a four year course, and boys knew that if they attended they would come out skilled journeymen to work for certain wages, the palace could not be filled; for humanity is the same the world over; there are few ambitious men, and even if all sorts of opportunities were supplied, advantage would not be taken of them.'[80]

The economic conditions that 'permitted the businessmen to use the state and identify themselves with the masses without anxiety and without fear of contradiction'[81] were the same that produced the working-class reformism that also made this possible. These conditions were not simply Canada's economic backwardness but also its particular type of capitalist development: the dominance of a financial bourgeoisie, its uneven extension of capital-intensive production, and the predominance of the petite bourgeoisie among the subordinate classes (a given of the Canadian class structure which formed the major backdrop to the reformism of Canadian working-class politics).[82] Yet reformism contains a rejection as well as an acceptance of the dominant class' values and practices. The very struggles of workers and farmers, the two major subordinate classes most affected by the new capitalism, were testimony to their resistance to the social and economic transformations which capitalism wrought. In spite of the dominant reformist character which this resistance eventually assumed, the oppositional strain in these struggles had its own internal dialectic. From the Nine

Hours Movement to the Social Credit and CCF parties in the 1930s and 1940s there existed both a continuity of leadership and a common source of oppression which generated these struggles.

A similar dialectic was at work in the educational reforms which stretched from 1870 to 1940. The reforms themselves were not merely the dominant class' response to increased class conflict generated by the transformations of Canadian capitalism. The class bias of the new educational reforms in turn generated opposition on the part of workers and farmers. Farmers, especially immigrants, were not willing to pay for reforms such as rural consolidation which were designed at heart to control them, just as in another context they did not respond to a conservation movement that cast them in the role of principal villain.[83] Similarly, workers, even when they accepted reforms like technical education, had different ideas about their purpose or utility. In Quebec demands for universal, free, obligatory education were part of the program of radical socialist workers' parties as early as 1900, whereas liberal educational reforms proposed by the Marchand government at the time were seen as a means of channelling popular aspirations into legitimate limits. Marchand's defence of these reforms against conservative critics rested on the argument that 'c'est en contrariant ces aspirations que nous le pousserions aux excès révolutionnaires, au mépris de l'autorité.'[84] When J.L. Hughes attempted to introduce manual training into the Toronto schools in 1886 he encountered trade union opposition on the grounds that it was a cover for trades schools.[85] Working-class testimony in 1891 on manual training and industrial schools indicated how working-class opposition to such reforms stemmed from a fear they would lead to 'a congested labour market [which] throws people out of employment' and therefore 'makes the struggle for life keener for those who are in it,' and the knowledge that youths trained in such schools 'are sent out with a knowledge ... that is necessarily imperfect.'[86]

There is a continuity to this working-class resistance to educational reforms imposed from above, a resistance that took the silent form of boycott as well as more overt protest, a resistance that worked itself out within a dominant reformist strain yet provided the basis for a radical tradition which would have a greater chance when the broader social structure had altered in its favour. For example, in the working-class opposition to technical education (in both its radical and reformist variants) can be seen that tradition which characterized the ambivalent working-class response to an earlier middle-class educational reform – the Mechanics' Institute, which, 'like the friendly society, was a "nursery for the industrious classes" of the community. Lessons learned in its halls would not be forgotten in later years.' Among these lessons were those of self-help, mutual aid, and 'the gains to be gleaned from literacy.' Not only did these lessons surface in future working-class responses to later educational reforms, they also formed part of that social and cultural matrix which provided the link between the craft organizations of the 1860s and 1870s and the rising labour movement at the turn of the century. Notions such as the rights of free-born Englishmen legitimized artisanal action opposing the rising industrial capitalism. Thus, the artisan was enabled to draw 'other segments of the working class and the community into battle with him.' These same notions in turn legitimized the actions of the new industrial working classes based on the demand for 'working class self-management of the production process' which posed to capital, in however implicit a form, the threat which led to reforms like technical education.[87]

The educational reforms of the progressive era must be seen, then, as the working out, within the relative autonomy of the school and, in a larger sense, the state, of the ongoing dialectic between capital and labour as it developed under Canadian capitalism. Educational reform therefore had its own dialectic; and just as the working class provoked reforms which it later resisted or only partially endorsed, the reforms engendered further reforms which only reinforced the social control functions of the school. The emphasis on child study, for example, became a justification for ability grouping based on psychological testing, which only increased the internal stratification of the schools on class, sex, and ethnic lines. Once again the educational bureaucracy was the key in providing the ideological legerdemain which translated the ideals of Dewey's progressivism into a reality of social control by ignoring, as Dewey himself did, the class nature of social reality.[88]

When fully developed, progressive education fused both reform and control into a single ideology which enabled educators to go about their business in full, if rather blithe, good faith. As the Alberta Department of Education explained in 1935, when outlining the thinking behind the practice of the new intermediate schools, an 'up-to-date programme' was both 'a reaction against the mechanized routine of formal instruction' and a 'recognition in the programme of training for personal and social efficiency, emotional control, and integration of personality.'[89] As such, progressive education was both a reformist response to growing social discontent manifested politically in the rise of the CCF and Social Credit and an adaptation of schooling to the new type of character formation required by the changes in corporate capital. These changes required a highly stratified work force that had internalized different norms of behaviour according to their place in the occupational structure. The task of producing and reproducing this work force fell to the schools, especially at the secondary level. It was reflected in both the expansion and internal stratification of the high schools in the decades following the First World War. Junior high schools were tried out in urban areas in the 1920s. Between 1921 and 1951 the percentage of males aged 15-19 enrolled in school increased from 22.86 to 40.89 per cent. By the 1940s educational reformers, still using their double-edged rhetoric, were pushing for composite high schools. Yet these schools had their roots in the Technical Education Act of 1919 which, by promoting vocationalism, helped, especially in Ontario, to 'break the "academic" monopoly of the high schools and collegiate institutes.'[90]

Once again members of the educational bureaucracy were instrumental in pushing through these reforms, while the reforms in turn consolidated the power of the educational bureaucracy. The logic of relative autonomy was at work. Reforms involving more sophisticated theory and methodology placed a premium on expertise. Many of the proponents of progressive education received their training at leading US colleges like Chicago and Columbia. These educators tended to concentrate in the upper reaches of the provincial departments of education. At the same time, the reforms they advocated generated pressures for the concentration of power in the hands of those very departments. Programs like technical education were costly and beyond the reach of rural areas. In the name of equalization, especially at the secondary level, leading educators advocated once again rural consolidation.[91] Administrative centralization also meant financial centralization, such that the provincial government would assume the total cost of education. Yet the financial weakness of the provinces was in large part responsible for the postponement of this administrative reform, just as it was responsible for the postponement of many other reforms during the 1930s such as junior high schools, extensive ability grouping, or expanded vocational programmes. Even university expansion suffered cutbacks in the 1930s, though some support came from the Carnegie and Rockefeller Foundations.[92]

Part of the reason for the cutbacks lay in the depression; part lay in the relatively less pressing need of the Canadian ruling class to use educational reform for social control, though educators through their international connections could see earlier their eventual utility. The state's delay in implementing such legitimation measures reflected once again the relative weakness of Canadian labour; and both derived from the relatively slow development of Canadian industrial capitalism. Yet in the long run the transformations in Canadian capitalism which such reforms presaged made themselves felt.[93] They also created another factor in the politics of educational reform to which administrative centralization and financial rationalization were central – the fiscal crisis of the state.

I V

Education no longer was the splendid deliverer. Davis sealed its fate by declaring it a non-growth industry; the media dropped its fascination with educational hardware and technique. In Toronto, the newspapers shifted their attention, as if on cue, to mass transit and city politics.[94]

The economic changes that underlay the reforms in post-war Canadian education involved not only the final transformation of the economy to industrial capitalism but also a shift in its internal composition: the growth of the tertiary sector, an increase in the white-collar proletariat, the integration of significantly more women into the labour force. Between 1941 and 1961 the white-collar component of the labour force increased from 25.2 to 38.6 per cent, while the primary occupational group declined from 30.6 to 13.1 per cent. Within the white-collar sector the biggest increase was in the clerical subgroup, of which women formed a disproportionate part. Between 1901 and 1941 women's percentage of the labour force increased from 13.3 to 19.8 per cent; between 1941 and 1961 from 19.8 to 27.8 per cent. This increase occurred disproportionately among the white-collar sector, and within that sector among the clerical subgroup (from 50.1 per cent of white-collar workers in 1941 to 61.5 in 1961). Professionals accounted for the second biggest increase in the white-collar sector, while the percentage of self-employed professionals declined.

These changes posed both staffing and legitimation problems for Canadian capitalism, not least of which was and is the integration of new strata into the labour force. In the case of women, for example, 'the rapid increase in the proportion of married women in the labour force has created deep strains in the basic unit of Canadian social organization, the male-dominated nuclear family.'[95] Furthermore, women have joined in the main that clerical component of white-collar work which offers little upward mobility, considerable boredom, and relatively low salaries. The proletarianization many white-collar workers face has resulted in increased militancy and the proliferation of white-collar unions. The tension arising from the discrepancy between the promise of upward mobility offered by the expansion of white-collar occupations and current reality was especially acute for native Canadian workers, in view of the fact that immigrants tended to fill disproportionately the ranks of professional and skilled occupations during the fifties.

Part of the increase in white-collar work has meant an increase in control functions, as the shift in the 1950s from a predominantly goods-producing to a predominantly service-producing economy was reproduced within the manufacturing sector. A study of the automobile and automobile parts manufacturing industries showed that 'in one large fabricating and assembly plant the salaried staff increased by 116 per cent over ten years. Here the number of foremen tripled, and the number of graduate engineers increased by 60 per cent. Modern manufacturing has brought with it increasingly complex administration which in turn requires employees with special qualifications, particularly in production planning, quality control, and inspection.'[96] As in an earlier period of capitalist development, the most important aspect of these qualifications is their reliability to turn out profitable production within the hierarchical division of labour. This qualification is no less important for those who hold the technical positions that have been created as a result of post-war developments in technology. The problem for capital is not simply one of finding suitable candidates for that occupational level but also one of legitimating a situation where even technical and, in certain cases, professional occupations are becoming increasingly regimented. The tension becomes especially acute as former members of the petite bourgeoisie become integrated into this segment of the white-collar salariat.[97]

These contradictions are especially manifest in the state sector, where 'public employees have become "dirty workers" ... who are used to clean up or control our social problems.'[98] Training suitable candidates for these control functions is in itself a problem, which is exacerbated by the fact that these positions are defined publicly in terms of welfare. As a result these workers experience daily the tension arising from the contradiction between the ostensible and real nature of their work; and the dissatisfaction which it sparks poses further management problems for the ruling class. The situation of white-collar workers holds equally well for blue-collar workers. Mechanization has reduced mainly unskilled labour anywhere from 33 to 50 per cent, while 'at the level of skilled trades some occupations increased while others contracted.'[99] Automation, however, has not measurably improved the lot of even the more highly paid blue-collar workers in capital-intensive industry. If anything, the increased fragmentation and control has only produced more alienation and worker resistance at the shop floor level.[100]

A concomitant feature of these transformations in capital, especially the division into a capital-intensive monopoly sector and a labour-intensive competitive sector, has been an increase in the surplus labour population, more and more dependent on the state.[101] Workers in this secondary labour market where 'jobs usually offer low wages, unstable employment, poor working conditions, exhausting work, and little opportunity for advancement,'[102] are drawn disproportionately from native people, Québécois, women, teenagers, recent immigrants, migrant Maritimers, and exiled prairie farmers. As such, they reflect the regional distribution of economic activity within Canada, itself a product of Canada's hinterland status vis-à-vis the United States.

The growth of the surplus labour population has contributed in turn to the fiscal crisis of the state. In the first place, it has required increased outlays by the state sector to cover social expenses. These programs have led in turn to the growth of the state sector proletariat. 'By the decade of the 1970s, roughly 12% of the labour force was working directly for the State, while 18% of the labour force was directly or indirectly supported by Government payrolls. This becomes all the more important when we realize that between 1961 and 1970 the gross payroll of all public employees as a percentage of all wages, salaries and supplementary labour income increased from roughly 7% to 14.5%.'[103] As expenditures outstrip revenues, the state is faced with an ever-growing fiscal crisis that it has attempted to resolve at the expense of the public sector employees.

The fiscal crisis is especially acute at the provincial and municipal levels, where expenditures outstripped revenues between 1950 and 1970. The public debt increased by 505 and 511 per cent respectively compared to a 136 per cent increase for the federal government between 1950 and 1968.[104] Because the federal government has had greater access to tax resources it could finance its needs from domestic sources while provincial governments had to borrow in foreign markets. The growing involvement by the provinces in accumulation areas[105] has meant that they have had even less money to spend on legitimation functions, itself a legacy of the BNA Act and the structure of Canadian capitalism which gave rise to it. Consequently, Ottawa has often had to initiate legitimation programs and use its fiscal powers to induce the provinces to go along. The Canadian bourgeoisie therefore looked to the federal government to undertake these programs of general interest to the bourgeoisie as a class. Now, however, the monopoly capital sector looks to the provincial governments to carry out such programs, since the major investment areas for both legitimation and accumulation necessary to the growth of a 'social-industrial complex' – such as resource extraction, education, health – fall under provincial jurisdiction. As the growth of such a complex requires changes in monopoly capital-state relations in order to co-ordinate spending and policies and, it is hoped, avoid continuous direct state confrontation with the working class, the shift from Ottawa to the provinces of certain responsibilities represents an attempt to rationalize the Canadian bourgeoisie's response to the fiscal crisis at the provincial level.

These transformations, and their contradictions, provide the material backdrop to post-war changes in the education system which really got underway in the 1960s. The most noticeable of these changes were: the establishment of progressive education as the dominant ideology and its translation into practice, especially at the elementary level; the consolidation of school boards, especially at the high school level, and the development of composite high schools with the expansion of vocational education; the expansion of post-secondary education, especially the establishment of community colleges; increased teacher militancy and confrontation with the state; and rationalization of the education sector under provincial control.

As before, these changes emerged out of the logic of school reform. As the Hall-Dennis report remarked, virtually every idea in the Ontario Program of Studies for elementary years published in 1937 'might have been expressed by educationally enlightened and advanced authors today.'[106] By the time they were implemented, however, they had assumed additional significance in response to the economic changes whose relative lateness had delayed their earlier implementation. The progressive reforms at the elementary level – special classes, open classrooms, an abundance of technology, sophisticated streaming – were basically new socialization mechanisms to prepare students for eventual school failure and a job future in the surplus labour market. The expansion of the vocational/technical system served similar socialization functions. Skills learned in the vocational schools had very little correlation with future jobs, except in 'low-paying, dead-end clerical work, mostly for women, in the big offices of large financial and corporate concerns.'[107]

Most students in vocational schools were not even getting proper training in basic literacy skills, which deprived them even more of those tools necessary to understand the class origin of their position and to change it. Instead, schools provided socialization 'directed to the development of a properly subordinate character structure suitable for the dead-end work that awaits these kids – or for a life in which they will have no jobs at all.'[108] The guidance system was an important part of this process, helping to confirm the students in their overall class position and reproduce the existing class- and sex-stratified occupational hierarchy, in part through the use of tests which have the power of neutrality, in part through the type of advice given. 'They gave us advice but I found it inadequate; they don't seem to be qualified. What they say is too academic. It doesn't seem as if any one of them has ever really worked in industry. So you might say that they just don't know what they are talking about. At least, what they say hasn't been relevant to the bit of experience I've had. For instance, they don't describe the *reasons* for different systems. They might say there is an incentive system, but *why* piece-work pay rather than another system? Why an hourly wage rather than another system? And, of course, they have their own pet jobs they like to describe and leave out all kinds of other important jobs' (works in shipping room, Grade XI Technical, failed, left school at age 16, nine siblings).[109]

Class- and sex-based streaming within schools also helped legitimate the class and sex stratification at that level of the occupational hierarchy: 'Girls have been finding jobs in personal service, public service, finance institutions or big industry. Boys have found theirs in personal service, trade or small industry. With the exception of personal service, the two sexes have found their jobs in very different segments of the economy.'[110] The growth of vocational schools in the sixties only increased this trend. In Ontario, the federal Technical and Vocational Training Assistance Act (1960) led to a reorganization of the secondary school program so that the school boards could undertake construction of the new composite high schools, and thereby Ontario could maximize the use of federal largesse. The new course of study entailed the establishment of different streams with different educational and occupational futures for their students.[111]

The growth of vocational education in the sixties and associated reforms represented, therefore, a new development in progressivism, providing a response to the staffing problems posed by the new sectoral and occupational divisions brought about by the transformations in Canadian capitalism. The extension of these reforms to post-secondary education formed part of this process.

The growing need to prepare more and more students for positions in the increasingly regimented blue- and white-collar monopoly sector or in the secondary labour market was accompanied by the need to prepare a new stratum of salaried technicians and semi-professionals in the monopoly and state sectors. The growth of community colleges and the expansion of the university sector reflected the need to process 'large numbers of students to attain that particular combination of technical competence and social acquiescence required in the skilled but powerless upper-middle positions in the occupational hierarchy of the corporate capitalist economy.'[112] At the same time, 'the proletarianization of employees and technicians calls for a "multiplication of middle-level managers" to control the former' and whose function resides almost exclusively in that of control.[113] Among the principles governing the establishment of Colleges of Applied Arts and Technology in Ontario, for example, was one stating: 'The colleges must operate in the closest possible cooperation with business and industry, and with social and other public agencies to ensure that curricula are at all times abreast of the changing needs of a technological society.'[114] William Davis' speech in 1965 outlining the clientele of community colleges designated the semi-professionals and junior and middle-management as key targets in their program.[115] A study on the impact of community colleges in British Columbia revealed that community colleges, though not as selective as universities, contain a significantly greater number of students whose fathers hold professional or managerial positions; that these divisions are reproduced within the different streams of post-secondary education; and that the different streams contain students with different sets of expectations about future education, future jobs, and their present activities – all of which tend to reinforce the class system, as do the financial benefits derived from a college diploma.

The expansion of the education system at all levels also enabled reformers to claim that schools were delivering on their democratic promise. School consolidation had been justified, after all, as the logical consequence of a commitment to provide equally progressive resources to all. In their very definition of democratization as 'the process by which such education is made available to a broader socio-economic cross-section of the population than was the case in the past,' educators guaranteed that the real class functions which underlay school expansion would remain hidden, thus legitimating schooling as an explanation of economic success.[116] These reforms generated, in turn, their own contradictions. Educational opportunity in many cases became 'a millstone around the children's necks,' especially in the hinterland regions the reforms were designed to serve. The very lack of regional industry meant that higher education eventually entailed the forced abandoning of one's community.[117] In general, 'the "degreee of fit" between the product of the vocational school and the industrial world' was found to be far from perfect; and the same was true for the relationship between college studies and future destinies. There was 'a wide discrepancy between the proportion of students planning to continue to university and the 20% who actually do so,' while 'only half of the graduates employed were engaged in work directly related to their college studies.' The reactions of employers to community college graduates were also highly ambiguous.[118]

Ironically, the very transformations of capitalism which required the expansion of post-secondary education for new socialization tasks made it impossible for the schools to deliver on their promises to provide useful skills, job training, or occupational mobility. This was true for career education in the United States; and the subordinate position of Canada in the US economic empire only underscored this fact. The implementation of the Technical and Vocational Training Assistance Act was in part the result of a concern with a decline in the number of skilled European immigrants to Canada, but also the result of a concern over rising unemployment. As before, the reliance on immigrant skilled workers reflected the underdevelopment of the Canadian economy, while the sources of both stagnation and recovery lay in the capitalist nature of the economy, and the American economy at that. As if in recognition of this situation, Ontario, when building institutions under the Technical and Vocational Training Assistance Agreement, made 'little apparent use of manpower requirement forecasting data or future job trends.' Even the federal government had no clear estimates of the manpower requirements and capacity when it proposed the 1960 act.[119]

None the less, the justification for the expansion and consolidation of the secondary and post-secondary school system was everywhere made in terms of matching training with future job requirements, providing the skills needed for upward mobility in a technological society, etc. Human capital theory became the dominant ideology in spite of evidence to the contrary produced by its adherents;[120] and Canada invested accordingly. As Alexander Lockhart has shown, by 1969 Canada was investing 8.9 per cent of its GNP in education, more than any other leading industrial society, but when the justifications for such investment did not pan out, a legitimacy crisis ensued. Having ' "sold" the higher education package ... in terms of its potential for equalizing opportunity,' the state was incapable of keeping up its end of the implicit bargain in providing appropriate jobs for all those who 'agreed to accept a narrow, sometimes irrelevant, often alienating and increasingly prolonged educational confinement as the price paid in youth for privilege in later life.' The gap between supply and demand for university graduates in the early seventies may be 'as high as one third the annual production, perhaps more if unemployment is considered.' Though Canadian investment in education outstripped that of the United States, 'the proportional expenditure on R and D by Canadian industry has steadily declined, primarily as a result of foreign subsidiaries cutting back on their branch plant R and D activities.'[121] The contradictions resulting from the use of education to reproduce a labour force that suits the changing needs of capitalism were once again heightened in Canada by its dependent pattern of economic development.

Attempts to deal with the ensuing legitimacy crisis, especially manifest in the youth culture, have taken a number of forms, all of which amount to a rationalization of the education system. One response has been to take measures to improve the degree of fit between post-secondary institutions and the job market. The group that studied the impact of community colleges in British Columbia, for example, recommended that efforts should be made to inform the business community of the college programs and get them to recognize their importance.[122] The recommendations of the Nadeau report on the condition and needs of collegial education in Quebec are particularly interesting in that regard. As if in recognition of the student discontent, the authors proposed a redefinition of the college program which attempted to take into account recent critiques of the education system but integrated them into support for a more rationalized structure. On the ideological level, they recognized the adult status of the student, but used it to make him or her responsible for their program. The program itself they redefined in terms of a modular structure which would demand increased participation in its formulation from the community, but especially industry. In this way they hoped to get the students to internalize as their own the needs of society and avoid what the authors recognized at the beginning but quickly glossed over, the possibility that their needs and the needs of society may be incompatible. The redefinition of the college student's status, coupled with the provision of funds for economic independence, was in line with the personality requirements of the jobs they will be required to fill. It was accompanied, in turn, by a redefinition of the secondary school's purpose which amounts to deskilling and therapy under the guise of responding to the radical critique of high school.[123] This would parallel the actual 'déqualification au travail ... qui affecterait toutes les catégories occupationnelles' and which is reflected in 'la multiplication des fonctions subalternes de supervision et de contrôle.'[124]

All serious critical formation, on the other hand, is left to the university, such that the streaming within the colleges would become more pronounced. Within such a redefinition of the school system, it is conceivable that much of the 'expectational framework' could be removed without jeopardizing its reproductive functions. This is to a large extent what career education is all about, while the abandonment of rising expectations has itself become a major component of the new dominant ideology being fashioned to cope with the current crisis of capitalism.[125]

At the same time, the recommendations of the Nadeau report represent the thinking behind the dominant class' efforts at rationalization in view of the fiscal crisis of the state. Replacing established courses by a program worked out by the student and the community would permit not only greater control by industry over education but also permit a more rational use of resources which would keep costs within provincial budgetary constraints. One method is program budgeting; another is regional planning. Hence an essential part of the proposed reform is a form of decentralization which would provide for a special deputy ministry for post-secondary education and transform its role from bureaucratic control to program planning and research co-ordination. Decentralization would not really give increased power to students and professors, but rather permit the creation of regional and provincial committees which would avoid duplication of resources and maximize use of existing facilities throughout the community. These structures would eventually cover the entire educational system for a single region.[126]

Such reforms would parallel those that accompanied the expansion and consolidation of secondary education in the sixties throughout Canada.[127] Not only did the progressive reforms cost money; progressive rhetoric demanded that these reforms be made available to all. While school expenses rose, the local tax base was insufficient to provide the necessary funds. The increase in tax rates and in reliance on borrowing eventually led to demands for provincial intervention, demands that were first raised by the educational establishment. Paralleling early school reform, progressive education represented the interests of monopoly capital – as the Dennis-Hall report put it, 'the small school and the local school board have had their day' – while the opposition to these reforms came from more traditional sectors of the economy. Consolidation brought a change in the social composition of trustees, who now came from wealthier, professional backgrounds representing the interests of the monopoly sector oriented towards technical efficiency and the use of educational machines, technology, and services.[128]

In this sense the expansion of educational facilities in the 1960s also represented the growth of a 'social-industrial complex.' Education now became a source of investment for the dominant corporations in the monopoly sector. By 1968, for example, 14 per cent of Canadian cities with populations of more than 40,000 used programmed tests regularly and 48 per cent had adopted them experimentally.[129] Federal intervention into the field of vocational education on a serious level in the 1960s, while it did little to combat unemployment, did provide a tremendous source of investment in terms of construction of new schools and the provision of materials. Between 1961 and 1966, 278 new vocational or composite schools and 55 alterations to existing schools were undertaken in Ontario alone. Furthermore, the fiscal agreements were such as to encourage school boards to expand as much as possible as quickly as possible, yet once they had expanded the school boards were faced with increased operating costs that placed them at the mercy of the provincial government and gave the latter a powerful lever in pushing through consolidation.

Fiscal equalization had the same effect, for the increase in provincial grants led in turn to an increase in school board expenditures. This made the latter more reliant on provincial grants, whose percentage of expenditures increased from 39.1 in 1958 to 45.3 in 1967.[130] Increased fiscal control of education by the provincial government was extended to cover capital financing via the Capital Aid Corporation, the Treasury Department, and the Ontario Municipal Board. This was important because it enabled the provincial government to control as much as possible the sources of public investment and thus render it the most appropriate level of government to develop 'a social-industrial complex' that best fits the needs of monopoly capital, which is highly American based. One such example was the provincial government's support for SEF, a US school design agency backed with Ford Foundation funds. Although SEF was supposed to enhance the learning environment, there is little evidence that it did so. On the other hand, it did 'monopolize Metro's school building market' at the expense of independent builders. Furthermore, though more costly than other kinds of building, the Metro Toronto School Board justified it in 1970 on the grounds that 'Discontinuation of the SEF Building System would have a very detrimental effect on the progress of systems building development, not only in Ontario and Canada, but indeed for the entire North American continent, because of the impact of the SEF system on the North American building scene.'[131]

The provisions of control over capital financing meant, however, that the government had to intervene to authorize school projects for those boards whose municipalities were too much in debt to undertake them. This highlighted the need for school reorganization and the 1968 legislation did give school boards the power to issue their own capital debentures. This in turn created pressures for increased expenditures, which the provincial government proceeded to control in two ways. First, it made capital projects subject to provincial approval in design, construction, and financing. This meant that school reorganization was accompanied by a reorganization of the Department of Education whereby curriculum and inspection were transferred to the consolidated boards while the department assumed policy planning and development, with the school-administration branch emerging as the central control agency. Experts both in the capital and in the regions became the most efficient defenders of the new reforms. Second, the government used its power to set the proportion of total approved expenditures to be supported by provincial grants, in order to control local expenditure. Though it increased the share of provincial grants in school board expenditures, it also prevented local tax rates from rising accordingly by empowering the minister to make regulations governing school board expenditures. This centralization of power in the hands of the provincial government meant that it could control the rate of expansion of the education sector within politically acceptable limits, and in general determine the extent to which it was willing to invest in this particular sector. The federal abandonment of educational programs and its transfer to the provinces of tax points was an equally important part of this process, for the concentration of power at the provincial level will enable the state to shift priorities from one legitimation area to another, as education becomes a 'non-growth industry.'[132] Furthermore, the shift in state sector–monopoly capital relations signifying the growth of a social-industrial complex was underscored by the increasing participation of corporate foundations, especially US ones, in educational research and university planning.

This rationalization process is also not without its contradictions, the most noticeable of which is the rising militancy of teacher unions. The school's clients are also becoming more vocal and some links are emerging between state workers and state clients in this sector, that is, between teachers and students and parents.[133] Whether or not these contradictions will lead to a radical restructuring of schools and, beyond them, of society is ultimately a question of praxis. Revolutionaries working around the school issue must demand both socialist content and democratic control; yet even that is not the main stumbling block. Part of the problem is working on terrain where 'revolutionary reforms' meet up with the reformism of capitalist society in all its facets, while beyond that are all the practical problems involved in translating theory into practice in situations that have their own historical constraints, as the history of Canadian school reform shows. Not the least of these constraints is the absence of a mass socialist party and all that that absence has signified. What is needed is the theoretical working out of questions of revolutionary strategy on the basis of continuous praxis, but that is the beginning of another chapter.

NOTES

This article is the result of many conversations. The notes acknowledge most of them, but there are others who contributed in a different way: Leo Panitch, who long ago waited for me to work out my own approach to Marxism; John Thompson, who gave me my first bibliography on Canadian education; George Smith, who talked with me over a summer about the whole article while it was still half-baked and sent me detailed criticisms of the first draft; and other friends and colleagues who suffered to listen and raised some interesting questions.

1 Ryerson to W.H. Draper, 20 April 1846, cited by S. Houston, 'Politics, Schools and Social Change in Upper Canada,' in M. Katz and P. Mattingly, eds., *Education and Social Change* (New York 1975), 47 (emphasis in original)
2 M. Katz, *The People of Hamilton, Canada West* (Cambridge 1975), 64
3 Houston, 'Politics, Schools,' 46. For the history of Irish labourers, see H.C. Pentland, 'The Development of a Capitalistic Labour Market in Canada,' in *Canadian Journal of Economics and Political Science*, xxv, 4 (Nov. 1959), 460-1.
4 T. Naylor, *The History of Canadian Business* (Toronto 1975), I, 24, 4
5 See the testimony of the Swiss Poor Law Commissioner Escher that Ryerson quotes in his report published in 1847, cited in A. Prentice and S. Houston, *Family, School and Society in Nineteenth Century Canada* (Toronto 1975), 71-2.
6 See H. Bamman, 'Patterns of School Attendance in Toronto, 1844-1878,' I. Davey, 'School Reform and School Attendance,' M. Katz, 'Who Went to School?' all in Katz and Mattingly, *Education and Social Change*, especially 219-20, 239, 302-7, 282-3. See also Katz, *People of Hamilton*, especially 285-7 and chap. 2 *passim*.
7 For examples, see Houston, 'Politics, Schools,' 33-7, and W.B. Hamilton, 'Society and Schools in New Brunswick and Prince Edward Island,' in J.D. Wilson *et al.*, eds., *Canadian Education: A History* (Scarborough 1970), 115-16 and 120-1.
8 H. Graff, 'Respected and Profitable Labour,' in G. Kealey and P. Warrian, eds., *Essays in Canadian Working Class History* (Toronto 1976), 81-2
9 Cited in Prentice and Houston, *Family, School and Society*, 97
10 Houston, 'Politics, Schools,' 33-48; P. Ross, 'The Free School Controversy in Toronto, 1848-52,' in Katz and Mattingly, *Education and Social Change*, 61-70
11 Cited in S. Houston, 'Victorian Origins of Juvenile Delinquency: A Canadian Experience,' in *ibid.*, 89. See also Ross, *ibid.*, for an account of the struggle in Toronto.
12 W.B. Hamilton, 'Society and Schools in Nova Scotia,' in Wilson, *Canadian Education*, 99-100
13 For Upper Canada, see Houston, 'Politics, Schools,' 37; for Quebec, see D. Lawr and R. Gidney, eds., *Educating Canadians* (Toronto 1973), 43-6, 54-5; for

Nova Scotia, see *ibid.*, 46-8, and Hamilton, 'Society and Schools in Nova Scotia,' 100; for PEI, see Hamilton, 'Society and Schools in NB and PEI,' 111-21; for New Brunswick, see Lawr and Gidney, *ibid.*, 61-5.

14 Hamilton, 'Society and Schools in NB and PEI,' 111-13

15 Katz, *People of Hamilton*, 183

16 Cited in Prentice and Houston, *Family, School and Society*, 95-6

17 Katz, *People of Hamilton*, 189 ff.; see also Naylor, *Canadian Business*, I, *passim*, and Davey, 'School Reform,' 297-306

18 See R. Gidney, 'Elementary Education in Upper Canada: A Reassessment,' in Katz and Mattingly, *Education and Social Change*, 3-26; H. Graff, 'Towards a Meaning of Literacy: Literacy and Social Structure in Hamilton, Ontario, 1861,' in *ibid.*, 256, 260-1, and 'Respected and Profitable Labour'; and, more broadly, see C. Jencks *et al.*, *Inequality* (New York, 1973); I. Berg, *Education and Jobs: The Great Training Robbery* (Boston 1971); and M. Katz, *The Irony of Early School Reform* (Cambridge 1968).

19 Cited from Ryerson's annual report of 1851 in Houston, 'Politics, Schools,' 46

20 'Egerton Ryerson on the Need for Central Control,' in Prentice and Houston, *Family, School and Society*, 81

21 For examples, see *ibid.*, 104-27.

22 D. Cameron, *Schools for Ontario* (Toronto 1972), 43

23 Bamman, 'Patterns of School Attendance,' 227

24 'A Local Superintendent Advises,' in Prentice and Houston, *Family, School and Society*, 118 (emphasis in original)

25 S. Bowles and H. Gintis, *Schooling in Capitalist America* (New York 1976), 26

26 Houston, 'Politics, Schools,' 41

27 See Houston, 'Victorian Origins,' 87-8, and Katz, *People of Hamilton*, 194-206, for some case histories.

28 Davey, 'School Reform,' 306-12, for corroborating evidence; see also Katz, 'Who Went to School?' 284

29 Bamman, 'Patterns of School Attendance,' 228-30. For the class bias of Toronto trustees, see Ross, 'Free School,' 69; Davey, *ibid.*, 296.

30 Bamman, *ibid.*, 240

31 See Barber's report in Prentice and Houston, *Family, School and Society*, 101-3.

32 P. Bourdieu and J.-C. Passeron, *La Reproduction* (Paris 1970), 234 – although the authors also tend to stress the conservative nature of the education system.

33 'A Provincial Reformatory for Incorrigible Pupils,' Nova Scotia Provincial Educational Association Report, 1885, cited in Prentice and Houston, *Family, School and Society*, 283

34 Graff, 'Respected and Profitable Labour,' 62. For a contemporary exploration of this theme, see R. Sennett and J. Cobb, *The Hidden Injuries of Class* (New York 1973).

35 Royal Commission on Industrial Training and Technical Education, *Report of the Commissioners*, Part IV (Ottawa 1913), 1708-9 (hereafter *Report*)

36 Graff, 'Respected and Profitable Labour,' 62

37 M. Robin, *Radical Politics and Canadian Labour* (Kingston 1968), 103

38 E.P. Audet, 'Education in Canada East and Quebec, 1940-75,' in Wilson, *Canadian Education*, 175

39 See *Schooling*, 239 and chap. 9, for the development of their argument.

40 G. Kealey, ed., *Canada Investigates Industrialism* (Toronto 1973), 39-40; cf. R. Stamp, 'Evolving Patterns of Education: English Canada from the 1870s to 1914,' in Wilson, *Canadian Education*, 327; Lawr and Gidney, *Educating Canadians*, 66; Bamman, 'Patterns of School Attendance,' 238-40; Katz, *People of Hamilton*, 303-8

41 See Ivan Illich's remarks about the myth of obligatory schooling in *Deschooling Society*, (New York 1970).

42 'The Bane of Irregular Attendance,' in Prentice and Houston, *Family, School and Society*, 165

43 J.D. Wilson, 'The Ryerson Years in Canada West,' in Wilson, *Canadian Education*, 226

44 For Ontario, see 'The Ambitions of the Teaching Professions,' in Prentice and Houston, *Family, School and Society,* 175-8; for Nova Scotia, 'Educators Debate the Meaning of Incorrigibility,' *ibid.*, 280-6.

45 Words of a prominent Catholic philanthropist, cited in Houston, 'Victorian Origins,' 86

46 Cited in Prentice and Houston, *Family, School and Society*, 282-4

47 Houston, 'Victorian Origins,' 134

48 Kealey, *Canada Investigates Industrialism,* 42. As for Canadian business cycles, after an upswing following the National Policy of 1878 the Canadian economy took a downswing in the 1880s and only fully recovered with the 'wheat boom' of 1896. See Naylor, *Canadian Business*, II.

49 'The Elusive Image of Home,' in Prentice and Houston, *Family, School and Society*, 287. For evidence on Hughes' reforms see Stamp, 'Evolving Patterns,' 318-20. For a variety of views on the new pedagogy, see Lawr and Gidney, *Educating Canadians*, 179-88.

50 Lawr and Gidney, *ibid.*, 165

51 Cited from an 1860 speech by Ryerson in Houston, 'Victorian Origins,' 93

52 A. Prentice, 'Education and the Metaphor of the Family: The Upper Canadian Example,' in Katz and Mattingly, *Education and Social Change*, 116-17

53 Cited in Prentice and Houston, *Family, School and Society*, 250, 261

54 See Stamp, 'Evolving Patterns,' 317; 'The Social Value of Practical Training: Homemakers and Wage Earners,' in Lawr and Gidney, *Educating Canadians*, 171-3; N. Sutherland, 'To Create a Strong and Healthy Race: School Children in the Public Health Movement, 1880-1914,' in Katz and Mattingly, *Education*

and Social Change, 145-6 and 150-1.

55 R. Stamp, 'Education and the Economic and Social Milieu: The English Canadian Scene from the 1870s to 1914,' in Wilson, *Canadian Education*, 300-3

56 Katz, *People of Hamilton*, 290, 303-8

57 On the intensity of the conflict, see S. Jamieson, *Times of Trouble: Labour Unrest and Industrial Conflict in Canada, 1900-66* (Ottawa 1968), especially 65-76, 147-8. For an example of a particular dispute, see J. Morrison. 'Ethnicity and Violence: The Lakehead Freight Handlers before World War I,' in Kealey and Warrian, *Essays*, 143-60.

58 L. Johnson, 'The Development of Class in Canada in the Twentieth Century,' in G. Teeple, ed., *Capitalism and the National Question in Canada* (Toronto 1972), 169, 164-76; cf. Naylor, *Canadian Business*, II, 186-93

59 Cited in D. Young and A. Machinski, *An Historical Survey of Vocational Education in Canada* (Ottawa n.d.), 17-18

60 *Report*, I, 19; see also 9, 13, 23, 63-5

61 Lawr and Gidney, *Educating Canadians*, 137, 128-9

62 *Report*, 47, 1710, 41-3; cf. Bowles and Gintis, *Schooling*, chap. 5

63 'Extending Education to the Adolescent,' in Lawr and Gidney, *Educating Canadians*, 177-8

64 Lawr and Gidney, *ibid.*, 168; cf. 110-12 and 175-6; 196, 117-18. Bourdieu and Passeron, *La Reproduction*, have also pointed out the class role of language in schools.

65 See, for example, G. Martell, 'The Schools, the State and the Corporations,' in Martell, ed., *The Politics of the Canadian Public School* (Toronto 1974), 22. See also Bowles and Gintis, *Schooling*, 287-8. None the less, even today local control is invoked by traditional elites, as was the case in the conservative resistance to consolidation in the sixties (see Part IV of this article).

66 Cited from *Industrial Canada* (July 1913), and TLC *Proceedings* (1913), in R. Stamp, 'Technical Education, the National Policy, and Federal-Provincial Relations in Canadian Education, 1899-1919,' in *Canadian Historical Review*, LII, 4 (Dec. 1971), 417; Lewis cited in Robin, *Radical Politics*, 143, from the report in the *Labor News*, 5 April 1918

67 Stamp, *ibid., passim*

68 Johnson, 'Class,' 169-70; Naylor, *Canadian Business*, II, especially chaps. 10, 11, and 14. For other evidence about the overall open attitude of the Canadian bourgeoisie to foreign investment, see H.V. Nelles, *The Politics of Development* (Toronto 1974), 146, 149. For evidence about educational policy, see P. Ross, 'The Establishment of the PH D at Toronto: A Case of American Influence,' in Katz and Mattingly, *Education and Social Change*, 205-6.

69 Nelles, *ibid.*, 146, 330

70 *Report*, 15, 65; 1705-6, cf. 1729; 2087

71 Besides Robertson, members of the commission included the president of the Royal Society of Canada, two other leading educators, the secretary of the CMA, a member of the Nova Scotia legislature connected with the coal-mining industry, and one representative of labour. See Stamp, 'Technical Education,' 415-16.

72 T.W. Acheson, 'The Changing Social Origins of the Canadian Industrial Elite, 1880-1910,' in G. Porter and R. Cuff, eds., *Enterprise and National Development* (Toronto 1973), 54-5

73 Naylor, *Canadian Business*, I, 233

74 Stamp, 'Technical Education,' 421

75 W.N. Grubb and M. Lazerson, 'Rally 'Round the Workplace: Continuities and Fallacies in Career Education,' in *Harvard Educational Review*, XLV, 4 (Nov. 1975), 458

76 Jamieson, *Times of Trouble*, 158-9; Robin, *Radical Politics*, 118-73

77 Stamp, 'Technical Education,' 422-3

78 Young and Machinski, 'Historical Survey,' 18-19

79 Nelles, *Politics of Development*, 253, 254

80 *Report*, 1678

81 Nelles, *Politics of Development*, 255

82 Johnson, 'Class,' 146-7

83 For the reaction of farmers to rural consolidation, see Stamp, 'Education and the Economic and Social Milieu,' 298-300 and 304-5. For their reaction to the conservation movement, see Nelles, *Politics of Development*, 192.

84 For the program of radical parties, see A. Charpentier, 'Le mouvement politique ouvrier de Montréal (1883-1929),' in P. Harvey, ed., *Aspects historiques du mouvement ouvrier au Québec* (Montreal 1973), 151. For Marchand's remarks, see his speech to the Quebec legislature, 28 Dec. 1897, cited in a paper by James Kelly on the history of education in Quebec in the twentieth century, unpublished, presented for a course at the Université du Québec à Montréal.

85 Stamp, 'Evolving Patterns,' 320

86 'Organized Labour Protests: The Testimony of D.J. O'Donoghue (1891),' cited in Prentice and Houston, *Family, School and Society*, 277-8

87 B. Palmer, 'Give Us the Road and We Will Run It! The Social and Cultural Matrix of an Emerging Labour Movement,' in Kealey and Warrian, *Essays*, 113-24; see also Bowles and Gintis, *Schooling*, 59-63, 73-9, 182-6, for a similar discussion in the American case.

88 See the evidence and thinking of the Putman-Weir Report, *Survey of the School System of British Columbia* (Victoria 1925); see also Lawr and Gidney, *Educating Canadians*, 213-19.

89 Lawr and Gidney, *ibid.*, 220; cf. R.S. Patterson, 'The Establishment of Progres-

sive Education in Alberta,' unpublished PH D thesis, Michigan State University, 1968

90 Stamp, 'Technical Education,' 423; for corroborating evidence, see Young and Machinski, 'Historical Survey,' 21-2; for the educators' rhetoric, see Lawr and Gidney, *ibid.*, 221-4; for enrolment figures, see G.W. Bertram, *The Contribution of Education to Economic Growth*, Staff Study no. 12, Economic Council of Canada (Ottawa 1968), Table 18, p. 30; for junior high schools, see R.S. Patterson, 'Society and Education during the Wars and Their Interlude: 1914-45,' in Wilson, *Canadian Education*, 372.

91 Lawr and Gidney, *ibid.*, 202-6. See also the 1934 King report in British Columbia for an illustration of the way consolidation would increase the control of the provincial Department of Education.

92 Patterson, *ibid.*, 381. For the postponement of other reforms, see *ibid.*, 372, and Young and Machinski, 'Historical Survey,' 23.

93 Johnson, 'Class,' 170-1, pointed out that 'with the huge expansion of physical plant created in the over-speculation of 1920-30, the basic facilities were established which would allow their [manual labourers'] incorporation within the capital intensive industrial sector when economic conditions warranted it. The depression delayed that process for a decade ... It was the Second World War, and C.D. Howe's program of industrialization and rapid expansion of the capitalist sector through guaranteed wartime profits, which finally completed the transformation of the Canadian economy to industrial capitalism and finally incorporated most of Canadian labour into advanced modes of industrial capitalist production.'

94 J.L. Lind, *The Learning Machine: A Hard Look at Toronto Schools* (Toronto 1974), 148

95 Johnson, 'Class,' 164-76, 178

96 J. Porter, *The Vertical Mosaic* (Toronto 1965), 46-50, 152

97 Johnson, 'Class,' 167-8. See also the study by D. Brunelle, 'La structure occupationnelle de la main-d'œuvre québecoise 1951-1971,' in *Sociologie et Sociétés*, VII, 2 (Nov. 1975), 83, where he also documents this situation, yet warns against confusing the situation of technical and professional workers with proletarianization. G. Carchedi has also made this distinction. In defining proletarianization as the disappearance of the function of capital he has explained how dequalification, proletarianization, and the proliferation of new control positions affect simultaneously the new middle class. See 'On the Economic Identification of the New Middle Class,' in *Economy and Society*, IV, 1 (Feb. 1975), 63-6.

98 See R. Deaton, 'The Fiscal Crisis of the State,' in D. Roussopoulos, ed., *The Political Economy of the State* (Montreal 1973), 47; see also p. 48 for the discussion that follows.

99 Porter, *Vertical Mosaic*, 152-3
100 Johnson, 'Class,' 173-4. There is a growing body of literature on blue-collar dissatisfaction and resistance. See, for example, S. Faber, 'Working Class Organization,' in *Our Generation*, XI, 3 (Summer 1976) or Martin Glaberman's review of *Labour and Monopoly Capital* by Harry Braverman in the same issue.
101 See J. O'Connor, *The Fiscal Crisis of the State* (New York 1973), for a development of this argument with concrete application to the United States. Johnson, *ibid.*, 172-4, advances a similar argument for Canada.
102 C. Gonick, *Inflation or Depression* (Toronto 1975), 152
103 Deaton, 'Fiscal Crisis,' 35
104 *Ibid.*, 38-9
105 See G. Stevenson's article in this volume.
106 Cited in Lawr and Gidney, *Educating Canadians*, 254
107 See Martell, 'Schools,' 9 and 11-12; cf. the study by C. Reich and S. Zeigler, City of Toronto Board of Education, Research Department, *Report 102* (April 1972).
108 Martell, *ibid.*, 11
109 Quoted in O. Hull and B. MacFarlane, *Transition from School to Work*, Report no. 10, Department of Labour (Dec. 1962, Ottawa 1965) 69
110 *Ibid.*, 77
111 Cameron, *Schools for Ontario*, 167-8; see also Lind, *Learning Machine*, 71-3
112 Bowles and Gintis, *Schooling*, 212 and chap. 8 in general
113 Carchedi, 'Economic Identification,' 83-4, n 81
114 Young and Machinski, 'Historical Survey,' 46
115 Cited in Lawr and Gidney, *Educating Canadians*, 244-5
116 J. Dennison *et al.*, *The Impact of Community Colleges* (Vancouver 1975), especially chaps. 5 and 6, pp. 184, 45-6; cf. 'School Consolidation in the Sixties' in Lawr and Gidney, *ibid.*, 250-1
117 A. Cohen, 'The Political Context of Childhood: Leaders and Anti-Leaders in a Changing Newfoundland Community,' in E. Zureik and R. Pike, eds., *Socialization and Values in Canadian Society* (Toronto 1975), I, 179-80. For an idea of the contradictions this entails within the working class, see Sennett and Cobb, *Hidden Injuries*, especially 27.
118 Dennison *et al.*, *Impact of Community Colleges*, especially 61, 87, 107-9; cf. Hull and MacFarlane, *Transition*, 64
119 See Young and Machinski, 'Historical Survey,' 46; cf. p. 35 for the general argument, as well as Lind, *Learning Machine*, 58; Gonick, *Inflation or Depression*, 110-29; Grubb and Lazerson, 'Rally 'Round the Workplace'; Cameron, *Schools for Ontario*, 165.
120 See Bertram, *Contribution of Education*, 58, where the author points out that

educational changes in the United States have not led to changes in the income gap between the United States and Canada, yet he goes on to affirm (p. 62) that increased investment in education will lead to a narrowing of the income gap.

121 Lockhart, 'Future Failure: The Unanticipated Consequences of Educational Planning,' in Zureik and Pike, *Socialization*, II, 195-9

122 Dennison *et al.*, *Impact of Community Colleges*, 87-8, 108

123 For the recommendations of the Nadeau report, see *Le Collège: Rapport sur l'état et les besoins de l'enseignement collégial* (Quebec 1975). For a discussion of some of their implications, see D. Ethier, 'Le rapport Nadeau ou le programme "de crise" du Ministère de l'Éducation du Québec,' in *Chroniques*, nos. 8-9 (Aug.-Sept. 1975), 33-46. For evidence of what 'deskilling' and therapy have meant in Toronto schools, see Martell, 'Schools.' I am obliged to George Smith for first directing my attention to the concept of 'deskilling.'

124 Brunelle, 'La structure,' 78

125 *Le Collège*, 38-9, 48-9; Grubb and Lazerson, 'Rally 'Round the Workplace,' 473. I am obliged to Marvin Lazerson of the Foundations of Education Department, UBC, for a discussion where this idea became clarified. See also Lockhart, 'Future Failure,' 203.

126 *Le Collège*, 96-7, 130-2, 154-70

127 Stamp, 'Government and Education in Post-War Canada,' in Wilson, *Canadian Education*, 449-50

128 For accounts of provincial fiscal reform and school consolidation, see Cameron, *Schools for Ontario*, especially 53-104, and chap. 10; and Lind, *Learning Machine*, 207-14.

129 H. Stevenson, 'Crisis and Continuum: Public Education in the Sixties,' in Wilson, *Canadian Education*, 497-8

130 Cameron, *Schools for Ontario*, 153

131 Lind, *Learning Machine*, 181-96

132 See Martell, 'Schools,' 24-9, for a discussion of the trade-offs.

133 For examples, see the articles in Martell, *Politics of the Canadian Public School*, 172-257. This strategy was part of the document that the CEQ proposed to its members in 1972. Centrale des Enseignants du Québec, *L'Ecole au service de la Classe Dominante* (Quebec 1972), 30-6. The Mouvement de Démocratisation Scolaire and increased support for the Common Front strike of 1976 in Quebec are other signs of this process.

14

Art and accumulation: the Canadian state and the business of art

ROBIN ENDRES

In 1949 five cultural organizations received $21,000 from the federal government, which also gave $356,876 to fairs and exhibitions and $115,200 to military associations and institutes.[1] In 1975 the federal government gave $57 million to the arts (of which $23.7 million came from the Canada Council).[2] The background to this extraordinary increase in state financing of the arts can be briefly sketched, beginning with the formation in 1949 of the Royal Commission on National Development in the Arts, Letters and Sciences (known as the Massey Commission), which heard and received briefs from hundreds of groups and individuals and reported in 1951. Its major recommendation was the establishment of a national arts council, modelled on the Arts Council of Great Britain, which would carry out the threefold purpose of subsidizing the arts in Canada, promoting Canada's cultural image abroad through tours and exchanges, and acting as a national commission for UNESCO. The Canada Council was duly formed in 1957 with a $50 million endowment, and proceeded to engender a new era of state spending on the arts and a new area of state bureaucracy. The beginning of the end of this development came in 1975 when the government partly subsidized the Council for Business and the Arts in Canada, a move which indicates a trend away from state and towards private spending, and an overall cutback in subsidies.

This article will explore the motives of the state in financing the arts, examine the effects on the artists and the public, and outline a possible strategy. It will attempt to answer such questions as: Was it (and is it) necessary for the state to exercise control, through funding, over potentially disruptive artists? Was it (and is it) necessary to react to the cultural demands of the Canadian working class? In what ways can funding the arts be profitable for the bourgeoisie? What are the relative strengths of the accumulation and legitimation functions of the state in this area?

Works of art are commodities. Their production and consumption are economic facts. However, the effects which works of art have on us, the audience, are ideological; they are part of the ideological superstructure. Both aspects of art are related in exceedingly complex ways, the mysteries of which have been pondered by Marxist aestheticians since Marx himself raised the question in the Preface to the *Critique of Political Economy* in 1859. When we consider the issue of state financing of the arts, the two functions of the capitalist state, accumulation and legitimation, are in this field likewise related in complex ways. Just as it is possible to stress the content of art (its 'eternal message') and overlook the social context in which it is produced, it is possible to overstress the hegemonic benefits to the state when it funds the arts. At first glance, it would appear that the major role of the state here is legitimation. It is well known that the live performing arts are immensely unprofitable.[3] There are certainly historical precedents for the predisposition of states to build cultural monuments to commemorate themselves. Artists are frequently mystified as an iconoclastic, anarchic force, an element so inherently disruptive to society that the state must co-opt them. The main reason for stressing the legitimation function, however, comes from the large body of theory (mostly Marxist) which emphasizes the ways both the state and the ruling class (through, for example, ownership of the media) use ideology as a means of social control.

John Porter, in his discussion of media elites in Canada (which with slight modification could be extended to apply to the artistic elite) gives an adequate summary of this view: 'Besides providing cohesion and unity, value systems give a sense of rightness to the social order and legitimacy for particular practices and usages, including class and power structures, within a given society ... To ensure that a value system does not become so vague that it ceases to perform its social function of providing cohesion, it is necessary to build into certain social roles the task of restating and generalizing values. Individuals who have a particular facility with the written and spoken word and who *can manipulate symbols* assume these ideological roles.'[4]

Althusser, building on Gramsci's theory of the hegemony of the ruling class, distinguishes between the repressive and the ideological apparatuses of the state (which he calls 'ISAS'). The former, such as the military and police, maintain class society through violence; the latter's function is to aid in the reproduction of labour power through 'a reproduction of its submission to the rules of the established order, i.e. a reproduction of submission to the ruling ideology for the workers, and a reproduction of the ability to manipulate the ruling ideology correctly for the agents of exploitation.'[5] Since culture is one of the ISAS which Althusser lists, he would probably claim, for example, that television reproduces workers' submission, and so-called 'high culture' (ballet, opera, classical theatre, and music) reproduces the ability of the ruling class to rule.

These and similar theories are valuable analyses. Their assumption, however, that social control and the reproduction of labour power are sufficient benefits for the state to engage in financing of the arts, does not give the whole picture, and therefore cannot yield an adequate strategy. In Canada, ideological manipulation of the cultural needs of the working class is carried out so well by the American-owned electronic media that there is no need for the state to play a role. Between the Second World War and the upsurge of left cultural nationalism – the period of greatest spending – artists tended to be politically conservative. Thus, with one possible exception (the Canada Council's Senior Arts Grants, which are subsidies to a handful of individual artists and which represent a tiny percentage of its overall budget), each state expenditure on the arts has directly or indirectly fostered accumulation of capital and/or has been remunerative for the state itself. In this field, where one would consider legitimation to be the primary function of the state, there has been virtually no 'social expenses' such as welfare payments constitute. Of course, the legitimation function cannot be entirely overlooked by the state. To some extent and in limited ways, funding the arts has at least curtailed the mass emigration of Canadian artists to the United States and England. The state's main legitimation function, however, appears to be promoting its own image (and that of those corporate elites whose patronage to the arts the state obviates) as 'civilized' and 'cultured.' Ultimately there can be almost no payment to the arts which does not foster accumulation and which does not also make the state look good and, to some extent, give 'a sense of rightness to the social order.'

In periods of state expansion (of spending and bureaucracy) both functions operate at a maximum, a situation which characterized the last twenty-five years or so. However, in periods of cutbacks in state spending, and when, for reasons largely peculiar to the live performing arts, the accumulation function becomes limited, there is a possible crisis of legitimacy. Were the state able or willing to finance the arts purely for legitimation purposes, no such crisis would occur. There are few areas where the state's relationship to the capitalist class is more mystified than in the field of the arts. As long as arts spending is increasing, the state can make, and gain credibility for, claims for its humanitarianism, its concerns for the spiritual richness of the nation, for encouraging the creative potential of the country's artists, and for making it possible for everyone to appreciate the arts. When spending decreases, which means that it is less profitable for capital, there is some danger that these claims will be exposed as the rags and tatters of bourgeois ideology which they in fact are.

There are several ways in which the Canadian state, through subsidies to the arts, directly or indirectly fosters accumulation. The building of cultural hardware – chiefly the provincial arts centres or 'regional theatres' – like the building of community colleges and universities in the sixties, constitutes direct accumulation. Indirectly, the state fosters accumulation by giving grants to arts organizations rather than artists. Since the former are made up of members of the corporate elite, the Canada Council gives them public money to administer as they see fit, thus freeing them from having to make donations themselves. An indirect accumulation function is also fulfilled by various efforts by the state to make corporate giving attractive through a network of tax loopholes. Subsidizing annual festivals or financing the arts in small towns helps to attract investment and stimulates the tourist industry. Finally, funding the arts actually benefits the state itself through the returns of direct and indirect taxes.

DIRECT ACCUMULATION: CULTURAL HARDWARE

We can begin to ascertain the nature of the state's accumulation function by examining the assumptions of the Massey Report and the discrepancies between what many of the submissions requested and what the Canadian people actually got. Subsequent government publications issued by the Canada Council also illuminate the issues. The Massey Report, of course, is not exactly a document which throws crumbs to the masses in order to disguise the cakes it offers to the corporations. One of its legitimate and praiseworthy concerns was the attempt to limit American cultural domination in Canada and the notorious 'brain drain' of the late forties and fifties when talented Canadian scholars and artists flocked to the United States. The following statement has often been quoted by left cultural nationalists to indicate that the cultural elite of the day was 'progressive': 'a vast and disproportionate amount of material coming from a single alien source may stifle rather than stimulate our own creative effort; and, passively accepted without any standards of comparison, this may weaken critical faculties. We are now spending millions to maintain a national independence which would be nothing but an empty shell without a vigorous and distinctive cultural life. We have seen that we have its elements in traditions and in our history; we have made important progress, often aided by American generosity. We must not be blind, however, to the very present danger of permanent dependence.'[6] However, a more pervasive (and curiously antiquated) concern of the report, coming as it did shortly after the end of the war, was that a national culture is a vital aspect of national defence. Churchill, the authors say, would not have been able to rally the British people to their self-sacrificing war effort had he not been able to appeal to a centuries-old cultural tradition.

Although this concept of culture as defence is dated, its broader implication, that the state should finance culture in order to foster national unity, has been and continues to be a central alleged purpose of state subsidies. Both the Massey Report and subsequent funding patterns of the Canada Council assume, however, that the way to develop national unity through the arts is to emulate established European models of ballet, opera, music, and theatre, rather than to fund local, regional indigenous cultures and then send them touring the nation. Closely related to 'national unity' is 'Canada's cultural image abroad,' the promotion of which is one of the founding principles of the Canada Council. Twenty-five years later these aims have, in their own terms (but probably not in anyone else's), come to fruition. A handful of principal dancers with the National Ballet have become media stars, photographed constantly for the press and interviewed regularly on television and radio. Two of them, Karen Kain and Frank Augustyn, were invited to dance with the Bolshoi, and ten others were asked by Nureyev himself to dance in Paris. The *nature* of the state's legitimation function – the ways in which 'national unity' and 'Canada's cultural image abroad' are promoted – is itself a function of capital accumulation.

Ballet, theatre, and music, in order to measure up to the 'best' of European models, need training schools, large operating budgets, and, above all, large performing areas in large auditoriums. Significantly, the majority of theatre groups who submitted briefs argued against the construction of new theatre buildings. At the time of the report, most small cities and large towns in Canada had playhouses which had been built in the late nineteenth century for touring players. Many had become movie houses, but several were being used by local amateur dramatic groups. Some felt that even funds spent to restore existing facilities would be less useful than giving money to the artists themselves; others were adamant that if funds *were* to be spent on buildings, they should only finance restorations: 'There is no doubt that the expenditure of adequate sums of money could restore suitable and numerous playhouses, but whether this would mean a renaissance of the theatre in Canada has been sharply questioned. *Les Compagnons de St-Laurent* agreed with the Western Stage Society that the construction of theatres and halls on a grand scale is not necessary or advisable but that much could be done to make existing accommodation more suitable for theatrical performances if competent advice on this matter were available from a central agency.'[7]

These recommendations were, in a word, ignored, and under the guise of the need for 'better facilities' the state financed the building of one or more arts centres or regional theatres in every province except Newfoundland. Even Prince Edward Island has its own concrete cultural white elephant, the Confederation Centre, whose imposing and pretentious architecture is no doubt intimidating to most islanders but not to wealthy tourists. A subject of much well-known controversy is the fact that such institutions tend to hire British or American artistic directors, or even directors from Toronto, who are, it is claimed in many quarters, unresponsive to the cultural needs of the community.

The case of Newfoundland is instructive. Throughout the country, dedicated theatre people devoted to creating new, experimental, and often politically radical Canadian plays rejected the large theatre companies and formed what are known as 'alternate theatres' to distinguish them from 'regional theatres.' In Newfoundland there are three small theatre groups, one which tours commercial comedies, a satirical revue (Codco), and a militant and very progressive group which creates plays in small communities based on local political issues (the Newfoundland Mummers' Troupe). However, since they are the *only* theatre groups in the province, they can hardly be called 'alternate' theatre. The secretary of state decided that, once again, what was needed was a big building housing a regional theatre company, to which the existing groups would be the alternative. When the three groups joined together and submitted a brief demanding artistic control, the project was dropped, at least temporarily. Newfoundland is the last province where state subsidies to the arts can directly foster accumulation of capital through cultural hardware. Therefore it is unlikely that such a building will not, sooner or later, be constructed to display, for example, the National Ballet to the local bourgeoisie and the tourists.

The case of the National Arts Centre is even more decisive proof that the state was more interested in accumulation than in responding to the stated needs of theatre groups. According to the Massey Report: 'Repeatedly at our sessions throughout Canada the question of a National Theatre was discussed. Almost invariably the view was expressed that a National Theatre should consist not in an elaborate structure built in Ottawa or elsewhere, but rather in a company or companies of players who would present the living drama in even the most remote communities of Canada and who would in addition give professional advice to local amateur dramatic societies ... It would, of course, be disastrous to conceive of the National Theatre merely as a playhouse erected in the capital or in one of the larger centres.'

In its proposals for the aims of the Canada Council, the report says nothing about buildings, either regional arts centres or a National Arts Centre. It recommends 'The encouragement of Canadian music, drama and ballet (through the appropriate voluntary organizations ...) by such means as the underwriting of tours, the commissioning of music for events of national importance, and the establishment of awards to young people of promise whose talents have been revealed in national festivals of music, drama or the ballet.'[8] That the state ignored the warnings of the Massey Report concerning buildings is one of the few indications of disagreements within the bourgeoisie as far as culture is concerned. What the Canadian people got was a 'playhouse in the capital,' whose touring record is dismal, and which, most of us would agree with the Massey Report, is a disaster. Thus, in the case of the state financing cultural facilities, the direct accumulation function was primary, the legitimation function fairly limited to making the state and the elitist patrons of high culture 'look good,' more in their own eyes than in the eyes of the public. The artists were not pacified with concrete buildings, and their protests, over the years, have gained some measure of public support, including the beginnings of support from the labour movement.

Nevertheless, *direct* capital accumulation is a limited function of the state in financing the arts. The state cannot continue to build arts centres the way it can roads or military hardware. Empty auditoriums would assuredly be an embarrassment, not to mention being unprofitable from the point of view of *indirect* capital accumulation.

Before discussing the complexities of indirect accumulation, however, it can be noted that it is a little-known fact that the Canada Council Act made provision, in addition to its $50 million Endowment Fund to subsidize the arts, for a University Capital Grants Fund of an additional $50 million. This fund, which was intended for the building of universities and community colleges, was paid to the council by the minister of finance out of the Consolidated Revenue Fund – and was entirely spent by 1972. [9]

INDIRECT ACCUMULATION: SUBSIDIZING THE PATRON

The United States is the only country where corporate funding of the arts far exceeds state funding, a fact which the Massey Report attributed to its immense wealth, claiming that 'other countries cannot afford to follow their example.'[10] Certainly there are many Canadian-owned corporations wealthy enough to finance a large share of the arts in Canada. Nor did it ever seem to occur to either the authors of the report or the cultural bureaucrats that at the very least American-owned subsidiaries should contribute a proportion of what the parent company donates in the United States. Taxation benefits aside, there are considerable intangible benefits to corporations, in terms of corporate image, to be gained from donating to the arts. Nevertheless, until very recently, the Canadian state has made few efforts to encourage the private sector to give to the arts. On the contrary, the practice has been to take public money and give it to the so-called 'voluntary arts organizations' (or arts boards) to administer as they see fit, with virtually no accountability to the state, let alone the public. Although members of these organizations are responsible for private fund-raising (mostly they raise funds from each other through a network of corporate friendships, for a particular 'worthy cause') this constitutes only 11 per cent of the operating funds for the live performing arts.[11] Funding boards rather than artists is not only a way of preserving 'establishment' forms of culture; it is also an indirect means of capital accumulation since it obviates the necessity of corporate subsidies.

There is no confusion or mystification in the Massey Report on this question. It is simply taken as a given throughout that not artists, but voluntary organizations (perceived as composed of hard-working, self-sacrificing citizens), should receive state money. 'We consider that the relation of voluntary effort to governmental activity is the focal point of the work of this Commission ... the democratic form of government is made practicable through the work of voluntary organizations ... ' Judging from the alacrity with which the authors of the report responded to the demands for money from such organizations, the latter must have been quite convincing in their claim that they could not raise money from the private sector – that is, from each other. In outlining its reasons for recommending the establishment of the Canada Council, the report states: 'There are in Canada many voluntary bodies whose work is of national importance but whose resources are inadequate for their growth or even for their survival ... There does not now exist in Canada any Board or Council to advise the Government on this matter ... We believe that a Board or Council competent to advise the government on its present and future subvention lists for voluntary organizations concerned with the arts and letters and with the humanities and social sciences would be a useful innovation and an administrative improvement.' The report's first, and presumably most important, proposal is 'the strengthening, by money grants and in other ways, of certain of the Canadian voluntary organizations on whose active well-being the work of the Council will in large measure depend.'[12] Once again, we have the state giving a subsidy to the capitalist class, then expanding its own bureaucracy to do the paperwork and establish the myths of legitimacy necessary to disguise the real nature of the subsidy.

INDIRECT ACCUMULATION: STIMULATING LOCAL INDUSTRY

Another indirect capital accumulation function is the stimulation of local industry and the ability of a 'cultural drawing card' in smaller cities to attract investment. According to an American study: 'A ... materialistic set of indirect benefits which flows from the arts is the advantage that the availability of cultural activity confers on business in its vicinity – the fact that it brings customers to shops, hotels, restaurants and bars. On a national level, distinguished performing arts organizations may serve, analogously, as a significant tourist attraction.'[13] According to a Canadian study undertaken for the Canada Council by a firm of management consultants: 'there is repeated evidence ... that industry, especially larger organizations, welcomes the presence of the performing arts and that the arts can be a major source of strength for the business community. Increasingly, with rising standards of education and widening interest in the arts, companies find it easier to attract young executives (and their wives) to communities where the arts contribute significantly to the quality of life. This factor assumes increasing importance as industry tends in many cases to decentralize to smaller communities.'[14] Clearly, attracting capital will be a major criterion of funding at the municipal level in smaller cities: 'many Maritime cities were trying to attract industry and consequently the main rationale was to improve the cultural environment to satisfy corporate executives and their families.'[15] Again, the type of art produced and performed when this is the motivation will be unlikely to be responsive to the indigenous cultural needs of the community.

The most striking example is certainly Stratford, Ontario, transformed from an obscure rural community to a thriving industrial and tourist centre by the Stratford Shakespearean Festival. The festival receives the largest single subsidy of all the performing arts organizations (it has been said that their costume budget alone would finance two or three 'alternate theatres'), yet it remains inaccessible to the majority of Canadians. Even people living in Toronto find the costs of transportation, expensive tickets, and accommodation prohibitive.

INDIRECT ACCUMULATION: PROVIDING TAXATION BENEFITS

A final method of indirect accumulation concerns various taxation benefits available to wealthy individuals and corporations donating to the arts. In its 1969 brief, *Taxation and the Arts* , the Canada Council began with its usual alleged concern for the fate of the poor artist, then proceeded to list a series of recommended corporate tax write-offs. Of eighteen proposals, only six applied to individual artists, and were intended to redress minimally some rather egregious hardships for self-employed artists rather than to aid them materially. It was proposed, for example, that artists be allowed to average their income over five years, deduct expenses of materials and tuition fees (the latter already a right for all post-secondary students), and be exempt from federal and provincial sales tax on the purchase of materials and the sale of works of art, and from import duties on materials.

The other twelve proposals constituted some extremely generous inducements to the wealthy donor. For example, corporations and individuals would deduct 100 per cent of the value of works of art donated to museums and galleries, both privately and publicly owned. Funds given to the arts would be considered charitable donations, permitted 20 per cent deduction, extended up to five years if the gift exceeds the maximum price. Businesses which purchase works of art for their premises would be eligible for unspecified tax benefits, and the council recommends that 'a specific provision be made in the income tax regulations to codify the present practices' because 'business enterprises generally are unaware of the tax benefits which can be derived from purchases of this kind.' Works of art are excellent investments, especially in times of recession, because their value appreciates. The Canada Council, however, advocated that 'sculptures, murals, architectural engravings and other artistic works incorporated into buildings should be eligible for *depreciation* for income tax purposes at a rate of 20%.' Another series of proposals concerned bequests, suggesting, for example, that bequests be exempt from estate taxes and succession duties even when they will not be received by public institutions until after the deaths of the donor's children.

The most generous proposal was that gifts or donations of a 'capital nature' should be 150 per cent deductible. 'Projects of a capital nature' means anything except 'projects of a labour nature,' that is, anything which is not a donation to an actual artist. 'Essentially, the type of projects envisaged should be of a capital nature. Expenditures to cover the cost of materials in the production of new operas, plays and ballets would qualify for the 150% deduction proposed on the same basis as outlays made towards museums, opera houses, art galleries, cultural centres, or other similar projects. Extension of existing facilities should equally qualify. Contributions of important works of art and other objects to furnish or adorn such centres should also be eligible.' Since this 150 per cent deduction would mean that corporate profits could actually increase as a result of 'donations' to the arts, the council acknowledged the fact and proposed some limitations. The phrasing of its qualifications is instructive: 'For individuals whose marginal personal income tax rates may rise as high as 80%, some limitations are necessary to ensure that contributions do not have the effect of actually increasing residual income after taxes and after the special deduction. While *some tenable arguments might even be made to the contrary*, we are also of the view that *at least some element of private generosity* must be involved.'[16] Nevertheless, there can be no doubt that a corporate tax lawyer could easily have juggled enough of the council's recommendations to allow his client to 'actually increase residual income after taxes.'

Not all of the Canada Council's recommendations have been legislated; however, they are interesting from the point of view of the extent to which the state *desires* to help capital. One piece of tax legislation which has been given royal assent and for which proclamation is forthcoming is Bill C-33. This bill, 'an act respecting the export from Canada of cultural property,' is designed to encourage individuals and corporations to sell or donate works of 'national importance' to Canadian rather than foreign museums, galleries, and so on.[17] Again, 'works of national importance' refers to just about everything – cultural, archaeological, historical, and other works and collections' – including works less than fifty years old, made by living persons. The bill specified initially that all works should be designated as of national importance by yet another group of cultural bureaucrats, the Canadian Cultural Property Review Board. Then it was amended so that works did not have to be on the review board's list to qualify – although the board, of course, will continue to function.

The loopholes include exemption from capital gains tax for sales of works, and up to a 100 per cent deduction of income for works donated – in the year of the donation and the preceding year. Since works of art appreciate, and since the larger the corporation (or the wealthier the individual) owning them, the bigger the rewards from this tax legislation, a corporation collecting Canadian art can increase profits considerably through carefully selected donations. And if executives of such corporations sit on publicly funded boards of galleries and museums, they are in an optimal position to make Canadian 'national treasures' put hard cash into their own coffers. The artist who produced the work has in all probability received little or no subsidization from the state and little or no profit from the sale of his work.

Corporations, like the state, use rhetoric which indicates that legitimacy is a more important consideration than profit. G. Hamilton Southam, of the newspaper Southams and director-general of the National Arts Centre, states it rather baldly: 'Capitalism is now in the position of having to justify

itself, not only in respect to other economic systems, but, even more important, in respect to its own people and to itself. It is important to stress this
point. For most major private contributors and industrial or corporate arts
supporters I am sure this, rather than possible tax or other immediate benefits, welcome as they may be, is the deciding factor.'[18] He may be right to
some extent. However, we may be certain that without various material incentives provided by the state there would be substantially less 'good corporate citizenship' in the field of spending on the arts. If corporations are so
desperate to shine their image with a few ballets and operas, why has private spending decreased substantially in recent years? Between 1972 and
1975, corporate giving to the arts increased overall ($6 million in 1974, rep-
resenting 10 per cent of corporate charitable donations), but decreased as a
percentage of pre-tax profits from 1.5 to 0.8 per cent. It was partly as a result of this decrease that the state began increasing taxation benefits.

HOW THE STATE BENEFITS

A significant and little-known aspect of state financing of the arts in Canada is that such funding is remunerative for the state itself. The most obvious example is the often very high rent paid by performing arts companies
for the state-owned buildings in which they rehearse and perform. A Canada Council study on the economic impact of the Toronto Symphony Orchestra, the Royal Winnipeg Ballet, and the Théâtre du Nouveau Monde
concludes that 'support of the arts comprises no net burden on the public
treasuries since tax receipts from artistic endeavours, at the very least, balance the funds dispersed.' Direct taxes paid back to all three levels of government include property tax, personal income tax of employees, taxes paid
by suppliers on materials and services, amusement taxes on ticket sales, and
annual depreciation on capital assets. Additional monies are returned to the
state through government services, chiefly postage and electricity. Also,
there is an indirect taxation multiplier effect, whereby spending of disposa-
ble income by performers and other employees results in indirect taxes.
Thus, for example, returns to each level of government of direct and indirect taxation and government services, expressed as a ratio of grants to the
Royal Winnipeg Ballet in 1971-2 were 74 per cent of the federal grant, 194
per cent of the provincial grant, and 70 per cent of the municipal grant. The
returns constituted 96 per cent of combined state subsidies. The figures for
the Toronto Symphony are more surprising. Returns to the state were 191
per cent of the federal grant, 225 per cent of the provincial grant, and 96 per
cent of the municipal grant, for a total return of 185 per cent of all subsidies. This represented a return to the state in 1972-3 of $735,000.

The study also documents some of the indirect capital accumulation of these three organizations. For example, 'associated costs of attendance' such as babysitting fees, dinner, liquor, and transportation account for almost half the ticket cost. 'Residual economic multiplier effects' are expenditures such as income spent by employees minus direct and indirect taxation, funds paid out in purchases by the organization, and the various associated attendance costs paid by the audience. If these factors are included in the case of the Toronto Symphony, 'the resulting grand total contribution to the economy is seen to amount to nearly four (3.94) times the sum total of grants received by the organization,' or roughly $2,615,000 for the year.[19]

Another area in which subsidizing the arts is remunerative for the state is the investment possibilities in purchasing works of art. The visual arts are far less capable than the performing arts of providing the state with opportunities to foster capital accumulation or to benefit directly itself. Subsidies to individual artists in the form of grants or a minimum income constitute purely social expenses. Therefore, 'faced with the alternatives of subsidy or purchase, government ... has chosen to buy.'[20] In 1973, after selling its modest collection of Canadian art (purchased for $90,000 and sold for $120,000) to the Department of External Affairs, the Canada Council set up the Art Bank to purchase works from Canadian artists. As of the fall of 1975, the Art Bank had spent $5 million on 5500 paintings, graphics, and sculptures, all of which are available for lease to government offices at one per cent per month of the purchase price. About half have been rented, almost all to government offices in Ottawa, bringing in annual rental fees of $175,000. This represents an internal transfer inside the state. The real investment, though, is in the future, when at least 15 per cent of these works, it is estimated, will 'survive' – that is, appreciate.

The two ostensible purposes of the Art Bank, enthusiastically proclaimed in government brochures, are to help the artists and make art works more accessible to the public. The latter aim is surely a travesty, with half of the works buried in a warehouse and the other half mostly in the offices of government bureaucrats wherein the public seldom ventures (most government buildings do not have large foyers). Institutions in which art would be seen by the public, such as hospitals and schools, do not qualify to lease because they are in the jurisdiction of the provinces. Furthermore, amassing a collection of Canadian art in Ottawa does very little to help the artist: 'for the artist, purchase provides a windfall but it offers no sustained support for his work ... In fact, purchase does not even ensure exposure.' 'Windfall' is an aptly chosen word. 'For the six hundred or so artists who have been purchased it has meant only an average of $1,300 or so a year additional income. Yet the majority of purchases have been under $500, a thin layer of jam, indeed.'[21] Judging from reproductions of examples of art purchased, the taste of government art buyers is identical to that of corporations – the majority are large, abstract, or 'minimal' paintings and sculptures which have, in fact, been labelled 'corporate art.' Artists are thus subtly encouraged (and it is difficult to blame them, given the fact that only a very few make a living by their work) to create works too large and expensive for average houses and apartments, works drained of content and destined to be non-distracting decorative designs on office walls. Most criticism of the Art Bank has come from the right (especially from petit-bourgeois gallery owners when the government buys directly from the artists' studios) because of fears it will inflate the Canadian art market. That there has been no movement of the left to demand genuine accessibility or a guaranteed income for artists allows the state to continue to benefit and mask this process with the most transparent of legitimation claims.

THE STATE BUREAUCRACY

A few words on the nature of the state bureaucracy in the arts field are in order here, although little analysis from a Marxist point of view has been done in this country on the meaning of bureaucracy. The Canada Council is an 'independant' body which reports to the cabinet through the secretary of state. The chairman, vice-chairman, and nineteen-member board are all appointed by the Governor-in-Council, and the council appoints and pays employees and technical and professional advisers. Its original endowment fund yields about $4 million annually and it receives an annual grant from the government – $40,987,000 in 1975. Since 1968, however, some of the traditional areas of the council's jurisdiction have been taken over by the secretary of state. For example, the National Museums of Canada Corporation was established in 1972, and funds for films and publishing are administered by agencies directly under the government. 'Political observers saw the changes in the Council as yet further evidence of Trudeau's streamlining of the government, the effort to establish parallel management in all branches. According to insiders, the Council was intended to become like the National Research Council, with the humanities and social sciences separated from the arts.'[22] Although directors of the council have always been 'cultivated' men in the sense of having familiarity with the 'high culture' of Europe, their advisers have increasingly tended to be technocrats with degrees in economics, political science, and sociology.

The relationship between the three levels of government also has interesting features and also needs further analysis. It had been the intention of the Massey Report that the federal government would subsidize the 'professional' arts, the municipalities the more amateur, community-oriented projects, with provincial governments somewhere in between. This has hardly been the case. Instead, funding by the Canada Council has bestowed credibility on the recipients, thus qualifying them for provincial and municipal funding as well. The funding patterns of all three levels of government differ by only a few percentage points. 'Without exception, municipalities did not assist individuals because of the difficulty of evaluation. They preferred organizations that had a long-standing reputation within the community, and they were not particularly disposed to new and amateur groups ... when private arts organizations apply for a municipal grant they are often required to have high standards of excellence, a great reputation in the community, other sources of support, a high earned income, an up-to-date administration, and an audited financial statement before they are actively considered for a grant.'[23] Obviously, a newly formed group of modern dancers, for example, would not possibly be able to fulfil most of these criteria and would have inordinate difficulty obtaining the small grant needed to perform its works. In the absence of more detailed information, we can surmise that the accumulation function takes precedence with all three levels of the state.

THE CULTURAL ELITE

Although neither John Porter nor Wallace Clement document the composition of the elites of artistic boards, an article by Christina Newman in *Chatelaine* magazine leaves no doubt that boards are made up of some of the highest ranking members of the corporate establishment: 'Until the last dozen years or so, when governments began to support the arts with public funds, the Cultural Establishment was the special preserve of the Anglo-Saxon-Anglican, Scottish-Presbyterian upper-middle-class ... These people still dominate the boards ... They still dress up, in jewelled pantsuits and ruffle dress shirts, and go to opening nights. They still attend auctions for the opera guild in the autumn wearing ocelot hats, give luncheons for the museum in the springtime ... and dance at medieval balls in the inner courts of art galleries in costumes that probably cost enough, en masse, to add half a dozen paintings to the collection they're benefiting. They still defend staunchly the fact that the only way to join most symphony or art gallery women's committees is to be 'put up' by two members ...'
Newman distinguishes between the 'old rich' on the boards and the

'corporation men.' In the first category are the Winnipeg Richardsons (Royal Winnipeg Ballet, Manitoba Theatre Centre), the Eatons (National Youth Orchestra, Canadian Opera Company, Art Gallery of Ontario), the Davies family in Kingston, and the Olands in Halifax. 'Corporation men' include D.S. Anderson, vice-president of the Royal Bank of Canada (St Lawrence Centre), Walter Bean, deputy chairman and vice-president of Canada Trust (Stratford Festival Board), Edmund C. Bovey, president of the Northern and Central Gas Company (Toronto Symphony, Art Gallery of Ontario; owner of one of the largest collections of Canadian art; chairman of the Council for Business and the Arts), and various executives of breweries and advertising agencies. With the exception of a handful of very wealthy Jews, virtually no other ethnic group is represented. 'When asked why this should be so, one Cult. Est. ['Cultural Establishment'] member responded with surprise, "Well, nobody knows who they *are,* for heaven's sake." '

Apart from the obvious cachet involved in sitting on these boards (there is, apparently, a hierarchy of boards, with the Stratford Festival at the top), there are the expected economic advantages. As Newman has a mythical but typical corporate member of an arts board say, ' ... anyway, it's good for business. You know what I mean? You meet a man on one of these boards, a vice-president of a bank, say, and you talk symphony deficits half a dozen times a year and who knows what might come out of it?'[24] Members of arts boards wield influence and power (that is, direct funds to their own organization) through the usual interlocking pattern of state and corporate elites. Susan Crean, author of the first major study of the economics of the arts in Canada, documents the phenomenon for Ontario: ' ... arts councils allied themselves closely with the big organizations, so closely that it is not unusual for them to have board members in common. The tradition is especially strong in Ontario, where the moving force behind the establishment of the Ontario Arts Council in 1963 was ... Arthur Gelber, who was then serving as president of the CCA [Canadian Conference of the Arts] ... Christina Newman described him ... as a unique figure in the Canadian cultural establishment, holding more important positions on more important boards than anyone else. Gelber has been a member of the Ontario Arts Council since 1963 and is now its vice-chairman. The chairman, Frank McEachern, is the other remaining member of the original Council; he is director of community relations for Eaton's of Canada Limited (and is married to Florence Mary Eaton). Through Gelber, McEachern, Stratford physician Ian Lindsay, and Lanfranco Amato, former president and general manager of Olivetti Canada Limited, the council maintains direct connection with the boards of the National Ballet, the Toronto Symphony, the St. Lawrence Centre, the Stratford Festival, the Shaw Festival and the Canadian Opera Company. That list includes all of the big-money clients of the council (which receive annual grants in excess of $50,000, most of them in the neighbourhood of $200,000). In 1974, these six clients accounted for $1,245,000 (roughly 30 per cent) of the Council's grants, which went to 686 individuals, organizations, and programs. Furthermore, since the outset, managers and artistic directors of major arts institutions have also done long stints on juries and advisory panels of funding bodies. Oddly enough, none of this is said to constitute conflict of interest.'

Members of boards of museums and galleries are able to profit even more directly than those on boards of performing arts organizations. According to Crean, they can influence acquisitions in such a way as to increase the value of their own collections; they are in close contact with dealers and various experts and thus can often purchase art works cheaply; and by making donations of collections they can pass the sometimes very high costs of insurance and upkeep on to the taxpayer.[25]

From the outset of the era of state financing of the arts to the present, there has been, on the part of both state cultural bureaucrats and the corporate elites of arts boards, a thoroughly hidebound determination to keep actual artists out of decision-making in the state bureaucracy and off the boards of arts organizations. These bodies have been closing their doors to artists (sometimes slamming them) since the recommendations of the Massey Report. Once again, reversing the wishes of the people whose opinion they had 'democratically' solicited, the report stated: 'We have given great care, in our deliberations, to the many submissions made to us concerning the appropriate composition of such a Council, notably from Canadian artists and writers who have urged that a Council be established which would be representative of their professional organizations. With this view we are unable to agree. We judge that the members of a policy-making body to be concerned with many complex aspects of Canadian life should be free to consider all problems before them without the restraints which normally would bind them too closely to the organization or to the group which they would represent.'[26]

If one were to believe in conspiracy theories, one would have to assume that the foregoing is meant tongue-in-cheek. What the tactfully worded message conceals, of course, is the worry that artists would allocate money to themselves or their friends. That this is exactly what is advocated for the corporate elite and their representatives in the state bureaucracy does not seem to cause any alarm. In fact, the state and the arts boards capitalize on the image of the artist as feckless with money. As one artistic director said to Newman, the boards 'treat us with a mixture of obsequiousness and scorn. Obsequiousness because they figure talent is some kind of occult phenomenon they don't understand and scorn because they figure that we are completely impractical in financial terms.'[27] As several commentators have pointed out, keeping artists out of these organizations is like keeping doctors out of hospitals. To give it some credit, the Canada Council regularly consults an Artists Advisory Committee. It is, however, just that – advisory – with no real influence or power, and several artists have resigned or ended their terms in frustration.

Arts boards do not even attempt this semblance of democracy. When an American was appointed curator of the Art Gallery of Ontario in 1972, several artists realized that if they were to prevent such appointments, or have any influence on the policies of the gallery, they would have to obtain representation on the board. The board's nominating committee accepted the nomination of one artist (Joyce Wieland) but asked a second (Robert Bailey) to withdraw. When he refused, the board was forced to have an election – the first in its history. The artists then began to question the use of proxy ballots, and membership meetings became, for a time, heated political debates with the board using as many legalistic arguments as their corporate lawyers could invent. 'When it was finally put to Crashley [president of the Board of Trustees] that the election patently favoured one particular group over all others, he agreed ... remarking that it was "normal" for corporations to operate to the advantage of management. Later another Trustee also pointed out that signing ballots was a regular procedure at Imperial Oil and Noranda.'[28]

Confrontations such as these inevitably lay bare the workings of arts boards, demonstrating that not only do the policy-makers of a publicly funded cultural institution operate like a corporation, they don't blush to admit it. Artists' representation on such boards would threaten the status quo, not only of the corporate executives but also of the state which supports such organizations. Neither can afford to have this relationship exposed. Artists influencing the type of art produced and subsidized would undoubtedly favour new, experimental, and sometimes radical works; would perhaps advocate democratization of the arts through free performances, lower ticket prices, costly tours. Such changes would seriously undermine the current profitability of the arts in Canada.

THE CRISIS OF LEGITIMACY

So far we have listed the ways in which state funding of the arts directly or indirectly aids capital accumulation and/or is lucrative for the state, keeping in mind that every state expenditure on the arts also performs a certain legitimation function. The features outlined have characterized state spending on the arts for the last twenty-five years or so. However, in the current economic situation, there is a crisis of state spending in all areas, and the area of financing the arts contains some special contradictions. If the general crisis occurs when state expenditures outstrip state revenues, the problem in the arts is made more extreme by non-productivity, particularly in the live performing arts. The labour power required to perform a symphony, for example, can hardly be reduced through the introduction of new technology. It takes the same number of people the same amount of time to perform it as it did when the symphony was written. That the electronic media can increase productivity astronomically attests to the non-productivity of the live performance: '... an orchestral performance on television, which, we are told by the professionals, takes less than twice the man-hours of a live performance, can reach an audience of 20 million instead of the 2,500 persons who occupy a concert hall, thus yielding an increase in productivity of four hundred thousand per cent.'[29]

Building ever larger concert halls has only a limited ability to increase productivity because of acoustical problems and because of the attendant loss of 'intimacy.' Air-conditioning halls to make them available for use year-round and buying more expensive sets and costumes are likewise limited possibilities of a 'one-shot' nature. Were the rest of the economy to remain the same in terms of productivity, the problem would not be so acute. Since the opposite is the case, and given inflation, the 'income gap' in the live performing arts is constantly widening. In 1971-2 in Ontario, for example, the income gap is a percentage of total budget was 55 per cent for all arts organizations – 35 per cent for the performing arts and 83 per cent for museums and galleries.[30] Figures for projected percentage increases are not available, but it is estimated that the total cost of financing the arts in Canada will reach $175 million by 1980, compared to $45 million in 1972.[31] It is safe to assume that by the end of this decade, because of the unproductive nature of the arts and inflationary costs, state funding will no longer be able to increase the overall rate of profit in the economy through facilitating direct or indirect capital accumulation via the arts.

Large performing arts organizations have a life – and an audience – of their own. It is extremely difficult for the state to cut back their grants, at least more difficult than to cut back in those few areas which constitute social expenses alone, such as small experimental groups and subsidies to individual artists. In the case of museums and galleries, cutbacks have not so far affected acquisitions (such as the Henry Moore collection, purchased by the AGO for $20 million), but take the form of decreases in accessibility, as indicated by the current recommendations to charge admission to the Art Gallery of Ontario and to close the Royal Ontario Museum at night, the only time most of the working population can visit. The inability of the state to increase the rate of profit through spending on the arts thus creates a possible crisis of legitimation.

The state is now rather frenetically attempting to find ways to make direct corporate funding more attractive through the tax loopholes described above, and through the establishment of the Council for Business and the Arts. Given the widening income gap, however, it must cut back on those areas associated with legitimation, namely assistance to artists and accessibility to the public. Even though these have received relatively limited funding in the past, they have given rise to certain expectations which cannot now be denied without protest. It is this contradiction now facing the state – the contradiction that as possibilities for accumulation decrease, the legitimation function is weakened – that must be exploited by cultural workers and the socialist movement in general in Canada. Before discussing how this is to be done, however, it may be helpful to discuss some of the social consequences resulting from the nature and patterns of state spending on the arts.

THE TRUE SUBSIDIZERS

We cannot separate state intervention in the arts from the state of the arts and of culture generally. The fact that the state funds arts organizations and not artists has far-reaching implications for the type of work that gets produced and the type of audience that sees it. The artist always works, consciously or unconsciously, with an audience in mind. When that audience is also the patron or of the same elite as the patron (members and friends of the arts board or the Art Bank) the artist will create work that will get funded by pleasing the taste of this audience/patron, taste which will be conservative in the performing arts in the sense of copying established foreign models and conservative in the visual arts in the sense of 'corporate art.' When the motive for municipal funding is to attract investment to the area, art which reflects local culture will be passed over in favour of art with 'universal' – read bourgeois – appeal. Even if some small percentage of the art subsidized is Canadian, it will tend to reflect the values of the class of the audience/patron.

Since 1957 the Canada Council has spent $120 million on the arts in Canada. No figures are available on exactly how much of this went directly to artists themselves, but while there is no doubt that more artists than pre-

viously make some income from their work, state funding has not significantly increased the number able to actually make a living from their art.
One study of professional artists (defined as holding membership in a union
or professional association) in music, dance, and theatre indicates that the
mean income for all three groups ($6500) was lower than the average for
the labour force ($6905) in 1971. Even these figures are misleading because
the majority of artists in these fields are not 'professional,' and because 75
per cent of the respondents were employed 'in a secondary arts occupation
which was categorized in the same sector as their primary arts occupations.'[32] Thus most of the artists surveyed did not make a living from their
work. In fact, there is only one Canadian playwright who has made a living
writing plays, and in any given week three-quarters of Actors Equity members are out of work. Writers and visual artists fare even worse, especially
when their work is reproduced without fees or royalties for 'educational
purposes.' 'Time and again, artists are asked to lend their works and their
talents as though these meant no more to their living than a cup of sugar ...
It happens when a public art gallery exhibits an artist's work and pays everyone connected with the show (curator, secretary, janitor, guards) except
the artist; it happens when newspapers and magazines ... reproduce an
artist's work without asking permission or without paying a royalty; it happens when journalists, researchers, academics, and producers in all media
ask artists to give interviews, information, advice, and ideas to their projects, but hastily claim that the budget is too small to pay an honorarium ...
And, almost always, the person who does the asking is being paid for his
job and would not dream of doing it for nothing.'[33]

In 1972, Actors Equity closed down a series of workshop productions by
Factory Lab Theatre in Toronto because the actors were being paid less
than scale. The actors eventually sided with management because they preferred to work for less on a project they were committed to than receive
scale in the regional theatres. That the union, and not state funding policies
which starve out smaller theatres, was made the villain, was a useful divide-
and-conquer tactic for the state. The economic reality of the case, and of
the other examples mentioned, is that *the artists themselves are the real subsidizers of art in this country.*

The other consequence of the state giving funds and control to elite arts
organizations boards is that *the public as excluded audience is also the real
subsidizer of the arts.* The vast majority of Canadians who pay for art with
their taxes are not the recipients of art. Even if ticket prices were made less
expensive this would be the case, for in the first place the art produced
speaks little to the concerns and does not reflect the values of the majority,

that is, the working class; and in the second place there are less definable but none the less real and powerful reasons why the houses of culture are seen to be the preserve of the bourgeoisie. Arts boards are accountable to no one but themselves. Peter Swann, director of the Royal Ontario Museum, probably did more than any artistic director to make that institution accessible and popular (he opened the museum at night and doubled attendance, among other things) and was eventually dismissed for his efforts. A public meeting at the St Lawrence Centre and delegations to Premier Davis and the minister for colleges and universities, George Kerr, were to no avail. Since fifteen of the eighteen members of the board were government appointees, the government confirmed the boards as 'supreme authority over all museum policy.'[34] As long as public funds are administered by corporate and state elites the public will continue as excluded audience. Tom Hendry, a playwright and director who has often served as the token artist on boards and Canada Council advisory committees, states the obvious corollary: 'It is not unreasonable to conclude that if we truly wish to expand the audience for the performing arts, we will have to find ways to include among decision-makers and policy-makers those who have an interest in satisfying the cultural needs of the 95% of Canadians who at present have nothing to do whatsoever with our productions.'[35] That state funding patterns have catered to the material and cultural interests of the ruling elite has resulted in three deformations: art which is undemocratic in its form and content; continuing economic privation of the artist and distortion of his creativity; and real but intangible sanctions against the participation of the vast majority of Canadians in their culture.

STRATEGY

Righting the wrongs in these three areas of culture will ultimately mean a state which funds working-class and progressive art, which guarantees an income for artists and which would encourage the use of the workplace and the community as the focus for the arts, thus raising the cultural level of all people and recruiting potential professionals from talented workers – the practice, in short, of socialist societies. What strategies should be developed to mobilize artists and the public as excluded audience in order to achieve these goals? How does a strategy for cultural workers fit into the overall strategy to overthrow the capitalist state? A useful beginning is to examine some of the existing proposals in the light of the analysis of the state's accumulation function in the financing of the arts.

It is fairly easy to discredit the naïve ultra-leftist view that all state grants to the arts should be refused because they automatically imply control of artistic freedom, in this case the freedom to be radical. This view is really not very far from the antediluvian bourgeois idea that artists can only create 'true' art when they are hungry. As Jack Pollock, an exception because he is both an artist and a successful arts entrepreneur, stated in the *Globe and Mail:* 'I find that continued financial support, with few or no demands, produces a kind of lethargy and does not seem to stimulate that competitive spirit so necessary for personal growth. It can also become relied upon, and expected, making artists, as someone recently commented, "no more nor less than civil servants." The creative minds of a country must be free of political ties, provincial attitudes, and above all, the overwhelming burden of obligation that total support demands. Freedom costs.'[36] The leftist version of this view, popular in the sixties under the influence of Marcuse's 'repressive tolerance' theories and at a time when LIP and OFY grants were indeed instituted to 'cool out' social protest, argues that truly radical art can only be created by the 'oppressed' (defined as those who are poor and do not work) who do not 'sell out' to the state.

Except in rare cases (say, theatre performed in parks by two or three actors) production costs for film, music, theatre, and dance make this ideal impossible. Even the visual artist, for whom expenses may be relatively low, needs funds to help make his work accessible to people, and of course all artists need money to provide time to create. Furthermore, the ultra-left analysis misses the point that cultural rights are political rights – that it is necessary to struggle with the state to provide funds for small experimental groups even where, in the case of dance, for example, the content of their work may not be ostensibly political. Legitimation measures taken by the state such as LIP and OFY grants to artists always create more problems for the state than they solve when it is forced to cut back, since amateurs who acquired skills under these programs are now prohibited from using them, and are a potential focus of more profound social protest. 'Radical' artists who moralistically refuse state funding and point the finger at those who do not, will not be able to organize (or even participate in) a movement which will exploit the contradictions of capitalism by demanding measures which the state cannot supply. The argument must always emphasize more, not less, state spending on the arts, in addition to qualitative demands concerning the nature of the art to be subsidized and the structures necessary to facilitate accessibility.

Althusser's more sophisticated analysis of the ideological role of culture as one of the 'ideological state apparatuses' is susceptible to somewhat similar errors when a possible strategy is considered. In attributing virtually all areas of life under capitalism to the state (education, family, law, politics, trade unions, communications, and culture) he fails to distinguish between the limited freedoms of a bourgeois democratic state and more repressive regimes. Thus he can offer no tactics for periods of economic stagnation when it is necessary to fight to preserve or regain limited freedoms while linking that struggle to more radical demands. For example, if the sole outlook of the state in financing the arts is to reproduce the submission of labour to the status quo of class society, there would be no point in labour attempting to establish unity with artists for the joint benefit of increased subsidies to artists and increased accessibility of culture to labour. This unity becomes feasible when the independent commodity production base of artistic work is undermined through the necessary dependence of artists on state support, and the artists' perspective hence becomes more working class. The cultural ISA reproduces submission to the status quo primarily in the sense that workers are excluded from appreciating the performing and visual arts because they are the preserve of the bourgeoisie as the artistic structures are now constituted. This situation creates and encourages the 'culture's not for the likes of us' mentality, which can only be overcome by the development of workers' culture. To some extent funds for such a culture can and will come from the trade union movement itself, but it will still be necessary, because of the high costs of artistic production, to demand funds from the state, and this will come about through trade union representation on the boards of arts organizations. Althusser, however, considers the trade unions as an ISA as well, and therefore offers us no possibility of finding ways in which power and control over funding – and hence over ideology – can be won. Finally, if the state's accumulation function is overlooked and we are simply concerned with ideological control, there can be no way of exploiting the contradiction of the state when it is no longer able to increase the rate of profit through financing the arts.

Far more influential among Canadian artists and audiences than either of the above analyses is that offered by the left cultural nationalists. Cultural nationalism has been the major ideological influence in the establishment of artists' organizations and unions such as Canadian Artists Representation and the Writers' Union, as well as the separation of Canadian Actors Equity from the American parent union and the current attempts by ACTRA to have a voice in limiting roles taken by foreign performers. The left-wing advocates of cultural nationalism have been responsible for almost all the criticism and analysis published in the field, and much of it is exemplary. There can be no question that the plight of the Canadian artist – whose works are overlooked in favour of those produced by non-Canadian artists, usually dead ones who don't ask for royalties, and who creates in a cultural climate permeated with the colonial mentality which says that no matter what he creates it probably won't measure up – is sufficient to arouse indignation on the part of all patriotic people. We must not be tempted, however, into a 'Canadian art for Canadian art's sake' stand, which is, in fact, the pitfall of the left cultural nationalists. No matter how much lip service is paid to the ideal of a people's culture, they invariably fall into the trap of a narrow nationalism which supports all Canadian art and every Canadian artist regardless of content or political practice.

Susan Crean, for example, whose analysis of the undemocratic nature of arts organizations in invaluable, never admits the possibility that Canadian commercial interests can, if given the chance, pervert culture just as effectively as any other capitalists. Nor is the Canadian state innocent of financing home-grown Canadian trash. The Canadian Film Development Corporation, for example, has subsidized those wonderful Canadian films 'Ilse, She-Wolf of the ss' and its sequel 'Ilse, Harem Keeper of the Oil Sheiks,' in addition to several execrable films in the horror, violence, and pornography categories – all paid for by the Canadian people. Rather than attacking this less than admirable practice of the state, however, Crean compares the film industry to military defence, mourning the demise of the AVRO Arrow and warning that the same fate awaits the Canadian film industry.[37]

Rick Salutin, perhaps the best-known exponent of left cultural nationalism, both in his plays and articles, is occasionally reduced to similar distortions. In one of his 'Culture Vulture' columns in *This Magazine* he describes a new Canadian comic book, *Captain Canuck*, in which the hero is an agent for the 'Canadian International Security Organization' whose mission is to fight the communist hordes invading Canada over the North Pole. That such a publication needs to be incorporated into the left nationalist position is itself significant, and Salutin's response cannot be considered entirely facetious: 'Ah well, if we're going to have crap, it might as well be Canadian. In fact that could serve as one of the guiding principles of Canadian cultural nationalism. I mean think of it. No wonder nations like the U.S., U.K., or Japan produce the odd cultural gem: they put out so much junk they *have* to hit once in a while.'[38] Unless the class question in the field of culture is made primary, unless nationalism is related to proletarian internationalism, the left cultural nationalist position will inevitably continue to make such errors.

A genuine Canadian culture would be working class and democratic both in terms of the type of art created and the type of audience which participates in it. While this cannot be achieved without a socialist revolution, we can build a base which will strengthen the working-class movement by directing demands to the state which will focus on both the quantity and quality of state funding of the arts, and raise the issues of who decides and who benefits. The first series of such demands should be concerned with the economic well-being of the artists themselves, for without creative people able to create in relative freedom from economic pressures, nothing else can follow. The present handful of Senior Arts Grants, for example, should be expanded and given to younger artists who face the same 'catch 22' situation confronting the job hunter told he won't be hired until he has some experience. Younger artists at present ineligible for funds have the greatest difficulty creating the works which will eventually make them eligible. 'Senior' artists should then be eligible for a guaranteed annual income, and the number of artists qualifying should be distributed demographically to ensure that regional cultures thrive. Artists would then be free to work together in groups without having to establish administrative staffs in order to get grants.

Our artists must no longer be forced to subsidize their own art while the state enables a parasitical elite to feed off their work. One possible demand is that the large performing arts organizations be made into Crown corporations administered by the state, thus freeing the Canada Council to fund smaller, more experimental groups, subject of course to the participation of artists and members of the community and labour movement on the decision-making bodies. Municipal governments especially should be required to fund the smaller, local community-oriented arts projects and not the large organizations already receiving funds from provincial and federal sources.

Such changes would also begin to tackle the question of democratization of the arts in terms of audience accessibility. Rather than funding the arts to attract investment, local councils must finance those groups and individuals whose art grows out of and reflects back on their specific community. Where performing organizations or institutions like museums and art galleries are large enough to need administrative boards, the composition of those boards should include artists, representatives of the labour movement, and those involved in the community, with corporate representatives in the minority. At present these boards are classified as non-profit corporations and thus do not pay salaries. This should be changed so that people who cannot afford to volunteer their services will be encouraged to participate. Such boards must also be made accountable to the public. At the federal and provincial level, a much greater proportion of funds should be given over to touring, not the productions of the large performing arts organizations or the collections of art held by corporations, but the works of local groups who can share their experiences with people living in other parts of the country. Factories and offices should be the sites of exhibitions and performances, both local and touring. Funds should be available to amateur groups of all kinds in addition to professionals.

Of course, the relevance of such demands really depends on the nature of the work of art produced. Indeed, neither analysis nor strategy is meaningful unless we ask ourselves what type of culture we want to promote in this country. This question has been and will continue to be the subject of debate as long as we recognize the distinctiveness of the form of expression we call art, and only some tentative suggestions are appropriate here. Probably more useful than entering into the debate about realism versus formalism is to locate art as a subsection of culture. If culture can be defined as that which transmits values, art transmits values specifically through the use of symbols (metaphors, visual images, and so on). The use of the symbols may be didactic but more often manipulates the emotions in a complex variety of positive and negative ways. In the nature of both the reasoned and the emotional response to art we can locate a value or values and decide if they are desirable or undesirable, that is, if they encourage or impede the development of the working class and its allies towards socialism. Until scientific tools are developed for such analyses there will be much unproductive controversy and disagreement; none the less we can work towards a general consensus based on the broadest anti-capitalist criteria. In order to ensure that such art is created and that it is available to the largest possible audience, there must be unity among progressive artists and the more militant sections of the trade union movement to attack the ideological hegemony of the state in the cultural sphere, and to force the state to subsidize our culture and our artists rather than the art of the ruling class whose profits it now helps to accumulate.

NOTES

This article discusses primarily live performing arts (opera, theatre, music, dance) and visual arts (painting, sculpture, graphics). Film, radio, television, and publishing and their relation to the state warrant separate studies.

1 *Report of the Royal Commission on National Development in the Arts, Letters and Sciences* (1951), 75 – hereafter *Massey Report*. Of the five cultural organizations, three were learned societies not concerned with the arts, leaving only the Canadian Writers' Foundation and the Royal Academy of Art as recipients of state funds.

2 Susan Crean, *Who's Afraid of Canadian Culture?* (Don Mills 1976), 116 and 132
3 As is the production of paintings and sculpture, their housing and exhibition to the public. However, individual works of art are highly profitable as investments to the private sector and the state.
4 *The Vertical Mosaic* (Toronto 1965), 459; emphasis supplied to stress the particular role of artists as manipulators of symbols
5 Louis Althusser, 'Ideology and Ideological State Apparatuses (Notes towards an Investigation),' in *Lenin and Philosophy and other Essays* (London 1971), 127-8
6 *Massey Report*, 381
7 *Ibid.*, 197
8 *Ibid*, 197 and 198, 381
9 The Canada Council Act, 1957, *Revised Statutes of Canada* (1970), I, Article 17
10 *Massey Report*, 273
11 Christina Newman, 'Who Runs Culture in Canada?' *Chatelaine Magazine* (June 1970), 80
12 *Massey Report*, 73, 372, 381
13 William J. Baumol and William G. Bowen, *Performing Arts: The Economic Dilemma* (New York 1966), 383
14 Urwick, Currie and Partners, Ltd., Management Consultants, *An Assessment of the Impact of Selected Large Performing Companies upon the Canadian Economy*, Canada Council (Ottawa 1974), 18-19
15 Frank T. Pasquill, *Subsidy Patterns for the Performing Arts in Canada*, Canada Council (Ottawa 1973), 31
16 *Taxation and the Arts,* Canada Council (Ottawa n.d.) , 33, 29
17 Zelda Heller, 'Business and the Arts,' *Financial Times*, 1 Nov. 1976
18 *Ibid.*
19 Urwick, Currie and Partners, *Assessment*, v, 14
20 Dale McConathy, 'The Canadian Cultural Revolution,' *artscanada* (Autumn 1975), 38
21 *Ibid.*, 8, 25
22 *Ibid.*, 3
23 Pasquill, *Subsidy Patterns*, 33
24 Newman, 'Who Runs Culture in Canada?' 79, 81, 26
25 Crean, *Who's Afraid*, 144-5, 153
26 *Massey Report*, 377
27 'Who Runs Culture in Canada?' 84
28 Susan Crean, 'Up Front with the Artists: The AGO Affair,' *Canadian Forum* (Nov.-Dec. 1973), 64
29 Baumol and Bowen, *Performing Arts*, 163

30 Sam Book, *Economic Aspects of the Arts in Ontario*, Ontario Arts Council (Toronto 1972), 31
31 Crean, *Who's Afraid*, 117
32 Christine Panasuk, *An Analysis of Selected Performing Arts Occupations*, Canada Council (Ottawa 1974), 1. This study also found that male artists earned an average of $2000 a year more than female artists in all three categories.
33 Crean, *Who's Afraid*, 160
34 *Ibid.*, 141
35 'The Acceptable Few: A Cursory View of the Position of Arts Boards of Directors in Canada,' in *Readings on the Governing Boards of Arts Organizations*, Canada Council (Ottawa 1971), 39
36 'Get Art to People – and Out of Art Bank Warehouses,' 7 Aug. 1976
37 *Who's Afraid*, 114
38 'Pickings by the Culture Vulture,' *This Magazine* (Sept.-Oct. 1975), 20

15

A political economy of citizen participation

MARTIN LONEY

Poverty as such never was and cannot be the driving force in the struggle for social change and liberation. It can become such a force only if the poor act not as under-privileged individuals, each looking for help from above (from the State, the wealthy, the welfare institutions), but as a cohesive group or community bent on winning the right of self-government, the power of changing a society that denies recognition to their needs.

During the 1960s and early 1970s the Canadian government introduced a variety of programs with the general, if none the less vague, purpose of pro-moting citizen participation. The government commissioned experts to study ways in which citizens' involvement could be encouraged and citizens' groups aided. A considerable increase in government funding of the voluntary sector and of various interest groups produced an apparent growth in the number of organizations representing citizens' views and de-mands in all areas of life. Notably, native groups, the poor, and youth groups found government funding much more accessible.

The purpose of this paper is not to document this growth but rather to suggest that it must be viewed at least in part as a program of social control. What Canada has witnessed is not a genuine increase in grass-roots democ-racy but a move to increasingly sophisticated strategies for reincorporating potentially dissident groups into the mainstream of society. Simultaneously, government funding has ensured the domination of ideas and practices which sustain the existing socio-economic order either directly or by maintaining the illusion of a genuine pluralism. It is worthwhile to review briefly the challenge to liberal notions of democracy inherent in such state activity.

The classic pluralist position is summarized by R.A. Dahl, who argues that in a pluralist society 'there are a number of loci for arriving at political decisions; that businessmen, trade unions, politicians, consumers, farmers, voters, and many other aggregates all have an impact on policy outcomes; that none of these aggregates is homogeneous for all purposes; that each of them is highly influential over some groups, but weak over many others; and that the power to reject undesired alternatives is more common than the power to dominate over outcomes directly.'[1] Clearly, when a situation arises in which an increasing number of the pluralist pillars of society are dependent to a greater or lesser extent on the state for their financial viability, the pluralist defence is undermined. Yet that is precisely what has happened – not only in the area of tax write-offs for those supporting established political parties (to the detriment of non-established parties) but also in the less publicized area of 'voluntary organizations,' long assumed to be one of the strengths of democracy.

It appears that there is now general acceptance of the idea that the welfare state plays a key role in protecting the social stability of Western capitalist societies. R. Titmuss, for example, argued against the 'assumption that the establishment of social welfare necessarily and inevitably contributes to the spread of humanism and the resolution of social injustice. The reverse can be true. Welfare, as an institutional means, can serve different masters. A multitude of sins may be committed in its appealing name. Welfare can be used simply as an instrument of economic growth which, by benefitting a minority, indirectly promotes greater inequality. Education is an example. We may educate the young to compete more efficiently as economic men in the private market one with another, or we may educate them because we desire to make them more capable of freedom and more capable of fulfilling their personal differences irrespective of income, class, religion and race ... Welfare may be used to serve military and racial ends – as in Hitler's Germany. More medical care was provided by state and voluntary agencies not because of a belief in every man's uniqueness but because of a hatred of men ... Welfare may be used to narrow allegiances and not to diffuse them – as in employers' fringe benefit systems. Individual gain and political quietism, fostered by the new feudalism of the corporation, may substitute for the sense of common humanity nourished by systems of non-discriminatory mutual aid.'[2]

In April 1976 the chief economist of Ford Motor Company bluntly observed: 'Unemployment insurance and welfare are two reasons why there isn't blood on the streets here.' Canadian cabinet minister Bryce Mackasey, addressing the elite Canadian Club in May 1976, advised that 'The stability of free enterprise depends on the welfare state ... As we face this capital crunch I hear business men saying, "Cut back on welfare and transfer payments." But a country whose living standards are falling *faces more unrest* than a much poorer country whose living standards are rising.'[3]

From a liberal perspective, S.M. Lipset has argued that the working class has been incorporated into Western capitalist societies on the basis of a welfare and trade union bargain.[4] J. Rex, from a more radical perspective, has provided a critical view of this argument: 'It is possible to argue against the so-called end-of-ideology thesis that it represents so much wishful thinking on the part of the bourgeoisie and their personal managers. In fact, the welfare state and full employment are likely to be maintained if, and only if, it is clear that workers are prepared to fight to defend them; and in most of the advanced industrial countries at the same time it seems clear that, whether through economic necessity or simply taking advantage of the temporary weakness of the working class, the political parties of the bourgeoisie have sought to undermine the welfare and trade union bargain and to fall back on an open class-rule. This, however, is really a matter for argument. It is also at least possible to argue that, for twenty-five years after the Second World War, the politics of countries like Britain, France, Germany, and the United States turned simply on the question of shares within the bargain. Conservatives would press the bargain one way, the forces of labour the other.'[5] Rex notes that, in any case, no matter what the strengths or dynamics of the 'welfare bargain' as it applies to the indigenous working class in Europe or the white working class in America, it certainly does not apply either to recent Third World immigrants into Europe or to the American black population. In the Canadian context we might wish to extend this caveat to cover the native population, groups trapped in what is loosely referred to as 'the poverty cycle,' and marginal youth groups – whose marginality has been increased by recent changes which make an increasing number of educated young people surplus to the needs of the economy.[6] The Canadian government's activities in the citizen participation field have been directed, in many ways, to providing an alternative means of involving these groups in the mainstream of society, without threatening the underlying stability or division of wealth and power in Canada. While a modified 'welfare bargain' concept may help to explain the continued acquiescence of organized labour, we have to look elsewhere for the social bonds which incorporate more marginal groups.

This paper is primarily concerned with a closer examination of one aspect of the incorporation of marginal groups – government programs to encourage citizen participation – and with the government's larger role in funding, and determining the nature of, the voluntary sector in Canada.

The government's activity in this area should first be placed in a larger context, and, secondly, it is necessary to refer briefly to the political dynamics at work in stimulating government intervention. The context of the discussion must first of all be the role of the state which is active, not simply in funding voluntary organizations and indirectly setting the parameters for their activity, but also of course in all areas of society. While it is beyond the scope of this paper to discuss in detail the social control aspects of all federal, provincial, and municipal government activity, the scale of direct state involvement is suggested by H. Armstrong's calculation that, as regards the potential labour force in 1971, 'there were 5,853,000 Canadians directly dependent on the state as clients or workers compared to 6,298,000 Canadians who were not.'[7]

A notional hierarchy of state involvement and the relative power of groups in society which enter into relationships with the state would place citizens' groups, for example, at a relatively low point. Unlike trade union groups, they enter into relationships with the government with little potential power; unlike industry, they do little to dictate the overall nature of state activity. Similarly, the amount of money involved in funding voluntary organizations is far below that expended on various programs available to industry. While the state in many ways becomes a servant of capital, and finds its behaviour (particularly when the political elite is socialist) circumscribed and curtailed by capital's attitudes and interests, the state, in dealing with most voluntary organizations, is clearly pre-eminent.

When we consider in more detail the nature and effect of state involvement in the voluntary sector, the comments which are made regarding the system-maintaining function of such involvement could be replicated elsewhere. The nature of the dominant order is capitalist, and any activities which threaten this order will meet opposition, which may take the form of inducements to co-operate, condemnation, or outright repression. Trade unions which step directly into the political arena, challenging not simply the share of gross national product received by labour but also the allocative mechanisms of a capitalist society, will encounter such opposition. At a higher level a government which itself seeks to change the terms on which capital operates will find itself the target of resistance and attack by international capital. The Chilean case provides a recent and dramatic example. In short, activity which is fundamentally oppositional in the sense of threatening the dominant socio-economic order, will always encounter considerable resistance. The ability to withstand such resistance will vary, but again we must suppose that disparate citizens' groups will have far less capacity than nationally organized trade unions. Similarly, groups without an independent economic base in the form of the ownership of capital, or, much less significantly, in the form of the receipt of regular dues from union members, must be far more circumscribed in their behaviour than groups which are not so directly in 'client' relationships to the state.

The political dynamics of state intervention are complex. It would be naïve to suggest that everything can be explained by an examination of the interests and actions of a ruling class which has a conscious master plan to meet all contingencies. Michael Kidron has offered a more accurate explanation of the changing role of the state: ' ... The state's growth has been in a series of disjointed steps that bear every sign of *not* representing a coherent attitude working itself out in institutional form, but rather a series of *ad hoc* responses to short-term problems which could not be dealt with in any other way.'[8]

The nature of the response may sometimes be primarily determined by the elite, sometimes by oppositional forces. Ian Gough argued: 'Since the last century the threat of popular discontent and mass struggle has led to important social concessions being made – for example unemployment insurance in the UK in 1911. At other times, social policies have been introduced by forward looking representatives of the dominant class to head off anticipated revolutionary demands. Many in Edwardian Britain were impressed by the success of the Bismarck model, among them Churchill, Chamberlain, Lloyd George, and Balfour. This was particularly important in the reform of the 1940s: it must be remembered that the Beveridge Report, the White Paper on Full Employment and the Butler Education Act were all drawn up during war-time by a Coalition government. They were consciously seen as a necessary part of the war effort by integrating all classes and alleviating discontent ... the social services have increasingly been viewed by labour movements as an integral part of wages, to be defended and increased in the same way as money wages. They are a *social wage* provided collectively by the state or some other body.'[9]

In fact, on any particular reform there may well be some difficulty in establishing a consensus as to the most powerful factor involved. Others would argue against Gough that, in the passage quoted, he both under-represents the role of the 'dominant class' in taking pre-emptive action in 1911, while he ignores the influence of the labour movement in the 1940s reforms which he cites. The point to be made is simply that the process is dynamic and dialectical, and that the role of non-elite groups in securing reforms or shifts in government policy must be taken into account.

Nicos Poulantzas has made a similar point, though at a more general and theoretical level: 'the state should be seen (as should capital, according to

Marx) as a relation, or more precisely as the condensate of a relation of power between struggling classes.'[10] In examining the growth in the Canadian state's involvement in the voluntary sector, we are viewing a process which was partly a 'pre-emptive' program by more enlightened elements of the elite, and partly a process initiated and influenced by grass-roots activity.

It is clear that one factor at work in the government's increased involvement in the citizen participation field was a desire to reincorporate newly dissident groups or to incorporate groups whose participation in the mainstream of Canadian society had always been marginal. This is not to argue that the growth of state involvement in the citizen participation field was the result of any master plan which sought to co-opt any and all groups of radical dissent which appeared. The process of government is not so attractively simple. Rather there appear to have been a number of factors which combined to encourage this thrust in government policy. The growth in federal revenue in the 1960s created the means for a general increase in federal spending in the social policy field and provided the material base for greater government action to combat what were defined as social problems.[11] This coincided with an increased concern to develop positive initiatives to strengthen the integrative mechanisms in Canadian society. This concern was prompted both by the specific and serious threat which political developments in Quebec posed to the maintenance of Canadian federalism, and by what was seen as the new social conflicts generated by a developed capitalist society. Historically in Canada, as Leo Panitch has argued in this volume: ' ... in terms of legitimation the state's role has not been comparatively active, imaginative, or large ... in the sense of concrete state activities ... directed at the integration of the subordinate classes in capitalist society either through the introduction of reforms which promote social harmony or through the co-option of working class leaders.' The considerable change which took place in the 1960s resulted in Canada shifting from a position where the state's legitimation function was relatively underdeveloped to one where, in some areas, the country pioneered new social programs which drew international attention. Canadian programs in job creation, for example, attracted attention both in the United States and Britain.[12]

There were a variety of motives at work in the Canadian government's designation of social problems and its formulation of a response. Some members of the elite were no doubt primarily concerned to take action which would undercut and pre-empt developments which might threaten social stability; others may have had a commitment to transform the image of the 'Just Society' from rhetoric to reality. Some target groups were readily identified in popular consciousness by their actions and the interpretation placed on these actions by the press and politicians. Youth appeared to represent a constituency whose views and lifestyle increasingly diverged from those of the mainstream – a phenomenon which, it was assumed, spread from Berkeley to Paris, and from Vancouver to Prague. Retrospectively we might question both the depth and the revolutionary nature of the 'youth revolt,' but for a government which deliberately sought to create a youth appeal and which was not presented with a plethora of competing 'problem constituencies,' initiatives directed towards youth were a logical priority. Equally, the increased militancy of the poor and native groups, coupled with the government's historic failure to resolve the problems faced by these groups or to achieve their full incorporation into society, identified them as targets for government action. American initiatives under Kennedy, which were continued under Johnson, also prompted Canadian interest, a point to which we shall return.

The government's programs in these areas were to a great extent based on *ad hoc* decisions, rather than any grand strategy. True, the government established a 'Committee on Youth,' which reported in 1971, to advise it on its relations with the younger generation. The committee saw its task as follows: 'An open breach of confidence exists between adults and youth. How can these conflicting views be ameliorated? How can the gap be lessened?'[13] The report of the committee, however, in no sense constituted a master plan, and indeed one of the government's largest initiatives in this field, the Opportunities for Youth program, was introduced before it reported.

There are no doubt specific issues of such a serious nature, from the perspective of the governing elite, as to necessitate a more coherent and co-ordinated approach. No less a strategist than Dalton Camp commented that history was likely to judge Trudeau's real success as his blunting of the separatist thrust in Quebec by policies not only of bilingualism and biculturalism but also of concrete material inducements. These inducements took the form of federal economic support and of programs specifically designed to incorporate individual French Canadians, particularly into the federal civil service.[14] One does not have to take Camp's rather sanguine view of the long-term stability of that achievement to recognize that by a combination of the carrot and the stick – in the form, among other things, of the War Measures Act – the Trudeau government has pursued a quite coherent and deliberate policy of recruiting the loyalties of the Québécois to a specific version of Canadian federalism and Canadian society.

Much government activity must be seen as more random than this, mediated by a number of factors including the well-intentioned activities of those within the state system who see themselves as 'radical.' In fact, state intervention in the voluntary sector generally will serve to maintain rather than challenge the existing social order, no matter what its particular origins. Intervention may be stimulated by the activities of 'go-betweens' who seek to bring disenchanted groups into the mainstream by way of providing them with the means to take part in activities leading to incremental change, or be encouraged by advocates of the status quo who, perhaps more cynically, perceive the advantage of incorporating dissident groups or the leaders of such groups by providing positive inducements to 'play the game.' In either case, state funding will have the same effect on the activities and internal structure of recipient groups. These points will be elaborated later.

State aid to minority and dissident groups plays an important role in legitimation, in sustaining the view that the state is not the agent of a particular social class but rather the benefactor of all. The acceptance of this view necessarily directs political activity towards conventional channels. These channels may at one level simply involve efforts to influence politicians and civil servants to produce a change in policy. Such efforts are, of course, premised on the assumption that the cause of present problems is not rooted in the very structure of society but is rather a function of particular decisions which are changeable by persuasion. Poverty is not rooted in the opportunity structures and labour markets of capitalist societies but rather in a failure of political will or imagination by politicians and their advisers. Hence, with different advice and stronger pressure effective steps can be taken to eliminate poverty. If the existing political elite is unwilling to take the necessary action, then efforts can be made to replace that elite with one of the available alternatives, through the ballot box. James O'Connor has argued the importance of maintaining the belief in the state's neutrality. While the state functions to preserve the conditions of the profitable capital accumulation, it must do so in a way which does not openly reveal its partisan nature: ' ... the state also must try to maintain or create the conditions for social harmony. A capitalist state that openly uses its coercive forces to help one class accumulate capital at the expense of other classes loses its legitimacy and hence undermines the basis of its loyalty and support.'[15]

In providing funds to the poor to help them protest welfare policies, or to native groups to help them fight land claims, the state asserts its independent role. Inevitably that role must be a difficult one, balancing the desire for legitimacy with the need to preserve the existing social order. When groups use state funds to begin to undermine the possibility of successful capital accumulation, as the native groups in the Northwest Territories have done in seeking to dictate the terms of resource development, pressure will be applied to restrain these activities and ultimately to sever funds (as indeed it has been). The problem is that each refusal of funds which is consequent to a political battle must erode the image of the state's neutrality, reducing its ability to play the role of arbiter. Ultimately the state may be forced to exercise coercion which will further undermine its neutral image. An understanding of this dilemma serves to clarify the state's otherwise ambiguous role in financing dissident groups. The concrete effects of this financing play an important role in enforcing acceptable political behaviour. None the less in some cases there will remain a doubt as to the overall impact. To what extent can state funding of native groups in the Northwest Territories be seen as responsible for furthering native militancy; to what extent has it enabled the federal government to establish some legitimacy which will facilitate further future resource exploitation without resort to overt coercion? An answer to such a question must in part depend on an estimation of what would have happened without government funding.

The political views of the group funded must also have an impact on the outcome, as must the group's structural situation and the range of political alternatives available. In practice, organizations of the poor will be much more readily incorporated in a situation where the possibility of fundamental political change is remote. Native groups with no viable strategy for independent survival must inevitably seek simply to influence the terms of their entry into settler society. It is precisely the possibility of maintaining a separate and relatively independent native society in northern Canada which makes the government's relationship with the native movement the more difficult. Similarly, it is the very political quiescence of English Canada which makes the task of co-optation so much easier.

The argument of this paper is that, while recognizing some ambiguity, overall government funding and involvement in the voluntary sector must be seen as a conservatizing force. In most cases political activity which falls outside the conservative paradigm will not be funded.

THE AMERICAN MODEL

The nature of the Canadian government's involvement in the citizen participation field was in part influenced by the very large programs initiated under John Kennedy and continued under Lyndon Johnson in the United States. These programs sought to tackle the problems of the American inner city. They were directed towards improving the economic position of inner city residents, creating new mechanisms of communication and involve-

BINS

ment between inner city residents and the larger society, and securing the Democratic party base in the northern cities where Kennedy had received key support in his presidential victory. F.F. Piven and R.A. Cloward, whose major analysis of the expansion of welfare programs in the United States in the 1960s, *Regulating the Poor*, won the C. Wright Mills award, argued that the programs could be seen in the context of regulation: 'When mass unemployment leads to outbreaks of turmoil, relief programs are initiated or expanded to absorb and control enough of the unemployed to restore order.' In a more recent work they stress the integrative results of the federal programs and their effectiveness in reducing social conflict: ' ... the very gains made in the sixties turned many blacks from group struggle to individual advancement. Thousands of veteran activists and hundreds of thousands of younger blacks from whom future activists might have been drawn were absorbed into colleges and universities, into industry and commerce, into the bureaucracies of government and into electoral politics. By this process, actual and potential activists were placated and isolated from the mass of blacks. In an increasingly hostile climate, they are preoccupied with consolidating their gains, not with mobilizing new waves of insurgency ... As for the majority of blacks who were left behind, they are quiescent as well. They have been calmed by the expansion of the relief roles and left leaderless by the expansion of the black middle class.'[16]

None the less, there was a certain duality to the programs in the United States, and while from one perspective we may judge them as efforts by a far-sighted political elite to undercut the growth of more radical protest movements, from another perspective they frequently appeared as the irrational use of federal funding to mobilize dissent. In the summer of 1965 the United States Conference of Mayors accused the director of the Office of Economic Opportunity, Sargent Shriver, of 'fostering class struggle.' Shriver's defence of the programs against such criticisms is interesting: 'Recognizing problems before we are fully ready to deal with them on our own terms can generate heat. But ignoring those problems, tuning out the voice of the poor, clinging to our past methods and approaches – can produce even more heat. It can produce a holocaust as it did last summer in Watts. We can no longer play it safe – for soon there will be no safe place, no place to hide.'[17]

THE CANADIAN EXPERIENCE

Canada did not face the same level of urban conflict as the United States, but none the less there were many in government who saw the need for pre-emptive action in dealing with the urban issue. Quite specific support for this view can be found in a memorandum to the cabinet of 16 June 1969, signed by John Munro, minister of health and welfare, and Gérard Pelletier, secretary of state. The two ministers urged financial support for the Black United Front of Nova Scotia, *inter alia*, because 'agitation which began last fall has injected into this situation the potential for racial unrest and perhaps violence such as has been seen in similar situations in the United States.' The Black United Front was seen as representing 'the constructive and moderate elements within the black community of Nova Scotia' while 'the failure of this organization will result in the discrediting of these elements and the shift of power to more extreme elements.'

The middle 1960s saw the creation of a host of initiatives in the citizen participation field. A special planning secretariat was established in the Prime Minister's Office under Lester Pearson, which was intended to promote citizen participation elements in government programming. Subsequently the initiative passed to the secretary of state. Even the Department of Regional Economic Expansion was encouraged to make provisions for citizen involvement in some of its development programs, though its efforts in this area left much to be desired.[18] Some of the new initiatives by government had, like those in the United States, a social change orientation. The most famous of the early experiments in this direction was the establishment in 1965 of the Company of Young Canadians.

No figures are available on the total increase in the amount of money which was dispersed by various levels of government to voluntary organizations or in social programs aimed at citizen participation, but two sets of figures do give us some indication of the levels of magnitude involved. A study undertaken for the Canadian Council on Social Development of 304 non-government agencies in thirteen Canadian cities found that government funding rose from $9,578,115 in 1962 to $51,467,044 in 1972. In 1962 government funding accounted for 45 per cent of these agencies' budgets, in 1972 for 64 per cent.[19] The two departments most centrally involved in the new thrust – the Department of the Secretary of State and the Department of Health and Welfare – underwent dramatic expansion. Between 1968 and 1972 the number of employees in the former increased by 100 per cent, and in the same period the increase in the staff of the latter was 350 per cent.[20]

The penetration of the voluntary sector is by no means confined to established agencies, but includes such innovative and often apparently radical groups as rape crisis centres, 'hassle-free clinics,' tenants' and welfare rights organizations, and women's centres. Indeed it can be argued that the government, through programs which mushroomed in the 1975 International

Women's Year, substantially incorporated the women's movement into the mainstream of society, both through the funding of activities at all levels and through the powerful media campaign which backed these programs. Otto Lang's opposition to government funding for the Saskatoon Women's Centre, whose advice on abortion aroused his Catholic ire, was interesting largely because it drew public attention to the government's involvement in what most people previously viewed as an independent organization.

Government funding extends beyond the community-based organizations into the media. Many local community newspapers survive only on the basis of LIP (Local Initiative Projects) – and previously OFY – grants. The ethnic newspapers in Ontario survive on government advertising placed by a leading Tory,[21] and even some apparently radical publications receive financing from some level of government. The *Last Post* is in receipt of funds from the Ontario Arts Council, and the Canadian Women's Press, which publishes a combination of socialist and feminist literature, receives some $50,000 annually from various levels of government.

At the national level, a number of apparently independent organizations upon close examination again turn out to be dependent on state funding. These range from those which maintain a level of quasi-independence, such as the Canadian Council on Social Development, which, for example, in 1971, with an operating budget of almost $1 million received less than 10 per cent of its income from individuals or groups,[22] or the National Indian Brotherhood, which receives most of its funding from the federal government, to the National Council of Welfare, whose members can only be appointed on the recommendation of a cabinet minister, and which is totally financed by the federal Department of Health and Welfare. Even the Canadian Federation of Human Rights and Civil Liberties Associations, the watchdog of the individual citizen's rights, is largely government-financed. Still more surprisingly, the Canadian Organization of Public Housing Tenants is almost exclusively dependent for financial support on the Central Mortgage and Housing Corporation, which itself is the prime target for the organization's activities.

It could of course be argued that all of this represents no more than the laudable desire of the government to facilitate the fuller working of democracy. In fact, government funding has a very pronounced effect on the way in which democracy works, serving to contain the debate within broad, but none the less definable, parameters. Ralph Miliband has argued: ' ... the fact that governments accept as beyond question the capitalist context in which they operate is of absolutely fundamental importance in shaping their attitudes, policies and actions in regard to the specific issues and problems with which they are confronted, and the needs and conflicts of civil society. The general commitment deeply colours the specific response, and effects not only the solution envisaged for the particular problem perceived, but the mode of perception itself; indeed, ideological commitment may and often does prevent perception at all, and makes impossible not only prescription for the disease, but its location.'[23]

The Canadian Council on Social Development is a useful example of an institution with a public presence, which, in participating actively in debate on public issues, serves to sustain the illusion of a meaningful debate and to reinforce the very narrow ideological space within which that debate occurs. The objective of the council is not confrontation with government but collaboration. As two critics of the council note: 'One reason we may assume the Council has done so well, therefore, from a financial perspective, is that its research and criticism of government has dealt with administrative details rather than fundamental issues.'[24] This attention to administrative detail and particular programs rather than to fundamental study of the roots of inequality and poverty, strives to appear non-partisan and value-free, but such 'pragmatism' remains essentially conservative, drawing as it does on that brand of liberal sociology which A. Gouldner has so accurately criticized as the 'new "ombudsman sociology" whose very criticism of middle-level welfare authorities and establishments serves as a kind of lightning rod for social discontent, strengthening the centralized control of the highest authorities, and providing new instruments of social control for the master institutions.'[25]

The council and other similar institutions serve to maintain the dominant pragmatic paradigm and confine the debate within its boundaries. When debate threatens to overstep those boundaries, the council stands ready to step in to restore that paradigm. Faced with the minor uproar which greeted its green paper on immigration, the Department of Manpower and Immigration turned to the council with offers to finance the sounding of views on the paper from across the country. In announcing the project, council director Reuben Baetz said: 'We have heard the most emotional and most radical views on immigration and population policy ... We must ensure that the loudest voices are not the only voices heard.'[26] In short, it was time to hear from that old standby, the 'silent majority.'

THE OPPORTUNITIES FOR YOUTH PROGRAM

The Opportunities for Youth program provides an excellent example of an *ad hoc* response to a perceived social problem, but within that response we find a central concern to integrate the program's target group into the main-stream of Canadian society. The objective of the OFY was to provide employment for youth, predominantly students, during the summer months in projects initiated and controlled by young people themselves. It was started in 1971 as part of a $67.2 million package designed to provide jobs and 'meaningful activities' to some of the more than 2.4 million university and high school students who would be out of school during the summer; OFY received $24.7 million of the total package which was to be dispensed on 'community oriented' projects initiated by and employing youth (youths were defined as those under twenty-five though in fact a number of older people were also employed). Projects could cover a wide variety of activities from drug clinics to day-care centres. A total of 2312 projects were ultimately approved in 1971 employing 27,832 students. The program provided jobs for 2.3 per cent of the student labour force and other federal government programs provided jobs for another 3.3 per cent. A number of provincial governments also ran summer employment programs which further reduced student unemployment. The provincial programs, like the federal programs, were largely motivated by a desire to 'make work.' In 1975, for example, the Ontario provincial treasurer, Darcy McKeough, commented that his government had hired thousands of students for the summer, and 'we have a hard enough time keeping them busy.'[27]

In addition to the students who benefited directly by being paid by OFY, a number of others were involved peripherally in the projects as unpaid participants or as clients – as, for example, in the opening of drop-in centres. It is reasonable to assume that OFY was successful in employing a disproportionate number of activist youth since they were likely to be the ones with the 'good ideas' for projects and the initiative to get the project organized and funded.[28] The broad outlines which were established for project funding also explicitly recognized the interests of more deviant youth. To offer mundane employment to people who had already expressed some cynicism about society was hardly useful. Projects must be allowed to reflect 'the imagination of young people themselves.'[29] The 1971 evaluators noted: 'implicit in the concept of "meaningful activities" was the recognition of the relationship between high student unemployment and the possibility of student unrest, and the planners of Opportunities for Youth realized that no program providing simply meaningless make-work would be satisfactory.' And they concluded that 'the outstanding achievement of Opportunities for Youth was its ability to provide students, as a target group, with activities they considered worthwhile.'[30] The program, however, was not simply useful in providing meaningful work; it also had a powerful implicit ideological message: 'the government cares.' OFY's staff noted the enthusiastic attitude of many participants towards the program, and clearly the government gained credibility, not only from many of the youth who worked on the projects but from others aware of this 'pro-youth' government initiative.

The scale of the problem which the government faced is evident from the official figures. In 1971 the seasonally adjusted unemployment rate for teenage males stood at 19.8 per cent, and this figure itself probably underestimated the real rate of teenage unemployment by between 6 and 10 per cent. A total of 281,000 Canadians between the ages of fourteen and twenty-four were unemployed (13.5 per cent of the age group) and again these figures probably substantially underestimated the real problem. It was on this job market that 1.1 million students would arrive.[31] This unemployment fueled youth dissent, at least as much as the Vietnam war or the obvious futility of much of what was offered in the name of education, creating a constituency which could be reached by radical ideas by removing the conservatizing effect of a steady job. Post-secondary enrolment had risen from 163,143 in 1960-1 to 475,548 in 1970-1. Yet despite the removal of such a sizeable number of people out of the labour market onto the campus, or, as one commentator put it, into 'the new proletarian parking lot,' the magnitude of youth unemployment continued to increase.[32]

One danger was that a number of students unable to obtain employment in the summer would be unable to return to school in the fall, hence exacerbating the winter unemployment picture and, potentially, disrupting their links with 'straight society.' The direct relationship between OFY and the provision of financial support to enable students to continue their studies was demonstrated in the increase in the salary paid to post-secondary students in 1975 from $90 to $110, following the recommendation of the 1974 program evaluation that the amount be raised by a further $20 'to offset the higher educational cost of post-secondary students.'[33]

The evaluators of the first year of the OFY program (1971) noted that 'prior to late 1970 [the government] has been forced to the recognition of a variety of potentially critical problems: summer unemployment among students, youth discontent, transiency, alienation and rebelliousness, the fear of revolution in Quebec, and the sudden increase in demands for action on such issues as drugs, pollution, social welfare, poverty, discrimination against women, Indians, Eskimos and Blacks, and the Americanization of the culture and economy.'[34] The government had already responded to what it saw as the growing crisis of alienated youth by opening hostels to keep those travelling up and down the country off the roadside and, perhaps more importantly, safe from the hands of the local police forces. That proved insufficient to stem discontent and there was, for a while, even talk of a free bus service to transport young people to and fro across Canada. It was as if one of the richest countries in the world could think of nothing to do with its children except to drive them around in buses all summer. In fact, the bus proposal was dropped when a major work creation program, OFY, was set up. Prime Minister Pierre Trudeau announced the program thus: 'we are saying, in effect, to the youth of Canada that we are impressed by their desire to fight pollution; that we believe they are well motivated in their concern for the disadvantaged; that we have confidence in their value system. We are also saying that we intend to challenge them to see if they have the stamina and self-discipline to follow through on their criticism and advice.'[35]

There is nothing startling or even controversial in the claim that OFY was in many ways no more and no less in its conception than an elaborate strategy for social control and the incorporation of dissenting youth into the great liberal pluralist framework.[36] The first evaluation of the program could hardly be more explicit on the deliberate social control aspects of the program; indeed, it is a constant theme of the evaluation. Referring to the establishment and orientation of the program, the evaluators wrote: 'The decision to focus the Summer '71 effort primarily on students, and also to some small extent on the marginal youth subculture – as opposed to dealing with youth and other disadvantaged groups generally – must be examined in terms of the perceived relationship between unemployment, inactivity, and social unrest. For it was not unemployment *per se* which was seen as creating social unrest, but rather inactivity and non-participation in general.'

The evaluators had earlier noted that 200,000 young people were estimated to be on the roads in 1970 and that the figure was expected to rise to 300,000 in 1971. They further reported that 'it may be thought slightly ironic to describe these individuals as "inactive" since it was precisely their activity, rather than their idleness, which was of concern to the Committee.' The committee to which the evaluators referred was in fact the interdepartmental committee established to develop the government's Student Summer Employment Activity Program, which, in the words of the evaluation, 'identified two major problems ... The first was that of critical summer unemployment among students, which was expected to be highest in Quebec ... The second was the distinct possibility that high student unemployment, coupled with an increasing tendency towards non-participation on the part of youth, could lead to social unrest.'[37] Given the volatile state of Quebec politics, it is not surprising to find that some 40 per cent of all OFY funding in the first year went there.

A third objective which was subsequently introduced into OFY was the promotion of 'national unity,' and though this clearly related to the growth of the separatist movement in Quebec, Secretary of State Pelletier pointed out that this was by no means an exclusive focus. He defined 'national solidarity' not as 'French/English relations but solidarity between Canadians all over the Country.'[38] The evaluators in turn defined 'national unity' as 'the promotion and intensification of some sense of patriotism or national solidarity.' For our purposes it is sufficient to note the utility of such mystifying concepts in class divided societies.

That the priority of the OFY program was not the alleviation of poverty or unemployment *per se* is clear from the program's almost exclusive orientation towards students. The secretary of state's Committee on Youth noted that 'The entry of students into post-secondary school gives them social and economic advantages beyond those of most young persons; students are, in fact, a privileged class. In this sense, the program is simply a social injustice, a form of discrimination against their peers who face similar or higher rates of unemployment.'[39] For the government what is important is not unemployment or poverty but its probable social consequences, and in that sense money was directed to those groups who had shown the greatest capacity for the creation of critical life styles and disruptive activities.

The essentially political objectives of the OFY program can be demonstrated not only by pointing out that the program was hardly designed to help the most needy but also by pointing out that the projects funded were dictated not by the government's burning commitment to alleviate hardship, improve the environment, or provide new community services, but by a desire to employ a specific target group in 'meaningful activity.' As the Canadian Council on Social Development noted: 'Both LIP and OFY programs were set up with the primary objective of providing employment. There is little dispute that they have filled gaps in the social service field, but agencies can provide ample documentation indicating prior awareness of such gaps. They were unable to fill them because of lack of money.'[40] Requests for continuation funding for projects which had demonstrated a real need fell on deaf ears despite the heavy social costs which were incurred by clients who had come to depend on the new resources created by the projects.

Perhaps the final evidence that the OFY program was an *ad hoc* response to what was seen as a minor emergency in youth employment and youth allegiance, was the way in which the program was initially administered. The program was rushed into existence to meet the summer demand for jobs and a large number of problems emerged. The application form, for example, did not ascertain whether the applicants were students – though this was the target group, no adequate data existed to provide anyone with an overview of the program, cost accounting was minimal, many projects were funded without any prior investigation, and 10 per cent of those funded never had any contact with the staff from the secretary of state who were responsible for program administration.[41] All the normal rules of bureaucracy were waived in order to provide some concrete and immediate demonstration of 'government concern.'

THE PARAMETERS OF GOVERNMENT FUNDING

That government is prepared to fund only certain kinds of organizations is confirmed by a study of what happens to organizations which have stepped outside the dominant paradigm and attempted to substantially shift the allocation of power in society. D. Rosenbluth, in examining the role of the government in the granting process, notes the self-evident but often ignored point that 'the grant is provided because it fits into the general social schemes of the grantor ... If the government's policies are to encourage innovations within the social services, grants will reflect this; if the policies are to suppress change, or merely to maintain stable norms, grants will similarly be reflective of these policies.'[42]

It is not easy to delineate any clear overall government policy in grants to citizens' organizations. A great deal depends on such factors as patronage by the local MP, the attitude of the particular civil servants involved, popular fads in the bureaucracy, changing target groups – students, the rural poor, women, Indians, and so on. What is clear is that certain kinds of behaviour by recipient groups are intolerable. The government is prepared to fund only a certain kind of democratic participation, and, in making that argument, one can simultaneously raise very grave questions about the role of government in this field. If government is not prepared to fund some groups or certain kinds of activities, what we see is not the funding which, in the words of the 1972 secretary of state Barbolet Report, 'gives new citizen organizations the opportunity to control the resources they need to carry out their strategies and objectives,'[43] but rather a further step towards a carefully managed 'democracy.' In effect, the plethora of government funding becomes an instrument not for citizen control over government but for government control over citizens. Approved activities will be rewarded, and recipient groups will serve as poles of attraction for potential members. Favoured individuals will emerge through government funded groups to take their place on social planning councils as representatives of the poor or some other worthy minority, and in the process will themselves cease to be poor.

The fate of the Company of Young Canadians provided an early and clear indication of the limits government placed on the beneficiaries of its largesse. The company was established in 1965. The words used to usher in the CYC foreshadowed those which Trudeau would later use in announcing the much larger OFY program; 'you will be asked,' Parliament was told, 'to approve the establishment of a Company of Young Canadians, through which the energies and talents of youth can be elicited in projects for economic and social development both in Canada and abroad.'[44] The CYC was to be based on the recruitment of 'volunteers' who were to be paid a subsistence salary plus a $50 per month honorarium paid out at the end of a two-year contract. (At the peak of the company's activities in 1968 there were 225 volunteers mainly engaged in community organizing activities with groups which included tenants, welfare recipients, and unorganized workers.)

The CYC's formation was not a response to any imminent social crisis or widespread youth dissatisfaction. Visible extra-parliamentary dissidence was mainly concentrated in the Student Union for Peace Action (SUPA), an outgrowth of the Canadian University Campaign for Nuclear Disarmament, whose small membership and eclectic ideology could hardly pose a threat to the most paranoid MacArthyist. However, SUPA's existence was, as Margaret Daly has argued, of crucial significance in determining CYC's direction.[45] SUPA had already entered community organizing in search of a political base for its pacifist communitarian brand of socialism and in that sense provided a potential model for the CYC, whose aims and principles adopted by its first council included 'a society in which people are in charge of their own destinies' and a commitment to 'support projects which will hopefully help to alleviate the causes of problems and will not simply "bandage" a symptom.'[46]

Important in bringing the resources of the CYC together with the aspirations of some of Canada's burgeoning new left was the crucial figure of the 'go-between,' who in liberal societies objectively serves to keep the ship on even keel while in fact appearing to be in the forefront of radical change. The go-between is anxious to sell innovative ways of ripping off the government to youth and other dissenting groups. Simultaneously, he offers more subtle means of 'showing you really care' (and indirectly mechanisms of keeping close control) to the government. The go-between is forever solving other people's problems, the apparently irresolvable contradicition in his hands simply evaporates, leaving the two parties both happily pursuing the same projects, if for totally opposite reasons. The go-between can easily bring together federal resources and militant Quebec separatists eagerly working on the same project. The crisis passes, the dissenters disappear into the state apparatus and peace reigns – until the next time. The state of course is always there, as is its raison d'être, monopoly capitalism, and in that sense it might be said that there can be only one winner and equally only one loser. With the aid of the go-between, dissent serves not to subvert the system but, ironically, to strengthen it. In short, objectively the go-between is only on one side, though for a man committed to the notion that 'sides' are merely a product of the way we look at the world rather than the reality of the way the world is organized, this argument is unlikely to be convincing.

In the case of the CYC there were many would-be go-betweens. Daly writes of the inclusion on CYC's governing council of Art Pape, one of SUPA's major leaders: 'Bob Phillips [of the Privy Council Office] and Stuart Goodings were smart enough to know that without Pape on the Council, the Company could abandon any claims to credibility with activist youth.' Art Pape in turn explained the position of those radicals who did work for the council: 'Man, there's four million dollars on the table. If we don't pick it up, somebody else is going to.'[47] Goodings makes no secret of the importance he attached to winning over the left to the CYC, and indeed in many ways the co-optation of the left was not a result of any decision of the leading Liberal ideologues but rather a gut-level reflex action of those involved.

It is now part of the historical record that, to the extent that CYC volunteers actually sought to put people in 'charge of their own destinies,' they encountered intense hostility, and that in Quebec, the most politically sensitive Canadian province, the company was accused by the Chairman of the City of Montreal's executive committee of terrorism and subversion. This accusation led to a parliamentary enquiry and the removal of political power from the hands of the company's volunteer employees into the hands of those whose most subversive thoughts resembled those of Mitchell Sharp. More contentious than the government's blunt refusal to countenance any meaningful radical activity – which actually surprised some people – is the effect that CYC had on the left. Margaret Daly writes: 'Had Art Pape and Doug Ward [president elect of the Canadian Union of Students] decided to steer clear of the CYC, the history of the New Left in Canada would be entirely different today; so different, in fact, that it is impossible even to guess where radicalism in this country might be now. SUPA's collapse (in the fall of 1967) was no doubt inevitable; plenty of factors extraneous to the CYC were involved in that. But without the split down the middle of SUPA over whether or not to co-operate with the CYC, and without lucrative CYC consulting jobs to drain off the talents and time of so many SUPA members (as happened through 1967 and part of 1968), who knows what sort of independent New Left organization might have risen from SUPA's ashes?'[48]

While the CYC was the most dramatic of the government's overt political interferences with those who refused to play by the establishment rules, political restrictions on the use of government funding are manifest at both the local and provincial levels. The government's growing role in funding the voluntary sector led to a number of clashes. In Hamilton the Welfare Rights group used Health and Welfare funding to create a militant opposition to the inadequacies and inhumanities of the welfare system, much to the anger of municipal and provincial politicians. In terminating their funding in 1971, Hamilton MP and health and welfare minister John Munro, advised them: 'continuing alienation of the larger Hamilton population by the use of militant tactics and radical rhetoric will only cause the city's low income residents to lose public support for the progressive reforms ... which they require, and for which they have called on urgently ... Confrontation tactics by people on welfare do not work, they alienate Canadians who are asked to support those less fortunate than themselves.'[49]

In the same year the New Democratic Party came to power in Saskatchewan, and in a short-lived burst of reform fervour established the Human Resources Development Agency. Included in HRDA's objectives was 'assisting people to "take control of their own lives" and the promotion and facilitation of social change in institutions, to facilitate the participation of the "disadvantaged" in social, cultural, and economic development.' The agency took the mandate seriously. Whenever possible, the program was placed under the direct control of organizations of the disadvantaged. Agency staff assisted disadvantaged groups in formulating demands for increased government resources and action. In short, the agency staff quite consciously identified with the disadvantaged, and sought to help them articulate a program for structural change, which would end their disadvantaged situation. Their efforts produced increased pressure on various government departments, and ultimately on the NDP government itself. This led to the rapid reorganization of HRDA when the government forced the executive director's resignation and terminated the contract of most of HRDA's staff. Linda Sperling, evaluating this process, concluded: 'As the work of the Agency progressed, it became apparent that the government had no notion of what Community Development or Economic Development really meant. The government's priorities, therefore, were generally incompatible with the needs of the organizations of the poor. Groups in government soon realize that any real access or control of a segment of the economy that is taken by a group that did not previously have it, implies taking it away from those who currently control it. This kind of economic development was and is unacceptable to the NDP government ... As long as governments can fund group projects that do not challenge the present structure of the economy, they will continue to support community development. As long as groups continue to propose projects that do not challenge the existing economic structure, they will continue to get funded. Governments have consistently used community development programs as a response to protest and social unrest in certain segments of society. As long as the program quiets the protest, its objectives are considered compatible with government.'[50]

These cases serve to demonstrate the limits of government-sponsored participation. In practice, the more important point is not the fate of the minority of organizations which are terminated or deliberately reorganized, but rather the consequences which the continued receipt of government funding has on other organizations. What is involved in government funding is not only the effective creation of groups which would never exist without state patronage but also the transformation of groups whose existence is not rooted in government initiative, but for whom the attraction of government funding produces a slow erosion of their original purpose.

Low income groups are particularly susceptible to the attractions of government funding. Such groups do not have ready access to other material resources and, in addition, government funding often carries with it the promise of jobs which may not be otherwise available, and certainly will not be available in anything other than low-paid industries offering monotonous work. Receipt of government funding will not, however, provide adequate funds for the employment of all members of the organization, and an immediate conflict can be expected between the organization's members for those paid positions available. The consequence of this conflict may well be the alienation of those who fail to secure a job. Those who do succeed in getting themselves on the payroll will have every reason to seek to secure the permanence of their positions, in so far as that is possible. The primary group objective will then be to satisfy the donor's criteria, which will frequently conflict with the original group criteria. Group time and activities will be absorbed in accounting for the expenditure of the current grant and preparing the submission for the next. Those who develop skills in grantsmanship will come to play a pivotal role in the organization. Support will be sought from local 'influentials' in the form of the municipal council and local politicians or from individual dignitaries. Such 'influentials' must be expected to demand certain standards of political behaviour or 'responsibility' in return for their support. The Riverdale Community Organization in Toronto failed to secure support because it neglected to win the backing of the Toronto City Council, who saw it as a militant, confrontational organization.[51]

Rosenbluth, in his analysis of the effects of government funding on community associations, argued: 'Analytically, grants may be seen as having two roles for the association. It gives the leaders approval for their proposed actions (a legitimizing role), while also giving them the funds with which to achieve them (an efficacy role). Previously the association's leaders drew the legitimacy for their actions from the membership, where in theory at least, the membership collectively determined the policy and gave legitimation to the leaders of the association. But with government funding, such reliance on the membership is no longer necessary. The links and communication networks from the membership up, take on increasingly less significance, while those from the government down, become more significant. As the necessity for membership participation diminishes, there will occur simultaneously a withdrawal of commitment to the association. The increased wealth will also tend to have an oligarchial effect on the organization, for there is a strong tendency for those who receive salaries from the funds (i.e. are no longer volunteers) to try and hold on to their position.'[52]

In a country which, outside Quebec, has no strong radical movement, the incorporation of potentially dissident organizations presents no great problem. The argument is not that without state involvement there will be a plethora of grass-roots radical activity but rather that state involvement generally precludes that development. One National Health and Welfare grant officer summarized the process: 'The objectives of programs change as soon as they get money – They tend to shift in accordance with the outlines laid down in the funding process. They have to start making compromises when they get government money. They just can't cope. This is a condition of being funded.'[53] Association members with more radical commitments to militant activity in grass-roots organizing have to contend not only with the conservatism of other association members but also with the financial inducement of government funding. This funding will necessitate the organization shifting its attention away from generalized oppositional activities towards offering concrete programs which are in reality often little more than appendages to the existing social service delivery system. Once funding has been accepted, there will be a strong tendency by group members to evaluate the group's activities in the light of its ability to satisfy the donor and raise further funds. The views of association members will decline in importance as they cease to be central to the organization's survival, which is now seen as dependent on outside funding. Without outside funding, a group must mobilize members not only to support its continued formal existence but also to raise the funds necessary for its day-to-day operations. With outside funding, the mobilization of the membership may in fact jeopardize further funding support, unless the membership can be mobilized around issues acceptable to the grantor.

The last twenty-five years have witnessed a rapid growth in the activity of the state at all levels in Western capitalist societies, as the state has sought to maintain both full employment and the continued profitability of private enterprise.[54] The state's accelerating involvement in all areas of social life has paralleled its activity in regulating demand. Indeed the state's involvement with the voluntary sector in community employment projects, Opportunities for Youth, and the Local Initiatives Program, has had both economic and social control aspects. The recent cutbacks in state spending in the social services field in Canada, which have included the termination of the OFY program and the final closure of the CYC, do not necessarily indicate a return to the inactive legitimating role which historically characterized the Canadian state. Indeed the explanation for these developments would appear to lie in the narrowly political realm, rather than to indicate an underlying structural change.

In Ontario the minority Conservative government sought to locate an electoral majority by the simple tactic of appealing to a constituency which it is assumed will support 'welfare bashing' and other reductions in government expenditure – reductions of course which do not affect the profitability of private enterprise. Nationally, the Liberal government has sought to respond to public concern about inflation by taking dramatic action in one or two areas which have never enjoyed overwhelming support from influential sectors of the public. In that sense the demolition of the CYC and the OFY programs is better understood as a conciliatory gesture to groups like the Calgary Chamber of Commerce rather than as a harbinger of fundamental change. That the revenue saved is less than the price of two Orion patrol planes and indeed is insignificant compared to the increase in defence spending, is surely suggestive of such a view, as is the continued concern by the government to devise new strategies for dealing with youth unemployment.

The thesis of this paper, that government intervention serves an integratieve function, is none the less borne out by the opposition generated to the cutbacks. New levels of militancy are emerging among both social service workers and dependents. Students faced with increasing pressure on university facilities, fee increases, and declining employment prospects are, at least at the level of student councils and the National Union of Students, returning to the activist stance which characterized student politics in the late 1960s – though not perhaps with the same level of militance or rhetoric. These developments do not herald any sudden upsurge in radical activism in Canada. It is clear that in English Canada increased dissidence poses no immediate threat to the status quo. But in the long term, as governments seek to resolve the economic crisis by increasing state management of the economy, while continuing to try to secure their political constituency, a continued growth in the state's legitimation activities can be anticipated. One of the very real consequences of this must be a substantial transformation of the political system itself. As the state moves into new areas of society the notion that it is the citizens who govern through their elected representatives must surely give way to a more thorough exploration of how the governing apparatus of the state itself controls the citizens and moulds and determines their political behaviour.

NOTES

The introductory quotation is from A. Gorz, *Strategy for Labour* (Boston 1967), ix.
1 Dahl *et al.*, *Social Science Research on Business: Product and Potential* (New York 1959), 36
2 'The Limits of the Welfare State,' *New Left Review*, 27 (Sept.-Oct. 1964), 33
3 *Globe and Mail*, Toronto, 4 May 1976 (emphasis added)
4 *Political Man: The Social Basis of Politics* (London 1959)
5 *Race, Colonialism and the City* (London 1973), 287
6 For an exploration of this latter argument, see A. Lockhart, 'Future Failure: The Unanticipated Consequences of Educational Planning,' in *Socialization and Values in Canadian Society: Socialization, Social Stratification and Ethnicity*, ed. E. Zureik and R. Pike (Toronto 1975), ii.
7 'The Patron State of Canada,' unpublished MA thesis, Carleton University, Ottawa, 1974
8 *Western Capitalism since the War* (London 1970), 24
9 'State Expenditure in Advanced Capitalism,' *New Left Review*, 92 (July-Aug. 1975), 75
10 'The Capitalist State: A Reply to Miliband and Laclau,' *New Left Review*, 95 (Jan.-Feb. 1976), 74
11 Federal government revenue rose from $7323 million in 1963 to $15,523 million

in 1970. Canada, Department of Finance, *Economic Review* (April 1975), Reference Table 54

12 See, for example, *Achieving the Goals of the Employment Act of 1946 – Thirtieth Anniversary Review*, I – *Employment, The Canadian Job Creation Model and Its Applicability to the United States*, a study prepared for the use of the Subcommittee on Economic Growth of the Joint Economic Committee, Congress of the United States (Washington 1976).

13 Committee on Youth, *It's Your Turn* (Ottawa 1971), 3

14 *As It Happens*, CBC Radio, 4 May 1976, interview with Camp

15 *The Fiscal Crisis of the State* (New York 1973), 6

16 *Regulating the Poor: The Functions of Public Welfare* (New York 1971), 3; *The Politics of Turmoil: Poverty, Race, and the Urban Crisis* (New York 1974), xiv

17 P. Marris and M. Rein, *Dilemmas of Social Reform* (London 1972), 250

18 See 'The Enemies within Community Development,' Bert Deveaux with Kaye Deveaux, in *Citizen Participation: Canada*, ed. James A. Draper (Toronto 1971).

19 N. Carter, *Trends in Voluntary Support for Non-Government Social Service Agencies* (Ottawa 1974), 9

20 D. Rosenbluth, 'The Effects of Government Funding on Community Associations,' unpublished MA thesis, Carleton University, 1973, p. 33

21 See *Globe and Mail*, 13 May 1976.

22 G. Drover and L. Ouaknine, 'Social Policy in the Making: The Function of the Canadian Council on Social Development,' paper presented to 2nd Annual Social Policy Conference, Carleton University, Ottawa, April 1975, p. 25

23 *The State in Capitalist Society* (London 1969), 72

24 Drover and Ouaknine, 'Social Policy,' 21

25 *The Coming Crisis of Western Sociology* (London 1971), 501

26 Canadian Council on Social Development, Press Release, 23 June 1975

27 *Globe and Mail*, 24 June 1975

28 Discussions with OFY staff support this view.

29 Secretary of State, News Release, 16 March 1971

30 A. Cohen *et al., Opportunities for Youth 71* , Report of the Evaluation Task Force to the Secretary of State (Ottawa 1972), 68, 84

31 *It's Your Turn*, 16, 20; and Cohen, *ibid.*, 56

32 R. A. Lockhart, 'The Effects of Recent Techno-Economic Changes on the Mobility Pattern and Opportunities of the American Middle Class with Particular Emphasis on Emerging Contradictions between Occupational and Educational Factors,' unpublished MA thesis, Simon Fraser Univeristy, Burnaby, 1970, pp. 211-45

33 C. P. Morrison, *Evaluation of the 1974 Opportunities for Youth Program*, Manpower and Immigration (Ottawa 1974), 9

34 Cohen, *Opportunities*, 22

35 *Can. H. of C. Debates*, 16 March 1971, p. 4288
36 The analysis here of OFY and LIP programs has been made in slightly different form by Lorne Huston, in 'The Flowers of Power: A Critique of OFY and LIP Programs,' *Our Generation*, VIII, 4 (Oct. 1972).
37 Cohen, *Opportunities*, 16, 19
38 Speech to the National Council of YMCAS, Geneva Park, Ontario, 29 May 1971
39 *It's Your Turn*, 181
40 Carter, *Trends*, 56
41 Cohen, *Opportunities*, 68
42 'Effects of Government Funding,' 24
43 *Task Force on New and Emerging Citizen Groups*, Secretary of State (Ottawa 1972), 19
44 *Can. H. of C. Debates*, 5 April 1965
45 *The Revolution Game* (Toronto 1973)
46 I. Hamilton, *The Children's Crusade* (Toronto 1970), 8-9
47 *Revolution Game*, 28, 31
48 *Ibid.*, 29
49 *Globe and Mail*, 9 Dec. 1971
50 'Evaluation of HRDA,' unpublished paper, 1975
51 See J. Apostle, 'A Question of Autonomy,' *Canadian Welfare* (July-Aug. 1972)
52 'Effects of Government Funding,' 21
53 *Ibid.*, 50
54 For a recent exploration of this, see A. Gamble and P. Walton, *Capitalism in Crisis: Inflation and the State* (London 1976).

Contributors

HUGH ARMSTRONG is a doctoral candidate in sociology at the Université de Montréal and teaches at Marianopolis College in Montreal. He has written a number of articles with Pat Armstrong on women and work, and their book on this subject is scheduled for publication by McClelland & Stewart in the spring of 1978.

WALLACE CLEMENT is an assistant professor of sociology at McMaster University. His main publications are *The Canadian Corporate Elite* (1975) and *Continental Corporate Power* (1977). He is currently working on another book, *The Work Place: Changes in Canada's Class Structure*.

ROBIN ENDRES teaches humanities at York University. She has recently co-edited and introduced an anthology of Canadian plays from the workers' theatre movement, *Eight Men Speak* (1977).

ALVIN FINKEL is a lecturer in the Department of History at the University of Alberta. He was formerly editor of *Canadian Dimension* and his article, 'Saskatchewan: The Great Depression,' was published in Hugh Innis, ed. *Regional Disparities in Canada* (1971). He is currently revising for publication his recent PH D dissertation for Queen's University on 'Canadian Business and the Reform Process in Canada in the 1930s.'

MARTIN LONEY is currently a lecturer in community work at Polytechnic of the South Bank in London, England. In addition to several articles, he is the author of *Rhodesia: White Ransom and Imperial Response* (1975).

RIANNE MAHON teaches in the Social Science Department, Atkinson College, York University. She recently completed her doctoral dissertation at the University of Toronto on 'Canadian Textile Policy: A Case Study in the Politics of Industrial Formation in Canada' and is currently working on the role of regulatory commissions in the capitalist state.

HENRY MILNER teaches political science at Vanier College, Montreal. He is the co-author of *The Decolonization of Quebec* (1973) and the author of *Quebec Politics: Conflict and Contradiction* (forthcoming). He has also written several articles on urban politics and on Quebec for *Our Generation*.

DENNIS OLSEN teaches sociology at Carleton University. He is currently completing a PH D dissertation on the Canadian state elite since 1960, and is the co-author with Wallace Clement of an article on social and economic inequality in Canada, 'How Bad Is Bad,' in *This Magazine* (1975).

LEO PANITCH is associate professor of political science at Carleton University. His main publications are *Social Democracy and Industrial Militancy: The Labour Party, the Trade Unions and Incomes Policy* (1976), 'Ideology and Integration,' *Political Studies* (1971), and 'The Development of Corporatism in Liberal Democracies,' *Comparative Political Studies* (1977). He is a frequent contributor to *Canadian Dimension*.

LARRY PRATT is an associate professor of political science at the University of Alberta. He is the author of *East of Malta, West of Suez: Britain's Mediterranean Crisis, 1936-1939* (1976) and *The Tar Sands: Syncrude and the Politics of Oil* (1976). He is currently working on a book on the political economy of western Canada.

STEPHEN SCHECTER teaches sociology at the Université du Québec à Montréal and is active in Montreal urban politics. His article, 'Urban Politics in Capitalist Society,' appeared in *Our Generation* (1975).

GARTH STEVENSON is an associate professor of political science at Carleton University. He has published one book, *Mineral Resources and Australian Federalism* (1977), and co-edited *A Foremost Nation: Canadian Foreign Policy and a Changing World* (1977), as well as contributed chapters to various other books. He is now writing a book on Canadian federalism.

DONALD SWARTZ is an assistant professor at the School of Public Administration, Carleton University. He is the author of 'The Health Industry,' *This Magazine* (1976) and the co-author of 'The Structure and Behaviour of Canadian Regulatory Boards and Commissions,' *Canadian Public Administration* (1975).

REG WHITAKER is an assistant professor of political science at Carleton University. He is the author of *The Government Party: Organizing and Financing the Liberal Party of Canada, 1930-1958* (1977), and co-author of *The Biography of an Institution: The Civil Service Commission of Canada, 1908-1967* (1972). He is a regular contributor to *Canadian Forum* and is currently working on a book on the political ideas of Mackenzie King.

DAVID WOLFE is completing a doctoral dissertation on the economic role of the state in Canada at the University of Toronto. He currently holds the position of sessional lecturer in political science at Glendon College, York University. His article on "Economic Growth and Foreign Investment: A Perspective on Canadian Economic Policy, 1947-1957" is forthcoming in the *Journal of Canadian Studies.*